PDE SOFTWARE:
Modules, Interfaces and Systems

IFIP TC 2 Working Conference on
PDE Software: Modules, Interfaces and Systems
Söderköping, Sweden, 22-26 August, 1983

organized by
IFIP Working Group 2.5 (Numerial Software)
on behalf of
IFIP Technical Committee 2 (Programming)
International Federation for Information Processing

Programme Committee
J. R. Rice *(Chairman)*
A. Brandt, B. Einarsson, B. Gustafsson,
J. K. Reid, H. Stetter, N. N. Yanenko

NORTH-HOLLLAND
AMSTERDAM • NEW YORK • OXFORD

PDE SOFTWARE:
Modules, Interfaces and Systems

Proceedings of the IFIP TC 2 Working Conference on
PDE Software: Modules, Interfaces and Systems
Söderköping, Sweden, 22-26 August, 1983

edited by

Björn ENGQUIST and Tom SMEDSAAS
Department of Computer Science
University of Uppsala
Sweden

Dedicated to the memory of N. N. Yanenko

1984

NORTH-HOLLAND
AMSTERDAM • NEW YORK • OXFORD

© IFIP, 1984

ISBN: 0 444 87620 0

Published by:
ELSEVIER SCIENCE PUBLISHERS B.V.
P. O. Box 1991
1000 BZ Amsterdam
The Netherlands

Sole distributors for the U.S.A. and Canada:
ELSEVIER SCIENCE PUBLISHING COMPANY, INC.
52 Vanderbilt Avenue
New York, N.Y. 10017
U.S.A.

Library of Congress Cataloging in Publication Data

IFIP TC 2 Working Conference on PDE Software.
    PDE software.

    1. Differential equations, Partial--Computer programs
--Congresses. 2. Differential equations, Partial--
Numerical solutions--Computer programs--Congresses.
I. Engquist, Björn, 1945-   . II. Smedsaas, Tom,
1945-   . III. International Federation for
Information Processing. Technical Committee 2.
IV. Title.
QA377.I44 1983   515.3'53   84-16630
ISBN 0-444-87620-0

PRINTED IN THE NETHERLANDS

PREFACE

The objective of this conference was to explore modern approaches to software for solving partial differential equations with an emphasis on creating PDE software as a modular system with careful attention to the interfaces involved.

The working conference recorded here was held at the Söderköpings Brunn in Söderköping, Sweden, from 22 to 26 August 1983. It was the third organized by IFIP Working Group 2.5 (Numerical Software) on behalf of Technical Committee 2 of the International Federation for Information Processing. There were 75 participants from 20 different countries. In addition to the 23 regular papers, one open session was organized. All papers are included in the proceedings. Two informal evening sessions with posters and demonstrations of PDE software on a graphic terminal were also arranged.

One topic of great interest at the conference was the vectorization of PDE software for use on supercomputers, with both theoretical and practical contributions. Another important topic was the future forms of PDE software. One can already see some systems which use adaptive algorithms or which include some symbolic analysis and preprocessing of problems. An important area for the future will be the development of expert systems for PDEs which will evolve from these ideas.

Multigrid methods have shown to be efficient for a large class of problems. This technique is now so well understood that it is ripe for software development. Finite differences and finite elements were given equal attention, and new views and general advice on the design of PDE software were presented. Applications ranged from semiconductor device modelling to the study of air pollution in Scandinavia.

Plenty of time was used for discussion. Edited versions of these discussions, prepared by a discussant for each half-day session, are attached to the end of each paper. We would like to thank the discussants for their excellent work during and after the meeting.

The conference chairman was John R. Rice. The programme committee consisted of John R. Rice (*chairman*), Achi Brandt, Bo Einarsson, Bertil Gustafsson, John K. Reid, Hans Stetter and N.N. Yanenko. The local arrangements committee consisted of Bo Einarsson (*chairman*), Eva Edberg and Gunilla Sköllermo. They had arranged a pleasant cultural and social program in the lovely old city of Söderköping and its vicinity.

The conference was partially supported by grants from IFIP and the Swedish Institute of Applied Mathematics. Travel grants have been received from the US Army Research Office, the Royal Swedish Academy of Engineering Sciences, the Swedish Institute of Applied Mathematics, and the Swedish Institute. The committee gratefully acknowledges this support.

Finally the secretarial help at the conference was given by Lena Östling, University of Linköping. Administrative and organizational support has been provided by the Swedish National Defence Research Institute (FOA), the Linköping University Computer Centre (LIDAC), and the Stockholm University Computer Centre (QZ). We would also like to express our deep gratitude to Bo Einarsson for extensive help with the editorial work.

Björn Engquist and Tom Smedsaas
Uppsala

TABLE OF CONTENTS

PDE SOFTWARE: Modules, Interfaces and Systems
B. Engquist and T. Smedsaas (eds.)
Elsevier Science Publishers B.V. (North-Holland)
© IFIP, 1984

1

TREESOLVE, A FORTRAN PACKAGE FOR SOLVING LARGE SETS OF

LINEAR FINITE-ELEMENT EQUATIONS+

J.K. Reid

CSS Division
AERE Harwell
Oxon OX11 0RA U.K.

We describe the design of a package of subroutines
intended to solve efficiently very large sets of linear
finite-element equations whose matrix is symmetric
and positive definite. It uses tree-search techniques
to organise frontal elimination so that input-output
operations are not excessive, and finds a good
elimination order automatically. It is portable and
easy to interface to existing codes. We describe our
experience in its use, modifications made
in the light of this experience and give some performance
results on the UNIVAC 1100/83, IBM 3081K and
CRAY-1 computers.

1.   INTRODUCTION

We consider the efficient direct solution of very large sets of
linear equations

$$Ax = b, \qquad\qquad (1.1)$$

whose matrix A is symmetric and positive definite. We assume that A
and b can be expressed as the sums

$$A = \sum_{m=1}^{e} A^{(m)}, \qquad b = \sum_{m=1}^{e} b^{(m)} \qquad\qquad (1.2)$$

of matrices $A^{(m)}$ and vectors $b^{(m)}$ all of whose elements are zero
except for those corresponding to an index set $S^{(m)}$, i.e.

$$A_{ij}^{(m)} = 0 \quad \text{unless} \quad i,j \in S^{(m)} \qquad\qquad (1.3)$$

and

$$b_i^{(m)} = 0 \quad \text{unless} \quad i \in S^{(m)} . \qquad\qquad (1.4)$$

The index sets $S^{(m)}$ correspond to the variables belonging in the
finite elements.

We find it convenient to describe what we do in terms of Gaussian
elimination. In fact we produce a symmetric factorization of a
symmetric permutation of A,

+This work was partially supported by the US Air Force under grant
AFOSR-81-0040

$$U^T D U = PAP^T ,\tag{1.5}$$

where U is upper triangular, D is diagonal and P is a permutation matrix.

2.   IRONS' FRONTAL METHOD

Our method of solution is based on the frontal method of Irons (1970). This depends on the observation that the elimination step

$$a_{ij}^{(\ell+1)} = a_{ij}^{(\ell)} - a_{ik}^{(\ell)} \; a_{kk}^{(\ell)-1} a_{kj}^{(\ell)}\tag{2.1}$$

of Gaussian elimination may be performed before all the assembly steps

$$a_{ij}^{(\ell+1)} = a_{ij}^{(\ell)} + a_{ij}^{(m)} ,\tag{2.2}$$

provided assembly is complete for the pivotal row k in step (2.1). Delaying the assembly steps gives the same result in exact arithmetic because of the associativity of addition and subtraction. In floating-point arithmetic there will be roundoff differences, but these will be minor because of the following minor extension of the result of Wilkinson (1961).

<u>Theorem</u>   If frontal elimination is applied to the matrix
$A = \sum\limits_{m=1}^{e} A^{(m)}$, where each $A^{(m)}$ is symmetric and positive semi-definite, then all intermediate quantities $a_{ij}^{(\ell)}$ in steps (2.1) and (2.2) satisfy the inequality

$$|a_{ij}^{(\ell)}| \leqslant \max_{i,j} |a_{ij}| .\tag{2.3}$$

<u>Proof</u>   Suppose that the first ℓ steps consist of ℓ_a assemblies and ℓ_e eliminations, so that $\ell = \ell_a + \ell_e$. By the associativity of addition and subtraction, $A^{(\ell)}$ could have been obtained by application of ℓ_e steps of Gaussian elimination to the matrix $\sum\limits_{m=1}^{\ell_a} A^{(m)}$.   This matrix is positive semi-definite since each $A^{(m)}$ is positive semi-definite;   it therefore has its element of largest modulus on its diagonal and by the result of Wilkinson (1961), the inequality

$$|a_{ij}^{(\ell)}| \leqslant \max_{i} \sum\limits_{m=1}^{\ell_a} a_{ii}^{(m)}\tag{2.4}$$

is therefore true. Also on account of the positive semi-definiteness of $A^{(m)}$, this matrix has non-negative diagonal elements and therefore the inequality

$$\sum\limits_{m=1}^{\ell_a} a_{ii}^{(m)} \leqslant a_{ii}\tag{2.5}$$

is true. The result (2.3) is now an immediate consequence of inequalities (2.4), (2.5) and the fact that A is positive semi-

definite so it has its element of largest modulus on its
diagonal.   QED

    Irons' pivotal strategy is based on an order for the assembly
steps. He eliminates each variable as soon as its row and column is
fully assembled, and uses a full matrix to hold the rows and columns
of $A^{(\ell)}$ that contain non-zeros. These rows and columns correspond to
variables that have not yet been eliminated but have appeared in one
or more of the sets $S^{(k)}$ corresponding to assemblies so far performed.
As each elimination is performed, the pivotal row (a row of the factor
U in equation (1.5)) is moved to permanent storage. The technique
works well for a long thin problem, as illustrated in Figure 1, if the
elements are ordered from end to end. In this case the set of
variables which are associated with an assembled matrix $A^{(m)}$ but which
have not yet been eliminated is never large; it forms a "front"
between the assembled and unassembled elements and moves from one end
of the region to the other. This is why the method is called the
frontal method. The full work matrix is usually called the frontal
matrix.

    Figure 1 illustrates the situation. Each element has a variable
at each vertex. The elements marked a have been assembled. The front
consists of variables at nodes marked □ and the variables at nodes
marked O have been eliminated. Thus the frontal matrix contains
rows and columns 5,12,13,19 of $A^{(\ell)}$. The assembly of element
(12,13,19) adds no extra variables to the front but permits variable
13 to be eliminated so that the front becomes (5,12,19). If element
(5,6,12) is assembled next, variable 6 has to be added to the front
but variable 5 can be eliminated to give a new front (6,12,19).

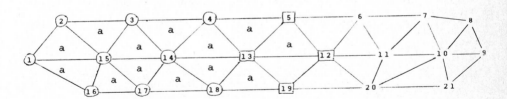

        Figure 1.   An illustration of Irons' frontal method.

3.   SUBSTRUCTURING

    If a variable is associated with only one of the matrices $A^{(m)}$,
then its row and columns is fully assembled within $A^{(m)}$ itself and it
may therefore be eliminated by performing the operations (2.1) before
$A^{(m)}$ is assembled into the frontal matrix. As ever, the pivotal row
is transferred to permanent storage. The process is known as "static
condensation". It means, for example, that the algebraic cost of
working with the 9-node biquadratic element illustrated in Figure 2 is
virtually identical to that of working with the 8-node element
illustrated in Figure 3.

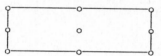

Figure 2.   9-node biquadratic element $\sum\limits_{i,j=0}^{2} a_{ij}x^{i}y^{j}$

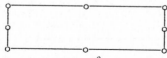

Figure 3.   8-node element $\sum\limits_{\substack{i,j=0 \\ i+j\neq4}}^{2} a_{ij}x^{i}y^{j}$

This idea extends naturally to groups of elements (sub-structures). Variables that appear within such a group but do not appear outside it may be eliminated by assembling the elements of the group by themselves. The grouping of elements in substructures and of substructures into larger structures, etc. is naturally represented by a tree. A simple example is shown in Figure 4. Such a tree may also be interpreted as a representation of an ordering for the assembly operations (1.2). For example the tree in Figure 4 represents the order

$$[\ [A^{(1)}+A^{(2)}]+[A^{(3)}+A^{(4)}] \ ] \ + \ [\ [A^{(5)}+A^{(6)}]+[A^{(7)}+A^{(8)}] \ ] \ .$$

To gain the full advantage of static condensation and substructuring, we must perform the summations from the inner brackets outwards and at every stage eliminate at once any variables that do not appear except within the element or substructure in hand. In fact each node of the tree corresponds to the assembly of the elements and substructures that are its children, followed by the elimination of variables contained in it but not appearing elsewhere.

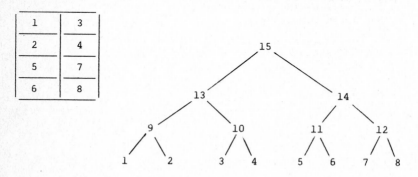

Figure 4.   An element problem and an assembly tree for it

The substructures may be natural (e.g. the wings, tail and

fuselage of an aeroplane) or may be artificially generated. Our
original hope with this work was to make good use of the user's
knowledge of the problem, perhaps thereby obtaining better
substructures than any automatic procedure could obtain. However our
experience has been that users are very reluctant to provide the
additional data and that when they do, the results are not necessarily
any better than our automatic procedure obtains.

We associate with each node of the assembly tree a square
symmetric "frontal" matrix $A^{(\ell)}$, which is obtained by assembly of the
frontal matrices $A^{(\ell)}$ associated with its children and elimination of
variables not involved elsewhere. The tree in Figure 4 is binary,
that is each non-terminal node has two children. In such a case, the
operations to be performed at each node are uniquely specified. If
the tree is not binary, there remains a choice at each node for the
order of assembly; we may

   i)   assemble first and then eliminate,
  ii)   assemble one-by-one eliminating each variable as soon as
        possible,
 iii)   assemble successive sets of frontal matrices, in each case
        performing eliminations to produce a new frontal matrix.

These three choices correspond to the three approaches for the overall
problem:

   i)   assemble overall matrix, then use band-matrix solution,
  ii)   frontal elimination,
 iii)   lower-level substructuring, as represented in Figure 4.

The conventional approach with substructuring involves approaches (i)
and (ii), which was the advantage of permitting standard codes to be
used for the operations at each node of the tree. However we explore
approach (iii). This actually includes approach (ii) because ordinary
frontal elimination is a special case of substructuring; we
illustrate this in Figure 5 for the problem of Figure 4. Other
possibilities are

   i)   nested dissection (George, 1973),
  ii)   one-way dissection (George, 1977),
 iii)   other automatic choices.

The tree in Figure 4 is an illustration of nested dissection with
three levels of dissection. Other choices (iii) are discussed in
section 5.

Figure 5. Frontal elimination tree for the problem of Figure 4

4.   DEPTH-FIRST TREE SEARCHES

Given an assembly tree such as that shown in Figure 4, there
remains considerable freedom over the order in which the operations
associated with the nodes are performed. It is necessary only that
for every node, its operations are performed after all those for its
children have been performed. A particularly convenient order when
intermediate results have to be held in auxiliary storage is that
associated with a depth-first search of the tree, which can be
expressed in an informal extension of algol 60 as follows

        mark all nodes as unused;
        set node i to the root;
        while node i is unused do
        begin if i has an unused child
              then replace i by its leftmost unused child
              else
              begin mark i as used
                    if i has a right-hand sibling
                    then replace i by its next right-hand sibling
                    else replace i by its parent
              end
        end

At each point when we replace i by its parent, we perform the
assemblies and eliminations associated with the parent node. For
instance the tree of Figure 4 leads to the following sequence of
values for i : 15,13,9,1,2,9,10,3,4,10,13,14,11,5,6,11,12,7,8,12,14,15
and the following sequence for the node operations:
9,10,13,11,12,14,15. The advantage of this order is that a stack may
be used to hold the element matrices generated at the nodes, because
those wanted at a particular node will always be those most recently
generated but not yet used. For example the successive stack contents
for the Figure 4 case are those shown in Figure 6.

										8		
			4			6		7	7	12		
	2		3	3	10		5	5	11	11	11	11	14
1	1	9	9	9	9	13	13	13	13	13	13	13	13	15

Figure 6.   Successive stack contents for the Figure 4 tree

We do not expect that there will be room in main storage for this
stack. We therefore organize it so that its top, the active part, is
always in main storage but that when necessary its bottom is moved to
auxiliary storage.

5.   AUTOMATIC CHOICE OF PIVOT SEQUENCES

In this section we consider the case when a non-binary tree has
been provided so that there remains some choice for the order of
assembly and elimination at the nodes, as discussed in section 3.
This includes the case when the user provides no substructuring
information since here we have a very simple tree consisting of its
root and all the elements as its sons.

A necessary first step in the analysis is to calculate index sets
$s^{(m)}$ for the non-terminal nodes of the tree. These consist of
variables involved in one or more elements that correspond to

descendants of node m and also in one or more elements that are not
descendents of node m. Such a set $S^{(m)}$ indexes the frontal matrix
$A^{(m)}$ created by the assembly of the elements of the substructure
represented by node m and the elimination of all variables internal to
it. Because there are such frontal matrices at every node, the method
is often called "multi-frontal". We find it convenient to regard the
original elements as being labelled by the integers $1,2,...,e$ and the
rest (including the root) to be labelled by integers $m \rangle e$.

Two depth-first searches of the kind described in the last
section permit the generation of such index sets $S^{(m)}$. During the
first search we record the position in the search at which each node
appeared for the last time. During the second search we hold the
least tree level, counting from the root, at which each variable has
appeared in an original element list or a list already found for a
non-terminal node. On returning to a parent node, we construct the
corresponding index list by merging the index lists of its children
and then removing any that are local to the corresponding
substructure. They may be recognized as non-local by having appeared
later in the first search or having already appeared at the same or
lesser (nearer the root) tree level in this search.

Figure 7.   A simple problem with non-binary tree

As an example, consider the problem illustrated in Figure 7. The
depth-first search returns to parents in the order 8,9,10,11.
Amalgamating the index lists of elements 5,6,7 yields the set
$(4,5,6,7,8)$; 7 and 8 do not appear later so may be eliminated to give
the set $(4,5,6)$; these variables are labelled as having least level
1. Next at node 9, amalgamating index sets yields the set
$(2,3,4,5,6)$; 2 and 3 appear later and $(4,5,6)$ are labelled at level 1
so none can be eliminated; 2 and 3 are labelled at level 2. At node
1 the variable 1 can be eliminated at once to give the set $(2,3)$. At
node 10 we merge lists 9 and 1 to give $(2,3,4,5,6)$; none appear later
and 2,3 are labelled at level 2 so may be eliminated to give the set
$(4,5,6)$. Finally $(4,5,6)$ are eliminated at node 11.

Once these index sets have been established, each node with more
than two children can be treated identically. Any variables in the
index set of one or more children but not in that of the parent is to
be eliminated. The aim is to add extra nodes to this part of the tree
in such a way that these eliminations are performed economically.

One possible strategy is a local "minimum-fill" algorithm. If
two frontal matrices with one or more variables in common are
assembled and we order the merged index set thus

   i)   variables in the first index set but not the second

  ii)   variables in both sets, and

 iii)   variable in the second index set but not the first

then the merged matrix, before any eliminations are performed, has the structure shown in Figure 8. If the numbers of variables in the three parts of the matrix are n_1, n_2 and n_3 then additional storage for $n_1 n_3$ zeros will be needed (because of symmetry only half of each matrix $A^{(m)}$ need be stored). Thus a possible strategy is to choose the pair of elements that yields the minimum value for the "fill" $n_1 n_3$, add a new tree node having these as its sons and the same parent as that of all the nodes under consideration. Following this we eliminate from the merged list any variables that we may, that is any not in the list of the parent or any of the other children. Following this we have a new tree with one more node and again all nodes having index lists. The new node has two children so needs no further treatment and the parent has one less child than before. We continue treating the parent until it has only two children, or (exceptionally) until no pairs of children have variables in common. In the latter case no further eliminations are possible, because if any were they could have been performed within the member elements since each involves a separate set of variables; thus any assembly order is equally satisfactory.

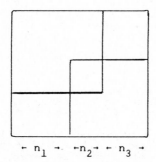

$\leftarrow n_1 \rightarrow$ $\leftarrow n_2 \rightarrow$ $\leftarrow n_3 \rightarrow$

Figure 8.   Merging two frontal matrices

It is interesting that here it is practicable to implement a minimum-fill algorithm, a rare situation for sparse matrix work. The reason is that for a large problem the number of pairs of elements with variables in common is likely to be a modest multiple of the number of elements, and for each pair the numbers n_1, n_2 and n_3 can be calculated in computer time that is proportional to the total number of variables (Gustavson, 1972) (e.g. given a vector of n integers none having value k, run through the first index list setting corresponding components to k then run through the second list testing corresponding components for equality with k). Following the merger of two element matrices, most fill-in values will remain unchanged; we have to perform recalculations only for those pairs of which one element has been merged into the new element.

Notice that this "minimum-fill" strategy has the merit of choosing at once any pair such that one index list is a subset of the other, for then the fill is zero, which is certainly minimal. Such no-fill choices are obviously desirable, since extra storage is certainly not needed, storage from the smaller element is saved and further savings result from eliminations that are possible following the merger.

Any eliminations performed after the merger must be of variables belonging to both index sets, because otherwise they could have been performed within the component element matrices. If both component matrices are full, then the resulting matrix after elimination will also be full (see Figure 8). If this situation pertains, then it will be economical to use full matrix storage for the matrices and minimizing the local fill will be a satisfactory algorithm. Unfortunately this is not always the case. In particular, when discretizing a partial differential equation by finite elements whose nodes are all at corners, merging two adjacent elements will not permit any eliminations except for those on the boundary in a two-dimensional problem, and not even then in a three-dimensional problem. This is reflected in our experience on actual problems, see section 7, table 1, example 3.

Fortunately the algorithm of minimum degree, called "scheme 2" when introduced by Tinney and Walker (1967), can also be implemented efficiently in this situation. Here we choose the next variable to be eliminated from those present in the lists of the children but not present in the index list of the parent. The degree of such a variable is the number of variables present in all the elements with which it is associated, i.e. it is the size of the assembled matrix that results from assembling all the elements to which it belongs. We add a new tree node that has as children all the nodes whose index lists contain this variable and has the original parent as parent. For convenience in our code we also introduce additional nodes if the new node has more than two sons, in order to construct a binary subtree that specifies the exact order of assembly of the corresponding elements; since no eliminations can take place until all have been assembled, the exact choice of binary tree is immaterial. It frequently happens that several variables are present in the same set of elements, have the same minimum degree and may be eliminated together once their elements are assembled; we exploit this in our code, calculating the degree only once for each such set. Note that by eliminating them together we are still keeping to the minimum degree algorithm because once one has been eliminated the rest have degree one less than previously and this is the new minimum, and similarly as the rest are eliminated. Following these assemblies and eliminations, new values for the degrees need only be calculated for the variables of the new element since the degrees of all other variables are unchanged.

6. SOFTWARE DESIGN

Our software package, which we call Treesolv, is designed for convenience of use and to partition its workspace automatically between main and auxiliary storage.

For convenient use, we require that the problem be specified by a sequence of calls to a small number of subroutines. They are the following

i)   INIT which must be called once before commencing any new problem;

ii) INELV which must be called once for each element to specify its index list;

iii) INELR which must be called at least once for each element to
specify the real values in its element matrix $A^{(m)}$; if $A^{(m)}$
is very large it may be specified in parts by consecutive calls;

iv) INSUP which must be called to specify that certain nodes are
children of a given node, thus permitting a user to provide
substructuring information;

v)   INSAME which must be called to specify that two substructures
(subtrees) are identical so that only one (the master) need be
processed;

vi) FACTOR which must be called to request that the structure of
the problem be analyzed (using the minimum-degree algorithm,
see section 5), the matrices assembled and all possible
eliminations performed and the factors stored on file; and

vii) SOLVE which is called to solve a set of equations whose matrix
has been specified and factorized by previous calls.

We permit considerable freedom over the order in which the
subroutines are called. INIT must be called first. Following this
INELV, INELR, INSUP, INSAME may be called in any order except where
several INELR calls are used for the reals of one matrix $A^{(m)}$ (such
calls must be consecutive). Only the topology of the problem, i.e.
the information passed through INELV, INSUP and INSAME, need be
specified before FACTOR is called. If the reals have not been
specified then FACTOR analyses the problem and makes available
information about the number of actual operations and the amount of
file space that will be needed for actual processing; it then returns
asking for appropriate INELR calls to be made prior to a recall of
FACTOR.

We use four random-access files. One holds integer information,
one holds real information, one is for integer workspace and once is
for real workspace. The integer file holds the index lists associated
with each node and specifies when each variable is eliminated. The
real file holds the reals of the original element matrices $A^{(m)}$, the
reals of a master copy of any substructure matrix $A^{(m)}$ that is
repeated in different parts of the tree and the reals of the rows of
the factor matrix U. The workfiles are needed principally because we
do not assume that we have enough main storage to store the biggest of
the matrices $A^{(m)}$. Its principal role is to hold the stack of
intermediate results generated during the depth-first search (see
section 4).

Our aim is for the most active part of the stack (its top) to
reside in main store while the less active part (its bottom) is moved
to auxiliary store. Although we could have used a fixed threshold
(actually one threshold for the reals and one for the integers) we
felt that it was very desirable to share main storage dynamically with
that needed for reading the frontal matrices $A^{(m)}$ from file and
performing the assembles, eliminations and forward and backward
substitutions. For example, during forward and backward substitution
the stack is not needed at all, so all the main storage can be used
for buffering the matrix factor U. A satisfactory way to handle this
is by using a single buffer for all four files, divided into fixed
length sections that we will call "pages", do all transfers by reading
or writing whole pages and let the demand control which are
transferred. For page management it suffices to use the simple rule

that when space is required, the page least recently accessed is filed (or overwritten if it has not been changed since it was read). It means that priority is given to supplying main storage for assembling a large element over holding the middle of the stack and that during forward and backward substitution as much as possible of the later rows of U, read during forward substitution, is retained for backward substitution. The package of subroutines that manages these paged transfers has been placed in the Harwell Subroutine Library (Hopper, 1984) under the name OF01.

Besides the paging buffer, other main memory arrays are needed by Treesolv, viz.

i)   an array holding four pointers for each tree node:

    a)   a pointer to the next right-hand sibling or to the parent if there is no such node

    b)   a pointer to the left-most child

    c)   a pointer to an entry in the file of integers

    d)   a pointer to an entry in the file of reals.

ii) an integer workarray of size the number of variables, used to enable rapid merging of lists of integers (see section 5)

iii) a full array to pass the vector b to SOLVE (or vectors, since SOLVE allows multiple vectors b) and return the solution x (or solutions).

iv) a few smaller arrays of size related to the number of tree levels (size that the stack may reach) and the maximum number of variables in an element matrix.

In our initial design, these arrays were all placed in COMMON, but this proved too awkward since it required the user to estimate good upper bounds on the sizes required. Therefore we have altered the package so that these arrays are all passed through arguments and a driver subdivides a large workarray dynamically; if an array proves to be too small the driver subdivides the array afresh and recalls the package.

7.   NUMERICAL EXPERIENCE

We summarize in Table 1 our experience in the use of Treesolv on four problems kindly supplied by A.J. Donovan of C.E.G.B. It may be seen that in all but the third case, the minimum-fill criterion gave slightly better results than the minimum degree criterion but it was disastrously much worse in the third case. The reason for this poor behaviour was explained in section 5. We have now replaced the minimum-fill strategy by the minimum-degree strategy because of this occasional very poor performance and also because it demands much more temporary storage if it is given a large problem with no substructures (because the number of adjacent pairs of elements can be rather large). Our original design was on the assumption that large problems would come naturally substructured, but in practice this appears not to be so.

Note in table 1 that the time for analysis (call to FACTOR without any reals) is always much less than the time to actually

J.K. Reid

factorize the matrix, particularly when the original elements are large (cases 1 and 4). This satisfactory situation pertains because during analysis we work with linear index lists symbolically representing operations on full triangular arrays of the same order. Thus an order-of-magnitude less operations are needed during analysis than during actual factorization.

	3D cylinder with flange	2D reactor core section	Framework: essentially in 2D	Turbine blade
Number of variables	2919	3024	3306	2802
Number of elements	128	551	791	108
Maximum number of variables in an element	60	16	12	60
Thousands of non-zeros in U	357 (374)	116 (122)	100 (69)	236 (276)
Millions of floating-point operations	56 (61)	6 (7)	8 (2.2)	23 (33)
Time (IBM 370/168 secs) Analysis	2	4	5	1
Factorization	71	13	26	32
Solution	3	1	1	2

Table 1   Performance on some structural problems from CEGB, using minimum-fill strategy, with minimum-degree results in brackets.

		2919	3024
Number of variables		2919	3024
Number of elements		128	551
Maximum number of variables in an element		60	16
Millions of floating-point operations		61	6.2
Inner loop time	seconds Mflops	2.4 25	0.4 14
overall processor time	seconds Mflops	4.2 14	1.6 4
Equivalent total time	seconds Mflops	11 5	2.3 3

Table 2   Performance of the first two cases from Table 1 on CRAY-1 computer

Note also the high overall execution rate, particularly in the first and fourth cases, despite all the data movement involved.

In Table 2, we show the result of running the first two CEGB problems on the CRAY-1 computer. Here we have separated out the time spent in the innermost loop (Gaussian elimination on a full symmetric matrix), the overall central processor time and the equivalent total time (where wait time, scaled by the average fraction of main store occupied, is included). It is the equivalent total time that is used for charging purposes and so it can be seen that the wait time gives rise to significant cost on the CRAY-1. Furthermore, it may be seen that the inner loop is gaining benefit from vectorization and executing at a speed comparable with that of full matrix code written in Fortran, but this leaves the remaining operations contributing significantly to the total time.

	Profile solvers			Treesolv
	Old	Old+ GPS	New+ GPS	
Matrix order		1074		
Maximum number of variables in an element		24		
Semi-band width	612	138	138	–
Storage $\times 10^4$	11	9	9	7
Central processor time (secs)	44	34	11	22
i/o $\times 10^6$	4.6	2.7	1.2	1.6
i/o time (secs)	73	51	16	145
Cost	130	98	37	176
Millions of floating-point operations	12	7	7	5

Table 3   Loden's UNIVAC 1100/83 comparison of an early version of Treesolv with profile solvers on giro problem

Loden (1980) compared the earlier minimum degree version of Treesolv (which he called SPARTA) with profile solvers available at Lockheed Palo Alto Research Laboratory. Shown in Table 3 are the results for his 'Giro' problem, whose geometry is essentially toroidal, but with additional structures. He used a long-established (old) profile solver without node reordering, he preceded this with node reordering using the algorithm of Gibbs, Poole and Stockmeyer (1976) and he used an improved (new) code also preceded by node reordering. It may be seen that for this problem Treesolv required less storage and less operations than the other codes, less central processor time than the old versions but its high input-output time meant that it was always more expensive to run. It was not using the present input-output package so some improvement in overall cost is possible but the reduction in number of operations is insufficient for any improved version of Treesolv to show dramatic gains on this problem over the best profile solver.

A larger problem, called "cross-cone" by Loden because its geometry is that of a cone attached to a cross, illustrates the potential of Treesolv's approach. Loden's results are shown in Table

4. Here Treesolv reduces the number of operations by the factor 6 and
storage by the factor 3. The overall cost is better than the old
profile program but is not better than the new one. However if the
input-output were performed as efficiently relative to the central
processor time as it is on the IBM or the CRAY-1 then Treesolv would
be the cheapest.

Finally we show in Table 5 some data on a very large problem
considered by Manteuffel (1979). His estimate of the magnitude of
direct solution is shown in column 1 and he decided that this approach
was impractical. By passing the structure of the problem (with one
variable per node instead of 3) to Sparspak (George, Liu and Ng, 1980)
we were able to estimate that node reordering would substantially
reduce the magnitude of the problem. The use of Treesolv would allow
a further worthwhile gain.

	Profile solvers		Treesolv
	Old	New	
Matrix order		3491	
Maximum number of variables in an element		24	
Semi-band width	958	958	–
Storage × 10^4	62	62	23
Central processor time (secs)	326	161	65
i/o time (secs)	289	117	415
cost	629	290	503
Millions of floating point operations	114	114	19

Table 4   Loden's UNIVAV 1100/83 comparison of an early version
            of Treesolv with profile solvers on cross-cone problem

	Profile approach		Treesolv
	Manteuffel estimate	Sparspak reordered	
Matrix order		17928	
Maximum number of variables in an element		60	
Semi-band width	~1300	~650	–
Storage × 10^6	~23	~12	4.8
Millions of floating-point operations	~30	~8	2.1

Table 5   A comparison of the profile approach and Treesolv
            on Manteuffel's problem

8. ACKNOWLEDGEMENTS

I would like to thank P.S. Jensen for his original interest in this work, without which I would not have begun, and the US Air Force for their partial support under grant AFOSR-81-0040.

9. REFERENCES

George, A. (1973). Nested dissection of a regular finite element mesh. SIAM J. Numer. Anal. 10, 345-363.

George, A. (1977). Numerical experiments using dissection methods to solve nxn grid problems. SIAM J. Numer. Anal. 14, 161-179.

George, A., Liu, J. and Ng, E. (1980). User guide for SPARSPAK: Waterloo sparse linear equations package. Report CS-78-30 (Jan. 1980 revision). Dept. Comp. Sci., Univ. of Waterloo.

Gibbs, N.E., Poole, W.G. Jnr. and Stockmeyer, P.K. (1976). An algorithm for reducing the bandwidth and profile of a sparse matrix. SIAM J. Numer. Anal. 13, 236-250.

Gustavson, F.G. (1972). Some basic techniques for solving sparse systems of linear equations. In Rose and Willoughby (1972), 41-52.

Hopper, M.J. (1984). (Ed.). Harwell Subroutine Library. A catalogue of subroutines (1984). Harwell report AERE-R.9185 (5th edition).

Irons, B.M. (1970). A frontal solution program for finite element analysis. Int. J. Numer. Meth. Engng. 2, 5-32.

Loden, W.A. (1980). A comparison of two sparse matrix processing techniques for structural analysis applications. In Jensen and Loden (1980), 27-64.

Jensen, P.S. and Loden, W.A. (1980). Supplementary study on the sensitivity of optimized structures. Report LMSC-D777859. Lockheed Palo Alto Research Laboratory.

Manteuffel, T.A. (1980). An incomplete factorization technique for positive definite linear systems. Math. Comp. 34, 473-498.

Rose, D.J. and Willoughby, R.A. Eds. (1972). Sparse matrices and their applications. Plenum Press, New York.

Tinney, W.F. and Walker, J.W. (1967). Direct solutions of sparse network equations by optimally ordered triangular factorization. Proc. IEEE, 55, 1801-1809.

Wilkinson, J.H. (1961). Error analysis of direct methods of matrix inversion. J. ACM. 8, 281-330.

DISCUSSION

Speaker: J Reid

Sewell: The simple frontal method can be thought of as imposing implicitly an
orderering on the nodes similar to that of the Cuthill-McKee ordering. Thus the
operations count for the simple frontal method (ignoring I/O operations) is of
order n^2 and the icore storage is of order n for an approximately square 2-D
finite-element problem with n unknowns. The multifrontal methods you discussed
are apparently the out-of-core analogues for minimum degree and nested
dissection algorithms. Thus the operation count is now of order $n^{3/2}$. What is the
storage (in-core) count order?

Sherman: The internal storage should be O(n) for a square problem using nested
dissection (and, most likely, for minimum degree). This is the storage for the
frontal matrix corresponding to the largest dissection separator (of size $O(n^{1/2})$
nodes) and to a subtree of the assembly tree rooted at the actual tree root.
Further storage reduction could only be achieved through more complicated I/O
involving the individual entries of this largest frontal matrix during assembly
and elimination. (This could also be done with the ordinary frontal method). As a
side remark, it can be shown that the largest frontal matrix will always have at
least O(n) entries for a square problem, independent of ordering.

Reid: I agree. In fact my code does not require that the frontal matrix resides
entirely in core when active, but other parts of the code require O(n) storage
in core.

Duff: A normal feature of sparse matrix work is the use of several indexing
(integer) arrays of length n, the number of variables. Since in your applications
n can be very large, these overhead vectors could contribute significantly to the
core requirements. Could you comment on this, in particular indicating how many
such arrays are required by your package?

Reid: There is only one integer array of length n, but other arrays may be of
comparable length. There is an array holding four pointers for each tree node.
There is an array whose length depends on the problem structure but must be at
least five times the number of "supervariables" in a substructure, where a
supervariable is a set of variables each of which is contained in the same set of
elements. And there is an array of length at least three times the greatest
number of variables in a frontal matrix. All these arrays are collected into a
single array that the user has to supply and this array is dynamically subdivided.

Hockney: The tree structure clearly lends itself to parallel computation and you
discussed the performance of TREESOLV on the CRAY-1. It would appear that data
movement is a much as determining factor in the overall efficiency as the actual
arithmetic. Hence the strict use of Megaflops to compare algorithms is wanting,
could you suggest a more appropriate measure for such machines?

Reid: For the floating-point operations it would be preferable to record the
number of vector operations (q, say) as well as the total number of floating-point
operations (s, say) for then the inner-loop time can be approximated by an
expression of the form $\alpha q + \beta s$ on vector machines.

Codes such as mine are also much affected by the costs of data movement. I do keep
some statistics on this and will include them for the examples in the final written
version.

Hockney: The formula $\alpha q + \beta s$ is exactly that which is used in the "$n_{1/2}$ method of
algorithm analysis" which is the subject of the last talk at this conference. In

my notation the run time of the algorithm is $T=r_\infty^{-1}(s+qn_{1/2})$ where $r_\infty=\beta^{-1}$ and $n_{1/2}=\alpha/\beta$. The value of the latter notation is that one finds it is $n_{1/2}$ (i.e. the ratio α to β) which is important in comparing the performance of alternative algorithms on the same computer, rather than the values of α and β separately. This allows one to draw simple "algorithmic phase diagrams" for choosing algorithms, some of which are given in the last talk.

Duff: Could you be more precise on the portability of your code? For example, how easy was it to move the code from the IBM to the CRAY?

Reid: It satisfies PFORT apart from direct-access I/O statements confined in one small subroutine. My friends at Lockheed were very agreeably surprised to fine it so easy to compile on CDC equipment and I have had no problems porting it to the CRAY, apart from the I/O operations. I did need to add a special comment in order to get the innermost loop to vectorize.

Sherman: Your experience on the CRAY parallels our own with a similar code operating entirely in-core. We find that most of the CPU time goes to operations (non-numerical, largely) not in the inner loop. Also, the inner loop is often executed for small subproblems for which it does not run at asymptotic rates.

Rice: Your performance data shows that I/O is a very significant factor in the total cost. Do you plan or hope to have better, special I/O to use with your package? Is it possible that the advantage of the other codes you mention comes from their assembly language I/O?

Reid: Iain Duff has recently been experimenting with the Cray Fortran 77 I/O facilities. He recommends non-standard I/O, but the loss in switching to Fortran 77 is typically about 35% which might in many situations be an acceptable overhead. Unfortunately the Lockheed experiments were outside my control so I cannot be sure, but it is my belief that some tuning for my code would have been possible.

Schönauer: In my experience direct methods for the solution of linear equations from pde's are mostly feasible in two dimensions. In three dimensions one should use iterative methods because they have no fill-in. The fill-in in direct methods not only affects the operation count but also the I/O. Do you have any comments on this?

Reid: In general, I agree. Note however that whether a single problem or a set of problems with the same matrix is to be solved has an important effect. If the factorization cost of a direct method can be shared over several problems then it will still be competitive for larger problems.

PDE SOFTWARE: Modules, Interfaces and Systems
B. Engquist and T. Smedsaas (eds.)
Elsevier Science Publishers B.V. (North-Holland)
© IFIP, 1984

SESAM'80 : A MODULAR FINITE ELEMENT SYSTEM FOR ANALYSIS OF STRUCTURES

Petter E. Bjørstad

Det norske Veritas
P.O. Box 300
N-1322 Høvik
NORWAY

SESAM'80 is a large commercial finite element package developed
by Det norske Veritas in the period 1979-1982. This paper will
describe the system with particular emphasis on the modularity and
the interfaces between modules. The implementation and some
capabilities of a few important modules will be outlined. Design requirements and tradeoffs between portability/efficiency and
generality/efficiency are discussed, together with the question of
code adaptability in a rapidly expanding field of computer technology and algorithmic development.

ACKNOWLEDGEMENT

The work to be described in this paper has been carried out by Det norske Veritas. A
large number of people participated in the SESAM'80 project group during the project
development phase. The author appreciates the information gained from numerous discussions with many individuals in the project group. Advice from the SESAM'80 project
leader, Dr. Nils Sandsmark, has been indispensable in the preparation of this work.

INTRODUCTION

SESAM'80 - Super **E**lement **S**tructural **A**nalysis **M**odules is a large commercial finite
element package developed by Det norske Veritas in the period 1979-1982.

Det norske Veritas is one of the leading societies in classification of ships and offshore
structures. All the activities of the institution are directed towards safeguarding of life, environment, and property at sea and ashore. In the quality assurance of structures, systems
and equipment, reliable analysis tools are vital. For this purpose Veritas started using the
finite element method as early as 1960. A large finite element package called SESAM'69
emerged and has been used by Veritas in the period 1969-1982. Unfortunately, SESAM'69
was not a modular design that easily adapted to new situations and extensions. As both
computer technology and our knowledge about software development advanced, it became
clear that a new, open-ended, modular finite element system would be necessary.

The development of SESAM'80 has been a very large project, the code contains several
hundred thousand lines of Fortran-77 code and has required approximately 130 man years
of effort. It is worthwhile to notice that this kind of development ideally involves many different kinds of professionals: structural engineers, specialists on the finite element method
as applied to engineering problems, computer scientists working with file systems, interactive graphics and high level command languages and numerical analysts working with reliability and efficiency of the numerical algorithms. This specialization within a software project
is a fairly recent phenomenon with its own difficult points. People from different fields
often face communication barriers due to different terminology and different points of view.
In a large project were more than 20 people working on the same system, it is almost
impossible to get a uniform standard. Very few people if any, will be able to understand
all the different subtasks and many project workers will need on the job training in order

to carry out their assignments.

PROBLEMS AND QUESTIONS

SESAM'80 is designed as a general purpose finite element system for use in structural analysis. The requirements in this field today, asks for special capabilities within every specific application area. This can most conveniently be satisfied by a modular collection of preprocessors and postprocessors interacting with the analysis modules.   SESAM'80 currently has special capabilities for the analysis and design of ships and offshore struc- tures. The design of the system makes it possible to add new application capabilities as required.

The largest structures that have been analyzed with the Sesam system, are North Sea oil production platforms. More than half a million unknowns can enter the finite element model and a complete analysis may require the equivalent of 1000 hours of cpu on a Vax-11/780.

Such an analysis have several problem areas. The structure itself may rest on the sea floor creating a structure - soil interaction problem. Furthermore, the ocean will exert forces on the structure due to current and waves. Finally the upper part of the platform will be affected by wind. These environmental forces must be calculated in order to carry out the structural analysis itself. The partial differential equations that enter the problem, come from continuum mechanics as well as fluid mechanics. The theory of beams, shells and solids are used in the structural analysis part while potential theory and Morrisons equation are currently used in the fluid mechanics problem area. Potential theory are used on large volume bodies. The vortex shedding problem and possible approximations of the Navier Stoke equations for solving slender body problems, are subject to active research, but the heuristic Morrison equation is still being used in applications. Finally, it should be pointed out that the differential equations may appear as a coupled system.

Given such a problem involving soil, fluids and structure, what answer should the computer ideally return? That is what questions are typically asked?

> Does this platform conform with the rules and standards of the AWS? (American Welding Society)
>
> In what locations of this concrete structure should more reinforce- ment be placed?
>
> When will this structure need inspection (or replacement) due to fatigue?

One easily understands that a solution to the core partial differential equations needs further processing in order to approach the type of questions asked.

AN OUTLINE OF THE SESAM'80 ARCHITECTURE

The modularity of the system extends over several levels. Each main module has an inter- nal modularity with internal interfaces. Figure 1 describes the main modules in the Sesam system.

One will notice from Figure 1 that the structural analysis part of the system is classified as one set of (central) modules surrounded by many more interacting modules. In fact, the main advance and effort in SESAM'80 lies in the development of pre- and postprocessing modules. Due to the complex geometries and the difficult modeling of real world problems by finite elements, it has been realized that this should be accomplished by interactive, graphics based, high level command languages.

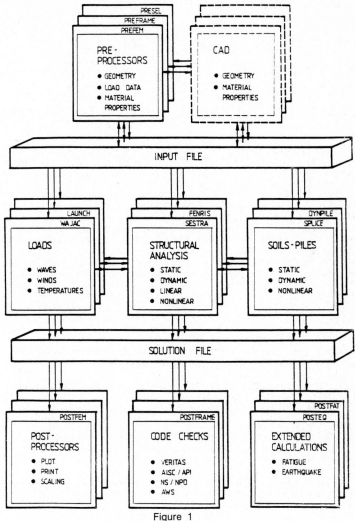

Figure 1
SESAM'80; Basic Architecture

Another important aspect of finite element analysis, is the often overwhelming amounts of output that can be produced. In order to extract useful information and to guarantee that all output data are consistent with predetermined rules and design criteria for a given structure, postprocessor modules are of utmost importance.

PREPROCESSOR MODULES

The objective of preprocessor modules is to convert a convenient problem description into a standard formulation that can be used as input to the finite element structural analysis programs. The key principle when designing a preprocessor is to minimize the total elapsed time of an analysis including human effort. In addition, the preprocessor provides a way of ensuring reliability of the input data.

Important aspects of preprocessor based work is the generation of geometrical data, node properties and external loads. A reordering of the internal node numbers in order to optimize the equation solvers is also performed as a preprocessing task. The main tools for validity checks within the preprocessors are graphics based. These modules are primarily designed as interactive programs, but a file containing the input commands are always created. This file provides a very compact way of storing information, it can later be modified and used to regenerate the same or slightly modified models for new analysis.

Another important concept in the SESAM'80 architecture, is the use of substructures or superelements throughout all phases of the analysis. A substructure is often a natural part of the structure to be modeled, but it is not restricted to be such a physical substructure. In general a substructure is defined to be any connected collection of finite elements in the model. This is often equivalently called a superelement. It is very fundamental that such a superelement can be treated in the same way as traditional finite elements. Internal degrees of freedom can be eliminated in each superelement and the superelements can be assembled into yet higher level superelements. In this way, a complete model can be built from the assembly of elements and superelements. This approach offers great advantages when modeling complex structures. Different engineers can work on separate parts of the structure, having discussed only the interface between the subparts. Also, a new analysis can be performed on a redesigned structure by only remodeling the structure that changed. Each substructure can be defined using a preprocessor to generate the finite element discretization. There is a special preprocessor available for putting different substructures together, forming a higher level superelement.

One advantage of this technique is the possible use of identical substructures (repeated superelements). Only one such substructure is created using the preprocessor and the corresponding Cholesky factorization is only computed once.

Figure 2 illustrates how a model of an offshore structure can be generated by first using a frame preprocessor to generate the deck and the legs separately. Next, the preprocessor for the superelement assembly has been used to create the global model.

INTERFACE FILES

There are two principal interface files. The input or preprocessor interface file is a card image oriented file containing the input to the analysis modules. This file is thoroughly documented and thus provide a way of coupling new programs to the system. In order to be flexible (and at a certain price in efficiency) records can come in almost any order. The file can be both formatted and unformatted.

Similarly there is an output or postprocessor interface file. The design of this file has been guided by the same principles. Together the two files give a complete decoupling of pre- and postprocessors from the analysis modules.

ENVIRONMENTAL MODULES

Environmental modules are computer programs that are used to compute the loads on the structure under consideration. In the linear case, this can be viewed as a special preprocessor, but since data from these modules may be needed at many stages in a nonlinear solution process, their organization must be different. Thus, the system is capable of solving problems involving fluid - structure interaction. The modules computing hydrodynamical loads are completely independent and are often operated as stand alone units. The communication between modules is by way of the file system. The numerical methods being used today, does not even use the finite element method. This flexible approach does have the drawback that extensive data transport and data conversion must take place between modules.

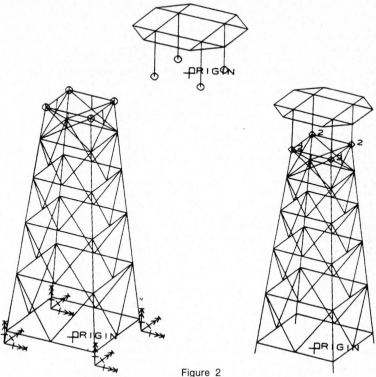

Figure 2
Automatic Generation of Substructures and Assembly

STRUCTURAL ANALYSIS MODULES

There are two principal finite element codes for structural analysis, depending on the analysis being linear or non-linear.

The linear program called SESTRA (Super Element STRuctural Analysis), is not restricted by problem size, even on fairly small computers. It is intended to solve a broad range of different problems both static and dynamic, selecting appropriate internal routines to carry out the required subtasks. The system is built on a number of basic libraries. There is a special element library performing standard calculations on a large number of basic elements. There are currently 33 different elements being used and the addition of new elements into the system is quite easy. Similarly, a general finite element programming system implementing the superelement technique, is used as the main programming tool in SESTRA. This system allows an arbitrary number of levels in the superelement hierarchy, in practice, the number is seldom higher than 5. These programming tools are managed from a set of SESTRA modules designed to carry out specific tasks that may be required in the full analysis. The execution path in SESTRA is controlled by a master program. The linear algebra is based on a block-matrix approach. A library of in-core routines has been built to do matrix operations, linear systems and eigenvalue calculations. A corresponding library of out-of-core routines (performing the same operations), uses the in-core library to implement block algorithms requiring only a few blocks in memory simultaneously. These blocks are transferred between memory and disk using an I/O system that can operate with buffered, nonbuffered and asynchronous transfers depending on efficiency considerations. The buffering system uses a shared pool of buffers implementing a least recently used strategy. A separate integer data structure containing address and pointer information is used to keep track of the floating point data. Thus, zero blocks are always treated implicitly and never operated on. The implementation of the Cholesky algorithm is therefore equivalent to a block profile algorithm. It should be stressed, that this system permits different data structures that do not depend on a sub-matrix formulation. The implementation of alternative numerical algorithms is therefore possible.

The nonlinear programming system FENRIS (Finite Element NonlineaR Integrated System) is a joint research development project between Veritas, The Norwegian Institute of Technology and The Society of Industrial and Technical Research. It is based on a continuum mechanics foundation allowing large displacements, rotations and strains in addition to material nonlinearities. The system does not use the superelement technique, but it can take advantage of the substructure formulation provided by the preprocessors. The linear equations being solved inside the nonlinear iterative loops, use a profile storage and solution scheme. Despite being an out-of-core based implementation, there are more assumptions on problem size related to the available computing resources. Efficiency and speed of execution are very important in a nonlinear code of this kind, this aspect has been given more weight in the efficiency/generality compromise than in the linear case. The code is oriented towards specific problem areas and theories by means of satellite programs, each satellite being set up to handle a smaller problem class. An element library is available in addition to a special material library, being able to take material nonlinearities into account.

POSTPROCESSING MODULES

The postprocessing modules are necessary to perform calculations and processing on the huge amount of data that are usually output from the finite element analysis program. In this way the results can be presented in an interactive session with a graphics terminal. The engineer can more easily select plots and prints that are interesting. A second very important objective is to perform automatic checks of the results with rules and standards that have been set for the given structure. With an increasing number of certifying authorities this task would have been extremely time consuming without special software modules. Lastly, postprocessors can perform further calculations on the output data. Fatigue and earthquake analysis are important examples of this kind.

DISCUSSION OF SYSTEM INTERFACES

The formulation of a physical problem in mathematical terms is today often hidden for the user. As the mathematical model is refined and specialized to include nonlinear phenomena, the underlying assumptions tend to be more complex and therefore more difficult to grasp for the user with a specific problem at hand. This can make interpretations of results more difficult and in the worst case, lead to wrong conclusions. The problem is indeed a challenging one; how can a software system guard against wrong use and possibly wrong conclusions due to limited understanding of the assumptions on the underlying mathematical model? This problem is getting more apparent as system complexity increases while at the same time they are being used by a larger and larger user group.

The representation and solution of a mathematical model, using discrete approximations and numerical methods on a computer, is crucial for any software system. This area is truly the domain of numerical analysts and mathematicians, large systems like SESAM'80 tend to use well proven, conservative techniques and methods. Thus this interface problem is normally of little concern, the price being a potentially loss in efficiency.

The transformation of numerical models and algorithms into production quality software, is the most demanding task as viewed from a large programming project like this. This is the area where most of the man effort (and money) is spent. The choice of Fortran as programming language, is without alternatives today and in the immediate future. It seems, that the only way to improve the programming environment imposed by Fortran, is by extensive use of software development tools and the slow evolution of the language itself.

The software must be modular, and several stages in the overall solution procedure naturally arise. Both the flow of the analysis through preprocessors, analysis modules and postprocessors, as well as the subdividing of the underlying problem into substructures are ways of breaking up the calculation into manageable pieces.

The interface between software system and computer system represents an area that is still quite unsatisfactory. There is a considerable difference between a fully .portable system of this size and complexity and the efficient implementation of such a system on any given computer. More standardization across machines with respect to operating systems, would be desirable. The I/O capabilities of the computer system can influence the performance of large finite element codes very dramatically. Computer graphics and special hardware architecture for efficient number crunching are also topics that currently must receive more attention.

The final interface between man and computer, has improved dramatically from the first finite element systems. This development seems certain to continue, making advanced tools more easily available to a larger group of people.

CONFLICTING REQUIREMENTS

The conflict between program generality and execution time when solving a specific problem is unavoidable. All problems in SESAM'80 are solved using I/O to disk. Also, being able to handle many different situations without any preset limits on the size of quantities that enter, leads to many branches and complex program logic. Small and medium sized problems will suffer at the expense of having a system capable of solving very large problems. Also, special problems are often solved inefficiently. The generality and flexibility of the system is considered more important than the ability to solve special problems in special ways. The goal will always be to solve the problems that are most often encountered in a time which is essentially equal to that of a specialized program for the same problem class.

SYSTEM ADAPTABILITY

The final test for a large software product like SESAM'80 is its ability to adapt and take advantage of new knowledge about the problems that are attempted solved, of new insights in software development and numerical algorithms, and of new computer architectures. In order to survive, the program must be able to change dynamically with time and in this sense it will never be completed. The answer to this challenge depends largely on the modularity. Modules can be added, changed or replaced, often without affecting the user interface at all. The resources committed to maintenance and extensions are presently of the order 5 man-year per year. Until now, the emphasis has been put on reducing the man-time required for a given problem. As a consequence, the development of pre- and postprocessors have been given a high priority. It is clear that more work on reducing the cpu- and elapsed time in the computer will receive more attention over the next few years. In order to take advantage of new hardware technology, the data structures and internal file systems are also likely to be modified.

The core linear equation solvers are all based on Gaussian elimination. A main reason for this is the frequent need to solve the same system with many, arbitrarily different, right hand sides. In many applications, the solution time for each new left hand side is significant, and an iterative method must be able to meet this time in order to be competitive. However, as larger and larger problems emerge, there might again be cases where iterative methods should be attractive. A very interesting and quite promising technique for the future, is the use of multigrid methods in these large finite element codes. In particular, the use of algebraic multigrid is a very attractive possibility.

DISCUSSION

Speaker: P. Bjørstad

Hockney: Apparently data transport is an expensive part of your runs. Do you
have ways of estimating these times a priori and hence of designing your
algorithms to minimize this cost?

Bjørstad: The data transport is performed by a selfcontained data handling system
using internal buffering. If one avoids interaction between this system and the
host computer paging system, the data transport can be estimated. Monitoring the
data transfer of the existing code is an important aspect of this task. We are
currently looking at the issue of optimizing the system with respect to data
transport.

Brandt: You stressed the advantages of direct-methods when one must resolve the
same system with many different loads. I should like to point out that multi-grid
techniques can also take advantage of previous solutions and perform subsequent
re-solutions even much more quickly than the initial fast solution. For example
relaxation on the finest grid should usually be performed only in neighbourhoods
where the problem data has changed.

Bjørstad: I do not know how this is possible for arbitrarily different right-hand
sides.

Brandt: This is possible if the right-hand side (or the left-hand side, for that
matter) changes are mostly local.

Madsen: Some of the difficulties you mention are associated with restrictions of
the Fortran programming language. Particularly problems of user interface. Have
you considered the use of other languages?

Bjørstad: The use of FORTRAN is dictated by economic considerations, there is
today no other programming language that can support a system like SESAM '80 on
different computers and with sufficient degree of standardization. The FORTRAN-77
standard was a step in the right direction, and in my opinion, an evolutionary
process changing FORTRAN into a better language is the only feasible way of
progress on this issue in this application area. I would like to add that the use
of advanced programming development tools can improve productivity and alleviate
some of the constraints imposed by the FORTRAN environment.

Lawson: You mentioned that a general solution scheme costs ten times that of a
specific scheme. Was this the cost for development of the codes or for the solution
using these codes?

Bjørstad: This cost estimate referred to the development of software and is
measured by project budgets. The measure is economic and order of magnitude only.
With respect to computer cost using a general code, it is a design goal that this
should be of the same magnitude as that of a special code provided the problem is
within the class of problems that motivated the development of the general code.

Rice: What are the sizes of the input file and solution file for large
applications?

Bjørstad: The input file will normally be proportional to the number of nodes in
the problem. The output file can be much larger since it is proportional to the
number of nodes times the number of quantities requested for each node. In a
dynamic analysis the solution file may therefore contain the time history of many

nodes in the model.
It is not unusual that these file can be 4-5 Megabytes. I would like to point out that a large application, using the superelement technique, will generate one input file and one solution file for each superelement of substructure thus limiting the size of the individual files.

Duff: You mentioned that you intend to investigate the solution of Navier Stokes equations further. Could you give some idea of the progress of work in this area particularly regarding vortex shedding? Presumably this would entail considerable changes to SESAM '80.

Bjørstad: This is indeed an area of active research at many institutions around the world. We are very interested in this research, but anticipate the most of the theoretical effort will be carried out at universities. Important work as it relates to the problem area of interest to Veritas is, in particular, carried out at NTH in Norway and at MIT.
New hydrodynamical load modules will be developed within the SESAM system as our knowledge of this problem area advances. The modularity and well-defined interfaces between the structural analysis modules and the environmental load modules should facilitate such extensions.

PDE SOFTWARE: Modules, Interfaces and Systems
B. Engquist and T. Smedsaas (eds.)
Elsevier Science Publishers B.V. (North-Holland)
© IFIP, 1984

A PORTABLE VECTOR-CODE FOR AUTONOMOUS MULTIGRID MODULES

P.W. Hemker, P. Wesseling & P.M. de Zeeuw

Centre for Mathematics and Computer Science, Amsterdam,

and University of Technology, Delft,

The Netherlands

The implementation is described of two multigrid algorithms for
use as standard subroutines for the efficient solution of linear
systems that arise from 7-point discretizations of elliptic PDEs
on a rectangle. For both algorithms a tuned scalar-version and a
tuned vector-version have been constructed and run on a CYBER 170,
a CRAY 1 and a CYBER 205. The CPU-times are given and compared.
The implementation is available in portable ANSI-FORTRAN.

INTRODUCTION

In this paper we describe software for the solution of discretized 2nd order linear
elliptic PDEs in two space dimensions. The domain of definition is assumed to be a
rectangle and the discretization is assumed to result in a regular 7-diagonal matrix.
The algorithms, based on multigrid cycling, are selected for efficiency. The aim
was to obtain software that is perceived and can be used just like any standard
subroutine for solving systems of linear equations. The user has to specify only
the matrix and the right-hand-side, and remains unaware of the underlying multigrid method. Such a subroutine, that operates without outside interference, will
be called autonomous. We find that a large class of equations can be solved efficiently by use of our autonomous multigrid subroutines. The equation may be non-
self-adjoint, and its coefficients are arbitrary.
The two algorithms use saw-tooth multigrid cycles [8,9]. One algorithm is based
on ILU-relaxation, the other on ZEBRA- relaxation [7]. The discretization on coarse
grids is provided automatically by means of a built-in Galerkin approximation.
Various scalar- and vector-versions of the code have been constructed and run on
a CYBER 170, a CRAY 1 and a CYBER 205. It appeared that a code written for automatic vectorization in portable ANSI FORTRAN runs efficiently in all cases.
Specially tuned versions are only a small fraction more efficient.
In section 2 we describe the class of problems that can be solved. In section 3
we describe the general algorithm for multigrid cycling. In the sections 4, 5, 6
we specialize the general algorithm and come to the various versions of the codes.
In sections 7, 8 we compare the various programs. In the last sections we formulate some conclusion.

2. THE PROBLEM

We consider the linear 2nd order elliptic PDE in two dimensions

$$(2.1.a) \quad \sum_{i,j=1,2} a_{ij}\left(\frac{\partial}{\partial x_i}\right)\left(\frac{\partial}{\partial x_j}\right) u + \sum_{i=1,2} a_i\left(\frac{\partial}{\partial x_i}\right) u + a_0 \, u = f \text{ on } \Omega \subset \mathbb{R}^2 ,$$

with variable coefficients and with boundary conditions on $\delta\Omega = \Gamma_N \cup \Gamma_D$

$$(2.1.b) \quad \left(\frac{\partial}{\partial n}\right) u + \alpha\left(\frac{\partial}{\partial s}\right) u + \beta u = \gamma \text{ on } \Gamma_N,$$

$$u = g \text{ on } \Gamma_D.$$

The coefficients are arbitrary but should satisfy the ellipticity condition. If this equation on a rectangle Ω is discretized on a regular triangularization of the form

(0,N₂)

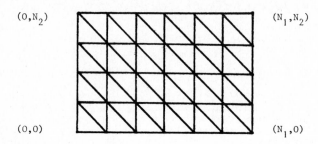

$(0,N_2)$ (N_1,N_2)

$(0,0)$ $(N_1,0)$

then the resulting discretization

(2.2) $A_h u_h = f_h$

can be a linear system with a regular 7-diagonal structure.

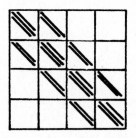

The shape of
a matrix A_h.

We consider codes for the solution of linear systems with a structure corresponding to this kind of 7-point discretization. On the rectangle Ω equidistant computational grids Ω^k, $k = 1,2,\ldots,\ell$, are defined

$$\Omega^k = \{(x_1,x_2) \mid x_i = m_i 2^{1-k},\ m_i = 0(1)N_i 2^{k-1}\}.$$

The user has to provide the discrete operator A_h and the data f_h only on the finest grid Ω^ℓ.
To solve the linear system efficiently, multigrid methods are used [2,7,8]. These methods make also use of Ω^k, $k = 1,2,\ldots,\ell-1$, but when using the autonomous subroutines the user remains unaware of this fact. Much effort has been spent in the search for efficient variants of the MG-method [3,4,5,6,7,8]. In this paper we consider only two variants that are found to belong to the more promising ones.

3. THE GENERAL MULTIGRID ALGORITHM

The general multigrid cycling algorithm for the solution of (2.2) is an iterative process, which makes use of a sequence of discretizations on the grids Ω^k, $k = 1,2,\ldots,\ell$.
Each multigrid iteration cycle consists of
(1) p relaxation sweeps, followed by
(2) a coarse grid correction, followed by
(3) q more relaxation sweeps.
The coarse grid correction consists of
a) the computation of the current residual $r_h = f_h - A_h \tilde{u}_h$;
b) the restriction of the residual to the next coarser grid $r_H = R_{Hh} r_h$;
c) the computation of $\tilde{c}_H$, an approximation to the solution of the correction

equation

(3.1) $\quad A_H c_H = r_H.$

This approximation is obtained by application of s multigrid iteration cycles to this equation, and

(d) updating the current solution $\tilde{u}_h$ by addition of the prolongated correction

$$\tilde{u}_h := \tilde{u}_h + P_{hH}\tilde{c}_H.$$

On the coarsest grid the correction equation (3.1) has to be (approximately) solved by another method (at choice). The coarse grid discrete operators A_H can be constructed by analogy to (2.2) or by Galerkin approximation:

(3.2) $\quad A_H = R_{Hh}A_h P_{hH}$

(cf. [8]).

4. THE ALGORITHMS

In this paper we consider the implementation of two particular instances of the multigrid algorithms: MGD1 and MGEOZ. Based on various comparisons [3,6,9], the parameters p, q and s are chosen to be 0,1 and 1 respectively. The resulting strategy is called a saw-tooth cycle [9]. For the prolongation and the restriction 7-point operators are chosen, that correspond to linear interpolation on coarse-grid triangles in the triangulation of Ω (for P_{hH}) and to its adjoint operator (for R_{Hh}). The Galerkin approximation (3.2) is chosen for the construction of the coarse grid operators A_H. For an approximate solution on the coarsest grid a single relaxation sweep is used. The two algorithms differ only with respect to he relaxation method.

In MGD1 the Incomplete LU (ILU-) relaxation is used [9]. For this relaxation the 7-diagonal matrix A_h is decomposed as

$$A_h = LU - C$$

where L is a lower-triangular matrix (with 1 for all main-diagonal elements) and U is an upper triangular matrix. The requirement that L and U have non-zero diagonals only where A_h has, determines L and U. The rest-matrix C has only two non-zero diagonals, of which the elements are easily derived from L and U. One relaxation sweep of the Incomplete LU-relaxation is now the solution of the system

$$LU\, u^{(i+1)} = f + C\, u^{(i)}.$$

After such a relaxation sweep a residual is efficiently computed by

$$r^{(i+1)} := f_h - A_h u_h^{(i+1)} = C(u_h^{(i+1)} - u_h^{(i)})$$

In MGEOZ the ZEBRA-relaxation is used [7]. This is a line-Gauss-Seidel relaxation in which first all points on even lines (lines that appear in the coarser grid) are simultaneously relaxed and secondly all points on the odd lines. An important advantage of this relaxation is the fact that many points can be relaxed simultaneously and that the residual computation simplifies, because the residual vanishes at all odd lines after a relaxation sweep. For ZEBRA relaxation tridiagonal systems have to be solved. The solution of these systems can be accelerated by storage of the decomposition of the tridiagonal matrices. We have chosen to do this at an extra storage cost of 2 reals per grid-point.

5. THE STRUCTURE OF MGD1 AND MGEOZ

The general structure of both MGD1 and MGEOZ is the same. First, in the preparational phase, the sequence of coarse grid discrete operators is constructed by

a subroutine RAP, according to (3.2). Then the decomposition is performed (in DECOMP or DECOMPZ) and the initial estimate of the solution is set to zero. Finally, in the cycling phase, at most MAXIT iterations of the cycling process are performed. On the basis of intermediate results the iteration can be stopped earlier; this necessitates the computation of a vectornorm (in VL2NOR).
In the following the structure of the cycling process of MGD1 is described in quasi-FORTRAN.

      DO 10 k=ℓ-1(-1)1

      CALL <u>RESTRICTION</u> (f,f,k). $f^k = R_{Hh}f^{k+1}$

  10 CONTINUE

C   START OF maxit MULTIGRID ITERATIONS

      DO 50 n=1, maxit

      IF (n.EQ.1) GO TO 30

      CALL <u>CTUMV</u> (C,u,v) $v^\ell = C^\ell(u^\ell - v^\ell)$

C v^ℓ IS THE NEW RESIDUE $f^\ell - A^\ell u^\ell$

      CALL <u>RESTRICTION</u> (f,v,ℓ-1) $f^{\ell-1} = R_{Hh}v^\ell$

      DO 20 k=ℓ-2(-1)1

      CALL <u>RESTRICTION</u> (f,f,k) $f^k = R_{Hh}f^{k+1}$

  20 CONTINUE

  30 CALL <u>SOLVE</u> (u,f,1) $u^1 = (L^1U^1)^{-1}f^1$

      DO 40 k=2 (1)ℓ-1

      CALL <u>PROLONGATION</u> (u,u,k) $u^k = P_{hH}u^{k-1}$

      CALL <u>CTUPF</u> (v,u,f,k) $v^k = C^k u^k + f^k$

      CALL <u>SOLVE</u> (u,v,k) $u^k = (L^kU^k)^{-1}v^k$

  40 CONTINUE

      CALL <u>PROLONGATION</u> (v,u,ℓ) $v^\ell = P_{hH}u^{k-1}$
      v^ℓ=v$^\ell$+u$^\ell$

      CALL <u>CTUPF</u> (u,v,f,ℓ) $u^\ell = C^\ell v^\ell + f^\ell$

      CALL <u>SOLVE</u> (u,u,ℓ) $u^\ell = (L^\ell U^\ell)^{-1}u^\ell$

  50 CONTINUE

In the actual implementation of MGD1, the matrix A_h is not kept in storage, but is overwritten by L and U. At minimal costs, the rest-matrix $C = LU - A_h$ is recomputed each time from L and U (in the subroutines CTUMV and CTUPF). All subroutines mentioned have their own particular features that make them more or less feasible for vectorization. This can be seen in table (8.2).
The structure of MGEOZ is more straightforward and follows directly from the MG-algorithm in section 3. Here the original matrix is not overwritten by the decomposition.
Two main alternatives exist for the implementation of ZEBRA relaxation. The lines in the grid can be relaxed successively and vectorization can be applied to speed up the solution of each tridiagonal system. However, because the solution of tridiagonal systems is not very suitable for vectorization, and all tridiagonal systems have the same size, we have chosen the other possibility to exploit vectorization, namely we solve all linear systems in each half relaxation sweep simultaneously by treating the even (odd) systems in parallel. Because of the rectangular shape of Ω the data-structure both in MGD1 and MGEOZ is simple. The grid-values of

u_h and f_h are stored sequentially in one-dimensional arrays. They are ordered by grid and in each grid they are ordered by meshline. The diagonals of A_h are stored similarly in a two-dimensional array; the columns of the array corresponding to the diagonals of the matrix.

6. VERSIONS OF THE PROGRAM

To investigate the advantages of vectorization, different versions of the programs have been constructed. One version is written in portable FORTRAN and is tuned for execution on sequential hardware (MGD1S and MGEOZS). Another version, also written in portable FORTRAN was tuned for vectorization (MGD1V and MGEOZV). To keep the FORTRAN portable, we had to rely on the automatic vectorization capabilities of the compilers at hand. All loops for which vectorization was required could indeed be expressed in standard ANSI FORTRAN.
Other versions of the programs were considered as well. An interesting variant was (not portable) MGD1D. This version is the same as MGD1V except for two statements, containing a call to a STACKLIB routine for the recursive parts of the routine SOLVE in MGD1. The STACKLIB library, supplied for the CYBER 200 series, contains particularly efficient routines for vector operations that are not vectorizable because of recursion. For the comparison of MGD1D and MGD1V see table (8.2) and (8.3). For details about the implementation of the vectorized versions cf. [10].

7. THE TEST PROBLEM

In this study we are not interested in the *numerical* behaviour of the algorithms for different problems. We consider here only the efficiency of their implementation. Therefore, we may restrict ourselves to a single testproblem: the solution of Poisson's equation on the unit square with Dirichlet boundary conditions. Of course, for this problem other alternatives exist for its efficient solution. A program implementing one cycle in a Full Multigrid (FMG) algorithm, specially tuned for this problem on a CYBER 205, is described in [1]. Such a program may run much faster than our general purpose code. They report the solution on a 129×129 grid (with the usual 5-point discretization) in 0.006 sec. However, we did *not* adapt our codes in any way to this particular problem. For our codes the cost of one iteration is the same for any 7-point discretization of a problem (2.1) on grids of a given size.
In all cases reported here, the problem was solved on a mesh with

$$(2^{\ell+1}+1)^2$$

meshpoints. The length of most vectors in the program is $(2^{n+1}+1)^j$, $n = 1(1)\ell$. $j = 1$ and $j = 2$ (i.e. they represent lines or complete grids on level n). We performed experiments for $\ell = 4,5,6,7$. For problems with $\ell > 5$ the size of the problem was too large to run on the available CYBER 170; for $\ell > 6$ The problem was too large for the available CRAY 1 (Daresbury 1983).

8. THE EFFECT OF VECTORIZATION

In the tables (8.1)-(8.5) we give CPU-times for the programs mentioned in section 6. On the CYBER 205 and the CRAY 1 the vector-tuned versions ran with the vector option, the CPU-times mentioned for the scalar-tuned versions ran without. If we run the portable vector-code in scalar mode we sacrify about 5% CPU-time on the CYBER 205 (CRAY 1: about 9%) when compared with the tuned scalar-code in scalar mode.
In the tables we give the total CPU-time in seconds spent in runs with 10 iteration cycles, including the preparational work. Also the time spent in the various subroutines is presented. From these numbers we derive the time spent in a single cycle. Additionally, we give the average convergence factor in the iterative cycling (CONV).

MGD1S	CYBER 170	CRAY 1		CYBER 205		
LEVEL	5	5	6	5	6	7
GRID	65 × 65	65 × 65	129 × 129	65 × 65	129 × 129	257 × 257
CONV	4.7E-2	4.7E-2	4.3E-2	4.7E-2	4.3E-2	4.3E-2
RAP	0.186	0.088	0.313	0.084	0.317	1.232
DECOMP	0.061	0.031	0.120	0.050	0.195	0.764
SOLVE	0.311	0.150	0.582	0.153	0.594	2.265
CTUMV	0.098	0.066	0.261	0.079	0.315	1.134
CTUPF	0.143	0.088	0.347	0.099	0.390	1.498
PROLON	0.041	0.030	0.113	0.024	0.093	0.360
RESTRI	0.066	0.017	0.062	0.014	0.054	0.202
VL2NOR	0.030	0.022	0.087	0.015	0.059	0.233
TOTAL	1.030	0.522	1.994	0.565	2.141	8.101
CYCLE	0.066	0.035	0.137	0.037	0.145	0.546

Table 8.1. CPU-times (in seconds) of the program MGD1S for problems with different sizes, run in scalar mode on different machines.

MGD1V	CRAY 1		CYBER 205		
LEVEL	5	6	5	6	7
GRID	65 × 65	129 × 129	65 × 65	129 × 129	257 × 257
CONV	4.7E-2	4.3E-2	4.7E-2	4.3E-2	4.3E-2
RAP	0.033 (2.7)	0.085 (3.7)	0.022 (3.8)	0.053 (6.0)	• 0.151 (8.2)
DECOMP	0.010 (3.1)	0.037 (3.2)	0.012 (4.2)	0.043 (4.5)	0.162 (4.7)
SOLVE	0.086 (1.7)	0.324 (1.8)	0.091 (1.7)	0.325 (1.8)	1.251 (1.8)
CTUMV	0.008 (8.2)	0.032 (8.2)	0.003 (26!)	0.010 (31!)	0.042 (27!)
CTUPF	0.011 (8.0)	0.043 (8.1)	0.004 (25!)	0.014 (28!)	0.059 (25!)
PROLON	0.007 (4.3)	0.018 (6.3)	0.009 (2.7)	0.022 (4.2)	0.061 (5.9)
RESTRI	0.004 (4.2)	0.011 (5.6)	0.012 (1.2)	0.031 (1.7)	0.092 (2.2)
VL2NOR	0.003 (7.3)	0.010 (8.7)	0.001 (15)	0.004 (15)	0.015 (16)
TOTAL	0.169 (3.1)	0.575 (3.5)	0.177 (3.2)	0.533 (4.0)	1.882 (4.3)
CYCLE	0.012 (2.9)	0.043 (3.2)	0.012 (3.1)	0.040 (3.6)	0.151 (3.6)

Table 8.2. CPU-times (in seconds) of the program MGD1V run in vector-mode. Between brackets: the acceleration factor by vectorization (compared with the tuned scalar version).

MGD1D	CYBER 205		
GRID	65 × 65	129 × 129	257 × 257
SOLVE	0.094 (1.6)	0.263 (2.3)	0.831 (2.7)
TOTAL	0.181 (3.1)	0.469 (4.6)	1.442 (5.6)
CYCLE	0.012 (3.1)	0.034 (4.3)	0.108 (5.1)

Table 8.3. CPU-times in seconds of the program MGD1D run in vector-mode

MGEOZS	CYBER 170	CRAY 1		CYBER 205		
LEVEL	6	6	7	6	7	8
GRID	65 × 65	65 × 65	129 × 129	65 × 65	129 × 129	257 × 257
CONV	2.3E-1	2.3E-1	2.2E-1	2.3E-1	2.2E-1	2.02E-1
RAP	0.188	⸙0.089	0.315	0.085	0.319	1.240
DECOMPZ	0.012	0.006	0.023	0.011	0.044	0.175
ZEBRA	0.333	0.135	0.511	0.148	0.585	2.309
RESIDU	0.106	0.049	0.191	0.045	0.180	0.733
PROLON	0.058	0.035	0.131	0.027	0.100	0.390
RESTRI	0.030	0.013	0.049	0.010	0.037	0.142
VL2NOR	0.018	0.013	0.048	0.008	0.033	0.128
TOTAL	0.797	0.348	1.286	0.353	1.333	5.216
CYCLE	0.053	0.023	0.088	0.023	0.090	0.357

Table 8.4. CPU-times (in seconds) of the program MGEOZS for problems with
different sizes, run in scalar-mode on different machines.

MGEOZV	CRAY 1		CYBER 205		
LEVEL	6	7	6	7	8
GRID	65 × 65	129 × 129	65 × 65	129 × 129	257 × 257
CONV	2.3E-1	2.2E-1	2.3E-1	2.2E-1	2.0E-1
RAP	0.033 (2.7)	0.085 (3.7)	0.022 (3.9)	0.054 (5.9)	0.151 (8.2)
DECOMPZ	0.006 (1.0)	0.023 (1.0)	0.010 (1.1)	0.040 (1.1)	0.158 (1.1)
ZEBRA	0.034 (4.0)	0.103 (5.0)	0.084 (1.8)	0.210 (2.8)	0.623 (3.7)
RESIDU	0.010 (4.9)	0.034 (5.6)	0.007 (6.4)	0.020 (9.0)	0.067 (10.9)
PROLON	0.008 (4.4)	0.022 (6.0)	0.013 (2.1)	0.032 (3.1)	0.093 (4.2)
RESTRI	0.004 (3.2)	0.009 (5.4)	0.009 (1.1)	0.022 (1.7)	0.059 (2.4)
VL2NOR	0.003 (4.3)	0.009 (5.3)	0.002 (4.0)	0.004 (8.3)	0.012 (10.7)
TOTAL	0.102 (3.4)	0.293 (4.4)	0.162 (2.2)	0.400 (3.3)	1.190 (4.4)
CYCLE	0.006 (3.8)	0.017 (5.2)	0.011 (2.1)	0.028 (3.2)	0.084 (4.3)

Table 8.5. CPU-times (in seconds) of the program MGEOZV run in vector-mode.
Between brackets the acceleration by vectorization.

We see that certain parts of the algorithms benefit greatly from vectorization viz.
CTUMV and CTUPF (a factor 25-30 on CYBER 205, a factor 8-9 on CRAY 1). Other parts
vectorize also well: VL2NOR, RAP, DECOMP, PROLON, RESIDU (on CRAY 1 also RESTRI and
ZEBRA, in which vectoroperations with stride 2 occur). Other parts hardly benefit
because of their recursive structure (DECOMPZ and SOLVE). If we give up portability,
SOLVE can be speeded up on the CYBER 205 by use of the STACKLIB library.

9. CONCLUSIONS

Implementation of general-purpose multigrid solvers on vectorcomputers is feasible.
Efficient programs in portable FORTRAN are now available for variable coefficient
elliptic problems in a rectangular domain, discretized by a 7-point difference mole-
cule. For the implementation implicit vectorization (auto-vectorization) can be used.
The effect of vectorization (the factor by which the program accelerates) depends
strongly on the size of the problem and, of course, on the algorithm used.
Our implementation with ILU-relaxation vectorized well on the CYBER 205 (factor 3.2-
4.3) but slightly worse on a CRAY 1 (factor 3.1-3.5). The implementation with ZEBRA
relaxation vectorized better on a CRAY 1 (3.4-4.4) and less well on a CYBER 205
(factor 2.2-4.4). The reduced vectorizability of MGEOZ on the CYBER 205 is due to
the frequent occurance of vectors with stride unequal 1. For MGEOZV the CRAY 1 is
faster than the CYBER 205; for MGD1V the CYBER 205 is faster for large problems.
We notice that for the determination of the efficiency of an algorithm on a vector-
machine the usual measure of complexity - the operations count - appears to be
completely irrelevant. Many more aspects have to be taken into account such as:
are the computations arranged in small or large do-loops, are they recursive, vectorizable, how are the data stored etc..
The relative efficiency of the various algorithms depends - of course - on the complexity of the algorithms and on the rate of convergence. The complexity of MGEOZ
is less, but generally MGD1 has a better convergence rate. Based on the present experiments we see that roughly one iteration with MGD1 takes twice the CPU-time of a
MGEOZ iteration. On the other hand, in our Poisson testproblem, the empirical convergence rate of MGD1 is twice the rate of MGEOZ, so that both algorithms appear

equally efficient in this case. In general, the relative efficiency of MGD1 and MGEOZ depends on the difference problem to solve, the size of the system of equations and on the machine used.

ACKNOWLEDGEMENT

We are indebted to Mr. W. Lioen who constructed different versions of MGEOZ.

NOTE

The codes discussed in the paper can be obtained by sending a tape to Mr. A. van Deursen, Dept. of Mathematics and Informations, Delft University of Technology, Julianalaan 132, 2628 Delft, The Netherlands.

REFERENCES

[1] Barkai, D. and Brandt, A., Vectorized Multigrid Poisson Solver for the *CDC CYBER 205*, In: Procs. Int. MG-Conference, Copper Mountain, Colorado, April 6-8, 1983.

[2] Brandt, A., Multi-level adaptive solutions to boundary-value problems, Math. Comp. 31, 333-390, 1977.

[3] Hemker, P.W., On the comparison of line-Gauss-Seidel and ILU relaxation in multigrid algorithms, In: J.J.H. Miller (ed.), Computational and asymptotic methods for boundary and interior layers, pp. 269-277. Boole Press, Dublin, 1982.

[4] Hemker, P.W., Multigrid methods for problems with a small parameter, To appear in: Procs. Dundee. Conf. 1983, LNM, Springer-Verlag.

[5] Hemker, P.W., Wesseling, P. and De Zeeuw, P.M., Multigrid methods: development of fast solvers. In: Procs. Int. MG-Conference, Copper Mountain, Colorado, April 6-8, 1983.

[6] Kettler, R., Analysis and comparison of relaxation schemes in robust multigrid and preconditioned conjugate gradient methods. In: W. Hackbusch and U. Trottenberg (eds.), Multigrid methods. Proceedings, Köln-Porz, 1981. Lect. Notes in Math. 960, pp. 502-534, Springer-Verlag, Berlin etc., 1982.

[7] Stüben, K. and Trottenberg U., Multigrid methods: fundamental algorithms, model problem analysis and applications. In: W. Hackbusch and U. Trottenberg (eds.), Multigrid methods. Proceedings, Köln-Porz, 1981. Lect. Notes in Math. 960, pp. 1-176, Springer-Verlag, Berlin etc. 1982.

[8] Wesseling, P., Theoretical and practical aspects of a multigrid method. Siam J. Sci. Stat. Comp. 3, 387-407, 1982.

[9] Wesseling, P., A robust and efficient multigrid method. In: W. Hackbusch and U. Trottenberg (eds.), Multigrid methods. Proceedings, Köln-Porz, 1981. Lect. Notes in Math. 960, pp. 614-630, Springer-Verlag, Berlin etc., 1982.

[10] De Zeeuw, P.M., Lioen, W. and Hemker, P.W., Vectorized Multigrid Codes, To appear as Mathematical Centre report, Amsterdam, 1983.

DISCUSSION

Speaker: P. Hemker

Gorenflo: You intend your method to be robust. Then it should also work when in your equation convection is large compared to diffusion, that is in the nearly singular case. But I do not see how. Can you comment on this?

Hemker: We have to distinguish between nearly singular and singularly perturbed problems. In the first case (an eigenvalue almost equal zero) any iterative solver will run into problems. In the second case, for instance for the convection-diffusion equation, if properly discretized (e.g. by an upwind discretization), the Incomplete LU relaxation and even more the Incomplete Line LU relaxation have execellent smoothing properties.
References:
P. W. Hemker: On the comparision of line Gauss-Seidel and ILU relaxation in multigrid algorithms. In: J. J. H. Miller (Ed.). Computational and asymptotic methods for boundary and interior layers, pp. 269-277, Boole Press, Dublin, 1982.
P. W. Hemker. Multigrid methods for problems with a small parameter in the highest derivative. To appear in: Numerical Analysis, Proc. of the Dundee 1983 Conference, D. F. Griffiths (Ed). Springer-Verlag.

Brandt: You gave examples of computing times for your software. For some of these problems there are vectorized multi-grid algorithms which are ~ 100 times as fast. Considering relaxation methods, I should like to emphasise that when one wishes to solve only to truncation error level then simple direction free, high vectorizable point relaxation (e.g. red-black ordering) is quite sufficient and adequate when the equations are highly anisotropic, unless there is one dominant (i.e. throughout most of the domain) alignment between one particular characteristic direction and a specific grid direction. Such dominant alignment must be known to the user and can be communicated to the system, in which case the latter would use simple, highly vectorized line relaxation.

Hemker: As far as I know there is one program, which has been referenced in my paper (Barkai and Brandt), which is specially designed for the CYBER 205 and solves the Poisson equation up to truncation error with a speed of 0.36 µsec/grid point. This is about 30 times as fast as our program. When we take into account that our program is designed for variable coefficient problems (and hence all the matrix entries have to be used explicitly) and that it is written in portable FORTRAN (and hence is not bound to one particular machine), we see that its existence is sufficiently justified. Possibly/probably you are right. However, we want to make available a routine which yields the solution of the linear system up to an arbitrary small residual, that can be specified by the user.

Hockney: It would appear that quite different strategies are best for different machines. For example, on the CYBER 205 it may pay to iterate more in the fine mesh because of the greater length of vectors involved. Have you any theory for estimating the run time on vector processors a priori?

Hemker: Indeed we find that different variants of the MG-method are best for different machines. So we find that the variant with ZEBRA-relaxation runs better on a CRAY 1, whereas the variant with ILU-relaxation runs better on the CYBER 205. We have no general theory for estimating the run time on vector processors, neither do we search for the optimal variants (or strategies) for the various different machines.

Duff: Your package is designed for linear problems but unfortunately life is nonlinear. In the solution of a nonlinear problem would you advocate using your package on the linearized problem obtained, for example, through a Newton-type solution scheme? How would this compare with solving the nonlinear problem on each grid as recommended by Achi Brandt.

Hemker: Both approaches are possible. It is claimed that the FAS multigrid approach can be more efficient. On the other hand there are arguments in favour of the Newton approach. In the latter case, if the iterative process does not converge - as sometimes happens for nonlinear problems - one may obtain better insight of the reason for the divergence.

Young: You talked about achieving 50% vectorization using the LU algorithm. Since the solution of a triangular system is not inherently vectorizable how were you able to achieve this?

Hemker: In the solution process for the LU-relaxation forward and backward substitution are performed with L (or U) being 4-diagonal triangular matrices. If we execute the substitution blockwise, the two diagonals in the off-main-diagonal blocks can be eliminated by vector-operations. Only the (non-vectorizable) solution of simple bidiagonal systems is left.

Reid: I am on the X3J3 Fortran committee and have a special interest on the incorporation of array facilities in the future Fortran (8X) standard. You seemed to have some trouble with differences between the scalar and vector versions of your routines. Do you think that facilities such as array or array section assignments could help you to avoid some of these problems?

Hemker: Yes, I think they may do so. But there is more to say about this. In my opinion a real programming language should in the first place provide a level of abstraction (abstraction from the machine architecture), in such a way that we can conveniently express our mathematical, algorithmical and "software engineering" thoughts in it. In this sense FORTRAN is a poor language. Therefore, for research work we prefer ALGOL 68. We use FORTRAN only because it is - unfortunately - the only language that is widely available for numerical computation. We would not be helped at all by FORTRAN extensions that would not be widely used and certainly not by extensions that would be implemented only on vector machines. In the present work we could write our program in a most elementary but portable FORTRAN and on the vector machines the compilers were clever enough to vectorize where it was necessary.

Reid: We are not designing extensions for a manufacturer or set of manufacturers, but for the standard itself and our hope and belief is that by the 1990s Fortran 8X will be as widely available as Fortran 66 was in the 1970s. Brian Smith, Laurie Schonfelder and I are the only representatives of the mathematical software community on the committee and our aim is to add to Fortran those facilities that have proved valuable in more powerful languages. One cannot "wipe the slate clean" because of the vast number of large working Fortran programs, whose owners are desperately anxious to continue to use them for ten or even twenty years. We need support and constructive criticism from those who are daily using other languages.

Rice: My experience of vectorizing compilers is that they are not very clever and many loops are not vectorized automatically. One must then rewrite the non-vectorized loops so that they can be recognized as vectorizable. This is rather inelegant. Have you encountered this problem?

Hemker: Yes, we have indeed. However, in our case, we were able to rewrite the programs in a portable FORTRAN in such a way that all the necessary vectorization was recognized by the compiler. In this sense the compiler was clever enough: we did not have to resort to special machine/compiler dependent vector language.

Brandt: It is at the algorithmic design stage that one thinks about vectorizability. It would be very good to have facilities to communicate these

design features directly to the machine. I would welcome features in extensions
to Fortran to accommodate this.

Hockney: It is not only vectorization which is important but also how long the
vectors are. This effect is characterized by the $n_{1/2}$ parameter of the computer,
about which I will talk more later this week.

Hemker: This is perfectly true. In the given examples this also explains the
behaviour of the speed-up factors on the CYBER 205, in particular for the
prolongation and restriction routines.
Further, for the CYBER 205, it is important whether the vectors are contiguously
stored or not.

PDE SOFTWARE: Modules, Interfaces and Systems
B. Engquist and T. Smedsaas (eds.)
Elsevier Science Publishers B.V. (North-Holland)
© IFIP, 1984

41

THE REDESIGN AND VECTORIZATION OF THE SLDGL-PROGRAM
PACKAGE FOR THE SELFADAPTIVE SOLUTION OF NONLINEAR
SYSTEMS OF ELLIPTIC AND PARABOLIC PDE's

W.Schönauer, E.Schnepf, K.Raith

Rechenzentrum der Universität Karlsruhe
Postfach 6380, D-7500 Karlsruhe 1, West-Germany

The basic ideas for the design of a variable step
size/variable order difference method for nonlinear
systems of elliptic and parabolic PDE's, with optimal balancing of all the relevant errors (including
the Newton-Raphson residual), are presented. The resulting SLDGL program package is critically reviewed
and the design goals for a complete redesign for full
vectorization, including efficient iterative linear
solvers for large 3-D problems, are discussed.

1. INTRODUCTION

This paper gives a <u>survey</u> of the research for the development of general purpose software for nonlinear systems of elliptic and parabolic PDE's which has been carried out at the computing center of the
University of Karlsruhe. It is impossible to present in this paper
<u>all</u> the details of this research and program development. Therefore
we try to make visible the <u>main</u> ideas and the reader may consult the
references for more details.

The user of a computer wants to find in the program library a black
box solver for nonlinear systems of PDE's (most technical problems
are nonlinear) of the type shown in Fig. 1.1a. He wants to deliver
in some form his PDE's and B.C.'s (boundary conditions) and an <u>accu-
racy requirement</u> to this black box solver and expects either a solution or a reasonable error information. Our research is directed
towards this goal.

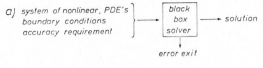

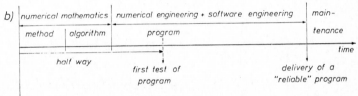

Figure 1.1
a) black box solver,   b) development of a PDE solver

The user expects from the black box solver also high efficiency: His PDE's should be solved with a minimum of computational cost. But at this point we find a basic problem in the design of PDE software, namely the problem of

efficiency versus robustness.

A highly efficient program uses all the special properties of a problem, thus cannot be robust (e.g. a fast Poisson solver cannot be used for arbitrary nonlinear PDE's). At the other hand, a robust program does not use all the special properties of a problem, thus cannot be highly efficient. Good software is always a compromise between the two contradictory properties of efficiency and robustness. Therefore the user of PDE software must also make a compromise between

hardware cost and software cost.

General purpose software needs more hardware cost (computer time), because it is not highly efficient. At the other hand it saves software cost, because only the subroutines for the PDE's must be programmed. The decision will largely depend on the quality of the PDE software and on the nature of the special problem.

The development of a PDE solver is depicted in Fig. 1.1b. The designer develops a method and an algorithm, which is mostly the domain of numerical mathematics. Then he develops a program, which is the combination of what H. Stetter [1] calls "numerical engineering" and of software engineering. The experience has told us that at the first test of a program we have gone only half the way until the delivery of a reliable program. Thus half the time of development of a PDE solver is devoted to reliability.

2. ACCESS TO THE ERRORS

The key to a selfadaptive difference method is the access to the discretization (or truncation) error. We use families of centralized equidistant or nonequidistant difference formulae of arbitrary order q for the BVP-directions (x,y,z) and nonequidistant backward difference formulae of order $p \leq 5$ for the IVP-direction (t), see Fig. 2.1. The formulae are computed by subroutines from Newton interpolation polynomials with the aid of "influence functions" [2,3].

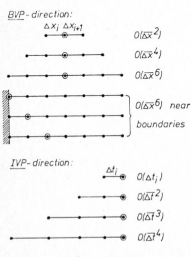

Figure 2.1
Families of difference formulae

We define e.g. for a derivative u_{xx} the discretization (or truncation) error d_{xx} by

$$d_{xx} := u_{xx,d,next} - u_{xx,d},$$

$$\left\{ + d_{xx,next} \right\} \qquad (2.1)$$

where $u_{xx,d}$ is the difference formula for u_{xx} (the index d means "discretized") of the actual order

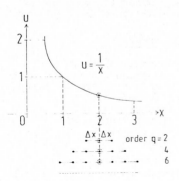

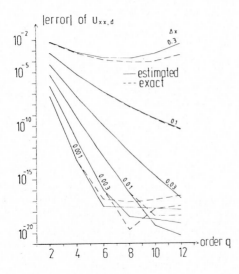

and $u_{xx,d,next}$ is the difference formula of the next member of the family. By this estimate we have neglected the error of the higher formula. For comparison we may compare (2.1) to the exact error

$$e_{xx} = u_{xx} - u_{xx,d} \qquad (2.2)$$

which shows that we have replaced for the estimate u_{xx} by $u_{xx,d,next}$. From (2.1) also follows that this estimate is useful only as long as the error decreases with increasing order (else the order would be "overdrawn"). Fig. 2.2 shows the quality of the error estimate (2.1) for the family of central difference formulae for $u_{xx,d}$ for the function $u = 1/x$. For very small errors the round-off error region is reached. For $\Delta x = 0.3$ the error increases for orders $q > 8$: there the **order is overdrawn. For** less smooth functions the order is overdrawn already for much lower orders. In the difference method we replace derivatives by a difference formula and its corresponding error estimate, e.g.

$$u_{xx} \Leftarrow u_{xx,d} + d_{xx} , \qquad (2.3)$$

where $u_{xx,d}$ serves for the computation of the solution and d_{xx} for the error control.

Figure 2.2
Absolute error of $u_{xx,d}$ for the family of equidistant central difference formulae.

Now we want to derive the <u>error equation.</u> The most general operator for a system of nonlinear <u>PDE's</u> which we consider is

$$Pu \equiv P(t,x,y,z,u,u_t,u_x,u_y,u_z,u_{xx},u_{yy},u_{zz}) = 0 . \qquad (2.4)$$

We introduce a Newton-Raphson (NR)-ansatz

$$u \Leftarrow u^{(\nu+1)} = u^{(\nu)} + \Delta u^{(\nu)} , \qquad (2.5)$$

where ν is the iteration index, which is dropped for simplicity.

Putting (2.5) into (2.4) and linearizing in the NR correction <u>function</u> Δu results in the following linear PDE for Δu:

$$Q\Delta u \equiv -\frac{\partial P}{\partial u}\Delta u - \frac{\partial P}{\partial u_t}\Delta u_t - \frac{\partial P}{\partial u_x}\Delta u_x - \dots - \frac{\partial P}{\partial u_{zz}}\Delta u_{zz} = Pu \ , \qquad (2.6)$$

where $\partial P/\partial u$, $\partial P/\partial u_t$,... are Jacobian matrices. This equation is solved by the difference method, replacing derivatives similarly to (2.3) and linearizing in the error terms d_ϕ. There results the error **equation**

$$\Delta u_d = \Delta u_{Pu} + \Delta u_{D_t} + \Delta u_{D_x} + \Delta u_{D_y} + \Delta u_{D_z}$$

$$= Q_d^{-1} \ [(Pu)_d + D_t + D_x + D_y + D_z] \ , \qquad (2.7)$$

where Q_d is the matrix resulting from the discretization process, $(Pu)_d$ is the discretized NR residual, D_t, D_x, D_y, D_t are discretization error terms, where e.g. for D_x holds

$$D_x = \frac{\partial P}{\partial u_x}d_x + \frac{\partial P}{\partial u_{xx}}d_{xx} \ . \qquad (2.8)$$

The error terms in the brackets are errors on the consistency level which are transformed by Q_d^{-1} to the level of the solution. The overall error Δu_d has been split up into its parts corresponding to the terms in the brackets. The x-discretization error e.g. is

$$\Delta u_{D_x} = Q_d^{-1} \ D_x \ . \qquad (2.9)$$

The NR correction Δu_{Pu} is according to (2.7) computed as the solution of

$$Q_d \ \Delta u_{Pu} = (Pu)_d \ . \qquad (2.10)$$

The error equation (2.7) tells us how we should compute efficiently: all the terms in the brackets should be balanced to nearly equal magnitude: if one of the terms is large, it destroys the accuracy, if one of them is small, it merely wastes computation time. Therefore the NR iteration is stopped, if

$$\| (Pu)_d \| \ < \ 0.1 \ \| D_k \| \qquad (2.11)$$

holds, where D_k is a key discretization error, e.g. $D_k = D_x + D_y + D_z$. The convergence of the NR iteration for a bad initial guess is favored by a relaxation factor ω which is determined that $\| (Pu)_d \|$ decreases. Instead of (2.5) we then use

$$u^{(\nu+1)} = u^{(\nu)} + \omega\Delta u^{(\nu)} \ . \qquad (2.12)$$

For "good" convergence, if $\| (Pu)_d \|_{\nu+1} < 0.1 \ \| (Pu)_d \|_\nu$ we use the simplified NR method with Q_d = const.

3. ELLIPTIC PDE's

The simplest "elliptic" problem is the <u>ordinary BVP</u> for a system of n nonlinear ODE's:

$$Pu \equiv P(x,u,u_x,u_{xx}) = 0 \ , \qquad (3.1)$$

with B.C.'s $Gu \equiv G(x,u,u_x,u_{xx})$ on the boundaries of the domain, but we assume Gu to be included in Pu. The operator (3.1) is a special form of (2.4) and consequently from (2.7) follows the error equation

$$\Delta u_d = \Delta u_{Pu} + \Delta u_{D_x} = Q_d^{-1} \; [(Pu)_d + D_x] \; . \tag{3.2}$$

The solution method is the key method for elliptic PDE's. If we have a system of n ODE's (3.1), the solution has n components

$$u_d = (u_{d,j}) \; , \quad j = 1,\ldots,n \; . \tag{3.3}$$

We introduce the following norms

global norm: $\qquad \|u_d\| = \max_{i,j} \; |u_{d,j}(x_i)| \; , \tag{3.4}$

relative local norm: $\qquad \|\Delta u_d\|_{rel,i} = \max_j \dfrac{|\Delta u_{d,j}(x_i)|}{\max_i |u_{d,j}(x_i)|} \; , \tag{3.5}$

relative global norm: $\qquad \|\Delta u_d\|_{rel} = \max_i \; \|\Delta u_d\|_{rel,i} \; . \tag{3.6}$

The selfadaptation of **order** and **grid** follows the scheme given below:

1. Compute basic solution for given initial order q_i and grid, stop if $\|\Delta u_{D_x}\|_{rel} <$ tol, where tol is a prescribed relative tolerance.

2. Compute estimates of the error norms for the orders $q = 2,4,\ldots.$ by

$$\|\Delta u_{D_x}(q)\|_{rel} \approx \|Q_d^{-1}(q)\|_{rel} \cdot \|D_x(q)\| \; , \tag{3.7}$$

   using the coarse estimate

$$\|Q_d^{-1}(q)\|_{rel} \approx \|Q_d^{-1}(q_i)\|_{rel} \tag{3.8}$$

$$\approx \|\Delta u_{D_x}(q_i)\|_{rel} \; / \; \|D_x(q_i)\| \; .$$

3. Global optimization of step size and order: Compute

$$\Delta x_{new} = [(tol/3)/\|\Delta u_{D_x}(q)\|_{rel}]^{1/q} \Delta x \; , \tag{3.9}$$

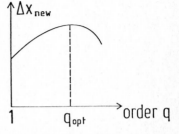

   check if Δx_{new} increases with the order. If it does not increase, the last order is $q = q_{opt}.$

   For an equidistant grid we compute $\Delta u_{D_x}(q) \approx Q_d^{-1}(q_i)D_x(q) \Rightarrow \Delta x_{new}$ from (3.9).

4. (only for nonequidistant grid) Compute local step sizes

$$\Delta x_i = [(tol/3)/\|\Delta u_{D_x}\|_{rel,i}]^{1/q} \cdot 0.5(x_{i+1} - x_{i-1}) \tag{3.10}$$

and put the Δx_i together either directly with priority for smaller step size or by cubic spline function smoothing (maintains even order) [15].

5. Now a new order and a new grid has been determined. Interpolate the old solution to the new grid and go back to 1.

It should be mentioned that only in the first and second pass a new order is determined. There is some similarity to the method of deferred corrections [4].

Now this solution method is extended to 2-D elliptic PDE's on a rectangular domain. The system of n nonlinear PDE's is

$$Pu \equiv P(x,y,u,u_x,u_y,u_{xx},u_{yy}) = 0 \qquad (3.11)$$

with B.C.'s Gu = 0 on a rectangular domain, which we assume to be included in Pu = 0. The error equation is

$$\Delta u_d = \Delta u_{Pu} + \Delta u_{D_x} + \Delta u_{D_y} = Q_d^{-1}[(Pu)_d + D_x + D_y] . \qquad (3.12)$$

For the determination of the orders qx and qy and of the x- and y-grid we want

$$\|\Delta u_{D_x}\|_{rel} < tol \quad \underline{and} \quad \|\Delta u_{D_y}\|_{rel} < tol . \qquad (3.13)$$

For the determination of qx and of the x-grid we project the maxima of the x-errors for each x_i onto the x-axis, see Fig. 3.1 and apply now for this error distribution the method of the ODE's. Then the same procedure is made in the y-direction, giving independent values for the order qy and the y-grid.

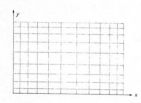

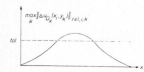

Figure 3.1
Projection of x-errors onto x-axis.

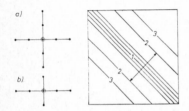

Figure 3.2
Illustration of semi-iterative method.

An essential part of a 2-D PDE solver is the solution of the linear equations (2.10) for the computation of the Newton correction Δu_{Pu}. For the example of the 4th order difference star of Fig. 3.2 a direct solver would give fill-in between the outer diagonals 3-3. Therefore we introduced a semi-iterative method by direct solution of the difference star with minimum order in the y-direction (b in Fig. 3.2) with fill-in between the diagonals 2-2, and then iterating to the full star (a in Fig. 3.2.), details are given in [2,3]. The essential idea is that the solutions for the minimum and full star differ "only" by the difference of the discretization error, which proved to be more than 100% of the solution in "critical" cases, thus the iteration may diverge, above all for Neumann B.C.'s. We also programmed an ADLI method, which needs diagonal dominance for convergence. The situation turns out to be not at all satisfactory: The two linear solvers are neither efficient nor robust enough.

For <u>3-D elliptic PDE's</u> the system of n nonlinear equations has the
general form

$$Pu \equiv P(x,y,z,u,u_x,u_y,u_z,u_{xx},u_{yy},u_{zz}) = 0 \ . \tag{3.14}$$

For 3-D problems the essential difficulty is the <u>immense</u> amount of
data. We consider the following example, e.g. for a fluid dynamic
problem:

$$\left.\begin{array}{l}
\text{system of 6 PDE's} \\
\text{4th order difference star} \\
50 \times 50 \times 50 \text{ grid} \\
\underline{\text{unknowns:}} \quad 50 \cdot 50 \cdot 50 \cdot 6 = 750.000 \\
\underline{\text{nonzero elements:}} \quad 50 \cdot 50 \cdot 50 \cdot 6 \cdot 6 \cdot 13 \approx 60 \text{ mio}
\end{array}\right\} \tag{3.15}$$

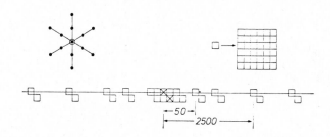

Figure 3.3
Structure of the matrix Q_d for (3.15)

In Fig. 3.3 there is depicted the structure of the resulting matrix
with 13 block diagonals, each "element" is a 6×6 block. We programmed a "block point" Jacobi method with selfadapted relaxation factor
(resolution to central block ☒), which needs block diagonal dominance for convergence and is neither robust nor efficient. Seeing the
size of a typical problem (3.15) we recognized that on a general purpose computer a selfadaptive (repetetive) solution would not be possible, we programmed only a nonselfadaptive method with prescribed
grid and order.

4. INITIAL AND INITIAL BOUNDARY VALUE PROBLEMS

The solution method for the ordinary IVP is the key method for the
t-direction (IV direction). The system of n nonlinear ODE's is

$$Pu \equiv P(t,u,u_t) = 0 \ , \tag{4.1}$$

the error equation is

$$\Delta u_d = \Delta u_{Pu} + \Delta u_{D_t} = Q_d^{-1} \ [(Pu)_d + D_t] \ . \tag{4.2}$$

We use the family of backward difference formulae of Fig. 2.1 of
order $p \leq 5$.

Replacing the derivative Δu_t in the linear differential equation resulting from (2.6) for the special operator (4.1) needs some explanation. If we compute the NR corrections the foregoing "profiles"

are not changed, therefore the corresponding terms vanish in the difference formula. But if we compute the discretization error, there
are foregoing errors which determine a global error (history). Therefore for t_i we have for the order p

$$\Delta u_{t,d,i} = \underbrace{a_i \, \Delta u_{d,i} + a_{i-1} \Delta u_{d,i-1} + \cdots + a_{i-p} \Delta u_{d,i-p}}. \qquad (4.3)$$

$$= 0 \text{ for local NR correction}$$
$$= \text{s-term for global error}$$

The step size is determined by

$$\Delta t_{i+1} = \left[(tol/3)/\max_j \left| \frac{\Delta u_{D_{t,j}}}{\max(u_{d,j}, rel)} \right| \right]^{1/p} \Delta t_i \,, \qquad (4.4)$$

where tol is a given relative tolerance, $1 \le j \le n$ denotes the component of the solution vector for a system of n ODE's and rel avoids
division by zero for a compo-
nent crossing the zero. The
choice of the order is made by
comparison of the discretiza-
tion error terms $\|D_t\|$ for
the orders p and p $+$ 1 according to Fig. 4.1. The method
starts with the order p = 1.
We use a polynomial extrapolation with order p as a "predictor". Finally the global
error is computed by

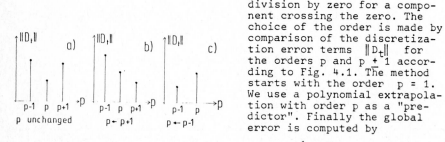

Figure 4.1
Determination of the order p.

$$\Delta u_{dg} = Q_d^{-1} [(Pu)_d + D_t + s] \,, \qquad (4.5)$$

with s given by (4.3).

The solution method for the parabolic IBVP's is a mere combination
of the IVP solver for the t-direction and the BVP solver for the space directions x,y,z. E.g. the solution method for the most general
operator (2.4) combines the IVP solver with the 3-D elliptic solver,
for details see [2,3]. Also for parabolic PDE's optionally a global
error is computed.

5. SURVEY OF SLDGL AND EXAMPLE

Fig. 5.1 gives a survey of the SLDGL-program package with its main
parts and examples of possible difference stars of the related families. But for the main parts there are mostly several versions, e.g.
for SL2E (2-D elliptic) there are 6 versions, which are different
combinations of the properties: equidistant/nonequidistant, selfadap-
tive/nonselfadaptive, semiiterative linear solver/ADLI linear solver.

The different versions are created by changing the corresponding statements in the original version, leading to 70.000 lines of Fortran
code and 50.000 lines of program documentation (user's guide). This
large amount of code introduced severe maintenance problems.

As a typical example we consider the flow in the "heat driven cavity", for details see [5]. The nondimensional equations and boundary
conditions are shown in Fig. 5.2. The PDE's result from the

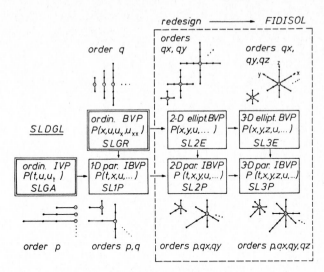

Figure 5.1
Survey of the SLDGL-program package

continuity equation, the definition of the vorticity $\zeta = v_x - u_y$, the Navier-Stokes equations and the energy equation. R_A and P_R are Rayleigh- and Prandtl number. The results are depicted in Fig. 5.3 and demonstrate clearly what we consider to be a **real** PDE solver: together with the solution there is computed a reliable error estimate. How to test the reliability of the error estimate (not only of the solution) is explained for this example in [5]. In a similar way only the global error can test the reliability of an IBVP.

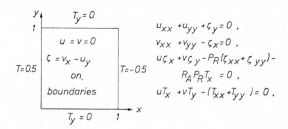

Figure 5.2
Boundary conditions and differential equations
for the heat driven cavity.

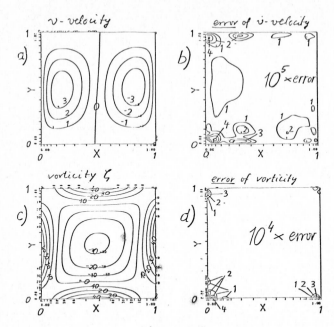

Figure 5.3

contour plots of   a) v,   b) $10^5 \cdot |\Delta v|/\|v\|$,   c) ζ,
d) $10^4 \cdot |\Delta\zeta|/\|\zeta\|$.   The "scale" indicates the selfadapted
grid.

6. ARBITRARY DOMAIN

The preceding 2-D and 3-D parts of the SLDGL-program package are designed only for a rectangular domain. The great advantage of the FEM
over the FDM is the easy treatment of arbitrary domains. Therefore
we developed an experimental version of our solution method (without
selfadaptation) for arbitrary 2-D domains by superposition of a rectangular grid on an arbitrary domain, see Fig. 6.1. The intersections of the boundary with the grid lines result in "irregular"
points which introduce a severe "bookkeeping" problem. Near the boundaries we must use 2-D "area formulae"
(2-D interpolation polynomials) instead of
the onedimensional formulae of a rectangular grid, for details see [6]. The resulting matrix has "scattered elements" as in
the FEM and not "scattered diagonals" as
in the FDM. The method works rather satisfactorily, but we consider it to be inefficient. Many technical problems have boundary layers for which a rectangular grid
is not well suited and boundary oriented
grids are necessary.

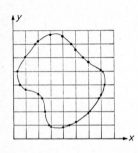

Figure 6.1
Arbitrary 2-D domain

Therefore we did not further follow this
line. We believe that the transformation
of the arbitrary domain to a rectangular
domain is the only possibility to preserve
all the advantages of the selfadaptive FDM.

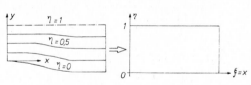

Figure 6.2
Transformation to a rectangular domain for half-diffusor

Such a transformation automatically generates body-oriented meshes in the physical plane (which could also be used as grid in a FEM). Fig. 6.2 shows the transformation of a half-diffusor to a rectangular domain. But this results in a nonorthogonal transformation, where <u>mixed derivatives</u> appear in the transformed equations. These can be treated easily by auxiliary variables. If we have e.g. u_{xy} then we introduce $v = u_x$ as new variable and $v - u_x = 0$ as new PDE and B.C. and then $u_{xy} = v_y$. Naturally the increased system is more expensive to be solved, but the method is standard.

We consider it as a separate task to make available the necessary tools for the transformation of usual types of 2-D and 3-D domains to rectangular domains.

7. REDESIGN SLDGL → FIDISOL

The SLDGL-program package has been developed in parallel with the development of the solution method itself. Therefore SLDGL cannot be well structured. It has been designed for general purpose computers because at the time of fixing the structure of the program vector computers were rare exotics. Now the situation has completely changed and vector computers are spreading in a great number in the field of scientific computing and they allow for the first time to attack realistic 3-D problems.

So we decided to start a <u>complete redesign</u> of the 2-D and 3-D parts of SLDGL, leading to the FIDISOL (finite difference solver) program. In SLDGL we extended the method from 1-D to 2-D to 3-D. But in FIDISOL we wanted to start directly with 3-D and get 2-D as a special case. We also wanted to include periodic boundary conditions, which are necessary e.g. for polar or cylindrical coordinates (they are not included in SLDGL). The basic ideas have been sketched in [7].

Before we started with FIDISOL we reevaluated the basic decisions from the very beginning. The results are as follows:

<u>FDM</u> (not FEM): The access to the error, opening the possibility for the choice of order and grid for a given accuracy, was decisive for the choice of the FDM. The resulting matrix has scattered diagonals (not scattered elements as in the FEM) which avoids the bookkeeping problem. The domain is rectangular, which needs transformation of arbitrary domains to rectangular domains.

<u>Newton-Raphson method:</u> We consider the NR method as the best compromise between efficiency and robustness for the solution of nonlinear PDE's. This necessitates the programming of the Jacobian matrices, but they are nevertheless necessary for the computation of the errors.

<u>Linear solver:</u> Only fully iterative methods (without fill-in) based on diagonal storing (no address calculation) should be used, see section 8.

<u>Modularization:</u> Design of very few very general modules which are
designed to be usable as far as possible for 3-D and 2-D. The structure of the 3-D problem has priority. Repetition of code should be
avoided.

<u>Vectorization:</u> Priority of data flow control, i.e. the algorithm
must be adapted to data flow, not data flow to the algorithm. The
design must be made for extremely large data sets. The modularization and vectorization are closely connected and are discussed in
section 9.

8. LINEAR SOLVER (LINSOL)

The basic ideas for the solution of large linear systems with scattered diagonals have been presented in [8,9]. For the discussion of the
solution method it is necessary to consider the environment in which
the linear solver LINSOL is used, see Fig. 8.1. For the designer of
LINSOL neither the differential operator Pu nor the B.C.'s are
known in advance, nor the structu-
re of the diagonal pattern which
results from the selfadapted order
of the method. Therefore we assume
that the linear system (2.10) which
we write now as

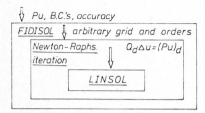

$$Q_d \Delta u = (Pu)_d \qquad (8.1)$$

Figure 8.1
Environment of linear solver

has an extremely large matrix Q_d
of scattered diagonals.

For such a matrix the only
useful storing without address
calculation is <u>storing by dia-
gonals</u>. The matrix is stored
as a linear "file" of its diagonals, see Fig. 8.2.

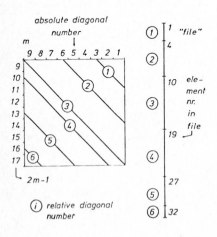

The consequence of diagonal
storing is that we now need
algorithms which can be formulated in diagonal form. These
are algorithms of the Jacobi or
CG (conjugate gradient) type
which are based on matrix-vector multiplications. Fig. 8.3
illustrates the computation of
Ar for the example of the matrix of Fig. 8.2. The rules are
given in [8,9]. It should be
mentioned that for $A^T r$ only the
rules for upper and lower diagonals must be interchanged.

Figure 8.2
Storing by diagonals
for a 9×9 matrix

Before we proceed **further** we consider the diagonal storing for the 3-D example (3.15). In Fig. 8.4 the "regular" 6×6 diagonal blocks are indicated. The end blocks have 11 instead of 6 diagonals. But there are additional diagonals because of the unsymmetric formulae near the boundaries. Therefore for the worst case of Neumann B.C.'s in all 3 space directions 21·11+10·6 = 291 diagonals with 291·750.000 ≈ 220 mio storage locations for the 60 mio nonzero elements result. Thus because of the block diagonals and of the end formulae also diagonal storing produces an "overhead" for the storing. But this is the price to be paid for the evasion of all address calculation.

For the efficiency of an iterative linear solver the <u>stopping criterion</u> plays an important role. The iteration is stopped if the following condition holds:

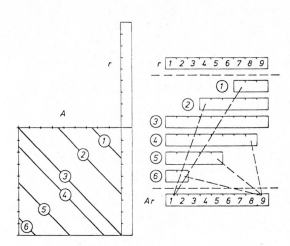

Figure 8.3
Illustration of the diagonal algorithm for the multiplication Ar

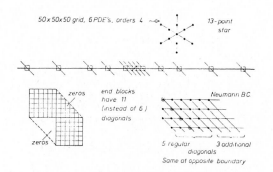

Figure 8.4
Illustration for the diagonal storing of example (3.15)

$$\frac{\left\| Q_d \Delta u^{(\nu,\mu)} - (Pu)_d \right\|}{\left\| (Pu)_d \right\|} \leq \varepsilon^{\ast}$$

(8.2)

$$= 0.1 \max \left[\left(\frac{\left\| \Delta u^{(\nu-1)} \right\|}{\left\| u_d^{(\nu-1)} \right\|} \right)^2 , \frac{\left\| D_k \right\|}{\left\| (Pu)_d \right\|} , \frac{\left\| Q_d^{(\nu-1)} \right\| \text{tol}}{\left\| (Pu)_d \right\|} \right] ,$$

limitation $0.1 \leq \varepsilon^{\ast} \leq 10^{-4}$, $\varepsilon^{\ast} = 0.1$ for $\nu = 1$,

with ν, μ iteration index for NR iteration and linear iterative solution, D_k key discretization error, e.g. $D_k = D_x + D_y + D_z$, tol is the given relative tolerance and for $\| Q_d^{(\nu-1)} \|$ we use the approximation $\| (Pu)_d^{(\nu-1)} \| / \| \Delta u^{(\nu-1)} \|$. The three terms in the brackets in (8.2) mean that the residual of the linear system on the consistency level should be small compared to the required accuracy of the NR correction, to the discretization error and to the given relative tolerance. The first term is explained in [2], the other two terms will be explained in a forthcoming paper.

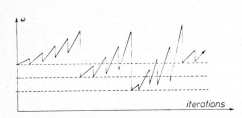

Figure 8.5
Meandering of ω for MJOR

As a consequence of diagonal storing we take as candidates only such iterative methods which are based on matrix-vector multiplications. We consider the following three methods:

Meander Jacobi overrelaxation (MJOR):

The method has been presented in [10], comparison tests have been presented in [8,9]. The idea is to use the classical JOR with a relaxation factor ω which is continuously varying like a meander, see Fig.8.5, and is controlled by a sophisticated strategy. If we want to solve

$$Ax = b , \quad r = Ax - b , \tag{8.3}$$

we define a JOR method by

$$D = \text{main diag } A , \quad A^* = D^{-1}A , \quad b^* = D^{-1}b ,$$
$$r^{*(\mu+1)} = r^{*(\mu)} - \omega A^* r^{*(\mu)} , \quad x^{(\mu+1)} = x^{(\mu)} - \omega r^{*(\mu)} . \tag{8.4}$$

The essential operation is $A^* r^{*(\mu)}$ .Presently we are testing new meanders (2/2 meanders in the terminology of [10]). The result of the meandering ω is a surprising efficiency which is far better than with the classical JOR. The disadvantage of MJOR is that it needs a "certain" (less than classical) diagonal dominance for convergence.

Preconditioned Jacobi conjugate gradient (PJCG): We assume in (8.3) A to be a general matrix. Therefore we cannot directly apply CG which assumes A to be symmetric positive definite, but we have to use the least squares method:

$$\underbrace{A^T A}_{B} x = \underbrace{A^T b}_{c} . \tag{8.5}$$

We apply a symmetric Jacobi preconditioning by

$$D = \text{main diag } B , \quad \underbrace{D^{-1/2} B D^{-1/2}}_{\hat{B}} \underbrace{D^{1/2} x}_{\hat{x}} = \underbrace{D^{-1/2} c}_{\hat{c}} \tag{8.6}$$

and solve $\hat{B}\hat{x} = \hat{c}$ by CG. Comparison tests have been presented in [8,9]. The matrix B is not explicitly computed, see [8,9]. The essential operations are two matrix-vector multiplications per iteration step. The disadvantage of PJCG is the squaring of the condition number in (8.5)which means a considerable loss of efficiency.

Biconjugate gradient method (BICO): The method of Fletcher [11] has been discussed in [12] and can be considered as the "CG" for indefinite linear systems. (8.3) is solved directly by an algorithm based on Lanczos' algorithm. The essential operations are two matrix-vector multiplications per iteration step. There is no squaring of the condition number. But theoretically the algorithm may fail for "critical" matrices A.

The problem is now to select the optimal algorithm out of these three and eventually further algorithms. This cannot be done by the user and cannot be done once because the properties of the matrix A may change during the PDE solution process (e.g. change of order). We believe that a continous dynamic choice in the form of a polyalgorithm gives the best compromise between efficiency and robustness.

The basic ideas have been presented in [8,9]. We make ml steps with method ℓ and determine a "normalized" (to equal computational amount) convergence factor k_1 for each method, then choose the best method i and make mi steps, check again and so on. If one method runs into an inefficient period, an automatic switch to another method is made. But there are problems because the CG type methods at first oscillate and then suddenly "fall down the cliff".

Another problem is that during the solution process only the L_2-norm of the pseudoresidual (transformed residual) is available. Therefore we check $\|\text{relat.pseudoresidual}\|_2 < \varepsilon$, in the affirmative check also if $\|\text{relat.residual}\| < \varepsilon^{\times}$ (8.2), put $\varepsilon = \varepsilon^{\times}$ at the beginning and adapt ε if necessary during the iteration process.

$\Downarrow$ $Ax=b$, stop if $\dfrac{\|Ax^{\mu}-b\|}{\|b\|} < \varepsilon^{*}$

LINSOL		
Nr.	conv. fact.	method
1	k_1	MJOR
2	k_2	BICO
3	k_3	PJCG
⋮		
		last method : emergency exit

Figure 8.6
Polyalgorithm

| B.C. | order | R | MJOR | | | BICO | PJCG | estimatet max. relative error |
			3/2,GF=2.9	2/2,GF=2.9	2/2,GF=3.0 AF=2.9			
Dir.	3	1	72	94	78	111	772	0.03 %
		10	106	130	106	90	870	0.02 %
		100	div.	div.	div.	77	1606	0.04 %
Neu.	3	1	516	356	534	244	3730	0.5 %
		10	414	398	474	212	3776	0.35 %
		100	div.	div.	div.	363		87 %
Dir.	5	1	321	284	342	230	1664	0.003%
		10	288	172	324	195	1228	0.003%
		100	div.	div.	div.	210		0.54 %
Neu.	5	1	1479	1760	1750	450	>7308	0.05 %
		10	1062	784	922	361	>9010	0.05 %
		100	div.	div.	div.	507		0.54 %

Table 8.1
Comparison tests, number of matrix-vector multiplications

Presently we are still running numerical experiments with different candidates for the individual components of LINSOL. Recent test results which use the new criterion (8.2) and include now BICO are presented in table 8.1. We use the test PDE

$$au_{xx}+bu_{yy}+cu_{zz}+R(du_{xx}+eu_y+fu_z)+gu+h = 0 \ , \tag{8.7}$$

the coefficients and the solution (trigonometric functions) are given in [8,9]. The coefficients of the linear system are computed by SLDGL. The domain of solution is the unit cube, the B.C.'s are either Dirichlet (Dir) on all 6 surfaces or Neumann on 3 surfaces and Dirichlet on the 3 opposite surfaces (Neu). We use an equidistant 18×18×18 grid and the orders 3/3/3 or 5/5/5 in the 3 space directions (FIDISOL would give the even orders 4 and 6 in these cases). The parameter R simulates a Reynolds number for a flow model: small R means diffusion dominated flow with diagonal dominant matrix, large R means convection dominated flow and complete loss of diagonal dominance. The three examples for MJOR in Table 8.1 designate three different control parameters for the ω meander.

The results of Table 8.1 indicate that for small R MJOR is the best method, but for higher values of R BICO is clearly superior. For R = 10^4 also BICO fails to produce a solution within 1000 matrix-vector multiplications (we stopped there the iteration). It is interesting to see the influence of the B.C.'s and of the order on the number of matrix-vector multiplications but also on the estimated relative error (which is close to the exact error). We believe that we are now only at the beginning of the development of efficient linear solvers. The multigrid methods are also promising, but presently are not yet robust enough to be included into such a general purpose program.

9. MODULARIZATION AND VECTORIZATION

A theoretically oriented program designer would try to optimize the use of the arithmetic units, ignoring the data transfer. A practically oriented designer gives absolte priority to data flow control because in present vector computers the arithmetic speed by far exceeds the i/o for large data sets (remember Fig. 8.4). Therefore in FIDISOL the arrangement of the data in the store is the key to all algorithms. The background has been presented in [13],[14]. We want to demonstrate some of the related ideas by examples.

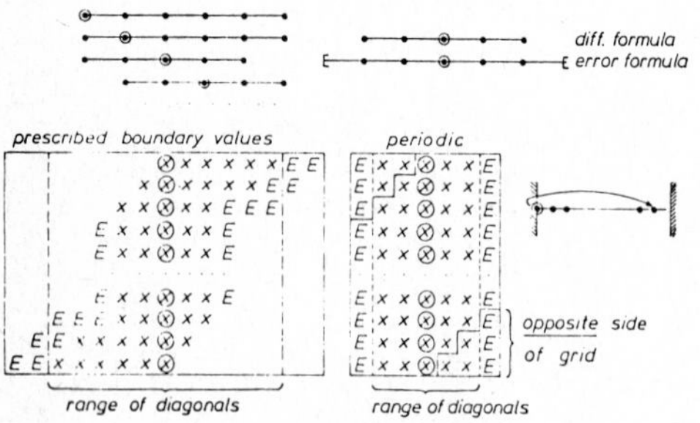

Figure 9.1
Arrangement of the coefficients
of difference formulae

In Fig. 9.1 there is depicted the arrangement of the difference formulae and error formulae (with additional points E) for prescribed boundary values and for periodic boundary conditions, from which also the diagonal pattern can be seen. There is no difference for equidistant and nonequidistant grid. If we want to compute a deriva-

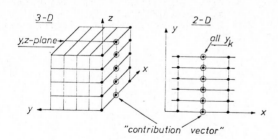

Figure 9.2
Illustration for the computation
of a derivative

tive by the evaluation of
a difference formula,
e.g.

$$u_{xx,d} = \sum_j a_j u_j , \qquad (9.1)$$

we can do this with the
same program for 3-D and
2-D, if in 3-D the u's
are arranged as "vectors"
in planes x=const and in
2-D on lines x=const, see
Fig. 9.2. Then we have
the following nested
loops:

loop over all x_i
    loop over all points of formula (j)
        loop over "contribution vector".

For the computation of y- and z-derivatives <u>sorting</u> in planes/lines
y=const and z=const is necessary. But with <u>large data sets</u> this sorting is a "controlled" access to the data in contrast to "random"
access without sorting.

An **essential part** of FIDISOL is **the generation of the matrix** Q_d.
Usually the matrix is generated by lines, see Fig. 9.3a, but

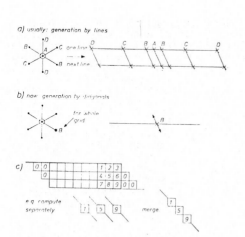

for diagonal storing and vectorization the generation
now is directly by diagonals,
see Fig. 9.3b. But if we have a system of PDE's we compute at first the "diagonal
parts" and merge them to the
final diagonal, see Fig.9.3c.
In the following we consider
for simplicity only a single
PDE.

In Fig. 9.4 there is depicted the composition of the
matrix elements for a 4th
order difference star, $a_{x,o}$
e.g. is the **central**
coefficient of the difference
formula $u_{x,d}$, $a_{x,1}$ is the
next right coefficient etc.
Fig. 9.4 illustrates the
<u>simultaneous</u> (fully vectori-
zed) computation of the main
diagonal coefficient A of
Fig. 9.4 over the whole grid.
All contributing terms must
be "prepared" and stored as
"vectors" over the whole

Figure 9.3
Generation of matrix elements,
a) by lines, b) **by diagonals,**
c) for a system of 3 PDE's

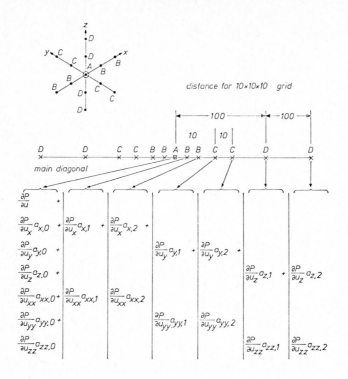

Figure 9.4
Composition of the elements of the
matrix Q_d for a 4th order difference star

grid. Coefficients of x,y,z-formulae change with i,j,k. But in the
vectors $\partial P/\partial u$, $\partial P/\partial u_x$,... there are contained the B.C.'s at boundary
points. Therefore in an expensive merging the B.C.'s $\partial G/\partial u$, $\partial G/\partial u_x$,...
are stored in the appropriate locations. Then the operations of the
first line of Fig. 9.5 can be executed as vector operations.

But there is for large data sets i.e. usual 3-D problems the difficulty that the main storage (CRAY) or the address space (IBM) or the
maximum vector length (CYBER 205) is to small. Therefore we offer
the possibility to subdivide the length of the vectors in Fig. 9.5
into parts of length mv and a remainder. But this automatically induces that also all terms which enter into the computation of the
$\partial P/\partial u$, $\partial P/\partial u_x$,... the solution and the preevaluated derivatives,
must be subdivided in the same way.

The consequent modularization of FIDISOL aims at the development of
modules which can be used as far as possible for elliptic and parabolic PDE's, for 3-D and 2-D PDE's, for prescribed and periodic
B.C.'s, for selfadaptive and nonselfadaptive solution method. Fig.
9.6 shows a coarse scheme for the modularization of the elliptic solver. The parabolic solver is an easy extension. The NR method is the

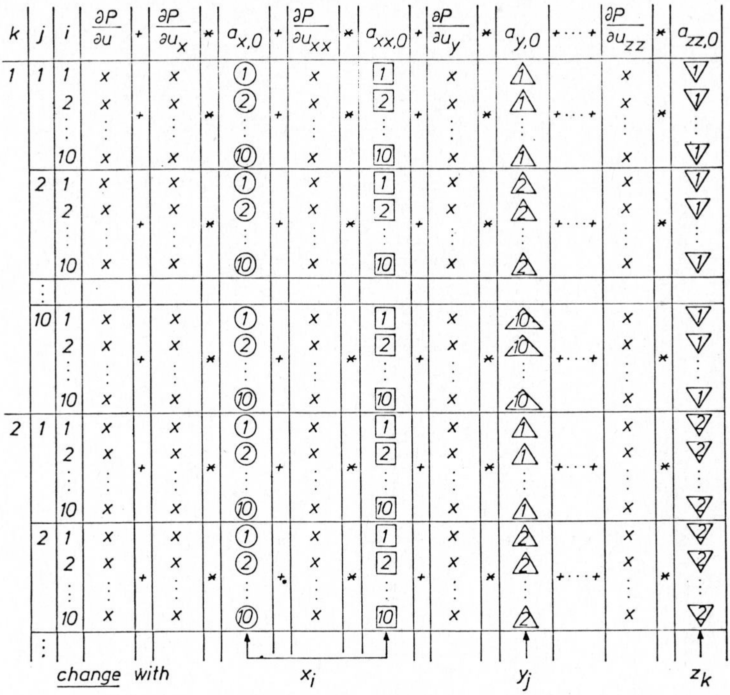

k	j	i	$\dfrac{\partial P}{\partial u}$	$+$	$\left\|\dfrac{\partial P}{\partial u_x}\right\|$	$*$	$a_{x,0}$	$+$	$\dfrac{\partial P}{\partial u_{xx}}$	$*$	$a_{xx,0}$	$+$	$\dfrac{\partial P}{\partial u_y}$	$*$	$a_{y,0}$	$+\cdots+$	$\left\|\dfrac{\partial P}{\partial u_{zz}}\right\|$	$*$	$a_{zz,0}$
1	1	1	x		x		①		x		⬜1		x		△			x		▽
		2	x	$+$	x	$*$	②	$+$	x	$*$	⬜2	$+$	x	$*$	△	$+\cdots+$	x	$*$	▽
		⋮	⋮		⋮		⋮		⋮		⋮		⋮		⋮		⋮		⋮
		10	x		x		⑩		x		⬜10		x		△			x		▽
	2	1	x		x		①		x		⬜1		x		△			x		▽
		2	x	$+$	x	$*$	②	$+$	x	$*$	⬜2	$+$	x	$*$	△	$+\cdots+$	x	$*$	▽
		⋮	⋮		⋮		⋮		⋮		⋮		⋮		⋮		⋮		⋮
		10	x		x		⑩		x		⬜10		x		△			x		▽
⋮																			
	10	1	x		x		①		x		⬜1		x		△10			x		▽
		2	x	$+$	x	$*$	②	$+$	x	$*$	⬜2	$+$	x	$*$	△10	$+\cdots+$	x	$*$	▽
		⋮	⋮		⋮		⋮		⋮		⋮		⋮		⋮		⋮		⋮
		10	x		x		⑩		x		⬜10		x		△10			x		▽
2	1	1	x		x		①		x		⬜1		x		△			x		▽
		2	x	$+$	x	$*$	②	$+$	x	$*$	⬜2	$+$	x	$*$	△	$+\cdots+$	x	$*$	▽
		⋮	⋮		⋮		⋮		⋮		⋮		⋮		⋮		⋮		⋮
		10	x		x		⑩		x		⬜10		x		△			x		▽
	2	1	x		x		①		x		⬜1		x		△			x		▽
		2	x	$+$	x	$*$	②	$+$	x	$*$	⬜2	$+$	x	$*$	△	$+\cdots+$	x	$*$	▽
		⋮	⋮		⋮		⋮		⋮		⋮		⋮		⋮		⋮		⋮
		10	x		x		⑩		x		⬜10		x		△			x		▽
⋮																			

change with x_i y_j z_k

Figure 9.5
Composition of the main diagonal coefficient A
of Fig. 9.4 over the whole grid x_i, y_j, z_k

central module, whose kernel is depicted in more detail in Fig.9.7, but without max iterations and without simplified NR. It is essential for the whole program that this kernel is very carefully designed, with reasonable error information if it fails. This is what H.Stetter [1] calls numerical engineering, see Fig. 1.1b.

It is trivial, that the problem of <u>vectorization</u> is closely related to the modularization, which came out clearly in the preceding text. But there are·still some further remarks worth while to be mentioned.

One problem is the delivery of the PDE's, of the B.C.'s and of the corresponding Jacobian matrices, i.e. $(Pu)_d$,$(Gu)_d$, $\partial P/\partial u$, $\partial P/\partial u_x$,..., $\partial G/\partial u$, $\partial G/\partial u_x$,... to the PDE solver. In SLDGL this is made by subroutines which are called by SLDGL in the innermost do-loop. But subroutine calls prevent vectorization. Therefore in FIDISOL the user has to enter his formulae into given fully vectorizable <u>program frames</u> (into the innermost loop) which are called by FIDISOL with presorted vectors. If the user's formulae are vectorizable, these whole program frames are vectorizable.

Another problem is that of sorting. If we have a system of n=3 PDE's we may have two sortings of the 3 unknown functions u, v, w namely

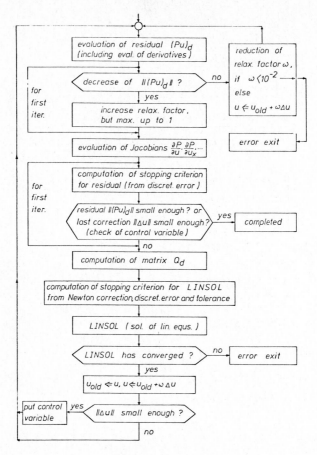

Figure 9.6
Coarse scheme for the modularization of the elliptic solver

$$u_1v_1w_1u_2v_2w_2 \cdots \longleftrightarrow u_1u_2 \cdots v_1v_2 \cdots w_1w_2 \cdots$$

Sorting of one form into the other corresponds to transposing a matrix, see Fig. 9.8a,b. If we assume that e.g. on a CYBER 205 we want to sort form a → b and the matrix needs 3 large pages we proceed always by lines in form a and by columns in form b, see Fig. 9.8c,d, thus minimizing the number of page faults. Therefore we use for c,d two different sorting algorithms. The same problem arises in a computer with fixed storage if the matrix exceeds the storage which is available to the user.

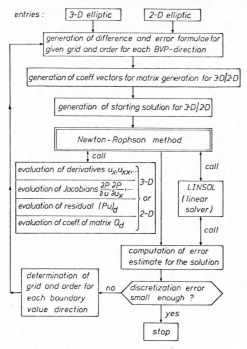

Figure 9.7
Structure of the kernel of the Newton-Raphson module

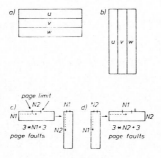

Figure 9.8
Illustration of the sorting process

10. A FIRST TEST RESULT AND CONCLUSION

Presently we have only a first test version of FIDISOL, including a
test version of LINSOL which contains only MJOR with the 3/2 meander
(first MJOR column in Table 8.1). Nevertheless it is interesting to
follow the progress in problem solving for the first example of
Table 8.1: Solution of the test PDE (8.7) with R = 1 for 18×18×18
grid with Dirichlet B.C.'s on the unit cube.

On SIEMENS 7880 (≈0.83×IBM 3081, measured for matrix multiplication)

1. Standard SLDGL (has nearly classical Jacobi linear solver),
   order 3: 36 min 32 sec CPU.

We introduce a new linear solver LINSOL (as mentioned above) into
SLDGL and the new stopping criterion (8.2) (the last two terms in
the brackets are new ones).

2. SLDGL (modified) with LINSOL, order 3:
   69.08 sec CPU.

Now we switch to FIDISOL, i.e. the matrix is generated by FIDISOL:

3. FIDISOL with the same LINSOL, now the order is 4:
   60.2 sec CPU.

On CYBER 205 (1 pipe, 1 megaword)

We take the program of point 3 on the vector computer, but choose
the scalar mode:

4. FIDISOL (same as 3.), in scalar mode:
   33.79 sec CPU, 312.8 SBU.

SBU = system billing units of CYBERNET convention.
Now we choose the vector option for compilation:

5. FIDISOL (same as 4.) with autovectorization:
   4.07 sec CPU, 73.9 SBU.

Two loops with suspicion of a recursion could not be vectorized automatically, therefore they are vectorized by explicit vector instructions:

6. FIDISOL (same as 5.), with two explicit vector operations:
   3.82 sec CPU, 70.29 SBU.

The choice of a better algorithm on the same computer took us from
36 min 32 sec to 60.2 sec, increasing the speed by a factor of 36.4.
The switching to the vector computer then took us to 3.82 sec, increasing the speed by a factor of 15.8 or a total of 574 compared to
the original value. It is remarkable that the autovectorizer reduced
the time from 33.79 sec to 4.07 sec, indicating that the program vec-
torizes excellently, i.e. that our design goal has been fully
achieved.

In conclusion we may make the following rather trivial statements:

- PDE software should give an information about the accuracy of the
  solution.

- For large 3-D problems the efficiency of the whole program depends on the efficiency of the linear solver. There further essential improvements are needed.

- A careful design of the whole program leads to full vectorization on vector computers. The key to vectorization for large 3-D problems is the data flow control.

11. ACKNOWLEDGEMENT

The SLDGL project has been supported by the Stiftung Volkswagenwerk, the FIDISOL project (including LINSOL) is supported by the Deutsche Forschungsgemeinschaft.

12. REFERENCES

[1] H.Stetter, Modular analysis of numerical software, Lecture Notes in Mathematics 773, Springer 1980, pp. 133-145.

[2] W.Schönauer, K.Raith, G.Glotz, The principle of the difference of difference quotients as a key to the selfadaptive solution of nonlinear partial differential equations, Computer Methods in Applied Mech. and Eng. 28 (1981), pp. 327-359.

[3] W.Schönauer, K.Raith, G.Glotz, The SLDGL-program package for the selfadaptive solution of nonlinear systems of elliptic and parabolic PDE's, Advances in Computer Methods for Partial Differential Equations - IV, edited by R.Vichnevetsky and R.S.Stepleman, IMACS 1981, pp. 117-125.

[4] M.Lentini, V.Pereyra, An adaptive finite difference solver for nonlinear two-point boundary problems with mild boundary layers, SIAM J.Num.Anal., vol 14 (1977), pp. 91-111.

[5] W.Schönauer, K.Raith, G.Glotz, The selfadaptive solution of 2-D boundary value problems in a rectangular domain, Numerical Methods in Laminar and Turbulent Flow, edited by C.Taylor and B.A.Schrefler, Pineridge Press, Swansea 1981, pp. 943-953.

[6] K.Raith, W.Schönauer, Ein Differenzenverfahren zur Lösung zweidimensionaler elliptischer Randwertprobleme auf allgemeinen Gebieten, ZAMM 61 (1981), pp. T307-T309.

[7] W.Schönauer, K.Raith, E.Schnepf, Basic ideas for the design of general purpose engineering software for nonlinear systems of elliptic and parabolic PDE's, Proceedings Third Int.Sympos.on Num.Methods in Engin., edited by P.Lascaux, Pluralis, Paris 1983, pp. 865-873.

[8] W.Schönauer, K.Raith, A Polyalgorithm with diagonal storing for the solution of very large indefinite linear banded systems on a vector computer, Proceedings of the 10th IMACS World Congress on System Simulation and Scientific Computation, vol 1, IMACS (1982), pp. 326-328.

[9] W.Schönauer, The efficient solution of large linear systems, resulting from the FDM for 3-D PDE's, on vector computers, Proceedings First Intern.Cooloqu. on Vector and Parallel Computing in Scientific Applications, edited by A.Bossavit, E.D.F.Bulletin de la Direction des Etudes et Recherches, Serie C, 1983,pp.135-142.

[10] W.Schönauer, Numerical experiments with instationary Jacobi-OR methods for the iterative solution of linear equations, ZAMM 63 (1983), pp. T380-382.

[11] R.Fletcher, Conjugate gradient methods for indefinite systems, Proc. of the Dundee Biennial Conference on Numerical Analysis, edited by G.A.Watson, Springer (1975), pp. 73-89.

[12] Y.Saad, The Lanczos biorthogonalization algorithm and other oblique projection methods for solving large unsysmmetric systems, SIAM J. Num.Anal. 19 (1982), pp. 485-506.

[13] W.Schönauer, E.Schnepf, K.Raith, Modularization of PDE software for vector computers, to appear in ZAMM 64, Sonderheft der GAMM-Tagung 1983.

[14] E.Schnepf, W.Schönauer, Parallelization of PDE software for vector computers, to appear in the Proceedings of "Parallel Computing 83", Berlin 26.-28.9.1983.

[15] K.Raith, E.Schnepf, W.Schönauer, A new automatic mesh selection strategy for the solution of boundary value problems with selfadaptive difference methods, Notes on Numerical Fluid Mechanics, vol 5, Vieweg (1982), pp. 261-270.

13. INTERNAL REPORTS

For the customars of the SLDGL-program package there is available a detailed documentation of the different parts of SLDGL. These are the following Interne Berichte des Rechenzentrums der Universität Karlsruhe (Nr./year):

13/79 K.Raith, W.Schönauer, G.Glotz, SLGA, ein selbststeuerndes Lösungsverfahren für Anfangswertprobleme bei gewöhnlichen Differentialgleichungen.

16/80 G.Glotz, K.Raith, W.Schönauer, Die Lösung großer linearer Gleichungssysteme mit dem Programmpaket WAVE.

18/80 W.Schönauer, K.Raith, Skizze der Arbeitsweise des SLDGL-Programmpakets.

19/81 K.Raith, G.Glotz, W.Schönauer, Differenzenformeln aus dem Newtonschen Steigungsschema.

20/81 G.Glotz, W.Schönauer, K.Raith, SLGR: Ein Programmpaket zur selbstadaptiven Berechnung von Randwertproblemen bei gewöhnlichen Differentialgleichungen 2.Ordnung.

21/81 E.Schnepf, Untersuchungen zu optimalen Stützstellenverteilungen bei der Lösung von Randwertproblemen mit Hilfe von selbststeuernden Differenzenverfahren.

22/82 K.Raith, G.Glotz, W.Schönauer, SLxP-Programme zur Lösung von nichtlinearen Systemen von parabolischen Differentialgleichungen im Rechteckgebiet.

23/83 K.Raith, G.Glotz, W.Schönauer, E.Schnepf, SLxE-Programme zur Lösung von nichtlinearen Systemen von elliptischen Differentialgleichungen.

DISCUSSION

Speaker: W. Schönauer

Pridor: Do you intend to treat irregular boundaries in FiDiSol?

Schönauer: Presently we recommend only to transform the irregular domain to a
rectangular domain. There is the excellent book of J. Thompson "Numerical grid
generation" which gives the actual state of the art in this field. But if you
read this book carefully you find still a lot of open problems.

Sherman: You use finite difference methods. Central difference do not work very
well, e.g. with large Reynolds number. Why don't you run into stability problems?

Schönauer: We have also problems with high Reynolds number, and therefore we
shall program an upwind differencing method, with the same error philosophy.

Young: In your talk you mentioned a method based on the Jacobi method. I suspect
that the parameters involved could be determined on the basis of Chebyshev
polynomials and that the scheme would be closely related to Chebyshev acceleration
applied to the Jacobi method (a two -term form). Can you tell how the parameters
were determined and what the resulting convergence rates were?

Schönauer: We solve arbitrary (indefinite, non-symmetric) linear systems. In our
Meander Jacobi Overrelaxation (MJOR) method the relaxation parameter is determined
by the residual itself and not predetermined (see reference in the paper). There
is presently no theory of MJOR. The convergence rate strongly depends on the
diagonal dominance and the structure of the matrix (e.g. the order of the
difference star or the type of boundary conditions).

Trottenberg: In my opinion, there is a big gap between the efficiency of the
solution methods that you use in your codes and for instance, the efficiency of
multigrid methods. Do you see any possibility to improve your solution methods
substantially?

Schönauer: We have just started to look for better methods. But the methods must
be robust enough for our environment. We look e.g. with great interest at the
multigrid methods or at algebraic multigrid, but presently these methods are not
robust enough for our black box solver.

Zlatev: How is the discretization error analysis organized? Do you attempt to
control both the errors in the space and the errors in the time dimension?

Schönauer: Both errors are controlled: The space grid and order are determined
for the given accuracy requirement at the initial profile and then remain fixed.
The time discretization error then is adapted to the space discretization error.

Zlatev: Could you solve problems containing first order space derivatives only
(hyperbolic equations) with your package?

Schönauer: No. But we intend to program an upwind differencing version and with
this one it might be possible (but without discontinuties).

Hemker: The matrices you consider have many diagonals because you use high order
difference schemes. Can you not use low order difference methods to set up a
simpler system of equations and apply defect correction to improve the accuracy of
the method?

Schönauer: In our semi-iterative method for the solution of the linear equations in 2-D, we do a similar thing, but directly from the lowest order to the highest order, which might be more than 100% change of the "low order solution" and might cause the method to diverge. But for the solution itself (in contrast to the iterative determination of a Newton correction) we never add an error estimate to the solution, because we then have no information about the accuracy of this solution.

Leaf: Is the mesh restricted to be uniform in your program?

Schönauer: The time mesh is always non-equidistant. The space mesh may be equidistant or non-equidistant, but the meshlines must go always from boundary to boundary (a purely local concentration of the points is not possible).

Duff: The Newton-Raphson iteration is not noted for its robustness on general nonlinear systems. Even the damped (underrelaxed) method wich you mentioned is not always efficient or robust. Have you encountered problems with this, how does your software handle it, and have you considered employing a more robust technique (such as a sparse version of Powell's dogleg algorithm or Levenberg-Marquardt)?

Schönauer: We willingly do not consider other methods. If the damping factor is less than 0.01 we give up and print out to the user that he should think about a better initial solution or a finer initial grid. If the user has proposed to the PDE solver a problem which is not well posed, no better method can furnish a solution. Our experience has been very favorable with our method, mainly because we accept a solution only if the Newton residual is decreased.

Machura: Could you comment on the "black box" feature of the system you have designed. You seem to have assumed that the user does not want to have a deeper insight into the solution process and that he expects you to make right decisions for him. This approach is in contradiction to the present trend to decompose the "black box" software into "black box" parts, which the user can use as building blocks to compose his program.

Schönauer: The users of our system will be mostly engineers, who have not been educated enough neither in numerics nor in computer science. For them the system should take all the decisions itself. For a more sophisticated user it is possible to influence the solution procedure by modifying the corresponding "program parts", whose documentation is given in a very detailed description.

PDE SOFTWARE: Modules, Interfaces and Systems
B. Engquist and T. Smedsaas (eds.)
Elsevier Science Publishers B.V. (North-Holland)
© IFIP, 1984

PARTITIONING AND ALLOCATION OF PDE COMPUTATIONS
IN DISTRIBUTED SYSTEMS

C. E. Houstis

Department of Electrical Engineering
University of South Carolina
Columbia, South Carolina
U.S.A.

E. N. Houstis

Department of Applied Mathematics
University of Thessaloniki
Thessaloniki
Greece

J. R. Rice

Department of Computer Sciences
Purdue University
West Lafayette, Indiana
U.S.A.

A methodology of partitioning PDE computations into computational
modules is introduced and applied to several examples. The problem
of allocating these modules to the processing units of a distributed
system is formulated and a heuristic algorithm for its solution is
presented. The algorithm's objective is to minimize interunit
communication overhead and to exploit the parallelism of the partitioned computation.

INTRODUCTION

The operation of a distributed system for the execution of a PDE computation requires first the partitioning of the computation into parallel computational
modules (CMs) and then their allocation to the physical processing units (PUs) of
the system. The two problems addressed in this paper are: (1) how to identify
the CMs most suitable for a distributed computation, and (2) how to allocate the
CMs to the PUs. The objectives in the allocation problem are to (a) exploit the
inherent parallelism of the PDE computation, (b) preserve the computational
order where necessary (synchronization), and (c) minimize the communication cost
between PUs.

In section two, we present a methodology for partitioning PDE computations that
tries to achieve a balance between the parallelism and overhead requirements.
This methodology is applied to the discretization and solution process of an
elliptic boundary value model. In principle, this partitioning is made independently of the eventual execution environment; in practice a good partitioning
often reflects this environment. Along with partitioning the computation there
is also the partitioning of the problem data into data blocks (DBs).

In section three, we formulate the problem of allocating the computational modules
to the processing units. In this study we assume that the PUs are in a homogeneous distributed system, a D-system. We assume that each PU has its own local
memory and that there are also global memories which are connected by an inter-

connection network. The traffic in the D-system is modeled by a <u>delay function</u>, d(u), where d is the delay per <u>information transfer unit</u> (ITU) and u is the network utilization. The objective of the allocation problem is to allocate the CMs and problem data to the PUs and memory so that the performance (measured by communication cost) is minimized subject to certain constraints. A heuristic algorithm is presented to solve this problem which is based on a clustering technique.

The combination of partitioning the PDE computation and its data and then allocating the parts to processing units and memories defines an algorithm for the computation. We call such algorithms <u>D-algorithms</u>.

THE PARTITIONING OF PDE COMPUTATIONS

The design of a D-algorithm for a given computation is viewed here as consisting of two distinct phases: the partitioning and allocation. The <u>partitioning phase</u> consists of subdividing the given computation into computational modules and clustering them into disjoint subsets for parallel or independent execution. This phase is based upon the relative strength of relationships between them. The <u>allocation phase</u> deals with grouping subsets of CMs and data blocks and then assigning them to physical processing units of the D-system. We deal with the second phase in section three.

Our objectives in the partitioning phase are:

(1) To partition of the computation into an appropriate number of communicating processes to be executed concurrently in a D-system.

(2) To keep overhead involved in implementing the algorithm as low as possible.

We assume that these objectives are met when a D-algorithm satifies the following design criteria:

(i)   Numerical stability is achieved.

(ii)   The required synchronization among processes is kept to a minimum.

(iii) The interprocess communication required by D-algorithms which satisfy (i) and (ii) is minimized.

(iv)   The algorithm is computation bound (i.e., not communication intensive).

To illustrate the design of a D-algorithm we consider the solution of an elliptic problem:

$$\frac{\partial^2 u}{\partial x^2} + \frac{\partial^2 u}{\partial y^2} = f \quad , \; x \in R \subset R^2$$

subject to Dirichlet boundary conditions

$$u = 0$$

The numerical solution of such a PDE involves

(i)   The discretization of the PDE to obtain a system of algebraic equations.

(ii) The solution of the algebraic system.

Numerous techniques exist for these two stages of the computation. For stage (i) we consider two finite element techniques: Galerkin based on linear quadrilateral elements and a collocation method based on bicubic-Hermite polynomials. For stage (ii) we consider an SOR type iterative method.

Example 1. A distributed Galerkin discretization algorithm

Consider a rectangular grid overlay Ω of R such as generated by the ELLPACK domain processor [Rice and Boisvert, 1984]. Denote by Ω' the elements of Ω that intersect R. Then the quadrilateral finite mesh D of R is obtained by mapping the boundary elements of Ω' to the domain R, see [Houstis et al, 1983]. Then the computation of the discretized Galerkin equations of the PDE problem is described as follows:

>   for e ε D do
>   begin
>   compute element stiffness matrix K_e;
>   Replace - Add (K,K_e);
>   end

where K is the global stiffness matrix over the entire discretization region. The operation Replace-Add (v,e) is indivisible and yields $s = v+e$ as its value and replaces the value of v by the sum s.

To construct a D-algorithm for Galerkin discretization, we partition D into M sets S_1, S_2, ... , S_M such that

(1) for any element e in D there is an index i in $\{1,...,M\}$ such that
$$e \in S_i. \quad \text{Thus} \quad \bigcup_{i=1}^{M} S_i = D.$$

(2) for any i from 1 to M and any pair e_1, $e_2 \in S_i$ we have $e_1 \cap e_2 = \phi$

(3) M is the minimum value so that (1) and (2) hold.

Assuming the existance of such a partition then Galerkin discretization can be expressed as M sequential steps. The ith step consists of K_i identical computational modules where K_i is the cardinality of S_i. Each module is expressed by

>   process stiffness (e)
>   begins
>   compute element stiffness matrix K_e;
>   Replace-Add (K,K_e)
>   end

The entire discretization computation is thus

>   For i=1 to M do
>   For all e ε S_i do
>   process stiffness (e);

Note that the element stiffness matrices K_e, e$\in$D could be computed in parallel in one time step and then the assembly phase can be partitioned as above. This alternate computation can be expressed by

```
For all   e ε D  do
         compute K ;
                  e
For   i: = 1 to M  do
      For all  e ε S   do
                    i
           begin
           Replace-Add (K,K )
                          e
           end
```

We believe that such a partition can have larger overhead requirements than the
first one which we have chosen to analyze.

We now show that this D-algorithm for Galerkin discretization satisfies the four
design criteria stated above.

(i) Stability

The usual sequential execution of these processes is well known to be
numerically stable. It is clear that the stability of the computation of the
stiffness matrices is order independent; there is no interaction between these
computations. The Replace-Add operation essentially involves the cumulative
addition of numbers as the elements of the global stiffness matrix. This phase
is also numerically stable because (a) the number of terms added into any one
matrix element is bounded and (b) the magnitudes of the terms are similar in
each individual element's stiffness matrix. Harmful round-off effects could
occur because of the cancellation of terms, but the size of this effect does not
depend on any predictable way on the order of the addition so that the probability of numerical difficulty here is the same as with the usual sequential method.

(ii) Minimum Synchronization Requirement

It is easy to see that the required synchronizations in the above algorithm
are:

(i)   The synchronization imposed by the partition of D into M sets.

(ii) The synchronization among processes associated with elements of S_i due
      to the Replace-Add operation.

The synchronization due to source (ii) depends very much on the implementation of
the Replace-Add operation. [Gottlieb et al, 1983] present an efficient hardware
implementation of this operation which efficiently handles simultaneous Replace-
Adds on the same variable. We view this synchronization requirement to be similar
to the one in a producer/consumer mechanism and consider it as minimizing. The
synchronization requirement for (i) depends very much on the value of M, the
number of disjoint subsets of elements. Next, we present an algorithm for
partitioning D, we call it the row (or column) coloring algorithm. A coloring of
a partition if D is the assignment of a unique color to each element S_i in the
partition.

Row (or column) Coloring Algorithm

```
/*  Color each element of a row (or column) of Ω using two colors with consecu-
    tive rows (or columns) having different pairs of colors.  The number of rows
    in Ω is nrow.   */
```

Step 1: <u>loop</u> : row : = 1 to nrow step 2

        color each element in the row (or column)
        using two colors α,β alternately;

        <u>end</u> <u>loop</u>

Step 2: loop : row : = 2 to nrow step 2

        color each element in the row (or column)
        using two colors γ,δ alternately;

        <u>end loop</u>

The number of colors used is called the chromatic number. This algorithm subdivides the mesh D into at most four subsets of disjoint elements. In fact, the following lemma suggests that the minimum M is exactly four. For simplicity, we prove the lemma only for rectangular regions. The extension to general domains follows easily.

<u>LEMMA</u>

Let Ω' be the rectangular overlay used to generate the mesh D consisting of M rows and n columns. If $M,n \geq 2$ then the chromatic number of the mesh D is four. Furthermore, every coloring of D with four colors can be obtained by the row (or column) coloring algorithm.

<u>Proof of the Lemma</u>

The chromatic number is at least four since each block of four squares is a set of four mutually adjacent regions. The chromatic number is at most four since it is clear that every rectangular overlay can be colored using the coloring algorithm. This establishes that the chromatic number is four, we next show that every coloring with four colors is one obtained from the coloring algorithm.

Suppose there is a four colored mesh with one of its rows having elements with three or more different colors. Then it follows immediately that there are three consecutive elements in this row which have distinct colors. Consider the 3 × M submesh determined by these three elements. It can be shown that its coloring is completely determined. For instance, consider the row immediately below (or above) row r

row r →

| 1 | 2 | 3 |
| ϱ_1 | ϱ_2 | ϱ_3 |

labeled as shown. Notice that the elements ϱ_1, ϱ_2 must be assigned colors three and four but ϱ_2 cannot be three because of the requirements of the partition. So ϱ_1 is three and ϱ_2 is four. Thus ϱ_3 is one, and by using an induction argument one can determine the 3 × M mesh. Now, consider the column immediately to the left (or right) of the submesh. It follows that in each two consecutive squares in this column, we must have the colors two and four. Thus, by induction on the columns we determine coloring similar to the one described by the column algorithm.

Thus, if one row has three or more colors, the mesh can be colored by the column coloring algorithm. If no row has three or more colors, then it is obvious that the row coloring algorithm can be used to obtain the coloring. This concludes the proof.

This lemma also verifies criterion (iv) for this D-algorithm.

   (iii)   Intermodule Communication

      The interrelationships of the computational modules in the D-algorithm imply that there is zero intermodule communication among pairs of modules associated with elements of the same subset. The communication cost involved due to the Replace-Add operation can be computed from the interconnection delay function d = d(u) once the number of information transfer units (ITUs) per module is determined. The computation of this communication cost is discussed in section three.

      [Bokhari, 1981] presents a different coloring algorithm to partition a triangular mesh and studies various MIMD processing techniques for the generation of the finite element equations.

Example 2. A distributed Collocation discretization algorithm

Assuming the rectangular mesh Ω' of R obtained from the ELLPACK domain processor, we can describe the collocation discretization as follows:

> for e ε Ω' do
>
>> begin
>>
>> compute element stiffness matrix K_e;
>>
>> Replace-Add (K, K_e);
>
> end

For detail description of the method, see [Houstis et al, 1983]. The design of a D-algorithm for this computation is based on the observation that the computation of each K_e uses only information local to e while the updating of the global stiffness matrix does not require any synchronization. The discretization can in fact be expressed as follows:

> for e ε Ω' do
>
>> process global stiffness (e)
>
> end

where we use

> process global stiffness (e)
>
>> compute element stiffness matrix K_e
>>
>> Replace-Add (K, K_e)
>
> end

Thus, no real synchronization conditions exist beyond those of the Replace-Add and we have a D-algorithm consisting of M = cardinality of Ω' identical processes.

To verify the conditions (i) to (iv) we can apply the arguments used earlier for the Galerkin method D-algorithm. Furthermore, in this case there are no synchronization requirements due to interrelationships among computational modules.

Example 3. A distributed SOR algorithm for finite differences

Assuming for simplicity that R is the unit square and Ω' is an N × N grid in R, then the finite difference approximation to Poisson's equation at a mesh point (x_i, y_i) in Ω' may be written as follows:

$(h = 1/N-1, \; x_i = i*h, \; y_i = i*h)$

$4 \, u_{i,j} - u_{i+1,j} - u_{i-1,j} - u_{i,i+1} - u_{i,j-1} = h^2 f_{i,j} \; . \; 1 \le i,j \le N$

where u_{ij} is the estimate of $u(x_i, y_j)$. The SOR iteration method is defined by

$u_{i,j}^{(n+1)} = w \, [u_{i+1,j}^{(n)} + u_{i-1,j}^{(n+1)} + u_{i,j+1}^{(n)} + u_{i,j-1}^{(n+1)} - h^2 f_{i,j}]/4 + (1-w) \, u_{i,j}^{(n)}$

To develop a D-algorithm for SOR, we consider a partition of the grid points of Ω' into $p \times q$ disjoint subsets $b_{i,j}$, $i = 1$ to p, $j = 1$ to q, of grid points where each subset has cardinality $\frac{N}{p} \times \frac{N}{q}$. The subset $b_{i,j}$ contains all those points

$x_{\ell,m}$

for $\quad \ell = 1 + (i-1)p$ to ip

$\qquad m = 1 + (j-1)q$ to jq

See Figure 1.

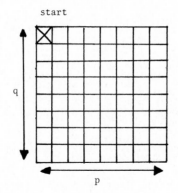

start

q

p

Figure 1

Partition of an N by N mesh into a p by q set of blocks of mesh points.

The synchronization of the D-algorithm for SOR is represented by the dependence graph in Figure 2 for the case $p = q = 3$. The i,j in Figure 2 represents the computational module involving the block $b_{i,j}$ of mesh points.

[Takahashi, 1982] presents a similar partitioning of the SOR computation for Laplace's equation. However, our allocation strategy is completely different from Takahashi's. The verification of the design criteria for this D-algorithm follows as in the previous two cases. In this case of the interprocess communication due to relationships between CMs may be significant. In fact, it is easy to observe each block $b_{i,j}$ must transfer $n = \frac{N}{p}$ ITU's and $m = \frac{N}{q}$ ITU's to neighboring blocks. One of the objectives of the allocation phase is to distribute the computation in a way that will minimize the total communication cost.

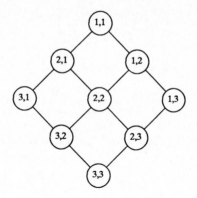

Figure 2
The dependence graph of the D-algorithm for SOR when p = q = 3.

Example 4. Finite Element Orderings

Figure 3 shows a finite element decomposition of a rectangular domain with two
slots (crossed areas). The domain is decomposed into 64 elements with a rectangular grid overlay, the elements are numbered from 1,1 to 8,8 as shown.

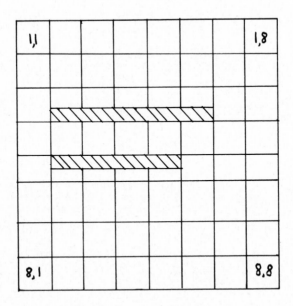

Figure 3
Finite element decomposition of rectangular domain with two slots removed (hashed
areas).

One may apply the frontal method to such problems to simultaneously form the stiffness matrix and carry out Gauss elimination to solve the PDE. The communication between elements depends on the finite element method used; common methods and basis functions require communication with the neighboring elements or elements one neighbor away. For simplicity here, we assume the simplest case of communication requirements only with the nearest neighbors.

A parallel approach to these computations is to start several processors at different points and let each create a "computational front." Such approaches are called multi-frontal methods. Figure 4 shows the synchronization graph that arises for a multi-frontal algorithm that starts one front at each of the four corners of the domain. This graph shows that the parallelism is almost complete at the start and then there is some synchronization required near the end when the four fronts collide near the center of the domain.

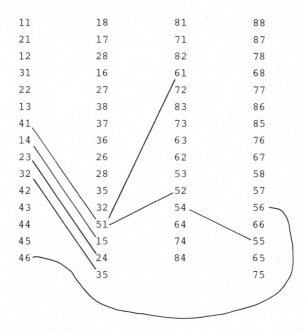

Figure 4

Synchronization graph of a multi-frontal algorithm using 4 fronts, one starting from each corner.

Figure 5 shows the synchronization graph that arises for a multi-frontal algorithm based on a nested dissection decomposition of the domain. Here fronts are started in 18 elements. Immediate collisions reduce the number of fronts to seven and then there are some later collisions that reduce the number of fronts to four. At the end there are quite complicated interactions as the fronts collide and coalesce at various places in the domain.

For the 4-front method of Figure 4, one could easily allocate the computation to four processing units by hand. It is not so clear what to do for this computation if one has fewer than four processors. More than four processors are unlikely to provide much benefit. For the nested dissection method of Figure 5, one is unlikely to be able to make a rational assignment of processors without considerable analysis. While 18 processors would provide the fastest execution and one the slowest, it is unclear how execution time and overall efficiency behave as the number of processors and varies from 18 down to one.

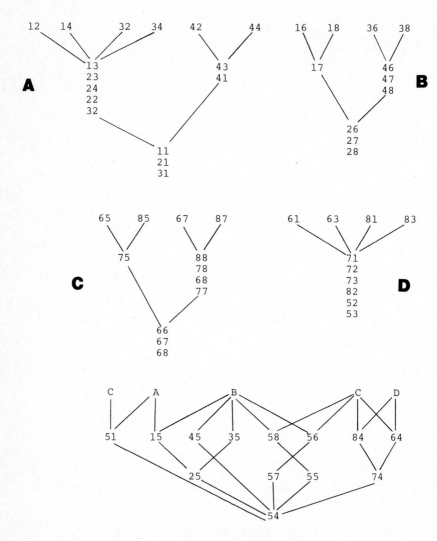

Figure 5
Synchronization graph of a multi-frontal algorithm based on a nested dissection ordering of the elements. The top four subgraphs labeled A,B,C and D are connected as shown in the bottom subgraph.

[Adams, 1979] presents a partitioning of the solution of the linear equations arising from some finite element or finite difference methods. His partition is a generalization of the classical red/black ordering of the grid points.

THE ALLOCATION PROBLEM

The implementation of a D-algorithm in a D-system requires an allocation of the computational modules to the processing units (PUs). Ideally, this involves the optimization of a performance measure under certain constraints imposed by the properties of the algorithm and architecture. The performance measure selected in this paper is the processing time of the D-algorithm. We assume that it is composed by the following three cost factors:

    (i)   execution of modules
   (ii)   interprocessor communication
  (iii)   common data reference

All the other possible cost factors (i.e., operating system cost) are assumed to be constants.

The constraints considered are the allowed work level of the D-system and the parallelism of the D-algorithm. For a given algorithm/architecture pair the allocation adopted tries to reduce (i) by exploiting the parallelism of the algorithm and to reduce (ii) and (iii) by clustering related computational modules with associated data blocks to the same PU.

This allocation is formulated mathematically by a cost function and constraints. The following quantities are used in this model.

D-algorithm quantities:

N_m = Number of computational modules

m_i = Storage used by the i-th module

t_i = Execution time of the i-th module

N_D = Number of global data blocks

M_i = Storage used by the i-th data block

X = Matrix representation of the synchronization graph

    x_{ij} = 1   means the i-th and j-th modules may be executed in parallel, otherwise x_{ij} = 0.

V = Matrix representation of the inter-module communication graph.

    v_{ij} = number of information units passed when module j follows module i.

        = 0 if both modules are on the same PU.

H = Matrix representation of the data communication graph.

    h_{ij} = number of information units that the i-th module requires from the j-th global data block.

D-system quantities:

N   = Number of processing units

P_i = Local storage capacity of i-th processor

g_i = Global storage capacity of the i-th processor

d(u) = Function which models the delay on the global communication bus as a function of the utilization u. An information unit is delayed by d(u).

u   = Utilization of the global bus, the number of information units being transferred over the bus divided by the total capacity C of the bus.

The allocation proposed in this paper is to minimize the communication costs under the artificial constraint that no processor execute more than time T. This provides an indirect method of minimizing the usual objective of total execution time. The advantage of this approach is that we have an efficient heuristic algorithm for solving this optimization problem. In practice this approach allows one to vary T and observe the change in the number of processors required to execute the D-algorithm.

Thus, the objective is to minimize:

communication cost between computation modules and communication cost between CUs and global data blocks

subject to the constraints:

(i) Module programs must fit into memory of PU.
(ii) Data blocks must fit into global memory of PU.
(iii) Must have enough time to execute all CMs allocated to a PU.
(iv) Execution time of the i-th PU is limited to T.

We note that the time limit T can be made non-uniform by replacing T by $r_i T$ in constraint (iv) where r_i is a constant. The analysis and heuristic algorithm may be modified in a straightforward way to handle this variation.

The strategy for allocating the D-algorithm to a D-system in this framework is expressed as follows:

Choose T

Do until satisfied

Solve the allocation problem

Observe (a) The number of PUs used

(b) The total computation time taken

Adjust T

end do

The mathematical formulation requires further quantities to express the allocation:

Q = Matrix representation of assignment of CUs

q_{ij} = 1 if the i-th CM is assigned to the j-th PU.

P = Matrix representation of assignment of data blocks

$p_{ij} = 1$ if the i-th data block is assigned to the j-th PU.

R = Auxilliary matrix

$$r_{ij} = 1 - \sum_k q_{ik} q_{jk}$$

= 0 if CMs i and j are assigned to the same PU

S = Auxilliary matrix

$$s_{ij} = 1 - \sum_k q_{ik} p_{ik}$$

= 0 if the i-th CM and the j-th data block are assigned to the same PU.

The three times associated with the computation on the k-th PU are:

$$T_e = \text{Execution time} = \sum_{i=1}^{N_m} t_i q_{ik}$$

$$T_c = \text{Communication time} = \sum_{i=1}^{N_m} q_{ik} \sum_{j=1}^{N_m} r_{ij} v_{ij} d(v_{ij}/(CT))$$

$$T_d = \text{Data time} = \sum_{i=1}^{N_m} q_{ik} \sum_{j=1}^{N_D} s_{ij} h_{ij} d(v_{ij}/(CT))$$

The three constraints for the k-th PU are:

Module storage: $\sum_{i=1}^{N_m} m_i q_{ik} \leq P_k$

Data storage : $\sum_{i=1}^{N_m} M_i p_{ik} \leq g_i$

Processing time: $T_e + T_c + T_d \leq T$

In addition to the three constraints on individual PUs there is also the synchronization constraint represented by X; two CMs to be executed in parallel cannot be assigned to the same PU. More explicitly,

If $X_{ij} = 1$ then $r_{ij} \neq 0$

This assures the exploitation of the parallelism in the D-algorithm.

For simplicity, we assume that P can be determined in advance. The reasoning is that the D-system is homogeneous, so we might as well assign the data blocks and then determine where to assign the CM's. If there were only one data block assigned per PU, then this assumption would be completely correct. This is a very likely situation, but not required. The analysis and heuristic algorithm can be extended in a straight forward manner to determine P. For simplicity, we have not done that here.

HEURISTIC ALGORITHM FOR THE ALLOCATION PROBLEM

There are two classes of algorithms for problems such as this allocation
problem: one is based on mathematical programming or exhaustive searches, the
other class uses heuristics. The disadvantage of the first class is that the
solution time may be too long and the disadvantage of the second class is that
one might not obtain an optimal solution. We present a heuristic algorithm here
and give some evidence that it is efficient and produces good solutions for PDE
computations.

[Ma et al, 1981] presents a similar allocation model for time critical applications. Their model uses different measures and they are a branch and bound
method to solve the allocation problem. [C. Houstis, 1984] uses a variant of our
model in a real-time application. [Gylys and Edwards, 1976] present a similar
model for the study of partitions of workloads in a D-system. Their model does
not use exclusive type constraints and they use distance measures for the interprocessor communication cost. [Li, 1981] presents an allocation model based on
an information transfer matrix and exploits its sparsity to study the impact of
processor interconnection on the global bus architecture. He uses a dynamic
programming algorithm to solve the allocation problem. Both [Bokhari, 1981] and
[Tukahaski, 1982] present allocation models for nearest neighbor D-systems.
Their solution of the allocation problem is equivalent to a well known NP-complete
computation. See [Hoversty and Jenny, 1980] for a study of the partitioning and
study of allocation of computational objects in networks of loosely coupled
processors.

Our algorithm for the solution of the allocation problem stated earlier is an
iterative method based on a heuristic cluster analysis approach. The basic idea
of the algorithm is group pairs of eligible computational modules or data blocks
into clusters such that the level of communication among clusters is minimized.
These clusters are then assigned to processing units and thus must meet the size
and synchronization constraints. This algorithm is described as follows:

      Algorithm

    INPUT: T = total time allowed for execution of any PU
              D-algorithm quantities = N_m, m_i, t_i, N_D, n_i, X, V, H

              D-system quantities = N_p, p_i, g_i, d(u), C

    OUTPUT: Q = Assignment matrix for computational modules
              P = Assignment matrix for data blocks

METHOD:

/* Initialization */

1. Set N_u: = N_M ; Allocate one CM per PU; Allocate each non-shared data
   block to a private memory unit and each shared data block to a common memory
   unit; Identify the pairs of CMs that are eligible for allocation to a
   single PU by testing the synchronization constraint X;

/* Select a pair of modules/data blocks to merge */

2. For the eligible pair search V to find the eligible pairs whose merging
   (allocation into a single PU) potentially eliminates the most information
   processing cost (IPC). If more than one eligible pair require the same IPC,
   select the pair which references the most shared data blocks; if this does
   not provide a unique pair, select one at random from these.

/* Check constraints */

3. If the three constraints are satisfied by the selected eligible pair then go
    to step 4 otherwise go to step 5.

/* Do the merging */

4. For the pair of CMs selected do the following: Allocate the CMs to a single
    PU, modify X. Allocate the associated data blocks of these CMs which are in
    private memory to the private memory of the single PU, update V and H.
    Decrease N_u by one and remove this pair from the list of eligible pairs.
    Go to step 6.

/* Eliminate pairs that violate the constraints */

5. Remove this pair from the list of eligible pairs.

/* Algorithm termination test */

6. If the list of eligible pairs is empty then stop, otherwise return to step 2.

The allocation produced by this heuristic algorithm depends on the value of the
artificial variable T. If one wishes to obtain an allocation into K PUs (K is
normally either the number of PUs available or the number of "natural" parallel
clusters in the D-algorithm), then one starts with a large initial value T_0 for T
and successively reduces it until K PUs are used. The resulting value of T is
hoped to be a realistic estimate of the best performance for the D-algorithm
executing on the given D-system.

We give two examples of the application of this algorithm using a particular
D-system. In the first example, our algorithm obtains the optimal allocation.
The data strongly support the conjecture that this algorithm is linear in the
number of CM's and therefore adds a simple fixed overhead to the computing cost
of solving the PDE. The second example involves a complex artificial D-algorithm,
the algorithm runs efficiently and the allocation obtained appears to be quite
good (the optional solution for this allocation problem is unknown).

The multiprocessor system architecture assumed is shown in Figure 6. Each PU
includes a processor and a local memory which is (logically) divided into
private memory and a double port common memory. Each PU is connected to its
local and common memory via a local bus and its common memory is also directly
accessible from other PUs through the global bus. Processors are not allowed to
access the common section of their own memory through the global bus.

The operation of this D-system is analyzed by [Houstis, 1984] and a communication
delay function d(u) is obtained that models the traffic on its global bus. This
function is used in the two examples. For simplicity, we have assumed in these
two examples that all the common data blocks are stored in the private memories.
Thus we only allocate the CMs to the PUs (determine Q).

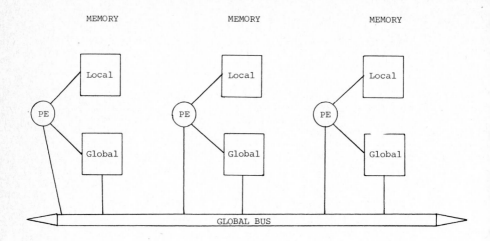

Figure 6

The multiprocessor system architecture (D-system) used in the two example applications of the heuristic algorithm.

Example 5. Allocation for the distributed SOR algorithm

We apply the heuristic allocation algorithm to the D-algorithm of Example 3 and
the D-system of Figure 6. If one has p PUs (i.e., Np = number p of column
partitioning) and then allocates one PU to each column block in the i-th row,
i = 1,2,...,q, then one has a natural and efficient allocation for this problem.
We calculate that the execution time for the i-th PU is the order of N^2/p (recall
that the SOR problem is N by N) and the communication cost is the order of N. We
see that the total computational cost is not affected by how the CMs are allocated
to the PUs and thus it is natural to try to minimize the communication cost. Our
assumption that the computation is not communication intensive is satisfied.

Table 1 shows the results of the heuristic algorithm applied to this example. It
obtained the natural allocation mentioned above.

Table 1. Execution time (sec.) of the heuristic allocation
algorithm for the distributed SOR algorithm.

# PU	# CM	Total time	Time per CM
9	81	0.47	.0058
16	256	1.33	.0052
25	625	4.77	.0076

Example 6. A general case

We next consider a general D-algorithm described by the graph model of Figure 7.
The numerical values on each arc indicate the v_{ij} in information transfer units.
For an initial value of T = 38,000, the algorithm produces the allocation of
Table 2, the actual time used is 5,333 units.

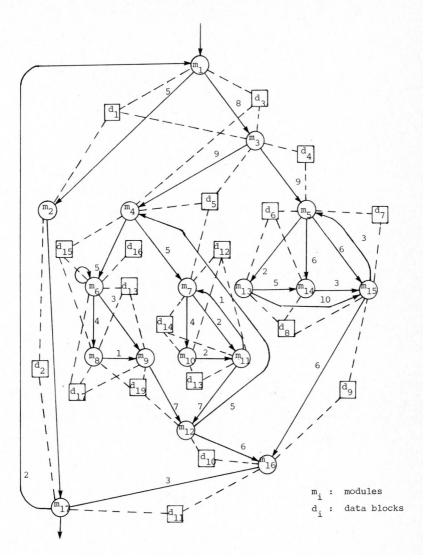

Figure 7
General case of Example 6. The m_i are computational modules, the d_i are data blocks and the values on the arcs are communication requirements.

Table 2. Allocation for Example 6.

Processor	Modules assigned	Data blocks assigned	(%) Utilization
PU #1	3,13,5,15,1,2,14	1,3,6,8,3,7	25.48
PU #2	6,16,8,12,4,9,17	15,17,18,10,16,19	27.12
PU #3	7,10,11	12,13,14	70.13
Common memory		2,5,9	

ACKNOWLEDGEMENTS

This work was supported in part by U.S. Army Research Office contract
DAAG29-33-K-0026 and National Science Foundation grant MCS 78-04878.

REFERENCES

[1]   Adams, L. and Ortega, J.M., Multi-color SOR method for parallel computation,
       ICASE Report No. 82-9, April 8, 1982.

[2]   Berger, P., Brounye, P. and Syre, J.C., A mesh coloring method for
       efficient MIMD processing in finite element problems, Proc. IEEE Conf. on
       Parallel Proc., Bellvue, Mich., (1982) 41-46.

[3]   Bokhari, H.S., On the mapping problem, IEEE Trans. Computers, 30 (1981)
       207-214.

[4]   Gottlieb, A., Lubachevsky, B.D. and Rudolph, L., Basic techniques for the
       efficient coordinations of very large numbers of cooperating sequential
       processors, ACM Trans. Prog. Lang. Systems, 5, (1983) 164-189.

[5]   Gylys, V.B. and Edwards, J.A., Optimal partitioning of workload for
       distributed systems, Proc. Compcon, (1976) 353-357.

[6]   Hoversty, K. and Jenny, C.J., Partitioning and allocating computational
       objects in distributed computing systems, Proc. IFIP 80, (1980) 593-598.

[7]   Houstis, C.E., An allocation algorithm for a real-time application to a
       multiprocessor system, Proc Intl. Symposium Performance of Computer
       Systems, Zurich, (1983).

[8]   Houstis, E.N., Mitchell, W.F. and Rice, J.R., Collocation software for
       second order elliptic partial differential equations, CSD-TR 446, Computer
       Science, Purdue University, (1983).

[9]   Li, H., The impact of process intercommunication on the global bus
       architecture, IEEE Proc. Real-time Systems, (1981) 29-31.

[10]   Ma, P., Lee, E.Y.S. and Tsuchlya, M., On the design of a task allocation
       scheme for time-critical applications, IEEE Proc. Real-time Systems, (1981)
       121-126.

[11]   Rice, J.R. and Boisvert, R.F., Solving Elliptic Problems Using ELLPACK,
       (Springer-Verlag, New York, 1984).

[12] Takuhaski, Y., Partitioning and allocation in parallel computation of partial differential equations, Proc. 10th IMACS World Congress, Vol. 1, (1982) 311-313.

DISCUSSION

Speaker: J. Rice

Delves: In practice, a given problem will need to be run on a given machine which has some fixed number N of processors; usually, the aim will be to minimise the total elapsed time spent in the machine. To compute this, you need to have in the model, both the communication costs and the cost per "piece of calculation". You have the latter in only indirectly, in the parameter T.

Rice: The execution time for each computational module is included in the module. The constraint that each processor can run only time T is enforced by requiring the times of those computation modules allocated to a processor to sum up to T or less. Thus, as T decreases, the number of processors required for the allocation increases. However, there is no direct minimization of the total elapsed time. Once N is fixed, one can adjust T to determine an allocation which uses just N processors. Our hope is that this allocation will be a good one; it is unlikely to be optimal in the sense you describe.

Leaf: Do I understand then that a search has to be made on top of your algorithm to find the minimal elapsed time? Did you do this?

Rice: Yes, a one dimensional search using the artificial variable T is made. We have done this in some examples and this phase could be automated easily once one decides on the exact objective.

Leaf: Did you consider machines where the global memory is structured so that "nearest neighbors" can communicate more directly than by the global bus?

Rice: The discussion presented here does not include "different" communication costs; only the global bus is used. When one looks at the details one sees that the heuristic allocation algorithm is applicable to more complicated communication structures. We are not sure of the limits of the structures that we can handle nor do we have any experience with effectiveness of the heuristics as the communication structure becomes more complex. We intend to explore these extensions. I would mention that there are some experimental computers being built with the communication structure described here. I expect some of the supercomputers of the later 1980's to have structures of this type.

Schönauer: The analysis with inclusion of the data transfer is much more realistic than those types of analysis: "How can I solve a linear system with n equations on a computer with n or n^2 or n^3 or n^4 processors; data transfer costs no time.
Schönauer: Can you analyse with this theory the behaviour of the HEP (Denelcor) computer?

Rice: We have not tried to analyze the HEP, so I am not sure. The HEP architecture is not exactly the same as assumed here, but it is not too far away. It would be an interesting application to attempt.

Pridor: The presented algorithm was interactive and heuristic; to be of practical use, the allocation of work to processors should be automated. There seems to be a chance in this direction, since there are efficient Graph-Theory based algorithms to solve assignment problems.

Rice: This algorihm does allocate the work (computational modules) to the processors. It is not difficult to automate the variation of the artificial parameter T to achieve some objective; we chose not to do this here because it seems to be an independent part of the allocation. I am not aware of solution algorithms that apply to this problem because of the nature of the global bus delay function. We hope that our algorithm is linear in the problem size, so you cannot expect to be much more efficient. Of course, if our algorithm produces poor results, we would have to replace it.

Pridor: There might be a way to minimize the total elapsed time by an iteration of standard assignment problems. Similar situations have been discussed in the literature on optimization.

Rice: We have not tried to minimize total elapsed time and this is a natural thing to do. If you know of a method in the optimization literature that solves this problem efficiently, you should bring it to the attention of the PDE software community as they will be facing this (and related) allocation problems.

Yanenko: Can you give some asymptotic evaluation of your method?

Rice: No. The algorithm is heuristic and we hope that it is linear in the number of computational modules. We have no analysis to support this and other people have not been sucessful in analyzing similar heuristic algorithms.

Yanenko: For real life problems it is important to be able to apply a variable, adaptive mesh method. This is for instance the case when there are singular points. This fact can have very important implications on the general structure of the algorithm.

Rice: It is not unfeasible to consider rectangular problems too. We have to take into account that the use of adaptive methods, in general, implies a messy programming.

Yanenko: It is important to equilibrate the accuracy and the amount of computation. The adaptive mesh is important to find a good partitioning of a complex boundary value problem into simpler boundary value problems.

PDE SOFTWARE: Modules, Interfaces and Systems
B. Engquist and T. Smedsaas (eds.)
Elsevier Science Publishers B.V. (North-Holland)
© IFIP, 1984

A SOFTWARE PACKAGE FOR STABILITY ANALYSIS OF DIFFERENCE METHODS

Michael Thuné

Department of Computer Sciences
Uppsala University
Sturegatan 4B 2nd floor
S-752 23 Uppsala
SWEDEN

A software package for automatic investigation of stability of initial-boundary value problems is presented. It is constructed for hyperbolic problems of first order in one space dimension. The package combines symbolic formula manipulation and numerical routines. Furthermore a user oriented problem description language is included. The software package is completely FORTRAN based, the symbol manipulation parts being written in LISP, using the FORTRAN coded LISP-F3 interpreter.

1. INTRODUCTION

Investigating the stability of difference approximations of linear initial value problems with no boundaries involved is fairly easy. However, when it comes to mixed initial-boundary value problems the analysis of stability is much more difficult. The theory, which is developed in general form for first order hyperbolic systems [3] and for second order parabolic systems [8], leads to complicated algebraic stability conditions. A final conclusion about the stability can therefore normally not be made by analytical methods, but numerical methods must be used.

In this paper we will describe the IBSTAB software package, which is designed for automatic stability analysis based on the general theory for hyperbolic problems in one space dimension. IBSTAB combines symbolic formula manipulations and numerical computations. The structure of the system is presented in section 3. Sections 4 to 6 present the different parts of the package and section 7 gives some test results for the numerical part of IBSTAB. To make the paper selfcontained the stability theory is reviewed in section 2.

2. THE STABILITY THEORY

The theory used for the stability investigation is the so called Normal Mode Analysis developed by Gustafsson, Kreiss and Sundström [3]. Here, it will just be described briefly, as the topic of this paper is not the theory in itself but the implementation of it.

We will present the stability theory for a quarterplane problem. In the following it is assumed that $t \geq 0$, $0 \leq x < \infty$. If there are two boundaries, e.g. $0 \leq x \leq 1$, then the theory shows that each boundary can be analyzed separately, "removing" the other boundary.

The grid is defined by

$$x_j = j\Delta x \quad , \quad j=-r+1, \quad -r+2,\ldots,$$
$$t_n = n\Delta t \quad , \quad n=0,1,\ldots \quad , \quad \lambda = \Delta t/\Delta x = \text{const.}$$

and the interior scheme has the general form

$$\sum_{\nu=-1}^{s} Q_\nu u_j^{n-\nu} = 0 \quad , \quad j=1,2,\ldots,$$

$$Q_\nu = \sum_{j=-r}^{p} A_{\nu j} E^j \quad , \quad Eu_j^n = u_{j+1}^n$$

By formally introducing $u_j^n = z^n \cdot v_j$ we arrive at a resolvent equation.

It is assumed that the coefficient matrices in the operators Q_ν can be diagonalized by one and the same transformation

$$T^{-1}A_{\nu j}T = D_{\nu j} = \mathrm{diag}(a_{\nu j}^{(1)},\ldots,a_{\nu j}^{(d)})$$

The assumption is not a severe restriction since in most cases the matrices $A_{\nu j}$ are powers of the coefficient matrix in the hyperbolic system

$$u_t = Au_x \quad ,$$

which can be diagonalized. With the transformation $w_j = T^{-1}v_j$ substituted into the resolvent equation we get the equation

(1) $$\sum_{\nu=-1}^{s} z^{s-\nu} \sum_{k=-r}^{p} D_{\nu k} E^k \cdot w_j = 0, \quad j=1,2,\ldots$$

(1) represents d scalar difference equations for the components $w^{(\tau)}$ of w. We seek the solution w which is bounded for $j \to \infty$. This solution is a combination of polynomials in the roots $\kappa_{\tau\mu}$, with $|\kappa_{\tau\mu}| \leq 1$, of the characteristic equations

(2) $$\sum_{\nu=-1}^{s} z^{s-\nu} \sum_{k=-r}^{p} a_{\nu k}^{(\tau)} \kappa_\tau^{k+r} = 0 \quad , \quad \tau=1,2,\ldots,d$$

corresponding to (1).

The solution w is substituted into the boundary conditions. This leads to a linear system of equations for the coefficients $\sigma_{\nu\tau}$ in w

$$M\underline{\sigma} = 0 \quad , \quad \underline{\sigma} = (\underline{\sigma}^{(1)},\underline{\sigma}^{(2)},\ldots,\underline{\sigma}^{(d)})^T$$

where $\underline{\sigma}^{(\tau)}$ contains the coefficients for $w^{(\tau)}$. Strong stability is established if the condition

$$\mathrm{Det}\, M \neq 0 \quad , \quad |z| \geq 1$$

is fulfilled. The determinant condition is

(3) $$\mathrm{Det}\, M(z,\underline{\kappa}_1,\ldots,\underline{\kappa}_d) = 0$$

where $\underline{\kappa}_\tau$ is a vector containing the $\kappa_{\tau\mu}$s corresponding to $w^{(\tau)}$. If (3) is satisfied for some value z, $|z| > 1$, $\max |\kappa_{\tau\mu}| < 1$, $\tau=1,\ldots,d$ then the scheme is unstable. The case $\mathrm{Det}\, M = 0$ for $|z| = 1$ can be separated into three cases

i) All the corresponding $\kappa_{\tau\mu}$s are less than one in magnitude. In that case the scheme is classified as weakly stable, cf. definition 3.2 in [3].

ii) One or more $\kappa_{\tau\mu}$s are on the unit circle. If these are all multiple roots of (2) then the scheme is classified as weakly stable.

iii) At least one of the $\kappa_{\tau\mu}$s is on the unit circle and is a simple root of (2). In that case the scheme is unstable.

If there is a case with $\kappa_{\tau\mu} = \kappa_0$, $|\kappa_0| = 1$, $z = z_0$, $|z_0| = 1$, it must be made sure that $\kappa_{\tau\mu}$ is the "right" root, i.e. for $z \approx z_0$, $|z| > 1$ it must be less than one in magnitude, and consequently approaches the unit circle from the inside when $z \to z_0$, $|z| > 1$. This behaviour is investigated by a perturbation calculation. z is modified such that $z = z_0(1+\delta)$, $0 < \delta < < 1$, and if one of the roots of (2) is such that $|\kappa - \kappa_0|$ is small and $|\kappa| < 1$, then κ_0 originates from the inside.

3. THE BASIC IDEAS OF IBSTAB

There are two difficulties in the theory just described, that motivate the use of software tools for the stability investigation. The main difficulty is of course the solution of the nonlinear system of equations ((2.2), (2.3)). We have to find all solutions with $|z| \geq 1$. To accomplish this we will normally need some numerical algorithm.

The other difficulty is the derivation of the nonlinear system (2.2), (2.3) from the difference approximation. This could be rather tedious if there are possibilities for multiple roots $\kappa_{\tau\mu}$ in the characteristic equations. In that case we will have to consider several constructions of the function w_j, each construction giving rise to a new determinant condition. Consequently a program for automatic derivation of (2.2), (2.3) would be of great help.

In the construction of IBSTAB the aim has been to apply the ideas of mathematical software used e.g. in the DCG-system [2]. The IBSTAB system thus combines symbolic manipulations and numerical routines. Furthermore it is intended to allow the user to present his problem in a "natural" manner that will not include the writing of FORTRAN subroutines or functions. Therefore IBSTAB contains an extended version of the problem specification language used in DCG [2], which makes it possible to present the stability problem in a notation which hopefully seems natural to a numerical analyst.

The structure of the system is presented in figure 3.1.

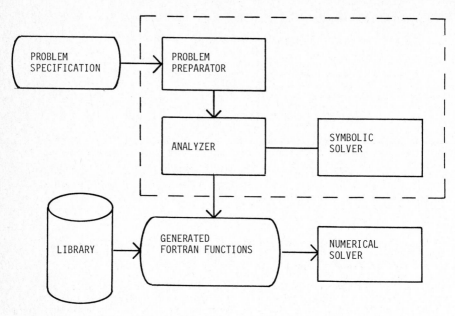

fig. 3.1

The symbol manipulation parts of the system are written in LISP, using the LISP-F3 interpreter [4], and the numerical part is written in FORTRAN. LISP-F3 is coded in FORTRAN and thus IBSTAB is completely FORTRAN based. Another advantage in using LISP-F3 is that it gives the possibility to make external calls to FORTRAN routines from LISP. This will be used e.g. when diagonalizing the matrices of the difference operators Q_ν.

Presently the parts of IBSTAB will only be introduced briefly. A closer description will be given in the following sections. The problem specification is given by the user. It is read by the problem preparator, which also generates the nonlinear system of equations ((2.2), (2.3)). The main task of the analyzer is to decide whether this system should be solved by a direct or by a numerical method. If the problem is simple enough to be solved analytically, then the symbolic solver takes over, making the stability analysis using symbolic manipulations.

If, on the other hand, the analysis shows that the numerical algorithm must be used, then the analyzer

1) symbolically calculates the jacobian of (2.2), (2.3)
2) generates FORTRAN functions for both (2.2), (2.3) and the jacobian.

The generated FORTRAN functions together with problem independent routines from a library make the numerical solver, which will now take over and perform the stability analysis.

4. THE NUMERICAL ALGORITHM

4.1 As said before the problem to be solved by the "numerical solver" part is:

Find all solutions of (2.2), (2.3) such that $|z| \geq 1$. To be able to do this we will have to invent some way of finding good initial guesses to all such solutions. When we have a good initial guess then we can use e.g. Newton's method to find the corresponding solution. We then check if that solution fulfills the stability criteria. If they are not fulfilled we conclude that the given difference scheme is not stable, otherwise we go on with the next initial guess.

One way of finding initial guesses is to use a continuation method. This approach was tried by e.g. Coughran [1] and Swenson [7]. Both experienced trouble at solutions where the jacobian was singular, i.e. at points where several continuation paths are crossing. Coughran, who made a more exhaustive study than Swenson, also noticed that a complete stability investigation using a continuation method, was very time consuming. The timing was furthermore sensitive to the choice of initial splitting in the continuation method. This is of course a serious drawback if the splitting is to be chosen automatically.

The drawbacks of continuation techniques motivate the development of some other algorithm for solving the stability problem. IBSTAB uses an iteration method which takes advantage of the special structure of the system (2.2), (2.3).

4.2 The IBSTAB numerical solver is based on the following two assumptions:

i) The non-linear system (2.2), (2.3) is generated from the diagonalized form of the difference equations.

ii) For $\lambda = 0$ all solutions (2.2), (2.3) have $|z| \leq 1$.

Assumption i) is fulfilled by letting the "problem preparator" diagonalize the difference scheme. Assumption ii) will be true if the difference approximation of the time derivative is stable when applied to the problem $u_t = 0$.

We also impose the restriction that for $\lambda > 0$ the number of solutions to (2.2), (2.3) is not greater than for $\lambda = 0$. This means that the number of time levels involved in the complete approximation must not be bigger than the number of time levels in the difference operator for the time derivative. This is no severe restriction, as most schemes currently in use fulfill it.

4.3 According to assumption i) our system (2.2), (2.3) has the following form:

$$f_j(\kappa_j, z) = 0 \qquad j = 1, \ldots, N$$

(1)

$$g(\kappa_1, \kappa_2, \ldots, \kappa_N, z) = 0$$

where the f_j:s correspond to characteristic equations and g is the determinant condition. In the simple case with one κ for each characteristic equation we will have $N=d$. The basic idea of the IBSTAB numerical algorithm is the following:

We know that for $\lambda_0 = 0$ all solutions to (1) have $|z| < 1$. Now choose $\lambda_1 = \lambda_0 + \delta\lambda_0$, where $\delta\lambda_0$ is a small stepsize, such that no solution will be perturbed by more than a "small" amount when we change from λ_0 to λ_1. Thus, for λ_1 no solution will have a z-part that is more than slightly outside the unit circle in the complex plane. We therefore "walk around" the circle $|z| = 1 + \xi$, where ξ is small and try to capture all solutions that crossed the unit circle when λ was changed from λ_0 to λ_1.

In other words: the algorithm only looks for solutions which have $|z|$ close to 1. In more detail the algorithm goes on as follows.

a) For λ_1 we choose z-values around the circle $|z| = 1 + \xi$. For each fixed z, we solve the f_j:s for corresponding κ_j:s. We thus get a possible solution $\alpha = (\kappa_1,\ldots,\kappa_N,z)$ to (1). To check if it is a true solution we insert α into g:

> if $g(\alpha) = 0$ then
>
> α is a solution

else

> if $|g(\alpha)| < \varepsilon$ then
>
> we assume that α is close to a solution and we use Brown's method to solve (2.2), (2.3) using α as initial guess

else we just go on to the next z-value.
The choice of the parameter ε will be discussed later.

b) If no instabilities are found for λ_1 then we set $\lambda_2 = \lambda_1 + \delta\lambda_1$ and repeat from a), replacing λ_1 by λ_2, e t c.

The algorithm is carried on until we find an instability or until we pass some limit λ_{STOP}. This limit should be set by the IBSTAB user.

The basic part of the numerical algorithm is shown in fig 4.1. The stepsizes in θ and λ are variable as is also ε. The calculation of these parameters will be described in the following sections.

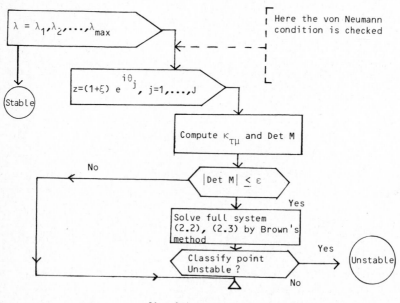

fig. 4.1

4.4 The choice of the step-size $\delta\theta$ in the angle of z is variable and governed by the following analysis. For z on the circle,

$$z = (1+\xi) \cdot e^{i\theta} \quad , \quad 0 < \theta < 2\pi,$$

the system 4.3.1 can be written in the form

$$f(\alpha) = 0$$

where the vector f has $d+1$ components and where $\alpha = (\kappa_1,\ldots,\kappa_N,\theta)^T$. Assume that at a certain point α we have $f(\alpha) \neq 0$, and we look for $\theta\delta$ such that $f(\alpha+\theta\alpha) = 0$. We perform the usual linearization, and obtain

$$0 = f(\alpha) + J(\alpha)\delta\alpha$$

where J is the Jacobian of f. Accordingly,

$$\delta\alpha = -J^{-1}(\alpha) \cdot f(\alpha).$$

In general even the last component $\delta\theta$ of $\delta\alpha$ is complex, but a reasonable choice is

$$(2) \qquad \delta\theta = \beta | [J^{-1}(\alpha)f(\alpha)]_{d+1} |$$

where $[\ ]_{d+1}$ denotes the last component of the vector, and where β is a constant which we in general choose less than one.

A simple calculation shows that (2) becomes

$$\delta\theta = \beta|g(\alpha) / (\frac{\partial g}{\partial \theta} - \sum_{j=1}^{d} \frac{\partial f_j/\partial\theta}{\partial f_j/\partial\kappa_j} \partial g/\partial\kappa_j)$$

The choice (2) is used in our algorithm together with a maximum limit

$$\delta\theta \leq \Delta\theta$$

Furthermore, even if $|g(\alpha)|$ was greater than ε we could still be close to a solution if g is "steep" near α. Therefore, if we get $\delta\theta < \mu$, where μ is small, we solve the full system by Brown's method.

4.5 Suppose now that for a certain λ-value the investigation is complete. Then λ must be increased by an amount δ as large as possible, but still small enough such that any possible z-solution near the unit circle is found. The choice of δ is based on the following analysis.

Assume that α_δ is a solution to 4.3.1 for the λ-value $\lambda + \delta$. We have

$$f(\lambda,\alpha_0) = 0$$
$$f(\lambda+\delta,\alpha_\delta) = 0$$

where α and f are defined above.

A Taylor expansion gives

$$0 = f(\lambda+\delta,\alpha_0+\alpha_\delta-\alpha_0) \approx f(\lambda,\alpha_0)+f_\lambda(\lambda,\alpha_0)\delta+J_\alpha(\lambda,\alpha_0)(\alpha_\delta-\alpha_0)$$

where f_λ denotes differentiation with respect to λ. J_α denotes the Jacobian with respect to α, and we assume that it is nonsingular.

For small values of δ we get

$$\alpha_\delta - \alpha_0 \approx -J_\alpha^{-1}(\lambda,\alpha_0)f_\lambda(\lambda,\alpha_0)\delta \quad .$$

Suppose that Δ_α is the maximum deviation (in the maxnorm $||\ ||_\infty$) of the starting point from the solution in order to get convergence for Brown's method. The choice of δ is then determined by

$$\delta \leq \Delta_\alpha \cdot \min_\alpha(||J_\alpha(\lambda,\alpha)||_\infty / ||f_\lambda(\lambda,\alpha)||_\infty)$$

where the denominator is maximized over those points where J_α was computed for the previous λ-value. We have used $\Delta_\alpha = \varepsilon$, where ε is defined in Fig. 4.1.

If J_α is singular or near singular, we use the value 0.1 of the right hand side.

4.6   The parameter ε is chosen to be some average size of g according to the following procedure:

a) For λ_1 we use
$$\varepsilon = \frac{1}{2}[|g(\alpha_1)| + |g(\alpha_2)|]$$

where α_1 and α_2 are two arbitrarily chosen points whose z-components fulfill $|z| = 1 + \xi$.

b) For the subsequent λ-values we take ε = average of the g-values for the "search points" generated for the preceding λ-value.

4.7   The sections 4.2 to 4.6 describe the numerical solver of IBSTAB as it is currently implemented. A possible improvement would be to change to a continuation method if for some λ we find all the solutions to (2.2), (2.3). We could then use these solutions as initial guesses for the next λ , thus taking λ as continuation parameter. This modification was studied by Swenson [7]. However, due to the difficulties which were discussed in section 4.1, this has not yet been included in IBSTAB.

Another improvement would be to implement the algorithm on a parallel processing machine. We could for example have all (or groups of) the z-values for a given λ examined independently of each other. This would be possible if we chose a fixed stepsize along the circle $|z| = 1 + \xi$, taking some "minimum" value of $\delta\theta$. If all the processors flagged stability then one processor could calculate a new λ-value e t c. We have not considered the details of such an implementation as we have no parallel processing machine to our disposition.

5.   THE LISP PART OF IBSTAB

5.1   We will now take a closer look at the LISP part of IBSTAB (see fig 3.1 above). The problem preparator reads the problem specification which is given in a user oriented problem description language. This language will be presented in section 6. The preparation consists in two parts. First the difference equations are parsed and if they contain matrix coefficients those are diagonalized by a call to an external FORTRAN subroutine. Secondly an internal form of equations (2.2), (2.3) is generated. Internally each polynomial is represented as a "binary tree list", i.e. a polynomial could be (loosely) described as

                    polynomial ::= atom | (operator polynomial polynomial)

For example, the expression
                    $z - 1 + \lambda(\kappa_1 - 1)$
is represented as

$$(+ (- z 1) (* L (- Kl 1)))$$.

This example also shows that λ is represented as L and κ as K.

5.2 The problem preparator thus produces an internal form of equation system 4.3.1. This is passed on to the analyzer. The analyzer just checks whether the system is simple enough to be solved by the direct solver. The criteria for this are

i) that there are only two equations in the system, i.e. that there is only one characteristic equation.

ii) that at least one of the equations is linear in one of the variables and that the coefficient in front of this variable is independent of the other variable.

iii) that substituting this "linear" variable in the other equation will yield at most a fourth degree polynomial in the remaining variable.

If these criteria are not fulfilled, then the analyzer symbolically calculates the jacobian of 4.3.1. Furthermore it generates FORTRAN functions of 4.3.1 and for its jacobian. If the characteristic equations are of degree less than or equal to 4 in κ, then FORTRAN expressions are also generated for the analytical formulas for solving for κ with fixed z. If on the other hand the degree should be greater than 4, then κ will instead be solved for by means of an iteration procedure. The analyzer then generates calls to that procedure.

5.3 The symbolic solver will take over if criteria i) to iii) are fulfilled. It will then first solve for the "linear" variable in terms of the other one. Thereafter it will make a substitution in the other equation thus obtaining a polynomial equation in one variable, this polynomial being of at most degree 4. This polynomial will then be solved by analytical formulas.

5.4 The basis of the problem preparator, the analyzer and the symbolic solver is a "toolbox" containing LISP-functions for symbolic manipulations such as symbolic arithmetics, symbolic derivation, complex arithmetics, substitution and polynomial equation solving. The toolbox has been jointly created by the DCG and IBSTAB projects. It should be noted that the symbolic manipulations are not strictly exact, because all numerical calculations that arise are done in finite precision floating point arithmetics.

6. THE PROBLEM DESCRIPTION

As stated in section 3, one of the intentions with IBSTAB is that it should have a user oriented problem description language. The user should be able to specify her problem in a manner that is natural to her. To illustrate how this goal has been approached we give a short example:

We wish to investigate the stability of a leap-frog approximation to

$$v_t = \begin{pmatrix} 0 & 1 \\ 1 & 0 \end{pmatrix} v_x \qquad 0 \leq x < \infty$$
$$v^I(0,t) = 0$$

with extra (numerical) boundary condition

$$w_0^n = 2w_1^n - w_2^n$$

where w_j^n is the approximation to $v^{II}(x_j, t_n)$. The investigation should be made for $0 \le \lambda \le 2$. The IBSTAB notation for this would be e.g.

```
DIFFERENCEEQS
U(J,N+1)-U(J,N-1)-L*A*(U(J+1,N)-U(J-1,N))=0.0
BOUNDARYCONDS
B1*U(0,N)-B2*U(1,N)+B3*U(2,N)=0.0
PARAMETERS
 DEPVAR=U;
 NDE=2;
 NBCND=2;
 DCOEFF= A : 0.0 1.0
             1.0 0.0;
 BCOEFF=B1 : 0.0 1.0
             1.0 0.0;
 BCOEFF=B2 : 0.0 0.0
             2.0 0.0;
 BCEOFF=B3 : 0.0 0.0
             1.0 0.0;
 LSTOP =2.0
END
```

This example shows the structure of the problem description language. It is based on selfexplaining section names. Expressions must be given with right hand side equal to zero. The difference equations and boundary condition should be presented in vector form. The name L for λ is fixed but the names of dependent variable (DEPVAR) and of difference equation and boundary condition coefficients (DCOEFF and BCOEFF) can be chosen freely. As shown by the example those are specified in the PARAMETERS section, where also the value of the coefficients are given. The other parameters are "number of difference equations" (NDE), "number of boundary conditions" (NBCND) and "stop-value of λ" (LSTOP). The example is not exhaustive: there are also sections for describing the polynomial equations if you have already derived those by hand.

It seems that for a person working in engineering or numerical mathematics the notation adopted in IBSTAB is much more natural than for example a conventional FORTRAN notation. The size of the description program is also considerably smaller than for a corresponding FORTRAN program.

7. NUMERICAL RESULTS

7.1 We have tested the numerical solver on problems with known properties. In this section we give some examples of such test problems.

Testproblem I:

$$u_t = \begin{pmatrix} 0 & a(x) \\ a(x) & 0 \end{pmatrix} u_x \qquad u = \begin{pmatrix} u^I \\ u^{II} \end{pmatrix} \qquad 0 \le x < \infty$$

$$u^{II}(0,t) = g(t)$$

This is the wave equation written as a first order system. We apply the leap-frog scheme. With linear extrapolation as extra boundary condition and with $a(0) = 1$ the scheme is weakly stable for $\lambda < 1$. For $\lambda \ge 1$ the von Neumann condition is not fulfilled. The numerical solver found that the scheme is weakly stable for $\lambda \le 0.97850$ and that the von Neumann criterion is not fulfilled for $\lambda \ge 1.00350$.

Testproblem II:

$$\begin{pmatrix} \rho \\ u \\ p \end{pmatrix}_t + \begin{pmatrix} \hat{u} & \hat{\rho} & 0 \\ 0 & \hat{u} & \hat{\rho}^{-1} \\ 0 & \gamma \cdot \hat{p} & \hat{u} \end{pmatrix} \begin{pmatrix} \rho \\ u \\ p \end{pmatrix}_x = 0 \qquad 0 \leq x < \infty$$

These are the linearized Euler equations. We apply the Crank-Nicholson scheme on the subsonic inflow problem using

$$[\hat{\rho}cu-p]_0^{n+1} = [\hat{\rho}cu-p]_1^n$$

as extra boundary condition, $\hat{u}$, $\hat{\rho}$ and c are chosen to make the method stable for $\lambda < 2$, unstable for $\lambda > 2$. The numerical solver stated that the approximation is stable for $\lambda \leq 1.98749$ and unstable for $\lambda \geq 1.99999$.

Testproblem III:

$$u_t = a(x,t)u_t \qquad 0 \leq x < \infty$$

We apply the 4:th order Kreiss-Oliger scheme [5] and take $a(0,t) = 1$. Choosing extra boundary conditions according to Sloan [6] and Oliger [5], IBSTAB states that the scheme is stable for $\lambda < 0.65$ and unstable for $\lambda > 0.7$. This confirms the analysis made by Sloan and contradicts the one made by Oliger, who claims that the scheme is stable for $\lambda < 0.7287$.

7.2 To study the performance of the numerical algorithms we have studied the following parameters for each test problem:

N_λ = number of λ-values that was checked

N_z = total number of z-values checked

$\overline{N}_z$ = N_z/N_λ

N_{BM} = total number of calls to the Brown's Method routine

$\overline{N}_{BM}$ = N_{BM}/N_λ

The maximal stepsize for λ is set to 0.1. The following table shows the results for the algorithm implemented on the IBM 370/158 computer at Uppsala University Computing Center.

	N_λ	$\overline{N}_z$	$\overline{N}_{BM}$	CPU-time (min.)
Testproblem I	11	38	26	4.0
Testproblem II	20	27	17	1.5
Testproblem III	7	44	23	1.9

The rather small set of testcases presented here indicate that the timing of the numerical solver is quite low in relation to the complexity of the problem. Furthermore the maximum stepsize for λ is chosen in most of the steps. It is only in the neighbourhood of the stability limit that we get reduced stepsizes in λ.

A negative property shown by the table is that the Brown's Method routine seems to be called unnecessarily often. However, this is probably a price that has to be paid in order to make the algorithm robust.

ACKNOWLEDGEMENTS

I would like to thank my adviser Bertil Gustafsson who has guided me in my work on IBSTAB. I am also grateful to Tom Smedsaas for his advice on the symbol manipulation parts of the package.

REFERENCES

1. W. M. Coughran. Jr.: On the Approximate Solution of Hyperbolic Initial-Boundary Value Problems. Computer Science Dept., Stanford University, Report no. STAN-CS-80-806.

2. Engquist, B. and Smedsaas, T.: Automatic computer code generation for hyperbolic and parabolic differential equations, SIAM J. Sci. Stat. Comput., vol 1, pp. 249-259, 1980.

3. B. Gustafsson , H.-O. Kreiss and A. Sundström: Stability Theory of Difference Approximations for Mixed Initial Boundary Value Problems II. Math. Comp., vol. 26,no. 119 (1972), pp. 649-686.

4. M. Nordström: LISP-F3 User's Guide. Dept. of Computer Sciences, Uppsala University, Report no. DLU 78/4 (1978).

5. J. Oliger: Fourth Order Difference Methods for the Initial Boundary-Value Problem for Hyperbolic Equations. Math. Comp., vol. 28, no. 125, pp. 15-25 (1974).

6. D. Sloan: Boundary Conditions for a Fourth Order Hyperbolic Difference Scheme. To be published.

7. I. Swenson: Undersökning av en Inbäddningsmetod för Lösning av Icke-Lineära Ekvationssystem i samband med Stabilitetsundersökning av Differensapproximationer av Begynnelse- Randvärdesproblem. Dept. of Computer Sciences, Uppsala University, Internal Report no. 83-1 (1983).

8. J. M. Varah: Stability of Difference Approximations to the Mixed Initial Boundary Value Problems for Parabolic Systems. SIAM J. Num. An., vol. 8, no. 3 (1971), pp. 598-615.

DISCUSSION

Speaker: M. Thuné

Young: Could your technique be used to analyze linear- multistep-method methods, and possibly other methods, for solving systems of first order ordinary differential equations?

Thuné: No, it is not possible, because in our algorithm we use the hyperbolicity of the PDE when we diagonalize the matrices in the resolvent equation. The special structure this gives to the system of polynomial equations is essential to the IBSTAB algorithm.

Stetter: With a semi-infinite domain, some boundary conditions will have the form of boundedness conditions at infinity. Is your code able to analyze such cases?

Thuné: It is assumed that the solution belongs to $\ell_2(0,\infty)$ when we work for the quarterplane $t > 0$, $0 \leq x < \infty$. That is the reason why only cappas with $|\kappa| \leq 1$ are included in the formula for W_j.

Gorenflo: During your talk it was my impression that you only treat the case of constant coefficients; in your final example, however, your equation is $u_t = -a(x,t)u_x$.
Can you treat this equation efficiently? Do you then have to solve many algebraic equations, one for each spatial grid point?

Thuné: The GKS-theory covers the variable coefficient case as well. E.g. if the coefficient is x-dependent, you only have to make the analysis for the case $x=0$ (i.e. $a(x)$ could be replaced by $a(0)$ in the stability analysis).

Yanenko: Have you considered the case of branching? If, with the continuation of λ you meet a branching point, then you run into a problem.

Thuné: We don't use a continuation method, i.e. we don't trace the solution from one λ to another.

Yanenko: You can have a branching point in your case as well.
Your method seems to work for stable differential equations. What happens if the differential equation is not stable or weakly stable?

Thuné: IBSTAB works as well for those cases as for the case with strong stability.

Hindmarsh: Are there thoughts of extending this method of analysis to higher dimensional problems?

Thuné: Yes, we have thought of extending it to two-dimensional problems. However, we first wish to make a more exhaustive testing of the "one-dimensional" version of IBSTAB.

Gorenflo: What do you think about computing physicist's method of experimentally testing stability by giving a random function as initial condition and looking for evolution in time whether there arise growing oscillations? A random function should be taken as initial input because such a function has a high probability of containing each possible component of noise.

Thune: First, the aim of the analysis made by IBSTAB is broader than just finding some λ-values for which the difference method is stable. We wish to find the limit up to which we can choose λ without violating stability. Secondly, there are examples where it is really very difficult to see from experiments that you have an unstable scheme.

Sköllermo: If you want more accurate bounds for the regions of stability and instability, how does this influence your computing times?

Thuné: It would not be influenced much. The reason for this is that the final refinement of the "uncertainty" interval between stable/instable is made by a simple bisection.

PDE SOFTWARE: Modules, Interfaces and Systems
B. Engquist and T. Smedsaas (eds.)
Elsevier Science Publishers B.V. (North-Holland)
© IFIP, 1984

THE "VECTOR MACHINE": AN APPROACH
TO SIMPLE PROGRAMMING ON CRAY-1 AND OTHER VECTOR COMPUTERS

Alain Bossavit

Electricité de France, D.E.R.,
92141 Clamart
France

We propose a model of a large family of present vector computers, based on the definition of an appropriate abstract type.
The rationale behind the definition of this VECTOR type (or,
in other words, this abstract "vector machine") is this: among
operations on vectors (in the received, mathematical acception
of this word), identify those that are especially fast on
actual vector computers, and ignore others. By programming
"toward" this abstract machine, in a top-down fashion, one will
obtain efficient programs in a natural way. This is proposed
as an alternative to the process of vectorizing, either automatically or by hand, existing programs. This also has some
pedagogical implications, that we tried to suggest by shaping
the paper into a short tutorial on vector machines and
their programming.

INTRODUCTION

This paper is a sketch of what, in our opinion, a short introduction to vector
programming should be, when directed toward people who solve PDE's as part of their
main activity, though not being computer scientists or numerical software specialists. The following introduction is an attempt to clear up our motivation. The
last alinea describes the organization of the paper as a whole.

There are now several dozens of mainframe vector computers in use around the world,
and thousand of users have access to them. This contrasts with the not so remote
time when only a few specialists would work on an Illiac 4 or a Star. One can
easily appreciate already now the impact of this evolution on numerical software
as a field of research and as a professional activity. What the effects will be
on users is less obvious. By "users" we mean those who solve equations by numerical methods with the purpose of studying physical systems (either natural or
artificial ones). This class of problems lead to very large computations, so this
community has always pushed toward the acquisition of the most powerful computing
facilities available. At the same time, they do not think of themselves as professional programmers (even if they devote most of their working time to programming activities !), and are rather reluctant to invest too much in subjects like
computer architecture, software engineering, even algorithmics. Will they make
the best of the potential that parallel architectures seem to promise, and that
vector computers already provide ?

The question of using up hardware to the best of its efficiency is a permanent one,
but it really takes on a new acuity now. It has always been true that "careful" or
"clever" coding, with full awareness of the idiosyncrasies of the machine, could
improve very much on the efficiency of the methods. But "very much" meant for
instance 10 %, or 50 % more than what the correct use of standard tools (Fortran
compilers, subroutine libraries, etc.) would provide. Now it may mean a multipli-
cative factor of 10 or 50.

Since the end of the sixties, serious programmers have argued more and more for-
cibly that efficiency considerations were quite accessory in comparison with
other domains of the programming activity [12, 14, 15, 31] . The trend was
quite consistent: prefer portability to "optimal" (but machine dependent) coding,
prefer readability to "clever" coding, emphasize person-to-person rather than
person-to-machine communication, etc. The motto of the period was: let the hardware work more, but spare human time. It would really be a pity if the advent of
vector computers resulted in any curbing down of this trend, but it could very
well happen. If users, who have not yet fully received the message of the advocates of modern software engineering, feel some unresolved contradiction between
this gospel and the search for efficiency, they will stop listening. The problem
is to get these orders-of-magnitude improvements which are at stake, without re-
verting back to programming practices which seem, at last, on the verge of receding.

This is of course a marvelous opportunity for computer scientists and numerical
analysts. The former may at last see their ideas (concerning program transformations, optimizing compilers, automatic vectorization, vector languages, etc. [10,
18, 20, 23, 24, 19, 27]) widely implemented. The latter are motivated in looking
for new algorithms or new implementations that could "squeeze the most" [13] out
of the machine. Indeed these efforts have given remarkable results. (See [26]
for a recent survey, and [11, 17, 27, 28] among references where emphasis is put on
ad-hoc coding. As for algorithmics, a starting point is [1], to be completed with
proceedings of the numerous conferences held since [2, 3, 4, ...].).

Nevertheless, the involvement of users themselves remains necessary. Current
compilers on vector machines are far from being state-of-the-art. No other language than Fortran is generally available. (Interestingly enough, this conserva-
tism of manufacturers seems to pay off. The prospect to have to "convert" programs
into a new language, even in a Fortran dialect very much alike Fortran itself, is
a ghastly one for people who decide about new hardware investments). As for mathematical software, there are real possibilities to make it available, through libraries. But the Fortran environment imposes limitations on what can be expected
from routines coded in assembly language. And subroutine libraries, anyway, are
not as largely used as they should be. More importantly, even if specialists succeed
in making efficient and unobtrusive tools, and in having them accepted by potential
users, some awareness among these of what a vector computer is should exist:
slight mistakes count when they result in missing a potential improvement of a
factor 10 up to 50.

Users are obviously not set against such an involvement (as the success of conferences on vector computing testifies). But one should not be too optimistic.
First, the subject matter is not easy. A look at the pages in Cray manuals which
deal with vectorization conditions for loops is enough to establish this point.
Next, our own experience (in the multi-machine environment of a computing center
which caters for very diverse computing needs) seems to indicate this: once users
have obtained a good Cray version of their former code ("good" means competitive
with the existing versions on conventional main-frames, so this notion is highly
relative, depending on the environment, on the computing center policy, etc.),
they lose interest in vectorization, and care about more urgent problems. Considerable gains in efficiency thus remain virtual.

We now arrive at the following conclusion: users will make a heartful but definitely limited investment of time and effort in understanding how vector computers
work, and how to make good use of them. They should be given tutorial material
tailored to this reality. One should concentrate on disseminating the information
which has the best return-to-investment ratio, in terms of overall efficiency. We
do not believe that the usual low-level approach (do and do-not rules, or the
unlikely coding examples of the Cray manuals, for instance) is correct according to
this criterium. Instead, and in complete accordance with the trends of modern
programming methodology already mentioned, we think one should rely on high-level
abstractions: try to develop a concept of abstract vector machine, show what

rational programming could be when practised on such a virtual machine. Then one could discuss the relevance of these concepts with respect to a specific real machine (the Cray-1, in the subsequent exposition), and hope that useful and simple rules of behaviour will present themselves to the minds of those exposed to such ideas.

The plan is:

1. The Vector Machine
    1.1 A study of the performances of a vector computer (the Cray-1).
    1.2 Notions of vector extensions of scalar operations, pipe-lines, regular storage.
    1.3 The abstract vector machine (definition of the type "vector").

2. Programming on the vector machine.
    2.1 "Think vectors": vectorizing the sum of components, the dot product, cyclic reduction.
    2.2 Algorithms in linear algebra: matrix multiply, triangular systems, Cholesky factorization.
    2.3 The compilation problem and the vectorization rules in Cray Fortran.

Conclusion.

A few points have been sacrificed for concision. Hints as to the developments they would justify are occasionally given in footnotes, so as to keep the body of the paper in the form of a tutorial.

I owe many thanks to Bertrand Meyer, from whom I borrowed much more than the notation used here [22]. Many ideas are his. Weaknesses in their expression are mine.

1. THE VECTOR MACHINE

A new generation of machines exist, on which operations on arrays (of integers, reals, etc.) are much faster than their scalar counterparts. We first give some evidence of this, next we explain the "pipe-line" concept which makes it possible.

1.1 Performances of a Vector Computer: the Cray-1

Consider the Fortran instruction on entities of *REAL* type:

(1) $A = B + C$

and the following sequence:

(2)
```
        REAL A(...), B(...), C(...)
  C     -- N IS SOME INTEGER VALUE GREATER THAN 0
        DO 1 I = 1, N
  1         A(I) = B(I) + C(I)
```

and let us time these operations on a vector computer. A convenient unit in the case of the Cray-1 will be its "clock-period", or CP, worth 12.5 nanoseconds. Operation (1) needs about 30 CP. As for (2), the results of the timing, as shown on Fig. 1, can be reported by the approximate formula:

(3) $t(N) = I + N\,V$

where I is the *I*nitialization, or start-up time, and V the time necessary for each new addition, in *V*ector mode. Let S be the execution time for (1), i.e. for the same addition, but in Sequential mode. One notices that V is much smaller than S, so that the overhead I is compensated for if $N > \lceil (S - V)/I \rceil$. One can base a classification of computers on the knowledge of the three quantities S, V, I [16]. On purely sequential machines, $V = S$ and I is negligible. Pipe-line computers like the Cray-1 have a big I and a small ratio V/S. And multiprocessor machines are defined by $V = 0$. (This is only a first approximation; we neglect secondary features like the "restart" time apparent on Fig. 1, or the boundedness of the number of processors).

The three characteristic times depend on the expression within the loop. Fig 2. shows other timings. One can get a very rough estimate of the execution time for a more complex sequence of operations by assuming additivity (which is only approximately true).

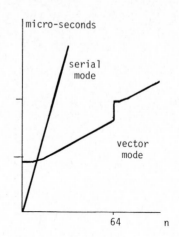

Figure 1
Timings for (1) and (2) on Cray-1

OPERATION	LOOP BODY	I	V	AVERAGE SPEED
assignment	$Y(I) = X(I)$	45	2	23
scalar + vector	$Y(I) = A + X(I)$	69	2	21
scal./vector	$Y(I) = A/X(I)$	111	2	19
add	$Z(I) = X(I)+Y(I)$	74	3	18
multiply	$Z(I) = X(I) \ast Y(I)$	76	3	18
	$Z(I)=X(I)+A \ast Y(I)$	86	4	28
sum	$S = S + X(I)$	339	3	8
dot product	$S = S+X(I) \ast Y(I)$	319	5	14
shift	$X(I) = X(I - 1)$	0	22	3.6
add·shift	$X(I) = X(I-1)+Y(I)$	0	32	2.6

Figure 2
Timings for a few operations on Cray-1. I and V (see text)
are in CP's of 12.5 ns each. Speeds are in MegaFlops.

This is enough to indicate that operations which, from a mathematical point of view, deal with vectors, fall into three different classes: the fast or good ones (in the upper part of the display), those that suffer from great initialization times (sum and dot-product), and finally those which are treated in scalar mode. This remark is basic to our approach: among vector operations (in the broad sense), we shall select the efficient ones, decide that only those deserve the "vector" label, and show that they form, taken together, an (abstract) "vector machine", rich enough to support all linear algebra algorithms. Programs written for this machine (i.e. avoiding the "bad" operations), should automatically benefit from high execution speeds.

1.2 Extensions, pipe-lines, regular storage

In order to follow the previous program, we have to know which operations should be discarded, and why. We need the theoretical concept of <u>extension</u> and the more ad hoc one of <u>regular storage</u> of vector entities.

1.2.1 Extensions of scalar operations

Let θ : *SCALAR* × *SCALAR* → *SCALAR* be a scalar operation (with two operands here, but this restriction is not essential). If u and v are two vectors of length n, the vector extension *VEθ* of *VE* is defined as the result of the program:

(4)

$$VE\theta \ (\underline{in}\ u,\ v:\ VECTORS,\ \underline{out}\ w:\ VECTOR)$$
$$\underline{for}\ i\ \underline{in}\ [1:n]\ \underline{do}$$
$$w(i) \leftarrow u(i)\ \theta\ v(i)$$

Let us suppose that θ is performed in m successive steps, or elementary actions $A^1, ..., A^m$, each requiring one CP to process the data. On a sequential machine, the assembly code for (4) would have the following structure:

(5)

$$\underline{for}\ i\ \underline{in}\ [1:n]\ \underline{do}\ \quad (1)$$
$$\underline{for}\ j\ \underline{in}\ [1:m]\ \underline{do}$$
$$A_i^j$$

and its execution would take nm CP. But obviously (5) is equivalent to:

(6)

$$\underline{for}\ j\ \underline{in}\ [1:m]\ \underline{do}$$
$$\underline{for}\ i\ \underline{in}\ [1:n]\ \underline{do}$$
$$A_i^j$$

If n identical processors are available to work on the n pairs of vector components, the inner loop will take only one CP. Total time: m CP. This is the mode of operation of multi-processor machines.

1.2.2 The "pipe-line" concept [25]

Another variant of (5) is:

(7)

$$\underline{for}\ i\ \underline{in}\ [1:n+m-1]\ \underline{do}$$
$$\underline{for}\ j\ \underline{in}\ [\max(1,\ i-n+1):\min(i,m)]\ \underline{do}$$
$$A_{i-j+1}^j$$

which a glance at Fig. 3 will help understand. Now the inner-loop actions can be done simultaneously, provided an assembly line of processors exist. This "pipe-line" is made of m contiguous processors, each specializing in one of the m steps of θ. Data enter the first one, are processed and passed on to the next one, up to the end of the line, from which results exit at the rhythm of one by CP. If instead of following i-components we look at what happens during a given clock period, we see that i-components undergo the first of the m treatments in the first processor, while the second processor executes step 2 on $(i-1)$-components, etc.

This results in an apparent speed of one component by CP, after a start-up time of $m-1$ CP, the total time being $n+m-1$. Therefore, we have an explanation for the shape of the timing-curve in Fig. 1. Now why should an addition, for instance, take 3 and not 1 CP at asymptotic speed, as Fig. 2 shows ? Because there are three pipe-lines involved, one to fetch the data from memory into a local register

(a "vector register"), one to add, one to store back the results. The length of
these vector registers is 64, and longer vectors are treated in several passes.
This accounts for the restart time we observed on Fig. 1.

Figure 3 is another way to display the
equivalence of (5), (6) and (7). What
we have in fact is a family of actions
which may depend on each other, in that
some need data that others provide.
This amounts to specify some partial
ordering on these actions (the graph of
this relation is the "dependence graph")
and our three programs were three total
orderings compatible with the given one.
They are in fact one and the same "program", from a functional point of view,
so one should speak of three different
sequential codings of the same thing.
The point is that a vector computer is
still a sequential machine in that it
decodes and executes a sequence of instructions. Only when a substring of
these happen to be independent, and if
separate pieces of hardware (the segments of the pipe-line) are there which
can take them in charge, can parallel
execution occur. The game is thus to
order the actions so that independent
ones are regrouped (in practice, this
means pushing them down to the inner-
mostloops). (2)

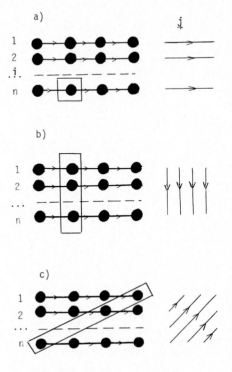

Figure 3
Three possible orderings for the
actions A^j_i. The actions in the
box are done simultaneously.

1.2.3 Regular storage

Pipe-lines are so fast that the rate
of transfer of the data from core
memory to the "functional units" (as
pipe-lines are called, when they perform an operation like +, *, etc.)
may have to be increased by a significant factor. Suppose 4 CP are
needed to fetch a number. If instead
of a single memory unit we have four, it becomes possible to activate one at every
clock, so that after some start-up time, data begin to flow in at the desired rate.
But they should also arrive in the desired order, thus be stored accordingly previous to execution. If one has:

(8)
$$DO\ 1\ I = 1,\ N$$
$$1 \qquad A(I) = B(I) + C(ADR(I))$$

this may well be a vector operation in the programmer's intent (if the integer
array ADR contains some permutation of 1, 2, ..., N). But it cannot be known at
compile time, thus the components of C cannot be stored in the right way, and (8)
will be executed in sequential mode. Compare now with:

(9)
$$DO\ 1\ I = 1,\ N$$
$$1 \qquad A(I) = B(I) + C(3*I + 2)$$

again a vector operation, but now the addresses are predictible.

Let us define, in the Fortran context, a "regular sub-array" of some array X, as the set of values $\{X(M + I*L) : L = 1, \ldots, N\}$ where L and M are constant integers. When mapping our vector machine onto the Fortran machine, we want extensions to be fast, so only regular sub-arrays can be considered as representations of vector entities. This is the "regular storage" rule, or implementation constraint. It has a corollary: not only should vectors be regularly represented, but they should *stay so*, which means that only operations which respect the representation constraints can be deemed "vector operations". This rules out permutations of indices, but allows shifts, truncations, and extraction of regular sub-vectors. In particular, operators *odd* and *even* (select odd or even components of a given vector to obtain a new, shorter one) are permitted.

Our bias toward the Cray-1 is apparent here. But even if other concepts than the division of the memory in banks and the "interleaving" just described are feasible, the problem with non-regular arrays is universal (it is known as the "gather-scatter" problem -- a short reflection about the implementation of sparse matrix methods is enough to realize its great importance). Manufacturers are at grips with it, and will eventually solve it. At this time, it will be possible to define a less restrictive vector machine than the one we now propose.

1.3 The Abstract Vector Machine

To describe the vector machine amounts to introducing a new type: *VECTOR*, with various operations. Operations which can be efficiently implemented on a vector computer are retained, others are ruled out. As we saw, two kinds of efficient operations exist: 1) Vector extensions of scalar operations, 2) Operations which respect the representation constraint. Should also be included operations which link the new *VECTOR* type with preexisting types, like *REAL* and *INTEGER*.

Let us display the "vector machine" (Fig. 4). (A more complete description can be found in [6]).

Remark Operations *odd* and *even* stem from a more basic one (sub-vector extraction, see (13) below). A few others of the same family may occasionally be useful, like for instance *head* and *tail* (first half and second half of a given vector), for the treatment of the Fast Fourier Transform (not included in this paper).

Remark All operations obtained by composition from the ones in the upper part of this table are also part of the vector machine. Properties of such combinations should be displayed, as part of a formal definition. Let us only examine the interplay between *odd*, *even* and *shift*:

(10) $E \tau^{-1} = \tau^{-1} O, \quad O \tau^{-1} = E, \quad E\tau = O, \quad \tau E = O$.

Remark It is a useful exercise to check that the three last operations in Fig. 4 are redundant, as far as they can be expressed from the ones above by composition. For instance, the sum of the components of a real vector can be recursively defined in the following manner:

(11) $sum(u) = if \ |u| = 1, \ then \ scal(u)$

                $else \ sum(odd(u) + even(u))$

From (11), one could derive an implementation of the dot product on the vector machine. This is not the one used on Cray-1, and next paragraph will comment a little on this.

NAME OF THE OPERATION	FUNCTIONALITY	ABBR.	COMMENTS
zero, one	→ VECTOR	0, 1	Vector constants
length	VECTOR → INTEGER	$\|u\|$	≥ 0; $\|one\| = \infty$; $\|zero\|=0$;
add	VECTOR × VECTOR → VECTOR	u + v	$\|u+v\| = max(\|u\|,\|v\|)$
multiply	VECTOR × VECTOR → VECTOR	u*v, uv	$\|uv\| = min(\|u\|,\|v\|)$
divide	VECTOR × VECTOR → VECTOR	u/v	partially defined
abs, sin, etc.	VECTOR → VECTOR		extensions of standard scalar functions and binary operators
sup, inf, etc.	VECTOR × VECTOR → VECTOR		
right shift	VECTOR → VECTOR	τ u	$(\tau u)_{i+1} = u_i \; ¥ \; i$
left shift	VECTOR → VECTOR	$\tau^{-1}u$	$\tau^{-1}\tau=id.$, $\tau\tau^{-1}=id.-\Pi_1$
even	VECTOR → VECTOR	E	
odd	VECTOR → VECTOR	O	see remarks on the previous page
mix	VECTOR × VECTOR → VECTOR		mixes two vectors u and v so that E mix(u,v)= v and Omix(u,v) = u
project	INTEGER × VECTOR → VECTOR	$\Pi_l u$	projection on the first l components
hom	REAL × VECTOR → VECTOR	λ u	
broadcast	REAL × INTEGER → VECTOR		"broadcast" creates a vector with all components equal to the given scalar
scal	VECTOR → REAL		value of u_1 if $\|u\| = 1$ (partially defined)
sum	VECTOR → REAL	Σ u	not a vector operation (stricto sensu)
component	VECTOR × INTEGER → REAL	u_i	
modify	VECTOR × INTEGER × REAL → VECTOR		let $v = modify(u, i, x)$: then $v_i = x$, and $v_j=u_j$ for all $j \neq i$

Figure 4

1.4 What About the Dot Product ?

The scalar product is a fundamental operation in linear algebra. As it is the composition of *multiply* (a bona fide vector operation) and *sum*, we shall examine the latter in what follows. The usual implementation:

```
        REAL S, REAL X(N)
        S = 0.
(12)    DO 1 I = 1, N
   1        S = S + X(I)
```

fails to be vectorizable. "To vectorize" has several distinct meanings, so a definition is needed here. In the context of a Fortran program like (12), it means that the compiler-generated code is such that the operations in the loop body will be executed by the appropriate pipe-line functional units (the "add" one, in this case). What would happen in this case if such vectorization would be performed is suggested by Fig. 5. At each clock, a pair $(S, X(I))$, coming from the scalar register S and from the i-th box of the vector register X, would be fed into the add pipe-line. Simultaneously, some result comes out of the pipe-line and goes into S. Obviously, the over-all result is <u>not</u> in conformity with the usual semantics for (12), because of the time-lag introduced by the journey through the pipe-line.

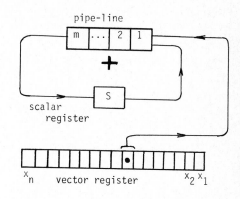

Figure 5
A wrong way of computing sum(s)

We have here a first exemple of "dependence" in an instruction: location S is used to store the result of a process which makes use of the present content of S. On detecting this dependence, the compiler restrains from using the vector register in association with the add pipe-line. To gene-rate purely sequential code (for each value of the index I, fetch $X(I)$ in some scalar register X, add the contents of S and X, store the result in S) would not do, in consideration of the frequent use which is made of *sum* and its parent *dot-product* in numerical analysis. The generated code would run at typical sequential speed (see last line of Fig. 2, where the loop body exhibits a similar kind of dependence) of a few millions floating-point operations per second (MFLOPS). The same figure shows a much more efficient dot-product, which is due to the following approach.

Since the time-lag between entry and exit was responsible for the wrong result in Fig. 5, some temporization of the same duration (m CP, for a pipe-line of length m) should correct this (Fig. 6). We now use m different scalar registers S_j to store the successive values of S. They all contain 0 at the beginning. At each clock period, one of these is asked to deliver its content at the entrance of the pipe-line, while at the same time the result coming from the other end of the pipe is put into the *pre-vious* register. When this is over, it remains to add together (at scalar speed) the contents of the S_j. We now see how the dot-product can achieve a high asymptotic speed, at the cost of a rather high start-up time.

We are not through. Instead of the "rotating register" device of Fig. 6, the Cray implementers have made use of the trick of "chaining" the add unit onto itself (Fig. 7). The output of the pipe-line is du-plicated and sent to two different destinations: the entrance of the pipe, and a passive vector register the m last locations of which play the role of the S_j's. From a func-tional point of view, Fig. 6 and 7 are equivalent, but the last one

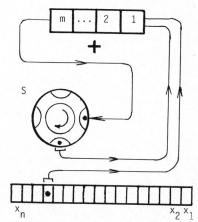

Figure 6
Principle of implementation of "sum".

avoids the necessity of a special
hardware device.

It is worth noting that many other
tricks exist (a different one is
announced for future Cray hardware),
so one would like a more abstract
and more general approach. This is
provided for in the next section.

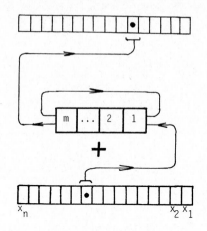

Figure 7
Actual implementation of "sum"
on Cray-1, using "self-chaining".

2. PROGRAMMING THE VECTOR MACHINE

The idea is simple: program <u>toward</u> the abstract vector machine, by stepwise refinement. The resulting code <u>makes</u> use of efficient operations only, by the very
definition of the vector machine. A last translation in Fortran yields a program
which is easily vectorized by the compiler.

Programming by stepwise refinement [31] can be conceived as the production of a
first program on a high level abstract machine, followed by a series of transcrip-
tions on machines of descending level (i.e. poorer in types). To support such an
approach, it is first necessary to build an appropriate pyramid of abstract machines. The one at the base is the vector machine. The one at the top depends on
the problem at hand, and may in some instances not allow more than a <u>specification</u>
of the problem.

We shall first deal with problems that do not need other levels than the vector
machine itself, then turn to algorithms in linear algebra. Finally, we survey the
problems met by the compiler (and thus, by people who write them) in dealing with
the Fortran code obtained as the result of the descending process.

2.1 <u>Don't Think Componentwise</u>

2.1.1 <u>*Sum* (of the components of a vector) on the vector machine</u>

Let us now define explicitly the aforementioned *extract* primitive. Its functionality is:

(13) $extract : VECTOR \times INTEGER \times INTEGER \times INTEGER \rightarrow VECTOR$

and *extract(u, b, e, s)* is the subvector of u which begins at rank b, ends at rank
e or less, with a stride of s. A way to <u>specify</u> *sum* on the vector machine is to
say (informally--formality does not bring anything useful there) that *sum* is dis-
tributive with respect to the vector addition, homogeneous (i.e. $sum(\lambda u) = \lambda\, sum(u)$)
and that $sum(u) = scal(u)$ <u>*if*</u> $|u| = 1$. Now apply this to a set of complementary
extractions of the given vector u. An application of this idea was (11). Another
one results in the following program:

$$
\begin{aligned}
&\underline{in}\ u\ :\ VECTOR,\ \underline{out}\ v:\ VECTOR\ ;\\
&\underline{parameter}\ m\ :\ INTEGER;\\
&\underline{local\ variable}\quad n:\ INTEGER\ ;
\end{aligned}
$$

(14)
$$
\begin{aligned}
&n \leftarrow length(u);\\
&v \leftarrow 0\ ;\\
&\underline{for}\ j\ \underline{in}\ [\,1\,:\,m\,]\ \underline{do}\\
&\quad|\quad v \leftarrow v + extract(u,\ j,\ n,\ m)\\
&\{sum(u) = sum(v)\}
\end{aligned}
$$

(The last line is an assertion on the state of the variables at this point of the program).

It remains to work on v by another method. The process described in § 1.4 is just this, with the same interpretation for m. Observe that there is independence in the j-loop, but this does not slow down the computation, since the addition in the loop-body operates on vectors, and will eventually be translated in Fortran by another, inner loop, where no dependence appears[3].

This idea of considering a vector as a set of shorter sub-vectors is very productive. It amounts, as one easily sees, to a renumbering of the components. It accounts for the "diagonal sweep", the "red-and-black" and other "coloring" schemes [5] in finite differences or finite element applications. This is the idea Calahan refers to with his aphorism "vectorize across the sub-systems". (In this sentence, "to vectorize" takes on a new meaning, namely "put the Fortran code in such a form that it is easily vectorized--in the first acception of the word--by the compiler").

2.1.2 The "odd-even" Paradigm

The idea behind (11) is also a very productive one. Consider the evaluation of a polynomial by Horner's rule, which seems to be a basically sequential process:

(15)
$$
\begin{aligned}
&\underline{function}\ Horner\ :\ REAL\ (\underline{in}\ a\ :\ VECTOR,\ x\ :\ REAL)\\
&\quad\underline{variable}\ i:\ INTEGER;\\
&\quad i \leftarrow length(a);\quad p \leftarrow a_i\ ;\\
&\quad\underline{while}\ i > 1\ \underline{do}\\
&\quad\quad|\quad i \leftarrow i - 1\ ;\\
&\quad\quad\quad p \leftarrow p * x + a_i
\end{aligned}
$$

But using odd and $even$ as defined above, we remark that:

(16) $\quad Horner(a,\ x) = Horner(odd(a) + x\ even(a),\ x^2)$

and this is the basis for a recursion, which can be nicely expressed on the vector machine by the recursion-free program:

(17)
$$
\begin{aligned}
&\underline{program}\ valpol(\underline{in}\ a:\ VECTOR,\ x:\ REAL,\ \underline{out}\ p:\ REAL)\\
&\quad\underline{variables}\ n:\ INTEGER,\ y:\ REAL,\ b:\ VECTOR\ ;\\
&\quad n \leftarrow length(a)\ ;\ y \leftarrow x\ ;\ b \leftarrow a\ ;\\
&\quad\underline{while}\ n > 1\ \underline{do}\\
&\quad\quad|\quad n \leftarrow \lceil n/2 \rceil;\\
&\quad\quad\quad b \leftarrow odd(b) + y * even(b)\ ;\\
&\quad\quad\quad y \leftarrow y * y\\
&\quad y \leftarrow scal(b)
\end{aligned}
$$

Is (17) more efficient than (15) ? There is a trade-of: (15) performs fewer floating-point operations, but at vector speed (time V of Fig. 2, instead of S).

But (17) uses up $I\log_2 n$ CP for the loop start-ups. The break-even point is at $n \simeq 12$ [7]. This way of evaluating polynomials is only of academic interest. A more interesting approach--when the polynomial is to be computed for several values of x-- consists in using (15) for an x of VECTOR type (x being of course the vector made from these values). Again we see there an instance of "vectorizing across the sub-systems".

As an exercise, one may work out the "renumbering" approach. The relation of this last program with (17) would be the same as the relation of (14) with (11). Of course, *sum(u)* is just *Horner(u, 1)* !

Let us look at a more interesting application (from a practical point of view) of the odd-even scheme: solving linear recurrences. The problem is to find a VECTOR x such that:

$$(18) \qquad x_i + a_i \, x_{i-1} = b_i, \quad i = 2, \ldots, n, \quad x_1 = b_1 ,$$

i.e., in our notation, such that $x + a \star \tau \, x = b$, where a and b are the data. Applying operators *odd* and *even*, we obtain:

$$(19) \qquad E x + E a \; O x = E b, \qquad O x + O a \; \tau \, E x = O b.$$

Elimination of Ox in (19) gives a problem similar to the original one, but of reduced order:

$$(20) \qquad E x - E a \; O a \; \tau E x = E b - E a \; O b$$

Once (20) is solved, giving Ex, (19) yields Ox. So there is a recursive solution:

```
       program linrec (in a, b: VECTORS, out x: VECTOR)
             variable y: VECTOR ;

       if length(a) = length(b) > 1 then
(21)   |     linrec(-Ea Oa, Eb - Ea Ob, y)
       |     x ← mix(Ob - Oa τy, y)

       else
       |     x ← b
```

The transformation into a recursive-free Fortran code is easy. See [8] for a detailed treatment.

What we have done is known as "cyclic reduction", and applies with slight modifications to the problem of tridiagonal systems [30]. It is fair to mention that the "renumbering" idea again gives a more efficient routine, but only if coded in assembler language [11].

Some algorithms of the Fast Fourier Transform family also rely on the odd-even approach. When the order is a power of 2, it is an easy exercise (use *head* and *tail*, as well as *odd* and *even*, to obtain a recursive definition of the vector function *fft: VECTOR → VECTOR*).

2.2 Linear Algebra

We now turn to algorithms which need a multi-level pyramid of abstract machines to be specified and developed. What is needed is essentially the MATRIX type, with the new operations:

```
       order: MATRIX → INTEGER
       col  : MATRIX → VECTOR
```

$$row \quad : MATRIX \rightarrow VECTOR$$
$$\times \quad : VECTOR \times VECTOR \rightarrow MATRIX$$

and the natural abbreviations a^j, a_i for $col(a, j)$ and $row(a, i)$. The dyadic product $\times$ is defined by $(u \times v)_i{}^j = u_i v_j$. Let us display a few algorithms on this machine (details about their derivation starting from specifications can be found in [9]).

(22)

$$program \; matrix\_multiply \; (\underline{in} \; a: MATRIX, \; x: VECTOR,$$
$$\{order(a) = length(x)\}, \; \underline{out} \; y: VECTOR)$$
$$\underline{for} \; j \; \underline{in} \; [1 : length(x)] \; \underline{do}$$
$$y \leftarrow y + a_j \; x^j$$

(This is the often quoted example of a variant which works better on a vector computer than the standard way of coding, which would be row by row, instead of column by column, and using dot products. Version (22) is more efficient because of the relatively great start-up time of scalar products.)

Next example:

(23)

$$program \; triangular \; system \; (\underline{in} \; a: MATRIX, \; b: VECTOR, \; \underline{out} \; x: VECTOR,$$
$$\{a \; is \; inf\text{-}triangular \; and \; regular\})$$
$$variable \; xj: REAL \; ;$$
$$x \leftarrow b \; ;$$
$$\underline{for} \; j \; \underline{in} \; [1 : length(b) \; \{ = order(a)\}] \; \underline{do}$$
$$xj \leftarrow x_j/a_j{}^j \; ;$$
$$x \leftarrow x - xj \; a^j \; ;$$
$$x \leftarrow modify(x, \; j, \; xj)$$

Now the Cholesky factorization:

(24)

$$program \; Cholesky \; (\underline{in} \; a: MATRIX, \; \underline{out} \; s: MATRIX)$$
$$variables \; pivot: REAL, \; c: MATRIX \; ;$$
$$c \leftarrow a \; ;$$
$$\underline{for} \; j \; \underline{in} \; [1 : order(a)] \; \underline{do}$$
$$pivot \leftarrow sqrt(s_j{}^j) \; ;$$
$$s^j \leftarrow c^j/pivot \; ;$$
$$c \leftarrow c - s^j \times s^j$$

Program (24) works on the matrix machine: the last instruction involves a dyadic product and a matrix addition. (To be completely correct, we should not assign directly, as done here, to the columns of s, but use instead an appropriate equivalent of the *modify* introduced above). One more step would translate (25) into a program which runs on the vector machine. Getting rid of the slack variable c, we obtain:

(25)

$$program \; Cholesky \; (\underline{in} \; a: MATRIX, \; \underline{out} \; s: MATRIX)$$
$$s \leftarrow inf\text{-}triangular \; part \; of \; a \; ;$$
$$\underline{for} \; j \; \underline{in} \; [1 : order(a)] \; \underline{do}$$
$$pivot \leftarrow sqrt(s_j{}^j) \; ;$$
$$s^j \leftarrow s^j/pivot \; ;$$
$$\underline{for} \; k > j \; \underline{do}$$
$$s^k \leftarrow s^k - s_j{}^k * (\Pi_k s^j)$$

A further translation leads down do the level of the serial (Fortran) machine. (For simplicity, the positivity test has been omitted, and should be introduced at this level). One can see from this example how the advocated process works. It guarantees that only efficient operations are invoked, so the final version is efficient on any vector computer (besides being correct as the result of stepwise refinement, provided no clerical errors slip in, and even these are more easily spotted in programs which result from such a process).

2.3 An Easy Task for the Compiler

Consider the <u>vector extension</u> (as defined in § 1.2.1) of some (possibly complicated) scalar expression. Its natural translation in Fortran is through a loop depending on some index I. Since vectors are not necessarily represented contiguously, the addresses of their components will be (integer) affine functions of I. Such quantities are referred to as "CII's" in Cray manuals, from "constant integer increments". So indices in array expressions will be CII's depending on I, and not I itself.

The compiler's task, when presented with a Fortran DO loop is to check whether this is the translation of the extension of some expression, and if so, to generate vector code, using vector registers and pipe-lines as we have already seen. This task--which amounts to a <u>decompilation</u>, a rather interesting activity from a compiler--may be quite complicated. Our approach is likely to produce Fortran instructions which do not cause trouble, for one will naturally comply with the following rules:

1) All array indices within the loop-body should be CII's. In the case of a multi-indexed array, all indices but one should be constant (with respect to the loop variable), the other one should be a CII.

2) There is at least one assignment to an array variable in the loop.

3) No *GOTO*, *DO*, *IF* or *CALL* is allowed within the loop.

4) No reference to non-standard functions (other than *sin*, *abs*, etc.) should appear.

5) There is no dependence in instructions of the loop-body.

These rules are often presented ex abrupto, as if they were some kind of taboos the programmer should respect. In fact, they are only <u>rules that the compiler makes use of</u>, in order to detect loops which are <u>not in an obvious (for it) way</u> the translation of some vector expression. A detailed study of these rules is unnecessary, especially the last one, which cannot be properly understood without a lengthy explanation of the difficult concept of dependence. (See [21] for a formal definition of dependence as implicitly defined by the Cray manual rules, and [18] for a much more general study of the concept). Here, we need not define dependence in detail: let it be understood as any instruction feature which is incompatible with the loop being the translation of the extension to vectors--all regularly represented--of some scalar expression. This negative definition is enough, since our way of writing programs cannot result in using any such feature. Of course the compiler has to know about dependence it the other way, but this is not the programmer's concern, and such specialized knowledge should not be imposed on her/him.

CONCLUSION

We have presented a concept of "vector machine" which, once mastered, could help a non-specialist to make efficient use of a vector computer like the Cray-1 without a too long study of its architecture and idiosyncrasies. In particular, it was assumed that only standard Fortran environment was used. This approach has its inherent limitations. In particular, it does not account for specific possibilities of the Cray-1 ("super-vector" speeds [17]) (and would similarly fail for other vector computers). Let us give an example. The machine code for the matrix-multiply program (22) would look like this:

(26)

$$y \leftarrow 0 \; ;$$
$$\underline{for}\ j\ \underline{in}\ [\,1 : n\,]\,\underline{do}$$
$$\quad load\ y\ in\ a\ vector\ register\ VR1\ ;$$
$$\quad load\ a^j\ in\ a\ vector\ register\ VR2\ ;$$
$$\quad VR3 \leftarrow VR1 + x_j * VR2\ ;$$
$$\quad store\ VR3\ into\ y$$

It is pure waste to store a vector which is loaded back immediately after. (But the Fortran compiler has to do it, if it is to run reasonably fast, since it cannot detect, without an expensive analysis, what is obvious to our eyes.) This is avoided in the following version:

(27)

$$load\ y\ in\ VR1\ ;$$
$$\underline{for}\ j\ \underline{in}\ [\,1 : n\,]\,\underline{do}$$
$$\quad load\ a^j\ in\ VR2\ ;$$
$$\quad \underline{if}\ j\ odd\ \underline{then}\ VR3 \leftarrow VR1 + x_j * VR2\ \underline{else}\ VR1 \leftarrow VR3 + x_j * VR2$$
$$store\ VR3,\ if\ n\ odd,\ or\ VR1,\ if\ even,\ into\ y$$

Thanks in particular to this simplification, (27) is quite fast (120 MFLOPS) on Cray-1. A few other algorithms similarly appear to be more efficient when coded in Cray Assembler Language than on the vector machine. An accurate model of the Cray-1 should thus incorporate a few operations of the "matrix machine" besides the vector operations considered so far. The advantages of such an approach should be carefully balanced against its main drawback: programs written for this "super vector machine" would depend on a Cray library and be non-portable.

FOOTNOTES

(1) It would be pointless to explicit here the background we need. But of course it goes a little beyond the familiarity with Fortran which the intended audience is supposed to have, and this gap should first be closed. Our stand is that one should welcome this opportunity to complete the curriculum of our users on software engineering, pass on the message that programming is not reducible to coding in some language, etc.

(2) Developments starting from this remark would lead to the "transformational approach" to vectorization [18, 19, 20], the paradigm of which is thus to be found in the pipe-line concept itself. But we do not want to follow this track.

(3) Again, as in § 1.2.2, the transformational approach applies there. The code derived from (14) is the same as (12), up to a change in the order of the atomic actions (here, the additions).

REFERENCES

[1]   Kuck, D.J. Lawrie, D.H. and Sameh, A.H. (eds.), High Speed Computer and
      Algorithm Organization (Ac. Press, New York, 1977).

[2]   Händler, W. (ed.), CONPAR 81 (Conference on Analysing Problem Classes and
      Programming for Parallel Computing, Nürnberg, June 1981) (Springer-Verlag,
      Berlin, A981).

[3]   Feng, T., (ed.), Proc. 1982 Conference on Parallel Processing (IEEE Computer
      Society Press, 1982).

[4]   Bossavit, A. (ed.), Actes du Colloque "Calcul Vectoriel et Parallèle"
      (AFCET-GAMNI-ISINA, mars 83, Paris), Bull., EDF-DER Série C, No 1 (1983),
      RGE SA, Paris.

[5]   Adams, L. and Ortega, J., A Multi-Color SOR Method for Parallel Computation,
      in. Ref. [3].

[6]   Bossavit, A., Présentation de la machine vectorielle, modèle abstrait du
      Cray-1, Bull. DER EDF, Série C (Math. Info.), No 1 (1982), pp. 55-69.

[7]   Bossavit, A., Un aspect de l'algorithmique vectorielle : l'heuristique pair-
      impair, in Les Mathématiques de l'Informatique (AFCET, Paris, 1982), pp. 549-
      561.

[8]   Bossavit, A., Comment j'ai vectorisé certains de mes programmes, Int. Report,
      EDF, 92141 Clamart, HI 4271/00, 1982.

[9]   Bossavit, A. and Meyer, B., The Design of Vector Programs, in: Algorithmic
      Languages (North-Holland, Amsterdam, 1981).

[10] Boyle, J.M., Program Transformations and Language Design, in: The Relation-
      ship between numerical computation and programming languages, edited by

      J. K. Reid (North-Holland, Amsterdam 1982), pp. 285-294.

[11] Calahan, D.A., Ames, W.G. and Sesek, E.J., A Collection of Equation Solving
      Codes for the Cray-1, Systems Eng. Lab. Report N. 133 (1979), the University
      of Michigan, Ann Arbor.

[12] Dijkstra, E.W., A Discipline of Programming (Prentice-Hall, Englewood Cliffs,
      N.J., 1976).

[13] Dongarra, J.J. and Eisenstat, S.C., Squeezing the Most out of an Algorithm in
      Cray Fortran, Report T.M. 9, Math. and Comp. Sc. Division, Argonne National
      Laboratory, Argonne (Ill.), 1983.

[14] Gries, D., The Science of Programming (Springer Verlag, Berlin, 1981).

[15] Hoare, C.A.R., An Axiomatic Basis for Computer Programming, Comm. ACM, 12, 10
      (1969), pp. 576-582.

[16] Hockney, R. and Jesshope, C.R., Parallel Computers (Adam Hilger, Bristol,
      1981).

[17] Jordan, T.L., A Guide to Parallel Computation and Some Cray-1 Experiences,
      Internal Report, Los Alamos National Lab. UR 71-247, L.A., NM 87545.

[18] Kennedy, K., Automatic Translation of Fortran Programs to Vector Form, Rice
      Tech. Report 476-029-4 (1980), Houston, Texas 77001.

[19] Kuck, D.J., Kuhn, R.H., Padua, D.A., Leasure, B. and Wolfe, M., Dependence Graphs and Compiler Optimization, Dpt. of Computer Science Report (1982), U. of Illinois at Urbana Champaign, Ill. 61801.

[20] Lamport, L., The Coordinate Method for the Parallel Execution of Iterative Loops, SRI International Report CA-7608-0221 (1976), 333 Ravenswood Avenue, Menlo Park, Cal. 94025.

[21] Meyer, B., Un calculateur vectoriel : le Cray-1, et sa programmation, Int. Report, EDF HI 3452/01 (mai 1982), EDF, 92141 Clamart, France.

[22] Meyer, B. and Baudoin, C., Méthodes de Programmation (Eyrolles, Paris, 1978).

[23] Paul, G., Wilson, M.W. (eds.), The Vectran Language: An Experimental Language for Vector/Matrix Array Processing, IBM Palo Alto Scientific Center Report G320-3334 (Aug. 75).

[24] Perrott, R.H., A Language for Array and Vector Processors (Actus), ACM Trans. on P.L.S., 1, 2 (1979), pp. 177-195.

[25] Ramamoorthy, C.V., Li, H.F., Pipeline Architecture, ACM Comp. Surveys, 9, 1 (1977), pp. 61-102.

[26] Sameh, A., An Overview of Parallel Algorithms in Numerical Linear Algebra, in Ref. [4], pp. 129-134.

[27] Rodrigue, G.H., Lectures at the "Atelier de Calcul Vectoriel", Dourdan (Oct. 1982), France.

[28] Schreiber, R., A New Implementation of Sparse Gaussian Elimination, ACM TOMS, 8, 2 (1982), pp. 256-276.

[29] Sedgewick, R., INRIA "Club Calcul Parallèle" Seminar talk, 19 April 1983,. INRIA, Rocquencourt, 78153 Le Chesnay, France.

[30] Stone, M.S., An Efficient Parallel Algorithm for the Solution of a Tridiagonal System of Equations, JACM, 20, 1 (1973), pp. 27-38.

[31] Wirth, N., Program Development by Stepwise Refinement, Comm., ACM, 14, 4 (1971), pp. 221-227.

DISCUSSION

Speaker: A. Bossavit

Reid: I am not familiar with the hardware details but I know from experience
that the dot product is computed on the CRAY at vector speed. Of course this may
not be true on future machines based on parallel rather than pipeline hardware,
but for the CRAY the dot product may be included as a basic vector facility.

Bossavit: There still is a greater start-up time for the dot product in FORTRAN.
And as for the CRAY library function SDOT, to include it would be against the
strict portability rules adhered to in this paper (FORTRAN and nothing else, no
penalty when the code comes back to a conventional machine). But I readily admit
the point. The matrix multiply example was there to show how the selection of
only the efficient operations in the abstract machine (excluding less efficient
ones, such as the dot-product in this case) would lead in a natural way to the
most efficient variant of a given algorithm, when several of such variants exist.

Duff: The point is that the CRAY-1 has only one pointer for each vector register,
and the pointer to V0 in V0 ← V0 + V1 is not moved until after 8 cycles, so a
recursive vector-add is possible. For example, the CRAY SCILIB routine SDOT runs
asymptotically at 74 Megaflops, i.e. at full vector speed.

Bossavit: Yes, the marginal time (the quantity V) is 2 for SDOT, because of
extensive chaining, so that a code based on SDOT may be more efficient than one
based on SAXPY (the vector operator y := ax + y). But the fair comparison would
be not with SAXPY but with what Dongarra and Eisenstat ("Squeezing the most of an
algorithm in CRAY FORTRAN", Argonne, TM9, Apr. 1983) calls a GAXPY, that is vector
accumulation (for which one can use the CRAY routine MXMA). Then it is again
apparent that SDOT has a greater start-up time.

Young: You showed a graph describing the Gauss-Seidel method applied to a
rectangle with the natural ordering of the points. The revised ordering which is
equivalent to the natural ordering for the Gauss-Seidel method is the "ordering
by diagonals" rather than the "red black" ordering as you stated. (This is not a
major point, especially since the convergence rates are the same for all three
orderings.)

Bossavit: You are right.

Duff: I would like to comment globally on portability. I think it is perfectly
fair to call a code portable if it calls a subroutine which may or may not be in
FORTRAN. For the whole package to be portable, a FORTRAN version should exist but
this does not preclude the use of specially coded versions for efficiency on
particular machines. A good example of this is the BLAS for which standard FORTRAN
versions exist but many of which have been included in the CRAY-1 CAL-coded
SCILIB. SDOT is one of these routines.

Bossavit: I agree that this is a quite acceptable approach to portability.
Anyway, what counts here is the concept of virtual vector machine, not the list
of operations included. The dot product may be acceptable in it at the present
time.

Schönauer: We must keep in mind what the main bottle necks are in present
vector-computation. For the CRAY-1 this is the one-word transfer between the main
storage and the vector register. The drawback of CYBER 205 is that it can
essentially handle only contiguous vectors. For a reasonable use of these vector
computers one should care for these drawbacks, e.g. only the so-called

super-vector-programming gives the 130 MFLOPS with the CRAY-1.

Bossavit: You pinpoint the weakness of my approach (at least when only the CRAY is considered). It is true that the vector machine concept does not give a complete image of the CRAY-1, since it fails to account for the super-vector speeds. In fact the CRAY is intermediate between a vector-machine and a matrix-machine. The concept of virtual vector machine is quite fit if the target class of (actual) vector computers is large enough. But for the CRAY alone, the right concept is rather a "boosted vector-machine", including some functionalities of the "matrix level".

Huang: I have a question related to the use of the SOR-like methods on a vector machine. According to the Four Colour Theorem, for an arbitrary planar graph, the set of grid-points can be divided into four groups such that no point is connected to any point in the same group. But is there an effective and simple algorithm giving this division?

Reid and Sherman: Essentially, the answer is yes, although we are aware of no published algorithm for this specific problem. There are a variety of theoretical results stating how many "colors" are required for a specific type of difference operator (or finite element basis-function) on a particular type of grid (e.g. [1]). For the example of two-dimensional rectilinear grids using five-point difference operators, the number is two (achieved by the standard "red-black" coloring). An appropriate coloring may be obtained by using a variant of the algorithm developed for the approximation of Jacobian matrices by finite difference calculations ([2,3]). These algorithms must be modified to group together those grid points that may be simultaneously updated with SOR, rather than those whose solution value may be simultaneously varied in a finite difference calculation. The details are different, but the principle is the same. The resulting algorithm may not always achieve the minimum number of colors, but it will be quite close.

References:

[1] R.E. Bank, A.H. Sherman and A. Weiser, "Refinement Algorithms and Data Structures for Regular Local Mesh Refinement". In: R.S. Stepleman (ed.), Numerical Methods for Scientific Computing, North Holland Publ. Comp., Amsterdam, 1983.

[2] A. Curtis, M. Powell, J. Reid, "On the estimation of sparse Jacobian matrices", J. Inst. Math. Applie. 13 (1974), 117-119.

[3] T.F. Coleman and J.J. More, "Estimation of Sparse Jacobian Matrices and Graph Coloring Problems", Report ANL-81-39, Argonne Nat. Lab. , SIAM J. Numer. Anal. 20 (1983), 187-209.

PDE SOFTWARE: Modules, Interfaces and Systems
B. Engquist and T. Smedsaas (eds.)
Elsevier Science Publishers B.V. (North-Holland)
© IFIP, 1984

SOFTWARE PARTS FOR ELLIPTIC PDE SOFTWARE

John R. Rice

Computer Science
Purdue University
West Lafayette, Indiana
U.S.A.

We examine the question of whether very high level elliptic problem
solvers can be built (in theory or in practice) from a collection of
software parts. In theory the answer is yes, in current practice the
answer is no, because most of the required software parts are missing.
The "levels" of software parts needed are identified and their contents outlined. There are isolated collections of parts currently
available (e.g. the high level problem solving modules in ELLPACK,
the low level vector processing routines in the BLAS), but their percentage of those needed is low, perhaps 10-20 percent. A set of
priorities for creating the needed software parts is given and sets
of software parts in the area domain processing are considered in detail.

INTRODUCTION

The establishment of a software parts technology has been proposed for some time
now, see [Rice, 1979], [Comer et al, 1980] and [Wasserman and Gutz, 1982]. A
major effort incorporating this concept is the US Department of Defense STARS
program, see [Druffel and Riddle, 1983] and [Batz et al, 1983] for more details.
The long term goal of this technology is to (a) dramatically reduce the cost of
software development by reusing high quality software parts and (b) to have the
software parts "standardized" for particular subdisciplines so as to form an
informal, but tacitly standardized, "lingua franca" for software construction.

There are three steps to the creation of a set of good software parts. The first
is to design the set; it requires considerable experience and good judgement to
define a set of parts which is general enough to be useful, natural in its functions, and consistent internally and externally. The second step is to implement
the set of parts and test the design. This step is more than an order of magnitude more work than the first. The third step is to refine the design based on
the testing and to make sure that all the parts are of high quality (reliable,
robust, efficient, well documented, accurate, etc.). The third step is again an
order of magnitude more effort than the second. This ever escalating amount of
effort required is the reason that many attempts at software parts have failed;
not enough effort and talent were invested.

The purpose of this paper is to discuss the progress and potential for software
parts needed for the construction of elliptic PDE software. Most of the required
sets do not exist now and we give our view of the priorities and difficulties in
creating them. We finally conclude with somewhat more detailed analysis of the
parts sets for domain processing.

THE IDEAL

We first present an ideal hierarchy for software construction, see Figure 1. The goal is to use parts from each level as the major components in building parts at the next higher level. There would, of course, be some general purpose algorithmic code used as well. In an ideal world, one merely replaces the bottom level of parts as one moves software from machine to machine. The levels of parts defined are:

Virtual Machine Parts. We include a standard algorithmic language here (e.g., Fortran or Ada) plus parts for operations that normally must be implemented in a machine dependent manner. This set of parts must contain all the functionality needed for the higher levels.

Basic Operations. These parts perform standard, relatively simple operations. Examples are: matrix multiplication, matching two character strings, evaluating a function for an array of arguments, finding the maximum element of an array.

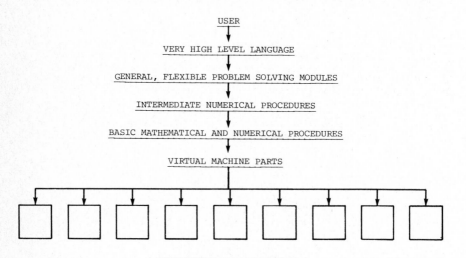

USER

VERY HIGH LEVEL LANGUAGE

GENERAL, FLEXIBLE PROBLEM SOLVING MODULES

INTERMEDIATE NUMERICAL PROCEDURES

BASIC MATHEMATICAL AND NUMERICAL PROCEDURES

VIRTUAL MACHINE PARTS

COMPUTERS OF ALL VARIETIES

Figure 1
The ideal hierarchy in creating very high level PDE solving systems upon layers of increasingly powerful software parts.

Intermediate Procedures. These parts perform somewhat more complicated, but still fairly standard, tasks. Examples are: tridiagonal linear system solver, intersection of a straight line and parameterized curve, evaluation of a B-spline and its derivatives on a standard domain, numerical integration on standard domains.

General Problem Solvers. These parts include complex algorithms for a general class of problems. Examples are: sparse matrix method for a linear system, integration over a general two-dimensional domain, Rayleigh-Ritz discretization of an elliptic operator on a partition of a domain, computing all eigenvalues of a band matrix.

Very High Level Languages. These are languages (systems) which allows one to state a problem and obtain its solution with very minimal effort. Examples are: ELLPACK, MATLAB, SAS, PROTRAN.

THE VIRTUAL MACHINE PARTS

We list 7 categories of parts and facilities that define a virtual machine for
PDE software. Table 1 lists them along their status and the extent that Fortran
provides the facilities. The categories listed in Table 1 are nearly self explan-
atory. By data structures we mean simple things like stacks, and records (a la
Pascal) and by algorithm construction we mean things like arithmetic on numerical
variables, control (IF, looping, etc.), subprograms with separate compilation and
declarations.

The conclusion to be drawn from Table 1 is that the algorithmic language and software parts needed to define the virtual machine are either already available or
rather well identified. However, to my knowledge, no one has presented a detailed
specification of the entire set of parts. This is a task that needs to be done;
one might view the current efforts of the Fortran standards committee, X3J3, as an
attempt to incorporate all these facilities within Fortran.

There is a danger in having the virtual machine parts incorporated within a complex language. One becomes dependent upon the compiler writer for the implementation of the facilities. The perennial inefficiency of Fortran I/O illustrates
the difficulty; it is inconvenient to extract the facility from the language and
almost impossible to improve it within the language. One would probably prefer a
leaner language that allowed parts to be easily incorporated, exchanged and rewritten.

Table 1. The 7 categories that define the virtual machine. The column Fortran
contains a brief comment on the extent to which the Fortran language
provides the required facilities.

Parts Category	Status	Fortran
Array Operations	Well identified, some sets of parts already exist	Nil
Functions	Usually part of the algorithmic language	OK
Graphics	Becoming standard, parts well identified	Nil
Character Operations	Often part of the algorithmic language, parts well identified	Poor(Fortran 66)
Text and Data I/O	Often part of the algorithmic language, often grossly inefficient	Inefficient
Data Structures	Often part of the algorithmic language, parts well identifed	Poor,only arrays
Algorithm construction	The essence of the algorithmic language, well identified facilities	OK

LEVELS OF SOFTWARE PARTS

We list additional sets of parts that are required to build elliptic PDE software.
Three "levels" are identified: *basic*, *intermediate* and *high level*. The dividing
line between these levels is not sharply defined, but the categorization is useful.

Basic Operations

These parts are somewhat of the nature of utilities that can be built out of
virtual machine parts. We list seven sets of such parts along with examples, six
of these sets also contain parts at the virtual machine level:

Array Operations   Matrix multiply, Transpose, Array multiply, Norms, Elementary
elimination steps, Permutations, Evaluation of array expressions.

Functions   Array arguments, Arrays of functions, Tensor products of
arrays of functions, Specific sets of polynomials in 1, 2 and
3 variables.

Graphics   Plots of $y=\oint(x)$, Contour plots of $\oint(x,y)$, Contour sections of
$\oint(x,y,z)$, Domain plots.

Characters   Matching word from list, Conversion of expressions from infix
to Polish and back, Aliasing in tables and lists, Arrays of
messages.

I/O   Tables of arrays, Global control of output (put switches on
generation and destination of output), Tables of functions.
Zero structure of arrays.

Data Structures   Sparse matrix representation of matrices e.g., (coef, idcoef)
vectors, (a_{ij}, i, j) vectors, (A, row_mark, col_mark) vectors,
Transformations between array representations, Basic symbol
table (name, id, value), Storage allocation stack.

Differentiation   Local univariate derivative estimates of functions, Creation
and application of finite difference stencils.

Intermediate Facilities

These parts are more complex and more specific to PDEs than the basic operations,
the four sets include some of the simpler numerical solution methods. As above,
we list the sets of parts along with examples.

Array Operations   Tridiagonal solvers, Gauss elimination for standard representations, FFTs, Inverses.

Domain Processing   Definition facilities, Gridding, Triangulation, Inside/outside
determination, Point location (relative to a grid, triangulation, etc.), Line and curve intersection, Normal to a curve or
surface, Mappings of standard domains.

Integration   Over standard domains, Along parametric curves, Handling of
standard singularities.

Basis Functions   Splines, Piecewise polynomials, Triangular elements, Compositions and transformations.

High Level Modules

These parts solve particular elliptic problems or carry out a major step in the
solution. The ELLPACK system [Rice and Boisvert, 1984], for example, divides
these into categories such as *Discretization* (of an elliptic problem), *Solution*
(of a linear system), *Indexing* (transformation of a linear system) and *Triples*
(complete solution of an elliptic problem). At this time, ELLPACK has 58 modules
identified at the user level; 51 of these are high level, 6 are intermediate
facilities and one is a dummy. ELLPACK also contains numerous intermediate level
facilities in its I/O and domain processing programs. We list the names of some

of the ELLPACK modules to illustrate the variety of software parts at this level:

5 POINT STAR	LINPACK BAND	FFT 9 POINT
HODIE HELMHOLTZ	JACOBI CG	DYAKANOV CG
NESTED DISSECTION	SPARSE LU PIVOTING	MULTIGRID MGOO
SET U BY BLENDING	REMOVE BICUBIC BC	FISHPAK HELMHOLTZ

It is easy to identify another 20-30 modules that would be appropriate to include in ELLPACK; this suggests that there are at least 100 high level modules for elliptic PDEs that are interesting and important.

PROSPECTS AND PRIORITY

A start has been made on a set of software parts adequate for elliptic PDE software, but it is a small one. The number of parts required in even a very narrow area is surprisingly large; recall that there are 38 BLAS and 52 programs in EISPACK. There are literally hundreds of software parts yet to be written which are relevant to elliptic PDE software.

All of the functionality needed in the sets of software parts is in existing programs, it just has not been isolated, organized, parameterized and made robust. The amount of effort needed to design and implement a set of software parts has always been surprising. The design of the BLAS took over four years and while this was a low level activity, this does show that one cannot sit down and make a finished design in an afternoon or two. It takes considerable experimentation and reflection to arrive at natural names, a set of parts that is natural to use, with neither too few nor too many parts.

The past experience shows that useful sets of software parts can be constructed and that they are expensive. The return on the investment far exceeds the cost, so the creation of software parts is economically the right thing to do. One economic difficulty is that there is no straight forward mechanism for the beneficiaries of software parts to defray the initial investment in creating the parts.

A software parts technology will not arrive full blown; this technology can be adopted piecemeal. Indeed, the current ideas about modular programming, etc. are naturally condusive to a software parts technology. Given that one can proceed piecemeal, the natural question is:

What are the priorities in developing software parts for PDE software?

Most people will single out array and vector operations at all levels, as the area with the highest priority. I agree with this assessment; the primary computational bottleneck is in manipulating and solving linear systems of equations. Furthermore, people already are trained to think in terms of vectors, matrices, etc., so there is an existing natural framework within which to develop these parts.

I group the following sets of parts as next most important:

    Functions (Basic operations)
    Basis Functions
    Domain Processing
    Differentiation

Their importance stems from the following: (a) the evaluation and manipulation of functions is often the second most computationally expensive part of solving elliptic problems, and (b) the algorithmic language facilities for functions, domain processing and differentiations are usually primitive so that a lot of

the obscurity in PDE software comes from these sources. Right behind these sets
of parts I place

    I/O Facilities
    Graphics

These are not particular to PDE software, so one can hope that other groups will
develop most of the software parts for these two areas.

I do not discuss further software parts for array and vector processing because
there is already so much activity in this area. I note that basis functions is
an area where there is a lot of natural scientific notation and background and
thus one already has a framework within which to work. This appears to be an
"easy" set of software parts to create. Domain processing is an area where one
draws pictures easily and writes corresponding programs with great difficulty.
There is no standard framework here and thus this area provides a test of our
capability to creat a useful set of parts in an "unstructured" or "novel" area.
Furthermore, some of the basic processes are computationally complex, so this
appears to be a "hard" set of software parts to create. I believe that creating
parts for differentiation is somewhere between basis functions and domain processing in difficulty. Generality in sets of parts for basis functions or
differentiation requires domain processing capabilities, but useful sets of such
parts could be built for specific classes of domains and partitions without
explicit domain processing facilities. I discuss in some detail sets of software
parts for domain processing.

SOFTWARE PARTS FOR DOMAIN PROCESSING

The first task in creating a set of software parts is to define the conceptual
framework. For a specific set, this means precise formal definitions of a number
of terms, objects, procedures, etc. However, there is also a need for closely
related specific sets to be in a common, but more intuitive, framework. Consider
one set of parts for the triangularization of general two-dimensional domains and
another set for rectangular grids in three-dimensional boxes. There might be no
overlap in specific software or facilities, yet a software parts technology needs
to have these two sets closely related at the conceptual level.

The principal objects in the conceptual framework are:

1. Domain. This is a general geometric entity such as a disk in the plane or a
    box in 3-space. Domains have boundaries, interiors and exteriors.

2. Elements. This is one of a small set of standard domains such as triangles,
    boxes, boxes with one curved side, etc.

3. Partition. This is a collection of elements which covers a domain and which
    overlaps only on element boundaries.

To simplify the discussion, we assume that there are just two domains of interest:
the problem domain, associated with the elliptic PDE, and the frame, a domain
that contains the problem domain. All processing is done within the frame, for
some parts sets the frame and problem domain may be the same. There is a natural
hierarchy of subsets of domains, namely:

    interior/exterior
    boundary = faces + edges + vertices

The elements are related to standard representations, one for each element type in
the partition. A standard representation may be parameterized such as the case of
the unit square with the (1,1) vertex cut off by a curve. There is a "simple"
mapping between each actual element and its standard representation. Thus, a

"simple" mapping will preserve geometric features (e.g. edges and vertices) and not unduly distort shape or area. The mapping may be more than just linear; one of the features of a specific set of parts is how the relevant mappings are made.

The general functionality of domain processing parts sets consists of

Creation: Objects are initially defined.

Information: Itemized or collective information is provided about one or a group of objects.

Operations: Manipulate the objects (e.g. split or merge two elements), provide new information (e.g. where is the inside of a domain or what is the map between a given element and its standard representation).

Many of these functions can be defined across all sets of parts for domain processing, most of them can be defined with natural analogy across all sets of parts.

The partition has certain rules about the nature of the elements (it might require uniform size or that no more than five elements meet at a point), and about neighbors (it is common to assume that a point which is a vertex of one element is a vertex of all elements containing it). Specific sets of parts will incorporate specific sets of rules to define the class of partitions involved.

The conceptual framework for domain processing should encompass the following provisions and specific instance.

Domains:
(a) 1, 2 and 3 dimensional.

(b) Defined by a set of boundary pieces or as unions/intersections from a small catalog of shapes or by the truth of a logical function of position.

(c) Interior defined by orientation or connectivity to a specified point.

Boundaries:
(a) Defined by a set of points (with tacit linear interpolation) or by an ordered set of pieces (faces, edges or vertices).

(b) Boundary pieces may be defined parametrically or by an implicit standard (e.g. linear interpolation).

Elements:
(a) May be based on rectangles (or boxes), on triangles (or simplices), or on stencils (as in finite diferences).

(b) A wide variety of irregular elements are included to accommodate general domains.

Partitions:
(a) Includes completely uniform partitions or somewhat irregular sizes.

(b) Rules for neighbors give some flexibility in the partition.

(c) Allow multiple partitions of a given domain.

Creation:
(a) Can define large numbers of objects at once or add a new object to a given collection.

(b) All types of objects can be created and named.

Information:
(a) Provide various levels of information about a single element, a group of
     elements (or subdomains) or the whole problem.

(b) Provide functions or notations for specific information (e.g. location,
     vertices, type, neighbors) that can be used freely in composition.

(c) Provide for a reference grid within the frame.

Operations:
(a) Provide considerable power in splitting, merging, discarding, mapping, etc.

Within this conceptual framework, there will be several, even many sets of parts
for particular choices of element shape, domain structure, etc. Figure 2 shows
element data structures for quadrilateral, point and triangular elements which
fit into this framework. For each case, the "basic" standard domain is shown
along with one "variation" standard domain needed to handle boundary/domain
interaction. The compass point labeling is useful for visualization but we propose a more uniform labeling as follows. Each element has a name (normally a
numerical index), then each component of an element (face, edge or vertex) is
identified by the elements to which it belongs. For the grid stencil element
this just gives a label to each point; for the others one has also pieces named
by element intersections (without repeating the element). Figure 3 shows pieces
of two domains with partitions; the names of the objects are listed:

Element   16   (basic quadrilateral element)
Edges   17,8,15,24
Vertices   17+9+8, 8+7+15, 15+23+24, 24+25+17

The plus sign + is actually a set intersection operator. A standard ordering is
used for the components of an object; here we chose starting with EAST and
proceeding clockwise.

Element   92   (one vertex cut off a triangle)
Edges   107,91,93,Null
Vertices   107+106+105+90+91, 91+78+79+80+93, 93,107

The second example assumes that the element is on the boundary of the domain and
there are no outside elements. We assume that element components can also have
individual names, thus vertex 87 might equal 107+106+105+90+91+92.

A set of parts thus is based on specific choices of

     1. Domain representations allowed
     2. Standard element domains
     3. Operations on elements and domains

The third group of choices defines both the general nature of the partition as
well as its interaction with the domain. Each set consists of a large number of
parts; we give a parts list (see Table 2) with about 30 generic items. We expect
actual sets to have more parts. For example, the GRIDPACK system [Brandt and
Ophir, 1984] has 56 "parts" that are identified for general uses; persumably
there are many more used to build GRIDPACK which that system does not provide to
the user. On the other hand, some GRIDPACK parts are for basis function rather
than pure geometry as discussed here.

STANDARD QUADRILATERAL ELEMENTS

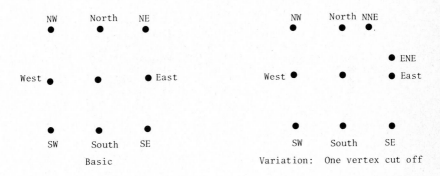

STANDARD GRID STENCIL ELEMENTS

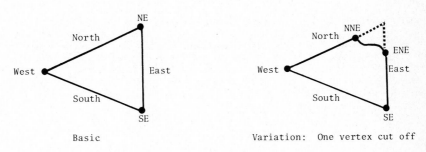

STANDARD TRIANGULAR ELEMENTS

Figure 2

Example standard domains for three element types. The compass point labeling is for visualization purposes.

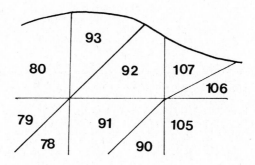

Figure 3
Two examples of domains partitioned into elements. The numbers are the names of
the elements.

Table 2. Generic parts list for domain processing. Most of these software parts
should be present in any set for domain processing.

NAME	BRIEF DESCRIPTION

Informational

DISPLAY ELEMENT(i)	Basic information about the element
DISPLAY FACE(i)	Basic information about the face
DISPLAY EDGE(i)	Basic information about the edge
DISPLAY VERTEX(i)	Basic information about the vertex
DISPLAY BOUNDARY(i)	Basic information about the boundary piece
ID OF (x,y)	Locates elements containing the boundary piece

Analogs of the following functions are needed for faces, edges and vertices also

INOUT(i)	True if i is inside domain
BOUNDARY(i)	True if i is adjacent to the boundary
TYPE(i)	ID of corresponding standard element domain
FACES(i)	Produces list of faces
EDGES(i)	Produces list of edges
VERTICES(i)	Produces list of vertices
LOCATION(i)	Produces standard (x,y) point in element
SIZE(i)	Approximate volume/area of element
DIAMETER(i)	Approximate diameter of element
FRAME(i)	Location relative to frame

The following functions are for boundaries

START(i)	(x,y) coordinates of initial point
STOP(i)	(x,y) coordinates of final point
PIECES(i)	Number of pieces of boundary

Creative

The following parts have complex input not specified in detail here.

DOMAIN	Define a domain
PARTITION	Create a set of elements that form a partition
BOUNDARY	Create a boundary
STANDARD ELEMENT(t)	Create an instance of a standard element domain of type t
ELEMENT	Create an actual element as prescribed

Operational

ADD ELEMENT	Add element to a partition
DISCARD ELEMENT	Discard element from partition
ADD PIECE	Add piece to a boundary
DISCARD PIECE	Discard piece from a boundary
MERGE ELEMENT	Create one element out of two
MERGE PIECE	Create one piece out of two
SPLIT ELEMENT	Create new elements from old using boundary intersections
INSERT BOUNDARY	Compute all boundary/partition intersection information
SET INSIDE	Specify interior of domain
MAP INTO	Create mapping of standard element to actual element
MAP OUTOF	Create mapping of actual element to standard element

ACKNOWLEDGEMENTS

This work was supported in part by U.S. Department of Energy contract
DE-AC01-ER81-01997 and U.S. Army Research Office contract DAAG29-83-K-0026.

REFERENCES

[1] Batz, J., Cohen, P., Redwine, W., The STARS program, IEEE Computer, 16,
     (1983), to appear.

[2] Brandt, A. and Ophir, D., GRIDPACK: Toward unification of general grid
     programming, these proceedings, (1984), p 269-288.

[3] Comer, D., Rice, J.R., Schwetman, H. and Snyder, L., Project Quanta, CSD-TR
     300, Computer Science, Purdue University, (1980).

[4] Druffel, L. and Riddle, W., The STARS program, IEEE Computer, 16, (1983), to
     appear.

[5] Rice, J.R., Software for Numerical Computation, in: Wegner, P. (ed.),
     Research Direction in Software Technology, M.I.T. Press, (1979), 688-708.

[6] Rice, J.R., Numerical computation with general two-dimensional domains,
     CSD-TR 416, Computer Science, Purdue University, (1982).

[7] Rice, J.R. and Boisvert, R.F., Solving Elliptic Problems Using ELLPACK,
     (Springer-Verlag, New York, 1984).

[8] Rice, J.R., Gear, C.W., Ortega, J.M., Parlett, B., Schulz, M., Shampine, L.F.,
     and Wolfe, P., Numerical Computation, in: Arden, B. (ed.), What Can be
     Automated (COSERS), M.I.T. Press, (1980), 51-136.

[9] Wasserman, A.I. and Gutz, S., The future of programming, Comm. ACM., 25,
     (1982), 196-206.

DISCUSSION

Speaker: J. Rice

Madsen: On one of your slides you have indicated a number of the difficulties encountered in software development. I would suggest that many of these difficulties can be attributed to the use of Fortran, which has many shortcomings. Is Fortran the wrong tool for PDE software development?

Rice: It is certainly true that Fortran could be improved. A number of the proposals tentatively adopted for the next Fortran will help, but we cannot wait that long.
Most of these deficiencies can be overcome by creating the virtual machine in Fortran. This then defines a "new" language in which programs are written. Although Fortran has been used historically for PDE software, the use of software parts is not directly connected to Fortran. Fortran is not the main difficulty, but right now there is not much alternative; Pascal is not that much better and probably even worse. Algol 68 is not that widely available and Ada is not available at all.

Madsen: I would like to make three observations in response.
(1) One area in which Fortran is deficient is error checking. A strongly typed language like Ada would correct 80% of the errors that should be checked.
(2) The number of software parts needed for a particular application depends on the language in which they are written. With a better language than Fortran, the number of parts would be much smaller.
(3) Fortran is very poor at character-handling, which can be important in PDE software. In my opinion, many of the deficiencies that you mentioned are language-dependent.
The results would be quite different with a different language.

Rice: Ada is a much younger language than Fortran (by about 30 years). This means that it has the potential to overcome some of the deficiencies that I mentioned. However, strong type checking does not avoid 80% of the errors, but perhaps only 30%.
The new Fortran may have additional useful capabilities similar to those of Ada. However, I believe that we should give up on Ada, Fortran, and other simple general-purpose languages. The solution is to develop preprocessors for each application area that contain features of special value and interest to the application area.

Delves: I would like to agree with Madsen. Although the extra cost of producing usable parts will never be negligible, your quoted factor of 10 comes partly from your implicit assumption that the underlying language is Fortran.

Rice: I don't agree. Fortran is not the problem. The problem with software parts is a failure to anticipate difficulties. No programming language would have helped in handling certain geometric cases. Something unexpected always happens. I mentioned that strong type checking might cover 30% of the validations needed to be done by a software part. However, this is the easiest part of the validation; it can be done systematically and routinely and constitutes perhaps 5 or 10% of the effort to make a reasonable validation. People are fooling themselves if they believe that strong type checking will solve the argument validation problem. It will not do so and it gives people a false sense of security.

Delves: In suggesting that you write a preprocessor to overcome the deficiencies of Fortran, you are in a real sense "writing your own linear equation solver". A number of better languages have been developed: Ada, Algol 68, and perhaps

Fortran 8x. These are "re-usable parts", and you should be insisting that they be used. In my opinion, it is not appropriate to suggest writing a preprocessor.

Rice: I have a preprocessor generator, which means that it does not take long to generate a language suitable for a given application. A general-purpose language cannot provide facilities for all applications. When better languages become widely available (and I expect this to happen someday), then I can write my preprocessor using them.

Delves: Pascal is a poor example to quote because it is not substantially better than Fortran, and is in some respects worse. What is required is a language which has an extensible syntax, so that objects "natural" to the field (here, PDE's; elements; grids; boundary conditions; e t c) can be defined together with operations on those objects. The languages that I mentioned previously let the user do this.

Sewell: In this context, I would like to mention IMSL's Protran products, which include substantial error checking (of dimensions, types, e t c). A core preprocessor is available, and it is easy to add extensions. Eventually (if there is enough demand), the user will be able to add his own facilities to Protran.

Rice: Much of the design of Protran reflects my own views and experience. However, I want to emphasize again that type checking is not enough; there must be checks on whether the problem is well formulated. Some properties can be checked easily. In other cases, complicated computation may be required to check in advance. For example, if one is solving a linear system which should have a symmetric positive-definite matrix, it would not be sensible to check this property of the matrix before beginning to solve the system. The check should be included in the central computational routine.

Schönauer: I would like to remark that in teaching programming, I tell my students to distinguish between programming and coding. Programming is the clear specification and description of how to solve a problem (independnent of the language). Coding is the implementation in a specific language. I believe that this distinction would be useful in this discussion.

My question concerns the effect on domain description of the trend toward parallel computing. Much of domain description involves address lists, e t c. Can you please comment on this problem on parallel machines?

Rice: Domain description is not particularly compatible with parallel processing. However, arbitrary shapes can be subjected to further processing so that it becomes practical to run on parallel machines.

As an aside, I want to mention that the advantages of software parts will be multiplied many times on parallel machines.

Concerning the comment given in the question, let me say that your distinction between programming and coding is not so clear to me. If the program, as you describe it, is complete and unambiguous, then it must be expressed in a language that has precise meanings. If this is so, then the step you describe as coding is simply language translation and one can see several levels of language translation take place in some cases. Many authors present method descriptions in English, German, jargon, e t c, which are neither complete nor unambiguous, and then imply that these are programs which are clear specifications and descriptions of how to solve a problem. It seems unlikely to me that one can give clear specifications and descriptions of how to solve a problem without using a language with an unambiguous definition.

Lawson: Could you comment on the extent to which the PDE community might be able to acquire technology and software parts from the computer-aided geometric design community?

Rice: CAD people have tended to stick to simple representations (e.g., all surfaces are planar, curves are a sequence of small lines). There is a great deal of technology for putting pieces together properly. The catalogue of possible shapes is very large, but there are not many parameterized descriptions. Sometimes the exact shape is not important (e.g., inside a washing machine). In other cases, however, much more precision is required - for instance, the hood of an automobile. The PDE software community should adopt the knowhow that the CAD people have developed. It is quite adequate for many applications, but I believe that a substantial amount of additional work is needed.

Reid: I am disturbed at the bifurcations in the higher (algorithmic) levels of your diagram on software part structure caused by hardware changes at the lowest level. I believe that the main problem is our long history of scalar computing. Would it not be preferable if higher-level algorithms were based on the assumption of underlyting vector hardware? The lower-level transformation of a vector algorithm to a scalar one is possible, whereas the reverse often is not.

Rice: I simply did not want to be overoptimistic. I would be pleased if one could keep bifurcation only at the low levels. However, I wonder whether we can maintain the same general methods (even at higher levels) as architectures change. I sympathize with Reid's view, and hope that it will be possible to avoid differences until we reach the virtual machine level. Different architectures of the future may necessitate quite different high-level approaches.

Delves: Which vector machine do you mean? The higher algorithmic levels are affected by the machine architecture.

Reid: The biggest difference happens when changing from a scalar machine to any vector machine.

Rice: I believe that there will be less effect from different vector and parallel machines than I fear. I am deliberately being pessimistic because I think it will be delicate to find the right language constructs, software parts, e t c, that will allow us to express an algorithm so that it will run efficiently on widely different architectures.

Duff: We might claim that subroutines such as those in the NAG or IMSL libraries are software parts. What are other examples?

Rice: The high-quality mathematical software libraries such as you mention are close to forming sets of software parts for some areas. The most common weaknesses are: (a) Even more emphasis is needed on robustness, but many routines still assume that the user is more clever and careful than he really is. They also seldom check for instances of total misuse. (b) More quantitative measure should be provided for the performance to be expected. (c) The libraries generally do not reflect a systematic study of some application area followed by the creation of a complete set of software parts, carefully coordinated to build higher-level software in the application area. I view the first two weaknesses as rather straightforward to remedy. There are some systematic packages (such as EISPACK and LINPACK), but this is unusual.

Delves: Other examples of software parts are structures with Gaussian points and weights, collections of finite elements, and lexical analyzers.

Rice: I see that I misunderstood Duff's question.A further example of a software
part is one that provides physical data values. This would allow one to obtain
high-quality data in the same way as one expects to obtain high-quality algorithms
from good math software parts. Note that some physical data is quite complex
(with three or four independent variables from an irregular domain) and has been
reported in the literature with widely varying values.

PDE SOFTWARE: Modules, Interfaces and Systems
B. Engquist and T. Smedsaas (eds.)
Elsevier Science Publishers B.V. (North-Holland)
© IFIP, 1984

AN EFFECTIVE METHODOLOGY FOR PDE SOFTWARE DEVELOPMENT

Li-Kuan Chen
Thomas K. Eccles
Juan C. Meza
Glenn O. Morrell
Andrew H. Sherman
William J. Silliman

Exxon Production Research Company
Houston, TX

One of the most challenging tasks in scientific computation is the construction of large software systems to
solve partial differential equations. In the petroleum
industry such software is required for the numerical simulation of petroleum reservoirs. In the past, most simulators
were developed in a manner that led to programs that were
efficient but that were extremely difficult to debug,
maintain, and modify. At Exxon Production Research Company
we have recently released the first version of a new multiple
application reservoir simulator (MARS) that was designed and
implemented with the avoidance of these difficulties firmly
in mind. Our simulator, which comprises over 550 subroutines
and 130,000 distinct lines of code, has performed reliably
and efficiently on both CRAY and IBM computers and at several
geographically separated sites around the world. It has also
successfully run the largest simulation model of which we are
aware (over 30,000 cells in a three-dimensional grid). In
this paper we describe the software methodolgy that has
worked so well for us in this project.

1. Introduction

One of the most important tools now used to assist in the development of
the world's petroleum resources is the numerical reservoir simulator. Essentially, such a simulator is a very large, complex piece of computer software
designed to solve a system of coupled partial equations. In this paper we
describe a methodology for the construction of software of this type that has
proven to be extremely successful in the development of a multiple application
reservoir simulator (MARS) at the Exxon Production Research Company (EPR).

Reservoir simulators model the fluid flow in a porous rock formation (the
reservoir) by formulating a system of partial differential equations whose
independent variables are fluid pressure and phase saturations. In the most
common type of model, the socalled black oil model, three phases (hydrocarbon
liquid, hydrocarbon vapor, and water) are included and limited mass transfer
between phases is permitted [1]. The MARS simulator employs a compositional
formulation described by Kendall et al [2] that is an extension of that proposed
by Acs et al [3]. For the full threephase black oil model, the MARS formulation
requires the solution of a system of three partial differential equations, most
often in the variables pressure (p), vapor saturation, and water saturation. In
simplified form using vector notation for saturation ($\underline{s}$) and the saturation
equations, these may be stated as:

$$C(p,\underline{s}) \ \frac{\partial p}{\partial t} = \ R_p(p,\underline{s}) - \sum_{m=1}^{3} V_{fm}(p,\underline{s}) \ \nabla \cdot \left[\sum_{r=1}^{3} X_{rm}(p,\underline{s}) \nabla p \right] \qquad (1.1)$$

$$\frac{\partial \underline{s}}{\partial t} = \ \underline{R}_s(p,\underline{s}) - \sum_{m=1}^{3} \underline{V}_m(p,\underline{s}) \ \nabla \cdot \left[U(p) \sum_{r=1}^{3} \underline{F}_r(p,\underline{s}) \right] \qquad (1.2)$$

The PDE's can be solved in a number of ways. Most frequently in MARS, the sequential semiimplicit procedure of Spillette, Hillestad, and Stone [4] is used. In this case, two sets of discrete equations are solved at each time step. First, the pressure partial differential equation (1.1) is solved, and the new pressures are used to compute the total (over all three phases) fluid velocity field U. The new pressures and the total velocity field are then used to discretize the two saturation equations (1.2), which are solved to obtain the fluid saturations at the end of the time step. In this sequential approach the PDE's are decoupled and linearized by making several simplifications. First, the dependence of each set of equations on the variables of the other is lagged in a Gauss-Seidel-like manner: that is, the most up to date values are used. Next, all fluid and reservoir properties used in constructing the coefficient functions are time-lagged in both pressure and saturation. Last, first-order Taylor series extrapolations are used to remove nonlinear dependencies in the resulting lagged equations.

In MARS (and the industry in general), both sets of equations are spatially discretized using a standard block-centered finite difference operator for second derivatives combined with an upstream-weighted onesided operator for first-order terms. Backward differences are normally used in time. The resulting sets of discrete equations may be quite large (upwards of 30,000 variables in the pressure equation, for instance) and have quite different characters. The pressure equation is essentially elliptic and, in principle, can be solved using standard differencing and linear algebraic techniques for such equations. Experience has shown, however, that the discrete pressure equation is often extremely difficult to solve, and the industry is devoting a significant research effort to this task. In contrast, the saturation equations behave hyperbolically, and the major difficulty encountered in practice is not solving the discrete equations, but in formulating the discretization so that the computed saturations are meaningful. This is particularly true in situations where sharp saturation fronts are to be expected, such as in the use of water flooding to increase oil recovery.

Additional complexity in the construction of a reservoir simulator is introduced by the fact that the fluid flow equations are not solved in isolation from some model of surface facilities and activities. For example, one major use of a simulator is to predict future reservoir performance under a variety of possible operating strategies. Such strategies are usually implemented in a set of well management or rate routines and generally enter the flow equations in the form of boundary conditions at wells. The interface between the rate routines and the flow package requires careful attention, and, in any case, the rate routines significantly increase the amount of code in a simulator.

From the foregoing it is clear that the development of a reservoir simulator is not a simple matter. A great deal of code must be written, and many
individuals are involved in design and implementation. The MARS simulator, for
example, contains over 550 subroutines and 130,000 lines of code. The team that
developed it consisted at one time or another of 18 Ph.D.-level engineers,
scientists, and mathematicians, most of whom were involved at essentially all
levels of the development process from program or module design to final coding,
testing and documentation. The development of MARS was further complicated by
the constraint that it run reliably and efficiently on a wide range of sizes and
types of simulation problems in two rather different computing environments: the
large IBM mainframes (such as the 3081) located both at EPR and at Exxon sites
around the world and the CRAY1-S computer at EPR. This last point, in particular, presented some potential compatibility problems such as the maintenance
of separate libraries and executable modules on the two machines and the
construction of overlays on the IBM.

All these considerations led us to impose the following requirements on the
design of the MARS program:

Modularity: Insofar as possible, the rate and flow packages would communicate only through a well-defined interface, and both would be independent of an underlying data management package used to move data between
main memory and auxiliary storage media such as disk and tape.

Reliability: Where necessary, less efficient, but more robust algorithms
would be used in order to reduce the chance of failure on difficult models
in the field. In addition, automatic program test and update facilities
would be developed in order to ensure the correctness and compatibility of
modifications and enhancements.

Maintainability: A single source code would be maintained using special
pre-compilation directives to include machine-dependent features. Also,
extensive internal documentation and optional debugging output would be
built into the code.

Efficiency: Inherently vectorizable algorithms would be provided for all
major tasks in the program, with unvectorized implementations used in IBM
code only where significant gains in efficiency would result. Also,
efforts would be made to allow for relatively easy replacement of
algorithms as better ones became available.

In the remainder of this paper we discuss the techniques and tools that we
have used to achieve our design goals. The discussion is divided into two parts
that cut across the boundaries suggested by the individual goals as listed
above. In Section 2, we discuss the overall structure of MARS, concentrating on
the underlying data management package and module interfaces and their effects
on modularity, reliability and efficiency. In Section 3, we describe a number
of tools and procedures used to enhance the reliability of the code and to
assist in maintenance. Finally, in Section 4 we briefly assess our experience
in developing MARS.

2. Program Structure

From a user's point of view, the MARS simulator divides quite naturally
into three functional sections: a flow package (FLOW) to solve the PDE"s
described in the Introduction, a well management package (RATE) to handle the
wells and surface facilities, and an edit package (EDIT) to generate reports and
data printout. A major design goal for MARS was to make each of these packages
as independent as possible so that changes in one part of the program would not
ripple through the entire code. This has been achieved by glueing the program

together with a data management package (CONTROL) containing rather sophisticated capabilities for inter-module communication and memory and disk management. Figure 2.1 illustrates the structure of MARS at this level.

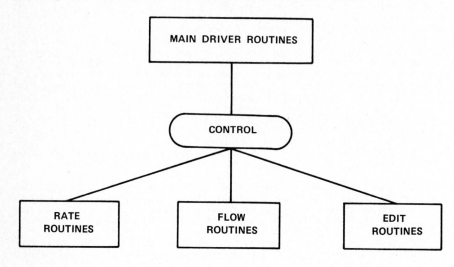

FIGURE 2.1: OVERALL STRUCTURE OF MARS

FLOW, RATE, and EDIT communicate primarily through data arrays managed by
CONTROL and, to a more limited extent, through COMMON blocks. In concept,
interfaces are quite straightforward, with CONTROL passing appropriate input
data to calculation subroutines and receiving output data from them. The
situation is complicated by the fact that practical reservoir models often lead
to computations that cannot be completely corecontained, and CONTROL must handle
any necessary transfer of data between core memory and auxiliary storage.

The overall execution of a simulation is driven by a small set of main
driver programs that use CONTROL to invoke required computational subroutines.
When a main program invokes a subroutine through CONTROL, it merely provides to
CONTROL the name of the desired subroutine, the names of the arrays to be used
for input and output data, and some auxiliary information that is used by
CONTROL to identify the particular invocation for later storage management (i.e.
paging) optimization (see below). CONTROL then performs the tasks of an
automatic paging system, except that, since the context is rather specialized,
it can be more efficient than more general systems. In particular, CONTROL
determines the location in core or on disk of the required arrays, loads appropriate segments of them while saving arrays that must be overwritten, sets up
integer pointers that indicate the boundaries of the in-core portions of the
arrays, and passes control to the actual computation subroutine. If there is
insufficient core memory to contain all of the array data, then CONTROL sets up
a loop in which the computation subroutine is called repeatedly until all of the
array data has been processed. In order to handle a variety of different types
of computations, provisions have been made to handle arrays that are required in
their entirety and to allow for overlap between successive segments of the array
data.

With respect to the issues addressed in this paper, the most important design feature of the CONTROL interface with the other packages is that CONTROL handles data transfer in such a way that the other subroutines in MARS can be largely coded as if they were passed whole arrays instead of only pieces. Most of the subroutines in MARS look as if they operated on arrays that were always entirely in core; the only evidence that this is not the case is that computations that might otherwise range from 1 to N, say, range instead from IJKLO to IJKHI, where these are two variables whose values are set up by CONTROL to indicate the portion of the data that has been passed. This makes it relatively simple to design, code, and test subroutines in MARS without worrying about data management issues, and we believe that it has significantly increased programmer effectiveness and program reliability and efficiency.

As an aside here, we might comment on the "paging" strategy employed by CONTROL. Since the application is so specialized, it is possible to improve significantly on the standard types of paging strategies used in general paging systems. CONTROL uses a form of predictive paging in which the entire history of subroutine invocations through CONTROL is used to predict what arrays are most likely to be needed next; these arrays are kept in core in preference to other, less likely candidates whenever arrays must be written to disk to free up space in core memory. The reason this scheme works so well is that a typical simulation consists of a long sequence of essentially identical time steps. Once the data flow is known for the first time step, it is usually correct to assume that subsequent time steps follow the same pattern. Only time step cuts or forced output points cause interruptions, and both types of events are relatively infrequent. In a variety of practical examples, CONTROL has demonstrated an ability to handle its paging task extremely efficiently.

Because CONTROL is a cut point for inter-package communication, the individual packages FLOW, RATE, and EDIT are inherently modular in the sense that no routines in any of these packages need make any assumptions about the internal workings of routines in any of the other two. This modularity is further enhanced by restricting most communication between routines in each of the three main packages to also go through CONTROL; the main exceptions are subpackages that consist of a number of closely-tied subroutines that together solve some important task. An example of this is the set of fluid property routines that must pass information among themselves below the level of CONTROL in order to avoid the use of excessive temporary storage. Even here, however, care has been taken to reduce inter-module communication and preserve top-down structure.

Another important result of using CONTROL to invoke computational subroutines is that it is possible to provide a common set of debugging facilities that allow monitoring of the data passed to each subroutine. These facilities are discussed in some detail in Section 3, but we wish to note here that this type of feature would be impossible if subroutines could obtain input data from a multitude of sources. In fact, though, almost all MARS subroutines receive all of their data in arrays passed by CONTROL, with the most notable exception of data reading routines whose sole function is to read user-supplied data from a standard input dataset. (However, these routines, too, are invoked through CONTROL.)

A third advantage of the central role of CONTROL is the isolation of hardware-dependent code in a single place. A number of routines do contain compiler-dependent code related to the use of vectorized algorithms on the CRAY1-S, but essentially all of the code that depends on the precise characteristics of the hardware or operating system (such as efficient disk input and output) is located in the CONTROL package itself. More specifically, this sort of code is restricted to a small number of mainly assembly language routines that perform certain specialized tasks. The largest part of the CONTROL package itself, and all of the rest of MARS, is written in standard conforming Fortran. This is a significant improvement in MARS over previous Exxon simulators which should make it much easier to port the simulator to the various sites worldwide where it will be run.

Finally, the last benefit of the use of CONTROL to handle intermodule interfaces is that it allows us to carry out smaller-scale simulation research and development projects using MARS without impacting production users of the simulator. The basic requirement for this is an environment in which it is straightforward to interface independently-developed modules into the simulator without making extensive permanent changes. New modules can be usually be interfaced to MARS simply by modifying two subroutines: a subroutine assignment routine that describes the calling sequence to CONTROL and a main driver program that actually calls the new module (usually in place of some other existing module). In most cases no changes are required to input or output processing routines, since the debugging facilities described in the next section provide a means of controlling the use of the new module. As an example of this type of effort, we have examined a number of sparse Gaussian elimination packages as optional methods for equation solution in MARS, and we shortly plan to use this approach to evaluate a variety of conjugategradienttype iterative methods. In both cases, the use of MARS as a test site facilitates comparison of new methods with existing ones on realistic problems reflecting actual simulator applications.

3. Development Aids

A program as large as the MARS simulator would be extremely difficult to develop without software tools to assist in coding, debugging, and maintenance. Some of the things that we found most useful were standard items provided as part of the basic computing environment at EPR (e.g., the PANVALET source management facility [5]), but we did develop a number of tools and procedures that proved extremely important in achieving the goals set forth in the Introduction. In this section we describe three of the ones that seem central to developing and maintaining a reliable software product.

3.1 A Fortran Preprocessor

A basic tool developed for the MARS project is a simple type of Fortran preprocessor. Not so general as some described in the software tools literature [6], it still provides us with the capability of maintaining a single source code containing compilerdependent Fortran and code intended only for use in debugging. When placing such code in the program, the programmer brackets the code with special comment statements that identify the conditions under which the code is to be included in the preprocessed source. For example, if a piece of code were intended for use only on the CRAY1-S computer, it would be preceded by the comment "CIF CRAY" and followed by the comment "CENDIF". Semantically, this is interpreted by the preprocessor to mean that the code is to be included if the keyword "CRAY" is included in the control input stream for the preprocessor. The basic syntax recognized by the preprocessor allows for if-then-else constructions, negation, conjunction, and disjunction.

The preprocessor keywords themselves are not special, and it is occasionally useful for programmers to define personal keywords during the testing process. However, the keywords most widely used in MARS allow for machine-specific code ("CRAY" or "IBM") and two types of debugging code ("DEBUG" or "SUPERBUG") distinguished by their costs during execution (see below). Other keywords control the disposition of code that is preprocessed out of the source: it or the special comments surrounding it may be retained in the form of Fortran comments. We anticipate that in the future we may wish to use keywords to allow custom tailoring of MARS to handle the special needs of users at remote sites throughout the world.

3.2 Debugging Facilities

MARS is large and complex enough that we have no realistic expectation that it will ever be entirely bug free, so as a consequence we view the inclusion of flexible diagnostic features as extremely important. The preprocessor has enabled us to do this quite conveniently, since it is possible to include a substantial amount of debugging code in the archival source for MARS without any requirement that it be included in production versions.

Initially we had intended to produce two versions of MARS: a production version stripped of all debugging code and a debugging version incorporating extensive diagnostic facilities. However, it has turned out that much of the debugging code amounts to little more than printing of array or scalar data that takes up little space in the compiled module and has essentially no effect on compiler optimization of the program. Since such code can usually be bypassed with simple and cheap logical tests, we have found it more convenient to normally include such code even in versions of MARS used for actual production simulation runs. This allows us to more easily track down any problems that our users encounter when running the program.

There is debugging code, however, that either cannot be included cheaply in a production version or is extremely unlikely to be useful in most circumstances in the field. We have dubbed such code "SUPERBUG" to distinguish it from the "DEBUG" code just discussed. "SUPERBUG" code is normally deleted from the source except when its use is absolutely necessary since its inclusion may substantially degrade the performance of the simulator. Examples of such code include computation of various algebraic residuals in iterative method subroutines, printing of variables inside of certain loops, and printouts that would generate very large amounts of output.

To control the use of the debugging code in MARS, we have provided two distinct facilities through which users can specify what diagnostic information is desired and, to a large degree, the form in which it is presented. First, in the block-structured input data for MARS, users may include a DEBUG block of the form shown in Figure 3.1. The three subblocks of this data specify information that is used by the program to determine whether a particular piece of debugging code is to be executed and, if so, to limit the amount of array data printed out. The SUB-ENDSUB block contains keywords that designate particular subroutines or groups of subroutines in the program. The KEY-ENDKEY block contains keywords that specify which of several pieces of debugging code is to be executed by the designated subroutines. Finally, the RANGE-ENDRANGE block contains information that can limit the portions of arrays that are printed out in debugging code. (Recall that some arrays in the simulator may have tens of thousands of entries.) For example, if it were desired to print residuals every iteration of the iterative method LSORC, the user would specify the subroutine "LSORC" and the keyword "RESIDUAL". Frequently used keywords include those that cause the printing of various internal tables and control variables used by the CONTROL data management package, since many of the program failures encountered during development turn out to be due to some difficulty in the interfacing of a subroutine with CONTROL. It is also possible to use keywords to control the use of nonstandard code that is included for research or testing purposes only.

```
DEBUG
     SUB
          LSORC
     ENDSUB
     KEY
          RESIDUAL
     ENDKEY
     RANGE
     ENDRANGE
ENDDEBUG
```

Figure 3.1:   Example of DEBUG Data

A second facility is provided for user-controlled printout of subroutine array arguments. Here we have exploited the fact that most subroutines are invoked through CONTROL, so there is a well-defined place in the program where most array arguments are processed. CONTROL maintains a table of array arguments that are to be printed and can print them either before or after invoking a subroutine as required. If an array is too large to fit entirely in core memory, then, as noted in Section 2, CONTROL will invoke a subroutine more than once to process pieces of the array. In this case the array will also be printed in pieces corresponding to the individual subroutine invocations; this would clearly be extremely difficult without a centralized data management package.

The user controls diagnostic argument printout by including a PRINT-ENDPRINT block as illustrated in Figure 3.2. When the program encounters such a block in the input data stream, CONTROL's argument printing table is updated. The user can specify the names of the subroutines for which arguments are to be printed, the names of the array arguments, whether the arrays are to be printed before or after the subroutine, the index range over which the arrays are to be printed, and the format of the printout (sequential or grid-oriented, standard formatted Fortran output or hexadecimal dump). Internally, arrays must be assigned before use, and CONTROL retains information concerning the datatype of an array (e.g. single or double precision, integer, alphanumeric). As a result the printout can be provided in a compact and highly readable form.

```
PRINT
     SUB = LSORC
     ARR = DELP   PRHS
     WHEN = AFTER
     I = 1,5    J = 2,4    K=1,3
ENDPRINT
```

Figure 3.2:   Example of PRINT Data

The same printing facilities that are used by CONTROL to print array arguments are also used by individual subroutines to print all or part of their argument arrays at intermediate points in their computations. As a result, diagnostic array printouts throughout the program have a uniform appearance and, in certain cases, can be controlled with the PRINT-ENDPRINT data block. This often alleviates the difficulty of extracting a small amount of useful information from a large amount of data printed in diverse formats by different subroutines. In addition it relieves each programmer from having to provide extensive output formatting facilities in each subroutine.

3.3 Library Management Procedures

Maintaining the integrity of the program is a major difficulty with any large program that will exist at a number of remote sites and will be undergoing frequent modification. In particular, we are concerned that the version of MARS released to users be as reliable as possible and that it conform to the capabilities announced in the user"s guide. Yet, at the same time, we need to be able to make changes in the program to fix bugs or to add new features. In order to reconcile these requirements, we have devised a library management and update procedure that is quite robust and largely automatic.

We maintain versions of the source and object libraries at three levels (designated "T", "X", and "Y") and executable modules at two levels (T and X). The T version is the oldest version of the program and should correspond exactly to the current release of the user's guide. In general it is expected to be the most reliable version as well, since it will be the most widely used and tested. However, when bugs are discovered in the T version it is not feasible to correct them immediately, since that would require an entirely new program release. Such bug fixes are introduced into the younger X or Y versions, and as a result, a small fraction of users may actually not use the T version for production simulations.

The X version of the program represents a fairly stable version of MARS that is available to users but may have capabilities that are somewhat different from those documented in the user"s guide. It will also be the version of the program in which important bugs in the T version are fixed. We expect that the X version of the program will be updated approximately monthly, but that release of a new T version will occur less frequently (say every three to six months).

The Y version of MARS is a test version that is not available to most users. This version undergoes almost daily change and, in spite of our best efforts, may contain a number of bugs. Most changes to the program, including most bug fixes to the X and T versions, start out in the Y version and migrate to the X and T versions as part of the normal update process described below. Since the Y version changes so rapidly, there seems to be little point in trying to keep an up-to-date executable module, so only source and object module libraries are maintained.

We have developed formal procedures for program updates that incorporate a substantial number of automatic program tests. Four basic steps are involved in updating the Y version of the MARS. First, an automatic module checkout procedure is used to secure exclusive access to each subroutine that is to be modified. Next, the required changes are coded and debugged. Third, an automatic procedure is run to check that the changes do not introduce bugs into the existing version of the program. This procedure compiles the modified subroutines, runs a series of approximately 20 test examples, and automatically compares key portions of the output with saved corect output. If this is successful, then the last step, the actual update of the libraries, is performed, and the exclusive access is relinquished. The first two steps in the update process are generally done in parallel with other programmers, but the last two are executed by just one programmer at a time in order to avoid conflicting modifications. In most cases all testing is performed on the CRAY1-S computer due to faster turn-around and the fact that most code is common to the IBM and CRAY environments. In some cases, however, automatic tests are run on both machines when there is reason to expect that the changes might cause different performance on the two machines.

Periodically (currently monthly), the Y version libraries are integrated into the X version libraries. Most of this update is done automatically in a number of steps that perform extensive tests, rename source code datasets, update the libraries, and construct executable modules for both the IBM and CRAY1-S computers. In addition, a number of detailed global crossreference listings are produced for both the source code and the executable modules; these have been of great assistance in making program modifications. The testing performed in a Y-to-X update is far more extensive than that required to update the Y version: upwards of 60 different test cases are run on each computer. Ideally we would hope to complete a Y-to-X update in a single day or two at most, but we have found that three to four days seems to be more typical so far.

Infrequently, the X version must be updated to fix a critical bug that has shown up in the X or T versions. Such an X-to-X update involves less extensive testing than a Y-to-X update because the code changes are usually very limited. X-to-X updates can usually be completed in a matter of hours, so it seems quite reasonable to use them to incorporate emergency bug fixes into the program.

At scheduled intervals we plan to issue new releases of the T version of MARS. Such releases entail significantly more work than the other program updates since updates to the user"s guide must be issued at the same time, and new versions of the program must be sent to all remote sites running the program. (This would not necessarily be the case with Y-to-X updates, which might affect only local users on the EPR computers.) In other respects, the X-to-T update procedure is almost identical to the YtoX update procedure.

4. Assessment and Concluding Remarks

By most reasonable standards, the MARS project has been very successful, and we believe that this is largely due to the methodology used in developing the program. In approximately two years a relatively small team was able to produce a large complex software product that works well now and promises to be fairly easy to upgrade and maintain. One indication of the success of the methodology is our experience with the initial release of the program. We adopted a phased approach to release in which we began by working closely with just a single user. Within six weeks of the release for that user, MARS was regularly running the largest reservoir simulation study ever attempted (so far as we know): a model containing over 30,000 cells in a three-dimensional grid system for a full threephase black oil system. Shortly thereafter, MARS was released to all of the engineers at our location in Houston, and it has run reliably and efficiently on a variety of simulation models since then. We are now in the process of making MARS available to users at a number of other sites worldwide; we expect to be able to support and maintain the program from Houston with only a minimum of difficulty.

Apart from its contribution to the rapid development of a reliable new program, the MARS design has also turned out to be flexible enough to simultaneously support ongoing simulation research and development projects. This is extremely important to us because the current black oil MARS is only the first step along the road to an integrated simulator including black oil, compositional/miscible, and thermal modelling capabilities. In the past adding new modelling capabilities of this scale would have required extensive redesign and recoding of the simulator, but based on our experience so far with compositional features, this will not be true of MARS. We believe, therefore, that we have hit upon a methodology for PDE software development that will serve us well for some time to come.

Acknowledgments

We wish to acknowledge the contributions of our colleagues on the MARS development team in helping to design and refine the methodology and tools described in this paper. Much of what we have accomplished required their patience and willingness to work with earlier versions of software, particularly CONTROL, that lacked the generality of the current products. We are also grateful to Exxon Production Research Company for permission to publish this paper.

References

[1] Peaceman, D. W.: <u>Fundamentals of Numerical Reservoir Simulation</u>. Elsevier Scientific Publishing Company, Amsterdam, 1977.

[2] Kendall, R. P., Morrell, G. O., Peaceman, D. W., Silliman, W. J., and Watts, J. W.: Development of a multiple application reservoir simulator for use on a vector computer. Paper SPE 11483 presented at the Middle East Oil Technical Conference, Manama, Bahrain, March 14-17, 1983.

[3] Acs, G., Doleschall, S., and Farkas, E.: General purpose compositional model. Paper SPE 10515 presented at the Sixth SPE Symposium on Reservoir Simulation, New Orleans, LA, Jan. 31-Feb. 3, 1982.

[4] Spillette, A. G., Hillestad, J. G., and Stone, H. L.: A high-stability sequential-solution approach to reservoir simulation. Paper SPE 4542 presented at the SPE 48th Annual Meeting, Las Vegas, Sept. 30-Oct. 3, 1973.

[5] Pansophic Systems, Inc.: <u>PANVALET User Reference Manual</u>. 1978.

[6] Boyle, J. and Dritz, K.: An automated programming system to facilitate the development of quality mathematical software, in <u>Information Processing 74</u>, proceedings of IFIP Congress 74, Editor J. L. Rosenfeld, North-Holland, pp. 542-546, 1974.

DISCUSSION

Speaker: A. Sherman

Duff: Early in your talk you indicated that relatively little time was spent in the actual solution of the discretized equations. Our experience at Harwell is that the solution of linear equations accounts for 40-50% of the total run time. Is this because the PORES package at Harwell is a fully implicit simulator as opposed to your sequential formulation, or is there another explanation?

Sherman: First, I said that about 35% fo the total run time was spent on equation solution, split into about 15% for solution of the discrete pressure equation and about 20% for the discrete saturation equation in a three-phase simulation. This is only a slightly smaller relative cost (as compared to the PORES times that you cited) and is largely due to our sequential formulation, as you noted. We solve one block 1×1 system and one block 2×2 systems as opposed to the solution of a block 3×3 system in PORES. Moreover, the variables in each of our systems are comparably scaled, whereas the PORES system has variables of vastly different sizes (pressures and saturations). This undoubtedly has some effect on the amount of iteration required.

Yanenko: Can you explain the use of a physical data bank? Are the physical properties not known? Are experiments needed to determine them?

Sherman: There are two types of physical properties that enter into reservoir simulations: fluid and rock. Fluid properties such as compressibility, density, e t c, can usually be measured fairly accurately in the laboratory using fluid withdrawn from the reservoir.

Rock properties are less well known. In the first place, the wells penetrate only a tiny portion of a reservoir, so we can have no direct information about most of the rock. Second, it may not be possible to obtain rock samples without changing their physical properties during the sampling process, particularly for unconsolidated (i.e. loose) rock formations. Finally, it is extremely difficult to accurately measure certain properties that may vary depending on the composition of the fluid flowing through the rock. An example of this is relative permeability, which is used to characterize the interference among simultaneously-flowing fluids in the reservoir, when more than two phases (e.g., liquid oil, hydrocarbon vapor, and water) are present.

Leaf: I have two questions. First, what is the feedback between the decoupled equations? Which determines the step size? Second, since you have 600 subroutines, it would appear difficult to nail down the communication between subroutines. The problem is that interfaces tend to evolve, and changes propagate throughout all the subroutines.

Sherman: In answer to the first question, the pressure and saturation equations are related in two basic ways. The pressure equation depends on the saturations through the fluid properties that help to determine the coefficients of the pressure equation. The saturation equation depends on the old pressures through the pressure-dependent rock and fluid properties, and it depends on the newly computed pressures through the total fluid velocity computed after pressures have been advanced in time. The time step for the simulator is determined by comparing actual changes in pressure and saturation over a time step to user-specified target values. (Certain measures of residual error are also taken into account.) If the changes in variable values exceed user-specified tolerances, the entire time step is repeated.

With respect to the second question, our general approach has been similar to that in ELLPACK. We decided early on the forms in which certain data would be passed, and we have stuck to these decisions. For example, there are a number of routines to solve linear equations, and at the interface level they all are given the matrix and righthand side in a standard form. Some of the routines need a different form internally, and they must bear the cost of carrying out the necessary data structure transformation. Similar routines may vary widely in their specific interface data needs, but any given piece of data is always passed in the same format. Since we were careful initially to choose data formats appropriate for our workhorse routines, we have not been forced to make the sort of interface changes that, as you suggest, might ripple through the entire program.

Vouk: Could you please comment on the standards used in testing the code? With such a vast amount of code, it is probably impossible ot test all the code.

Sherman: In general we test capabilities rather than actaul branches of the code. We depend on the programmer of each module to test the details of that module thoroughly. Our automatic testing procedures are designed to ensure that the overall program continues to be able to solve a variety of reservoir models successfullyand that each of the various program options and features works on at least one problem. We have made certain that each new feature added to the program is exercised in at least one test problem, and we have added several test problems that replicate conditions in which earlier versions of the program failed. (These latter problems are intended to prevent reintroduction of bugs that we have fixed.)

Duff: The compositional model is considerably more complex than the black oil model and, to my knowledge, there are few simulators currently using this more complicated approach. In terms of the added information one obtains about the reservoir being modeled, is the extra effort in developing the compositional model justified?

Sherman: It is true that compositional simulations are quite a bit more complicated than black oil simulations. However, certain physical processes in reservoirs simply cannot be modeled accurately using black oil models. Examples include many proposed enhanced oil recovery techniques, such as injection of gas that is miscible with resident reservoir fluids. In other situations it is necessary to model the movement of certain hydrocarbon components accurately in order to divide income equitably among companies holding joint interest in a reservoir. At the present time the industry's ability to obtain accurate results from compositional models is severely limited by a number of problems, most notably high computational cost for fine grids and unphysical dispersion introduced by the numerical methods in current use. However, these problems are being attacked by Exxon and others, and one may expect significant improvements over the next several years.

Schönauer: For an engineer, the simulator is a black box, You have mentioned formal testing of the code itself. What help is provided for the engineer to determine the accuracy of the computed solution?

Sherman: The engineer is helped in assessing the solution by graphical aids and other post-processing calculations. However, in fact the reservoir simulator cannot help very much in determining the accuracy. The definition of "accuracy" is partly an engineering question, and partly a question of what management will accept. It is not really a mathematical question because there is often not enough information to make a meaningful mathematical statement.

For example, I have looked at pressure matchings that compare computed and observed values. To me, as a mathematician, the values do not look at all close; however, an engineer may say that this is the best fit that he has seen in 20 years! A mathematical assessment of accuracy would require information and definitions that are not typically available in the industry for real problems.

<u>Simpson</u>:   How many sites use your code? Is it difficult to synchronize the user library and the T-library?

<u>Sherman</u>:   At present the MARS code is in use in Houston and Australia. Next month we plan to install it in Calgary, and I expect that it will be installed in Europe by sometime next year.

In response to the second question, I would say that we don't have the same kind of problem that many other software distributors face in this regard. We expect to have a relatively small number of installations (at most 10-15), and we expect that each of these sites will, in fact, be anxious to use new releases as they are made available because of the additional capabilities that will be provided. We are hopeful that we can avoid the proliferation of specially-modified versions of MARS that would make synchronization difficult. Also, since all of our remote sites will be IBM installations, we will be able to provide executable load modules for each update, thus reducing to almost nothing the effort required to bring up the new version.

PDE SOFTWARE: Modules, Interfaces and Systems
B. Engquist and T. Smedsaas (eds.)
Elsevier Science Publishers B.V. (North-Holland)
© IFIP, 1984

P A C K A G E   A D M

FOR STUDYING LONG-RANGE TRANSPORT OF POLLUTANTS IN THE ATMOSPHERE

Zahari Zlatev, Ruwim Berkowicz and Lars P. Prahm
Danish Agency of Environmental Protection
Air Pollution Laboratory, Risø National Laboratory
DK-4000 Roskilde, DENMARK

The long-range transport of pollutants in the atmosphere
is an important environmental problem. Mathematical models are commonly used to study this phenomenon. These
models are often described by systems of partial differential equations (PDE's). The systems of PDE's are normally solved numerically. A package of subroutines, which
can successfully be used in the numerical treatment of
the models describing long-range transport of air pollutants, has been developed at the Danish Agency of Environmental Protection. Some features of this package are
described in the present paper.

1. INTRODUCTION

Many meteorological phenomena (as, for example, long-range transport
of air pollutants) are studied by the use of mathematical models containing advection-diffusion partial differential equations. ADM
(Advection-Diffusion Modelling) is a package of FORTRAN subroutines,
which are designed to solve efficiently some special advection-diffusion equations that appear often in atmospheric environments. The
package attempts to exploit some salient features of these partial
differential equations (as e.g. the fact that the influence of the
advection terms on the behaviour of the solution dominates clearly
over the influence of the diffusion terms).

The basic ideas used in the solution process can briefly be described
as follows. The discretization of the space derivatives is carried
out by trigonometric interpolants which are truncated Fourier series
(pseudospectral discretization). The time-integration algorithm can
be chosen among 8 different schemes. An option, where a variable
stepsize variable formula time-integration scheme can be specified,
is also available. The diffusion terms are treated separately from
the advection terms. The subroutines of the package can be used in
the solution of equations (or systems of equations) on 1-, 2- and
3-dimensional space domains. Graphical output with FORTRAN-callable
subroutines can be obtained.

The performance of the package has been studied by many numerical
examples, which are typical for the area under consideration. Some
long runs with realistic meteorological data prepared at the WESTERN
METEOROLOGICAL SYNTHESIZING CENTRE (MSC-W) in Norway have also been
carried out. These data have been collected within the project EMEP
(European Monitoring and Evaluation Program), in which practically
all European countries participate. Some numerical results will be
presented. These results demonstrate the efficiency of the variable
stepsize variable formula option of our package in the simulation of

long-range transport of air pollutants. The calculated (by the mathematical model) results will be compared with results obtained in the
observations in different EMEP stations located in the countries that
participate in the EMEP project.

2. THE MATHEMATICAL MODELS HANDLED BY PACKAGE   ADM

The long-range transport of sulphur pollutants is modelled by a system of two partial differential equations (PDE's) of the following
type:

(1) $\frac{\partial c}{\partial t} = - u \frac{\partial c}{\partial x} - v \frac{\partial c}{\partial y} + K_x \frac{\partial^2 c}{\partial x^2} + K_y \frac{\partial^2 c}{\partial y^2} + \frac{\partial}{\partial z} \left(K_z \frac{\partial c}{\partial z} \right) + Q ,$

(2) $\frac{\partial c^*}{\partial t} = - u \frac{\partial c^*}{\partial x} - v \frac{\partial c^*}{\partial y} + K_x \frac{\partial^2 c^*}{\partial x^2} + K_y \frac{\partial^2 c^*}{\partial y^2} + \frac{\partial}{\partial z} \left(K_z \frac{\partial c^*}{\partial z} \right) + Q^* ,$

where the space domain $\mathcal{D}$ is defined by

(3) $x \in [a_1, b_1], \quad y \in [a_2, b_2], \quad z \in [a_3, b_3],$

while the time-unknown t is varied in the finite interval

(4) $t \in [a, b].$

The system, (1) - (2), of PDE's is considered with the following
boundary and initial-value conditions:

(5) $c(a_1, y, z, t) = c(b_1, y, z, t), \qquad c^*(a_1, y, z, t) = c^*(b_1, y, z, t);$

(6) $c(x, a_2, z, t) = c(x, b_2, z, t), \qquad c^*(x, a_2, z, t) = c^*(x, b_2, z, t);$

(7) $\frac{\partial c(x, y, a_3, t)}{\partial z} = \frac{\partial c(x, y, b_3, t)}{\partial z} = 0, \qquad \frac{\partial c^*(x, y, a_3, t)}{\partial z} = \frac{\partial c^*(x, y, b_3, t)}{\partial z} = 0;$

(8) $c(x, y, x, a) = f(x, y, z), \qquad f \quad being \ a \ given \ function;$

(9) $c^*(x, y, z, a) = f^*(x, y, z), \qquad f^* \quad being \ a \ given \ function.$

3. INTERPRETATION OF THE QUANTITIES INVOLVED IN THE MODEL

In our special case (where long-range transport processes of air pollutants in the atmosphere are studied) the different quantities involved in the mathematical model (or, in other words, in the system
of PDE's given by (1) and (2)) are interpreted as follows:

> *(i)* *The unknown functions,* $c(x,y,z,t)$ *and* $c^*(x,y,z,t)$, *are*
> *concentrations of sulphur di-oxide,* SO_2 , *and sulphate,*
> SO_4 , *in the atmosphere.*

> *(ii)* *The coefficients before the first-order space derivatives,*
> $u(x,y,z,t)$ *and* $v(x,y,z,t)$, *are wind velocities along*
> *the Ox axis and Oy axis respectively.*

(iii) The coefficients attached to the terms containing second-order space derivatives, K_x, K_y and K_z, are diffusion parameters.

(iv) The inhomogenity functions, $Q(x,y,z,t,c)$ and $Q^*(x,y,z,t,c,c^*)$, represent different sources and/or sinks.

4. BASIC ASSUMPTIONS

Experience with mathematical models describing long-range transport of air pollutants in the atmosphere (especially, long-range transport of sulphur pollutants) indicates that the following assumptions are realistic.

(A) The diffusion parameters K_x and K_y are <u>positive constants</u>.

(B) The third diffusion parameter, K_z, is a <u>piece-wise constant in z function</u>. This means that if x^*, y^* and t^* are fixed and if $0 \leq z \leq h$, then $K_z(x^*,y^*,z,t^*)$ does not vary in z. In our model it is also assumed that if $z > h$, then $K_z(x^*,y^*,z,t^*) = 0$ for $\forall(x^*,y^*,t^*)$. The special meteorological parameter h is called the mixing height.

(C) There is <u>no vertical advection</u>. This means that $w \equiv 0$, where w <u>is the vertical</u> component of the wind velocity.

5. NUMERICAL ALGORITHMS IMPLEMENTED IN PACKAGE   ADM

The computational work at an arbitrary time-step consists of the following major stages:

(a) discretization of the first-order space derivatives ("the advection terms"),

(b) calculation of the contribution corresponding to the horizontal diffusion (i.e. corresponding to the terms containing K_x and K_y),

(c) performance of the time-integration,

(d) calculation of the contribution due to the vertical diffusion (i.e. due to the terms containing K_z).

The numerical algorithms used in each of these   4   stages of the total computational work at the time-step under consideration are briefly described below.

(a) <u>Discretization of the first-order space derivatives</u>
The discretization of the first-order space derivatives is carried out by applying trigonometric interpolants, which are truncated Fourier series. This method is well-known under the name "<u>pseudospectral Fourier discretization</u>". A similar approach is used in   [2,3]. The computational speed of the process is

increased by the use of 1-dimensional FFT subroutines. Swarztrauber's package, [4], is attached to our subroutines and used as a "black" box to perform forward and backward Fast Fourier Transforms. The algorithm used during the first stage of an arbitrary time-step is described in [9-14].

(b) *Calculation of the contribution corresponding to the horizontal diffusion. The contribution corresponding to the horizontal diffusion (i.e. corresponding to the terms containing K_x and K_y) is calculated by the use of the Fourier components of the involved functions. The assumption that both K_x and K_y are positive constants is exploited in the calculation of this contribution. The approach used in the second stage is described in [15] (see also [10-14])*

(c) *Performance of the time-integration process. Explicit formulae are used in the time-integration process. Special algorithms designed for the PDE's under consideration have been developed (using the ideas and the methods described in [5-7,17-19]) and implemented in package ADM. There are 8 different time-integration algorithms. Each of them can be specified by the user before the run. In addition, a variable stepsize variable formula option of package ADM has been constructed. An attempt to determine the "best" time-stepsize and the "best" formula is carried out at each time-integration step (automatically by the code) when the latter option is in use. The time-integration part is fully described in [16] (see also [10-14]).*

(d) *Calculation of the contribution due to the vertical diffusion. The contribution due to the vertical diffusion (i.e. due to the terms containing K_z) is calculated by the use of the fact that the diffusion parameter K_z is a piece-wise constant in z function. This fact and the boundary condition (7) allow us to apply even Fourier expansions (i.e. expansions expressed by cosines only) on each grid-line perpendicular to the horizontal plane in order to calculate the contributions corresponding to the terms containing K_z. This method is justified in [15] (see also [13]); however, it has been used in a previous study, [1], by Berkowicz and Prahm.*

It should be mentioned here that both a stability control and an accuracy control are carried out in the time-integration part when the variable stepsize variable formula option is specified. Moreover, the stepsize can be changed at each time step when the latter option is in use. In the general-purpose software for solving ODE's by explicit methods the same stepsize must always be used several steps after the last stepsize change. This is rather inefficient in our special case, where in general the stability requirements are clearly dominating over the accuracy requirements and the stepsize should follow the variation of the norm of the wind velocity vector (see [16]). The usefulness of the above rules in the numerical treatment of models describing long-range transport of air pollution is demonstrated in [16].

6. CHECKING THE CORRECTNESS OF THE IMPLEMENTATION OF THE ALGORITHMS

Many experiments (several hundreds; see [9-16]) have been performed to check the correctness of the implementation of the algorithms in the package. A special set of rules for choosing test-examples has been proposed in [12]. Special tests which illustrate the advantages of using 3-dimensional models (both in order to take into account the variation of the mixing height h and in order to take into account the changes of the wind direction and the speed of the wind at the different atmospheric levels) have been suggested in [13]. Many numerical results obtained during this experimental phase are reported in [9-15]. Graphical representations, including three-dimensional plots, are also given in the above references. It must be emphasized that the experimental phase indicated that package ADM provides a reliable and a very efficient solution of many problems arising in our field. It must also be emphasized that the variable stepsize variable formula option of package ADM has been checked very carefully during the experimantal phase.

Some results obtained in the runs with the well-known (especially in meteorology) rotation test are given in Fig. 1 and Fig 2 as an illustration. The rotation test is defined by (see, for example, [14]):

$$(10) \quad \frac{\partial c}{\partial t} = (1-y)\frac{\partial c}{\partial x} + (x-1)\frac{\partial c}{\partial y}, \quad x \in [0,2], \quad y \in [0,2], \quad t \in [0,20\pi];$$

$$(11) \quad x_0 = 0.5, \quad y_0 = 1.0, \quad r = 0.25, \quad \bar{x} = \sqrt{(x-x_0)^2 + (y-y_0)^2};$$

$$(12) \quad c(x,y,0) = 100(1-\bar{x}/r) \quad \text{as} \quad \bar{x} < r,$$

$$(13) \quad c(x,y,0) = 0 \quad \text{as} \quad \bar{x} \geq r.$$

The cone defined by (12) rotates with a constant angular velocity around an axis perpendicular to the (x,y)-plane and cutting this plane at the point (1.0,1.0). A full rotation is performed for any time-interval with length 2π. This means in particular that

$$(14) \quad c(x,y,0) = c(x,y,2k\pi) \quad (\text{ for } \forall x \in [0,2] \quad \text{and for } \forall y \in [0,2])$$

is satisfied for $k = 1,2,\ldots,10$. The exact solution (according to (14) this is also the initial distribution) and the calculated solution of the rotation test (after 10 rotations) are presented graphically in Fig. 1 and Fig. 2.

7. RUNS WITH REAL METEOROLOGICAL DATA OVER TWO-DIMENSIONAL SPACE DOMAINS

Of course, all runs of test-examples during the experimental phase are needed only as a preparation of the package for long runs with real meteorological data. The preparatory runs(described in [9-15]) showed that the software is able to solve some problems, which may appear under some rather special circumstances in practice. Moreover, the tests illustrated the great efficiency of package ADM in the solution of such problems. Nevertheless, we considered the success of the use of package ADM in the experimental phase only as an indication that the package will also perform well in the solution of problems with real meteorological data. Therefore we felt it is necessary to run such problems also. We have done this. Many runs with meteorological data prepared at the Western Meteorological Synthesizing Centre (MSC-W) in Norway have been carried out. These data have

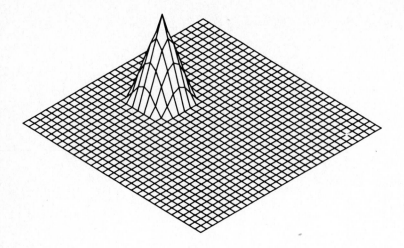

<u>Fig. 1</u>

The exact solution of the rotation test-example after 10 rotations of the cone
(in fact, the exact solution after k rotations, k being an arbitrary positive integer, is identical with the initial distribution defined by (11)-(13);
see (14)).

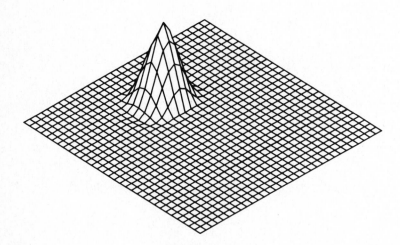

<u>Fig. 2</u>

The calculated solution of the rotation test-example at t=20π (i.e. after 10
rotations). The calculations were carried out with a constant stepsize and with
an Adams-Moulton predictor-corrector scheme (the predictor being of order 3, the
corrector being of order 4). The CPU time was about 347 seconds (including
the computing time taken for the preparation of the three-dimensional plots); in
other words, the package uses about 35 seconds CPU time per rotation; see **[11]**.

been collected within project EMEP (European Monitoring and Evaluation Program), in which practically all European countries participate. Two-dimensional runs (i.e. no vertical diffusion) over a time
interval covering the period from December 25 1978 to January 10 1980
(i.e. a little more than a year) have been performed using about 90
minutes CPU time on IBM 3033 with a constant time-stepsize $\Delta t = \frac{1}{2}$
hour. Many runs, covering short periods of one or two weeks, were
carried out using a time-stepsize $\Delta t > 1$ hour. This indicated that
if the code is optimized so that an algorithm for automatic choice
of the time-stepsize and the formula is built-in in the time-integration subroutines, then the CPU time for the whole run (from December 1978 to January 1980) can be halved (approximately). Therefore
we developed a variable stepsize variable formula option (see [16])
in package *ADM*. The efficiency of the new option of the code is
illustrated by the fact that the long run described above (with the
use of the meteorological data from December 1978 to January 1980)
is completed in 46 minutes CPU time when this option is applied on
the IBM 3033 computer at our disposal. The average time-stepsize
is about 65 minutes when the variable stepsize variable formula option is specified.

8. RUNS WITH REAL METEOROLOGICAL DATA OVER THREE-DIMENSIONAL SPACE DOMAIN

The meteorological data prepared at MSC-W in Norway have also been
used in several three-dimensional runs (i.e. runs in which the vertical diffusion is taken into account). The space domain (which covers all European countries has been discretized by the use of a
$32 \times 32 \times 9$ grid. This means that 9 horizontal levels are considered.
The distance between two adjacent grid-points on a grid-line perpendicular to the horizontal plane is $\Delta z = 0.3$ km. The distances between two adjacent grid-points on the grid-lines parallel to the Ox
axis and the Oy axis are $\Delta x = 150$ km. and $\Delta y = 150$ km., respectively. This means that the system of PDE's (1) - (2) is transformed
into a system of 18432 ordinary differential equations (ODE's) at
each time-step. A typical run covered a time-interval of about 42
days. If the constant stepsize constant formula option is used, then
the CPU time is about 75 minutes (with a time-stepsize $\Delta t = \frac{1}{2}$
hour). If the variable stepsize variable formula option is used, then
the CPU time is about 40 minutes (with an average time-stepsize
$\Delta t > 1$ hour). All runs described in this paragraph were carried out on
the IBM 3033 computer at NEUCC (Northern Europe University Computing Centre, Lyngby, Denmark).

It should be mentioned here that we are able to use <u>explicit</u> time-
integration algorithms in the three-dimensional runs <u>only</u> because
the vertical diffusion is treated in a special way (see §4 and [15]).

9. PRESENTATION OF THE RESULTS

The presentation of the results depends on the answer to the following question: *How will the results be used?* As a rule it is convenient
to present the calculated results graphically (note that the amount
of the calculated results is enormous; this is especially true for
the runs over three-dimensional space domains, where the output data

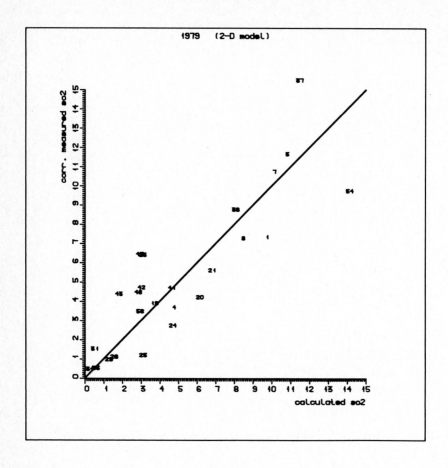

Fig. 3

Comparison of the mean values (for 1979) of sulphur di-oxide calculated by package ADM and the mean values (for 1979) of sulphur di-oxide observed at different EMEP stations (the EMEP stations are denoted by integer numbers and two coordinates are attached to each station; the abscissa is the calculated mean concentration, while the observed mean concentration is the ordinate). The run is carried out over a two-dimensional space domain.

have often magnitude $O(10^9)$ and the graphical presentation is the only possible). Moreover, in our case a comparison with measured values of sulphur di-oxide and sulphate is also needed in order to check the reliability of the model. Therefore the mean year (or month) values of the computed concentrations of sulphur di-oxide and sulphate were plotted against the mean year (or month) values of the measured concentrations of sulphur di-oxide and sulphate at the meteorological stations located in different countries participating

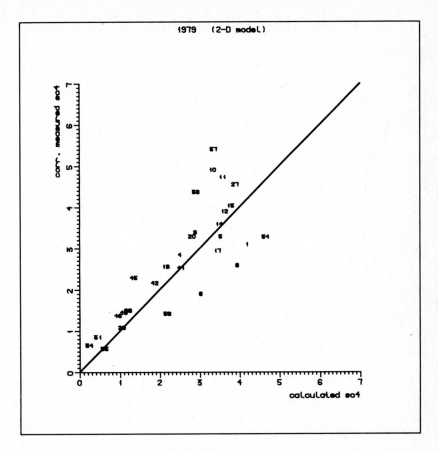

Comparison of the mean values (for 1979) of sulphate calculated by package ADM and the mean values (for 1979) of sulphate observed at different EMEP stations (the EMEP stations are denoted by integer numbers and two coordinates are attached to each station; the abscissa is the calculated mean concentration, while the observed mean concentration is the ordinate). The run is carried out over a two-dimensional space domain.

in the EMEP project. In the same way the calculated and the measured results concerning the wet deposition of sulphur (i.e. due to deposition of both sulphur di-oxide and sulphate) were plotted. The results of this comparison will be reported in the near future. We are ready to emphasize now that the calculated concentrations and wet depositions are in a god agreement with the measured concentrations and depositions (this is illustrated in Fig. 3 - Fig. 5). *This indicates that both the mathematical model defined by (1) - (2) and the numerical algorithms implemented in the software are very reliable for our class of problems.*

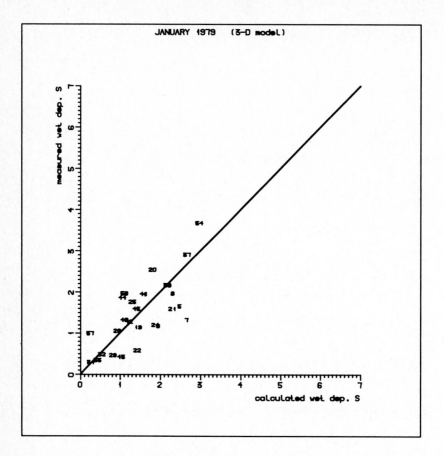

Fig. 5

Comparison of the mean values (for January 1979) of the "wet deposition" (concentration in precipitation) of sulphur calculated by package ADM and the mean values (for January 1979) of the "wet deposition" (concentration in precipitation) of sulphure observed at different EMEP stations (the EMEP stations are denoted by integer numbers and two coordinates are attached to each station; the abscissa is the calculated value of the "wet deposition", while the observed value of the "wet deposition" is the ordinate). The run is carried out over a three-dimensional space domain.

The fact that the results calculated by package ADM are quite reliable indicates that the package can be used in many different situations, where experimental data is not available. As an illustration of this statement let us mention that the software has been used to estimate the contribution of sulphur pollution due to the Danish sources only to the total sulphur pollution in Denmark and in the

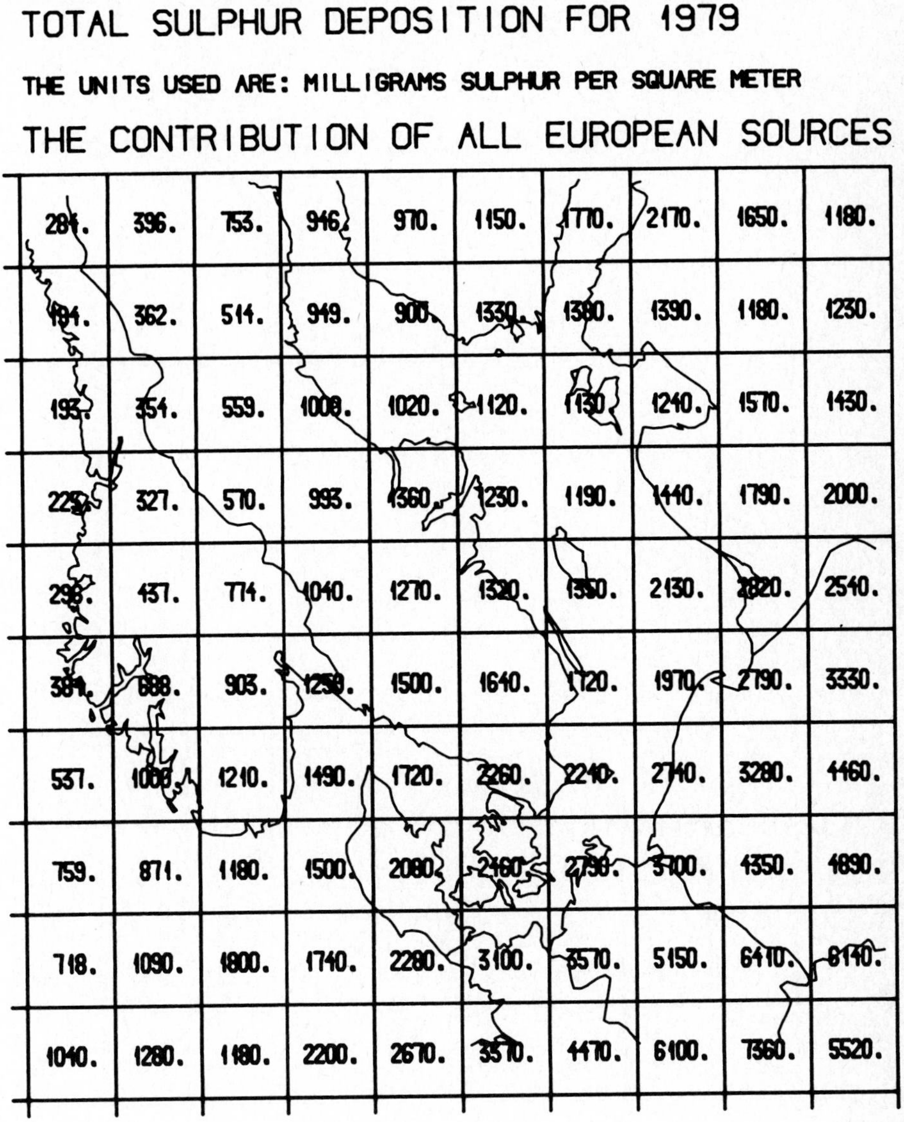

TOTAL SULPHUR DEPOSITION FOR 1979

THE UNITS USED ARE: MILLIGRAMS SULPHUR PER SQUARE METER

THE CONTRIBUTION OF ALL EUROPEAN SOURCES

284.	396.	753.	946.	970.	1150.	1770.	2170.	1650.	1180.
194.	362.	514.	949.	900.	1350.	1380.	1390.	1180.	1230.
193.	354.	559.	1008.	1020.	1120.	1150.	1240.	1570.	1430.
225.	327.	570.	993.	1360.	1230.	1190.	1440.	1790.	2000.
296.	431.	774.	1040.	1270.	1320.	1550.	2130.	2820.	2540.
381.	688.	903.	1250.	1500.	1640.	1720.	1970.	2790.	3330.
531.	1000.	1210.	1490.	1720.	2260.	2240.	2740.	3280.	4460.
759.	871.	1180.	1500.	2080.	2460.	2790.	3700.	4350.	4890.
718.	1090.	1800.	1740.	2280.	3100.	3570.	5150.	6410.	8140.
1040.	1280.	1180.	2200.	2670.	3570.	4470.	6100.	7360.	5520.

Fig. 6

The total sulphur deposition in Denmark and in the region around Denmark for 1979 calculated by package ADM. The values of the total sulphur deposition are obtained as sums of the values of the wet deposition and the values of the dry deposition.

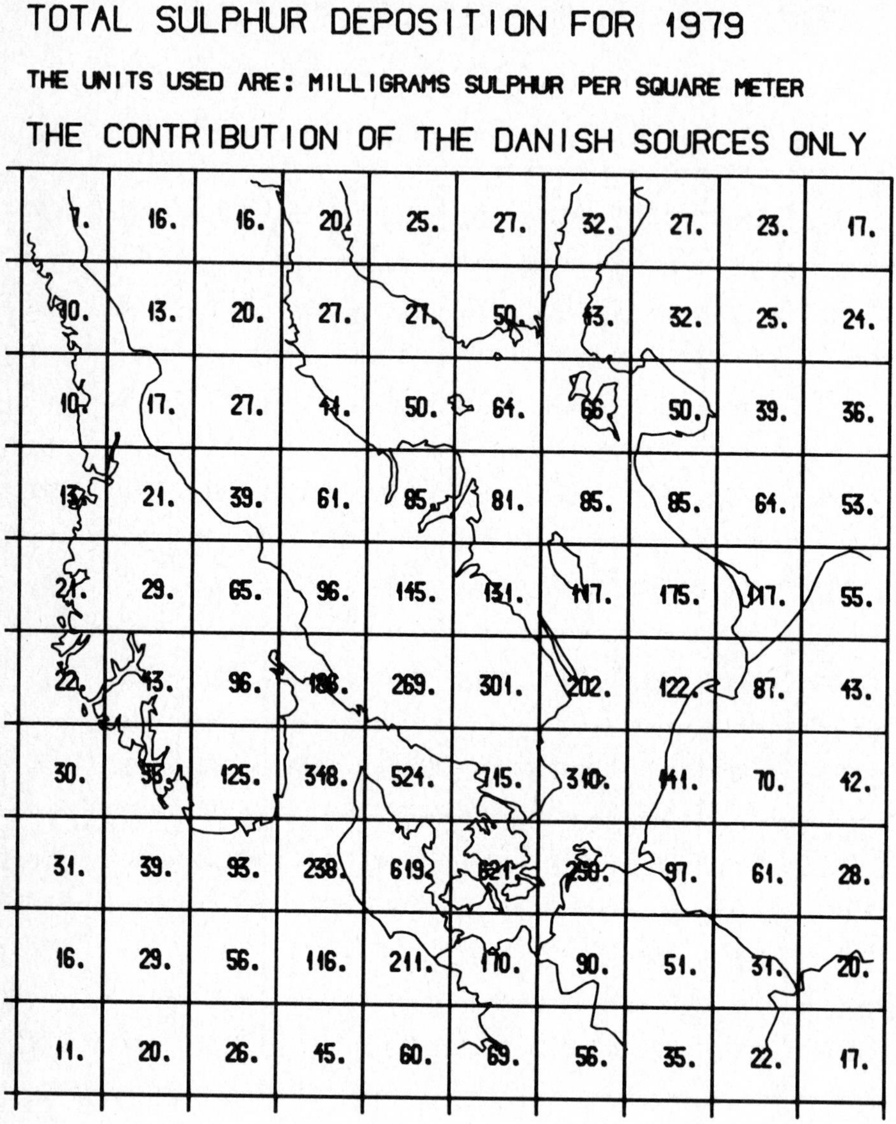

TOTAL SULPHUR DEPOSITION FOR 1979

THE UNITS USED ARE: MILLIGRAMS SULPHUR PER SQUARE METER

THE CONTRIBUTION OF THE DANISH SOURCES ONLY

7.	16.	16.	20.	25.	27.	32.	27.	23.	17.
10.	13.	20.	27.	27.	50.	43.	32.	25.	24.
10.	17.	27.	41.	50.	64.	66.	50.	39.	36.
13.	21.	39.	61.	85.	81.	85.	85.	64.	53.
21.	29.	65.	96.	145.	131.	147.	175.	117.	55.
22.	43.	96.	186.	269.	301.	202.	122.	87.	43.
30.	58.	125.	348.	524.	715.	310.	141.	70.	42.
31.	39.	93.	238.	619.	821.	290.	97.	61.	28.
16.	29.	56.	116.	211.	170.	90.	51.	31.	20.
11.	20.	26.	45.	60.	69.	56.	35.	22.	17.

Fig. 7

The total sulphur deposition in Denmark and in the region around Denmark for 1979 calculated by package **ADM**. The values of the total sulphur deposition are obtained as sums of the values of the wet deposition and the values of the dry deposition. The emission from all sources but these in Denmark is set equal to zero in this experiment.

region around Denmark. Some results, which have been obtained in these experiments, are presented in Fig. 6 and Fig. 7.

10. PORTABILITY OF THE PACKAGE

No machine-dependent constants are used in the code. No special features of the computer at our disposal (the IBM 3033 computer at NEUCC; the Northern University Computing Centre, Lyngby, Denmark) are applied in the subroutines. Therefore the subroutines should work on many large computers. We have already run the subroutines on the following computers:

IBM 3033   at NEUCC (Northern Europe University Computing Centre, Lyngby, Denmark);

UNIVAC 1100   at RECKU (Regional Computing Centre at the University of Copenhagen, Copenhagen, Denmark);

CYBER 175   at ECMWF (European Centre for Medium Range Weather Forecasts, Reading, England);

CRAY 1   at ECMWF (European Centre for Medium Range Weather Forecasts, Reading, England);

11. VECTORIZING OF THE CODES

All loops in the subroutines are fully vectorized. The same is true for Swarztrauber's package [4], some subroutines of which are used to carry out forward and backward FFT's during the space discretization. Therefore the subroutines should be efficient when they are used on vector processors (as CRAY 1 or CYBER 205). Our experiments on the CRAY 1 computer at ECMWF (see above) confirm this statement. The CPU times have been reduced by a factor 6 - 8 when CRAY 1 has been used instead of IBM 3033.

12. DOCUMENTATION OF PACKAGE ADM

The main drivers in the constant stepsize constant formula option of *ADM*, the three subroutines: ADM01, ADM02 and ADM03, are fully documented in [10]. The rules used in the documentation of package Y12M in [20] are also applied in the documentation of package *ADM*.

The subroutines which are internally called are not documented in [10]. It is assumed that the user will never directly refer to these subroutines. Nevertheless, a short description of the function of each of these subroutines is given in [10].

The different stages of the computational process are well structured in package *ADM*. This means that separate subroutines have been written for the different parts of the computational process. This can be exploited to develop some drivers for situations which are not covered by the above-mentioned three drivers.

All subroutines are written in two versions: *a single precision version* and *a double precision version*. The sixth letter in each subroutine in package ADM indicates the version: S for the single precision versions and D for the double precision versions. For example, ADM01S, ADM02S, HELP3S are single precision versions, while ADM01D, ADM02D, HELP3D are the corresponding double precision subroutines. The sixth letter is always omitted when a statement, which is true both for the single precision version and for the double precision version, is made.

Mixed arithmetic is not used in the package. This meeans that only single precision operations are used in the single precision versions, while only double precision operations are used in the double precision versions. The use of mixed arithmetic operations may cause difficulties on some computers.

The variable stepsize variable formula option of package ADM will be fully documented in the near future.

The codes of all subroutines of the constant stepsize constant formula option of package ADM with full documentation are at the *Air Pollution Laboratory, National Agency of Environmental Protection, Risø National Laboratory, DK-4000 Roskilde, Denmark*. This option is prepared for distribution. All requests for tapes with the codes of the constant stepsize constant formula option (supplied with some demonstration programs) as well as the technical questions concerning the performance of the subroutines should be addressed to the authors. Advances in theory and the experience of the users may prompt alterations in these codes. Readers and/or users are invited to write to the authors concerning any changes they may advocate.

R E F E R E N C E S

[1] Berkowicz, R. and Prahm, L. P., Presentation of inter-grid sources in pseudospectral dispersion models, Appl. Math. Modelling, 2 (1978) 205-208.

[2] Christensen, O. and Prahm, L. P., A pseudospectral model for dispersion of atmospheric pollutants, J. Appl. Meteor., 15 (1976) 1284-1294.

[3] Prahm, L. P. and Christensen, O., Long-range transmission of pollutants simulated by a two-dimensional pseudospectral method, J. Appl. Meteor., 16(1977) 896-910.

[4] Swarztrauber, P. N., Vectorizing FFT's, in: Rodrigue, G. (ed.), Parallel Computations (Academic Press, London-New York, 1982).

[5] Thomsen, P. G. and Zlatev, Z., Two-parameter families of predictor-corrector methods for the solution of ordinary differential equations, BIT, 19 (1979) 503-517.

[6] Zlatev, Z., Stability properties of variable stepsize variable formula methods, Numer. Math., 31 (1978) 175-182.

[7] Zlatev, Z., Zero-stability properties of the three-ordinate variable stepsize variable formula methods, Numer. Math., 37 (1981) 157-166.

[8] Zlatev, Z., Consistency and convergence of general multistep variable stepsize variable formula methods, Computing, 31 (1983) 47-67.

[9] Zlatev, Z., Berkowicz, R. and Prahm, L. P., Numerical treatment of the advection-diffusion equation. Part 1: Space discretization, Report No. MST LUFT-A47, Air Pollution Laboratory, Danish Agency of Environmental Protection, Risø National Laboratory, DK - 4000 Roskilde, Denmark (1981).

[10] Zlatev, Z., Berkowicz, R. and Prahm, L. P., Numerical treatment of the advection-diffusion equation. Part 5: Documentation of ADM01, Report No. MST LUFT - A58, Air Pollution Laboratory, Danish Agency of Environmental Protection, Risø National Laboratory, DK - 4000 Roskilde, Denmark (1982).

[11] Zlatev, Z., Berkowicz, R. and Prahm, L. P., Choice of time-integration scheme in pseudospectral algorithm for advection equations, in: Morton, K. W. and Baines, M. J. (eds.), Numerical Methods for Fluid Dynamics, pp. 303 - 321 (Academic Press, London-New York, 1982).

[12] Zlatev, Z., Berkowicz, R. and Prahm, L. P., Testing subroutines solving advection-diffusion equations in atmospheric environments, Comput. Fluids, 11 (1983) 13 - 38.

[13] Zlatev, Z., Berkowicz, R. and Prahm, L. P., Three dimensional advection-diffusion modelling for regional scale, Atmos. Environ., 17 (1983) 491 - 499.

[14] Zlatev, Z., Berkowicz, R. and Prahm, L. P., Stability restrictions on time-stepsize for numerical integration of first-order partial differential equations, J. Comput. Phys., 51 (1983) 1 - 27.

[15] Zlatev, Z., Berkowicz, R. and Prahm, L. P., Numerical treatment of the advection-diffusion equation. Part 6: Special treatment of the diffusion terms, Report No. MST LUFT - A72, Air Pollution Laboratory, Danish Agency of Environmental Protection, Risø National Laboratory, DK - 4000 Roskilde, Denmark (1983).

[16] Zlatev, Z., Berkowicz, R. and Prahm, L. P., Numerical treatment of the advection-diffusion equation. Part 7: Selfadaptive time-discretization, Report No. MST LUFT - A74, Air Pollution Laboratory, Danish Agency of Environmental Protection, Risø National Laboratory, DK - 4000 Roskilde, Denmark (1983).

[17] Zlatev, Z. and Thomsen, P. G., Application of backward differentiation methods to the finite element solution of time-dependent problems, Internat. J. Numer. Meth. Engng., 14 (1979) 1051-1061.

[18] Zlatev, Z. and Thomsen, P. G., Automatic solution of differential equations based on the use of linear multistep methods, ACM Trans. Math. Software, 5 (1979) 401 - 414.

[19] Zlatev, Z. and Thomsen, P. G., Differential integrators based on linear multistep methods, in: Absi, E., Glowinski, R., Lascaux, P. and Veysseyre, H. (eds.), Méthodes numérique dans les sciences de l'ingénieur - G. A. M. N. I. 2, Vol. 1, pp. 221 - 231, (Dunod, Paris, 1980).

[20] Zlatev, Z., Wasniewski, J. and Schaumburg, K., Y12M - solution of large and sparse systems of linear algebraic equations (Springer, Berlin-Heidelberg-New York, 1981).

DISCUSSION

Speaker: Z. Zlatev

Schönauer: Does your physical model include information about rain, e t c?

Zlatev: Yes, all this information is contained in the model, which is very complete, and is part of a very ambitious project.

Duff: It seems that most countries in Western Europe are trying to prove that they are not primarily reponsible for poisoning the Swedish lakes with acid rain. Clearly, as in the previous talk by Sherman on oil reservoir models, there is much political interest in the results of your simulation vis-a-vis simulation by other countries and groups. Have you any experience of this?

Zlatev: Our results are prepared for the Ministry of the Environment, which has asked us to perform calculations considering both all of Europe, and Denmark only. Many more results will be obtained, since we have only recently begun using real rather than simulated data.

Madsen: Do you consider the chemical interaction between species, or just transport?

Zlatev: Our model includes only simple (linearized) reactions. In the future, we plan to use more complicated chemistry. The results so far are quite satisfactory using only the linear model. However, when we consider a smaller area, we shall be urged to include more detailed chemistry.

Madsen: This may force a change in your algorithm.

Zlatev: With more complicated chemistry, we shall probably not be able to use explicit methods. Explicit methods have been successful because of the large distances between any two adjacent grid-points of the space domain.

Gorenflo: In the z-boundaries (floor and ceiling) you take Neumann boundary conditions, which are physically very plausible, but in the x and y directions you assume periodicity. Is there a physical justification for this?

Zlatev: We use a special procedure to damp the concentrations at the boundaries. In particular, we create false, more extended boundary, which allows us to simulate the boundary conditions artificially. The concentration is nearly zero along two of the edges, and we place artificial boundaries well outside the other two edges. In this way we achieve periodicity on the vertical sides of the space domain, which is necessary for the Fourier transformations.

Grossmann: How do you treat near-singularities that arise because the diffusion coefficients are small relative to the velocities? The stepsizes are heavily dependent on the velocities. Can you use an "upstream" concept to enlarge the stepsizes?

Zlatev: The stability checks involve only the wind velocity vector. The natural assumption is that the main part of the transport is the wind. The diffusion coefficients are small. We do not try to approximate the space derivative. We are trying to calculate a correction to be incorporated in the solution vector, and take apart the terms with both horizontal and vertical diffusion. Thus, we can remove restrictions on the stepsize caused by these terms. For smaller regions, we can probably not make these assumptions, and hence new algorithms are needed.

Lawson: I question your statement that general-purpose software is not adequate because it favors keeping the same time step. This is not true in state-of-the-art ODE software, which changes the step frequently, and also the order. For example, the package of F. Krogh includes stability as well as accuracy test, and other packages also include this feature.

Zlatev: My assumption that the same stepsize is used as long as possible is based on a statement in the book by Shampine and Gordon (1975). In the software with which I am familiar, the control parameters are based on accuracy requirements only. In this case, error estimators will not give good results if the time step changes quickly. In our package, the stability requirement can cause a quick change in the time step. The simple formula used in our work is *not* general. General software controls stability by checking the largest eigenvalues; we don't need such a complicated test.

Madsen: To follow up Chuck Lawson's comments, I would like to mention that a general-purpose ODE code (of Hindmarsh) underlines the ARAC project in the United States, which uses an atmospheric transport code.

Zlatev: What method is used in the ODE code? The use of implicit methods is not efficient, for several reasons. In our application, we must read the data every six hours. We can use a time stepsize of more than one hour with explicit methods. The use of implicit methods in this context seems unjustified to me because there must be an upper bound of six hours on the time stepsize. The price that has to be paid for this reduction is solving systems of algebraic equations at each time step. It is obvious that this is a very high price, and the use of implicit methods in the time-discretization is prohibitive for our special problems.

Madsen: The code uses Adams or backward differentiation methods and a $PE(CE)^n$ method similar to the one described.

Zlatev: We must use methods with good stability properties along the imaginary axis. It is not impossible to use general-purpose software, but it is better for our application to use special code. The stability properties of the predictor-corrector schemes especially constructed for the package ADM are better than those of predictor-corrector schemes of Adams type that are implemented in the software you mentioned. Moreover, for our special problem we are able to use a very reliable and very simple stability control parameter. Such a degree of simplicity and reliability may be achieved only when the special features of the problem under consideration are exploited in a proper way.

Stetter: Your stepsize procedure could be exchanged for the one included in the general-purpose software package.

Zlatev: Yes, but this would still be more complicated than the procedures that we use.

PDE SOFTWARE: Modules, Interfaces and Systems
B. Engquist and T. Smedsaas (eds.)
Elsevier Science Publishers B.V. (North-Holland)
© IFIP, 1984

PROBLEM SOLVING ENVIRONMENT FOR PARTIAL
DIFFERENTIAL EQUATIONS: THE USER PERSPECTIVE

Marek Machura

Institute of Atomic Energy
Computing Centre
05-400 Otwock-Swierk
POLAND

This paper proposes a coherent approach to the task of designing general purpose software for partial differential
equations (PDE). It describes problem solving environments
and discusses the different requirements of end-users, con-
tributers and maintainers of PDE-software . Specially, it em-
phasizes the importance of open-endedness in order to provide an evolution capability.

1 INTRODUCTION

With recent and forthcoming hardware and software advances which aim at improving
programmer productivity and software quality, we are facing a breakthrough in the
utilization of computers. There is a general consensus among computer scientists
and software developers that the traditional ad hoc procedures should be replaced
by a systematic professional approach to software development. This means that in
the nearest future we ought to drastically revise our ways of thinking as to how
the computer software should be implemented, disseminated and kept abreast of the
state-of-the-art. The present trends in software development allow us to believe
that the most probable path to be taken will be creation of a diversity of user-
friendly software environments. This is undoubtedly a great challenge to the
software developer community. Organized research and massive effort on an unprecedented scale will be needed in the years to come.

The above remarks can equally well apply to the development of mathematical software. Scientific computing constitutes a substantial fraction of computer applications. It is the responsibility of our community to meet the growing demand for
a versatile and reliable mathematical software, and to transfer as quickly as
possible into the public domain what has been newly invented and proved useful.
Our major goal should be to design a development strategy which will meet the
requirements of the modern user demanding up-to-date high-quality mathematical
software.

In this paper, I will try to show what future software for the numerical solution
of partial differential equations /PDEs/ might look like. Though the paper contains no substantially new ideas, it proposes a coherent approach to the task of
designing general-purpose PDE software. A no less important objective is to stimulate discussion and call for closer co-operation among those involved in the development of PDE software.

The difficulties we encounter in the development of general-purpose PDE software
are very well known:

1. PDE problems allow a considerable freedom of formulation.

2. Certain features of PDE problems require individual treatment.

3. There exist many numerical methods designed to deal with small classes of problems, none being truly universal.

4. The change in user demands and the development of new algorithms cause general PDE software to become obsolete within a few years after completion.

5. Pre- and post-processing is usually required in order to facilitate preparation of input data and interpretation of output data.

6. The development of general-purpose PDE software is a costly and time-consuming task.

As a consequence of these difficulties, one is not surprised to find that:

1. The solution of PDEs usually concerns one narrow class of problems or one highly specialized application area.

2. The resulting PDE software usually lacks flexibility in changing its structure or even parameters.

3. General PDE software often has an experimental character, low reliability and primitive input/output facilities.

4. A lot of duplicative effort is involved in developing PDE software.

5. As a result of dispersed activities, many of the general-purpose PDE packages remain unknown to users or are hardly accessible.

6. The user lacks performance assessment of the available PDE packages and the numerical methods they are based on.

Thus what is needed is a co-ordinated effort to develop versatile, reliable, portable and user-friendly general-purpose PDE packages. Particular attention should be directed towards:

- meeting the requirements of end-users, contributors as well as maintainers of PDE software,
- making provision for different levels of user interest and expertise, and
- providing a built-in mechanism to ensure continuous evolution of PDE software.

In this way we arrive at an idea of designing future PDE software as complete problem solving environments. Fortunately we do not have to start from scratch, for our undertaking can be based on the extensive experiences gained during the development of PDE program systems, notably ELLPACK /1/ and DCG /2/. Another source of helpful solutions can be found in advanced structural analysis systems.

Section 2 of this paper contains a discussion of the reasons behind the development of problem solving environments. A model of an environment for the solution of PDEs is presented in Section 3. The problem of ensuring open-endedness is outlined in Section 4. Sections 5 and 6 describe end-user, contributor and maintainer interfaces. The discussion of problem analyzers for PDEs can be found in Section 7. Finally, some aspects of the project co-ordination are discussed in Section 8.

Because a general-purpose problem solving environment for PDEs does not yet exist, much of the paper is of necessity speculative and leaves many questions still open. The paper attempts to present a synthesis of users' balanced expectations that seem feasible to be realized. Since the user's viewpoint on PDE software has been adopted no attempt will be made to discuss the design of numerical algorithms and the technical aspects of implementation.

2 ADVANTAGES OF PROBLEM SOLVING ENVIRONMENTS

A problem solving environment /PSE/, regarded as a generalization of conventional application software, is an integrated collection of programs designed to be employed in a consistent way by all interested parties. A specific PSE does not merit the name unless it provides a uniform support for the entire process it is inteded to facilitate. In general, the user population of a PSE encompasses not only end-users who make direct use of the supplied software in order to solve their problems, but it also includes PSE contributors and maintainers. This collective purpose seems to be the main cause of the impetus towards the development of PSEs. They are meant to be useful to wide user communities, to solve great ranges of problems by up-to-date methods, and to maximize the user productivity.

It is probably best to define a PSE by enumerating its characteristics:

1. Breadth of scope and applicability.

2. User-friendliness / easy-to-use input language, robustness, a catalogue of available capabilities, tutorial facilities, different levels of user expertise, human factors/.

3. Flexibility in constructing programs from program units /composability/.

4. Integration of capabilities /co-operation of program and program units/.

5. Use of central information repository /storing input data, intermediate results, output data, test data, control sequences, programs, e t c/.

6. Open-endedness /improvements, updates, changes, incorporation of new programs/.

7. Portability.

It is clear that a PSE promotes the use of application software by activating the user and making his task easier, as well as by providing a mechanism for continuous software evolution. The user is no longer a passive element in the solving process. The concept of full automation has been abandoned in favour of closer man-machine interaction. In order to give the user a greater control over the computational process, 'black-box', programs are decomposed into 'black-box' modules which the user can employ as building blocks. On the other hand, the user has no longer to deal with a static piece of application software. Traditional monolithic software has been replaced by an open-ended one which enables a PSE to evolve as research and development permit.

We are now able to summarize the benefits we hope to derive from creating a general-purpose PSE:

1. It offers specialized services to a large user community.

2. It increases user productivity in that it ensures simplicity of use, provides flexibility of application, and avoids unnecessary programming.

3. It is attractive to beginners or casual users as well as to experienced specialists.

4. It provides a common framework for all those interested in using and developing software in a given application area.

5. It propagates up-to-date quality software by integrating existing software and consolidating dispersed development activities.

6. It establishes the channels for software developers to share their knowledge and skills.

7. It lays down rules for software development and documentation.

8. It sets up standard testing strategies and performance evaluation schemes in order to compare rival methods and implementations.

9. It can be used as a testing lab in implementing highly specialized application software.

Before completing this section, it seems appropriate to briefly comment on general programming environments. Both general programming environments and applications software undergo nowadays similar qualitative evolution. The former are gradually being transformed into automated software developmentenvironments /3/; the latter - as indicated above - is expected to assume the shape of PSEs. Since this paper deals with the prospect to creating a PSE, it is of great importance to be aware of the developments taking place in the field or programming environments. Firstly, developers,contributors and advanced end-users of PSEs are expected to take full advantage of the available programming capabilities, so that they can minimize their efforts. Secondly, some ideas put forward by the designers of software development environments could be of great value to the designers of PSEs. This should surprise nobody since in the end, advanced programming environments are intended to facilitate the implementation of modern application software.

3 GENERAL MODEL OF A PSE

Before embarking on a costly, large-scale program like the development of a software environment for PSEs, it is essential to answer a number of basic questions. First, we have to identify users to whom a given PSE will be addressed. Secondly, we have to select those user demands which we are able to fulfill. And thirdly, we have to decide on a structure of the PSE as an ultimate goal of our endeavours. These three elements constitute a logical model of the PSE we intend to develop. As to the technical model, it will be discussed very briefly, since technical aspects are not dealt with in this paper.

Each software system adopts - if only implicitly - som model of its users. So we begin the discussion with presenting a model of the users who are meant to work within the PSE. We have already emphasized that a complete PSE should meet the demands of three user groups: end-users, contributors and maintainers.

There is no need to recall that end-users are the main customers of the PSE. They can be further subdivided into other groups according to the different levels of competence they represent. We defer further discussion of this subject until Section 5. As to the other two user groups, we must realize that it is very important to ensure appropriate facilities to both contributors who influence the scope of applicability of a given PSE and maintainers who are responsible for its smooth running. Present-day application software too often tends to neglect the roles of those two user groups whose participation is vital during the entire lifetime of the software.

Let us also mention that in addition to the three main user groups, it is possible to distinguish a fourth one, namely that of external users. These are users who solve their problems outside the PSE. They work within some general programming environment, but occasionally extract ready-made modules from the PSE and incorporate them in their programs.

Apart from the above function-oriented model of the PSE users, it is important to consider another model which will enable us to determine more precisely the population of potential end-users. Such an end-user oriented model is of considerable significance since it can conclusively answer the question of the usefulness of the PSE.

This matter is unfortunately not so clear in the case of the numerical solution of PDEs. The long-standing controversy on general-purpose and special-purpose software for PDEs has always caused great excitement among software developers. The advocates of specialized software argue that real-life PDE problems are so complex that they can only be solved by finely tailored algorithms and related programs. The advocates of general-purpose software, on the other hand, do not claim that they produce a panacea but programs which can prove useful to many users solving typical problems. In a sense, the attitude of the former tends to undermine the purposefulness of designing large-scale general software for PDEs. It is an open secret that general-purpose software is doomed to be criticized each time one wishes to solve a problem which does not fall within the admissible problem class. Irrespective of these biased objections, I believe it is our major goal to transfer into the public domain as much general-purpose software for PDEs as possible. Only this type of software can substantially increase the general user's solving capabilities.

We return now to the task of indicating potential end-users of the proposed PSE. I think they will count among educational workers and students, research workers, and to a lesser extent among those working in various branches of industry. The role of the PSE as an educational and training tool is evident, since those interested will have easy access to a variety of algorithms and their implementations. Numerical analysts will use the PSE as a test-bed for designing and testing their algorithms, as well as for carrying out performance studies. In the first place, however, they will enrich the domain of mathematical software with general-purpose programs based on proved numerical techniques. Representatives of chosen branches of science and technology, as well as of industry, will solve typical PDE problems which do not require special treatment. They will also use the PSE to perform pilot studies by simplifying first the structure of their problems, or experimenting with different methods prior to freezing them within special-purpose programs. In my opinion, the future general-purpose PSE will also have some limitied production applicability. However, there will always be much room left for the development of highly specialized application software.

As a part of the PSE model, we naturally have to determine <u>user requirements</u>, and subsequently select those requirements that we are able to <u>meet</u>. At this point, I do not intend to enumerate the general demands, since they have already been specified at different places in the previous sections. Other, more specific demands will be described later on when we proceed to discuss user interfaces.

Now let us outline the <u>overall structure</u> of the proposed PSE. In general, a PSE may be viewed as a <u>consistent collection</u> of tools. A tool is a self-contained program designed to perform a clearly defined function, and communicate with other tools by means of data files only.

From the point of view of a PSE, it is important to differentiate between main tools and support tools. Main tools are used directly in the solution process; they reflect the scope of applicability of a given PSE. Support tools are utilities which serve to facilitate the work of environment users. Whereas main tools are problem processing tools, support tools are auxiliary tools. We postpone the discussion of the support tools until Sections 5 and 6, and concentrate on the main tools for a while.

What we need in a software environment for PDEs are three basic types of main tools enabling the end-user to prepare input data, define a problem, and interpret results. The tools meant for the data preparation will be called <u>geometry processors</u>. They will facilitate the task of constructing a mesh for a given domain by enabling the user to specify, generate, check and modify his input data. The user will define a problem by means of a tool called <u>problem analyzer</u>. The problem analyzer, based on some special input language, will comprise three phases: PDE problem statement, algorithm specification, and output specification. The third group of main tools will consist of output processors, and will be subdivided into tabulation tools and graphics tools.

Both the geometry processor and problem analyzer serve the purpose of problem definition, and provide the necessary input information for the computational process. The output processor edits the output information produced by the computation. However, in order to start the actual computations, the user needs yet another tool, a so called computation controller. The computation controller integrates such operational tasks as selection of solving modules, specification of parameter values, and link-load-run actions. A typical sequence of tool activations required for the solution of a PDE problem is shown in Fig. 1. A double-line arrow denotes invocation of the corresponding tool by the user, as well as interaction of the user with this tool.

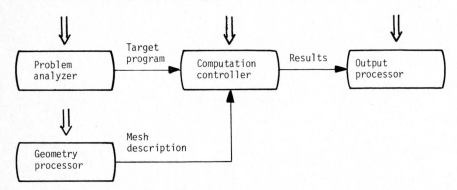

Fig. 1 Typical sequence of main tool actications

It is very unlikely that the PSE for PDEs will be based on a single problem analyzer. The variety of PDE problems and numerical methods will certainly force the PSE developers to construct a series of problem analyzers. A number of geometry processors and output processors will be associated with each problem analyzer. A combination of problem analyzer, geometry processors and output processors will constitute the core of a PSE package designed to solve some general class of PDE problems by means of a chosen numerical method. Within a package, a set of uniform rules will be in force, contributing to its integrity. This concerns, in the first place, the standardization of data structures and program structures generated by the problem analyzer.

In contrast to the traditional software packages, the packages included in the PSE will not be stand-along ones. On the contrary, being self-contained collections of tools, they will at the same time constitute a family of packages, sharing among themselves many common tools. In this way a lot of duplication of software development effort will be avoided. It is clear that this benefit is due to the fact that the proposed PDE software is organized as a PSE.

In the model presented so far, we focused the attention on the functions which the environment tools are intended to realize. An equally important part of the model is how the management of information within the environment is to be organized. Though this aspect is sometimes overlooked by application-centered users, it is vital for each software environment.

Thus from the developer standpoint, a software environment may be seen as an information utility. At the centre of the environment is a data base of all information

being processed within the environment. Surrounding this data base is an information management system which ensures access to the data base in response to
requests made by the tools. Such a central information repository will enable the
environment user to automatically manage all information pertinent to his problem,
i.e., input data, intermediate results, output data, test data, source programs,
object code, e t c. An environment repository could be implemented as a conventional file directory system, giving the user protection from unauthorized access
and erroneous modifications.

Having discussed the set of the basic tools and the concept of central file repository, we can describe, in a general way, the control structure of the PSE.
All environment functions will be activated by a command language processor. The
command language processor analyzes user-supplied commands. Since the typical
command is simply a tool invocation, it consists of the tool name and a sequence
of input and/or output files:

  <tool name> <file 1>..... <file n>

The command language processor manages the execution of user-selected tasks and
the definition of files associated with these tasks.

One of the characteristics of a PSE is an intensive exchange of information between the user and the environment. This results from the requirement that the
user take an active part in the solution process. We assume therefore that the
PSE for PDEs will be interaction-oriented. Consequently, the command language
processor will be an interpreter, and the user will communicate with the tools
interactively. This means that all interactive tools must have built-in support
for control and tutorial purposes.

The proposed PSE can, in addition, take advantage of another present-day hardware
development, namely distributed processing methodology. The PSE can be implemented
as an interaction-rich workstation, based on a minicomputer, equipped with the
necessary devices such as disks, graphics displays, keyboards, data tablets,
plotters, e t c. Due to its computing power and storage facilities, this specialized computer system will enable the user to accomplish the bulk of pre- and
post-processing work locally. The actual computations, on the other hand, will be
carried out on a large computer or, if feasible, on a minicomputer. If the workstation were connected to a network of various computers with a broad variety of
PDE software, the user would have a full range of solving tools at his disposal.
Eventually, we would arrive at a distributed PSE for PDEs.

4 OPEN-ENDEDNESS

One of the prerequisites of a true PSE is the provision for an evolution capability. This requirement is of paramount importance since a PSE is not a static
type of software, but undergoes continuous improvements, changes and enlargements.
Actually, general-purpose software by its very nature should be designed to
facilitate the incorporation of /i/ general enhancements developed by contributors, and /ii/ replacement modules developed by skilled users with special requirements.

As alluded to in Section 3, the PSE for PDEs can be envisaged as a set of packages
self-contained, yet sharing common capabilities. This represents one possible
method to ensure the open-endedness of the PSE. Instead of trying / provided it
were feasible at all / to construct a single, monolithic, all-purpose problem analyzer for PDEs, we assume that the PSE will consist of an unspecified number of
problem analyzers. It does not of course mean that the number of difference
packages will grow without limit. On the contrary, we must exercise restraint in

choosing candidates for individual implementation. The decision to construct a new problem analyzer should be justified by the generality of a PDE problem class that is to be solved and a numerical method that is to be employed.

It is the underlying numerical method which dictates implementation principles for a given package, enhancing its integrity simultaneously. Each package will be built around one of the basic methods: finite difference method, finite element method, method of lines, adoptive mesh refinement method, e t c. Based on different methods, data structures and program structures, a series of selfcontained packages will be designed to solve elliptic, parabolic and hyperbolic equations in one, two and /if practicable/ three space dimensions. A separate problem analyzer will have to be developed for each package.

In addition to ensuring open-endedness of the PSE on the package level, we have to ensure an evolution capability within the packages themselves. A package is usually designed to handle a broad class of PDE problems. This class is further subdivided into narrower subclasses, in order to enable contributors to take into account specific elements of the PDE structures.

Analogously to the partition of the PSE into packages, we can envisage packages themselves as being subdivided into a series of problem solvers. A problem solver is a program realization of a numerical algorithm handling a specific class of PDE problems. A solver is composed of user-visible and user-invisible modules. The former are also called user-selectable modules.

Designers of a new general-purpose package should never restrict the class of different PDE problems by fixing their number in advance. On the contrary, they should incorporate in the problem analyzer a mechanism enabling the package to readily accept new solvers.

In order to meet the above requirement, the concept of a problem description record /PDR/ can be introduced /4/. A PDR is a standard data structure containing a description of a class of problems that can currently be solved by one of the solvers from the package run-time library. A PDR fulfils the following tasks:
- enables the problem analyzer to check whether a user's problem can be solved by the package,
- supplies information necessary for the problem analyzer to generate a target program, and
- enables package contribution to add new solvers in a standard way.

Each solver contained in the package run-time library must have an associated PDR. All PDRs constitute the PDR set. Before the analysis of a user's problem can begin, the PDR set is searched for an appropriate PDR. A PDR basically contains two kinds of information: /i/ master equations, and /ii/ the names of the solver and its user-visible component modules.

The intentional open-endedness of the PSE packages influences the way users solve their problems. Prior to making use of a package, the user must consult an associated solver catalogue. Only when the user finds that his problem can be solved by one of the available solvers, he may activate an appropriate problem analyzer. The chosen problem analyzer takes then the initiative and prompts the user for information needed to define the problem. The user must always specify the name of the solver he wants to employ. Note that in reality, the name of the solver is the name of the related PDR. It is only the selected PDR which specifies the name of the solver and its user-visible modules /see section 7/.

Fig. 2 shows schematically the basic idea behind an open-ended package. Adding a new numerical algorithm to the package requires: /i/ including a new description in the solver catalogue, /ii/ including a new PDR in the PDR set, and /iii/ including new modules in the package run-time library.

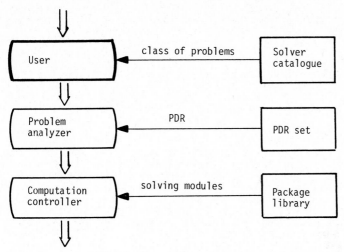

Fig. 2 Open-ended package

5 END-USER INTERFACE

A careful design of user interfaces has top priority among the tasks developers of
a PSE must face. After all, it is through the interfaces that users see and understand a PSE. Functionality and versatility of user interfaces will in the end decide whether users will feel encouraged or discouraged to work within a given environment.

PSE users can choose to have the status of an end-user, contributor or maintainer.
The end-user status allows users to solve PDE problems. The contributor status is
intended for those who want to construct special-purpose /private/ or general-purpose /public/ solvers and/or modules. The maintainer status is meant to be used
by those authorized to install general-purpose software. So for example, a skilled
user may choose the contributor status to develop a piece of general software; the
end-user status to perform test calculations; and - provided he is given authority
- the maintainer status to install the software within the PSE.

According to the selected status, the user has access to the PSE through the end-
user interface, contributor interface, or maintainer interface, respectively. All
three interfaces constitute a coherent collection of tools. Each interface comprises the tools specific to its purpose. However, some general tools belong to
more than one interface.

In this section we present a general description of the end-user interface for the
proposed PSE. The spectrum of end-users, in their knowledge of numerical analysis,
of programming, and of problem solution, will be very broad. For our purposes,
we divide end-users into three classes: /i/ amateur users with no knowledge of numerical methods, /ii/ informed users with some basic knowledge of numerical
methods, and /iii/ specialist users with extensive expertise of both numerical
analysis and programming.

Amateurs users are recruited from beginners and casual users, as well as from
users who have neither interest nor time to experiment with available software.

They usually need nothing more than predetermined solution paths. After having gained some experience, amateur users will certainly demand more flexibility in specifying the component modules of the solvers, and thereby will gradually become informed users.

Specialist users will want to incorporate their own modules in the existing solvers, implement their own solvers using existing component modules, or even develop complete solvers. For that reason, the work of the specialist user is very much like that of the contributor. However, the specialist user is usually motivated by some special application, and therefore makes only local contributions to the environment.

Apart from the main tools designed to be directly employed in problem definition and solution /see Section 3/, the end-user interface comprises a number of support tools. They are briefly described in this section. Other support tools, meant for specialist end-users with contributor status, will be described in Section 6.

TUTORIAL TOOL

The work of users within an interactive environment should not be based on hardcopy documentation only. Environment users would rather expect to have interactive access to the information they need in their work. Therefore a tutorial tool should be one of the basic environment tools. Combined with graphics, it will quickly convey a broad view of the PSE and ensure general guidance for the user. The tutorial tool supplies the information which is necessary to ensure the user's access to the basic capabilities of the environment. On the lower level, all other tools will have their own built-in tutorial facilities.

PROBLEM CATALOGUE TOOL

This facility is very important in all open-ended PSEs. It enables the user to find out if his problem can be solved by one of the available packages. The central problem catalogue contains general information on the classes of PDE problems handled, and specifies the names of problem analyzers as well as the names of the related geometry processors and output processors. This information allows the user to select and activate an appropriate problem analyzer. Further information about solvers and their component modules can be found in a solver catalogue associated with each package.

PROBLEM ANALYZERS

A problem analyzer constitutes the core of each package. Its purpose is to aid the user in formulating a problem, selecting a solver, and presenting results. A detailed description of the functions of a PDE problem analyzer can be found in Section 7.

    Input file: empty or old problem specification.

    Output files: new problem specification, target source program.

GEOMETRY PROCESSORS

The task of constructing complicated meshes for general domains is cumbersome and prone to errors, therefore it is usually separated from problem definition. Geometry processors enable the user to specify, generate, check and modify data necessary to define the geometry of a domain. In order to simplify the tedious specification of mesh points, geometry processors should be provided with some auxiliary facilities, such as definition of repetetive data patterns, specification of the domain's regularity and symmetry, automatic mesh generation. Each geometry processor is associated with one or more problem analyzers.

Input file: empty or old mesh specification.

Output file: new mesh specification.

COMPILER

This is a standard tool from the encompassing programming environment. It translates the target source program generated by a problem analyzer into object code.

Input file: target source program.

Output file: object code.

COMPUTATION CONTROLLER

This is a specialized loader which is used to perform the link-load-run actions. It enables the user to indicate component modules that set up a solver, and automatically links them with the object code. It then urges the user to specify the values of parameters /if there are any present in the problem formulation/, and starts the execution. The computation controller can be employed to solve the same problem with different combinations of component modules. It also enables the user to resume an interrupted computation, provided the solution has been saved before.

Input files: object code, mesh specification, saved solution.

Output files: results, saved solution.

TABULATION TOOLS

These are output processors aimed at interpreting the results from the solution process. They will enable the user to review the solution tables, 'zoom' in on the area of interest, provide headings, determine printout formats, and produce print-ready output for the selected table parts. A number of different tabulation tools will be developed, each being associated with one or more problem analyzers.

Input file: results.

Output file: print-ready output.

GRAPHICS TOOLS

Graphics tools are generally recognized facilities designed to enhance human comprehension of large volumes of data. They play a substantial role in the solution of PDEs. Some of the graphics tools can be used for checking input data /graphical representation of mesh specifications generated by geometry processors/. Other graphics tools can be used to analyze the results generated in the solution process. The results are first reviewed on a display device, and subsequently the graphical information, extracted from the areas of interest, is used to produce a hard copy for documentation. A variety of graphics tools will be developed, each being related to one or more problem analyzers or geometry processors.

Input file: results.

Output file: control commands for a graphical device.

FILE REPOSITORY TOOL

We have already stressed the central role of a file repository within the PSE. The file repository tool helps users to manage files which are created, manipulated and deleted during the solution process. For each PDE problem being solved, the user can create a protected set of files, called a notebook. The objects /files/ contained in a user's notebook are problem specification, mesh specification, target source program, object code, computational results, saved solution, print-ready output, control commands for a graphical device, e t c. In addition to having a name and content, each object has a predefined attribute. This allows for an automatic association of each file with the task that created it and tasks

which use it. The file repository tool should provide for the following notebook
maintenance functions: creating and destroying a notebook, opening and closing
a notebook, including and deleting an object, and listing the names and attributes of objects.

Input file: file to be included.

FILE COPY UTILITY

This utility integrates basic copy functions needed by environment users. It
serves to copy a disk file onto a disk file, save a file or a notebook on magnetic
tape, make hard copies of the contents of print files, e t c.

Input file: old file.

Output file: new file.

6 CONTRIBUTOR AND MAINTAINER INTERFACES

The remaining two interfaces can be described together, since both contributors
and maintainers employ the same set of basic tools. The selected user status determines how these tools may be used. The contributor status gives the user
access to all the information which is necessary to develop new modules within
the environment. It also enables him to incorporate new capabilities locally,
without affecting the public libraries of the environment. The maintainer status,
on the other hand, allows the entitled user to include the relevant extensions
and modifications in the public libraries.

Libraries are open-ended, homogeneous collections of pieces of information. In
the proposed PSE, we expect to have the following five types of libraries:

1. Central problem catalogue

   Contains general information on the classes of PDE problems handled by all
   environment packages.

2. Module catalogue

   Contains a record of all modules setting up a given package. They are classified as solvers, visible modules and invisible modules.

3. PDR set

   Contains a list of PDRs associated with all solvers of a given package.

4. Module source library

   Contains the source text of all modules setting up a given package.

5. Package run-time library

   Contains the object code of all modules setting up a given package.

There is one central problem catalogue in the PSE. As to the other libraries,
their number is equal to the number of available packages. They are all public
libraries in that they are available to all environment users. However, only users
having the maintainer status are authorized to modify them.

Users with the contributor status may create and manipulate their own libraries
which are local to a given package. These are called private libraries. Such private libraries as PDR sets and run-time libraries are automatically used by appropriate tools during the computational process.

Since libraries are nothing but data files, they can be treated as objects of the
file repository. All public libraries of a given package will constitute a single
public notebook. Similarly, all private package libraries which belong to a

specialist user or a contributor can be combined to form one <u>private notebook</u>.

What contributors and maintainers need is a set of library support tools that internally make user of the file repository utilities. Each of these tools imposes some structure upon the corresponding library, which otherwise is merely a sequence of bytes or words. The library support tools accomplish the following tasks:

- creating and destroying a library,
- including, deleting and changing a library object,
- listing the contents, and
- setting up a library search path.

In order to ensure proper management for all environment libraries, we need the following library support tools:

- problem catalogue utility,
- module catalogue utility,
- PDR set utility,
- module source utility, and
- run-time library utiltity.

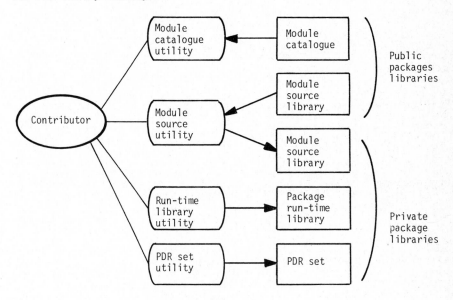

Fig. 3 Contributor interface

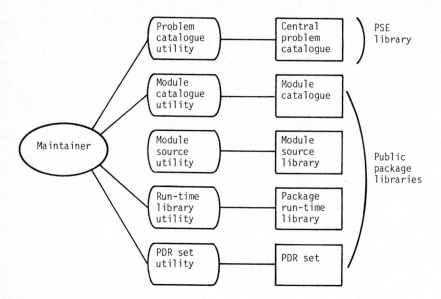

Fig. 4   Maintainer interface.

The way these tools may be employed by users with the contributor and maintainer status is shown in Fig. 3 and Fig. 4, respectively. The arrows pointing towards library support tools indicate that these tools may only be used to consult the related libraries. The arrows pointing towards libraries indicate that these libraries may also be modified.

Apart from the library support utilities, the contributor and maintainer interfaces encompass the environment's tutorial tool, file repository tool and file copy utility. In addition, careful consideration should be given to the selection of adequate programming aids, such as text editors, compilers, formatters, e t c. They can usually be transfered unchanged from the surrounding programming environment.

Finally, note that the tools presented in this section enable the user to introduce extensions solely to the existing packages, and do not assist directly in developing packages built around new problem analyzers. One cannot rule out, however, that in the future a number of useful support tools will be constructed to ease this task. An example of such a tool could be a generator of new problem analyzers, or a utitlity to modify the command language interpreter.

7   PDE PROBLEM ANALYZERS

Problem analyzers are of fundamental importance in each PSE. They are complex tools equipped with problem description languages. In general, an input language intended for a problem analyzer should encompass the following three steps: /i/ problem statement, /ii/ algorithm specification, and /iii/ output specification.

A variety of special languages has been defined for PDE program packages and systems. These languages differ in the extent they support the three steps needed to formulate a user's problem. Most of them cover adequately the first step, i.e., problem statement, neglecting to some extent output specification and algorithm specification. A notable exception among these languages is the input language for ELLPACK /1/ which gives equal importance to all the three formulation steps.

It does not seem reasonable at this point to discuss various syntactic constructs introduced by designers of PDE languages, and ultimately to define a model language for all problem analyzers. Instead, we will rather concentrate on the functional requirements a typical language for PDEs should meet.

The problem statement phase should enable the user to specify symbolically all typical elements of the mathematical formulation, such as PDEs, domains, boundary conditions and initial conditions. This task is quite straightforward, except for the domain specification. One should carefully investigate the possibility of defining boundaries in a simple and efficient way. For the immediate future, we will probably deal with planar domains. The definition of domains in three space dimensions needs still further investigation.

The problem statement should also encompass the definitions of all constants, variables and functions occurring in the problem formulation. The PDE language should provide for the specification of

- independent and dependent variables,
- constants,
- parameters,
- coefficients,
- tabulated functions, and
- high-level programming language functions.

Constants are arithmetic expressions which are evaluated once at the beginning of computations and therefore need not be recalculated each time they are referred to. The user may wish to repeat the calculation of his problem for different values of chosen variables /parameters/. The parameter values are introduced by means of the computation controller. Coefficients are functions which are defined and used without specifying their arguments. They occur first of all in PDEs and boundary conditions, and are employed to make the problem formulation more transparent. Tabulated functions can be used when no analytical forms of functions are available. The user may also wich to define a complicated function as a subprogram written in some high-level programming language /most probably it will be Fortran/.

As described in Section 5, general meshes for finite element methods are expected to be constructed outside problem analyzers by means of appropriate geometry processors. For finite difference methods, however, there is no need to design special geometry processors. Instead, a mechanism to define rectilinear meshes should be provided by the problem description language. Apart from space meshes, the user should also be able to specify a series of time steps for evolutionary problems.

The second phase in the problem formulation is algorithm specification. Recall that each algorithm handling a certain class of PDEs is realized as a problem solver composed of user-visible and user-invisible modules. Though it seems impossible to define one modular structure for all PDE solvers implementing different methods, we can envisage a typical PDE solver as the one in Fig. 5. The control module of a solver may activate its component modules only once in the prescribed order /elliptic PDEs/, or it may contain a complicated activation scheme corresponding to the numerical method employed /time-dependent PDEs, nonlinear problems, eigenvalue problems/.

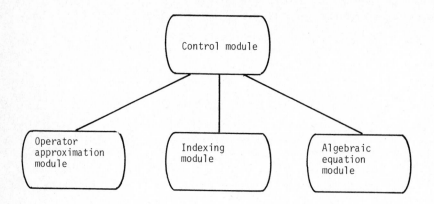

Fig. 5 Structure of a typical solver.

A solver presents itself to the user as a collection of visible modules. By indicating a solver, the user actually indicates its control module. This control module will be called from within a driver program generated by the problem analyzer. Selecting a solver without specifying its component modules means that default modules will be included. Otherwise, the user may specify any admissible component module he wishes to incorporate in the selected solver. If the user intends to solve his problem with different combinations of component modules, he must specify them all in advance. This makes it possible for the problem analyzer to check the legality of module use and generate proper module calls. Additionally, the user is expected to specify the values of all module parameters, unless he wishes the default values to be valid.

The third phase in the problem formulation is output specification. Since the actual analysis and interpretation of results is done by specialized output processors, the purpose of this phase is to prepare computational results for later processing and request some operational information.

In order to prepare data for output processors, the user must specify the name of a file which will contain all results of interest, and determine the contents of the file. The user may indicate solutions to be transferred to the result file. He may also choose to calculate residuals or error /provided he supplies the true solution/, and place this additional information together with appropriate identification on the result file.

Operational information enables the user to gain more insight into the computational process. The user may wish to examine performance statistics of the chosen solver /execution time used, central memory used, e t c/, or he may request intermediate results to learn how the solution process was carried out The user should also be able to control the level of diagnostics produced by solvers and their component modules.

8 NEED OF CO-ORDINATION

Since the construction of an environment for PDEs must of necessity be a co-operative effort, it is of great importance for software designers to decide on a joint
development strategy.

Before we attempt to discuss this issue, it is perhaps purposeful to briefly investigate the development of finite element software systems /5/. It is a well
known fact that specialized finite element software has reached - due to a massive
funding - a relatively high level of sophistication and popularity. In its in-
fancy, finite element software was implemented as specialized program packages.
As the years went by, program packages gradually matured into a variety of general program systems. In addition, many new packages and systems were derived from
the old ones, contributing to software duplication and users' confusion. When it
became apparent that finite element software could be best implemented as an
open-ended PSE, it was soon discovered that - due to the enormous manpower investment needed - it was impossible to replace the established systems by completely
new ones. Thus the only feasible approach left was to resort to the difficult
task of building upon the existing systems and integrating their capabilities.

As far as general-purpose PDE software is concerned, the question is whether we
will be able to benefit from the experience gained in the development of large
finite element systems. In my opinion, the delay in the development of general
PDE software, in comparison with the development of specialized finite element
software, can be used to the advantage of the former. We do not necessarily have
to go the same way. On the contrary, if we succeed in establishing a common development strategy at the right time, there are good chances that in the future
our joint effort will result in creating a complete environment for PDEs.

Two opposite strategies can basically be taken into consideration: decentralized
development and centralized development.

Decentralized development strategy is based on a belief that the size and scope
of the enterprise make it unlikely to be carried out successfully under central
co-ordination. This work is more likely to be successful if it is done piece-
meal by a number of independent organizations. It is expected that - in response
to initiative taken by interested organizations - an evolutionary development of
small prototype environments will ensue. In the end, it is hoped that somebody
will make the final effort and synthesize a larger, more encompassing environment
from smaller ones. The drawbacks of this approach are that /i/ progress may be
too slow due to the lack of funds and the orientation towards local applications,
/ii/ a lot of duplicative effort will be involved, and /iii/ evolution difficulties, similar to those of large finite element systems, seem probable to arise.

Centralized development strategy, on the other hand, is intended to help co-ordinate a massive development effort, and thereby avoid the drawbacks of decentralized approach. On its part, however, this strategy is endangered by severe organizational and financing problems, as well as by its inherent tendency to exert
too much control over the co-ordinated process.

In practice, we should strive to strike a balance between these two opposing
approaches. Appreciating the benefits of co-ordination, we should not neglect the
significance of developers initiative. Thus a compromise solution might be to
set up a development co-ordination centre that would centralize general developments and promote decentralized software contribution. Its role would be to design a framework within which all development activities would take place.

The work of the co-ordination centre can be divided into two consecutive phases:
initial phase and operational phase.

The initial phase encompasses the following tasks:

- designing a PSE,
- implementing the PSE infrastructure, and
- providing standards.

The co-ordination centre is expected to work out a detailed proposal for a PSE and submit it to a critical examination by the user and developer communities. If this proposal passes the test of public scrutiny, all general tools and basic utilities of the PSE can be implemented.

The purpose of standards is to impose regularity and consistency on solvers, their component modules and other tools constituting end-user interface /in the first place problem analyzers/. The co-ordination centre should establish a set of implementation standards, such as module classification, naming schemes, error handling mechanisms, performance monitoring, intermodular communication, save capability, portability, e t c.

Good documentation is vital to the success of a software project. It assists and encourages use of the software. Different levels of documentation should be provided for different users. Documentation standards are particularly important in a project involving many collaborators.

The co-ordination centre could also produce standard development aids. Examples of such aids intended for solver and module devlopment could be standard error handling utilities and a virtual memory facility. The latter would enable developers to manipulate common data structures, using out-of-core storage. Tool generators /for instance a problem analyzer generator/ could also be considered as desired development aids.

This preparatory phase will be followed by the operational phase. It will in general encompass the following tasks:

- software acquisition,
- software quality control,
- software dissemination, and
- software performance studies.

The co-ordination centre is expected to acquire software and check its quality by considering such issues as adherence to implementation and documentation standards, case of use, portability, e t c. Contributed software will be classified as educational, research or production one. In addition, if a piece of software undergoes a successful attestation, it will be identified as certified. Uncertified software will also be distributed to propagate the latest research in numerical analysis. The sequence in which the PSE will be enriched with new features, will be determined by the needs and interests of those users who will want to make a contribution.

The co-ordination centre will also assume that responsibility of disseminating software. This will include both the infra-structure software and contributed software. The co-ordination centre will distribute on request the entire PSE or selected PDE packages together with the related utilities. Software distribution will of course involve distribution of associated information, such as installation manuals, tuides for users, contributors and maintainers, various forms of documentation, software updates, newsletters for users and contributors, e t c.

One may justifiable say that it is easy to demand a co-ordinated strategy like this, but very difficult to carry it into effect. Construction of the software environment for PDEs will be an unprecedented enterprise in the development of application software, requiring organized research, substantial capital investment, and many person-years of design and implementation.

Obviously, the biggest question is, who will do the work. Though it is impossible to definitely answer this question at present, we could try to indicate potential developers who might become engaged. The most difficult development phase is un-' doubtedly the initial one, centralizing all preparatory activities. The co-ordinator of this phase might possibly be found among the established numerical groups with much experince in developing general-purpose software for PDEs. After the PSE has been designed, basic tools implemented and standards defined, the co-ordination task might be taken over by some non-profit, self-supporting software organization that would carry on with the operational phase.

One of the purpose of the PSE is to avoid the escalation of development costs by minimizing the total costs of dispersed activities. Undoubtedly, it will be difficult to find appropriate funding for the initial phase of the project, since the payoff for this effort is long-term and partially intangible. If, however, some organization decides to sponsor this phase of the project, the whole enter-prise has every chance of being successfully completed because the development costs of the operational phase will be shared among all future contributors.

9 CONCLUSION

The requirements set forth in this paper outline   plan for the development of a problem solving environment for partial differential equations. The individual requirements can all be regarded as being within the state of the art at the pre-sent time and therefore contain no specific high-risk features. Nevertheless the set of requirements taken as a whole presents a substantial technical and orga-nizational challenge to developers.

In my opinion, this challenge will sooner or later be accepted due to the two very important features such an environment provides:

1. It ensures a continuous development based on constant consultation with both user and contributor communities.

2. It offers the possibility of significant improvement in the problem solving process.

The evolution of traditional application software will be enhanced by the current hardware and software developments. Sharp decreases in the cost of computing equipment, escalating costs for personnel and advantages of distributed processing entitle us to believe that the futere user and software developer will be provided with a variety of personal problem solving and software development environments.

REFERENCES

1. Rice, J.R.: ELLPACK 77 User's Guide, Rep. CSD-TR 289, Comput. Sci. Dep., Purdue Univ., 1978.

2. Engquist, B. and Smedsaas, T.: Automatic computer code generation for hyper-bolic and parabolic differential equations, SIAM J. Sci. Stat. Comput., vol 1, pp. 249-259, 1980.

3. Osterweil, L.: Software environment research: Directions for the next five years, Computer, Vol. 14, pp. 35-43, 1981.

4. Machura, M.: DEP Contributor's Guide, ISD Report No. 285, Univ. Stuttgart, 1980.

5. Schrem, E.: Trends and aspects of the development of large finite element soft-ware systems, Computers and Structures, Vol. 10, pp. 419-425, 1979.

DISCUSSION

Speaker: M. Machura

Schönauer: Your ideas are in some sense idealistic, although I agree with them. In the real world, there is a problem in doing what you suggest. In Germany, there would be no chance of getting money for a long-range project like the one you have described. The research foundations only support short-term projects, e.g. for one year. Therefore one needs to produce results in less than a year.

Machura: The proposal to construct a PSE for PDEs may seem to be somewhat idealistic at present. Nevertheless I think that a framework of this kind can be regarded as a long-term goal in our efforts to develop general-purpose software for PDEs. Finding appropriate financial support for the development of general application software has always caused much trouble. I believe, however, that the technical, organizational and financial challenge to develop a PSE for PDEs will sooner or later be accepted by our community.

Yanenko: Do you think that your structure can be applied in a general way to a wide class of problems? You did not indicate the set of algorithms and problems to be included. There is no universal system for all problems.

Machura: I agree that there is no universal system for all PDE problems, but we are certainly able to build a versatile system that will handle broad classes of problems. It was not my intention to discuss algorithms and problem classes in this paper. My goal was rather to present a general view of PSE. It is problem analyzers associated with different PSE packages that will reflect various structures of PDE problems and related algorithms.

Delves: At least for elliptic PDEs, ELLPACK seems to fit your criteria for being called a PSE. Can you comment on how well ELLPACK represent the kind of package you have in mind, or what additional features you think a PSE should have.

Machura: The proposed PSE has to some extent been influenced by the ELLPACK approach, and in fact can be regarded as its generalization. In terms of the presented PSE, ELLPACK qualifies as a PSE package designed to solve elliptic problems. The PSE will comprise a series of such packages.

Rice: The weak link in ELLPACK is the lack of problem analysis. It was not an ELLPACK goal to provide this, but it would make sense to include a much more careful analysis of coefficients, boundary conditions and of the domain. This would be helpful to the user and many modules could perform better if the resulting information were passed on to them.

Ophir: In Israel we have developed a system based on other principles. Our system supplies tools which enable users to manipulate grids and boundaries, to choose algorithms to treat grids; etc. These tools provide a set of software parts for the user. Our system is only for two-dimensional domains, but will be developed for three-dimensional problems.

Machura: There are essentially two types of general-purpose software for PDEs. One is based on fixed structures of the solving programs, enabling the user to specify parameter values and to indicate component modules to be employed. This approach has been favoured in the proposed PSE. The other type of PDE software enables the skilled user to construct an application-tailored program from the basic algorithms elements. Your system seems to be of the latter type. I would like to know what stage of development your system has now reached. As far as I know, some substantial difficulties to implement and to use similar systems have been reported (e.g., PDELAN, COMOL).

Lawson: Your interesting framework seems to apply to many fields, e.g. optimization. Could you remark on that?

Machura: Indeed, the idea of designing an open-ended PSE like the one presented in this paper lends itself to easy generalization. Similar models could be employed to construct multi-method PSEs that require co-operative effort and continuous evolution.

Ford: The next conference of the working group will be on problem solving environments so it seems very appropriate to mention them here as a bridge to the next working conference.

PDE SOFTWARE: Modules, Interfaces and Systems
B. Engquist and T. Smedsaas (eds.)
Elsevier Science Publishers B.V. (North-Holland)
© IFIP, 1984

THE ITPACK SOFTWARE PACKAGE*

David M. Young and David R. Kincaid

Center for Numerical Analysis
The University of Texas
Austin, Texas

ITPACK is a research-oriented software package for solving
large sparse systems of linear algebraic equations by iterative methods. The emphasis is on systems arising in the
numerical solution of partial differential equations. A
description is given of the current version of ITPACK, which
has been made available to the scientific community. Future
plans for ITPACK are outlined including the development of
additional iterative algorithms with faster convergence and
with the capability to handle more general linear systems.
A version of ITPACK for vector computers is also discussed.

1. INTRODUCTION

For several years the Center for Numerical Analysis has been involved in a project,
known as ITPACK, which is concerned with the iterative solution of large sparse
systems of linear algebraic equations. The emphasis is on systems arising in the
numerical solution of partial differential equations by finite difference methods
or by finite element methods. A major goal of the ITPACK project is to carry on
research on iterative algorithms. This research includes studies of existing
methods, the development of new methods, and the comparison of iterative methods
with direct methods. The research involves both theoretical analysis and numerical
experimentation. Another goal of the ITPACK project is the development of research-
oriented software, based on iterative methods, for solving large sparse linear
systems. While these computer programs are intended to be reasonably efficient,
the primary emphasis is on flexibility and usability. The programs are primarily
intended for use in academic research and teaching. While they are not production-
oriented, they can be used for moderate-size industrial problems. They may also
be useful for solving pilot problems, thus providing a guide for the construction
of large tailor-made production programs.

One of the major accomplishments of the ITPACK project has been the development of
the ITPACK software package. The current version of this package, ITPACK 2C, is
described in [14] and is available through the International Mathematical and
Statistical Libraries (IMSL).

A brief description of the iterative algorithms used in ITPACK 2C is given in
Section 2. The routines of ITPACK and their usage are described in Section 3.
The use of the ITPACK code to provide solution modules to the ELLPACK software
package for partial differential equations is described in Section 4.

*This work was supported in part by the National Science Foundation through Grant
MCS 79-19829 by the Department of Energy through Grant DE-AS05-81ER10954 and by
the Control Data Corporation through Grant 81T01 with the University of Texas at
Austin.

A brief review of the ITPACK project is given in Section 5. In Section 6 we describe work which is being done to develop an expanded ITPACK package. The objectives are to develop a more flexible package containing additional and more powerful iterative algorithms which can also handle a wider class of problems including strongly nonsymmetric problems. Finally, in Section 7, we discuss the impact of vector computers in the area of iterative algorithms and software. Some of the problems involved in rewriting the ITPACK software for vector computers, such as the Cyber 205, are discussed.

2. ITERATIVE ALGORITHMS

In this section we describe a class of iterative algorithms for solving the linear system

(2.1) $Au = b$

where the coefficient matrix A is a given real nonsingular N x N matrix, is a given N x 1 column vector and the N x 1 column vector u is to be determined. The matrix A is assumed to be large and sparse.

The iterative algorithms which we consider include four components:

     (a)   a basic iterative method
     (b)   an acceleration procedure
     (c)   an adaptive procedure for automatically determining
           any necessary iterative parameters
     (d)   a stopping procedure

A <u>basic</u> <u>iterative</u> <u>method</u> for solving (2.1) is a method of the form

(2.2) $u^{(n + 1)} = Gu^{(n)} + k$

where $u^{(o)}$ is arbitrary. As shown in [19] a basic iterative method can be defined in terms of a nonsingular matrix Q, referred to as a "splitting matrix." Thus, if we represent A in the form

(2.3) $A = Q - (Q - A)$

we can write the system (2.1) in the form

(2.4) $Qu = (Q - A)u + b$

If we define the iterative method by

$$Qu^{(n+1)} = (Q - A)u^{(n)} + b$$

then we obtain (2.2) with

(2.5) $G = I - Q^{-1}A, \quad k = Q^{-1}b$

In order that the basic iterative method be feasible, it must be easy to solve any linear system of the form Qx = y for x given y. Examples of suitable splitting matrices are matrices which are diagonal, tridiagonal, upper triangular, and the product of a lower triangular matrix and an upper triangular matrix.

We list below the splitting matrices for several standard basic iterative methods. Here we have represented A in the form

(2.6) $A = D - C_L - C_U$

where D is a diagonal matrix and where C_L and C_U are strictly lower and strictly upper triangular matrices, respectively.

Method	Splitting Matrix Q
Richardson	I
Jacobi	D
Gauss-Seidel	$D - C_L$
SOR (successive overrelaxation)	$\omega^{-1} D - C_L$
SSOR (symmetric SOR)	$(2-\omega)^{-1}(\omega^{-1} D - C_L)D^{-1}(\omega^{-1} D - C_U)$

Here the real number ω is an iteration parameter which is chosen to make the convergence of the basic iterative method as fast as possible.

In many cases a basic iterative method can be speeded up using an acceleration procedure. Let us consider the case where the basic iterative method is symmetrizable in the sense that $Z(I - G)$ is symmetric and positive definite (SPD) for some SPD matrix Z. For a symmetrizable iterative method the eigenvalues of G are real and less than unity. Evidently if A is SPD then Richardson's method, the Jacobi method and the SSOR method (if $0 < \omega < 2$) are symmetrizable with Z = A or Z = Q. The Gauss-Seidel and SOR methods are not symmetrizable and are used without acceleration, in most cases.

Two acceleration procedures are used in ITPACK 2C, namely, Chebyshev acceleration and (the three-term form of) conjugate gradient acceleration. In either case the procedure is defined by

(2.7) $u^{(n+1)} = \rho_{n+1}\{u^{(n)} + \gamma_{n+1}(Gu^{(n)} + k - u^{(n)})\} + (1 - \rho_{n+1})u^{(n-1)}$

In the case of Chebyshev acceleration $\gamma_1 = \gamma_2 = \ldots = \gamma$ and $\rho_1, \rho_2, \ldots$ and γ can be computed in terms of m(G) and M(G), the smallest and largest eigenvalues of G, respectively. In the case of conjugate gradient acceleration the $\{\rho_i\}$ and the $\{\gamma_i\}$ can be computed explicitly in terms of certain inner products involving the pseudo-residual vectors

(2.8) $\delta^{(n)} = Gu^{(n)} + k - u^{(n)}$

The amount of work required per iteration with conjugate gradient acceleration is somewhat greater than with Chebyshev acceleration. However, the convergence is always at least as fast (measured in a certain norm) and in many cases is very much faster. Also the fact that no iteration parameters involving m(G) and M(G) are required is a big advantage for conjugate gradient acceleration.

The use of an acceleration procedure yields a very large increase in the rate of convergence especially for problems where the unaccelerated method converges very slowly (or even fails to converge). Thus the factor of improvement is approximately $\sqrt{K(I - G)}$, or greater, for large K(I - G). Here K(I - G) is the condition number of I - G.

For a linear system arising from a 5-point finite difference discretization of a second-order elliptic partial differential equation over a square mesh of length h the factor of improvement for the acceleration of the Jacobi method would be of order h^{-1}.

In order to carry out an iterative procedure involving a basic iterative method and an acceleration procedure several iteration parameters may be required. Thus, for Chebyshev acceleration one needs estimates for m(G) and M(G). Also for the SSOR method the parameter ω is required. With conjugate gradient acceleration there is no adapting of iteration parameters required except in the case of the SSOR method where ω must be estimated.

The sensitivity of the iterative procedures to the choice of iteration parameters is usually so great as to make it impractical, in general, to estimate them a priori. Fortunately, adaptive procedures are available to determine the parameters automatically. With these procedures one estimates very crude initial values of the iteration parameters and begins the iteration process. If, at any stage, the observed convergence rate is appreciably less than the anticipated convergence rate then the iteration parameters are modified. Details of the procedures used are given in [5] and [6].

An often neglected problem with iterative algorithms is that of deciding when to terminate the iteration process. In other words, when is the vector $u^{(n)}$ a sufficiently accurate approximation to the true solution $\bar{u} = A^{-1}b$? Ideally, we would like to stop the iterations when

$$(2.9) \qquad \| u^{(n)} - \bar{u} \|_{\alpha} / \| \bar{u} \|_{\alpha} \leq \zeta$$

where $\| \cdot \|_{\alpha}$ is a suitable norm and ζ is a stopping number in the range, say, $10^{-3} \leq \zeta \leq 10^{-8}$. It can be shown that (2.9) is satisfied if the condition

$$(2.10) \qquad (1 - M(G))^{-1} \| \delta^{(n)} \|_{\alpha} / \| \bar{u} \|_{\alpha} \leq \zeta$$

is satisfied where $\delta^{(n)}$ is given by (2.8). Actually, we use the test defined by

$$(2.11) \qquad (1 - M_E)^{-1} \| \delta^{(n)} \|_{\alpha} / \| u^{(n)} \|_{\alpha} \leq \zeta$$

For adaptive Chebyshev acceleration M_E is the latest estimate for M(G). For conjugate gradient acceleration M_E is the largest eigenvalue of a certain tridiagonal matrix of order n whose elements involve the $\{\rho_i\}$ and the $\{\gamma_i\}$. The test (2.11) has been found to be satisfactory in a wide class of cases.

3. THE ITPACK PACKAGE

The ITPACK 2C package contains the following seven main routines:

Name	Method
JCG	Jacobi Conjugate Gradient
JSI	Jacobi Semi-iteration
SOR	Successive Overrelaxation
SSORCG	Symmetric SOR Conjugate Gradient
SSORSI	Symmetric SOR Semi-iteration
RSCG	Reduced System Conjugate Gradient
RSSI	Reduced System Semi-iteration

For the above methods the term "semi-iteration" is equivalent to "Chebyshev acceleration."

No adapting of the iteration parameters is needed for the JCG method. In the JSI method there are actually two iteration parameters which are needed, namely $m(G)$ and $M(G)$. In the current version of ITPACK it is assumed that a number $\underline{m}$ is available such that $\underline{m} \leq m(G)$. An adaptive procedure is used to find $M(\overline{G})$. (A later version of ITPACK will provide for the adaptive determination of $m(G)$ as well as of $M(G)$.)

No acceleration procedure is involved in the SOR routine. The parameter ω is determined adaptively following a procedure described in [6].

For the SSORCG method the parameter ω is determined adaptively. In the SSORSI method it is known that $m(G) \geq 0$ for all ω. Hence, it is only necessary to find $M(G)$ and ω using an adaptive process. The adaptive processes used for the SSORCG and the SSORSI methods are described in [8] and [5].

The RSCG and RSSI routines can be used if the system (2.1) can be written in the red-black form

$$(3.1) \qquad \begin{bmatrix} D_R & H \\ K & D_B \end{bmatrix} \begin{bmatrix} u_R \\ u_B \end{bmatrix} = \begin{bmatrix} b_R \\ b_B \end{bmatrix}$$

where D_R and D_B are square diagonal matrices. We remark that a linear system obtained by solving a standard five point finite difference equation over a rectangular grid can be put into the red-black form by suitable reordering of the equations and by a corresponding relabelling of the unknowns. By the elimination of the sub-vector u_R one obtains the reduced system

$$(3.2) \qquad (I - D_B^{-1}KD_R^{-1}H)\, u_B = D_B^{-1}(b_B - KD_R^{-1}b_R)$$

If we apply Richardson's method to the reduced system (3.2), we obtain the RS method. Conjugate gradient acceleration and Chebyshev acceleration applied to the RS method yield the RSCG method and the RSSI method, respectively. No adapting of the iteration parameters are involved in the RSCG method. For the RS method it can be shown that $m(G) \geqq 0$; hence the RSSI method only involves the adaptive determination of the parameter $M(G)$.

A typical calling sequence for using ITPACK 2C with the SSORCG method has the form

        CALL SSORCG(N, IA, JA, A, RHS, U, IWKSP, NW, WKSP, IPARM, RPARM, IER)

To use another method simply replace SSORCG by the name of the other method. Here N is the order of the system and IA, JA, A are single-dimensional arrays used to represent the matrix A of (2.1) in the sparse matrix format used in the Yale sparse matrix package [3]. In this representation the nonzero elements of the matrix A are stored row-wise in the array A. The corresponding column numbers are stored in the array JA. Pointers to the ends of the rows are provided by the array IA.

The arrays RHS and U give the vector b of (2.1) and the initial approximation $u^{(0)}$ to the true solution $\bar{u}$, respectively. Usually, $u^{(0)} = 0$. The arrays IPARM and RPARM contain parameters with which the user can choose to control the iterative process. For example, if one wants the maximum number of iterations to be 250, then one would set IPARM(1) = 250. Otherwise the default value of 100 would be used. Similarly, if one wanted the stopping number ζ of (2.11) to be 10^{-8}, then RPARM(1) would be set to 1.0E-08; otherwise, the default value of 5×10^{-6} would be used. The user can also specify estimates for $M(G)$ and, for the JSI method, $m(G)$. Also, one can specify ω for the SOR and SSOR methods. Options are available to fix the estimates of $M(G)$ and/or ω instead of having them be determined adaptively. Further details of the usage of ITPACK 2C are given in [14].

4. THE USE OF ITPACK WITH ELLPACK

The ELLPACK software package, see, e.g., Rice [16], is a collection of routines for solving a class of partial differential equations by various procedures. The user provides information, using a special language, to specify such things as the differential equation, domain, boundary conditions, mesh discretization, solution of the algebraic system, etc. A preprocessor constructs a FORTRAN program using various modules. Included among the solution modules for ELLPACK are seven modules based on the seven ITPACK 2C routines. These routines were modified so as to use the ELLPACK data structure, which is described in Section 7.

The use in ELLPACK of the seven solution modules corresponding to ITPACK 2C is very convenient. For example, suppose one wants to use the JCG method with a maximum of 125 iterations, with the stopping number $\zeta = 10^{-7}$ and with all other controllable parameters set to their default values. One simply writes the following ELLPACK statements after the discretization statement.

        INDEX.   AS IS

        SOL.   JACOBI CG (ITMAX = 125, ZETA = 1.0E-7)

The first statement indicates that the ordering used by ELLPACK in carrying out the discretization process is not to be changed. To use the RSCG method one would write

        INDEX.   RED-BLACK

        SOL.   REDUCED SYSTEM CG (ITMAX = 125, ZETA = 1.0E-7)

Before beginning the iteration process the program would first permute the rows and columns of the coefficient matrix to yield a red-black matrix. If that is not possible, then the run will terminate and an error message will be given.

At the end of the ELLPACK run, printed output is given describing the performance of the iterative procedure in terms of number of iterations and timing.

More information on the use of ITPACK in ELLPACK is given in [13].

5. THE ITPACK PROJECT

In 1974 Garrett Birkhoff suggested that software be developed for solving elliptic partial differential equations. He proposed that the user have the option to use either iterative methods or direct methods to solve the resulting systems of linear algebraic equations. Discussions were held with John Rice, Robert Lynch, and the authors, as well as with others which led to the establishment of the ELLPACK project and the ITPACK project. The first version of the ITPACK software package was completed in 1978 and was distributed by IMSL. Several revised versions have since been written. A writeup of the current version, ITPACK 2C, appeared in 1983 in the Transactions of Mathematical Software [14].

A number of people, in addition to the authors, have contributed to ITPACK. Dr. L. A. Hageman collaborated with Dr. Young on the book [6] which contains the theoretical basis for the algorithms of ITPACK. In addition, Dr. Hageman contributed the SOR algorithm which is used in ITPACK. The first version of the ITPACK package was programmed by Roger Grimes. Other contributions have been made by John Respess (modifications of ITPACK), Bill MacGregor (sparse storage systems), K. C. Jea (research on nonsymmetrizable iterative methods), Tom Oppe (vectorization), and T. S. Mai (modularization and expansion of ITPACK).

The work on the ITPACK project has been supported by grants from the National Science Foundation since 1976. Support has also been received from the Department of Energy and from Control Data Corporation.

6. WORK IN PROGRESS

The current work on the ITPACK project has three primary aspects: the development of a greatly expanded software package; research on iterative algorithms; and vectorization. In this section we will discuss the first two aspects; vectorization will be discussed in the next section.

We are in the process of developing an expanded ITPACK package which will be written in a modular form. This will permit any component of the algorithm to be changed without affecting any of the other components. Thus, for example, any one of several basic iterative methods can be used with any one of several acceleration procedures. This will provide greater flexibility than is possible with the current ITPACK package where there is a separate subprogram for each basic method/ acceleration procedure combination. The expanded package is designed to handle linear systems where the matrices are not necessarily symmetric and positive definite (SPD). The current version of ITPACK is designed for linear systems with SPD matrices although the routines will work on many problems where the matrix is "nearly" SPD.

Modules are being prepared for the expanded package for various basic iterative methods in addition to those currently used in ITPACK (Jacobi, SOR, SSOR, and RS). Several basic iterative methods based on approximate matrix factorization techniques will be included. Modules are also being prepared for several acceleration procedures which can be applied to nonsymmetrizable iterative methods. Such procedures include three generalized conjugate gradient acceleration procedures,

called ORTHODIR, ORTHOMIN, and ORTHORES as well as three versions of the Lanczos
method; see [20] and [9]. In addition, we plan to include an adaptive Chebyshev
acceleration procedure developed by Manteuffel [15]. The programs of the expanded
ITPACK will be tested over a wide variety of problems including many generated by
ELLPACK. We plan to prepare documentation which will describe the algorithms used
and the uses of the package.

In parallel with the software development we are carrying on research on iterative
algorithms. Particular emphasis is on the convergence properties of generalized
conjugate gradient acceleration procedures and other procedures for speeding up
the convergence of nonsymmetrizable iterative methods. While the behavior of many
of these methods in their unmodified forms, is fairly well understood, it is
usually necessary to modify, or truncate, them in order that the machine time and
storage required are reasonable. The truncated procedures are much less well
understood. We plan to study breakdown, convergence, and rate of convergence for
these methods using numerical experiments as well as theoretical analysis where
feasible.

Another primary focus of the research is a comparative study of a number of basic
iterative method/acceleration procedure combinations and their effectiveness over
a wide class of problems involving partial differential equations. Special
attention will be given to cases where the matrix of the system is symmetric and
positive definite (SPD), nearly SPD, symmetric indefinite, etc. Besides basic
methods based on approximate factorization, we plan to consider the method of
Concus and Golub [1] and of Widlund [17] as well as methods based on the use of
normal equations and modified normal equations; see, e.g., Dongarra et al. [2]
and Elman [4].

7. VECTORIZATION

The advent of high-performance vector computers such as the Control Data Cyber 205
and the Cray 1 is having a profound effect on iterative algorithms and software.
As an example, consider the problem of solving the linear system

(7.1) $Lu = b$

for u where L is a lower triangular matrix. With a scalar computer this could be
solved very easily by forward substitution. One could get u_1, u_2, ..., explicitly;
however, one cannot compute u_i until u_{i-1}, u_{i-2}, ..., u_1 have been computed. This
means that the process is not vectorizable and is thus not efficient for a vector
computer. Because of the need for vectorization, some iterative methods which are
effective on conventional, or scalar, computers may not be effective on vector
computers and vice versa. Thus, for instance, the Jacobi method, which is generally
not highly regarded as an iterative method for scalar computers, is well adapted
for a vector computer. This is also true of the RS method, which can be used if
the matrix A of the system (2.1) is a red-black matrix. However, the SOR and SSOR
methods are, in general, not well suited for vector computers. On the other hand,
if A is a red-black matrix or can be made so by permuting the rows and corresponding columns of A, then the SOR method with the red-black ordering is vectorizable.
This is also true for the SSOR method. However, for a linear system derived from
a five-point difference equation with a rectangular mesh, the SSOR method is much
less effective, in terms of number of iterations, with the red-black ordering than
with the "natural" ordering. The use of the natural ordering does not lead to good
vectorization for the SSOR method. However, if one orders the mesh points "by
diagonals," one can obtain some degree of vectorization for the SSOR method; see
Hayes [7]. Numerical studies have shown that the accelerated SSOR method with
the red-black ordering on a vector computer can be faster than with the natural
ordering in spite of the greater number of iterations; see Kincaid and Oppe [11].

Vectorization considerations make various methods based on approximate matrix factorization procedures less attractive than for scalar machines. Various modifications have been proposed to improve the vectorization of such methods without substantially increasing the number of iterations; see, e.g., Van de Vorst [18] and Johnson, Micchelli, and Paul [10].

The problems of vectorization is being kept in mind as we develop the expanded version of ITPACK and in our research on iterative algorithms. In the meantime we have taken the current version of ITPACK, which we refer to as "scalar ITPACK 2C," and prepared a vector version, which we refer to as "vector ITPACK 2C." As described in [11] and [12], two major changes were made for the vector ITPACK 2C. First, many of the DO loops which had been unrolled for scalar optimization were rewritten as tight DO loops so that they would be executed efficiently in the vector mode. Second, the data structure was changed from the row-oriented structure of the Yale sparse matrix package to a column-oriented data structure similar to that used in ELLPACK. In this new structure two two-dimensional arrays, COEF and JCOEF, are used to represent the coefficient matrix A. The array COEF contains the nonzero elements of A and JCOEF contains the column numbers. Thus, the matrix

$$A = \begin{bmatrix} a_{11} & a_{12} & 0 & a_{14} \\ a_{21} & a_{22} & a_{23} & 0 \\ a_{31} & 0 & a_{33} & 0 \\ 0 & a_{42} & 0 & a_{44} \end{bmatrix}$$

is represented by

$$COEF = \begin{bmatrix} a_{11} & a_{12} & a_{14} \\ a_{22} & a_{21} & a_{23} \\ a_{33} & a_{31} & 0 \\ a_{44} & a_{42} & 0 \end{bmatrix}, \quad JCOEF = \begin{bmatrix} 1 & 2 & 4 \\ 2 & 1 & 3 \\ 3 & 1 & 1 \\ 4 & 2 & 1 \end{bmatrix}$$

With this structure the product of a matrix times a vector can be computed much more efficiently on a vector computer than it can with the other data structure; see [11], [12], and [13].

As described in [11] and [12], for a set of test problems a substantial reduction in time was obtained using vector ITPACK 2C as compared to scalar ITPACK 2C on both the Cyber 205 and the Cray 1.

REFERENCES:

[1] Concus, P. and Golub, G. H., A Generalized Conjugate Gradient Method for Nonsymmetric Systems of Linear Equations, Report Stan-CS-76-535, Computer Science Department, Stanford University, California (1976).

[2] Dongarra, J. J., Leaf, G. K., and Minkoff, M., A Preconditioned Conjugate
     Gradient Method for Solving a Class of Non-symmetric Linear Systems, Argonne
     Nat. Lab. Rep. ANL-81-71 (1981).

[3] Eisenstat, S. C., Gursky, M. C., Schultz, M. H., and Sherman, A. H., Yale
     Sparse Matrix Package, II, The Nonsymmetric Codes, Research Report No. 114,
     Department of Computer Science, Yale University, New Haven, Connecticut
     (1977a).

[4] Elman, H. C., Iterative Methods for Large, Sparse, Nonsymmetric Systems of
     Linear Equations, Res. Rep. 229, Department of Computer Science, Yale
     University, New Haven, Connecticut (1982).

[5] Grimes, R. G., Kincaid, D. R., and Young, D. M., ITPACK 2.0 User's Guide,
     Center for Numerical Analysis Report No. 150, The University of Texas at
     Austin, Austin, Texas (1979).

[6] Hageman, L. A. and Young, D. M., Applied Iterative Methods (Academic Press,
     New York, 1981).

[7] Hayes, L. J., Comparative Analysis of Iterative Techniques for Solving
     Laplace's Equation on the Unit Square on a Parallel Processor, M.A. Thesis,
     Department of Mathematics, The University of Texas at Austin, Austin, Texas
     (August 1974).

[8] Hayes, L. J. and Young, D. M., The Accelerated SSOR Method for Solving Large
     Linear Systems: Preliminary Report, Center for Numerical Analysis Report
     No. 123, The University of Texas at Austin, Austin, Texas (1977).

[9] Jea, K. C. and Young, D. M., On the Simplification of Generalized Conjugate
     Gradient Methods for Nonsymmetrizable Linear Systems, J. of L. A. A. (to
     appear).

[10] Johnson, O. G., Micchelli, C. A., and Paul, G., Polynomial Preconditioners
     for Conjugate Gradient Calculations, SIAM J. Numer. Anal. 20 (1983), pp.
     362-376.

[11] Kincaid, D. R. and Oppe, T. C., ITPACK on Supercomputers, Center for
     Numerical Analysis Report No. 178, The University of Texas at Austin, Austin,
     Texas (1982).

[12] Kincaid, D. R., Oppe, T. C., and Young, D. M., Adapting ITPACK Routines for
     Use on a Vector Computer, Center for Numerical Analysis Report No. 177, The
     University of Texas at Austin, Austin, Texas (1982).

[13] Kincaid, D. R. and Young, D. M., The ITPACK Project: Past, Present, and
     Future, Center for Numerical Analysis Report No. 180, The University of Texas
     at Austin, Austin, Texas (1983).

[14] Kincaid, D. R., Respess, J., Young, D. M., and Grimes, R., ITPACK 2C: A
     FORTRAN Package for Solving Large Sparse Linear Systems by Adaptive
     Accelerated Iterative Methods, T.O.M.S. 8 (1982), pp. 302-322.

[15] Manteuffel, T. A., Adaptive Procedure for Estimating Parameters for the
     Nonsymmetric Tchebyshev Iteration, Numer. Math. 31 (1978) 183.

[16] Rice, J. R., ELLPACK, Progress and Plans, in: Schultz, M. (ed.), Elliptic
     Problem Solvers (Academic Press, New York, 1981), pp. 135-162.

[17] Widlund, O., A Lanczos Method for a Class of Nonsymmetric Systems of Linear
     Equations, SIAM J. Numer. Anal. 15 (1978), pp. 801-812.

[18] Van der Vorst, H. A., A Vectorizable Variant of some ICCG-methods, Academisch Computer Centrum Utrecht, Utrecht, The Netherlands (1979).

[19] Young, D. M., Iterative Solution of Large Linear Systems (Academic Press, New York, 1971).

[20] Young, D. M. and Jea, K. C., Generalized Conjugate Gradient Acceleration of Nonsymmetrizable Iterative Methods, J. of L. A. A. 34 (1980) 159.

DISCUSSION

Speaker: D. Young

Hindmarsh: In the user interface, suppose a user can supply only a module for Ax (given x), not the elements of A. Some subset of ITPACK methods can be adapted to this situation, and I wonder if any thought has been given to it. (I mean here the extreme case that only a module for Ax is given, no other information about A, and no matrices are to be stored - only a modest number of vectors; hence any preconditioning is precluded, for example.)

Young: We have been discussing the possibility of specifying, not the matrix A and the preconditioning matrix Q, but rather procedures for computing such matrices as Ax, $Q^{-1}x$, etc. for a given vector x. We have not considered a scheme which you suggest where no preconditioning is allowed since it would limit the flexibility of ITPACK, which is a research-oriented code. However, the matrix-free idea would certainly be attractive for a _production_-oriented code.

Duff: You discussed some methods appropriate for unsymmetric problems, eg. ORTHOMIN, ORTHORES, CHEBYSHEV etc. Since, in the symmetric case, it is only preconditioning that makes conjugate gradients practical on large problems, is is natural to assume that a good preconditioning will be required when using the above methods on unsymmetric systems. Could you comment on preconditioning in the unsymmetric case?

Young: It is certainly important to have a good preconditioning in the unsymmetric case as well as in the symmetric case. (In an extreme case where all of the eigenvalues of the iteration matrix lie on a circle in the complex plane, no acceleration of the method is possible.) In the case of a "nearly symmetric" problem it would be logical to use a preconditioning based on the symmetric case (e.g. the symmetric SOR matrix, an incomplete factorization procedure, etc.) We plan to carry on research using the expanded version of ITPACK to try various preconditioner/acceleration procedure combinations for various nonsymmetric systems.

Hockney: You mentioned at the beginning that you had planned some comparisons between iterative and direct methods. Would you care to comment on this?

Young: A number of numerical experiments were carried out for some model problems using ELLPACK with a variety of linear equation solvers including the iterative methods of ITPACK as well as several direct methods. A paper with authors Sherman, Kincaid, and others was published a few years ago. Only the results were presented, and the reader was free to draw his own conclusions. A great deal more work remains to be done in this area. At least we now have a tool to use.

Rice: I would like to answer Hockney's question. I wrote a paper (The performance of 13 methods to solve the Galerkin equations, Linear Algebra and Its Applications, 1983) which compared 13 linear equation solvers for the Galerkin equations. Iterative methods became more efficient at a crossover point which was usually about 200-400 equations. Thus direct methods were more efficient only for smaller problems where the computational cost is rather low anyway.

Yanenko: Research in USSR shows that the stability of the Chebyshev method depends on the ordering of the parameters. For some orderings the method is unstable.

Young: We use the three-term form of Chebyshev acceleration rather than the two-term form. With the former, the error after n steps is equal to the optimum Chebyshev polynomial of degree n multiplied by the initial error vector. This may not be true for the two-term form. We are aware, however, of work which has been done in the USSR on the ordering of the parameters for the two-term form which avoids instability.

Simpson: I would like to add a comment on the comparison of direct and iterative solution techniques. Actually, it is primarily a comment on the usefulness of convenient, compatible interfaces. We have at Waterloo a finite element package which uses SPARSPAK, the package of sparse matrix direct solvers by Alan George and Joseph Liu. We also recently obtained ITPACK2. The user interfaces of these packages are very similar, and both conveniently allow an incremental specification of the global matrix, from a fill of local stiffness matrices, i.e. an assembly facility for the FEM. A few terms ago, I gave as a course project for a graduate student the task of replacing SPARSPAK by ITPACK2 in our FEM package and running some comparisons. The comparisons confirmed what I think Professor Rice has just said, i.e. roughly speaking, for moderate sized problems (several thousand unknowns) there was little difference in the times, but the storage was significantly less for the iterative methods (typically, about a half).

The point I would like to emphasize, however, is that the interfaces that these two packages present are simple and compatible, so that a student with relatively little familiarity with either was able to unhook one and hook up the other in a few days, with no significant debugging problems. I feel that this is an example of an interface design that has been successful in making these two general purpose package pleasant to use.

Young: I welcome this comment and have nothing to add.

Duff: In response to John Rice's comment, the size at which iterative methods become superior will be dependent both on the computing environment and whether the equations are being solved once only as for several source terms. Of course, as we saw from the talk, there is only a subset of PDE's on which iterative methods are currently reliable. Many problems, in fluid flow for example, can give rise to unsymmetric problems.

Young: I agree with the first sentence. Concerning the second sentence I agree that iterative methods are not currently completely reliable and efficient for unsymmetric problems. However, for many problems they are indeed effective.

Schönauer: We still have to learn a lot about iterative methods. When we built in arbitrary order approximation in our system we found that the time of iteration went up with the order. Similarly, when we went from Dirichlet to Neumann boundary conditions the number of iterations went up by as much as a factor of ten. This shows that the crossover point is problem dependent.

Young: I heartily agree that we still have a lot to learn about iterative methods. One of the main objects of our work on the ITPACK package is to facilitate research in this area. The ordering of the equations may or may not be important. For example, for the SOR method with a five-point difference equation the convergence rate may be the same for the natural ordering and for the red-black ordering. On the other hand, for the symmetric SOR method, the convergence may be much slower with red-black ordering than with natural ordering. On the basis of certain model problems I would expect that the convergence with Neumann boundary condition would be much slower than with Dirichlet boundary conditions.

Reid: Are you planning to put multigrid methods into ITPACK?

Young: In the current phase on an extended version of ITPACK we do not plan to include multigrid methods. However, these methods may well be included in later phases.

Miller: Do you agree with a previous speakers comment that iterative methods are not appropriate for general purpose finite element programs, especially when the linear system is non-positive definite and non-symmetric?

Young: I do not agree with the above comment. There are undoubtedly many finite element problems where direct methods would be more appropriate than iterative methods. However, for many large finite element problems, especially those involving three dimensions, the use of iterative methods would be appropriate. Very reliable programs are available for positive definite problems. Even for non-positive definite and non-symmetric problems there exist iterative methods which, though not guaranteed to work effectively, may be quite effective in some cases. It may well be that it would be more appropriate to try such a method and then switch over to a direct method if the iterative method should fail.

Duff: At Harwell our oil group solve large PDE where the matrix is often unsymmetric. Even though iterative methods might have convergence difficulties, extensions of conjugate gradients (preconditioned ORTHOMIN) are nevertheless commonly used. There is, however. a direct solution option in the code for cases where iterative methods fail. Thus we at Harwell find both iterative and direct solvers useful in the solution of large systems of PDEs.

Sherman: I second what Iain has pointed out. In our reservoir simulators, iterative methods are the usual solution techniques employed. We find methods such as line SOR extremely effective, and we fall back on direct methods mostly in the rare cases where iterative methods fail. (Often, in fact, we find those failures due to errors in the input data for the model, not to properties of the linear system for the proper model.)

Young: These are good comments and I have nothing to add!

PDE SOFTWARE: Modules, Interfaces and Systems
B. Engquist and T. Smedsaas (eds.)
Elsevier Science Publishers B.V. (North-Holland)
© IFIP, 1984

MOLAG: A Method Of Lines Adaptive Grid Interface for
Nonlinear Partial Differential Equations*

Niel K. Madsen

Lawrence Livermore National Laboratory
Livermore, California 94550
USA

We describe an adaptive grid or moving node method wich can be used
to solve systems of nonlinear partial differential equations. The
method is implemented in the form of a method of lines software
interface. When this interface is combined with a reliable ordinary
differential equation solver, one obtains the capability to adaptively
solve systems of partial differential equations. Numerical results
are presented.

INTRODUCTION

Over the past several years, adaptive numerical techniques for solving partial
differential equations have received considerable attention. These techniques
have the promise for obtaining more efficient and accurate numerical solutions
for partial differential equations. The moving finite element method [1] is
perhaps the most noteworthy and has been used to obtain dramatically improved
solutions for some difficult problems. Even in the light of the successes of
the moving finite element method, we have been motivated to consider other
alternatives. The moving finite element method is not particulary easy to
implement and is rather expensive computationally. Although it is based on rather
conventional Galerkin finite element mathematical ideas, people have found the
technique difficult to understand and accept. Also, even though numerous papers
discuss the subject of adaptive methods, very little (if any) software is
available for general use.

There are several purposes for this paper. First, we wish to present a simple and
understandable adaptive grid (moving node) solution method which has a reasonable
computational cost and which may be easily implemented and applied to a broad
variety of problems. Second, we wish to make our techniques readily available to
any interested party and have therefore implemented our ideas in the form of a
method of lines software interface similar in nature to a previous fixed grid
interface PDEONE [3,4]. Third, we want to encourage people to use, to evaluate,
and to improve upon the ideas and software we present.

CLASS OF ALLOWABLE PROBLEMS

We will consider systems of partial differential equations (PDEs) which have the
following form:

$$(1) \qquad u_t = f(t,x,u,u_x,u_{xx}) \quad , \quad x_L < x < x_R \quad , \quad t > t_0 \quad ,$$

* Work performed under the auspices of the US Dept of Energy by the Lawrence
Livermore National Lab under contract W-7405-ENG-48.

where   u   is the solution vector with NPDE components, and u_x and u_{xx} are
its first and second derivatives, respectively. We will allow boundary conditions
for the kth PDE equation to be of the form:

(2) $a_k u_k + b_k (u_x)_k = g_k$,   at $x = x_L$ and x_R ,

and require initial conditions $u = u_0$ at $t = t_0$. If $b_k \neq 0$ for some k,
then a_k, b_k, and g_k may be nonlinear functions of t and u, otherwise they
may be functions of t only. We also allow for the possibility that no boundary
condition is specified for a particular solution component. This would be
signaled by setting $a_k = b_k = 0$ for that component at the desired boundary. It
is of course very clear that the equations (1) and (2) are so general that they
include PDE systems which may not be well-posed.

We assume that at $t = t_0$, a grid or mesh is specified, which consists of a
sequence of NPTS ($>$ 5) points in $[x_L, x_R]$ such that $x_L = x_1 < x_2 < ... < x_{NPTS} = x_R$.
We will adopt the method of lines approach for solving (1)-(2) and use centered
finite differences for u_x and u_{xx} to convert the PDE system to a system of
ordinary differential equations (ODEs). These ODEs will then be solved with an
ODE integrator package. The boundary conditions are treated as in PDEONE [3,4].

ADAPTIVE GRID METHOD

For many problems it is the case that the solution components vary in a smooth
manner over the entire domain. When this occurs, it is reasonable to simply use
a fixed mesh or grid and solve the problem in the usual manner. However, for
many problems the solution components may exhibit extreme variation in quite
localized regions (such as with propagating wave pulses or shock fronts). For
these types of problems, it would be very useful to be able to dynamically
adjust or adapt the mesh or grid so as to have small zones in the localized
regions where extreme solution variation is occuring and to allow for coarse
or large zones in regions where the solution is changing very little. The grid
points should then dynamically follow the changes in the solution as time
evolves.

Using the method of lines philosophy together with the centered finite difference
approximations mentioned above, our PDE system is approximated with the semi-
discrete ODE system:

(3) $\dfrac{du_{k,i}}{dt} = f_{k,i}(t, u_{1,1}, ..., u_{NPDE,NPTS})$, $\begin{array}{l} k = 1 \ \ \text{to} \ \ \text{NPDE} \ , \\ i = 1 \ \ \text{to} \ \ \text{NPTS} \ , \end{array}$

where $u_{k,i}$ denotes the kth solution component associated with the grid point
x_i. We now wish to allow the grid points to move with time, i.e. $x_i = x_i(t)$.
Changes with time in $u_{k,i}$ will now occur because of the differential equation
(3) and also because of the movement of the grid point x_i. In order to account
for these changes, the governing equations (3) must be modified to be (dropping
the arguments of $f_{k,i}$):

$$\frac{du_{k,i}}{dt} = f_{k,i} + (u_{k,i})_x \frac{dx_i}{dt} \quad , \qquad k = 1 \text{ to } NPDE \quad ,$$

(4)

$$\frac{dx_i}{dt} = (\text{to be specified}) \qquad , \qquad i = 1 \text{ to } NPTS \quad .$$

We will use the same difference approximations for the term $(u_{k,i})_x$ in (4) as are used to obtain the semi-discrete ODE system in the beginning. We remark now that at any given grid point x_i we will have $NPDE + 1$ ODE equations as given by (4).

In order to completely specify our adaptive grid method, we must develop a strategy for moving the grid points, i.e. we must specify dx_i/dt for each grid point. There are many possible strategies to accomplish this. The moving finite element accomplishes this by minimizing PDE residuals over the finite element test space as well as over the grid point locations. We have adopted the concept of defining a mesh function which will in some sense measure the local adequacy of the current node locations. We will then dynamically adjust the grid point locations so as to equalize the mesh function over the entire mesh. This approach was first brought to our attention by J.M. Hyman (Los Alamos National Lab). We will define a nonnegative function which will have the following properties:

$$\lim_{h_i \to 0} m(i) = 0 \quad ,$$

$m(i) << 1$ implies good resolution ,

$m(i) = O(1)$ implies resolution is OK ,

$m(i) >> 1$ implies poor resolution ,

where $h_i = x_{i+1} - x_i$, and $m(i)$ is the mesh function value associated with the ith grid interval. Our fundamental grid point moving strategy is to define motion of the grid points so as to equi-distribute the mesh function values over all the mesh intervals.

We will require that the two grid points, x_1 and x_{NPTS}, at the ends of our domain remain fixed for all time. Therefore, we have that

$$\sum_{i=1}^{NPTS-1} (h_i) = x_R - x_L .$$

As the nodes move, the rate of change of the ith mesh zone length is $dh_i/dt = dx_{i+1}/dt - dx_i/dt$. Because the entire domain length is fixed, we have that $SUM(dh_i/dt) = 0$. We will adaptively move the grid points by requiring that

(5)

$$\frac{dh_i}{dt} = \frac{dx_{i+1}}{dt} - \frac{dx_i}{dt} = M - m(i) \quad ,$$

where

$$M = [\sum_{i=1}^{NPTS-1} m(i)] / (NPTS - 1)$$

is the average mesh function value over all of the mesh zones. Since $dx_1/dt = dx_{NPTS}/dt = 0$, we can easily solve (5) for each dx_i/dt once the mesh function values $m(i)$ are determined.

To complete the definition of the adaptive grid strategy, we must define the mesh function. Three specific goals are important in defining the mesh function: 1) the PDE right hand side f should be well approximated, 2) the PDE solution u should not change greatly (in some sense) over any one zone, and 3) excessive adjacent zone distortion should be avoided. We have found the following five different mesh functions to be quite useful depending upon the particular type of node positioning we are trying to achieve

$$m_1(i) = \sum_{K=1}^{NPDE} W_K \left| (f_K)_h - (f_K)_{2h} \right|_1 / T_1$$

$$m_2(i) = \sum_{K=1}^{NPDE} W_K \left| u_{K,i+1} - u_{K,i} \right| / T_2$$

(6)

$$m_3(i) = \sum_{K=1}^{NPDE} W_K \left| (u_x)_{K,i+1} - (u_x)_{K,i} \right| / T_3$$

$$m_4(i) = \sum_{K=1}^{NPDE} W_K \left| K_{K,i+1} - K_{K,i} \right| / T_4$$

$$m_5(i) = \left| x_{i+1} - x_i \right| / T_5$$

In (6), $(f_K)_h$ and $(f_K)_{2h}$ represent the values of the Kth PDE right hand side evaluated for the current zone size h_i and for a zone size twice as large, respectively. W_K is a user specified component weight, $K_{K,i}$ is the curvature of the Kth solution component at x_i, and each T_p is chosen so that $SUM(m_p(i)) = 1$. The first mesh function m_1 is designed to insure that the right hand sides of the PDEs are well approximated. The second, third and fourth mesh functions are designed to control the amount of change of the solution u according to three different measuring criteria. The fifth function in (6) is to allow control over excessive adjacent mesh zone distortion.

In actual calculations, we have found all of the above mesh functions to be effective and useful. The fourth mesh function involves second derivatives of the solution and therefore has the potential for introducing stiffness [3] into the ODE system. In our implementation, we define the <u>total</u> mesh function to be a linear combination of the five functions in (6), i.e.

(7) $$m(i)_{TOTAL} = Am_1(i) + Bm_2(i) + Cm_3(i) + Dm_4(i) + Em_5(i)$$

where A, B, C, D and E are user specified constants.

In computing with adaptively moving nodes, it is essential that the grid does not tangle, i.e. grid points must not cross over each other. In order to guarantee that this does not occur, algorithmic constraints must be applied. When a zone reaches a small size and the mesh function is still trying to force the zone to a smaller size, we must override the desires of the mesh function. Our philosophy is to keep the average mesh function value M fixed (and known) and to change the m_i for those zones which we feel are too small. We will replace m_i with some m_i^*, where $m_i^* < m_i$. In order to preserve the value of M, we must make compensating changes to other zones by redistributing $m_i - m_i^*$ over other larger zones. To achieve smoothness in this control algorithm, we begin modifying m_i in small amounts when the zone size reaches $2h_{MIN}$. We distribute the excess $m_i - m_i^*$ over zones larger than $2h_{MIN}$ in proportion to their size in excess of $2h_{MIN}$. The precise algorithm is shown in the interface listing.

USE OF MOLAG

The purpose of MOLAG is to form and evaluate the right hand side of the semi-discrete ODE system (4) which approximates the original PDE system (1)-(2) and to define the motion of the grid points so that they will adapt to the solution being computed. MOLAG is structured and used very much like PDEONE [4]. If the grid point moving algorithms were removed, MOLAG would essentially be the PDEONE interface routine. There is one possible point of confusion in the descriptions which follow. Heretofore in our presentation, NPDE has denoted the number of PDEs in our original system (1). Hereafter, NPDE will denote the old NPDE plus 1, because adding the node moving algorithm has given us one extra equation at each node as is reflected in (4).

We must first construct a main program which sets parameters and allocates storage for the ODE integrator to be used. (We have used the LSODE ODE integrator [2] and recommend it). The main program must define the initial conditions for the PDE solution components and also define the initial grid point locations. MOLAG assumes that the solution values and grid point values are ordered and placed into an NPDE by NPTS array U such that

$$U(K,I) = u_{K,I} \quad \text{for} \quad K = 1,\dots,\text{NPDE-1} \quad \text{and} \quad I = 1,\dots,\text{NPTS} \quad ,$$

and

$$U(\text{NPDE},I) = x_I \quad \text{for} \quad I = 1,\dots,\text{NPTS}.$$

The main program must initialize the ODE integrator and provide for the output times and for the printing or plotting of results. We remark that the integrator may have to be trivially modified so as to properly call MOLAG.

The use of MOLAG requires the construction of two additional routines, F and BNDRY, which define the PDE right hand side and the boundary conditions, respectively. In the descriptions which follow, T and X are scalar quantities which represent the current values of the time t and spatial variables x, respectively; U is a vector with entries u_K for K = 1 to NPDE - 1; UX is a vector with entries $(u_K)_x$ for K = 1 to NPDE - 1; and UXX is a vector with entries $(u_K)_{xx}$ for K = 1 to NPDE-1. The values of U, UX and UXX are associated with the time T and point X. Stated briefly, the purposes of the routines F and BNDRY are as follows. For given values of the quantities T, X, U, UX and UXX: the routine F is to compute appropriate values of the vector function f in (1); and BNDRY is to compute appropriate values for the boundary condition functions a_K, b_K and g_K in (2) at the left or right boundary as determined by the input value of X.

Subroutine F   is constructed as follows:

SUBROUTINE F(T, X, U, UX, UXX, UDOT, NPDE)
DIMENSION U(NPDE),UX(NPDE),UXX(NPDE),UDOT(NPDE)

Here the user must define UDOT(K) for K = 1 to NPDE-1.
These are the values of the functions f in (1). The values for
T, X, U, UX, and UXX are provided by the interface routine
MOLAG.

RETURN
END

Subroutine BNDRY is constructed as follows:

SUBROUTINE BNDRY(T, X, U, A, B, G, NPDE)
DIMENSION U(NPDE),A(NPDE),B(NPDE),G(NPDE)

Here the user must define A(K), B(K) and G(K) for K = 1 to NPDE-1 at the
left or right boundary as determined from the incoming value of X. These are the
values of the functions a_K, b_K and g_K in (2). Setting A(K) = B(K) = 0 will
signal MOLAG that no boundary condition is desired for the Kth PDE component
at this particular boundary.

RETURN
END

NUMERICAL EXAMPLE

We will consider a simple test problem which involves two opposite travelling
wave pulses which collide, interact and then separate. The PDE system is as
follows:

$$u_t = - u_x - 100\ u\ v$$
$$v_t = v_x - 100\ u\ v$$

$$\text{for } x \text{ in } [-.5, .5\ ]$$

with boundary conditions

$$u(t, -.5) = v(t,-.5) = u(t,.5) = v(t,.5) = 0\ ,$$

and with initial conditions $u(0,x) = r(x)$ and $v(0,x) = s(x)$ where

$$r(x) = \begin{cases} 0.5\ (\ 1 + \cos(10\ \pi\ x)\ ) & x \text{ in } [-.3,-.1] \\ 0 & \text{otherwise} \end{cases}$$

$$s(x) = \begin{cases} 0.5\ (\ 1 + \cos(10\ \pi\ x)\ ) & x \text{ in } [.1, .3] \\ 0 & \text{otherwise.} \end{cases}$$

The figures show the results obtained by using MOLAG with the mesh function
parameters A = 1, B = 0, C = 0, D = 1, E = 1, and DELTA = h_{MIN} = 0.002,
and also the results obtained from the use of a non-moving grid.

Shown below are all of the user required routines that are required to adaptively
solve this problem using MOLAG and the integrator LSODE. LSODE was modified

slightly so that it would call MOLAG with the proper calling arguments.

```
        PROGRAM WAVE( MOLIN, TAPE2=MOLIN, MOLOUT, TAPE3=MOLOUT )
        COMMON /MESHFN/ A, B, C, D, E, DELTA
        COMMON /PARAMS/ NPDE, NPTS
        DIMENSION IWORK(350), RWORK(2750), U(3,101)
        EXTERNAL MOLAG, JAC
C
C   READ INITIAL GRID AND VALUES
C
        NPDE = 3
        NPTS = 101
        READ(2,1) A, B, C, D, E, DELTA
      1 FORMAT(6E10.3)
        READ(2,2) ( (U(K,I),K=1,NPDE), I=1,NPTS )
      2 FORMAT(3E10.3)
C
C   SET UP LSODE PARAMETERS
C
        NEQ = NPDE * NPTS
        T = 0
        ITOL = 1
        RTOL = .00001
        ATOL = .00001
        ITASK = 1
        ISTATE = 1
        IOPT = 0
        LIW = 350
        LRW = 2750
        MF = 20
        TOUT = 0.05
C
C   CALL ODE INTEGRATOR
C
     10 CALL LSODE( MOLAG, NEQ, U, T, TOUT, ITOL, RTOL, ATOL ,
      *     ITASK, ISTATE, IOPT, RWORK, LRW, IWORK, LIW, JAC, MF )
        IF( ISTATE .NE. 2 ) CALL EXIT
C
C   OUTPUT RESULTS AND LOOP BACK UNTIL DONE
C
        WRITE(3,11) TOUT, ( (U(K,I),K=1,NPDE), I=1,NPTS )
     11 FORMAT(3HT =, E10.3 / (3E20.6) )
        TOUT = TOUT + 0.05
        IF( TOUT .LE. 0.4 ) GO TO 10
        CALL EXIT
        END
        SUBROUTINE F(T,X,U,UX,UXX,UDOT,NPDE)
        DIMENSION U(NPDE),UX(NPDE),UXX(NPDE),UDOT(NPDE)
C
        UDOT(1) = -UX(1) - 100.0 * U(1) * U(2)
        UDOT(2) =  UX(2) - 100.0 * U(1) * U(2)
C
        RETURN
        END

        SUBROUTINE BNDRY(T,X,U,A,B,G,NPDE)
        DIMENSION U(NPDE),A(NPDE),B(NPDE),G(NPDE)
C
```

```
      NPDEM1 = NPDE - 1
      DO 10 K=1,NPDEM1
        A(K) = 1.0
        B(K) = 0.0
        G(K) = 0.0
   10 CONTINUE
      RETURN
      END
```

REFERENCES

[1] Gelinas, R. J., S. K. Doss and K. Miller, The Moving Finite Element
    Method, J. Comp. Phys., 40, No. 1, March 1981.

[2] Hindmarsh, A. C., LSODE and LSODI, Two New Initial Value Ordinary
    Differential Equation Solvers, ACM-Signum Newsletter, 15, No. 4 (1980) 10-11.

[3] Sincovec, R. F. and N. K. Madsen, Software for Nonlinear Partial Differential
    Equations, ACM Trans. Math. Software, 1, No. 3, (1975) 232-260.

[4] Sincovec, R. F. and N. K. Madsen, Algorithm 494, PDEONE, Solutions of Systems
    of Partial Differential Equations, ACM Trans. Math. Software, 1, No. 3,
    (1975) 261-263.

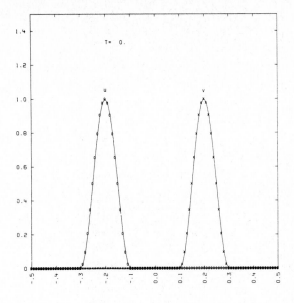

Non-moving grid

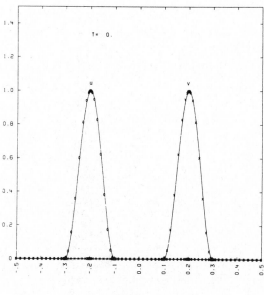

MOLAG

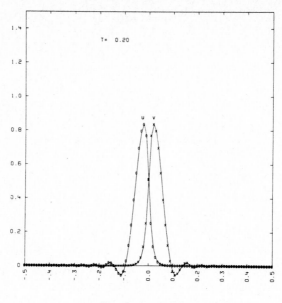

Non-moving grid

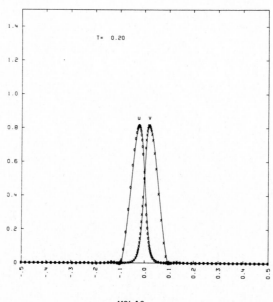

MOLAG

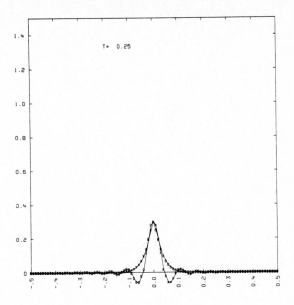

Non-moving grid

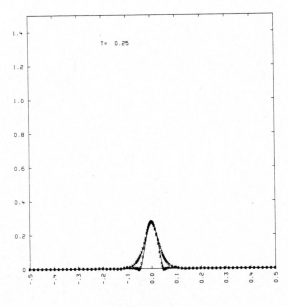

MOLAG

N.K. Madsen

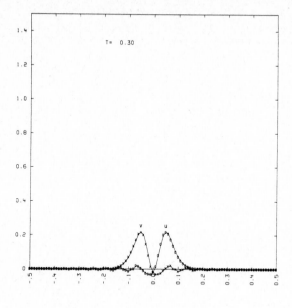

Non-moving grid

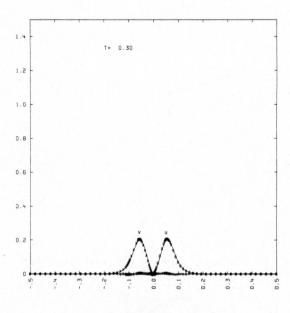

MOLAG

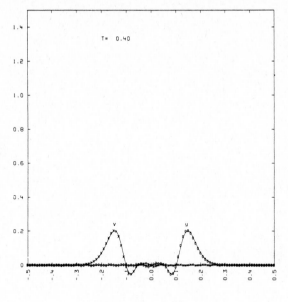

Non-moving grid

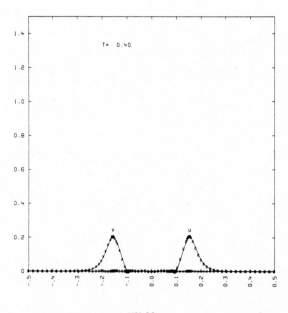

MOLAG

DISCUSSION

Speaker: N. Madsen

Furzeland: We have been experimenting with the method of lines and adaptive meshes and, in general, agree with your conclusions. Have you tried propagating shocks in the form of step functions rather than smooth pulses? We have found the under/over shoot problem to be far more serious in this case unless one forces the mesh-points to follow the characteristic paths as done in the moving finite element method.

Madsen: The moving finite element method is successful for these problems because the grid points are allowed to move very close together. This introduces a tremendous amount of stiffness (caused by the grid point control techniques) into the problem and a stiffly stable solver must be used. We have been motivated to try to use non-stiff methods and have not attempted these step function solutions as yet. With the MOLAG interface and the LSODE stiff solver we now have the capability to solve these problems but have not done so as yet.

Yanenko: For your method stability is a crucial point, especially for singular perturbation problems. If boundary layers arise and you have to refine your mesh then stability restrictions become very strong. Your package cannot solve such problems. van der Houwen has proved that in the case of 2D heat equations the best method based on ODE approach gives rise to the ADI method. This works for two dimensional heat conduction problems. Do you know this work?

Madsen: I disagree. The stability question is not an issue since implicit methods are used in the LSODE package and work well for such problems.

I am not specifically familiar with the work you mentioned of van der Houwen.

Hockney: Is there any objection to introducing more mesh points when needed, or removing them when they get too close? If so what is it?

Madsen: ODE integrators with their error control algorithms and past time history vectors do not cope well with discontinuities that could be introduced by the addition or deletion of points in the grid. In principle one could probably do this if sufficient care is taken to do it smoothly - but we have chosen not to do it. It would also disrupt the matrix data structures if one is using an implicit method.

Hockney: The ratio of h_i to h_{i+1} near the peak of the wave appeared to be about 1 to 4 in some places. Is not this rather large, in view of the fact that one objective of the formulation was to keep such changes small?

Madsen: Whether or not a 4 to 1 ratio of zone sizes is large is a rather relative question. We could have easily made these ratios smaller or larger by a different choice of the mesh function parameters.

Hockney: Do the grid points move with the wave, or does the wave move through the grid points? If the latter then the grid points appear to move rather like the particles of the fluid. The method then begins to look a bit like a particle in cell (PIC) or Lagrangian method. Would you care to comment on the relation between these methods and yours.

Madsen: Depending upon the current solution conditions, both situations can occur. In principle - for the problem results shown, the grid points should move with the fronts following characteristic paths in the (x,t) plane.

However, when the minimum grid point separation algorithm becomes involved as the waves collide and points become close together, the waves pass through the grid points. The PIC and Lagrangian methods are related but not in a precisely clear manner.

Gorenflo: Does your program provide for a proper balancing of space discretization accuracy and time discretization accuracy? In case of a coarse spatial grid you may waste a lot of computer time when using a high-order time discretization.

Madsen: The program does not directly balance the space and time errors. The space error will be determined by the mesh functions used, the minimum grid point separation allowed, and the total number of points allowed in the adaptive grid. I agree that a proper balancing of the space and time errors is desirable.

Grossman: Our experiences with the method of lines applied to a diffusion problem indicated that it is not effective to use the LSODE-code without modifications. These modifications should take into account the special structure of the ODEs obtained from PDEs by semidiscretization. Did you use a modified version of LSODE to take advantage of the specifics of the PDE?

Madsen: The MOLAG interface is totally equivalent to our original PDEONE interface and does not make use of any Jacobian structure other than its bandedness. With the adaptive methods, the Jacobian structure is more complicated and we plan to take advantage of the detailed Jacobian structure when our studies have been sufficient to decide upon the best techniques. LSODE was used in the standard form other than for some slight modification, which were required to properly call MOLAG.

Zlatev: In your time-discretization procedure you use the implicit version of LSODE. This time-integration code is based on backward differentiation formulas. This means that your time-integration code uses a "history" (at time-step k your time-subroutines use the values of the right-hand side vector of the system of ODEs that have been calculated and stored at previous steps, say,k-1, k-2, ..., k-p). When you change your space-grid at step k, you in fact change the system of ODEs by which you attempt to approximate your PDE. The fact that you are solving at steps k-p, k-p+1, ..., k-1, k systems of ODEs defined on different grid-spaces (though of the same dimension) should in some way be taken into account when you use the "history" at step k. How do you take into account this fact?

Madsen: All of the necessary past history is taken care of automatically by the LSODE integrator. The basic equations being solved properly account for the grid notion and the ODE solver does the rest.

Sherman: You suggested that the extension of your method to higher dimension was straightforward. However, in 2-D the problem class you treat includes problems with expanding fronts. Can you comment on the extension of your methods for such problems (which seem to require the introduction of additional grid points not originally present)?

Madsen: One would have to insure that one started with a sufficient number of grid points so as to be able to resolve the solution adequately for the time lengths under consideration. With due care, one could probably develop the capability to add additional points as needed - but when using implicit methods it would be preferable to stay with the same points.

Brandt: The difficulties in higher dimensions seem to me to be very great. Another point is that in most cases it is pointless to make a small mesh spacing when the time step is not adjusted too.

Madsen: Rodrigue and Oliger and Berger have looked at local refinement
methods where different time steps are used on different parts of the grid.
For our adaptive technique, the ODE integrator will undoubtedly cut the
time step when the small mesh spacings occur.

Rice: First, let me note that a student, Steven Pruess, of Carl de Boor
studied "moving finite elements" in the late 1960's for two point boundary
value problems. de Boor then presented a slightly different version of this
theory in one of his papers a few years later. The approach was to choose
the points of the mesh to be nearly optimal from the approximation theoretic
point of view. It is known, that the density function of the optimal point
distribution is the "sigma-norm" of the solution u of the problem. This norm
involves the (k+l)st derivatives if one is using k-th degree polynomials.
This suggests that one should perhaps use higher derivates in the mesh function.
If, for example, the spatial discretization was quadratic polynomials
(ordinary finite differences), then the sigma norm of the third derivative
would be appropriate to use. de Boor and his student both presented ways to
estimate the required derivatives in practice (as they are usually not readily
available).

This viewpoint explains why mesh functions using the first derivative are not
reasonable; such mesh functions would provide good points for methods that
use piecewise constants to approximate the solution. Since no one uses such
a crude method, it is no surprise from this perspective that Miller's original
mesh functions for the moving finite element method has not proved to be useful.

My question is: Have you considered or experimented with mesh functions involving
higher derivatives?

Madsen: As I pointed out in the presentation, one way to determine the grid
motion would be to try to minimize the local truncation errors which would
involve these higher derivatives. The first mesh function of our five is
directed toward this end - but as the direct computation of higher derivatives
is more difficult, we have not done it yet.

Rice: My impression from your presentation is that there is considerable
uncertainity about the proper mesh function to use. The final remarks of the
discussion of your paper quoted an experimental study which was supposed to
have concluded that one particular mesh function was the "best" and suggested
that the issue is resolved. Do you believe the question is resolved or not?

Madsen: The use of the word "best" was intended only as a comparison between
those five mesh functions we implemented. What is ultimately the best mesh
function is definitely still an open question.

Walsh: I want to emphasize a point made earlier. Moving mesh points around
is not what you want to do if you want to achieve a certain accuracy. Until
we can tie together time and space accuracy the choice of weight function
for the space mesh is not very important.

Madsen: The philosophy of moving the mesh points around is aimed at producing
the "best" (in the sense of smallest error) solution with the resources (i.e.
the number of points you can afford to use) you have available. This is a
good approximation philosophy. Rigorous error estimates are going to require
a lot more development of theory. The mesh function is to some extent a
measure of the spatial error.

<u>Schönauer</u>: That is what I tried to say earlier. Also, what you should do is control the global error. We balance time and space errors and also compute the global error.

<u>Madsen</u>: The theory does not exist to compute rigorous global error bounds or estimates for nonlinear problems. Heuristic estimates can be formed and I think that is what you have done. Balancing time and space errors, as stated before, is a good approach.

PDE SOFTWARE: Modules, Interfaces and Systems
B. Engquist and T. Smedsaas (eds.)
Elsevier Science Publishers B.V. (North-Holland)
© IFIP, 1984

APPLICATIONS OF TWODEPEP

Granville Sewell

IMSL, Inc. and
The University of Texas at El Paso
El Paso, Texas   79968

IMSL's TWODEPEP solves a very wide range of time-
dependent, steady-state and eigenvalue PDEs in general two.
dimensional regions, using up to fourth order isoparametric
elements on a triangulation which is generated and graded
automatically. A preprocessor supports a simple problem
description language and a graphical output program post-
processes TWODEPEP output.

While it is impossible to write a general purpose PDE
program which is state-of-the-art in all its application
areas, TWODEPEP has proven to be useful in such diverse
applications as solid elasticity, fluid flow, diffusion,
heat conduction and semiconductor transport problems.

1. INTRODUCTION

The field of partial differential equations is far too vast, and special
features are far too prevalent, for us to harbor any hope that a "general
purpose" package will be developed in the forseeable future which will solve all
PDE applications (even if we, say, restrict ourselves to 2D problems) using
"state of the art" techniques to handle the special features of each problem.

I do not believe, however, that this should discourage us from attempting to
design "general purpose" programs. Several years consulting with IMSL customers
in various areas of mathematical software have convinced the author that computational efficiency is generally far less important to the end user than most
numerical analysts tend to imagine. This is naturally less true when we are
dealing with expensive problems such as PDE applications than, for example,
quadrature problems. However, even when choosing a PDE package, users are
generally more interested in ease of use and flexibility than speed.

IMSL's TWODEPEP represents one attempt to design a general purpose PDE package.
TWODEPEP solves time independent, time dependent and eigenvalue PDE's in general
two dimensional regions. Some of its features might be considered "state of the
art" while others clearly are not—we will discuss examples of each below. We
have operated under the theory that the TWODEPEP subscriber would not want us to
ignore an important area of application simply because TWODEPEP cannot solve
problems in that area as efficiently as could be done with a program tailored to
that application.

2. ALGORITHMIC FEATURES OF TWODEPEP

For time dependent, time independent and eigenvalue problems, TWODEPEP provides
optional quadratic, cubic and quartic isoparametric triangular elements and

automatic mesh refinement and grading, the latter feature being absolutely
indispensible for a general purpose program. Newton's method (with optional
stepsize limitation) is used to solve the resultant nonlinear systems and the
linear equation solution is done by a band elimination method using the reverse
Cuthill-McKee ordering, with a check for zero multipliers (which makes the band
method competitive with envelope solvers). A frontal method is used to organize
the out-of-core storage operations for large problems.

The choice of solution method was motivated primarily by considerations of
generality and storage. Iterative methods, such as successive overrelaxation,
were rejected because they may fail on general, indefinite problems and it is
not known theoretically what class of finite element equation sets can be solved
efficiently using iterative methods (although emperical results [1] suggest a
fairly large class). Sparse direct methods, such as the minimal degree
algorithm, are a more promising alternative, since they are also faster than
band elimination for large problems. ELLPACK comparisons [1] indicate that such
methods (e.g. the Yale Sparse Matrix Package minimal degree codes [6]) are
better than band elimination only for very large problems. In our own comparisons (Figure 8) the minimal degree algorithm appears to be faster even for
moderate size problems, but it requires about 10 times more core storage than
the frontal method used by TWODEPEP, and even for very large problems (200 quartic triangles with 1505 unknowns) the linear equation ordering, factoring and
solution phase represents only about 50% of the total CPU time. In addition, a
band solver is much better suited to parallel computation and works efficiently
in a virtual storage environment.

For time dependent problems, TWODEPEP's primary disadvantage is its lack of
automatic stepsize and error control features available in most method of lines
codes. A variable stepsize is permitted, but it must be specified a priori by
the user. A conversion to a method of lines approach with a Gear's method ODE
driver has long been contemplated, but some major modifications to existing ODE
codes would have to be made to accommodate some of TWODEPEP's current desirable
features, particularly the frontal method, which requires that assembly and elimination calculations be done simultaneously. TWODEPEP is able to achieve a
time discretization error of order $DT{**}4$ using Crank-Nicolson on two separate
runs combined with Richardson extrapolation, which also provides a global error
estimate. Gear's methods cannot provide higher than $DT{**}2$ accuracy with
"A-stability" [2, p. 365], although for nearly all practical applications the
higher order Gear's methods are stable. In addition, it can be argued that if
we assume that the user is able to supply a reasonable a priori stepsize
variation, a method of lines code designed for general stiff ODE's might make
substantially more function and Jacobian evaluations, the latter being very
expensive.

For eigenvalue problems, the inverse power method is used to find the eigenvalue
(and corresponding eigenfunction) closest to a specified number. The inverse
power method is probably competitive with other methods [3, p. 238] for finding
a single eigenvalue of a large sparse matrix, but its main advantage for
TWODEPEP is the fact that, as for time dependent problems, each iteration (step)
involves solving a linear system very much similar to the system solved for a
time independent problem. In fact the time independent, time dependent and
eigenvalue calculations are not done by separate routines within TWODEPEP but
share the same assembly and elimination codes, with only slight variations made
according to which case is being treated.

Of course, for the eigenvalue problem the matrix is not updated after the initial decomposition, and for the time dependent problem updating is done only
when convergence slows.

Two features very important for ease of use are the TWODEPEP preprocessor, which allows the problem description to be input in a simple, readable format, and the TWOPLOT graphical output program, which plots the output from TWODEPEP.

3. PROBLEM DESCRIPTION

The partial differential equations which TWODEPEP can (formally) solve are exhibited below, for a system of two PDE's. (TWODEPEP can solve systems of up to 9 PDEs.) The system is written as a parabolic problem, but TWODEPEP also solves the time independent case where C1=C2=0 and the eigenvalue case where F1 and F2 involve the terms lambda*P1(X,Y)*u and lambda*P2(X,Y)*v. This divergence formulation is appropriate for elasticity, fluid flow, diffusion, heat conduction, and many other applications, as will be seen in Section 4.

$$C1(x,y,u,v,t)\frac{\partial u}{\partial t} = \frac{\partial}{\partial x} \; OXX(x,y,u_x,u_y,v_x,v_y,u,v,t)$$

$$+ \frac{\partial}{\partial y} \; OXY(x,y,u_x,u_y,v_x,v_y,u,v,t)$$

$$+ F1(x,y,u_x,u_y,v_x,v_y,u,v,t)$$

$$C2(x,y,u,v,t)\frac{\partial v}{\partial t} = \frac{\partial}{\partial x} \; OYX(x,y,u_x,u_y,v_x,v_y,u,v,t)$$

$$+ \frac{\partial}{\partial y} \; OYY(x,y,u_x,u_y,v_x,v_y,u,v,t)$$

$$+ F2(x,y,u_x,u_y,v_x,v_y,u,v,t)$$

for (x,y) in the region R
with

$$u = FB1 \;(s,t)$$
$$v = FB2 \;(s,t) \text{ for s on part of the boundary } (\partial R_1)$$

and
$$OXX \cdot n_x + OXY \cdot n_y = GB1(s,u,v,t)$$
$$OYX \cdot n_x + OYY \cdot n_y = GB2(s,u,v,t)$$
$$\text{for s on the other part } (\partial R_2),$$
$$\text{where } (n_x,n_y) \text{ is the unit outward normal}$$

and
$$u = U0(x,y)$$
$$v = V0(x,y) \text{ for } t = T0$$

4. APPLICATIONS AREAS

Some of the more important TWODEPEP applications areas are listed in what follows. TWOPLOT output for several example problems is also given. These examples are described more completely in the TWODEPEP User's Manual.

4a. ELASTICITY

The two dimensional elasticity equations may be written:

$$0 = \partial(\sigma_x)/\partial x + \partial(\sigma_{xy})/\partial y + F1(x,y,u,v)$$

$$0 = \partial(\sigma_{xy})/\partial x + \partial(\sigma_y)/\partial y + F2(x,y,u,v)$$

where (u,v) is the displacement vector, (F1,F2) is the body force vector (force per unit volume) and σ_x, σ_y, σ_{xy} are the tensile stresses in the x and y directions and the shear stress, respectively. The stresses may be fairly general functions of the strains $\varepsilon_x = \partial u/\partial x$, $\varepsilon_y = \partial v/\partial y$, $\varepsilon_{xy} = \partial u/\partial y + \partial v/\partial x$.

For example, the plane stress relations are:

$$\sigma_x = E(\varepsilon_x + \nu\varepsilon_y)/(1-\nu^2)$$

$$\sigma_y = E(\varepsilon_y + \nu\varepsilon_x)/(1-\nu^2)$$

$$\sigma_{xy} = 0.5E(\varepsilon_{xy})/(1+\nu)$$

where E=elastic modulus and ν=Poisson ratio. These material parameters may be variable and even discontinuous to model interfaces between different materials. On part of the boundary the displacements may be given:

$$u = FB1(s)$$

$$v = FB2(s)$$

On the other part the boundary forces may be given:

$$\sigma_x{}^*n_x + \sigma_{xy}{}^*n_y = GB1(s,u,v)$$

$$\sigma_{xy}{}^*n_x + \sigma_y{}^*n_y = GB2(s,u,v)$$

where (GB1,GB2) is the boundary force vector (force per unit area).

Figures 1 and 2 show the TWODEPEP preprocessor input and TWOPLOT output for a simple elasticity problem.

4b. DIFFUSION AND HEAT CONDUCTION

The diffusion equation may be written:

$$\partial u/\partial t = \partial(-J_x)/\partial x + \partial(-J_y)/\partial y + F1(x,y,u,t)$$

where u is the concentration, (J_x,J_y) is the flux vector and F1 is the generation rate for u due to sources and sinks. The flux may be a function of x, y, t, u and the gradient of u.

For the steady-state problem, the left-hand side of the differential equation becomes 0.

On part of the boundary the concentration may be given:

$$u = FB1(s,t)$$

On the other part of the boundary flux may be given:

$$-J_x{}^*n_x - J_y{}^*n_y = GB1(s,u,t)$$

where GB1 is the inward boundary flux of u.

For the isotropic case, the flux is parallel to the gradient of the concentration, and the above equations reduce to:

$$\partial u/\partial t = \partial/\partial x(D(x,y,u,t)\partial u/\partial x) + \partial/\partial y(D(x,y,u,t)\partial u/\partial y) + F1(x,y,u,t)$$

$$u = FB1(s,t)$$

$$D^*\partial u/\partial n = GB1(s,u,t)$$

The diffusion coefficient, D, can be a step function to model interfaces between different materials. To model convection in the presence of a velocity field $\vec{V}$, the flux is $\vec{J} = -D\vec{\nabla}u + u\vec{V}$.

The heat conduction problem is a special case of diffusion but merits special attention:

$$C_p{}^*\rho^*\partial u/\partial t = \partial/\partial x(K\partial u/\partial x) + \partial/\partial y(K\partial u/\partial y) + F1(x,y,u,t)$$

Here u is the temperature, C_p is the heat capacity, ρ is the density, K is the conductivity and F1 is the heat generation rate due to sources and sinks. C_p, ρ and K may be functions of x, y, u and t. On part of the boundary the temperature may be given ($u=FB1(s,t)$) and on part the heat flux may be given ($K\partial u/\partial n=GB1(s,u,t)$). The heat flux, GB1, might be zero at an insulating boundary, or proportional to U_0-u if the surrounding medium is at temperature U_0.

Figures 3 and 4 show the velocity and temperature distributions for a heat conduction/convection example.

4c. SCHRODINGER EQUATION

The Schrodinger equation, which is at the foundation of quantum mechanics, has the form:

$$0 = \partial/\partial x(\partial u/\partial x) + \partial/\partial y(\partial u/\partial y) - kP(x,y)u + k\lambda u$$

where u is the probability amplitude (its square is proportional to the probability density), P(x,y) is the potential energy function, k is a constant and λ is the energy eigenvalue. The boundary condition is usually $u = 0$.

4d. MINIMAL SURFACE PROBLEM

If U(x,y) is the vertical height of a surface above the point (x,y), then the surface which has height FB1(s) above the boundary and which minimizes its surface area satisfies:

$$0 = \partial/\partial x\left[\frac{U_x}{\sqrt{1 + U_x^2 + U_y^2}}\right] + \partial/\partial y\left[\frac{U_y}{\sqrt{1 + U_x^2 + U_y^2}}\right]$$

U = FB1(s) on boundary.

4e. NAVIER-STOKES EQUATIONS

TWODEPEP can solve many fluid mechanics problems. As an example, consider the Navier-Stokes equations for an incompressible viscous fluid. These equations can be written:

$$\rho U_t = \partial(\sigma_x)/\partial x + \partial(\sigma_{xy})/\partial y - \rho(UU_x + VU_y) + f_1$$

$$\rho V_t = \partial(\sigma_{xy})/\partial x + \partial(\sigma_y)/\partial y - \rho(UV_x + VV_y) + f_2$$

where (U,V) is the velocity vector, (f_1,f_2) is the body force vector (force per unit area), ρ is the density and σ_x, σ_y, σ_{xy} are the stresses. The stresses are given by ("penalty method" formulation [4]):

$$\sigma_x = \alpha(U_x + V_y) + 2\mu U_x$$

$$\sigma_y = \alpha(U_x + V_y) + 2\mu V_y$$

$$\sigma_{xy} = \mu(U_y + V_x)$$

where μ is the viscosity coefficient and α is a large "compresibility" parameter. Notice that the pressure has been replaced by $-\alpha(U_x + V_y)$, which forces the continuity equation to be approximately satisfied.

On part of the boundary, the velocity vector (FB1, FB2) may be given and on the other the tractions (GB1, GB2) may be given. For the time dependent problem the initial velocities should be given.

For steady-state problems the left-hand sides are zero, of course. At low Reynolds numbers (low velocities) the terms $UU_x + VU_y$ and $UV_x + VV_y$ may be neglected.

See Figure 5 for the output from a fluid flow problem at low and moderate Reynold's number.

4f. SEMICONDUCTOR PROBLEMS

The semiconductor transport equations may be written as:

$$\frac{\partial}{\partial x}(\varepsilon u_x) + \frac{\partial}{\partial y}(\varepsilon u_y) + q(n_i e^{\frac{w-u}{V_T}} - n_i e^{\frac{u-v}{V_T}} + N) = 0$$

$$\frac{\partial}{\partial x}(-J_{nx}) + \frac{\partial}{\partial y}(-J_{ny}) + qR_n = 0$$

$$\frac{\partial}{\partial x}(-J_{px}) + \frac{\partial}{\partial y}(-J_{py}) - qR_p = 0$$

where $J_n = (J_{nx}, J_{ny})$ is the electron current density and $J_p = (J_{px}, J_{py})$ is the hole current density. The current densities are usually modeled as:

$$J_n = -q\mu_n n_i e^{\frac{u-v}{V_T}} \nabla v$$

$$J_p = -q\mu_p n_i e^{\frac{w-v}{V_T}} \nabla w$$

Here the unknowns represent:

        u – electrostatic potential (volts)
        v – electron quasi-Fermi potential (volts)
        w – hole quasi-Fermi potential (volts)

The electron and hole charge densities may be found from u, v, and w by the for-

mulas $n = n_i e^{\frac{u-v}{V_T}}$, $p = n_i e^{\frac{w-v}{V_T}}$ respectively. The other variables are material or universal constants.

On the boundary, the values of u, v, w or of their normal derivatives are usually known. See Figure 6 for the electron density field calculated by TWODEPEP for a semiconductor example.

4g. SHELL PROBLEMS

A linear thin shell model (Mushtari-Vlassov theory), taken from [5] is outlined here.

It is assumed that the surface of the thin shell (thickness=h) is described by an orthogonal coördinate system,

$$x = x(\alpha, \beta)$$
$$y = y(\alpha, \beta)$$
$$z = z(\alpha, \beta)$$

with $x_\alpha x_\beta + y_\alpha y_\beta + z_\alpha z_\beta = 0$. Let a_0 and b_0 be unit vectors in the directions of $(x_\alpha, y_\alpha, z_\alpha)$ and $(x_\beta, y_\beta, z_\beta)$ respectively and let $n = a_0 \times b_0$ be the unit normal to the shell. Then we call u,v,w the displacements parallel to a_0, b_0, n, respectively, and $A(\alpha,\beta) = \sqrt{x_\alpha^2 + y_\alpha^2 + z_\alpha^2}$, $B(\alpha,\beta) = \sqrt{x_\beta^2 + y_\beta^2 + z_\beta^2}$. The equilibrium equations of the shell consist of two second order equations for u and v and one fourth order equation for w. The fourth order equation can be broken into two second order equations by use of an auxiliary variable p. These four coupled equations for u,v,w,p, written in a form appropriate for TWODEPEP, are:

(1) $\dfrac{\partial}{\partial \alpha}(BN_\alpha) + \dfrac{\partial}{\partial \beta}(AN_{\alpha\beta}) - \dfrac{\partial B}{\partial \alpha} N_\beta + \dfrac{\partial A}{\partial \beta} N_{\alpha\beta} + Y_\alpha AB = 0$

(2) $\dfrac{\partial}{\partial \alpha}(BN_{\alpha\beta}) + \dfrac{\partial}{\partial \beta}(AN_\beta) + \dfrac{\partial B}{\partial \alpha} N_{\alpha\beta} - \dfrac{\partial A}{\partial \beta} N_\alpha + Y_\beta AB = 0$

(3) $\dfrac{\partial}{\partial \alpha}(BQ_\alpha) + \dfrac{\partial}{\partial \beta}(AQ_\beta) + AB\left(\dfrac{N_\alpha}{R_\alpha} + \dfrac{N_\beta}{R_\beta}\right) + Y_n AB = 0$

(4) $\dfrac{\partial}{\partial \alpha}\left(\dfrac{-DB}{A}\dfrac{\partial w}{\partial \alpha}\right) + \dfrac{\partial}{\partial \beta}\left(\dfrac{-DA}{B}\dfrac{\partial w}{\partial \beta}\right) + ABDp = 0$

where

$N_\alpha = \dfrac{Eh}{1-\nu^2}(\varepsilon_\alpha + \nu\varepsilon_\beta), \quad \varepsilon_\alpha = \dfrac{1}{A}\dfrac{\partial u}{\partial \alpha} + \dfrac{v}{AB}\dfrac{\partial A}{\partial \beta} - \dfrac{w}{R_\alpha}$

$N_\beta = \dfrac{Eh}{1-\nu^2}(\nu\varepsilon_\alpha + \varepsilon_\beta), \quad \varepsilon_\beta = \dfrac{1}{B}\dfrac{\partial v}{\partial \beta} + \dfrac{u}{AB}\dfrac{\partial B}{\partial \alpha} - \dfrac{w}{R_\beta}$

$N_{\alpha\beta} = \dfrac{Eh}{2(1+\nu)}\varepsilon_{\alpha\beta}, \quad \varepsilon_{\alpha\beta} = \dfrac{1}{A}\dfrac{\partial v}{\partial \alpha} + \dfrac{1}{B}\dfrac{\partial u}{\partial \beta} - \dfrac{u}{AB}\dfrac{\partial A}{\partial \beta} - \dfrac{v}{AB}\dfrac{\partial B}{\partial \alpha}$

$Q_\alpha = \dfrac{-1}{A} Dp_\alpha + D\dfrac{(1-\nu)}{A^2 B}\left\{\left(\dfrac{\tfrac{A}{\beta}}{B}\right)_\beta + \left(\dfrac{\tfrac{B}{\alpha}}{A}\right)_\alpha\right\}w_\alpha$

$Q_\beta = \dfrac{-1}{B} Dp_\beta + D\dfrac{(1-\nu)}{AB^2}\left\{\left(\dfrac{\tfrac{A}{\beta}}{B}\right)_\beta + \left(\dfrac{\tfrac{B}{\alpha}}{A}\right)_\alpha\right\}w_\beta$

and where Y_α, Y_β, Y_n are the components of the surface force (per unit area) in the directions of a_0, b_0 and n, respectively. $R_\alpha(\alpha,\beta)$, $R_\beta(\alpha,\beta)$ are the radii of curvature in the directions of α and β, being positive when the center of curvature lies in the positive direction of n. E is the elastic modulus and ν is the Poisson ratio, and

$$D = \frac{Eh^3}{12(1-\nu^2)}$$ is the modulus of rigidity, and all are assumed constant. The

above problem is symmetric.

For fixed, clamped boundaries, u,v,w and $\frac{\partial w}{\partial \gamma}$ may be given. Otherwise,

$$GB1 = H \cdot hF_\alpha \qquad H = \sqrt{(An)_\beta^2 + (Bn_\alpha)^2}$$

$$GB2 = H \cdot hF_\beta$$

$$GB3 = H \cdot hF_n \qquad (n_\alpha, n_\beta) = \text{unit outward normal}$$
$$\text{to boundary at } (\alpha,\beta)$$

$$GB4 = -DH \frac{\partial w}{\partial \gamma}$$

where F_α, F_β, F_n are the boundary force (per unit area) components parallel to a_0, b_0 and n, and $\frac{\partial w}{\partial \gamma}$ is the normal derivative of w.

See Figure 7 for the vertical displacement, w, as calculated to TWODEPEP for a half dome with vertical loading.

References

1. "Performance Analysis of 13 Methods to Solve the Galerkin Method Equations," John Rice, Purdue University Computer Science Tech. Report CSD-TR 369, May, 1981.

2. An Introduction to Numerical Analysis, Ken Atkinson, John Wiley & Sons, 1978.

3. An Analysis of the Finite Element Method, Gilbert Strang and George Fix, Prentice-Hall, 1973.

4. "Newtonian and Non-Newtonian Viscous Incompressible Flow...", O. C. Zienkiewicz, R. H. Gallagher and P. Hood, in The Mathematics of Finite Elements and Applications II, Academic Press, 1976, pp. 235-267.

5. Variational Methods in Elasticity and Plasticity, Kyuichiro Washizu, Pergamon Press, 1975, Appendix H.9.8.

6. "The Yale Sparse Matrix Package II: Nonsymmetric Matrices," S.C. Eisenstat, M.C. Gursky, M.H. Schultz and A.H. Sherman, Research Report 114, Dept. of Computer Science, Yale University, 1977.

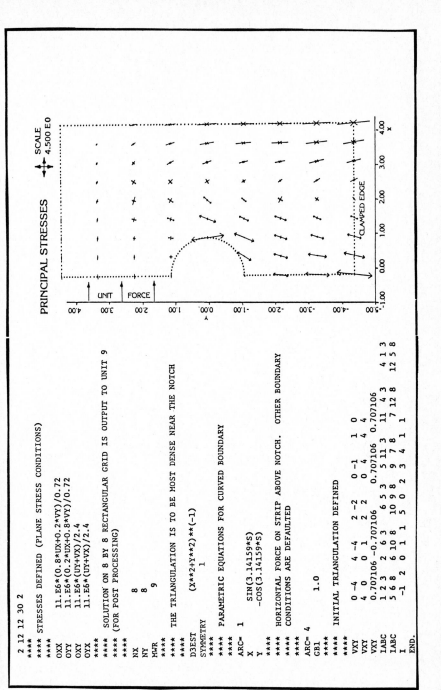

```
2 12 12 30 2
****
**** STRESSES DEFINED (PLANE STRESS CONDITIONS)
****
OXX        11.E6*(0.8*UX+0.2*VY)/0.72
OYY        11.E6*(0.2*UX+0.8*VY)/0.72
OYX        11.E6*(UY+VX)/2.4
OXX        11.E6*(UY+VX)/2.4
****
**** SOLUTION ON 8 BY 8 RECTANGULAR GRID IS OUTPUT TO UNIT 9
**** (FOR POST PROCESSING)
****
NX         8
NY         8
MWR        9
****
**** THE TRIANGULATION IS TO BE MOST DENSE NEAR THE NOTCH
****
D3EST      (X**2+Y**2)**(-1)
SYMMETRY   1
****
**** PARAMETRIC EQUATIONS FOR CURVED BOUNDARY
****
ARC= 1
X          SIN(3.14159*S)
Y          -COS(3.14159*S)
****
**** HORIZONTAL FORCE ON STRIP ABOVE NOTCH. OTHER BOUNDARY
**** CONDITIONS ARE DEFAULTED
****
ARC= 4
GB1        1.0
****
**** INITIAL TRIANGULATION DEFINED
****
VXY        0 -4    4 -4    2 -2    0 -1    1 0
VXY        4  0    0  1    2  2    0  4    4 4
VXY        0.707106 -0.707106  0.707106  0.707106  0.707106
IABC       1 2 3    2 6 3    6 5 3    5 11 3    11 4 3    4 13
IABC       5 6 8    6 10 8   10 9 8    9 7 8     7 12 8    12 5 8
I         -1 2 0    1 1 5    0 2 3    4 1 1
END.
```

FIGURE 1.   INPUT FOR ELASTICITY PROBLEM

PRINCIPAL STRESSES

FIGURE 2.   OUTPUT FOR ELASTICITY PROBLEM

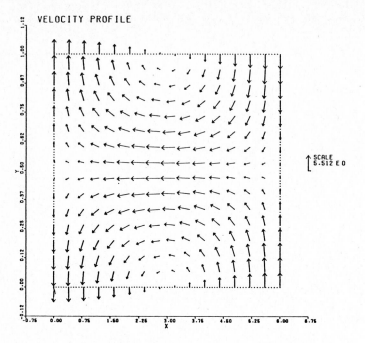

FIGURE 3.   VELOCITY PROFILE FOR SWIRLING LIQUID

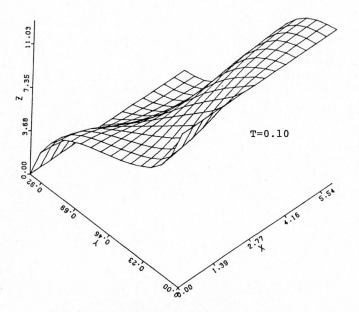

FIGURE 4.   TEMPERATURE DISTRIBUTION AT T = 0.10.
INITIAL DISTRIBUTION WAS 13(1-Y)
(EXAMPLE 5.13 IN USER'S MANUAL)

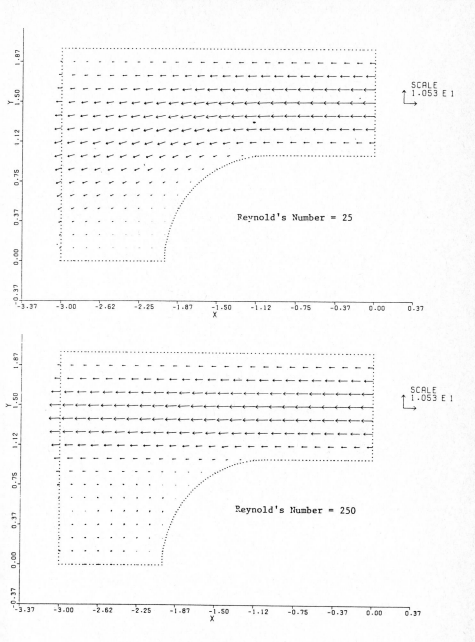

FIGURE 5. VELOCITY DISTRIBUTION AT LOW AND MODERATE
REYNOLD'S NUMBERS FOR FLOW PAST AN OBSTACLE
(EXAMPLE 5.8 IN USER'S MANUAL)

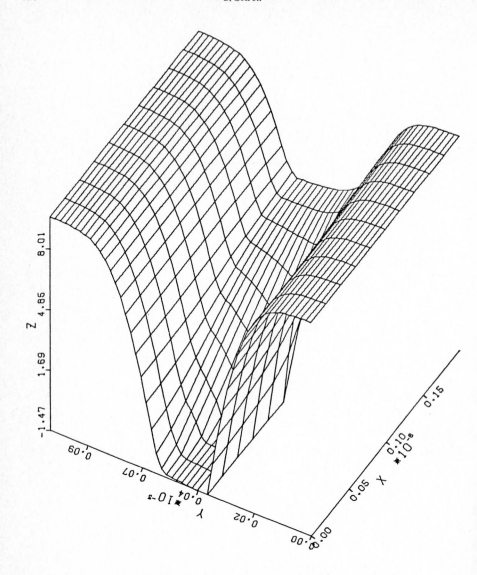

FIGURE 6.   ELECTRON DENSITY IN AN N-SEMICONDUCTOR-METAL STRUCTURE
            (EXAMPLE 5.11 IN USER'S MANUAL)

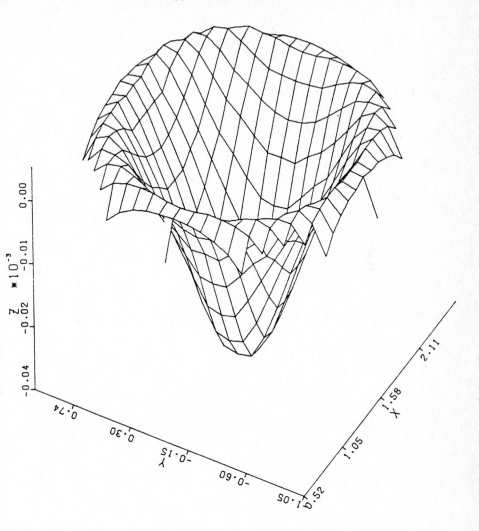

FIGURE 7.   VERTICAL DISPLACEMENT OVER PART OF DOME-SHAPED SHELL
(EXAMPLE 5.13 IN USER'S MANUAL)

G. Sewell

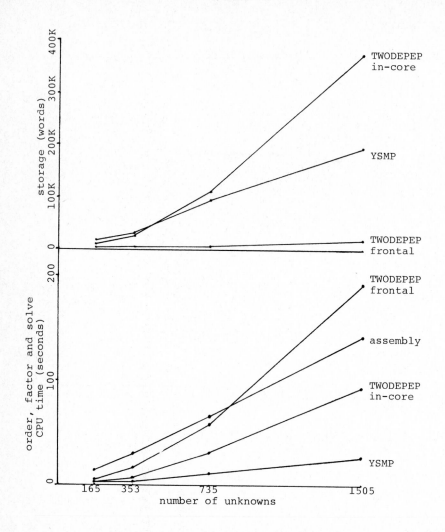

FIGURE 8. STORAGE AND CPU TIME REQUIREMENTS TO SOLVE LINEAR EQUATIONS FOR
SOLUTION OF LAPLACIAN(U) = F ON 1 BY 5 RECTANGLE, USING UNIFORM
QUARTIC ELEMENTS. (YSMP = ODRV, CDRV FROM YALE SPARSE MATRIX PACKAGE
(MINIMAL DEGREE ALGORITHM) USED TO REPLACE TWODEPEP BAND SOLVERS)

DISCUSSION

Speaker: G. Sewell

Schönauer: You mentioned automatic refinement of the mesh. How is that done?

Sewell: The refinement is not adaptive. The user simply provides a function of position which is largest where he wants the triangulation most refined. If the user knows something about the type of the singularities, it is possible for him to choose this function in such a was as to obtain "optimal" order convergence for problems whose solutions have derivative singularities. See article by Sewell in Angewandte Informatik, April 1982, p. 249.

Reid: I can answer your question to the audience about the use of a stiff ODE package. The Harwell package FACSIMILE written principally by Alan Curtis has the use of a sparse matrix solver built into it. It would be a lot of work to replace this by a frontal code, and I suspect that this is true of other stiff ODE solvers.

Miller: What does TWODEPEP do if and when overflow occurs when solving the sample problem for a semiconductor device shown during the talk.

Sewell: We try to avoid overflow during the Newton iteration by supplying our own exponential function which is defined something like $f(x) = \exp(\min(k,BIG))$. Hopefully by the time we are close to the solution, all exponential arguments are less than BIG. See Example 11 in the TWODEPEP User's Manual.

Duff: You showed a slide comparing your frontal solver with a general sparse matrix solver. Since the latter uses indirect addressing it will not vectorize whereas the frontal solver will. Hence, I imagine your timings would look quite different on a machine like the CRAY-1.

Sewell: Yes, I would expect TWODEPEP's frontal method to be more competitive on vector machines.

Yanenko: How can you detect singularities, e.g. transitions from elastic to plastic phase or the branching of flow? Can it be done automatically?

Sewell: The user must have some feeling for it and specify the correct grid. It is really up to the user and cannot be done automatically.

Brandt: An argument is that when the assembly is semidominant, taking more than 50 % of solution time say, it does not make much sense to develop fast solvers. However, if you want to re-solve, re-assembly is cheap (and sometimes not needed at all), and you gain a lot with a fast solver. This is especially important in design situations, optimization problems, etc.

Sewell: If the stiffness matrix is modified in one region, complete re-assembly must be done with TWODEPEP, anyway I believe the more important case is where the right hand side varies with a constant stiffness matrix. In this case direct solvers have an advantage.

Brandt: It is true that upwinding is equivalent to the use of artifical viscosity. But this is not a simple upgrading of the physical viscosity, because the latter is isotropic while the former is anisotropic. Sometimes the anisotropicity is very important; for example, near discontinuities aligned with the grid.

Sewell: As suggested in Section 3.14 of the TWODEPEP User's Manual, an "anisotropic" artificial viscosity term can be added which I believe removes this objection.

Furzeland: Practical users often have problems which involve more coupling between the unknowns than your master equations allow. How difficult would it be to extend TWODEPEP to equations where the left-hand side is, say, of the form

$$\text{NOPDES} \atop \sum_{i=1} c_i(t,x,y,\underline{u},) \frac{\partial u_i}{\partial t}$$

Sewell: For most time dependent applications, the time derivative of only the i-th variable appears in the i-th equation, or at least the equations can be manipulated into this form. I am not convinced that there are enough applications which cannot be put into this form to justify this generalization. I may be wrong.

Sherman: In regard to the use of artificial dispersion in place of upstream differences - upstream differences do introduce an anisotropic dispersion, as suggested by A. Brandt. In certain problems this may be advantageous; but in others, for instance certain petroleum problems, it is essential to avoid this anisotropicity. One way of doing this is the use of carefully chosen, velocity-dependent artificial dispersion. Thus it would seem that there are arguments on both sides in the comparison of the two techniques.

PDE SOFTWARE: Modules, Interfaces and Systems
B. Engquist and T. Smedsaas (eds.)
Elsevier Science Publishers B.V. (North-Holland)
© IFIP, 1984

SOFTWARE DEVELOPMENT BASED ON
MULTIGRID TECHNIQUES

Klaus Stüben, Ulrich Trottenberg, Kristian Witsch

Gesellschaft für Mathematik und Datenverarbeitung
Postfach 1240, D-5205 St.Augustin 1, West-Germany

1. Introduction and summary

One of the most important obstacles to the development of multigrid software -
and therefore also to the spreading of multigrid ideas and techniques - lies in
the fact that multigrid components can often hardly be incorporated into existing
non-multigrid PDE software. In many cases, these difficulties may have 'only'
technical reasons (irregular grid structures, multigrid-incompatible data structures etc.). This is valid, in particular, for certain large packages which are
designed for aerodynamics and structural mechanics. Several multigrid experts,
however, additionally claim that this way of developing multigrid software would
not at all lead to optimum, not even to really efficient multigrid codes, even
if the technical difficulties could be mastered.

One argument that is emphasized in this context is the following: the usual PDE
packages are modularly structured in particular with respect to the *discretization*
and the *solution* procedures, and this modular structure requires a clear distinction between both processes. Exactly this sharp distinction, however, is in con-
traction to a central element of the multigrid philosophy: According to Achi
Brandt, efficient *realization* of multigrid techniques requires, on the contrary,
a connection of both processes which is as strong as possible.

With this paper, we want to contribute to this discussion, namely to the question
as to whether there are natural (technical and/or more fundamental) design
requirements that are inherent to efficient multigrid software *("multigrid-specific
design principles")*.

The authors of this paper are neither software experts nor software "philosophers".
They have merely gained some practical experience in the development of certain
multigrid software. These software activities, which have been pursued in the
GMD multigrid group, have been:

(1) developing highly efficient codes for special scalar second order elliptic
     equations (MG00, MG01, etc.),

(2) writing a black-box (test-)program for the solution of a large class of
     sparse linear systems, based on the algebraic multigrid approach (AMG01),

(3) participating in the further development of the GRIDPACK system: providing
     tools for the convenient definition and handling of grid structures and
     grid routines (such as interpolation, restriction etc.).

Obviously, the three areas mentioned are characterized by very different objectives. In all three cases, the mathematical basis of the corresponding codes is
the multigrid principle. Our experience shows, however, that the influence of the
different objectives on the design of theses codes is much stronger than the fact

that all codes are based on the multigrid principle.

A typical "multigrid design" is realized only in the GRIDPACK system, not, however, in MG00 or AMG01. The GRIDPACK system assumes a certain discretization approach, whereas AMG01 can be employed independently from the underlying discretization. Of course, AMG01 may be incorporated into existing non-multigrid software very easily. So, our considerations make clear once more that the multigrid principle is conceptually very open and allows very different implementations.

In our presentation, we restrict ourselves to describing the MG00 package (Section 2) and the AMG01 code (Section 3). MG00 is regarded as to be representative for several other fast multigrid solvers for special equations like MG01 [24], SIHEM [23], COMFLO [4].As for the GRIDPACK system, we refer to the paper [9] contained in this volume.

For MG00 and AMG01, we will describe in some detail the objectives, design principles, data structures, etc. and give typical performance data.

2. MG00: a highly efficient multigrid solver for standard elliptic equations on rectangular domains

2.1 Range of applications

The MG00 modules treat general "Helmholtz-like" second order partial differential equations

$$- a(x,y)u_{xx} - b(x,y)u_{yy} + c(x,y)u = f(x,y) \qquad (\Omega)$$

or (in the self-adjoint form)

$$- (a(x,y)u_x)_x - (b(x,y)u_y)_y + c(x,y)u = f(x,y) \quad (\Omega)$$

on rectangular domains with general boundary conditions on each side

$$\alpha(x,y)u + \beta(x,y)u_n = g(x,y) \quad (\partial\Omega)$$

(where u_n denotes the normal derivative), i.e. Dirichlet, Neumann or more general boundary conditions with variable α and β. Periodic boundary conditions are allowed, too.

The differential equation is discretized by the standard second order finite difference method with a 5-point star. A uniform grid is used with grid lines matching the boundary of the rectangle Ω. The boundary conditions are treated in the following manner: The trivial case is boundary points with a Dirichlet condition. Otherwise an auxiliary point outside $\overline{\Omega}$ is used. (This allows one to discretize the normal derivative by the usual second order approximation (with meshsize "2h").) The approximation to the differential equation at the boundary point is used to eliminate the value in the auxiliary point. This yields a 4-point star for the boundary point. In the case of the self-adjoint form, however, this would require coefficient values outside $\overline{\Omega}$. Therefore a FEM-Ansatz is used to derive a second order discretization with a 4-point star for boundary points. This is achieved by using linear elements on triangles, approxmiate integration and an ad hoc symmetrization of the resulting difference star.

The modules work as

- iterative solvers ("MGI") with convergence factors of .01 - .1 per iteration

or as

- approximate direct solvers ("FMG") yielding an approximate solution for the given problem with an error of the magnitude of the discretization error.

Furthermore, the FMG version can be combined with additional iterations reducing the error to the exact solution of the discrete problem (but usually not to the solution of the continuous problem).

For all versions, the number of arithmetic operations and the CP-times are proportional to the number of unknowns.

Different MGOO modules are automatically invoked: M1,...,M4 in release 2. The coefficients of the differential equation, its form and the ratio of mesh sizes HX and HY determine the module:

a = b = 1, c const., HX=HY:	M1,
a = b = 1, c variable, HX=HY:	M2,
otherwise, if not self-adjoint form:	M3,
self-adjoint form:	M4.

The module M1 includes, for instance, Fast Poisson Solvers which compare favorably with highly specialized solvers as Buneman's or Total Reduction. The MG solvers allow, however, general boundary conditions with hardly any degradation of efficiency (see Table 2.3).

For all versions the essential restrictions are:

- no explicit first derivatives in the differential equation (to exclude singular perturbation instabilities),

- no mixed second derivative in the differential equation (for technical reasons: a 5-point approximation would not suffice in this case),

- smooth coefficients (For non-smooth coefficients a "Galerkin-type" coarse-grid operator would have to be used, cf. [26]. This approach is not used here in order to reduce the storage requirement.),

- second order discretization only (higher order discretizations or defect corrections are possible, cf. [1], [5] but are not included at the moment),

- no extremely high oscillating right hand sides for the default FMG version,

- the number of intervals should be equal to $p \cdot 2^q$ in each direction with integers p,q and p not too large ($p \leq 7$, say).

Further restrictions, namely

$$\text{positivity of a,b; nonnegativity of c and } \alpha \cdot \beta,$$

guarantee optimal MGOO results but they are not necessary. A warning is given if these conditions do not hold. In this case the user has to control MGI convergence factors (and FMG results). The advanced user can influence the MGOO modules to some extent to get good convergence factors even for (mildly) indefinite cases (see the description of MGOO parameters in 2.2) but highly indefinite problems cannot be treated by MGOO. Other solvers have similar problems in these cases.

2.2 Design principles, MG components

The essential design principles for the MGOO package are:

- optimal efficiency (measured in terms of CP-time and storage requirements) for the class of partial differential equations on rectangles defined above, in particular for treating very fine meshes,

- simplicity of user interface (ELLPACK version, cf. [19] and the extended default version),
- safe performance for standard cases, but more general applicability (with appropriate warnings, cf. the description above).

The simplicity of usage requires, in particular

- dynamic storage management by use of reusable workspace,
- unrestricted portability (achieved by using only the PFORT subset of FORTAN 66),
- error handling and output according to user specifications.

In contrast to other MG programs (e.g. Bank, Sherman [3], Dendy [12], Hemker et al. [15]), MGOO is designed to achieve highest efficiency for the special cases that can be treated. The different modules (M1-M4) are automatically called according to these cases. They use well known MG components within fixed algorithms. These components are chosen using theoretical predictions (based on model problem and local Fourier analysis [26]), and practical tests.

The details of the algorithms are as follows: The module M1 uses nearly the same algorithm as M2 and M3 uses nearly the same algorithm as M4. M1 (compared to M2) and M3 (compared to M4) allow a somewhat faster relaxation and need less storage since simpler difference stars can be used (constant central star element for M1, normalized western and eastern star elements for M3).

The "MG components" implemented are described in detail in [14]. Here we give only a short survey:

relaxation:

> *red-black relaxation* for M1/M2;
> *zebra line-relaxation* for M3/M4, either in rows (M3x/M4x), columns (M3y/M4y) or both alternatingly (M3a/M4a), with the appropriate direction chosen automatically.

MGI interpolation:

> always *bilinear*,

restriction of residuals:

> *half weighting* for M1/M2 (which is the same as half injection)
> *full weighting* for M3/M4 (which is the same as 3-point row or column weighting, depending on the previous relaxation),

solution on the coarsest level:

> *direct solution* using a precomputed LU-decomposition,

cycling:

> *fixed V-cycles* (but see MGOO-parameter IGAMMA),

FMG interpolation:

> *using the differential equation* on a semi-coarsened grid as known from MGR methods (cf. [20]) or from [17], i.e. red-black semi-coarsening in the case of M1/M2 and y-semi-coarsening for M3/M4.

The modules can be influenced to some extent by the follwing MG parameters:

M: 0 - FMG algorithm (default),
        1 - MGI algorithm.

N: 0 - Zero as initial guess for MGI,
        1 - user supplied initial guess.

ITER: Max(ITER,1) MGI cycles are performed in the MGI case. For FMG and ITER>1,
        additional ITER-1 MGI cycles are performed on the finest grid giving a better
        approximation to the discrete solution. For ITER=0 (default), a "cheaper"
        MGI cycle (less relaxation) is used compared to ITER>0. This cycle yields
        slower error reduction but is sufficient for FMG (see Table 2.3).

IGAMMA: 1 - V cycles in MGI and FMG (default),
        2 - W cycles.

NMIN: Minimum number of grid cells of the coarsest level in each direction. (The
        default value is 2.) By using a larger number of grid cells, mildly indef-
        inite problems can be treated.

IDCC: Specifies what to do for the singular case of a pure Neumann problem for
        Poisson's equation.

The additional parameter LPO gives an option for the amount of output (only fatal
error messages, debug modes etc.).

2.3 Data structure

Due to the restriction to boundary value problems on rectangular domains, data
structure in MGOO is not complicated. Relatively few pointers contain all necessary
information.

Since all grid functions are defined on rectangular grids (interior values) or
lines (boundary data), they can be stored as 2D or 1D arrays. 2D array indexing
is used in the innermost subroutines containing most arithmetic operations (relaxation, interpolation etc.). This facilitates extensions and was seen to be (a bit)
superior to 1D indexing for an optimizing compiler. The simple data structure is
essentially influenced by the need of coarser-grid functions due to the use of
different grids. For comparison with AMG01, the storage scheme is described in more
detail:

All non-local data are stored in the real workspace W and the integer workspace NW.
The only exceptions are some COMMON variables and the 2D array UH which contains -
on successful return - the discrete approximation. In this way the solution can
most easily be accessed by the user. The grids are numbered from 1 to M, 1 standing
for the given fine grid and M for the coarsest one. The information is stored in
this order. W contains the following arrays:

  - FH: fine-grid right hand side (2D),
  - BDd: (with d=S, E, W, N for south, east, west, north) fine-grid right hand
           side of non-Dirichlet boundary conditions (1D),
  - UHC: coarse-grid corrections for UH (2D); level 2,..., M,
  - FHC: coarse-grid right hand sides (2D); level 2,..., M,
  - BDdC: right hand side of coarse-grid boundary conditions (1D);
           level 2,...,M,
  - CEDS: center elements of difference stars (OD, 1D or 2D, see below);
           level 1,..., M,
  - AOB: (for a$\neq$const. or b$\neq$const.) western / eastern elements of difference
           stars (2D); level 1,..., M,
  - AM: LU-decomposition of the coarsest-level matrix, internal workspace for
           line relaxation etc.

The dimension of CEDS depends on the boundary value problem. More precisely, it depends on the number of different values of the central elements of the difference stars:

    0D - one variable: for a=b=1, c constant; Dirichlet, Neumann or periodic boundary condition

    1D - grid function on the boundary: for a=b=1, c constant; other boundary conditions,

    2D - grid function on the domain: otherwise.

Index bounds for all arrays are the variables NXPK(L) and NYPK(L), the number of points in x- and y-direction on level L, including boundary points. Starting addresses for all arrays are stored in some COMMON variables and (small) integer arrays contained in NW.

2.4 Performance

The high efficiency of MGOO can be demonstrated either by a theoretical analysis or by practical measurements and comparisons. The user is mostly interested in CP-time and memory requirements. Whereas the latter can easily be determined, CP-time comparisons are to some extent machine- and compiler-dependent (see e.g. [18]). Therefore also floating point operation counts are useful for a comparison.

The MGOO modules have a fixed predetermined cycling structure. Therefore it is easy to compute the number of floating point operations per unknown of the finest grid up to lower order terms. This operation count is independent of the boundary conditions and depends merely on the module (M1,...,M4) which is used. For FMG with V-cycles and ITER=0 - the default version - we get the numbers in Table 2.1.

	Floating point operations/point			words/point
	+/-	*	/	
M 1	18 1/2	6	-	2 2/3
M 2	19	3	4 3/4	4
M 3x	26 1/2	22 1/9	4 2/9	5 1/3
M 3y		25 4/9		
M 3a	30 8/9	29	5 1/9	5 1/9
M 4a	32 5/9	38 7/9	5 1/9	6 2/9

Table 2.1: Floating-point operation and memory count per point of finest grid for MGOO-FMG (default version)

The amount of storage depends on decisions taken in designing MGOO: Less storage would be necessary if the coefficients of the differential equation were re-evaluated but that would yield much larger CP-times. On the other hand, we do not store LU-decompositions of tridiagonal systems in M3 and M4. That would give a somewhat lower operation count but would increase the storage requirements by a larger amount. The compromise chosen seems to be the best one for large scale problems.

The theoretical predictions of Table 2.1 are confirmed by the following practical measurements. First, in Table 2.2 we give a comparison of different solvers for a model problem which can be treated by all of them. It is Poisson's equation on the unit square with Dirichlet boundary conditions, discretized with the usual 5-point star for h=1/N, N=256. The time measurements are made on an IBM 370/158 with the Fortran H-Extended compiler (OPT=2). More details about this comparison are given in [13]. One has to realize that all fast methods except MG require severe restrictions on the form of the differential equation and the boundary conditions.

method	complexity	CP-time	rcf.
Gauss-elimination	N^4	~ 1d (estim.)	
Gauss-Seidel	N^4	~ 1d (estim.)	
SOR	N^3	~ 30 min (estim.)	
ADI	$N^2 \log N$	4 min	
Buneman	$N^2 \log N$	16 sec	[10]
Total Reduction	N^2	10 sec	[22]
FACR(ℓ^*)	$N^2 \log(\log N)$	8 sec	[16]
KRFFT (marching)	$N^2 \log N$	7 sec[+)]	[2]
MGOO	N^2	7.5 sec	

Table 2.2: Comparison of several solvers for a model problem.
+) Note that KRFFT has to be run in double precision. That is no disadvantage as long as the IBM 370/158 is used because it favors double precision computations, but on other computers KRFFT would be slower than Buneman's algorithm.

Further comparisons of MGOO with other ELLPACK solvers will appear in [19]. On the basis of a private communication of J.R.Rice, MGOO is seen to be the fastest solver (among the second order ones). Additionally, we claim that the following statements hold:

- MGOO-FMG programs yield approximate solutions with an accuracy nearly equal to the truncation error,
- CP-times are (nearly) independent of the type of the boundary conditions and depend only on the module,
- memory requirement depends nearly only on the specific module,
- MGOO-MGI has a spectral radius which is between 0.01 and 0.1.

To demonstrate these properties, we here want to present only a few examples. Many more results are contained in [14] and in [28]. We have used the following differential operators on the unit square for the different modules:

$$M1: \quad - \Delta u,$$
$$M2: \quad - \Delta u + (x+y)u,$$
$$M3a: \quad - 100^{x+y-1} u_{xx} - u_{yy} + (x+y)u,$$
$$M4a: \quad -(100^{x+y-1}u_x)_x + ((4+\sin 2\pi x+\sin 2\pi y)/2u_y)_y + (x+y)u.$$

248   K. Stüben et al.

The boundary operators are

D: Dirichtlet boundary conditions,
M: mixed type boundary conditions: Dirichlet conditions on the southern and
eastern boundary, $u+\beta(s)u_n$ prescribed on the northern and western boundary with

$$\beta(s) = \max\{(s-1/2)^2 - 1/8, 0\}/8 \quad (s=x \text{ or } s=y, \text{ respectively}).$$

For FMG, the (continuous) solution was prescribed to be

$$u(x,y) = \sin 10x \, \sin 10y$$

and the right hand sides were chosen accordingly. In Table 2.3, we display:

t: the CP-times ([sec] on the IBM 370/158),
rt: the relative CP-times ([μsec per unknown] on the IBM 370/158),
δ_h: the relative accuracy of the FMG-solution $\tilde{u}_h$:

$$\delta_h := \| \tilde{u}_h - u \|_\infty / \| u_h - u \|_\infty$$

with the continuous solution u and the exact solution u_h of the
discrete problem,
w: the storage requirement ([words per unknown]),
$\tilde{\rho}$:   the empirical spectral radius of MGI (computed by the power method).

		t	rt	δ_h	w	$\tilde{\rho}$
M1	D	7.43	114	0.99	2.71	0.042
	M	7.60	116	0.96	2.74	0.049
M2	D	9.84	151	1.08	4.07	0.042
	M	10.05	153	1.00	4.07	0.049
M3a	D	24.9	380	1.35	4.44	0.068
	M	25.0	381	1.38	4.41	0.073
M4a	D	32.2	498	1.09	5.81	0.069
	M	32.7	499	1.20	5.76	0.074

Table 2.3: Properties of MGOO programs

The results in Table 2.3 fully justify the claims. We finally remark that the
CP-times of 114-500 μsec/unknown for the IBM 370/158 correspond to 18-86 μsec
on an IBM 3083 and approximately 10-45 μsec on a CYBER 170 (the latter are predictions obtained by comparing CP-times for FACR with Tempertons measurments [27].

3. Algebraic multigrid

Algebraic multigrid (AMG) characterizes the attempt to apply multigrid ideas to certain systems of linear equations

$$\sum_{j=1}^{N} L_{ij} u_j = f_i \quad (i=1,\ldots,N) \tag{3.1}$$

which do not need to have a continuous ("geometric") background. AMG has first been developed in [7] and more recently in [8],[6]. Here, we report on the code AMG01 [25] which has been written by the first author in close cooperation with A. Brandt, S. McCormick and J. Ruge. Meanwhile, certain parts of the code have been improved considerably by J. Ruge. As the resulting new code has, however, not yet been tested as systematically as the original one, we here refer only to AMG01.

We want to mention that - from a general point of view - the AMG concept has some similarities to the so-called "method of aggregation and disaggregation" [11]. The crucial differences between both concepts are

- AMG is to yield fully automatic algorithms for solving systems (3.1);
- AMG is to give the typical multigrid efficiency.

We describe the range of application and the basic ideas of AMG in Section 3.1 and 3.2, respectively. Section 3.3 treats the data structure used in AMO1. This description serves as an example of a general storage scheme which may be of interest also for other multigrid codes. In Section 3.4 we give some typical results on the performance of AMG01 and make some comparisons with the performance of geometric multigrid programs. Finally, in Section 3.5 we briefly describe an easy way of obtaining a posteriori error bounds for approximate solutions computed by AMG01.

3.1 Range of application; some general remarks

The algebraic multigrid methods which are considered here are conceived for the solution of certain (sparse) linear systems (3.1). So far, there is no concept of how to solve *arbitrary* systems of this kind by using multigrid principles. Extensive experience, however, has been gained in the application of AMG under the following assumptions:

$$L \text{ symmetric and positive definite, } L_{ij} \leqslant 0 \ (i \neq j), \ \sum_{j=1}^{N} L_{ij} \geqslant 0 \ (i=1,\ldots,N). \tag{3.2}$$

For this class of problems, AMG01 demonstrates extraordinary robustness (cf. Section 3.4) and multigrid-typical efficiency. In order to make AMG01 work efficiently, the assumptions (3.2) do *not* have to be satisfied strictly.

The above assumptions are known to be satisfied for many typical elliptic difference equations. From the application of usual "geometric" multigrid to such difference equations, it is known that - roughly speaking - pointwise Gauss-Seidel relaxation has good smoothing properties "in the direction of strong connections". In a general matrix of type (3.2), the strength of connections between unknowns is reflected by the size of the corresponding matrix coefficients. This fact is exploited in AMG, the main idea of which is as follows.

By applying a suitable Gauss-Seidel-type relaxation method to a system (3.1) with (3.2), error smoothing is obtained in the sense that was roughly described above. After smoothing, a reduced system of equations is constructed which plays the same role as the coarse-grid-correction equations in usual multigrid methods. The essential feature of this construction - and the construction of all other multigrid components - is that it is performed fully automatically using solely the algebraic information contained in the matrix L. In particular, the size of the matrix coefficients is taken into account in order to ensure that the reduced

system is suitable for correcting approximate solutions of the original system
(3.1).

This very rough description of the AMG idea already indicates that there are essential differences in the design of highly efficient multigrid solvers for special
problems like MG00 and the design of AMG solvers: In writing MG00, we took full
advantage of the geometrical background of the class of problems at hand. For
example, we assumed

- a regular rectangular finest grid;
- a fixed coarsening strategy (by doubling the mesh sizes);
- a fixed type of difference stencils (with at most 5 points), interpolation
  operators (linear interpolation) and restriction operators (half injection or
  full weighting).

In particular, the intergrid transfer operators used in MG00 (MGI-mode, see
Section 2.1) are oriented only to the coarsening process and do not involve the
difference equations. For the class of problems which are handled by MG00, these
special choices are known to be very good ones. Therefore it is reasonable
to incorporate them into the design considerations. Accordingly, the program
structure becomes relatively simple and the speed of performance becomes extraord-
inarily fast. As a consequence, however, the storage scheme used in MG00 is fixed
and rather inflexible: essential changes in the above multigrid components are
hardly possible without re-writing a good deal of the code. For example, the use
of different coarsening techniques (like red-black coarsening) or the use of
different coarse-grid operators (like Galerkin-type operators) would require such
changes.

For the treatment of more general cases, it is desirable to have a storage scheme
which is more flexible. In particular, no assumptions should be made on special
geometric situations, on the coarsening strategy, and on the form of the coarse-
grid operators used. In the context of AMG, one does not even know the coarser
"grids", the "coarse-grid" operators and the "intergrid" transfer operators in
advance. On the other hand, introducing more general (and more complicated)
structures will - clearly - lead to a loss of efficiency, either in terms of
storage or computational work or both.

3.2 Ideas of AMG

3.2.1 Grid terminology

As in usual multigrid methods, (3.1) is regarded as a system of fine-level equations
within a hierarchy of systems of coarser-level (residual) equations:

$$\sum_{j=1}^{N_k} L_{ij}^{(k)} u_j^{(k)} = f_i^{(k)} \qquad (i=1,\ldots,N_k). \qquad (3.3)$$

Here, (3.3) represents equations on increasingly coarser levels k (k=1,...,M),
with k = 1 being the original equation (3.1). We have $N_1=N$, $N_k < N_{k-1}$ (k=2,...,M).
The recursive construction of the systems (3.3) for k=2,...,M will be done such
that each of the coarse-level variables $u_i^{(k)}$ represents a certain variable $u_j^{(k-1)}$
on the next finer level. More precisely, $U_i^{(k)}$ is assumed to approximate the *error*
$u_j^{(k-1)} - U_j^{(k-1)}$ where $U^{(k)}$ and $U^{(k-1)}$ denote the exact solutions of the systems
of equations on level k and level k-1, respectively; $u^{(k-1)}$ denotes the previous
approximation on level k-1. Thus, the set of unknowns on each level k (k < M) can
be split into two subsets: a set of unknowns which are also represented on the next
coarser level k+1 (*C-variables* of level k), and a set of unknowns which are not
represented on level k+1 (*F-variables* of level k).

In this sense, we may still use the term "grid" if we interpret grids as sets of unknowns. For technical reasons, however, it is more convenient to think in terms of some ficticious grids and grid points which are associated with the unknowns. This will be done in the following. For this we renumber all the coarser-level unknowns (and correspondingly all related quantities) recursively for k=2,...,M: redefine the index of each k-level variable to be just the index of the corresponding C-variable on level k-1 which it represents. As a consequence, we may re-write (3.3) in the following form:

$$\sum_{j \in \Omega^k} L_{ij}^{(k)} u_j^{(k)} = f_i^{(k)} \qquad (i \in \Omega^k) \tag{3.4}$$

with $\Omega^1 := \{1,...,N\}$ and $\Omega^{k+1} \subset \Omega^k$ defined by

$$\Omega^{k+1} := \{i \in \Omega^k : u_i^k \text{ is C-variable}\}, \quad (k = 1,...,M-1).$$

Formally, we now interprete $u^{(k)}$ and $f^{(k)}$ as grid functions on the "grid" Ω^k with "grid points" $i \in \Omega^k$ and we interprete (3.4) as an operator equation on the space $\mathbb{G}(\Omega^k)$ of grid functions on Ω^k:

$$L^{(k)} u^{(k)} = f^{(k)} \text{ with } L^{(k)} : \mathbb{G}(\Omega^k) \to \mathbb{G}(\Omega^k).$$

More generally, we may think in terms of directed graphs instead of grids: Connections between grid points of Ω^k are given by the coefficients $L_{ij}^{(k)}$. In the simplest case, we define a point $i \in \Omega^k$ to be *connected* to a point $j \in \Omega^k$ if $L_{ij}^{(k)} \neq 0$.

In analogy to the definition of C- and F-variables, we introduce the notation of C- and F-points:

$$C^k := \Omega^k \cap \Omega^{k+1} : \qquad \text{set of } C\text{-points (of grid } \Omega^k),$$
$$F^k := \Omega^k \setminus \Omega^{k+1} : \qquad \text{set of } F\text{-points (of grid } \Omega^k).$$

Although C^k and Ω^{k+1} contain the same points, it is reasonable to distinguisch between these sets: Connections of points in C^k are always understood with respect to $L_{ij}^{(k)}$ while connections of points in Ω^{k+1} are understood with respect to $L_{ij}^{(k+1)}$.

3.2.2 AMG components

In the following we want to describe how AMG01 recursively constructs the different multigrid components, namely Ω^k, $L^{(k)}$ and the intergrid transfer operators I_{k-1}^k, I_k^{k-1} (k = 2,...,M). Using these components and a reasonable relaxation process for smoothing, a standard multigrid cycle can be defined as, e.g., described in [26]. As we are primarily interested in design questions here, we are not going to formally and fully quantify the respective components. Instead, we mainly describe which kind of quantities occur and hence have to be taken into account in making a decision about a reasonable storage scheme. As for more details about the specific algorithm used in AMG01, we refer to [25].

Let us assume that all multigrid components are known up to a level $k \geq 1$ so far. Then the (k+1)-level quantities are constructed as sketched in the following:

(1) <u>Construction of next coarser grid $\Omega^{k+1} \subset \Omega^k$</u>

The main goal is to contruct Ω^{k+1} in such a way that *Gauss-Seidel point-relaxation* on level k can be expected to have good smoothing properties with respect to Ω^{k+1}. As already mentioned earlier, the process of constructing Ω^{k+1} is guided by the fact that point-relaxation smooths "in the direction of strong connections". Therefore we have to distinguish between *weak connections* (small $|L_{ij}^{(k)}|$) and *strong connections* (large $|L_{ij}^{(k)}|$). Roughly speaking, we have to construct subsets $F^k \subset \Omega^k$ and $C^k \subset \Omega^k$ such that, for all $i \epsilon F^k$, those $j \epsilon \Omega^k$ to which i is most strongly connected, are contained in C^k. Clearly, there is much freedom in the concrete construction of these sets. As for the special algorithm used in AMG01, see [25]. Once C^k and F^k are constructed, Ω^{k+1} is defined to be just C^k.

(2) <u>Smoothing process on Ω^k</u>

As already mentioned above, we use Gauss-Seidel point-relaxation for smoothing. Usually, we first apply a partial Gauss-Seidel step to C-point equations only (in any order); afterwards we perform another partial step on the F-point equations *(C/F-relaxation)*. This corresponds to red-black relaxation in geometric multigrid. Usually, we apply one full C/F-relaxation step before and another one after the coarse-grid correction.

(3) <u>Interpolation operator $I_{k+1}^k : \mathbb{G}(\Omega^{k+1}) \rightarrow \mathbb{G}(\Omega^k)$</u>

Given a current approximation $u^{(k)}$ of the k-level equations, corrections from the coarser grid at points $i \epsilon C^k$ will be performed by simply using the corresponding coarse-grid values. On the other hand, corrections at points $i \epsilon F^k$ will require interpolation from "neighboring" coarse-grid points. In general, given any coarse-grid function $v^{(k+1)}$, the interpolated function $v^{(k)} := I_{k+1}^k v^{(k+1)}$ will be of the following form

$$v_i^{(k)} := \begin{cases} v_i^{(k+1)} & (\text{if } i \epsilon C^k) \\ \sum_{j \epsilon C^k} w_{ij}^{(k)} v_j^{(k+1)} & (\text{if } i \epsilon F^k) \end{cases} \tag{3.5}$$

Clearly, interpolation should be "local", i.e., for fixed $i \epsilon F^k$ only few of the weights $w_{ij}^{(k)}$ should be different from zero. In AMG01, the $w_{ij}^{(k)}$ are chosen to be proportional to $L_{ij}^{(k)}$ if this quantity is large, otherwise they are set to zero (cf. [25]).

(4) <u>Restriction operator $I_k^{k+1} : \mathbb{G}(\Omega^k) \rightarrow \mathbb{G}(\Omega^{k+1})$</u>

The operator I_k^{k+1} is chosen to be just the transpose of I_{k+1}^k. For positive definite problems, this is quite a natural choice (see the following paragraph). Explicitly, this means that, for any $v^{(k)} \epsilon \mathbb{G}(\Omega^k)$ (k < M), $v^{(k+1)} := I_k^{k+1} v^{(k)}$ is defined by

$$v_j^{(k+1)} := v_j^{(k)} + \sum_{i \epsilon F^k} w_{ij}^{(k)} v_i^{(k)} \quad (j \epsilon \Omega^{k+1}) \qquad (3.6)$$

with the same weights as in (3.5).

(5) Coarse-grid operator $L^{(k+1)} : \mathbb{G}(\Omega^{k+1}) \to \mathbb{G}(\Omega^{k+1})$

As for the coarse-grid operator, we define

$$L^{(k+1)} := I_k^{k+1} L^{(k)} I_{k+1}^k. \qquad (3.7)$$

This type of operator is used quite often in multigrid methods ("Galerkin-type operator"). For positive definite problems, the use of this operator - together with the restriction operator defined in (4) - has the advantage that corresponding multigrid coarse-grid-correction steps satisfy a discrete variational principle. Explicitly, the coefficients of $L_{nm}^{(k+1)}$ ($n, m \epsilon \Omega^{k+1}$) are given by

$$L_{nm}^{(k+1)} = L_{nm}^{(k)} + \sum_{i \epsilon F^k} (w_{in}^{(k)} L_{im}^{(k)} + w_{im}^{(k)} L_{ni}^{(k)}) + \sum_{i,j \epsilon F^k} w_{in}^{(k)} L_{ij}^{(k)} w_{jm}^{(k)}. \qquad (3.8)$$

3.3 Data structure

In a preparation phase, all multigrid components are computed, assembled and stored for later use, in particular, the coefficients $L_{ij}^{(k)}$ and the weights $w_{ij}^{(k)}$ of the interpolation. In this section we describe the storage scheme used in AMG01. Its basis is the well known sparse matrix storage scheme which is used, for instance, in the Yale sparse matrix package. This scheme is used not only to store the original matrix L, but also all the coarser-level equations. A similar scheme is also used to store the other quantities.

(1) Storage scheme for the original matrix

Only the non-vanishing entries of L are stored in a one dimensional array A, row by row. In order to identify the components of A with the matrix of L, we use two pointer vectors IA and JA:

- IA is of length N+1. For any I ($1 \leqslant I \leqslant N$), IA(I) points to the index position in A where the I-th row of L begins. IA(N+1) points to the index position just following the last entry of A. Thus the elements of the I-th row of L are stored at

$$A(J) \text{ with } IA(I) \leqslant J \leqslant IA(I+1)-1.$$

- JA is of the same length as A. For each J, JA(J) contains the column index of A(J) with respect to L. This means that

$$A(J) = L_{I,JA(J)} \text{ if } IA(I) \leqslant J \leqslant IA(I+1)-1.$$

Using this pointer JA, the elements of a fixed row of L can be stored in A in any order. We make, however, the convention that the diagonal element of each row is the first element to be stored (which is very convenient for relaxation) meaning that JA(IA(I)) = I for each I.

The unknowns u_i and the right hand sides f_i are stored in two vectors U and F, respectively, in consecutive order.

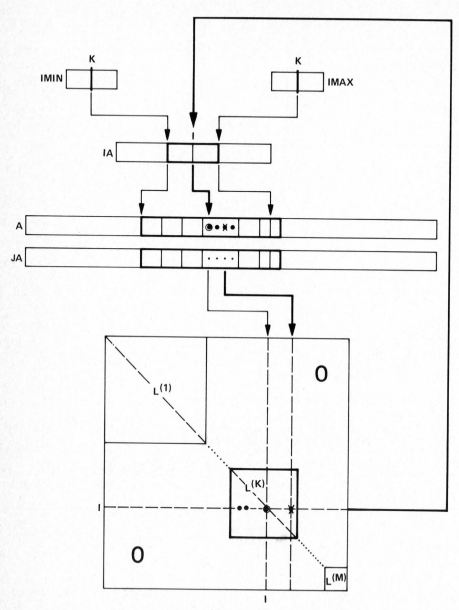

Figure 3.1: Use of pointers IMIN,IMAX,IA and JA to store the (non-vanishing) elements $L_{ij}^{(K)}$.

(2) Storage scheme for the multigrid hierarchy of systems of equations

The sequence of systems (3.4) is stored by extending the vectors A, U, F and the pointer vectors IA, JA in a straightforward manner and using the same technique as described above (cf. Figure 3.1). More specifically, U and F now contain all unknowns and right hand sides stored in consecutive order, grid after grid. Two small pointer vectors IMIN and IMAX are used to distinguish the different levels:

- IMIN, IMAX are both of length M. For any grid number K ($1 \leqslant K \leqslant M$), IMIN(K) and IMAX(K) point to the index positions of the first and last variable, respectively, belonging to that particular grid:

$$IMIN(K) := 1 + \sum_{i=1}^{K-1} N_i \ , \qquad IMAX(K) := \sum_{i=1}^{K} N_i \ .$$

The extended array A contains all (non-zero) coefficients of all systems (3.4). The extended pointer vector JA is of the same length as A, and IA is of length 1 + IMAX(M). These pointers have an analogous meaning as before. In particular, the K-th system of equations (3.4) can be written as

$$\left. \begin{array}{l} \sum_{J1 \leqslant J \leqslant J2} A(J) \ U(JA(J)) = F(I) \\ \\ J1 := IA(I) \ , \ J2 := IA(I+1)-1 \end{array} \right\} \quad IMIN(K) \leqslant I \leqslant IMAX(K).$$

(3) Intergrid transfer

First we use two pointer vectors ICG and IFG which connect unknowns on consecutive levels (we note that this way of connecting grids has already been used by J. Ruge in a previous version of AMG01):

- ICG is of the same length as U. If I is the number of any point on any of the grids Ω^K, K < M (i.e. IMIN(K) $\leqslant$ I $\leqslant$ IMAX(K), then ICG(I) is positive if I is a C-point and ICG(I) points to the corresponding point on the next coarser grid. In particular, ICG(I) is a number between IMIN(K+1) and IMAX(K+1), and the unknown U(I) is represented on the next coarser grid just by U(ICG(I)). If, on the other hand, I is an F-point, ICG(I) contains a non-positive value. (In this case, ICG(I) contains some information concerning interpolation, see below.)

- IFG is of the same length as U. For any coarser-grid point I, IFG(I) just points to the corresponding point on the next finer grid. In particular, U(I) represents the finer-grid variable U(IFG(I)).

Finally, all nonzero weights $w_{ij}^{(k)}$ ($i \varepsilon F^k$, $j \varepsilon C^k$; k=1,...,M-1) are stored in a one-dimensional array W, grid after grid. Weights which contribute to the same F-point I are stored in consecutive locations of W. Thus, the array W consists of a sequence of subarrays *(blocks)* each of which contains just all those weights which contribute to a fixed F-point (the *corresponding* F-point). We use a pointer vector IWF to build the link between these blocks and the corresponding F-points. Furthermore, we need pointer vectors IMINW, IMAXW, IW and JW which have an analogous meaning as the corresponding vectors IMIN, IMAX, IA and JA, respectively, from above:

- IWF is a pointer vector the length of which is given by the total number of blocks contained in W (which is some number less than but close to N). For the IB-th block, IWF(IB) points to the corresponding F-point.

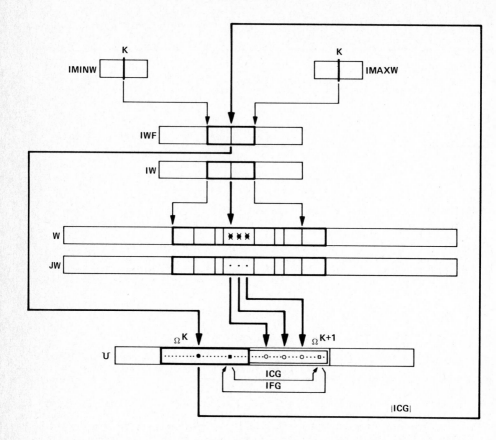

Figure 3.2: Use of pointers IMINW, IMAXW, IWF, IW, JW and ICG, IFG to store the
weights of interpolation from Ω^{K+1} to Ω^K and to connect the points
on Ω^{K+1} and Ω^K, respectively. Notation: • denotes the index of an
F-point of Ω^K which contributes in interpolation from the coarser-grid
points o with weight ✻ . ■ denotes a C-point of grid Ω^K which is
represented by the coarser-grid point □.

- In addition to what has been said in (2), the pointer ICG gives the reverse
  information of IWF: For each F-point IF, ICG(IF) is non-positive. If there
  is at least one coarser-grid point contributing to IF in interpolation,
  ICG(IF) is negative and its absolute value points to the number of the block
  in W containing the corresponding weights. In the exceptional case that no
  coarser-grid variable contributes to IF in interpolation, ICG(IF) is zero.

- IMINW and IMAXW are of length M-1. For any grid K < M, IMINW(K) and
  IMAXW(K) yield the first and last block number, respectively, containing
  weights which are needed in interpolating from grid K+1 to K.

- The length of IW is given by 1 + the number of blocks contained in W.
  For any IB, IW(IB) points to the index position in W where the IB-th block
  begins. The last entry of IW points to the index position just following the
  last entry of W.
- JW is of the same length as W. For any J, JW(J) points to the coarse-grid
  point the value of which has to be multiplied by W(J) in interpolation.

Using the above pointers, formula (3.5) for interpolation can be written in the
following way

$$V(I) \; := \; \begin{cases} V(ICG(I)) & (\text{if} \quad ICG(I) > 0) \\ 0 & (\text{if} \quad ICG(I) = 0) \\ \sum_{J1 \leqslant J \leqslant J2} W(J) \; V(JW(J)) & (\text{if} \quad ICG(I) < 0) \end{cases}$$

with J1 = IW(IB), J2 = IW(IB+1)-1 and IB = -ICG(I). I is the number of any grid
point on any of the grids K < M. Using this formula for interpolation in the
program however, is not efficient: at least two IF-statements are needed per point.
On the other hand, IF-statements can be avoided by looping over the blocks of W
and using the pointer vector IWF. This is demonstrated in the appendix where the
essential parts of a FORTRAN program are outlined (see, in particular, the SUB-
ROUTINE INTAD(K)). For an illustration of the above pointers, see Figure 3.2.

3.4 Numerical results

In this section we present some typical results obtained by AMG01. The main goal
here is to demonstrate the extraordinary robustness of the code compared to the
usual geometric multigrid methods. Therefore all test examples are discretized
elliptic partial differential equations. More examples, in particular certain artificial random systems of equations, are discussed in [25].

The particular problems tested are shown in the table below. All of them are defined
on the unit square using a square mesh of mesh size h=1/64 and Dirichlet boundary conditions (except for examples 11 and 12). These examples exhibit certain
different characteristics. In particular:

    examples 1-3:   different approximations to the Laplace operator;
    examples 4:   anisotropic operator;
    examples 5:   operator involving cross-derivative terms;
    examples 6:   singular operator;
    examples 7:   variable coefficients varying strongly in direction and size;
    examples 8:   like example 7; in addition highly oscillating;
    examples 9-12: piecewise constant, strongly discontinuous coefficient d .
                    The concrete coefficients d used are defined in the table.

Examples 4, 6-8 are discretized using the standard 5-point formula. Example 5 is
discretized by a 7-point stencil. The examples 9-12 use the same discretization as
in [25].

In writing geometric multigrid programs (using a fixed strategy of grid coarsening)
one has to take care of different situations like those arising in the above problems by choosing carefully the corresponding multigrid components: the interpolation operator, the coarse-grid operator and, in particular, the smoothing operator
(cf.[26]). On the other hand, the convergence factors (per iteration step of AMG01)
ρ given in the table show that the convergence behavior of AMG01 is essentially
the same for all the different situations. This is quite remarkable as AMG01

No.	problem	ρ	No.	problem	ε	ρ
1	$\dfrac{1}{h^2}\begin{bmatrix} & -1 & \\ -1 & 4 & -1 \\ & -1 & \end{bmatrix}$	0.095	4	$-\varepsilon u_{xx}-u_{yy}$	1.0 0.5 0.1 0.01	0.095 0.095 0.095 0.067
2	$\dfrac{1}{2h^2}\begin{bmatrix} -1 & & -1 \\ & 4 & \\ -1 & & -1 \end{bmatrix}$	0.145	5	$-\Delta u+\varepsilon u_{xy}$	0.5 1.5 1.7 1.95 2.0	0.120 0.120 0.099 0.068 0.0
3	$\dfrac{1}{h^2}\begin{bmatrix} -1 & -4 & -1 \\ -4 & 20 & -4 \\ -1 & -4 & -1 \end{bmatrix}$	0.115				

No.	$-(d_1 u_x)_x-(d_2 u_y)_y$	ρ	No.	$-(d_1 u_x)_x-(d_2 u_y)_y$	ε	ρ
6	$d_1=d_2=x^2+y^2$	0.100	8	$d_1=e^{\varepsilon \sin 60x \,\sin 60y}$ $d_2=1$	1 3 6	0.090 0.120 0.140
7	$d_1=10^{3(x-y)^2}$ $d_2=1+10^3\sin(\pi xy)$	0.130				

No.	$-\Delta(d\nabla u)$	ρ	No.	$-\Delta(d\nabla u)$	ε	ρ
9		0.140	11		1 10 100 1000 10000	0.154 0.139 0.147 0.147 0.143
10		0.110	12		1 10 100 1000 10000	0.135 0.130 0.130 0.120 0.115

Table 3.1: Comparison of convergence factors ρ of AMG01 (per iteration step) for several discretized elliptic problems.

uses only Gauss-Seidel point-relaxation for smoothing. As already explained earlier, the main reason for this robust behavior is the adaptive way in which AMG01 automatically constructs all necessary multigrid components: Strong dependencies in any direction are detected and properly handled.

3.5 An a posteriori error estimation

So far, there is no rigorous quantitative result proving the fast convergence of the AMG algorithm which has been used in AMG01. The theoretical approach to AMG in [6] gives some impression of how to treat the AMG concept principally. In particular, the smoothing can be understood rather well. The theorems obtained there are, however, not yet tailored to the algorithms used in practice.

In this situation, it is of particular significance that rigorous realistic error bounds for the obtained approximations can be provided without large additional numerical effort. A subroutine can be added to the AMG01 program which computes such error bounds automatically. The technique used is based on Schröder's inverse-positivity concept [21]. Here, we want to describe (one version of) this technique only principally. Technical details and numerical results will be given elsewhere.

We again consider the class of matrices which is given by the assumptions (3.2) in Section 3.1. These assumptions imply L to be an M-matrix. In particular, M is inverse-positive, so that any equation

$$Lz = r \quad \text{with strict positive} \quad r > 0^{*})$$

has a unique strict positive solution

$$z > 0.$$

In principle, any such z can be used for error estimation purposes: If $\tilde{u}$ is an approximation to the solution u^* of the equation $Lu = f$, the error estimate

$$|\tilde{u} - u^*| \leqslant \alpha\, z$$

holds with an α which satisfies the residual inequality

$$|d[\tilde{u}]| \leqslant \alpha\, Lz$$

[21]. Algorithmically, the construction of z and the error estimation can be carried out as follows:

Set $z^{(0)} = e$ $(e^T := (1,1,\ldots,1))$ and perform one AMG iteration step for the equation

$$Lz = e \tag{3.9}$$

yielding $z^{(1)}$. Compute $Lz^{(1)}$ and check whether

$$Lz^{(1)} > 0. \tag{3.10}$$

---

*) For $v \in \mathbb{R}^N$ the notation $v > 0$, $v \geqslant 0$, $|v|$ are to be understood componentwise:

$$v_i > 0 \ (i=1,..,N); \quad v_i \geqslant 0 \ (i=1,..,N); \quad |v| = (|v_i|).$$

If satisfied, compute

$$\alpha := \max_{1 \leqslant i \leqslant N} \frac{|(d[\tilde{u}])_i|}{(Lz^{(1)})_i} .$$

With these quantities, the inequality

$$|\tilde{u} - u^*| \leqslant \alpha \, z^{(1)}$$

is valid.

The numerical work to be carried out for the above estimation mainly is: one AMG iteration step, the computation of the residual $d[\tilde{u}]$ and the computation of $Lz^{(1)}$. If the condition (3.10) is not satisfied for $z^{(1)}$, another AMG iteration step should be performed yielding $z^{(2)}$. As the iteration is expected to converge rapidly to the solution $z > 0$ of (3.9), $z^{(2)}$ usually will satisfy the condition required for $z^{(1)}$ in (3.10) and thus can be used for the error estimation.

Appendix

In this appendix we sketch the structure of a FORTRAN subroutine for the performance of AMG cycles. The source text below is not complete. In particular, it does not include any declarations but shows only the most important steps. Its purpose is to demonstrate the ease of use of the storage scheme introduced in Section 3.3. All arrays used are described there and are assumed to be set up in a separate preparation phase.

```
      SUBROUTINE CYCLE(NCYC)
C
C     PERFORMS NCYC MULTIGRID CYCLES WITH FIRST APPROXIMATION ZERO. ALL ARRAYS
C     ARE ASSUMED TO BE SET UP IN A SEPARATE PREPARATION PHASE.
C
      CALL PUTZ(1)
      DO 100 NC=1,NCYC
C
C        GO DOWN TO COARSER GRIDS
C
         DO 10 K=1,M-1
            CALL RELAX(K)
            CALL RESCAL(K+1)
            CALL PUTZ(K+1)
10       CONTINUE
C
C        APPROXIMATE SOLUTION ON COARSEST GRID M
C
         DO 20 L=1,10
            CALL RELAX(M)
20       CONTINUE
C
C        GO BACK TO FINER GRIDS
C
         DO 30 K=M-1,1,-1
            CALL INTAD(K)
            CALL RELAX(K)
30       CONTINUE
100   CONTINUE
```

```
      STOP
      END

      SUBROUTINE RELAX(K)
C
C     PERFORM ONE (FULL) GAUSS-SEIDEL SWEEP ON GRID K
C
      DO 10 I=IMIN(K),IMAX(K)
        D=F(I)
        DO 20 J=IA(I)+1,IA(I+1)-1
          D=D-A(J)*U(JA(J))
20      CONTINUE
        U(I)=D/A(IA(I))
10    CONTINUE
      RETURN
      END

      SUBROUTINE INTAD(K)
C
C     INTERPOLATE CORRECTIONS FROM GRID K+1 TO GRID K
C     AND ADD THEM TO THE PREVIOUS APPROXIMATION OF GRID K.
C
C     COMPUTE NEW VALUES AT C-POINTS OF GRID K
C
      DO 10 I=IMIN(K+1), IMAX(K+1)
        U(IFG(I))=U(IFG(I))+U(I)
10    CONTINUE
C
C     COMPUTE NEW VALUES AT F-POINTS OF GRID K
C
      DO 20 I=IMINW(K),IMAXW(K)
        IF=IWF(I)
        DO 30 J=IW(I),IW(I+1)-1
          U(IF)=U(IF)+W(J)*U(JW(J))
30      CONTINUE
20    CONTINUE
      RETURN
      END

      SUBROUTINE RESCAL(K)
C
C     COMPUTE RESIDUALS ON GRID K-1 AND TRANSFER THEM TO THE NEXT
C     COARSER GRID K (USING THE TRANSPOSE OF INTERPOLATION).
C
C     TRANSFER C-POINT RESIDUALS
C
      DO 10 I=IMIN(K),IMAX(K)
        IF=IFG(I)
        D=F(IF)
        DO 20 J=IA(IF),IA(IF+1)-1
          D=D-A(J)*U(JA(J))
20      CONTINUE
        F(I)=D
10    CONTINUE
C
C     TRANSFER F-POINT RESIDUALS
C
      DO 30 I=IMINW(K-1),IMAX(K-1)
        IF=IWF(I)
        D=F(IF)
        DO 40 J=IA(IF),IA(IF+1)-1
          D=D-A(J)*U(JA(J))
```

```
40      CONTINUE
        DO 50 J=IW(I),IW(I+1)-1
        F(JW(J))=F(JW(J))+W(J)*D
50      CONTINUE
30      CONTINUE
        RETURN
        END

        SUBROUTINE PUTZ(K)
C
C       PUT ZERO TO THE VALUES OF GRID K
C
        DO 10 I=IMIN(K),IMAX(K)
        U(I)=0.0
10      CONTINUE
        RETURN
        END
```

References:

1. Auzinger, W.; Stetter, H.J.: *Defect correction and multigrid iterations.* Multigrid Methods. Proceedings of the Conference Held at Köln-Porz, November 23-27, 1981 (W. Hackbusch, U. Trottenberg, eds.). Lecture Notes in Mathematics, 960, pp. 327-351. Springer-Verlag, Berlin, 1982

2. Bank, R.E., and Rose, D.J.: *Design and implementation of an elliptic equation solver for rectangular regions.* Computers, Fast Elliptic Solvers and Applications (U. Schumann, ed.), pp. 112-124. Advance Publications, London, 1978.

3. Bank, R.E.; Sherman, A.H.: *PLTMG user's guide - July 1979 version.* Report CNA-152, Center for Numerical Analysis, University of Texas at Austin, 1979.

4. Becker, K.: *COMFLO- ein Experimentierprogramm zur Mehrgitterbehandlung subsonischer Potentialströmungen um Tragflächenprofile.* Preprint no. 604, Sonderforschungsbereich 72, Universität Bonn, 1983.

5. Brandt, A.: *Guide to multigrid development.* Multigrid Methods. Proceedings of the Conference Held at Köln-Porz, November 23-27, 1981 (W. Hackbusch, U. Trottenberg, eds.). Lecture Notes in Mathematics, 960. Springer-Verlag, Berlin, 1982.

6. Brandt, A.: *Algebraic multigrid theory: the symmetric case.* Appl. Math. Comp., Proceedings for International Multigrid Conference, April 6-8, 1983, Copper Mountain, CO. (S.F. McCormick, U. Trottenberg, eds.).

7. Brandt, A.; McCormick, S.F.; Ruge, J.: *Algebraic multigrid (AMG) for automatic algorithm design and problem solution. A preliminary report.* Report, Inst. Comp. Studies, Colorado State University, Ft. Collings, CO, 1982.

8. Brandt, A.; McCormick, S.F.; Ruge, J.: *Algebraic multigrid (AMG) for sparse matrix equations.* Sparsity and Its Applications (D.J. Evans, ed.), Cambridge University Press, 1984.

9. Brandt, A.; Ophir, D.: *Gridpack: Toward unification of general grid programming.* This volume, p 269-288.

10. Buzbee, B.L., Golub, G.H., and Nielson, C.W.: *On direct methods for solving Poisson's equation.* SIAM J. Numer. Anal., 7, pp. 627-656, 1970

11. Chatelin, F.; Miranker, W.: *Acceleration by aggregation of successive approximate methods.* Lin. Alg. Appl., 43, pp. 17-47, 1982.

12. Dendy, J.E. (Jr.): *Black box multigrid.* J. Comput. Phys., 48, pp. 366-386, 1982.

13. Foerster, H.; Witsch, K.: *On efficient multigrid software for elliptic problems on rectangular domains.* Math. Comput. Simulation XXIII, pp. 293-298, 1981.

14. Foerster, H.; Witsch, K.: *Multigrid software for the solution of elliptic problems on rectangular domains: MGOO (Release 1).* Multigrid Methods. Proceedings of the Conference Held at Köln-Porz, November 23-27, 1981 (W. Hackbusch, U. Trottenberg, eds.). Lecture Notes in Mathematics, 960. Springer-Verlag, Berlin, 1982.

15. Hemker, P.W.; Kettler, R.; Wesseling, P.; Zeeuw, P.M. de: *Multigrid methods: development of fast solvers.* Appl. Math. Comp., Proceedings for International Multigrid Conference, April 6-8, 1983, Copper Mountain, CO. (S.F. McCormick, U. Trottenberg, eds.).

16. Hockney, R.W.: *The potential calculation and some applications.* Meth. Comp. Phys., 9, pp. 135-211, 1970.

17. Hyman, J.M.: *Mesh refinement and local inversion of elliptic partial differential equations.* J. Comp. Phys., 23, pp. 124-134, 1977.

18. Rice, J.R.: *Machine and compiler effects on the performance of elliptic pde software.* 10 IMACS World Congress Proceedings. IMACS, New Brunswick, 1982.

19. Rice, J.R., and Boisvert, R.F.: *Solving Elliptic Problems Using ELLPACK.* Springer-Verlag, to appear.

20. Ries, M.; Trottenberg, U.; Winter, G.: *A note on MGR methods.* Linear Algebra Appl., 49, pp. 1-26, 1983.

21. Schröder, J.: *Operator inequalities.* Academic Press, New York, 1980.

22. Schröder, J., Trottenberg, U., und Witsch, K.: *On fast Poisson solvers and applications.* Numerical Treatment of Differential Equations (R. Bulirsch, R.D. Grigorieff, J. Schröder, eds.), pp. 153-187. Springer-Verlag, Berlin, 1978.

23. Solchenbach, K.; Stüben, K.; Trottenberg, U.; Witsch, K.: *Efficient solution of a nonlinear heat conduction problem by use of fast reduction and multigrid methods.* Numerical Integration of Differential Equations and Large Linear Systems. Proceedings of Two Workshops Held at the University of Bielefeld (J. Hinze, ed.). Lecture Notes in Mathematics, 968, pp. 114-148. Springer-Verlag, Berlin, 1982.

24. Stüben, K.: *MGO1: A multi-grid program to solve* $\Delta U-c(x,y)\ U=f(x,y)\ (\Omega)$, $U=g(x,y)\ (\partial\Omega)$, *on nonrectangular bounded domains* Ω. IMA-Report no. 82.02.02, Gesellschaft für Mathematik und Datenverarbeitung, St. Augustin, 1982.

25. Stüben, K.: *Algebraic multigrid (AMG): experiences and comparisons.* Appl. Math. Comp., Proceedings for International Multigrid Conference April 6-8, 1983, Copper Mountain, CO. (S.F. McCormick, U. Trottenberg, eds.).

26. Stüben, K.; Trottenberg, U.: *Multigrid methods: fundamental algorithms, model problem analysis and applications.* Multigrid Methods. Proceedings of the Conference Held at Köln-Porz, November 23-27, 1981 (W. Hackbusch, U. Trottenberg, eds.). Lecture Notes in Mathematics, 960, pp. 1-176. Springer-Verlag, Berlin, 1982.

27. Temperton, C.: *On the FACR(ℓ) algorithm for the discrete Poisson equation.* J. Comp. Phys., 34, pp. 314-329, 1980.

28. Tillmann, Ch.: *Beiträge zur effizienten Randbehandlung bei der Mehrgitterlösung elliptischer Randwertaufgaben im Rechteck.* Diplomarbeit, Institut für Angewandte Mathematik, Universität Bonn, to appear 1984.

DISCUSSION

Speakers: K. Stüben, U. Trottenberg and K. Witsch

Reid: I find your approach very attractive because it relieves the user of the tasks of choosing successive grids, choosing the smoothing operator and choosing grid-to-grid interpolating functions and getting them right. Some overhead in storage and operation count is certainly acceptable in exchange for these substantial gains. In fact, how big are these overheads?

Stüben: AMG01 does - in general - not compete with "optimal" geometric multi-grid solvers. Although the computing time for a cycle is close to optimal, the preparation time may take the time of several cycles. In the present version of AMG01, it may even take the time of up to 10 cycles. The preparation phase in this version of AMG01, however, is far from being optimized and we are hopeful to cut down the set-up time considerably.

Rice: We now have GM00 in the ELLPACK software and it outperforms all other fast methods. It is however, only an $O(h^2)$ method, have you applied AMG to high order methods?

Stüben: We have not yet applied AMG01 to higher order methods in a systematic way except in connection with the "Melustellenverfahren". In this case, the performance of the code was the same as for the second order examples. No serious problems should be introduced by the application of AMG to other standard higher order difference equations (although not all off-diagonal matrix entries have the same sign then). We have just started to apply AMG to different kinds of finite element matrices. However, there are no results so far.

Duff: I have two questions. The first is supplementary to that of John Reid and relates to storage. It would appear that you store all the h_{ij} for every level. Now, although as one moves to coarser grids the dimension of the h's reduce they will become denser and so the total storage required could be quite appreciable. How much storage is attributable to the h's and was all of this included in your answer to the previous question?

My second question relates to the generality of your method. Although you stated that the class of matrices for AMG01 was symmetric matrices with positive diagonal entries and non-positive off-diagonals, all the examples in your talk arose from the solution of elliptic PDE's. Could you comment on the performance of AMG01 on similar systems from other areas (for example, electric networks) and could you comment on the entension of AMG for the solution of more complicated PDE's, for example, fluid flow equations where the matrix may not even be symmetric?

Stüben: Without a reasonable control of the size of the coarser-grid matrices $L^{(k)}$, they indeed get denser and the total storage needed might become unaccept-able. There are, however, several ways to avoid this effect. In AMG01, the "radius of interpolation" is kept small by using only a few (usually 3) coarser-grid points to interpolate to a finer-grid point. By this, the size of the Galerkin-operators is cut down drastically. Additionally, the coarser-grid operators can be truncated by a good amount without affecting convergence too much. The latter possibility, however, has not yet been investigated systemati-cally. The total amount of storage actually need depends somewhat on the given problem. For the present version of AMG01, it typically ranges between 2 to 4 times the storage needed for the finest-grid matrix. One of the goals in the development of AMG01 is to reduce this further.

Concerning your second question, we started applying AMG01 to standard elliptic equations for natural reasons: for all the examples given, we know the per- formance and the difficulties with geometric multigrid methods which we wanted to compare AMG01 with. A series of experiments however, indicates that AMG01 performs about the same way for other sparse (symmetric) systems with positive diagonal entries and non-positive off-diagonals. In particular, we made computations with certain random systems of equations. (For reference, I refer to the proceedings of the 1983 International Multigrid Conference in Copper Mountain, Colorado, which will appear as a special issue of the Journal of Applied Mathematics and Computation.) Further results with AMG01 also indicate that symmetry is not really necessary (although the variational principle for the coarse-grid correction does not longer hold). How AMG should be applied to problems like those which arise from systems of PDE's (and which do not satisfy the sign condition mentioned above) is not yet investigated in details. AMG01 in the present form will - in general - not work efficiently for those equations. One reason is the use of Gauss-Seidel point-relaxation for smoothing which should be replaced by a more general scheme (a certain kind of block-relaxation, for example).

Hemker: For your routine AM00 you mention computing times from 140 to 500 μsec/point. In order to compare this with our routine MG01 which takes 16 μsec/point cycle, can you say on what computer your times were measured and how this machine compares to the CYBER 170?

Witsch: The time measurements were done on an IBM 370/158. I can't say anything about corresponding times for the CYBER 170.

Sherman: It was indicated that you felt it inappropriate to specialize multi- grid codes for vector machines because so little time was required to execute them on scalar machines. This seems to ignore the possibility that the multigrid code may be a (relatively small) part of a larger real-world program whose other parts can benefit substantially from execution on a vector machine. If multigrid codes are not vectorised, won't this tend to make them uncompetitive in such situations (since there may be a factor of 10 or more between the cost-per- operation of vectorised iterative methods and scalar multigrid codes)? I would make note of the fact that in time-dependent problems, more standard iterative methods can often achieve suitable convergence in 50-100 work units, even for difficult problems.

Witsch: I agree. If MG00 is run on a vector computer it should be vectorized as much as possible to achieve optimal efficiency. This is relatively simple since most operations (e.g. red-black relaxation, transfers etc.) can be done in parallel. For the case of the Laplacian with Dirichlet boundary conditions Barkai and Brandt describe an algorithm optimal for the CYBER 205 in the Proceedings of the Copper Mountain Conference on Multigrid Methods. Existing vector or pipeline machines have relatively different characteristics. Therefore, we decided not to invest work in adapting the code leaving that to interested users and waiting for better software tools for vectorization.

Existing MG software can be used to speed up the solution of (implicitely descretized) time dependent problems. The effect is not as tremendous as in the stationary case since classical iterative methods converge the faster the smaller the timesteps are. A larger saving can be achieved by using the MG idea also in time direction. A preliminary study of these questions for a simple nonlinear heat conduction problem has appeared in reference [23].

Young: Suppose we have Laplace's equation with Dirichlet boundary conditions on a rectangle and we use a five point finite difference discretisation. Is it possible, using multigrid with just two meshes, one twice the other, to obtain a rate of convergence which is independent of mesh size h? Or, do you need to use, in general, several different mesh sizes to do this?

Trottenberg: In order to obtain a convergence rate (convergence factor) that is bounded away from 1 independently of h it is not necessary to use more than two grids. The two grid method gives, on the contrary, a (slightly) better convergence factor than a real multigrid method. (This is due to the fact, that a multigrid method can be interpreted as a "disturbed" twogrid method.). However, if one takes work into account, a twogrid method is of no practical use. What one really wants is not only a convergence factor that is independent of h, but also the numerical work per iteration step should be proportional to the number of unknowns. This can, in general, only be achieved by a real multigrid method (going down to one fixed coarsest grid with meshsize h_0, and letting the finest meshsize h tend to 0.) A systematic rigorous analysis of the above mentioned problem has been given in reference [26].

Trottenberg: I should like to comment that I do not believe it to be wrong to solve non-linear problems by applying the multigrid method to a linearised problem (combination of Newton's method and one of the linear multigrid algorithms). Though the direct application of a nonlinear multigrid method will usually be more efficient and simpler.

Secondly I would like to add that there is a good book on the subject: [Hackbusch, Trottenberg (eds.): Multigrid Methods. Lecture Notes in Mathematics 960, Springer 1982].

Huang: Can one use extrapolation within the multigrid method?

Trottenberg: This is a very natural thing to do.

Yanenko: Surely this is not a stable process?

Brandt: One should extrapolate in the equations, not in the solution, and refer you to the so-called τ-extrapolation.

Hockney: You said that the number of arithmetic operations is proportional to the number of points in the (finest) mesh. What is the constant of proportionality?

Trottenberg: For Poisson's equation and the FMG version of MG00: 6 multiplications and 18 1/2 additions per point of the finest grid.

Schönauer: How do you get information about the discretisation error?

Trottenberg: Under certain (very natural) assumptions on the asymptotic behaviour of the discretization error one can prove that the Full Multigrid method ("FMG") gives a solution the error of which has the size of the discretization error. For the simple analysis see chapter 6 in reference [26].

Yanenko: You said, that the multigrid method is efficient but how do you apply this method to non-linear singular perturbation problems?

Trottenberg: There is a natural extension of the linear multigrid method (the so-called Full Approximation Scheme "FAS") to nonlinear problems.

The treatment of singular perturbation problems by multigrid methods is more difficult. One efficient approach is to combine the multigrid idea with artificial viscosity and defect correction techniques. The objective is here to obtain stable approximations which have nevertheless high order (2nd order) accuracy. This approach has been described and studied in detail in several papers as you can see, for example, from the multigrid bibliography.

Also in many other situations that are characterized by certain mathematical difficulties it seems useful too (for instance with continuation techniques in case of bifurcation problems).

PDE SOFTWARE: Modules, Interfaces and Systems
B. Engquist and T. Smedsaas (eds.)
Elsevier Science Publishers B.V. (North-Holland)
© IFIP, 1984

GRIDPACK: TOWARD UNIFICATION OF GENERAL GRID PROGRAMMING

Achi Brandt and Dan Ophir

Department of Applied Mathematics
Weizmann Institute of Science
Rehovot, Israel

GRIDPACK is a fully portable Fortran extension, including economic data structures, routines and macro-statements, for simplifying and unifying the programming of grid operations in general two-dimensional domains. These operations include the introduction and modification of grids, boundaries, inner and outer subgrids, grid functions, boundary functions and finite-difference operators, including operators near and on boundaries; interpolation between grids; sweeping conveniently and with full efficiency over grids; displaying grids, grid functions, boundary functions and boundary shapes; etc. The software will facilitate and modularize multigrid programming, permitting writing many processes once for all, including combinations of fast solvers with flexible local grid adaptations.

CONTENTS

1. INTRODUCTION

The main purpose of GRIDPACK is to supply the general Fortran programmer with convenient and fully efficient facilities for handling two-dimensional grids and for communicating grid routines to other programmers. The user of this software can, within his usual Fortran code and by means of simple macro-statements (or simple

calls to GRIDPACK routines), perform a variety of grid operations, such as:
− Create the logical structure (set of pointers) for a grid by specifying its domain (or boundary curves), meshsizes and ordering.
− Create similar structures for boundary grids (the intersections of any given
  boundary curves with given gridlines). Such structures can in fact be used for
  treating any other curves cutting through the grid, such as material interfaces
  and traced discontinuities (shocks, wakes, etc.).
− Create new grids from existing ones by various operations such as unions, intersection, transposition (changing row ordering into column ordering), coarsening
  and refinement; or create a new grid which is the "inner" part of a given grid
  (containing all gridpoints whose all neighbors with respect to a given templet
  are also gridpoints), or its "outer" part (the grid without its inner part).
− Define templets (neighborhoods of gridpoints).
− Allocate storage for grid functions, including boundary-grid functions. The
  resulting storage is fully efficient and flexible: the amount of pointers is
  small compared to the amount of real numerical data, but still allows grid
  changes costing small CPU times compared to the CPU times of numerical processes over the grids.
− Delete any of the above grids or storage allocations. Garbage-collection routines ensure deletion of holes in the data structure as soon as their total
  size becomes significant.
− Introduce numerical values, specified as Fortran functions, into the grid functions.
− Add, subtract or do any other arithmetic with grid functions.
− Interpolate from a grid function (or a boundary grid function) on a coarser
  grid to one on a finer grid, with any desired order of interpolation.
− Transfer information between the interior grid and the corresponding boundary
  grid.
− Sweep conveniently over grids, or parts of grids, or simultaneously over several grids, by various means, including various DO-like statements or calls to
  KEY routines which set up convenient-to-use arrays (see Fig. 1). The resulting
  sweeps are fully efficient, with single-indexed DO loops performing the sweeps
  over the inner strings. Inside the DO-like statements, grid functions can be
  programmed as if they were rectangular arrays and efficient automatic branching
  is available for separate treatment at irregular points (gridpoints some of
  whose neighbors, by a given templet, are not in the grid).
− Program, once for all grids and all programs, various tasks, such as various
  difference operators near boundaries involving both boundary and interior data,
  relaxation of general types of interior finite difference equations, relaxation
  of boundary conditions (independently or together with the interior relaxation),
  etc.
− Communication between curved grids (used locally, along boundaries or interfaces or discontinuities, in a multi-grid framework) and Cartesian grids. (This
  feature is still under development.)
− Display grids, grid functions, boundary shapes, templets, etc., showing also
  their relative geometric positions.

More important perhaps than any one of these specific operations is the fact that
the GRIDPACK software offers a general framework for communicating grid programs.
Any user of this software can program once for all various grid operations, that
can then be reused for any other grid in his program, or in any other program
using this software. Moreover, GRIDPACK routines can even be used by programs
which do not employ neither GRIDPACK nor its data structure, provided they incorporate some simple interface routines (the KEY routines; see Fig. 1, and Sec. 4.3).
Enormous programming repetition can thus be saved, and high degree of portability
gained.

To obtain full portability, GRIDPACK is entirely written in Fortran and as a Fortran extension. That is, the basic part of GRIDPACK is a collection of Fortran
routines which can serve any Fortran program. The current collection, described

in Sec. 4 below, can be expanded by user contributions. In addition, a special collection of macro-statements, called *Grid Language* (GL), has been developed (see Sec. 5), which can much simplify various programming tasks. These macro-statements can be used within a usual Fortran code: They are expanded into conventional Fortran statements, including calls to GRIDPACK routines, by a special preprocessor called PREPACK. The preprocessor itself is written in Fortran, thus maintaining the full portability of the system.

The development of GRIDPACK is of particular importance for the evolving technology of *multi-grid programming*. Multigrid techniques (or, more generally, Multi-Level Adaptive Techniques - MLAT) are already used quite extensively as fast (in fact, the fastest) solvers for discretized partial differential equations of general types on general domains. They can also be used for many other purposes, such as the flexible creation of locally refined discretization and local coordinate transformations, all integrated into the fast-solvers. (See, for example [8] for a brief discussion of multi-level capabilities, potential and research, and [7] for a more complete introduction and survey of recent developments. The geometrical capabilities of local refinement and coordinate transformation are described in [6, Sec. 9], as well as in previous publications [2], [3], [4].) All multigrid algorithms, and in particular those with highly developed geometrical capabilities, are based on standard grid operations, of the types mentioned above, which are used time and again, for different grids in the same program and in many different multigrid programs. Thus, the GRIDPACK system may very much facilitate programming in this field, encourage the use of its full potential, and promote portability, communication and cooperation.

Some multigrid algorithms are indeed provided together with GRIDPACK (see Sec. 4.8). A collection of other multigrid programs comes on the same magnetic tape, called MUGTAPE (multi-grid tape) on which GRIDPACK is distributed. The detailed description of GRIDPACK [1] appears as another file on that tape. The tape also includes MUGPACK, a precursor of GRIDPACK that can be used both for learning the programming techniques and as a special-purpose program for the multigrid solution of the 5-point Poisson equation on a general domain. Still much simpler programs, for rectangular domains, are also included on MUGTAPE. Some of them are very short and very suitable for first acquaintance with multigrid techniques.

```
SUBROUTINE PUTZ(N)
COMMON J1(65), J2(65), JR(65)
CALL KEYS (N,I1,I2,IR,J1,J2,JR)
DO 1 I=IR+I1, IR+I2
DO 1 IJ=JR(I)+J1(I),JR(I)+J2(I)
1 Q(IJ)=0
END
```

Figure 1

PUTZ: *An illustration of using a* KEY *routine*

PUTZ is a general routine for setting to zero the function defined on grid number N. Notice that this routine can be used for any uniform-grid function, and in any program which uses GRIDPACK; in fact, it is enough that the program includes KEYS. Routines like PUTZ, and far more complicated ones, can thus be written once for all; having been written by one GRIDPACK user, all others can benefit from them. Notice also the full efficiency of the central DO loop, and the ease of writing: $Q(IJ)$ stands for $U_{I,J}^N$. Generally, $Q(JR(IR+i)+j)$ would stand for any U_{ij}^N, with expressions like $JR(IR+i)$, for each i needed in a central loop, being evaluated before the loop. If the central loops are on i, the grid can be transposed (see Sec. 4.3).

A new version of MUGTAPE, including the completely revised version of GRIDPACK described in this article, will hopefully be released by the end of 1983. It will be available from the Department of Applied Mathematics, Weizmann Institute of Science, Rehovot, Israel.

The first description of GRIDPACK appeared as Section 4 in [3] and a complete description of its first phase was given in [5]. In addition to the present authors, several routines were contributed by Fred Gustavson and Alan Goodman (see Sec. 4.1), some boundary-treatment routines are modified ELLPACK routines [9], and some interpolation routines were contributed by Markus von Cube (see Sec. 4.6). The sponsors of this project, in addition to the Weizmann Institute of Science, are the United States Army, through its European Research Office under contract DAJA37-79-C-0504, and the Gesellschaft für Mathematik und Datenverarbeitung (GMD) in St. Augustin, FRG, through its Institut für Mathematik (IMA), where one of the authors (Ophir) worked for two years. The interest, assistance and encouragement of the entire GMD-IMA group is especially acknowledged.

2. DEFINITIONS

The following terms are used throughout GRIDPACK:

The *lattice* with *origin* (x_0, y_0) and *meshsizes* (h_x, h_y) in the (x,y) plane is the set:

$$L(x_0, y_0; h_x, h_y) = \{(x_i, y_j) \mid x_i = x_0 + ih_x, \ y_j = y_0 + jh_y ; \ i,j \text{ integers}\}.$$

A *uniform grid*, $G = G(D; x_0, y_0; h_x, h_y)$ is the intersection of the domain D and the lattice $L(x_0, y_0; h_x, h_y)$. A *uniform subgrid* G', of grid G, is a uniform grid defined on a subdomain D' of the domain D, with the same lattice. They are formally two different grids, but they may share functions (see routine POINTO in Sec. 4.2), in which case G is called the *parent* of G'.

The *column* i of grid G defined above is the set of gridpoints:

$$\{(x,y) \mid x = x_0 + ih, \ (x,y) \text{ is in } G\}.$$

The *row* j of grid G is the set of gridpoints:

$$\{(x,y) \mid y = y_0 + jh, \ (x,y) \text{ is in } G\}.$$

A *grid-line* is a grid column or a grid row. A grid-line is composed of strings. A *point string* is a sequence of consecutive gridpoints in a grid column (*vertical string*) or in a grid row (*horizontal string*). The internal GRIDPACK representation of any uniform grid is organized in terms of either vertical strings or horizontal ones. In the first case the grid is said to be *vertical* or *in column construction order*, in the latter it is *horizontal* or *in row construction order*.

A *column string* is a sequence of consecutive columns. A *row string* is a sequence of consecutive rows. For brevity, the term *set* is used in GRIDPACK for column string (in case of vertical grids), or for row string (in horizontal grids). See Fig. 2. A *single-string grid* is a uniform grid with only one string per line and only one set. A *multi-string grid* is any uniform grid which is not single-string.

The following terms are used by GRIDPACK in treating boundaries of two-dimensional domains.

A *continuous piece* P in the (x,y) plane is any set of the form

$$P = P(X, Y, t^B, t^E) = \{(x,y) \mid x = X(t), \ y = Y(t), \ t^B \leq t \leq t^E\}.$$

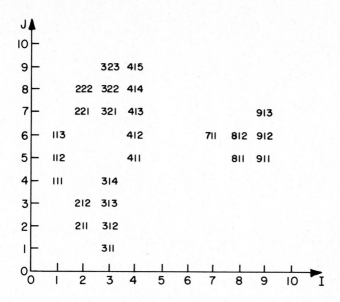

The structure of a vertical uniform grid and a function on it

The grid has two sets (strings of consecutive columns): (1,2,3,4) and (7,8,9). At gridpoint (I,J) the figure shows the value of a function $U_{IJ} = \nu_1\nu_2\nu_3$, where $\nu_1 = I$ is the column number, the digit ν_2 is the vertical string (or the corresponding data string) ordinal number within the column, and ν_3 is the gridpoint ordinal number within the string (<u>not</u> its row number J).

t is called *the piece parameter*. The piece *end-points* are the points

$$(X(t^B), Y(t^B)) \quad \text{and} \quad (X(t^E), Y(t^E)).$$

Each piece in a given program has a distinguishing *piece (ordinal) number*, which is independent of its placing in (possibly several) boundaries.

A *continuous curve* C is a union $\cup_{i=1}^{n}P_i$ of consecutive continuous pieces P_i; i.e.,

$$P_i = P(X_i, Y_i, t_i^B, t_i^E), \quad X_i(t_i^B) = X_{i-1}(t_{i-1}^E), \quad Y_i(t_i^B) = Y_{i-1}(t_{i-1}^E), \quad (i = 1, \cdots, n).$$

The curve is called *closed* if

$$X_n(t_n^E) = X_1(t_1^B) \quad \text{and} \quad Y_n(t_n^E) = Y_1(t_1^B),$$

otherwise the curve is called *open*.

A *boundary* B is a union $\cup_{i=1}^{m}C_i$ of continuous curves C_i. Sometimes there may be several boundaries in a program. A boundary is called *open* if at least one of its curves is open. The *boundary end-points* are the end-points of the boundary pieces.

A *boundary-grid* BG = $BG(B; x_0, y_0; h_x, h_y)$ is the intersection of the boundary B with the lines in the lattice $L(x_0, y_0; h_x, h_y)$. The intersection points are called *boundary-grid-points*. Those formed from intersecting vertical lattice lines are

called *vertical boundary points*, those formed from intersecting horizontal lines
are named *horizontal boundary points*. There may be points which are both vertical
and horizontal. A *discrete piece*, or briefly a *piece*, is the sequence of boundary-
grid-points on a given continuous piece, ordered in ascending values of the piece
(t). A *discrete curve*, or briefly a *curve*, is the sequence of discrete pieces
corresponding to the continuous pieces of a given continuous curve.

A *grid* is either a uniform grid (or subgrid) or a boundary-grid. In any given
program any number of such grids may be defined; each is given a unique number
called the *grid (ordinal) number*. We briefly say "grid n" instead of "the grid
whose number is n". When no confusion may arise, the general term "grid" is sometimes used for a uniform grid.

A *boundary point ordinal number* is the ordinal number of a boundary-grid-point
when they are all ordered in one natural sequence; i.e., in a natural order of
pieces (P_i coming right before P_j if $t_i^E = t_j^B$), and in ascending t within each
piece.

A *grid-function* is a function defined on a grid, i.e., an ordered set of values
with one to one correspondence to grid-points. Often it will represent some approximate solution of a discretized problem. There are two kinds of grid functions
corresponding to the two kinds of grids: a *uniform-grid-function* and a *boundary-
grid-function*. On any grid any number of grid functions may be defined. Each
grid function is thus uniquely specified by giving its grid number together with
its *grid-function index* (or *ordinal number*), the latter specifying its ordinal number relative to other functions defined on the same grid. A special grid function
is illustrated in Fig. 2 above.

A *data string* (or a *function-string*) is the sequence of function values that correspond to a point-string, which is a vertical string in case of a vertical uniform grid, a horizontal string in case of a horizontal uniform grid, and a discrete piece in case of a boundary grid. If several functions are defined on the
grid, all function values corresponding to the same gridpoint are taken consecuti-
vely, before all those corresponding to the next gridpoint in the string. We thus
view all the functions defined on the grid as a vector of functions, with a vector
of numerical values corresponding to each gridpoint. All these functions should
be of the same type: either real or integer. (The type can be changed, though.
It is determined at run time by using the QSPACE or LSPACE routines. See Sec.
4.2.) If both integer and real functions are desired on the same grid, it should
be treated formally as two different grids. (Similarly, an interior grid and its
boundary intersections are formally viewed as two different grids. Super-struc-
tures may later be defined for succinctly describing operations involving different but related grids.)

A *templet* is a set of shifts on a grid, used to describe the neighborhood of a
grid-point. For example, the neighborhood

$$\begin{array}{ccc} & \bullet & \\ \bullet & x & \bullet \\ & \bullet & \end{array}$$

(the standard 5-point neighborhood of the point x, used for example in approximating the Laplace or Poisson equation at x) is represented by the templet
((0,0),(0,1),(0,-1),(-1,0),(1,0)). Each templet in a given program has a unique
templet (ordinal) number (τ) by which it is defined and used.

The τ-*inner subgrid* of a given grid G is the grid composed of all the points belonging to G whose neighbors according to the given templet number τ are also all
in G. The τ-*outer subgrid* of a given grid G is a grid composed of all the points
of G without the points of the τ-inner subgrid. Note that if templet τ does not
include the (0,0) shift then the τ-inner subgrid of G will include points not in

G. These extra points form the τ-*ghost grid* of grid G.

3. INTERNAL DATA STRUCTURES

The internal structure is governed by a set of parameters given in, and partly calculated by, the initialization routine INIT (see Sec. 4.1). All the grids are organized using linked allocation in two general vectors ("garbage collectors"): The *L space* for all logical and integer data (mainly pointers), and the *Q space* for all type-real data (mainly numerical values of grid functions).

Most information related to grid n branches from a fixed list of integer parameters starting at L(L(n+LL)), where LL is fixed by INIT. This list, called the *grid L-squad* and fully described in [1, App. II], specifies the number NF of functions defined on the grid and their type (real or integer), the grid's type (a uniform or a boundary grid), its construction order (vertical or horizontal, if the grid is uniform), its parent grid m (i.e., the grid whose storage is used by grid n - see POINTO in Sec. 4.2; if regular storage was allocated by QSPACE(n,NF), then m = n; if no storage was allocated, then m = 0), various basic grid statistics (such as its total number of sets, columns and strings, or curves and pieces, total number of gridpoints, total L and Q spaces occupied by the grid and its functions, and its smallest and largest row and column numbers), and the addresses of its chief data structures: For a uniform grid the address is given of the first set-quad (see Sec. 3.1), for a boundary grid -- the address of the first curve-squad (see Sec. 3.2).

In addition there is a list of real parameters related to grid n, which starts at Q(L(n+LQ)) and is called the *grid Q-squad*. It specifies the lattice (origin and meshsizes) of the grid.

The length of each kind of grid squad is a system constant. It can be changed, if an extension of the system requires it, by changing the corresponding parameter in INIT.

3.1 Uniform-grid: The QUAD structure

A uniform grid is organized either vertically (in columns) or horizontally (in rows), depending on the order in which it is to be used. (See Sec. 4.3, including the remark about transposing from vertical to horizontal.) For definiteness, the *vertical* construction is here described.

Each vertical grid is described as a sequence of column strings (sets) with each column being described as a sequence of vertical strings (see Fig. 2). Each sequence, either of strings or of sets, is represented internally by a chain of *quads* (integer quadruplets), where each string (or set) is represented by a quad of the form

$$\text{QUAD} = \boxed{\text{LOC}\ \mid\ \text{INDEX}\ \mid\ \text{LENGTH}\ \mid\ \text{NEXT}}\ .$$

LOC is the location where the string (or the corresponding data string) is stored (in the L space if it is a set or a type-integer data string; in the Q space if it is a type-real data string). INDEX and LENGTH describe the lattice positions of the string. INDEX is its first index, i.e., the column number of its first column if this is a column string, or the row number of its first gridpoint if this is a data string. LENGTH is the cardinal number of columns or gridpoints in the string. NEXT is the location (in L) of the next quad in the chain; NEXT = 0 if the present quad is the last in its chain.

Thus, every grid is represented by a chain of *set-quads*, corresponding to its sequence of sets, and every column is represented by a chain of *string-quads*, corresponding to its sequence of vertical strings. Each set-quad points to a set (a sequence of consecutive columns), i.e., its INDEX and LENGTH pointers indicate which and how many columns are included in the set, and its LOC pointer show the address in L where the representation of that set starts. Namely, at L(LOC) a sequence of LENGTH string-quads starts, corresponding to the LENGTH columns of the set; each string-quad in that sequence is in fact the first in the chain of string-quads representing the corresponding column. Each string-quad points to a data string; i.e., its INDEX and LENGTH pointers indicate on which consecutive grid-points the data string is defined, while its LOC pointer shows the location in Q (or in L, if the data is type-integer) where the data string is stored.

This "QUAD structure" is relatively *inexpensive*, since a group of four integers represents a whole string of (possibly vectorial) function values. Moreover, it is very *efficient for grid sweeping operations*. If the sweep is made in the con-struction lines (e.g., in columns when the construction is vertical), then it can be made in terms of efficient singly indexed DO loops (see Fig. 1). To sweep that efficiently in the other direction, one can transpose the grid. The QUAD structure may be somewhat inefficient in separately accessing a single gridpoint of a multi-string grid, but this is an unlikely event. All the usual multigrid processes, for example, are sweep processes; an isolated access to a point is sel-dom needed.

Moreover, the QUAD structure is very *suitable for grid changes*, like those requi-red by adaptive-grid procedures. Every string can reside anywhere in the L or Q space, and its length can therefore easily be changed by reconstructing it in a new location if necessary. After many changes of this type, many gaps (unused locations) may appear in the Q and L spaces. The system can keep track of the total length of these gaps. When it accumulates to a serious proportion, the gaps can automatically be eliminated by one pass of "Garbage Collection" (described in [1, App. II]). This pass is very inexpensive relative to the numerical processes that would create those gaps (e.g., processes of grid adaptation, which normally follow at least a couple of relaxation sweeps over the adapted grids).

3.2 Boundary grid: Perimetric order

A boundary grid is organized as a sequence of curves, each curve being organized as a sequence of pieces for which data strings are given in the natural (ascending t) order. On each boundary grid a vector of special real-valued functions is automatically defined at construction time (but can be cancelled later). These are called the *Basic Boundary Functions (BBF)*. In the current system the vector includes four such functions, but this number can readily be changed (by changing the constant IBBFQ in INIT). The four functions are x, y, t and $\bar{k}$, in this order, defined for boundary gridpoints, where (x,y) are the Cartesian coordinates of the point, t is the value of the piece parameter there (hence $x = X(t)$ and $y = Y(t)$ in the notation of Sec. 2), and $\bar{k}$ indicates the kind of intersection: $\bar{k} = 1$ if the point is a vertical boundary point, $\bar{k} = -1$ if horizontal, $\bar{k} = 0$ if both.

Thus, this "perimetric" construction order starts internally with a sequence of lists in L, called *curve-squads*, corresponding to the sequence of curves of the grid. For each curve the corresponding squad specifies its closure type (open or closed), how many pieces it includes, and the addresses of two sequences of *"piece squads"*, one in L (*"L-squads"*) and one in Q (*"Q-squads"*), each sequence correspon-ding to the sequence of pieces in the curve. For each piece, its corresponding Q-squad gives the limits of its parameter (t^B and t^E in Sec. 2). Its correspon-ding L-squad specifies the piece ordinal number, the number of points in the piece, the type of its endpoints (whether they are gridpoints appearing in adjacent pieces), and a LOC pointer giving the address of its data string (in Q if the grid is type-real, in L if it is type integer).

The length of each kind of squad (curve squad, piece-L-squad and piece-Q-squad) is a system constant (currently 4, 4 and 2, respectively), which can easily be changed by changing the corresponding constant in the INIT lists.

Sometimes the Basic Boundary Functions of a boundary grid will not be directly part of its vector of function; e.g., when the grid is type-integer. Instead, a special parameter in the grid L-squad can be set to m, say, to indicate that the grid has the same Basic Boundary Functions as grid m. This parameter is set, e.g., by routines GRCOPY and BBFSTR (Secs. 4.1, 4.2).

3.3 Templet

The templet number τ is stored as a string of integers starting at $L(L(LNT+\tau))$, where LNT is fixed by the initialization routine INIT. The first integer in that string specifies how many shifts are included in τ, and the shifts themselves follow, each represented by a pair of integers.

4. GRIDPACK ROUTINES

In this section we briefly describe a selection of those GRIDPACK subroutines which are available to the usual user. Lists of routine parameters are sometimes abbreviated here for the sake of clarity. All parameters are allowed to be variables. We do not describe here error messages. For the full description of all GRIDPACK routines, including internal routines not normally accessible to the user, with the full lists of parameters and error messages, see [1, Appendix II].

4.1 Initialization and logical grid and templet operations

Logical grid operations are routines which deal with the logical structures (the pointers) of the grid, not with allocating or using storage for functions defined on the grid. Thus, the LOC pointers of the string quads remain undefined by these routines. (Routine LBRGRD is an exception.) The computer time expended by these routines (and also by those of Secs. 4.2 and 4.3) on uniform grids is negligible, because it is proportional to the number q of *strings* in the grid, whereas numerical processes (relaxation, etc.) expend many operations per *gridpoint*. Exceptions are routines LTPØSE, where the work is $O(q \log q)$, and LGRDCR, where the characteristic function should be evaluated at each lattice point in the rectangle $[x_1,x_2] \times [y_1,y_2]$.

As a general rule, all the routines below assume (and check) that when different grids participate in the same logical operation they have the same construction order and the same lattice (except in coarsening and refinement operations, of course). In grid operations creating new grids, if the new grid number coincides with a previously defined one, the old one is thereby deleted.

Several of the routines in this section and in Sec. 4.2 were designed in collaboration with F. Gustavson and written by him and by A. Goodman at IBM T.J. Watson Research Center, Yorktown Heights, New York. Some of the internal routines used by LGRDBR are modified ELLPACK routines [9].

INIT (MG,MT,MHL,MHQ) - Initialization routine, should be called before any other GRIDPACK routine. It gets from the user the values of MG and MT, the largest possible grid number and templet number, respectively, and MHL and MHQ, the maximal number of holes (deleted data) allowed before garbage collection should be performed in the L and Q spaces, respectively. The user can sometimes also make changes in a long list of GRIDPACK constants appearing in this routine. The INIT routine uses all these parameters and constants to set up various pointers into the L and Q spaces. (Cf., e.g., Sec. 3.3 and beginning of Sec. 3).

LGRDCR $(n,x_0,y_0,h_x,h_y,I_c,x_1,x_2,y_1,y_2,CHAR)$ - $\underline{Cr}$eate uniform-$\underline{grid}$ $G(D;x_0,y_0;h_x,h_y)$ with ordinal grid number n, where the domain D is defined by the cha$\underline{ra}$cteristic function CHAR(x,y):

$$D = \{(x,y) \mid x_1 \leqslant x \leqslant x_2 , y_1 \leqslant y \leqslant y_2 , CHAR(x,y) = 1\}.$$

I_c is the index of construction order; I_c = 1 if vertical, I_c = 0 if horizontal.

LGRD2F $(n,x_0,y_0,h_x,h_y,I_c,x_1,x_2,f_1,f_2)$ - Create uniform-$\underline{grid}$ number n given the $\underline{2}$ $\underline{f}$unctions $f_1(x)$ and $f_2(x)$. Similar to LGRDCR, except that

$$D = \{(x,y) \mid x_1 \leqslant x \leqslant x_2 , f_1(x) \leqslant y \leqslant f_2(x)\}.$$

LGRIJS $(n,I_1,I_2,IR,J_1,J_2,h_x,h_y,x_0,y_0,IC)$ - Create $\underline{s}$ingle-string $\underline{gr}$id number n by directly specifying the range of its $(\underline{i,j})$ positions, namely

$$I_1 \leqslant i \leqslant I_2, \quad J_1(IR+i) \leqslant j \leqslant J_2(IR+i).$$

LGRIJG $(n,\cdots)$ - Similar, for a $\underline{g}$eneral (possibly multi-string) grid.

LBRGRD $(n,h_x,h_y,x_0,y_0,NP,IP)$ - Create $\underline{b}$oundary-$\underline{grid}$ n which is the intersection of the lines of $L(x_0,y_0;h_x,h_y)$ with the NP continuous pieces whose ordinal numbers are given in the vector IP. The routine calculates points on piece number i by calling the earmarked, *user-written* Fortran Functions XCOORD(i,t), YCOORD(i,t), TBEGIN(i) and TEND(i), which give X(t), Y(t), t^B and t^E, respectively, for that piece (see Sec. 2). Together with creating the boundary grid logical structure, LGRDBR also automatically allocates storage and calculates the values of the four Basic Boundary Functions (cf. Sec. 3.2). These functions can of course be cancelled by QOFF (see Sec. 4.2), or be avoided when shared by formally different grids (see routines GRCOPY and BBFSTR).

LGRIDB (n,m,I_c,h_x,h_y) - Create the uniform-$\underline{grid}$ n bounded by the $\underline{b}$oundary-grid m, in construction order I_c. The meshsizes (h_x,h_y) of n should be integer multiples of those of m.

DELETE (n) - $\underline{Delete}$ grid number n.

LCOARS (n,m,I_x,I_y) - Create grid n which is the $\underline{coars}$ening of grid m by factors I_x and I_y in the x and y directions, respectively.

LGRDRF (n,m,NHL) - Create $\underline{grid}$ n which is the 1:2 $\underline{ref}$inement of uniform-grid m, with NHL additional h-$\overline{l}$ayers.

LUNION (n,ℓ,m) - Create $\underline{union}$ of two uniform grids: n = ℓ $\cup$ m.

LISECT (n,ℓ,m) - Create the uniform-grids $\underline{inter}$section n = ℓ $\cap$ m.

LMINUS (n,ℓ,m) - Create the uniform-grids difference n = ℓ - m.

BTEMPL (τ,IT) - $\underline{B}$uild $\underline{templet}$ number τ by the information in array IT, simply by copying from IT to $\overline{L(L(LNT+\tau))}$ (see Sec. 3.3).

DELTMP (τ) - $\underline{Dele}$tes $\underline{templet}$ τ.

LINNER (n,m,τ) - Create n as the τ-<u>inner</u> subgrid of grid m.

LOUTER (n,m,τ) - Create n as the τ-<u>outer</u> subgrid of grid m.

LGHOST (n,m,τ) - Create n as the τ-<u>ghost</u> grid of grid m.

LINRBT (n,m,τ_x,τ_y,I_c,h_x,h_y) - Create <u>internal</u> uniform-grid n bounded by <u>boundary</u>-grid m with construction order I_c and meshsizes h_x and h_y, "internal" being defined in terms of the <u>templets</u> τ_x and τ_y: An internal point is a grid point inside the domain bounded by m, whose all τ_x-neighbors and all τ_y-neighbors are also in that domain, and none of whose τ_x-neighborhood horizontal links and τ_y-neighborhood vertical links is intersected by the boundary grid. For these links to be well defined, τ_x and τ_y should respectively look like small horizontal and vertical *single-string* grids.

LTPOSE (n,m) - Create n as the <u>transpose</u> of m, i.e., the same uniform grid but in the opposite construction order.

RENAME (n,m) - <u>Rename</u> grid m as grid n, i.e., change the grid number.

GRCOPY (n,m) - Create <u>grid</u> n identical to (<u>copy</u> of) grid m. Grid *functions* are not copied, of course. In particular, in case these are boundary grids, the Basic Boundary Functions are not defined on the new grid. Instead the routine inserts the indication that grid n has the same BBF as grid m (cf. Sec. 3.2).

COMPAR (ℓ,m) - <u>Compare</u> the constants of grids ℓ and m (their origins, meshsizes, total number of points, strings and columns, etc.) and print them out, usually for debugging purposes.

ORIGIN (n,x_0,y_0) - Change the <u>origin</u> of grid n to (x_0,y_0).

Function NGFREE(n) is the smallest <u>grid</u> <u>number</u> greater than n which is <u>free</u> (not assigned to undeleted grid).

Function NTFREE(τ) is the smallest <u>templet</u> <u>number</u> above τ which is <u>free</u>.

4.2 Function storage allocation

The routines in this section specify, or change, the number NF of functions defined on a (uniform or boundary) grid, and allocate for them suitable Q or L storage, supplying accordingly the values for the LOC pointers in the string-quads or the piece-L-squads. Allocating storage in the Q space defines the functions, and hence the grid, to be type-real, while allocating in L defines them as type-integer.

QSPACE (n,NF) - Allocate <u>Q space</u> for a vector of NF grid functions on grid n. If NF has previously been set, it is changed through re-allocation in another part of Q (transferring the previously allocated space to the garbage collection lists).

LSPACE (n,NF) - Similar allocation in <u>L space</u>.

POINTO (n,m) - Set the pointers of uniform-grid n to <u>point into</u> the data strings of uniform-grid m. Usually grid n will represent a subgrid of grid m, created for example by LINNER(n,m,τ) or LISECT(n,ℓ,m). This routine thus enables us to operate on a proper part of a grid. The number of functions (NF) defined on n is automatically set to equal that of m.

BBFSTR (n,m) - Indicate that the Basic Boundary Functions of boundary grid n are identical to (hence <u>stored</u> with) those of grid m (cf. Sec. 3.2).

QOFF (n) - The same as QSPACE(n,o).

In addition to these routines, function storage allocation is also performed by LBRGRD.

4.3 <u>KEY interface</u>

Here is a collection of routines designed to interface between the user and the grid functions and other grid data. Starting from the grid number specified by the user, the KEY routines will trace various pointers, make some short calculations and then load convenient interface information into arrays named by the user. With this information the user can perform fully efficient DO loops over columns of vertical grids or over rows of horizontal grids. If the grid construction order is not compatible with the interior loops, one can obtain full efficiency by first transposing the grid (see LTPOSE in Sec. 4.1 and TFERTP in Sec. 4.4). The transposition is very inexpensive (relative to the cost of a relaxation sweep, for example).

The KEY routines are described here in terms of the *type-real* case (functions stored in Q). The same routines will similarly serve the type-integer case (functions stored in L). Only the basic part of the interface collection is shown below. More KEY routines exist in the system [1], and many others can easily be added based on the present ones.

KEYS $(n,I_1,I_2,IR,J_1,J_2,JR)$ - Load constants I_1, I_2, and IR, and vectors J_1, J_2 and JR so that if u is the only function defined on the *vertical* <u>s</u>ingle-string grid n, its value at the (i,j) gridpoint will be given by

$$u_{ij}^n = u(x_0+ih_x , y_0+jh_y) = Q(JR(IR+i)+j),$$

valid (i.e., (i,j) being indeed a gridpoint) for

$$I_1 \leqslant i \leqslant I_2, \quad J_1(i) \leqslant j \leqslant J_2(i).$$

See an example for the use of this routine in Fig. 1 above. For a *horizontal* grid n, KEYS$(n,J_1,J_2,JR,I_1,I_2,IR)$ would similarly give $u_{ij}^n = Q(IR(JR+j)+i)$.

KEYSV $(n,I_1,I_2,IR,J_1,J_2,JR,NF)$ - A <u>v</u>ectorial version of KEYS, where NF, another output parameter, is the number of functions defined on grid n. The ν-th function on vertical grid n can then be accessed by

$$u_{ij}^{n;\nu} = Q(JR(IR+i)+j*NF+\nu-1), \quad (1 \leqslant \nu \leqslant NF).$$

KEYGV $(n,\cdots)$ - Similar to KEYSV, but for a <u>g</u>eneral (possibly multi-string) grid n. In this case, for a vertical grid,

$$u_{ij}^{n;\nu} = Q(JR(KR(IR(\ell)+i)+k)+j*NF+\nu-1)$$

where k is the string number within the column and ℓ is the set number. NF, IR, KR and JR, as well as other vectors giving the ranges of j, k, i and ℓ in the grid, are all named by the user but loaded by KEYGV.

KEYI $(n,\tau,\cdots)$ - Similar to KEYGV, but giving the ranges for the τ-$\underline{inner}$ subgrid of n.

KEYBG (n,JR,NK,NF) - Access the functions on $\underline{b}$oundary $\underline{g}$rid n by loading vector JR so that the value of the ν-th grid function, at the point whose boundary ordinal number is k, is given by

$$u_k^{n,\nu} = Q(JR(k)+\nu), \quad (1 \leqslant k \leqslant NK, \ 1 \leqslant \nu \leqslant NF).$$

KEYBG1 $(n,\cdots)$ - Similar to KEYBG, but giving also detailed information concerning grid n and each of its curves and pieces.

KEYBI (n,IC,J_1,J_2,LR,L_2,K) - Access $\underline{b}$oundary grid vertical (if IC = 1) or horizontal (if IC = 0) $\underline{i}$ntersections. For example, if IC = 1 then J_1, J_2, LR, L_2 and K will be set so that, for $J_1 \leqslant j \leqslant J_2$ and $1 \leqslant \ell \leqslant L_2(j)$, the (perimetric) ordinal number of the ℓ-th (counting in ascending y) boundary point on column j is given by $K(LR(j)+\ell)$.

LAT (n,XO,YO,HX,HY) - Load the origin and meshsizes (i.e., the $\underline{lattice}$) of grid n into (XO,YO) and (HX,HY), respectively. (Some KEY routines output this information too.)

4.4 Function initialization, operation, transfer and save

The routines in this section and in the next are part of a growing collection of routines for putting values into, and transferring values between, grid functions. Routines mentioned in Sec. 4.5 are also part of that collection. Some of the routines are currently written only for type-real grids.

In the description below we denote the ν-th function defined on grid n by $u^{n,\nu}$, and its value at gridpoint (i,j) by $u_{ij}^{n,\nu}$. u^n stands for the whole vector of functions (or the single function) defined on grid n.

PUTSC (n,ν,C) - $\underline{Put}$ the $\underline{s}$calar $\underline{c}$onstant C into $u^{n,\nu}$.

PUTSF (n,ν,F) - $\underline{Put}$ the $\underline{s}$calar $\underline{f}$unction F(x,y) into $u^{n,\nu}$; i.e.

$$u_{ij}^{n,\nu} \leftarrow F(x_i,y_j) = F(x_0+ih_x, \ y_0+jh_y).$$

PUTVC (n,V) - $\underline{Put}$ the $\underline{c}$onstant $\underline{v}$ector V into u^n. The length of V is assumed to equal the number of functions defined on n.

PUTC (n,C) - Same as PUTSC(n,1,C).

PUTZ (n) - Same as PUTC(n,0).

PUTF (n,F) - Same as PUTSF(n,1,F).

In the following two transfer routines, it is assumed that the two participating grids have the same lattice and the same construction order. The transfer is made at all lattice points (i,j) common to the two grids.

TFERS (n,ν,m,μ) - $\underline{Transfer}$ (the $\underline{s}$calar function) $u_{ij}^{m,\mu}$ into $u_{ij}^{n,\nu}$. This can be used with m = n.

TFER (n,m) - $\underline{Transfer}$ u_{ij}^m into u_{ij}^n. It is assumed that grids m and n have the same number of functions.

TFERTP (n,m) - Trans_fer_ u_{ij}^m into u_{ij}^n, uniform grids m and n having opposite (_trans-_
posed) construction orders. By using this routine between two applications
of a line relaxation routine, for example, alternating-direction line relaxation procedure is automatically obtained. The transfer costs only one
addition per gridpoint, plus some operations per string.

WRITEF (n,LU) - Write the functions of grid n on logical unit LU.

READF (n,LU) - Read the functions of grid n from logical unit LU into their appropriate place in Q or L. It is assumed that they were written by
WRITEF(n,LU).

In the following routines, grids ℓ, m and n are assumed to be identical, and may
coincide.

SUBF　(n,ℓ,m) - Put $u_{ij}^\ell - u_{ij}^m$ into u_{ij}^n.

ADDF　(n,ℓ,m) - Put $u_{ij}^\ell + u_{ij}^m$ into u_{ij}^n.

PUTF2F (n,ν,ℓ,λ,m,μ,F) - Put $F(u_{ij}^{\ell,\lambda}, u_{ij}^{m,\mu})$ into $u_{ij}^{n,\nu}$.

4.5 Irregular and Boundary operators

One of the heaviest tasks usually confronted in general-domain grid programs is
that of storing and using the geometrical information related to the boundary,
producing, for example, difference approximations at the uniform-grid points right
near the boundary, or approximating Neumann boundary conditions, etc. The data
structures presented above, together with a library of routines, part of which has
already been written, can alleviate this task, and systematize it so that much of
the programming can be done once and for all. The main vehicle is the introduction of a collection of standard geometrical functions, some of which are boundary-
grid functions, others are τ-outer-subgrid functions.

First, the Basic Boundary Functions, produced during the construction of the boundary-grid (see Sec. 3.2), together with suitable interface routines (such as KEYBG
in Sec. 4.3), easily produce many new _boundary functions_, such as the slopes dx/dt,
dy/dt or dx/dy, or the curvature of the piece, or other higher-order derivatives,
etc.

Next, _boundary operators_ can be constructed, such as the finite-difference approximation to the normal derivative. For example, if the operator is linear, it has,
at each boundary-point k, the form $\sum_{\ell=1}^{L_k} \alpha_{k\ell} u_{(k,\ell)}$, where $\alpha_{k\ell}$ are fixed coefficients
and $u_{(k,\ell)}$ are values of a certain function (e.g., an approximate finite-difference
solution) defined either on the boundary grid itself, or on an associated uniform
grid (usually a grid with the same continuous boundary and the same lattice), or
(most often) on both. Thus, the internal representation of such an operator will
be a set of boundary-grid functions, some of which are type-real (e.g., the values
of $\alpha_{k\ell}$), others are type-integer (e.g., the _addresses_ of $u_{(k,\ell)}$), or the value of
L_k; because of the different type, these functions should be defined on a formally
different boundary-grid, which can be created by the GRCOPY routine). Each routine for constructing such an operator will have as input parameters all the relevant uniform-grid and boundary-grid numbers and function indices.

Operators defined on the outer points of uniform grids often require some boundary
information. The usual examples are finite-difference approximations to differential operators at irregular points, i.e., points without enough neighbors to form
the regular finite-difference approximation. Each such operator, generally called

irregular operator, is internally represented by a set of type-real (coefficients) and type-integer (mainly addresses) functions defined on a τ-outer subgrid. The construction of the GRIDPACK collection of irregular operators starts from the most basic ones, such as the following.

POINTE (n,m) - <u>Point</u> the (single) function on uniform-grid n to the east neighbor on boundary-grid m; i.e., for each gridpoint of n set the function value to be the address of the nearest boundary point lying east to the gridpoint, at a distance less than the meshsize. If the distance is greater than the meshsize, the value ITOP (a standard default integer, usually the largest integer defined on the computer) is instead inserted. Usually grid n for such a purpose will be a τ-outer subgrid, the templet τ containing (0,0) and the east shift (1,0).

POINTB $(n,m,\nu_E,\nu_W,\nu_N,\nu_S)$ - Similarly point the ν_E-th function on grid n to the east neighbor on boundary-grid m, the ν_W-th function to the west neighbor, the ν_N-th to the north, and the ν_S-th to the south.

Based on these routines and on KEYBG, and using the Basic Boundary Functions (see Sec. 3.2), functions giving the horizontal and vertical distances to the boundary are easily constructed. Then, with these elementary operators, it becomes easy to write routines which construct more advanced irregular operators. Once programmed, they can be used for any grid by any GRIDPACK user.

Similar general facilities can be developed to program *ghost* operators, i.e., operators defined on τ-ghost grids, such as extrapolation-from-the-interior operators.

Based on the boundary operators routines, a collection of boundary relaxation routines, for various types of boundary conditions, can be developed. Aided by the collection of irregular operators, interior-relaxation routines can easily be written. And so on. Finite-difference programming near curved boundary can thus be made more standard, easy and portable.

4.6 Interpolation

The collection of interpolation routines turned out to be perhaps the most difficult to develop, mainly due to the attempted generality. There are many possible cases to be considered regarding the relative positions of the involved grids and boundaries. Situations may arise, especially with very coarse grids and near special boundary configurations, where the desired order of interpolation is difficult, or even impossible, to achieve, since not enough points are available to interpolate from. Non-standard (e.g., non-central) interpolation formulas are then tried in various ways, searching for a rule as close to central as possible which still gives the highest possible interpolation order (up to the designated order). Therefore, uniform-grid interpolation routines have so far been developed only for the standard coarse-to-fine case, i.e., from a coarse grid m to a finer grid n where $(h_x^m:h_x^n , h_y^m:h_y^n)$ is either (2,2), (2,1), or (1,2), and where every coarse-grid line coincides with a fine-grid line. The routines are devised to have full speed at interior parts of the two grids, with fully efficient DO loops. Near the boundaries, however, the routines are still engaged in very inefficient searches. A different approach, similar to the templet-based operators described in Sec. 4.5, is therefore planned for the future. Detailed account and timing of the current interpolation algorithms is given in [1, App. II].

Routines INT2, INT2AD and INT4 were contributed by Markus von Cube at GMD, St. Augustin, Germany.

INTAD (n,m,ν,μ,I) - <u>Int</u>erpolate I-order bipolynomial interpolation from the μ-th function on the coarse grid m and <u>add</u> the interpolant to the ν-th function on the fine grid n. Both grids are uniform; this routine uses no boundary information, hence extrapolation would frequently be used at marginal points even for bilinear (I=2) interpolation. Special subroutines are used by INTAD for important cases which can be executed faster than the general case, such as single-string grids.

INTRB2 (n,m,ν,μ) - Perform linear (order <u>2</u>) <u>inter</u>polation from the μ-th function on <u>b</u>oundary grid m to the ν-th func<u>tion</u> on <u>b</u>oundary grid n, where both gri<u>ds</u> are defined on the same continuous boundary, but their lattices need not have any particular relation to each other. The interpolation is performed with respect to the piece parameter (t in Sec. 2). Near the piece endpoints interpolation is inevitably sometimes replaced by extrapolation, since no relation between adjacent piece parameters is assumed by this routine. (Other routines can be written with other assumptions, or with interpolation based on the (x,y) coordinates.)

INT2   (n,m,ℓ) - <u>Inter</u>polate linear (order <u>2</u>) interpolation from uniform grid m and boundary grid ℓ to uniform grid n, all assumed to have the same continuous boundary.

INT4   (n,m,ℓ) - Similar, with cubic (<u>4</u>-th order) interpolation.

INT2AD (n,m,ℓ) - Like INT2, but the interpolated function is <u>add</u>ed to the previous function on grid n.

4.7 Display and norms

The routines below are used for displaying grids (also showing the relative positions of several grids), grid functions, templets and boundaries.

DISPG (n,LW,ICAR,LU) - <u>Disp</u>lay uniform grid n by printing the character ICAR in page positions corresponding to grid positions. LW is the line width (number of characters per line); if it is not large enough, the grid is shown in bands of LW characters each. LU is the logical output unit.

DISPGS (N,NL,LW,ICAR,LU) - Similarly <u>disp</u>lay NL uniform grids simultaneously. N is a vector of NL grid numbers and ICAR is a vector of NL corresponding display characters. The grids are printed on top of each other, thus showing their relative positions. It is assumed that all grids have the same construction order and matching lattices; i.e., all lattices are subsets of one underlying lattice, used to determine the page positions.

DISPT (τ,LU) - Similarly <u>disp</u>lay <u>t</u>emplet number τ.

DISPF (n,ν,LW,IFE,w,d,LU) - <u>Disp</u>lay the values of the ν-th function on grid n, using Fortran format Fw.d (if IFE = 'F') or Ew.d (if IFE = 'E'), LW and LU meaning as above.

PLTLAT (n,XL,YL,IPEN) - <u>Plot</u> part of the <u>l</u>attice of boundary grid n, in IPEN color and on XL × YL paper. This is used as a background for other plots.

PLTBND (n,ν,IPL,INDB,IPEN,XL,YL) - <u>Plot</u> boundary grid n and the ν-th function on it. If INDB = 0, the ordinal numbers of the gridpoints are shown. If INDB = 1, their types of intersection are printed. if INDB = 2, the values of the function are printed. If INDB = 3, the boundary curves are drawn by straight segments joining their gridpoints. If INDB = 4, the continuous pieces are drawn and their ordinal numbers are marked. IPEN is the color and XL × YL is the size of the paper. If IPL = 1, this is the last plot on the present paper. It is thus possible to combine several such plots on top of each other, in a variety of colors.

PRINTQ (n) - Printout all the parameters of grid n.

DUMPQL - Dump the Q and L vectors (for debugging purposes).

Various GRIDPACK FUNCTIONs exist for calculating norms of functions, error norms, etc. Examples:

Function FNORMX(n,ν) - Gives $\|u^{n,\nu}\|_\infty$ (the maximum norm).

Function FNORM2(n,ν) - Gives $\|u^{n,\nu}\|_2$ (the L_2 norm).

Function DIFMX(n,ν,m,μ) - Gives $\|u^{n,\nu}-u^{m,\mu}\|_\infty$.

4.8 Multigrid drivers and subroutines

GRIDPACK comes with a collection of multigrid programs that are used for testing the whole package and are also useful for solving various PDE problems and can easily be extended to solve many others. An example:

MULTIG $(x_1,x_2,y_1,y_2,$CHAR$,x_0,y_0,$H$_x,$H$_y,$M$,\cdots,$RELAX,RESCAL$)$ - Solve a differential equation using M grids with lattices

$$L(x_0,y_0 ; H_x*2^{-k} , H_y*2^{-k}), \quad (1 \leq k \leq M).$$

A sequence of additional parameters specified by the user controls the algorithm to be an accommodative or fixed Full Multi-Grid (FMG) algorithm employing the Correction-Scheme (CS) or the Full Approximation Scheme (FAS). RELAX(n,RES) should be a routine that performs a relaxation sweep (thus also defining the difference equations, including boundary conditions) and outputs the residual norm RES. It should be written for a general grid number n (using a KEY routine, as in Fig. 1). RESCAL(n,m) should be a routine that computes residuals in a fine grid n and tranfers weighted averages of them to the coarser grid m.

Routines RELAX and RESCAL should generally be supplied by the user of MULTIG. Some fairly general routines of these kinds, called RELG and RESG, come with GRID-PACK and can be easily modified and generalized to various other cases. A library of such routines, all written in terms of general grid numbers, should, in time, be developed. Important aids for writing such routines are the boundary and irregular operators (Sec. 4.5) and the Grid Language (GL), described next.

5. GRID LANGUAGE (GL)

To facilitate the programming of grid "sweeping operations" (operations which are done sequentially at all or most gridpoints; e.g., a relaxation sweep), and to simplify various other aspects of using GRIDPACK and other grid-oriented programming, a special extention of Fortran called Grid Language (GL) has been developed. The GL macro-statements are written within the usual Fortran code, each macro being identified by "C*" in the first two columns, and may be continued to several card images by the usual Fortran continuation convention. These macro-statements are expanded into usual Fortran statements, including suitable calls to various GRIDPACK routines described above, by a special preprocessor named PREPACK. This preprocessor itself is written in basic Fortran, and thus enjoys full portability.

A representative list of GL macro-statements is given below. In addition to these, GL statements will also be used to have more convenient calls to GRIDPACK routines.

For example, n = UNION(ℓ,m) will be used instead of CALL UNION(n,ℓ,m). The list of such statements will not appear here since it is so far only partly implemented.

For a detailed list of limitations and restrictions currently placed on GL statements, and for a detailed description of PREPACK with its three modes, see [1, Appendix III].

5.1 GL DO statements

The three dots ($\cdots$) appearing in a statement below mean that indefinite number of additional groups, similar to the groups subscripted by 1 and 2, could be added to the statement. Also, we denote by (x_i^n, y_j^n) the values of the (x,y) coordinates at the (i,j) gridpoint of grid n.

DO 5 I = I1,I2,ΔI - The usual Fortran DO statement, except that I1, I2 and the increment ΔI may be any arithmetic expression, and may assume any (negative, zero or positive) integer value.

DO 5 (I,J) = GRID(n),ΔI,ΔJ,$n_1(I_1,J_1)$,$n_2(I_2,J_2)$,$\cdots$ - The row index I and the column index J traverse all the gridpoints (I,J) of <u>grid</u> n, in its construction order and in (positive or negative) increments ΔI <u>and</u> ΔJ, while (I_ℓ,J_ℓ) simultaneously traverse the corresponding gridpoints on n_ℓ, (ℓ=1,2,$\cdots$); i.e., at each pass of this DO loop (performing the statements following the DO, up to the statement labelled 5) (I,J) is another point on grid n, and (I_ℓ,J_ℓ) is set so that $(x_{I_\ell}^{n_\ell}, y_{J_\ell}^{n_\ell}) = (x_I^n, y_J^n)$, if this is possible. When impossible, close values are set by some rules [1, AIII-4.2.2]. The grid numbers n and n_ℓ can be integer constants or variables, but should not, of course, change inside the DO loop.

DO 5 I = GRID(n),ΔI,$n_1(I_1)$,$n_2(I_2)$,$\cdots$ - I traverses the lines of <u>grid</u> n, in increments ΔI, while I_ℓ traverses the corresponding lines of grid n_ℓ. The lines are columns if grid n is vertical, rows if it is horizontal. Grids $n_1,n_2,\cdots$ are assumed to have the same construction order.

DO 5 J = COL(I,n),ΔJ,$n_1(J_1)$,$n_2(J_2)$,$\cdots$ - J traverses the gridpoints of <u>column</u> I in grid n, J_ℓ assuming corresponding values on grid n_ℓ.

DO 5 I = ROW(J,n),ΔI,$n_1(I_1)$,$n_2(I_2)$,$\cdots$ - Similar.

5.2 Statements inside GL DO loops

The following GL statements can typically be used inside DO-GRID or DO-COL or DO-ROW loops. The ASSIGN statement can also be used outside the loop.

ASSIGN u AS ν ON n - Means that in the present subprogram, the letter(s) u stand for the ν-th function on grid n. The function index ν and the grid number n can be either constant or variable.

u(I,J) = u(I+1,J)+u(I-1,J)-$u_1(I_1,J_1)$*H2 - An example of a usual Fortran replacement statement, except that u and u_1 may be grid functions. u is defined as a grid function by an "ASSIGN u AS ν ON n" statement, in which case n should appear as a grid number in the preceding DO statement. Also, u is automatically designated as a grid function if it coincides with a (constant or variable) grid number appearing in the DO statement, in which case u stands for the *first* function of that grid. Expressions like u(IX,JX) can be used, with IX and JX any arithmetic expressions in I and J, respectively, where (I,J) are the indices in the DO statement traversing the grid on which u is defined.

REGULAR(τ)
IRREGULAR 15 - The sequence of statements between these two should be executed only for gridpoints of the τ-inner subgrid (of the principal grid in the DO statement), while the sequence between IRREGULAR and the statement labelled 15 should only be executed for the points of the τ-outer subgrid. This is a way to differentiate between the treatment of irregular and regular points while still maintaining high-speed DO loops for the latter.

IF((I_1+1,J_1).IN(τ_1).n_1) GO TO 5 - Test whether (I_1+1,J_1) belongs to the τ_1-inner subgrid of grid n_1. This is a slow way to differentiate types of points and should therefore usually be used only in the sequence following an IRREGULAR statement.

6. FUTURE EXTENSIONS

The GRIDPACK and Grid-Language system should be extended in many directions. First, improvement in the current routines, and chiefly in the interpolation collection (see Sec. 4.6) is needed, and the library of boundary and irregular operators (see Sec. 4.5) and multigrid programs (see Sec. 4.8) should significantly be expanded. Much of this may be contributed by various GRIDPACK users.

Next, *staggered grids* (interacting grids whose lattices are shifted a constant shift from each other) should be admitted. This would require an additional collection of interpolation routines, some additional GL DO statements to conveniently access shifted neighbors, and more boundary-operator programs. Then, *rotated grids* and *curved grids* should similarly be introduced. It is enough to introduce the simple family of curved grids described in [3, Sec. 2.3] or [6, Sec. 9.3], which are fully characterized by single-variable functions. This will make it possible to use *local* coordinate transformations in multigrid fast solvers, allowing very effective treatment of curved boundaries, interfaces, etc.

Moving boundary capabilities should also be added. This would make it possible to trace interfaces and interior discontinuities (e.g., shocks). Again, a collection of new interpolation and boundary-operator programs will have to be developed for this purpose.

Another, ambitious task is the extension of the current two-dimensional system to deal with *three-dimensional* grids.

REFERENCES

[1] Brandt, A. and Ophir, D., GRIDPACK SYSTEM, A detailed, voluminous description, to appear as a file on MUGTAPE84 (which will carry the system itself as another file, and some other files of various multigrid programs).

[2] Brandt, A., Multi-level adaptive solutions to boundary-value problems, Math. Comp. 31 (1977) 333-390.

[3] Brandt, A., Multi-level adaptive techniques (MLAT) for partial differential equations: ideas and software, in: Rice, J.R. (ed.), Mathematical Software III (Academic Press, New York, 1977, pp. 273-318).

[4] Brandt, A., Multi-level adaptive solutions to singular-perturbation problems, in: Hemker, P.W. and Miller, J.J.H. (eds.), Numerical Analysis of Singular Perturbation Problems (Academic Press, New York, 1979, pp. 53-142).

[5] Ophir, D., Language for Processes of Numerical Solutions to Differential Equations, Ph.D. Thesis, Dept. of Appl. Math., The Weizmann Institute of Science, Rehovot, Israel (1979).

[6] Brandt, A., Guide to multigrid methods, in: Hackbusch, W. and Trottenberg, U. (eds.), Multigrid Methods (Springer-Verlag, Berlin, 1982).

[7] Hackbusch, W. and Trottenberg, U., Multigrid Methods (Springer-Verlag, Berlin, 1982).

[8] Brandt, A., Introductory remarks on multigrid methods, in: Morton, K.W. and Baines, M.J. (eds.), Numerical Methods for Fluid Dynamics (Academic Press, New York, 1982, pp. 127-134).

[9] Rice, J.R. and Boisvert, R.F., Solving Elliptic Problems Using ELLPACK (Springer-Verlag, Berlin, 1984).

DISCUSSION

Speaker: A. Brandt

Brandt: The multigrid solution <u>can</u> be done in 5 to 10 work units, where a work unit <u>is</u> the number of operations appearing in the discrete equations. People who question this based on their own experiences have probably failed to implement the method correctly. For example early workers claimed that the method was good for Dirichlet problems but not for Neumann. They had, however, failed to transfer the boundary condition residuals to the coarser grids. Even when this is done, convergence rates may somewhat deteriorate if care is not taken to avoid interference between relaxation on the boundary points and in the interior. This knowlegde of how to treat non-Dirichlet boundary conditions is only one of many pieces of knowledge corresponding to various problem features, such as non-linearities, singularities, re-entrant corners, unbounded domains, non-ellipticity, discontinuities in data and discontinuities in solution, global and semi-global conditions, etc. Each one of these features requires a thorough understanding as to what it implies in terms of multigrid solvers. Mistreating just one of them may cause the solution time to increase dramatically. Since convergence will often still be obtained, due to the corrective nature of the fine-grid relaxation, the user may be misled to believe that nothing is wrong with his code. Even if he suspects errors, he is unlikely to discover them all, because they confusingly interact with each other, an impossible network of conceptual mistakes and programming bugs. To obtain full efficiency, the research should be very systematic, introducing one feature at a time accompanied by various simple-problem mini-studies. Many lessons have so been learned; many of them can already be studied from published papers.

Yanenko: You said that most of the time is spent on the finest mesh, what then <u>is</u> the role of the coarse meshes?

Brandt: The coarse meshes are used to accelerate convergence of the smooth components. The information about the size of smooth error components is necessarily obtained from many fine-grid points, and can therefore efficiently be used only when collected to just few coarse-grid points.

Schönauer: We have tried imposing rectangular grids on arbitrary domains and experienced severe book-keeping problems. How do you overcome these?

Brandt: This is explained more fully in my write-up.

Madsen: Could you tell us about the availability of multigrid software? Also, you indicated that the novice is prone to make mistakes in this area, how then should he introduce himself to the subject?

Brandt: A lot of multigrid software is either not documented or not user oriented and I agree that this can be confusing. Some of the better software, including GRIDPACK, MGOO and BBMG, will appear in the new version of the magnetic-tape MUGTAPE, which will hopefully be released early next year.

A video course of 24 lectures on multigrid techniques is readily available from Colorado State University, Office of Instructional Services, Fort Collins, Colorado 80523, phone 303-491-5416, Production Numbers L8101-110, M8111-114, M8166-175. Abstracts and copies of video transparancies can be obtained by writing to me. An updated (as of May 1982) "Guide to Multigrid Developments" contains a lot of information for somewhat advanced multigridders. The complete novice can read Secs. 2, 3.1, 4 and Appendix B in my 1977 paper (Math. Comp. 31, pp. 333-390), just 12 pages, describing the most basic concepts through a single example, with its mode analysis, Fortran code and output. Or he can read the extensive introductory paper of Stüben and Trottenberg. That paper, and the above "Guide", and many other multigrid articles, have appeared in the book "Multigrid Methods" (W. Backbusch and U. Trottenberg, eds., Springer Verlag 1982).

Simpson: I was quite interested to see in your grid system macros that you seem to have two types of grid distinguished by whether the grid is stored by rows or columns. I can see some difficulties of incompatibility in operations on grids like unions. What is the benefit of this explicit distinction?

Brandt: Sweeping operations (like relaxation) are performed much faster if their ordering conform with the internal structure. We have a routine (or macro) called TRANSPOSE, which changes column ordering to row ordering, and vice versa. This should be controlled by the user. When you try to take UNION of grids with different construction order, the system will first automatically use TRANSPOSE.

Grossman: Methods will need to know where neighbouring points are; for irregular points how does GRIDPACK provide this information?

Brandt: Initially we wrote routines to find out whether there were sufficient neighbours but this approach was not wholly satisfactory. We therefore adopted the template approach described in the paper.

PDE SOFTWARE: Modules, Interfaces and Systems
B. Engquist and T. Smedsaas (eds.)
Elsevier Science Publishers B.V. (North-Holland)
© IFIP, 1984

EFFICIENCY OF THE NUMERICAL ALGORITHMS AND
THE DECOMPOSITION PRINCIPLE FOR MODERN COMPUTERS

N. N. Yanenko

Institute for Theoretical
and Applied Mechanics
Institutskaya ul. 4/1
630090 Novosibirsk 90
USSR

The notions of the algorithm and its efficiency have changed
essentially in recent years due to the rapid development of
the mathematical modelling and growing complexity of the
computers. We focus our discussion on the algorithms
specifically oriented towards mechanics of continua, although
many points of view presented in the paper are of general
character. This orientation takes into account the
traditionally unified treatment of mechanical problems, which is
based on: i) conservation laws, ii) closure relations,
iii) interpretation of a global process as a sum of local ones,
iv) representation of the interaction of adjacent domains through
boundary conditions (autonomous or nonautonomous).

1. REAL COMPUTATIONAL ALGORITHM

Real computational algorithm (r.c.a.) executed on a computer consists of two
parts:
i) analytical algorithm (a.a.),
ii) cybernetical algorithm (c.a.).
An a.a. is a sequence of arithmetical, algebraical, symbolical operations
executed serially or in parallel on the logical elements (l.e.) of a computer.
The information connected with the a.a. is transformed on l.e. Sometimes this
transformation is followed by the loss of the information, for example in
arithmetical operations, due to round-off errors. On the contrary, there is no
loss of information in algebraic and symbolic manipulations.

The c.a. comprises the information transfer realized by elements, functional
units (F.U.) and interconnection networks, the manipulation of instructions, the
logical reconfiguration of the F.U.'s and their interconnections.

All these operations are information conserving.

As long as the computers were slow and their structure simple, the efficiency of
the r.c.a. was measured essentially by that of the a.a. In particular, the time
needed for the information transfer was not taken into account. Along with the
increasing speed and complexity of the computer the relative execution time of
the c.a. increases too.

In this way the efficiency of the r.c.a. structure is intimately connected not
only with the structure of the a.a. and that of the program, but also with the
architecture of a computer and the implementation of the r.c.a. on it too. The
need for harmony in the computation process, that is for good correspondence of
all its parts, becomes all the more insistent.

2. THE STRUCTURE OF THE COMPLEX ALGORITHM

The modular construction of the algorithm is universally acknowledged as the most efficient way of numerically solving large problems. An algorithm modelling the evoluation or the state of complex physical systems is divided into parts called modules, that correspond to those of the system. The modules are joined together with the aid of the matching module. This kind of modular construction we call the physical decomposition. There is another approach for constructing the modular structure.

The algorithm representing the behaviour of the system maps it by means of finite difference or finite element approximation on the system of linear algebraical equations, as a rule, with a big number of unknowns (global algebraic system, g.a.s.). The g.a.s. is divided into a set of simpler systems which are solved separately (serially or in parallel). After exchange of data these partial solutions are joined together into a global solution by means of the matching module.

The second approach will be called algebraical decomposition. This approach is more general, but the algebraic decomposition is not so clear as the physical one. Furthermore, the most important aim of an approximation is constructing an adaptive mesh and analytical representation in the numerical cells to get convenient structure of the global **algebraical matrix.**

Here we come to a very important problem of constructing the matrix by the choice of both algebraical algorithm and informational medium. We shall designate by $M(t_n, t_{n+1})$ a module representing a single step operator, by $M(t_o, t)$ the one representing a solution operator.

It is to be noted here that in order to facilitate the synthesis of a global algorithm its modules should be homogeneous and their basis relatively small. In the papers [1-4] we introduced the notions of the simple (homogeneous), autonomous, nonautonomous module and of modular basis, local, global algorithm.

3. THE SIMPLE MODULE

The simple module is a program realizing an analytical algorithm and having the following properties:
   i) control over the stability of the algorithm and, in particular, over the condition numbers of the matrices used in the algorithm,
   ii) control over the approximation and accuracy of the algorithm,
   iii) uniformity of the difference scheme,
   iv) homogeneity of the reference medium (regular curvilinear mesh, regular triangulation),
   v) correspondence of the analytical model to the physical one:
The algorithm approximates a boundary Cauchy problem globally or for one integration step, i.e. approximates solution or single step operator,
   vi) compactness: the program and data set associated with the simple module are mapped in some subdomain of the operational (homogeneous) memory fixed for the execution time,
   vii) completeness: the data set associated with the simple module consists of arbitrary functions belonging to some functional class.

This property guarantees flexibility and adaptivity of the modular system, which are essentially important for matching the modules in a large program and for the transportability of the modules,
   viii) the possibility of utilizing the module in both autonomous and nonautonomous modifications. For an autonomous module $M_i = M_i(t_n, t_{n+1})$ input data $I_n(M_i)$ are computed from output data $O_n(M_i)$ of the same module and the

data of other modules $M_j (j \neq i)$ are not used. For the nonautonomous modules M_i the transformation and/or the transfer of data from other modules belonging to $\{M_\alpha\}$ is necessary. The transfer and/or transformation of data is realized with help of a matching module. It is to be noted here that the notion of the simple module is mainly conncected with the properties of homogeneity and it doesn't imply that the simple module cannot be decomposed further into simple modules of smaller size. The process of decomposition can be continued up to the modules which cannot be decomposed further. These may be called basic ones and constitute the basis of the modular system. The main aim of a good modular design is minimizing the modular basis and facilitating at the same time a simple and clear macro language.

4. THE CLASSIFICATION OF ALGORITHMS FOR SIMPLE MODULES

Before considering the effectiveness of the analytical algorithm pertaining to a simple module, we shall introduce some notions and symbols relative to the structure of the module and of the modular system.

c_i - continous model used in the algorithm of M_i ,

d_i - discrete model,

n_i - the mesh pertaining to the algorithm of M_i ,

Ω_i - domain of initial value data of M_i,

ω_i - data set adjoining to Ω_i and used for matching a nonautonomous module M_i with the other ones from the set $\{M_\alpha\}$,

$\overline{\Omega}_i = \Omega_i + \omega_i$,

ψ_i - the data set of coefficient functions pertaining to M_i ,

z_i - the data set of boundary conditions pertaining to M_i,

Y_i - the data set $\{\alpha\}$ of undefined boundary conditions corresponding to a nonautonomous module M_i ,

y_i - the data set adjoining Y_i and defined by the condition:

$\overline{Y}_i = Y_i + y_i$, where $\overline{Y}_i$ is a minimal data set necessary for obtaining the numerical values of $\{\alpha\}$,

W_i - data set associated with the module M_i necessary for its computing.

The following relations are satisfiable

$W_i = \Omega_i + \psi_i + Z_i$ (autonomous module),

$W_i = \Omega_i + \psi_i + Y_i$ (nonautonomous module),

$W_i = \overline{\Omega}_i + \psi_i$ (nonautonomous explicit module).

There are two classes of nonautonomous modules: those with numerical boundary conditions and those with partly algebraical, partly numerical b.c.'s. The modules of the first kind will be called numerical, those of the second kind - the algebraical ones. M_i can be considered as a function of the data sets $\Omega_i, \psi_i, Z_i; M_i = M_i(\Omega_i, \psi_i, Z_i)$. Data ψ_i , Z_i fixed, the module M_i gets autonomous, realizes a step operator and can be considered as a function of Ω_i:

$M_i = M_i(\Omega_i).$

Let us introduce the notion of frame (pattern) module. A module $M(\Omega_i, \psi_i, Z_i)$ is called a frame module if the following conditions are valid:

i) ψ_i, Z_i are standard data sets ψ, Z,

ii) M is a standard representative module of a modular system $\{M_i\}$,

iii) matrices of $M_i(\psi_i, Z_i)$ are equivalent to that of M.

The representation ii) can be put into the form:

$$M_i(\psi_i, Z_i) = T(\psi_i \to \psi, Z_i \to Z) \cdot M(\psi, Z)$$

where

$T(\psi_i \to \psi, Z_i \to Z)$ is a transfer module.

We can consider, more generally, the module M_i as a function of the model and mesh:

$$M_i = M_i(c_i, d_i, n_i, \Omega_i, \psi_i, Z_i).$$

We put correspondingly

$$M_i = \pi(c_i \to c, d_i \to d, n_i \to n, \psi_i \to \psi, Z_i \to Z) \cdot M(c, d, n, \psi, Z)$$

where π is an operator of the transformation

$$c_i \to c, \; d_i \to d, \; n_i \to n, \; \psi_i \to \psi, \; Z_i \to Z$$

which comprises, in particular, the operators of analytical transformation and of transfer.

The notion of frame module originates from the theory of difference schemes and is intimately connected with that of local difference operator, (see [5]). The most important application of the frame module is connected with the transformation of coordinates and correspondingly with that of the difference scheme.

Let $\Lambda u - f = 0$ be

an original scheme (frame scheme) which has constant coefficients in some initial (e.q. Eulerian) coordinates. After a transformation of the coordinates it becomes a scheme with variable coefficients and may be considered as an image of the frame scheme under the transformation. Thus, the frame scheme is a prototype of a class of equivalent schemes. The frame prototype completely defines the type of a boundary value problem.

Note: By an appropriate choice of the coordinates a frame scheme with small parameters can be reduced to a regular one. In this case the small parameter is introduced into the transformation function. By tuning (or activating) a nonautonomous module we understand the preliminarily fixing of all its input data to prepare the module for further functioning as an autonomous model. These data can be obtained in many ways: through the direct transfer of output data within the modular system $\{M_\alpha\}$, through their intermediate transforming, by means of the matching module, by solving the set of equations for algebraical (nonfixed) parameters, (see fig. 1.).

Now let us formulate the conditions imposed on the algorithms and accordingly give their classification. The stability and consistence of an algorithm guarantees its convergence. The verification and realization of these conditions for an autonomous simple algorithm is based on the fundamental theorems of convergence (see [5]).

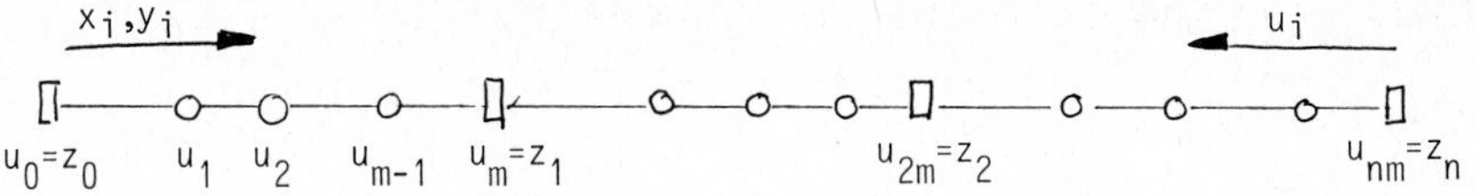

$$x_i, y_i \longrightarrow \qquad\qquad\qquad\qquad u_i \longleftarrow$$

$$[\!]\!\!-\!\!\!-\!\!\!\circ\!\!-\!\!\circ\!\!-\!\!-\!\!\circ\!\!-\!\![\!]\!\!\leftarrow\!\!-\!\!\circ\!\!-\!\!\circ\!\!-\!\!\circ\!\![\!]\!-\!\!-\!\!\circ\!\!-\!\!\circ\!\!-\!\!\circ\!\![\!]$$

$$u_0 = z_0 \quad u_1 \quad u_2 \quad u_{m-1} \quad u_m = z_1 \qquad\qquad u_{2m} = z_2 \qquad\qquad u_{nm} = z_n$$

$$A_i u_{i-1} + B_i u_i + C_i u_{i+1} = F_i \quad , \quad i = 1, \ldots, N = m \cdot n - 1$$

$$\overline{A}_1 u_0 + \overline{B}_1 u_1 = \overline{F}_1$$

$$\overline{B}_{N-1} u_{N-1} + \overline{C}_{N-1} u_N = \overline{F}_{N-1}$$

$$a_\alpha z_{\alpha-1} + b_\alpha z_\alpha + c_\alpha z_{\alpha+1} = f_\alpha \quad , \quad \alpha = 1, \ldots, n-1$$

$$\overline{a}_1 z_0 + b_1 z_1 = f_1$$

$$b_{n-1} z_{n-1} + \overline{c}_{n-1} z_n = f_{n-1}$$

$$a_1, b_1, c_1 \quad A_1 \ldots A_m, \quad B_1 \ldots B_m, \quad C_1 \ldots C_m;$$

$$A_{m+1} \ldots A_{2m}, \quad B_{m+1} \ldots B_{2m}, \quad C_{m+1} \ldots C_{2m}$$

Nonautonomous modules and their reducing to a system of autonomous modules by means of the matching module based on algebraical sweeps.

Fig. 1.

The analysis of the algorithm having the structure of a semigroup or that of its step operator generates a dichotomy of the difference schemes. These can be divided into the classes:
  i) absolutely or conditionally stable schemes,
 ii) absolutely or conditionally consistent ones,
iii) explicit or implicit ones.
The relations between these notions are formulated in the theorems as follows:

Theorem 1. Let

$$\frac{\partial u}{\partial t} = L(D)u = \sum_{\alpha=0}^{p} A_\alpha D^\alpha u \qquad\qquad (1)$$

be a correct system with constant matrices A_α. Then the explicit scheme

$$\frac{u^{n+1} - u^n}{\tau} = L(\tfrac{\Delta}{h})u^n, \qquad \Delta = \frac{T_1 - T_{-1}}{2} \qquad\qquad (2)$$

is absolutely consistent with (1) and conditionally stable if the condition

$$\frac{\tau}{h^{2p}} \le \text{const}$$

holds. Here p is the order of (1) and const is a positive constant.

Theorem 2. The implicit scheme

$$\frac{u^{n+1} - u^n}{\tau} = L(\frac{\Delta}{h})u^{n+1} \tag{4}$$

is absolutely consistent with (1) and is absolutely stable.

Theorem 3.

If:

   i) the differential operator $L(D)$ in (1) has unbounded spectrum,

  ii) the difference operator

$$\frac{T_0 - E}{\tau} - \Lambda_0(T_1) \tag{5}$$

is absolutely consistent with the differential operator $\frac{\partial}{\partial t} - L(D)$ then:
the explicit scheme

$$\frac{u^{n+1} - u^n}{\tau} = \Lambda_0(T_1)u^n \tag{6}$$

cannot be absolutely stable.

Theorem 3 states that no explicit scheme can be absolutely stable and absolutely consistent simultaneously. A scheme having both the properties must be implicit.

Theorems 1, 2 use the correctness and the stability in the sense of Petrovsky. It is to be noted that for large classes of Cauchy problems and difference schemes solution operators in the theorems (1-3) constitute the semigroup in some Banach space.

For the effectiveness of the simple autonomous module the number of operations in step operator per point is essential. We introduce into consideration a positive function $\phi(N)$ that signifies the number of operations corresponding to the step operator of a module containing N points.

Definition: If

$$\rho(N) \leq \text{const.} \cdot N \tag{7}$$

where const is independent of N , then the scheme is locally economical (economical on the step operator). The explicit scheme is always locally economical with $C = m_e$, where m_e is the number of operations per point.

The one-dimensional implicit scheme is locally economical too with $C = m_i$, where m_i is the number of operations corresponding to one point.

Let τ^s denote the maximal timestep admitted by stability conditions, τ^α - the maximal step admitted by the accuracy requirement. Then the expression

$$K_e^i = \frac{m_i}{m_e} \cdot \frac{\tau_i}{\tau_e}$$

approximatively represents the relative efficiency of the implicit scheme as compared to the explicit one.

In the ratio

$$\frac{\tau_i}{\tau_e} ,$$

τ_i is to be taken as a maximum value for all admissible τ_i^α, τ_e- as a maximum value for all admissible τ_e^S .

If

$$K_e^i \leq \text{const} , \qquad\qquad (9)$$

where const is independent of N, then the scheme can be called globally economical or efficient (economical on the solution operator).

Up to now we have considered the effectiveness in a fixed mesh. Applying the mesh transformation we can increase the effectiveness of the algorithm due to the homogeneity of local accuracy and the increasing maximum time step τ^S admitted by stability.

Let m_e, τ_e, m_i , τ_i denote the number of operations and the time step for an explicit scheme, and an absolutely stable implicit scheme respectively. Then the implicit scheme is preferable to the explicit one if

$$m_i \cdot \tau_i \leq m_e \cdot \tau_e , \ K_e^i \leq 1. \qquad\qquad (10)$$

Is it possible in the multidimensional case to construct simple autonomous efficient algorithms? Generally speaking, the following statement is true: there exists a decomposition of the multidimensional implicit, absolutely stable and consistent scheme into the product of one-dimensional schemes that are implicit, absolutely stable on each fractional step and absolutely consistent on the whole step. This decomposition can be realized as a splitting up scheme or as that of approximate factorization.

For large classes of the differential equations and the difference schemes this statement is exact and can be considered as a theorem (theorem 4). As one-dimensional implicit absolutely stable and absolutely consistent schemes are efficient, the theorem 4 asserts that there are multidimensional efficient simple modules. There arises a question: whether the decomposition of a one-dimensional implicit module into a set of one-dimensional implicit modules of smaller size is possible.

The following statement is valid:
Theorem 5. The system of three-diagonal equations with N×N matrix $(N = N_1 \cdot N_2)$ admits the decomposition into N_1 three-diagonal subsystems, each with $N_2 \times N_2$ matrix. The matching module is a $N_1 \times N_1$ three-diagonal system (see [15]). The result is valid for recurrent scalar and vector-relations, scalar and vector "sweeps".

The given analysis is related to the abstract (analytical) computational algorithms and abstract (analytical) modules. The computer architecture and the algorithm structure have not been taken into account. Notwithstanding, already on this level the possibility and efficiency of the algorithm decomposition into one-dimensional ones is evident.

Note 1. Not every splitting along the coordinate directions generates a decomposition into purely one-dimensional problems. Thus, when splitting a second order system with mixed derivatives, the latter are taken from a lower level, and fractional step modules are not onedimensional as regards the data sets. The full decomposition into onedimensional modules with one-dimensional data sets can be realized in the following manner:

i) by splitting along coordinate and diagonal directions (see [7]),
ii) by interpolating the mixed derivatives from the values on two adjacent
coordinate lines to the middle line. It is to be noted that the
interpolation operator can be considered as an additional fractional step
module or as a matching module,
iii) by expressing the values of mixed derivatives on the lower time level through
the data on three adjacent lines and by transferring these data as right hand
sides for the middle line [7].

The process of obtaining   the values of the right hand sides can be considered
as an additional fractional step module that serves as a matching one.

Note 2. According to basic properties of the schemes (stability, consistency,
explitcitness, efficiency) a dichotomic classification can be introduced.

Let us consider some class of problems. We shall write $S(\alpha_1,\alpha_2,\alpha_3,\alpha_4)$ iff for
every problem of this class there exists a scheme of some form with the properties
$\alpha_1,\alpha_2,\alpha_3,\alpha_4$; $\alpha_i = 0, 1$.

The properties of the schemes are supposed to be coded in the following form:
$\alpha_1 = 1$ iff a scheme is absolutely consistent.

$\alpha_2 = 1$ iff a scheme is absolutely stable,

$\alpha_3 = 1$ iff a scheme is implicit,

$\alpha_4 = 1$ iff a scheme is locally economical.

Then theorems 1 - 4 can be represented as:

Theorem 1 $S(1,0,0,1)$,

Theorem 2 $S(1,1,1,X)$,

Theorem 3   not $S(1,1,0,X)$, $x=0$ or $X=1$,

Theorem 4 $S(1,1,1,1)$.

This dichotomic classification can be enlarged by adding other properties
(group properties, conservativeness and so on).

Note 3. For the quality and effectiveness of the algorithm stability and
approximation control are very important. For this aim functions and parameters
of the algorithm have to be adaptive. For example, weight coefficients in a two
level implicit scheme should guarantee the maximum of dissipation in the region
of a shock wave (shock layer) and the maximum of accuracy in the region of smooth
solution.

The predictor-corrector scheme is especially adaptive and guarantees a
reasonable agreement between stability and accuracy, predictor ensuring the
stability, corrector ensuring the accuracy (see [7, 8] . Splitting up according
to physical processes enhances too the stability and accuracy control. I.e.,
splitting up a diffusion process in a reagent medium, described by the equation

$$\frac{\partial u}{\partial t} = \Delta u + f(u) \tag{12}$$

into two alternatively operating subsystems (see [7, 9])

$$\frac{1}{2}\frac{\partial u}{\partial t} = \Delta u \qquad \text{(diffusion process)}, \tag{13}$$

$$\frac{1}{2}\frac{\partial u}{\partial t} = f(u) \qquad\qquad \text{(reaction).} \qquad (14)$$

enables one to integrate diffusion equation by means of noniterative implicit scheme and correspondingly the reaction equation by stiff equation method.

The application of a homogeneous representation, in particular, the uniform order of a local approximation as well as constructing the adaptive mesh permits accuracy control of the algorithm.

The presence of the interior iterations in a step operator hinders the accuracy evaluation. Equally this is valid for interior iterations in an overlapping matching.

5. THE GLOBAL ALGORITHM

Now we shall consider the real computational process and modules. In the case of the global algorithm, which represents a composition of the simple nonautonomous modules, efficiency of the algorithm depends strongly on the architecture of the computer, on the structure of the modular system and that of a matching module in particular.

Let us compare the efficiency of the explicit and implicit schemes for the global algorithm. In the case of the explicit scheme the matching module consists simply of joining the domain Ω_i to the strip $\omega_i = \sum_j \omega_{ij}$ where ω_{ij} are adjacent strips, $\omega_{ij} \in \Omega_{ij}$; Ω_{ij} are adjacent domains. The data sets are taken for the same time level. This matching can be realized by a direct data exchange and by obtaining the solution in Ω_i on the upper time level (see fig. 2) with $\overline{\Omega}_i$ taken on the lower time level. In the case of the explicit schemes the matching module completely preserves the analytical algorithm and leaves it unchanged.

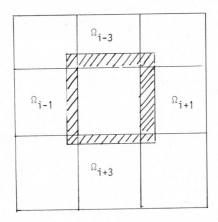

Matching of modules by a cover in the case of explicit difference schemes.

Fig. 2

Thus, the explicit matching causes no information loss and can be considered as a cybernetic one. It is to be noted that in the case of explicit matching the global algorithm is flexible as regards the algorithm decomposition in general and the choice of the domains Ω_i. The negative property of the explicit module structure is the rigidity of the stability criteria, especially for large problems and complex modular systems. For example, the profiles of the viscous flows with high Reynolds numbers have large gradients near the body. The conditions of the uniform local accuracy requests refining of the space mesh in the boundary layer domain. According to the Courant stability criteria for explicit schemes, the time step $\tau = \tau(h_{min})$ becomes very small and as a consequence the difference scheme is not efficient. The stability conditions imposed by an implicit scheme restrict less rigidly, if not at all, the step-size of the implicit scheme, but the matching algorithm is more complex than that for the explicit one. Furthermore, the global analytical algorithm changes because of the approximate factorization, iterations, interpolations (truncation error), solving the system of equations pertaining to the matching module (round off error). The analytical algorithm can loose a semigroup structure because of additional interior nonlinearity iterations. In the case of a module synthesis with the overlapping of neighbour domains, the algorithm looses a semigroup structure too, and this is true both for implicit and explicit schemes. If the application of a complete directional splitting up is possible, the matching module is reduced to transposing the matrix and/or to the algebraical sweeps. The efficiency of the implicit algorithms increases and attains the maximum for the homogeneous modular system.

6. HOMOGENEOUS MODULAR SYSTEM

The program that has a good modular structure can be effectively realized on the parallel computers. It is especially true in the case of the homogeneous modular system.

Definition. The set of homogeneous simple modules $M_i(N_i)$, $i=1,...,p$ (N_i - the number of points in a module's mesh) constitute a homogeneous modular system, if the following conditions are fulfilled:

i) $N_1 = N_2 = ... = N_p$,

ii) the continuous models C_i pertaining to the modules $M_i(i=1...p)$ are equivalent, i.e. become identical for equal coefficient functions. The same is valid for the discrete models d_i,

iii) the meshes are equivalent, i.e. become identical under piecewise smooth one to one transformation. The condition number of the transformation must be controlled in order that the machine implementation be possible. If the sets of exchange, turning and boundary value modules constitute separately (each for itself) homogeneous systems, we call the homogeneous modular system a homogeneous modular structure. For scalar computers the global computation process can be reduced to the cycle:

$$(M_1,E_1) \cdot (M_2,E_2) \cdot ... \cdot (M_p,E_p) =$$
$$= (MT_1,E_1)(MT_2,E_2) \cdot ... \cdot (MT_p,E_p) = \qquad (15)$$
$$= M(T_1,E_1) \cdot M(T_2,E_2) \cdot ... \cdot M(T_p,E_p)$$

where T_i is the module of turning (activating), E_i - that of exchange.

For parallel computers this cycle can be realized by concurrent implementation of the modules $M_1...M_p$ in SIMD type computing. If N_i are not equal, the macrocodes of M_i are essentially the same, but the input parameters of M_i are different. In this case the homogenization of the modular structure is necessary. For some cases of problems it can be realized, for example, by the method of fictitious domains (MFD) (see [10]).

7. THE EFFECTIVENESS OF THE GLOBAL ALGORITHM

The presence of the transfer operators complicates the global algorithm. Therefore the minimization of transfer operations is desirable. The optimal minimization is possible in directional splitting up. In this case the modules become onedimensional and autonomous, the transfer is reduced to matrix transposing. But such an optimum can be realized in special although typical cases of splitting (e.g. when a differential system contains only derivatives along the coordinate axes and no mixed ones). In a general case besides the matrix transposing, it is necessary to introduce exchange operators between neighbour modules in order to express mixed derivatives through the pure ones by means of interpolation.

Another approach is to compute the mixed derivatives on the lower time level t_n on the middle line and consider them as the right hand side to obtain the values of the pure derivatives on the upper time level t_{n+1}. Interpolation can be considered as a kind of an explicit scheme, and in this interpretation it reduces to the step operator which can be flexibly decomposed. The idea to realize a splitting up on parallel computers was presented in [11] . In Western publications the utilizing of the ADI methods for supercomputers became generally accepted in the seventies - eighties. More generally one can speak about realization of a fractional step method on parallel computers. For this aim the thorough classification and evaluation of the fractional step schemes (MFS) on parallel computers becomes a necessity. The econometrics of the global algorithm is not yet developed. Nonetheless, already now there are reliable qualitative evaluations of the different MFS-schemes.

When realizing the algorithms on parallel computers, the MFS-schemes, which are analytically equivalent, become nonequivalent in practical implementations on parallel computers. E.g. the heat equation

$$\frac{\partial u}{\partial t} = \Delta u, \quad \Delta = \sum_{i=1}^{m} \frac{\partial^2}{\partial x_i^2} , \quad m = 2 \qquad (16)$$

has two analytically equivalent schemes:

 i) directional splitting up scheme with weights,
ii) the alternating direction schemes,

but their realizations on parallel computers are different. In the first case the matching module reduces to matrix transposition, in the second case the additional exchange operators between every three adjacent modules are necessary. Both algorithms have the homogeneous modular structure. It is to be noted that for $m = 3$ the splitting up with weights and ADI schemes are even algebraically nonequivalent (the first scheme is absolutely stable and consistent, the second one is conditionally consistent and conditionally stable). The ADI mD scheme (m = 2,3) was utilized in a probe parallel computer ADINA (see [12 A,B]). It is clear that the corresponding splitting up scheme is more effective. Both algorithms can be utilized in a SIMD structure. The stabilizing correction scheme has nonequivalent fractional step modules and therefore cannot be realized in a SIMD structure (see [7]). The other examples and general considerations permit to conclude that the splitting up schemes are most effective in a real computational algorithm. They attain the minimal data exchange, maximal homogeneity and the simplest matching module. Some very important examples show that the efficiency ratio

$$\frac{T_{exp}}{T_{imp}}$$

evaluated on the scheme of a complete directional splitting up is of the same order for scalar and parallel computers. In [12] it was shown on the probe computer ADINA with N parallel processors and for a $N{\times}N$ global matrix that the coefficient of parallelism is approximately equal to 1. By its structure ADINA is an array computer with a buffer memory and a special switching network.

Another approach can be proposed. Each of N processors is a bundle of elementary vector processors functioning in the pipe line and chaining mode and constitutes a functional unit that realizes a vector recurrent relation. As a onedimensional implicit scheme for the differential equations of mechanics is computed by means of vector sweeps (vector recurrent relations), every sweep can be essentially speeded up by combining the pipe line and chaining.

We shall try to give an asymptotical evaluation for the parallelism coefficient of MFS schemes. Let p_1 be the number of subdivisions corresponding to the flow of arithmetical scalar operations in a pipe line; p_2 the additional gain of speed in the bundle of a vector pipeline processor due to the chaining. Then the overall gain in the speed of the bundle of the chained vector processors is approximately equal to

$$p = p_1 \cdot p_2 .$$

If the number of the bundles is N_2, where N_2 is the number of rows, the gain in speed on the first fractional step is equal to $p \cdot N_2$. For the first fractional step the ratio

$$\frac{T_{imp}}{T_{exp}}$$

has the order of M, where M is the number of operations for the inversion of the matrix of vector components in the recurrent relation. Taking into account that M is independent of N_1, N_2 we get to the conclusion that the global module on the first fractional step is effective. The same is valid for all the fractional steps. The transition from the first fractional step (x_1-direction) to the second one (x_2-direction) is realized by the transposition of the global $N_1 \times N_2$ matrix (the analogous situation is valid for a 3D case). The utilizing of the switching network and buffer memory was proposed in [12] . For scalar sweeps the switching time is negligible and the parallelism coefficient is near to 1. The system of bundle vector processors can be transformed to an array computer with additional speed gain. For this aim every pipe line processor of the bundle should be segmented into microprocessors, the processor bundle is segmented correspondingly into a bundle of microprocessors. This structure permits the application of algebraical sweeps (see [15]). If q - a number of points in each sement, $\frac{N}{q}$ is that of segments, the gain of speed due to the segmentation is proportional to the number of microprocessors and is represented by the ratio

$$K = \frac{N^2}{q}\, p \qquad\qquad\qquad (17)$$

where K is a constant independent of N, q, p and is connected with the algebraic sweeps and switching time.

As a final conclusion we can state that the efficiency relation between explicit and implicit schemes holds for scalar, vector and array processors to within a universal constant.

8. HETEROGENEOUS MODULAR SYSTEMS

Now we will consider the examples and types of the heterogeneous modular structures which can be realized on SIMD computers with relatively small coefficient of parallelism or on MIMD ones. The heterogeneity of the global algorithm is a negative property that has as a consequence the heterogeneity of the modular structure and the lowering of the parallelism coefficient. We will discuss some types of heterogeneity:

i) the heterogeneity of the continuous and/or discrete model. When splitting up according to physical processes, the approximated models on the fractional steps are essentially different and, consequently, so are the corresponding analytical algorithms. This heterogeneity requires quite different macrocodes and can be realized only on a MIMD computer. The typical example of this situation is splitting up of the system of equations governing the behaviour of a reagent gas.

$$\frac{\partial W_i}{\partial t} = \frac{\partial \Sigma^{\alpha}(\overline{W}, \frac{\partial \overline{W}}{\partial x})}{\partial x^{\alpha}} + F^i(W) \qquad \begin{array}{l} \alpha=1,\ldots,m \\ i=1,\ldots,n \end{array} \qquad (18)$$

On the first fractional step we have the system of gasdynamical equations

$$\frac{1}{2}\frac{\partial W^i}{\partial t} = \frac{\partial \Sigma^{i\alpha}(W, \frac{\partial W}{\partial x})}{\partial x^{\alpha}} \qquad . \qquad (19)$$

On the second fractional step the system of ordinary differential equations

$$\frac{1}{2}\frac{\partial W^i}{\partial t} = F^i(W) \qquad (20)$$

is to be integrated. The system (20) is in many cases stiff.

Another example is the decomposition of the problem of steady flow past a body. For the transonic flow the domain of integration is subdivided into two domains: I, II. In the domain I where the flow is subsonic an iteration algorithm is applied. In the domain II of the supersonic flow the marching method is applied (see fig. 3).

Traditionally, when considering the viscous flow past a body, two domains are introduced (I,II). In the domain I a gas is considered as frictionless and Euler's equations are to be integrated; in the domain II the equations of boundary layer hold. The dividing surface or line is obtained by iterations (see fig. 3).

ii) parametric heterogeneity. This kind of heterogeneity is typical of complicated domains. In this case even if the model is uniform, the directional splitting up generates onedimensional segments with different numbers of points or different analytical units.

iii) logical heterogeneity. If the algorithm has a nonlinear branching, the realizing program has logical loops, the chaining should be of variable structure. For the MFS algorithms a MIMD computer is necessary.

iv) the most typical example of a heterogeneous modular structure is the decomposition of a MFE algorithm into physical modules (a substructure or a

superelement method). In this case the integration domains Ω_i may have
topologically nonequivalent meshes, or the solutions may have quite different
analytical representations. As a consequence, the matching module becomes complex,
the method of algebraical sweeps should be replaced by a more general, but not
very efficient method of elimination.

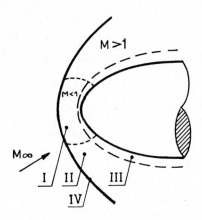

Calculation scheme for a blunted body flowed around in a supersonic
gas flow:

I - subsonic region,   II - supersonic region,
III - boundary layer, IV - shock wave.

Fig 3.

A MFE algorithm with a physical decomposition can be realized on a SIMD computer
with a small parallelism coefficient or on a MIMD computer.

There is a possibility for another algorithmic realization which is connected
with the decomposition of a global linear algebraical system. In this case the
method of algebraical substructures can be applied (see [13]).

   v) For a system of ordinary differential equations the decomposition of
integration algorithm can be reduced to the splitting up of the right hand sides.
The resulting subsystems are essentially different and the computer realization
is only possible with a rather small coefficient of parallelism.

   vi) Systems of linear network equations can be reduced by means of algebraical
sweeps to a parametrically heterogeneous modular structure, which consists of
linear onedimensional modules. Its matching module constitutes a system of
Kirchhoff's relations.

9. HOMOGENIZATION OF HETEROGENEOUS MODULAR STRUCTURE

According to our classification of heterogeneity we will consider the means of
the homogenization:

   i) in the case of a model heterogeneity the homogenization can be realized by
means of a generating model, i.e. the model which generates as special cases the
models c_i pertaining to M_i . For example, the system of Navier-Stokes equations
generates as particular cases the equations of an ideal gasflow, those of boundary

layer, detachment, reattachment flows, jets, wakes, coherent structures and so on. The system $c_i \in M_i$ of simple models is approximated everywhere for each $i=1,\ldots,p$ by the unique generating model, and a homogeneous system of modules is constructed on its base.

This homogeneization may enlarge the number of arithmetic operations in the global algorithm, but the number of basic modules diminishes, and the program becomes more clear and simple. It is to be supposed that enhancing the speed of the parallel computers will stimulate the utilizing of generating models, because of the simplifying of the macrolanguage and programming technology.

   ii) in the case of the parametrical heterogeneity there are several approaches to the homogenization problem. In a MFD method an arbitrary integration domain Ω is included in some simple domain Π : $\Omega \subset \Pi$, admitting the regular mesh, and the boundary conditions are transferred to $\nu\Pi$ (see [10]). All these transformations allow to approximate a heterogeneous structure $M_i[\Omega_i(N_i),A_i]$ by a homogeneous one $M_i[\Omega_i(N),A_i^\varepsilon]$, where each domain $\Omega_i(N)$ has an equal number of points N and algorithms. A_i^ε can be presented in the form

$$A_i^\varepsilon = A^\varepsilon B_i^\varepsilon .$$

Here B_i^ε is a rotation operator and A^ε is a pattern module, one for all simple modules M_i . Coefficient functions in MFD are singular and their computation is connected with a linear branching.

Another approach to treating the boundary value problems with an arbitrary domain is an appropriate choice of coordinates permitting a unified mesh.

iii) nonlinear branching and a lowering of the parallelism coefficient can be eliminated through approximating the algorithm with the branching by one. For example, the scheme of Latter, which is good to distinguish between the waves of rarefaction and those of compression can be replaced by a uniform scheme of Neumann -Richtmyer (see [5]). Linear branching conditions remaining in a linearized algorithm can be included in a homogeneous analytical algorithm as additional logical functions. In this way a mixed analytical-logical homogeneous algorithm can be constructed. The above mentioned approaches do not cover all possibilities, and the procedures problem of homogenization remains open. The effective homogenization reduces the number of basic modules, increases the parallelism coefficient, diminishes the number of logical configurations. In the strict meaning of the word one can speak about homogeneous modular structure only for a set of modules of the same dimension. FSM in combination with MFD allows another approach to homogenization to reduce the set of multidimensional modules to that of onedimensional and to minimize in such a way the module basis. A special place belongs to the modules of boundary conditions. For all the diversity of boundary conditions it is possible to represent the step operator as a product of two operators:

   a) a step of the first boundary problem,
   b) a correction operator of boundary conditions (see [1,7]).

This representation allows to bring to a standard form an arbitrary boundary value problem expressing its peculiarity through the correction operator of boundary conditions.

10.   CONCLUSION

From the preceding presentation the following conclusions can be drawn:
   i) the modern computers stressed the growing importance of the cybernetic

algorithm. For the complete evaluation of the global algorithm efficiency the real
time needed for executing the cybernetical algorithm should be taken into account,
  ii) for the parallel computers the relative efficiency of implicit and explicit
schemes remains principally unchanged as compared to scalar computers.

For many important problems the implicit schemes conserve their principal
advantages. It is true especially for the dynamic meteorology, stationary flows
past bodies e t c,
  iii) the modular structure of the algorithm became the necessary condition of the
efficient parallel computations. If the modular structure is heterogeneous, the
value of the parallelism coefficient diminishes. The maximum of the parallelism
coefficient is achieved on the splitting up schemes, when the modular structure
has a model and parametrical homogeneity,
  iv) homogenization - full or partly - of the modular structure can be obtained
by several approaches:
  a) the method of a generating model,
  b) the method of fictitious domains,
  v) approximation control is facilitated under the following conditions:
  a) homogeneous analytical representation of the solution,
  b) adaptive mesh securing the uniform distribution of the local truncation
error,
  c) the absence of inner iterations,
  vi) the efficiency of a real global algorithm (econometrics) becomes an important
branch of computational matehmatics, the development of which is only starting.

REFERENCES

1. A. N. Konovalov, N. N. Yanenko, Modular principle of a program design as a
   foundation of a program package for solving the problems of mechanics. In
   sbornyk "Program complexes of mathematical physics". Novosibirsk, 1972.

2. N. N. Yanenko, A. N. Konovalov, Technological aspects of numerical methods in
   mathematical physics, Acta Universitatis Carolinal, Mathematica of Physica,
   1974, N1, 2.

3. N. N. Yanenko, V. I. Karnachuk, A. N. Konovalov, Problems of mathematical
   technology. In sbornyk "Numerical methods for mechanics of continua".
   Novosibirsk, v. 8, N3, 1977.

4. N. N. Yanenko, Problems of modular analysis and parallel computations in
   mathematical physics. In sbornyk "Parallel programming and systems of high
   performance". Novosibirsk, CC DAN SSSR, v. 1, 1980.

5. B. L. Rozdestvenski, N. N. Yanenko, Systems of quasilinear equations and
   their applications to gasdynamics. Translations of Mathematical Monographs,
   American Mathematical Society, Providence, Rhode Island, v. 55.

6. A. M. Ilyin, Stability of the difference schemes for Cauchy's problem of
   differential equations in private derivatives, Report DAN SSSR, v. 164, N3,
   1965.

7. N. N. Yanenko, The method of fractional steps, Springer Verlag
   Berlin-Heidelberg-New York, 1971.

8. N. N. Yanenko, I. K. Yaushev, On an absolutely stable scheme for integrating
   gasdynamical equations, Trudy of Mathematical Institute SSSR, 1966, v. 74.

9. V. M. Kovenya, N. N. Yanenko, Splitting up method for the problems of gasdynamics, Nauka, Novosibirsk, 1981.

10. A. N. Konovalov, Method of fictitious domains for the problems of filtrations... In sbornyk "Numerical methods for mechanics of continua". Novosibirsk, 1972, v. 3, 5.

11. G. I. Marchuk, N. N. Yanenko, Application of a splitting up method (method of fractional steps to solving the problems of mathematical physics), Report on IFIP, New York, May, 1960, (see in sbornyk "Some problems of applied and numerical mathematics", Novosibirsk, 1966)

12. T. Nogi, ADINA Computer I and II. Reprinted from the Memories of the Faculty of Engineering, Kyotot University, v. XLIII, Part 3, July, 1981, see also

   "Parallel Machine ADINA". Computing methods in Applied Sciences and Engineering, North-Holland, 1982, edited by R. Glowinski and J. L. Lions.

13. Schrem, Programmbausteine und Datenstrukturen für die Implementation der Methode der finiten Elemente, Dissertation, Universität Stuttgart, 1978.

14. A. F. Voevodin, S. M. Shugrin, Numerical methods of solving onedimensional systems, Nauka, DAN SSSR, N83, 1981.

15. N. N. Yanenko, A. N. Konovalov, A. H. Bugrov, G. W. Shustov, On the organization of parallel computing and parallel mode of progonkas. In sbornyk "Numerical methods of continual mechanics". Novosibirsk, v. 9, N7, 1978.

Editors' comment: Due to the sudden death of Academician N. N. Yanenko on the 16th January 1984, some minor editorial changes have been done without his consent.

DISCUSSION

Speaker: N. Yanenko

Rice: I want to emphasize the important point that Yanenko made about the
effect of better algorithms. In some important areas, the development of better
numerical algorithms have done more to advance our abilities to solve problems
than has the development of larger and faster computers. This fact is quite
unexpected and unknown outside the numerical algorithms community. This fact
should be pointed out to those who are very willing to spend millions on new
computer development and yet not willing to spend thousands on new numerical
methods. A summary of the progress in algorithmic methods for elliptic problems
is given in my recent book: Numerical Methods, Software and Analysis, McGraw-Hill,
1983 (Chapter 10).

For example, in solving linear systems from ordinary finite difference methods,
the sequential development of SOR, ADI, FFT and multigrid techniques has led
to orders of magnitude of improvement in our numerical computing capabilities.
In another direction, the development of better discretizations (higher order
finite elements or finite differences) has led to similar improvement. When
these two thrusts are combined in the future, we can expect to obtain factors
of improvement in efficiency of up to 10^{12} (for 3-dimensional, general elliptic
problems). This improvement is as much as the total for going from mechanical
hand calculators to modern computers.

Hindmarsh: It has been observed that the use of operator splitting techniques
such as ADI works well sometimes and poorly other times - particularly when the
effects of the individual operators tend to cancel each other. Are you aware
of these examples and do you know of any theory which can predict when the use
of operator splitting techniques will be successfull?

Yanenko: Yes, I am aware of the difficulties you mentioned. They can occur
particularly when solving nonlinear problems and when boundary layers are
present. Splitting methods are not good for arbitrary nonrectangular domains
(such as with irregular finite element grids), if additionally the adapting
mesh approach is not used.

For boundary layer problems, if one uses adaptive mesh approximations, then
one should be able to make splitting methods work.

Implicit methods are always going to be necessary, but it is important to make
them simple. They can be used for probably 90 percent of the time, particularly
for modules.

Stetter: When you separate a large problem into smaller segments - how do you
introduce the free parameters into the calculation - particularly for nonlinear
problems?

Yanenko: For linear problems, it is easy to do and it can always be done. For
nonlinear problems, you can linearize (as with Newton's method) and introduce
them at each step.

PDE SOFTWARE: Modules, Interfaces and Systems
B. Engquist and T. Smedsaas (eds.)
Elsevier Science Publishers B.V. (North-Holland)
© IFIP, 1984

SOFTWARE FOR TIME-DEPENDENT PROBLEMS

M. Berzins and P.M. Dew
Department of Computer Studies, The University, Leeds LS2 9JT
and
R.M. Furzeland
Shell Research Limited, Thornton Research, P.O. Box 1, Chester CH1 3SH

The design of a new software package for the solution of
time-dependent ordinary and partial differential equations
using the method of lines is described. The modular
nature of the package makes it possible to solve a wide
range of problems by the interchange of different modules
in the areas of time integration, numerical linear algebra
and spatial discretisation. The design aims to provide
sufficient flexibility to cater for the wide range of
mathematical models that arise in industrial applications.

INTRODUCTION

The aim of this paper is to describe the design of general purpose computer
software for the numerical solution of mathematical models that involve a
wide range of time-dependent ordinary and partial differential equations
(o.d.e.s and p.d.e.s). The motivation behind the design is to provide a
flexible and open-ended software tool to enable the user to solve the varied
and complex mathematical models that arise in practice, see Furzeland (1982).

The design philosophy employed is that of a set of well-defined and independent
modules that are controlled by a supervisory program. The internal structure
of the package allows the individual modules to be easily replaced and in this
way provides the mathematical modeller with easy access to a number of
different numerical methods. This allows a wide range of problems to be tackled,
including coupled non-linear p.d.e.s of parabolic/elliptic/hyperbolic type
with complicated boundary conditions coupled to ordinary differential and
algebraic equations. The package is being written in standard FORTRAN 77, is
designed to be portable and attempts to take into account possible use on
vector and parallel processors.

Much of the software that is used for problems of this type is based on the
methods of lines and in particular on the time integration method of Gear,
see Hindmarsh (1981). An outstanding feature of the most versatile software
of this type is that it allows the user access to different numerical methods,
e.g. DSS/2, Scheisser (1976), FORSIM V1, Carver (1978) and/or allows one or two
sophisticated numerical methods to be applied easily to a wide range of
problems, e.g. POST, Schryer (1977) and DISPL, Leaf et al (1978). Our intention
is to provide a single framework that combines some of the best features of these
packages and also allows the user access to more recently developed methods in
the areas of differential-algebraic equations, Petzold (1982), moving meshes,
see Miller (1981) and Herbst et al (1982), and spatial discretisation methods,
see Berzins and Dew (1983). The overall aim is to provide the user with
flexibility both in the class of problems that can be solved and in the range of
numerical methods that can be employed. In particular the user should be easily
able to change a module from any of the four main areas in the package. These
are the time-integration method, the non-linear equations solver, the linear

algebra routines and the spatial discretisation method. This interchange is made more difficult in many existing packages because some of these modules may be nested and may lack clearly defined interfaces to the rest of the package. We shall allow easy replacement of these modules by providing them with clearly defined interfaces to the main driving program. Our design employs the concept of reverse communication to increase the flexibility of this approach by placing all these modules at the same level in the driving program. This allows the modules to communicate in a more flexible way.

At the core of the proposed software is a versatile o.d.e. integrator whose structure has the flexibility to deal with stiff or non-stiff o.d.e.s coupled with algebraic equations, full/banded/sparse Jacobian matrices computed analytically, numerically or not at all, Newton or other non-linear equations solvers, automatic step size selection and a wide choice of error control tests. P.d.e. problems are solved using the method of lines in which the problem is first discretised in space and then integrated in time using the core o.d.e. integrator. The finite-difference or finite-element spatial discretisation routines will be complemented by various remeshing techniques and will also allow coupled o.d.e.-p.d.e. problems (e.g. moving boundary problems) to be included.

STRUCTURE OF THE PACKAGE

In this section we shall consider the broad structure of the package. The outline of this modular structure is illustrated in Figure (1).

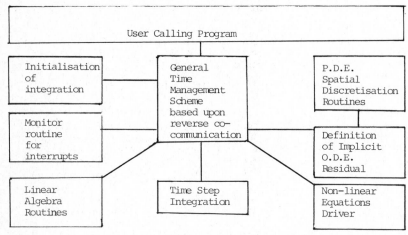

Figure 1

This structure is very general with regard to the possible communications paths between modules. In order to begin a more precise definition of the software we shall briefly describe how the modules communicate and what their main functions are.

Reverse Communication

The essence of this approach is that none of the main modules are nested in their calling structure, i.e. all calls and communications are made from the driving routine rather than at lower levels. The basic principle can be illustrated by considering the non-linear system of equations given by :

$$\underline{F}(\underline{U}) = 0 \tag{1}$$

A library program would normally require the name of the routine that computes the residual of equation (1). This routine would also have to have a fixed parameter list. Suppose that the non-linear equations solving routine is called SOLVER. In using reverse communication, SOLVER returns to the calling program when it requires the residual of equation (1). The user thus has to write code that is slightly different from the normal call to SOLVER. Suppose that the array R is given the values of equation (1) by the routine RESID. The code in the user's program then takes the form :

```
REPEAT
    CALL SOLVER(........,R,AGAIN)
    IF AGAIN THEN CALL RESID(U,R,NEQN)
UNTIL NOT AGAIN
```

This approach has long been advocated for FORTRAN libraries by Reid and Hopper (1980) and has been used for non-linear equation solvers, see Mallin-Jones (1978), and for parabolic equations, see Dew and Walsh (1981). The advantage of this approach is that the library program does not need to know anything about the call to the routine RESID. This shortens the parameter list of the library program and makes it much easier to change the user supplied routine (RESID). The disadvantage of this approach is that the internal structure of the library routine (SOLVER) must be more complicated and care must be taken to preserve any local variables that are needed both before and after the reverse communication call back to the user. In FORTRAN 77 this is accomplished by the use of a SAVE statement that allows local variables and/or COMMON blocks to be saved between one call of a routine and the next call. The simple example above uses only one level of reverse communication to communicate between SOLVER and RESID. In this package we shall use it to communicate between all the major modules.

In order to investigate the overheads of using this style of software design we · have carefully restructured the LSODI integrator of Hindmarsh and Painter, see Hindmarsh (1981), to work in the reverse communication form, which is described below. Timing experiments on a number of parabolic equations showed that the increase in c.p.u. time was less than five percent.

Module Outlines

We shall now briefly describe the tasks performed by the main modules that are called from the time management scheme, as shown in Figure (1). Before integration proper can commence all the control parameters and workspaces needed by the time integration routine and the problem definition (spatial discretisation routine) must be initialised. This is done by the user's calling program before the integration time management scheme is entered and is described further in section (3). The FORTRAN name of each module is given in brackets.

Initialisation of Integration (INITAL)

Once the time management scheme is entered the integration is initialised. This is done by calculating the initial values of the algebraic components, the time derivatives, the weights that are used in error norm formation and the stepsize. If the o.d.e. system is in normal form this is relatively straightforward. However, the situation is rather more complicated for systems of differential and algebraic problems, see Petzold (1982). This module also has an option to restart the integration when the o.d.e. problem has been changed. This allows p.d.e. mesh modification techniques to be included in the package.

Step (STEP)

Given a solution at time t the STEP module predicts the solution at a time t+h. A return is then made to the time management scheme, which calls the non-linear equations routines that set up and solve the system of non-linear equations for the solution at time t+h. Once the solution is found (or the non-linear equations solver breaks down) a return is made to STEP to continue the calculation. In the case when the non-linear equations solver repeatedly fails STEP decides on the strategy to be adopted (reduction in stepsize h, etc). As soon as integration reaches or passes the user-defined output point the STEP routine evaluates the solution at that point and returns to the driving program.

Non-linear Equations Driver (NLNSVR)

This routine controls the solution of the systems of non-linear equations that arise in the time integration. The standard module uses the modified Newton's method to solve these equations. In order to cater for implicit o.d.e.s there must be at least five modes of operation for this routine. Firstly, given an initial solution vector it must be able to solve the non-linear systems of equations for the values of the time derivative. Secondly, it must be able to solve for both a new solution vector and a new time derivative using the assumption

$$\dot{Y}_{n+1} = \frac{(Y_{n+1}-z)}{hd} \tag{2}$$

where the vector z and the constants h and d are already known. This may involve recalculating the Jacobian matrix. The third mode is just the second but using an already factorised Jacobian. Fourthly, for the purposes of error estimation the non-linear solver must be allowed to perform just one iteration using the already factorised Jacobian matrix. Finally, in the case when explicit methods of time integration are used it is only necessary for the step routine to be able to access the residual routine via NLNSVR. In all five cases, after the pass through the non-linear solver has been completed control is passed back to STEP.

Jacobian Matrix Formulation (JAC)

The Jacobian matrix of the system of non-linear equations being solved is evaluated by this module. This is done either by finite-differencing and repeated calls to the problem definition routines or by a user-supplied routine to supply the analytic Jacobian. In order to use efficient differencing it is necessary to have precise information on the structure of the Jacobian matrix. In the case of full, banded or block-banded matrices this is most conveniently done by the user specifying the bandwidth or blocksize in the calling program as the initialisation stage for this module. In the case when sparse matrix techniques are used the sparsity pattern is best generated internally prior to the formulation of the first Jacobian matrix. Alternatively the user may supply this information as part of the initialisation stage. In either case we have to take account of possible time dependencies in the sparsity pattern. The same sparsity information is used in forming the LU factors of the Jacobian; the call to the linear algebra modules to perform this factorisation is also made from this module.

Back Substitution (BACKSB)

The LU factors formed in the previous module are passed (via a workspace) into the routine that forms the next iterate in the standard manner used by Newton's method. As this backsubstitution function is performed far more frequently than the Jacobian evaluation it makes sense to have a separate module for this. Although designed primarily for the modified Newton's method this structure applies equally well to other iterative methods. In this case the Jacobian routine becomes the routine that initialises the method and the backsubstitution routine corresponds to the iterative part of the method.

O.D.E. Residual Formation (RESID)

We shall use the general implicit o.d.e. problem definition given by :

$$\underline{F}(\underline{Y},\underline{\dot{Y}},t) = O \tag{3}$$

This module returns the values of the residual of this equation by substituting the approximations to the vector $\underline{Y}$ and its time derivative. The calls to the p.d.e. spatial discretisation routines are made from this module. It is for this reason that the module has its own workspace, which may hold parameters such as the spatial mesh. The experienced user may also substitute his own version of this module, which could include his own spatial discretisation. There is also an option in the calling sequence to this module for it to return only those parts of the derivative that depend on the time derivative. This is used in the o.d.e. local error estimates suggested in Petzold (1982) for differential-algebraic equations.

Monitor Routine (MONITR)

The purpose of the monitor module is to enable the user to carry out any tasks that need to be performed at the end of each time step. For instance he may try to estimate the global error or in the case of a p.d.e. problem he may wish to refine the spatial mesh. In the case of remeshing a subsidiary calculation that creates a new mesh based on the current solution profile is needed. A further complication is that the number of mesh points and hence the dimension of the o.d.e. system being solved may change. It is for these reasons that the monitor routine has access to the workspace used in spatial discretisation and has the capability of restarting the integration when the mesh changes. The restart facility can also be used to accommodate discontinuities in the o.d.e. variables.

Module Intercommunication Paths

The way in which these modules work together in the normal course of a time integration is illustrated in Figure (2). Each of the modules also has the capability of terminating the integration when a fatal error occurs by calling an error-handling routine to process the appropriate error message and by then returning an error condition to the time-management scheme.

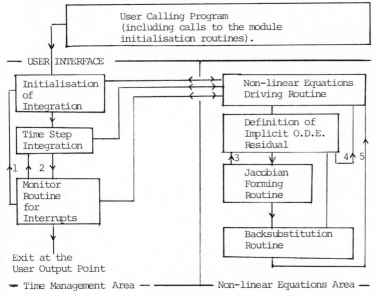

Figure 2

In Figure (2) :

Loop 1 represents the start, which can be forced by the monitor routine when the problem changes, for instance when mesh points are added by the mesh modification routine.

Loop 2 shows the usual step-monitor loop in time integration.

Loop 3 is the numerical differencing loop that may be used to form the Jacobian matrix.

Loop 4 illustrates the case when the linear equations area is accessed merely for the purpose of residual evaluation, e.g. explicit time-integration methods.

Loop 5 is the iteration loop for the solution of non-linear equations.

Each of the initialisation, step and monitor modules has access to the non-linear equations solver part of the package. This is described in section (2.2.3) above. The way in which control is passed between the time management area and the non-linear equations area is described by a simple system of reverse communication indicators.

Each of the main modules in the package has its own reverse communication indicator. These are:

MODULE	INDICATOR
STEP	ISTEP
RES	IRES
NLNSVR	INLN
JAC	IJAC
INITAL	INIT
MONITR	IMON

These indicators are on three communications levels; this is best illustrated diagrammatically.

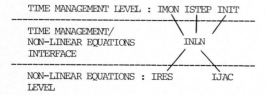

    TIME MANAGEMENT LEVEL : IMON ISTEP INIT

    TIME MANAGEMENT/
    NON-LINEAR EQUATIONS   INLN
    INTERFACE

    NON-LINEAR EQUATIONS : IRES   IJAC
    LEVEL

The non-linear equations part of the driver is accessed from the time management area by using INLN. The non-linear equations driver sets the values of IRES and IJAC needed in order to perform the task required of it by the time management part of the package. After the non-linear equations solver has completed its task control is transferred back to the appropriate part of the time management scheme.

USER INTERFACE

The next section of this paper describes how the user applies the package to his problem. This involves writing a simple calling program and specifying the problem to be solved. Problem specification may be done in one of two ways. The user can either write his own routine that forms the residual of the o.d.e. system (including the spatial discretisation for p.d.e. problems) or he can tailor his problem to the form required by a system routine.

CALLING PROGRAM

This program consists of the user's initialisation plus a call to the package main driving routine. The calling program may also contain calls to initialisation routines for some of the main modules in the package. This is necessary to accommodate a wide range of numerical methods. Consider for instance the wide range of o.d.e. integrators that one would like to include. This makes it difficult to design a common interface that fits many different integrators without being cumbersome. The work areas used by the integrators can be split into scalars and arrays. The arrays used in the internal interfaces (see Berzins, Dew and Furzeland (1983) from a subset of those required by most integrators; other arrays may be passed in through the STEP workspace WKSTEP. The first 2*NEQ elements of this array are assumed to correspond to the saved values of the solution and its time derivative by the driver. A wide range of scalar parameters may be accommodated by having an integrator-dependent initialisation routine that places these parameters in the relevant COMMON blocks. This routine also performs any necessary initialisation of the workspace WKSTEP.

The same approach can also be applied to the modules RESID, NLNSVR, JAC, MONITR. This allows flexibility with regard to the parameters and workspaces that are required by these routines while retaining a quite general but not overlong driver interface. Information is then passed to the main part of a module from its initialisation section by COMMON blocks or by the workspace that is passed through the body of the driver to the module.

The call to the time management scheme, the main driving part of the package, takes the form:

```
      SUBROUTINE DRIVER (NEQ, T, TOUT, Y, YDOT, IDAE, WKDRIV, NWKDRV,
     -         RTOL, ATOL, ITOL, INFORM, JNORM,
     -         RESID, WKRES, NWKRES, STEP, WKSTEP, NWKSTP
     -         MONITR, WYMON, NWKMON, NLNSVR,
     -         JAC, WKJAC, NWKJAC, JACPVT, JACFRM, BACKSB)
C******************************************************************
C
C  TYPE DECLARATIONS FOR DRIVER INTERFACE
C
      INTEGER NEQ, IDAE(NEQ), NWKDRV, ITOL, INFORM(13),
     -        NWKRES, NWKSTP, NWKMON, NWKJAC, JACPVT(1)
C
      REAL Y(NEQ),YDOT(NEQ),RTOL(1), ATOL(1),
     -        WKDRV(NWKDRV), WKRES(NWKRES), WKSTEP(NWKRES),
     -        WKMON(NWKMON), WKJAC(NWKJAC)
C
      CHARACTER*6 JNORM
      EXTERNAL RESID, STEP, MONITR, NLNSVR, JAC, JACFRM, BACKSB
```

Of these parameters seven are the names of routines: RESID, STEP, MONITR, JAC, JACFRM, BACKSB, NLNSVR. The parameters beginning with the prefix WK are the workspaces for these routines and the prefix NWK indicates the size of the workspaces. The array WKDRV contains the workspaces used in the driver modules. The routine JACFRM is an optional user-supplied routine to provide the analytic Jacobian matrix. The integer array JACPVT holds the pivot information for the decomposition of the Jacobian matrix. The parameters RTOL, ATOL and ITOL are similar to the parameters used by LSODI, see Hindmarsh (1981), for specifying the form of error test to be used. The array INFORM is used to input and output integration parameters and statistics, including optical inputs and outputs. The array IDAE is used to indicate whether or not each of the 'NEQ' equations that make up the differential-algebraic system is algebraic or differential in nature. IDAE(J)=1 indicates that the Jth equation contains time derivatives and IDAE(J)=0 indicates that the Jth equation is purely algebraic. The parameter JNORM specifies the type of error norm to be used in the error test (as in Dew and Walsh (1981)) with the options.

JNORM='MAXMUM' : Maximum norm.

JNORM='AVER12' : Averaged L2 norm

JNORM='L2NORM' : L2 Norm.

A more detailed description of the interfaces used by the routine whose names are passed into the driving program is given by Berzins, Dew and Furzeland (1983).

SPATIAL DISCRETISATION AND PROBLEM INTERFACE

These are two main ways in which a user can apply the package to his problem. One approach is for the user to write his problem in the 'master equation' form used by a package spatial discretisation routine. This 'master equation' needs to be rather general in order to encompass a realistic problem class. The alternative is for the user to write his own routine to form the residual of the o.d.e. system. This routine may include the user's own spatial discretisation or may make use of building blocks provided by the package.

The building block approach is employed by Scheisser (1976) to provide a good deal of flexibility in the package DSS/2. In this case finite-difference building blocks are used to form the spatial derivative approximations required to semi-discretise the p.d.e. This approach is very simple to use with finite-difference formulae as the difference approximations are substituted directly into the p.d.e. but cannot be used so easily with other discretisation methods. For example Galerkin methods usually semi-discretise the weak form of the p.d.e. by using quadrature rules. In this case it is not at all clear what the building blocks should be for what is quite a complicated process. Similar comments also apply to collocation methods although the complications here are caused by breakpoint and boundary conditions and by use of basis functions such as B-splines.

Regardless of which approach the user adopts the potential problem class is still restricted by the differential algebraic equations that can be solved by the o.d.e. integrator. When trying to solve differential-algebraic equations of the type used in our problem definition, i.e.

$$\underline{F}(\underline{Y},\underline{\dot{Y}},t)=0, \ \underline{Y}(0)=k \qquad (4)$$

there are a number of very difficult problems that can be encountered, see Fox and Mayers(1982) and Petzold(1982). At present very little general purpose software exists for this class of problems. Software has been written for the similar class of problems given by:

$$B\underline{\dot{Y}}=f(\underline{Y},t) \qquad (5)$$

where the matrix B may be singular, see Hindmarsh(1981). We shall include the techniques used by Hindmarsh and those described by Petzold(1982) in the modules that deal with differential-algebraic equations.

The ability to solve the class of o.d.e.s defined by equation(4) would allow us to semi-discretise a very broad class of p.d.e. problems. The restriction imposed by equation(5) limits us to equations that are linear in the partial derivative with respect to time of the solution, i.e. p.d.e.s of the form:

$$C(x,t,u,u_x)u_t - F(x,t,u,u_x) = x^{-m}\frac{\partial}{\partial x}[x^m R(x,t,u,u_x)] \qquad (6)$$

together with the boundary conditions

$$B(t)R(x,t,u,u_x)=G(x,t,u,u_x) \text{ at } x=a \text{ and } x=b. \tag{7}$$

where [a,b] is the spatial interval of interest, u,C,F,R, and G are vector valued functions. A class of equations that are also linear in the time derivative but have a more general dependence on the spatial derivatives than equation(6) is semi-discretised by the finite-difference code described in Sincovec and Madsen(1975). However, the advantage of considering equations such as (6) is that spatial discretisations that conserve the flux, R, may be applied and that Galerkin methods (lumped or unlumped) as well as finite-difference methods may be applied. Equation (6) is also the problem class used by Skeel(1981) in deriving new semi-discretisation formulae based upon difference approximations. These methods may also be viewed as lumped Galerkin methods using linear basis functions. Testing on a number of parabolic equations has shown, see Skeel(1983), that these methods are more accurate than the more traditional finite difference methods. A similar increase in accuracy can be gained by using the Chebyshev discretisation method of Berzins and Dew(1983). This method also has the option to use high order spatial discretisations as well as those based on low order finite-difference type approximations.

We can expect advances in o.d.e. software to solve equations of the form of (4) by allowing a more general p.d.e. problem interface given by:

$$C(x,t,u,u_x,u_t,u_{xt})=x^{-m}\frac{\partial}{\partial x}[x^m R(x,t,u,u_x,u_t,u_{xt})] \tag{8}$$

and for the moment restricting the functions $C(...)$ and $R(...)$ to be linear both in the time derivative and in its first spatial derivative. This restriction could easily be checked by the spatial discretisation routine. The natural extension of this class of problems is given by Schryer(1977) who considers mixed o.d.e./p.d.e. problems of the type that interest us. The problem class that Schryer's package can theoretically handle is given by:

$$C(x,t,u,u_x,u_t,u_{xt},v,\dot{v})=\frac{\partial}{\partial x}R(x,t,u,u_x,u_t,u_{xt},v,\dot{v}) \tag{9}$$

where v and $\dot{v}$ are the o.d.e. variables and their time derivatives that are coupled to the p.d.e. (e.g. as arises in moving boundary problems solved by the co-ordinate transformation method, see section (3,4)). This problem class (with its extension to the polar form) seems to be general enough to cover all of the problems that we have encountered at present. The flexibility inherent in this package would allow more general finite-difference or collocation methods to be incorporated at a later date should the need arise.

In order to illustrate how the p.d.e. is described, consider the flux function R as defined in equation(6). This function is defined by:

$$R(x,t,u,u_x)$$

The user interface for this function is given by:

PDEFUN(NPDE, IPTS, X, T, U, UX, RF)
INTEGER NPDE, IPTS
REAL X(IPTS), T, U(NPDE,IPTS), UX(NPDE,IPTS), RF(NPDE, IPTS).

The user is requested to provide the values of the flux function R for the Ith p.d.e. at the X(J)th mesh point, J=1,IPTS, which lies in the open interval (X(1), X(IPTS)). The number of mesh points, IPTS, and their positioning are provided by the spatial discretisation routine. The open interval defined by the discretisation routine usually corresponds to the interval between the breakpoints of the spatial piecewise polynomial approximation.

This interface is general enough to cover evaluating many function values at once (as in vector mode for the CRAY 1) and can also be extended to cover evaluation of the functions C and R simultaneously by adding an extra array CF, of the same dimension as RF, into the parameter list. Extra parameters will be needed if the functions C(..) and R(..) depends on the time derivative, on its first spatial derivative or on any o.d.e. variables (as in equation (9)).

Discontinuities in the function C(..) are handled by placing them at the breakpoints. In this case the user has to check the open interval supplied by the discretisation routine to determine whether or not the left or the right value of the function at the discontinuity must be supplied.

Boundary Conditions

The boundary conditions for the general class of p.d.e.s given by equation (9) can then be given by :

$$B(t)R(x,t,u,u_x,u_t,u_{xt},v,\dot{v})=G(x,t,u,u_x,u_t,u_{xt},v,\dot{v}) \qquad (10)$$

The flux function R(..) can be substituted from the boundary condition (10) into equation (9) and the boundary condition incorporated in this way. This is particularly advantageous if equation (9) is discretised in its weak form (as in Galerkin finite-element methods). The alternative is to solve algebraic equations at the boundaries. This can be done without too much trouble in the case of Dirichlet type conditions, see Berzins and Dew (1982), but may cause problems when used with other boundary conditions. In any case equation (10) is general enough to cover both these options depending on whether or not the function B(t) is non-zero. A further alternative is to differentiate the boundary conditions in time as in PDECOL, Madsen and Sincovec (1977), though it is not difficult to construct cases for which this is unsatisfactory, see Berzins (1982). In order to cater for hyperbolic equations it is necessary to allow for null boundary conditions by allowing both functions B and G to be zero for one or more components at either boundary.

Mixed O.D.E./P.D.E. Problem Interface

In practice many of the problems that we wish to solve involve mixed systems of o.d.e.s and p.d.e.s Such systems are generated by the moving boundary problems surveyed in Furzeland (1980) and by the moving finite element method of Miller (1981). Problems of this type may be split into three classes.

Problems that are purely o.d.e.s in time.

Problems that are composed of closely coupled systems of o.d.e.s and p.d.e.s as arise from the moving finite element method of Miller (1981). These are so specialised that they require separate modules to be written for them.

Lastly there are problems that consist of p.d.e.s with o.d.e.s coupled to them because the p.d.e. is part of some larger problem (e.g. the moving boundary problem in section 3.4). It is this case that we shall consider in greater detail.

In the interface the user has to specify the spatial coupling points at which o.d.e.s exist and to define the form of the o.d.e.s in terms of the o.d.e. variables v and $\dot{v}$ and the p.d.e. variables u,u_t,u_x,u_{xt},R,x,t defined at the spatial coupling points. Suppose that there are NV o.d.e. variables represented by a vector v; we have to introduce the variables u and $\dot{u}$ into the functions C and R as used in the p.d.e. problem definition in equation (9). The interface described for the flux function in section 3.2 must therefore be extended by three extra parameters in order to include problems of this type. These are the integer NV and the arrays V(NV) and VDOT(NV). The interface used by POST can be extended slightly to meet our needs. This extended interface uses the following parameters :

T :   The current time

NV :   The number of o.d.e. variables

V :   The o.d.e. variables

VDOT : The time derivatives of the o.d.e. variables

NXI :   The number of o.d.e./p.d.e. coupling points

XI :   A vector that details the coupling points

NVXI : A vector describing which o.d.e.s are at which spatial coupling points

UI :   The p.d.e. solution at the coupling points

UXI :   The spatial derivatives of the p.d.e. solution at the coupling points

UTXI : The spatial derivatives of the p.d.e. time derivatives at the coupling points

RI :   The p.d.e. flux values at the coupling points

UDOTI : The values of the p.d.e. time derivative at the spatial coupling points

VRES : The o.d.e. residual.

The o.d.e.s are allowed to have the same general form as those in equation (5); that is they are linear with respect to the time derivatives. We are still faced with the problem of describing which o.d.e.s exist at which coupling points. This can be done by the use of an indicator array. Let

$$NVXI(J) = K, J=1, \ldots, NXI$$

where K is the current sub-total of the o.d.e. variables up to and including the XI(J)th coupling point. Thus (NVXI(J)-NVXI(J-1)) is the number of o.d.e.s at the XI(J)th coupling point. The overall interface for the routine D(..) that the user supplies to describe the o.d.e. part of the problem is then given by :

$$D(T,NV,V,VDOT,NXI,XI,NVXI,UI,UXI,UTXI,RI,UDOTI,VRES) \ .$$

Example Problem

In this section we shall show how the software described above may be used to solve a practical problem. The problem considered is that of a general two-phase moving boundary problem in the spatial region a<x<b with the moving boundary x=s(t) fixed by a co-ordinate transformation. This transformation defines new variables.

$$x_1 = \frac{x-a}{x(t)-a} \quad \text{and} \quad x_2 = \frac{x-b}{s(t)-b}$$

and the problem can now be formulated as the mixed o.d.e.-p.d.e. problem, see Furzeland (1982), given by :

$$C_i(x_i,t,u_i)\frac{\partial u_i}{\partial t} = \frac{\partial}{\partial x_i} R_i(x_i,t,s(t), \frac{\partial u_i}{\partial x_i})$$

where i=1,2 and $0<x_i<1$.

The moving boundary condition is given by :

$$s(t) = f(x_1,x_2,t,s(t), \frac{\partial u_1}{\partial x_1}, \frac{\partial u_2}{\partial x_2})$$
$$\text{at } x_1 = x_2 = 1$$

At this boundary the solution values are specified :

$$u_1 = u_2 = U(t) \text{ at } x_1 = x_2 = 1.$$

The fixed boundary conditions at x=a and x=b take the form given by equation (10) in section 3.2.1.   This formulation means that we can solve the problem as a system of two coupled p.d.e.s on a fixed mesh with an additional o.d.e. that is coupled to both equations. Consequently the problem can be solved by any of the fixed mesh discretisation routines in the package because it is in the form of equations (9) and (10). This means that the user can describe the problem to the system spatial discretisation routine by writing :

A routine that describes the functions C(..) and R(..) in equation (9); see the example in section 3.2.

A routine that defines the functions B(..) and G(..) in equation (10) at the left and right boundaries of the transformed problem.

A routine that defines the o.d.e. system which is coupled to the p.d.e. This routine is described in section 3.3.

In addition the initial solution profile and the initial position of the moving boundary must be provided before the package is entered and passed to the set-up routine (SETDIS) along with the spatial mesh and the details of the o.d.e.-p.d.e. coupling. This routine then passes these details to the finite-difference routine (FINDIF). The o.d.e. solution vector used in the driver contains the o.d.e. and p.d.e. solution components in a combined form. One function of the spatial discretisation interpolation routine is to disentangle these components. For the example above this is done by the system routine INTERP.

The   o.d.e. system is in normal form and the Jacobian is formed numerically. The special form of the Jacobian matrix that results from the co-ordinate transformation is probably best treated using sparse matrix techniques but for simplicity we shall assume that full matrix techniques are employed. We shall suppose that the user elects to use the system routines DCFULL and BSFULL,which form the Jacobian and backsubstitute using its factored form. The size of the real workspace needed by these routines is 2*N*N where N is the dimension of the o.d.e. system. For this simple problem the monitor routine, MBPMON, is used to test the position of the boundary after each timestep. The only other code that the user then has to write is the calling program, which includes the calls to the initialisation routines for the version of LSODI used in the package and for the spatial discretisation routine.

Two-Dimensional Problems

Until now we have been mostly concerned with problems in one space dimension. The main reason for this is that many of the problems arising at Thornton Research Centre are complex systems of p.d.e.s in one space dimension with coupled o.d.e.s. The package discussed here can be used equally well for problems in two or more space dimensions. This is done by replacing the spatial discretisation modules with the appropriate two-dimensional routines. The user problem interface to these modules will be different and the user will call different workspace definition modules prior to entering the package. The other major change is that the o.d.e. and linear algebra modules may be changed to those that are more suited to problems in two space dimensions.

SUMMARY

In this paper we have described the general structure of a new package for the solution of complex, time-dependent o.d.e./p.d.e. problems. The package provides a high degree of flexibility with regard to both the range of numerical methods that may be employed and the class of problems that can be solved. A practical example of its application to a moving boundary problem is considered.

Acknowledgement

This two-year collaborative project is being funded by Shell Research Limited, Thornton Research Centre, Chester.

REFERENCES

[1]   Berzins, M. (1982). Chebyshev Methods for Parabolic Equations, (Ph.D Thesis), Dept. of Computer Studies, The University, Leeds.

[2]   Berzins, M. and Dew, P.M. (1982). A Generalized Chebyshev Method for Parabolic P.D.E.s in One Space Variable. IMA J. Numer. Anal., Vol. 1, pp.469-487.

[3]   Berzins, M. and Dew, P.M. (1983). C^o Chebyshev Methods with Error Indicators for Parabolic Equations. Report No. 170, Dept. of Computer Studies, The University, Leeds LS2 9JT.

[4]   Berzins, M., Dew, P.M. and Furzeland, R.M. (1983). Software for Time-Dependent Problems. Report No. 180, Dept. of Computer Studies, The University, Leeds.

[5]   Carver, M.B. et al (1978). The FORSIM VI simulation package for the solution of arbitrarily defined partial differential and/or ordinary differential equations systems. Rep AECL 5821, Chalk River Nuclear Laboratories, Ontario, Canada.

[6]   Dew, P.M. and Walsh, J.E. (1981). A Set of Library Routines for the Numerical Solution of Parabolic Equations in One Space Variable. A.C.M. Trans on Math Soft, Vol. 7, pp. 295-314.

[7]   Fox, L. and Mayers, D.F. (1982). IMA J. Numer. Anal., Vol. 1, pp.377-403.

[8]   Furzeland, R.M. (1980). A Comparative Study of Numerical Methods for Moving Boundary Problems. JIMA, Vol. 26, pp. 411-429.

[9]   Furzeland, R.M. (1982). The Numerical Solution of Some Practical Problems Involving Partial Differential Equations and Moving Boundaries. Paper presented at Recent Developments in Numerical Analysis Colloquium, Manchester University, 19th-21st April 1982.

[10] Herbst, B.M., Schoombie, S.W. and Mitchell, A.R. (1982). Int. J. Num. Meths. Engng., Vol. 18, pp. 1321-1336.

[11] Hindmarsh, A.C. (1981). ODE Solvers for use with the Method of Lines. Advances in Computer Methods for Partial Differential Equations IV. R. Vichnevetsky and R.S. Stepleman (Eds). Publ. IMACS 1981.

[12] Leaf G. et al. (1978). DIPL : A software package for one and two spatially dimensioned kinetics-diffusion problems. Rep ANL-77-12 Rev 1, Argonne National Lab., Illinois, U.S.A.

[13] Madsen, N.K. and Sincovec, R.F. (1979). PDECOL : General Collocation Software, ACM Trans. Math. Soft., Vol. 5, pp. 326-351.

[14] Mallin-Jones A.K. (1978). Non-linear Algebraic Equations in Process Engineering Calculations, (in) Numerical Software - Needs and Availability (Ed Jacobs D.), Academic Press, 1978, pp. 167-180.

[15] Miller, K. (1981). Moving Finite Elements I and II. SIAM J. Numer. Anal., Vol. 18, No. 6, pp. 1019-1057.

[16] Petzold, L. (1982). Differential/Algebraic Equations are not O.D.E.s. SIAM J. Scientific and Statistical Computing, Vol. 3, pp. 367-384.

[17] Reid, J. and Hopper, M.J. (1980). pp.19-41 in Production and Assessment of Numerical Software (Eds. Hennell M.A. and Delves L.M.), Academic Press.

[18] Scheisser, W. (1976). DSS/2. An introduction to the numerical method of lines integration of partial differential equations. 2 vols. Lehigh University, Bethlehem, Pa., U.S.A.

[19] Schryer, N.L. (1977). Numerical Solution of Time Varying P.D.E.s in One Space Variable, Bell Laboratories, Computing Science Technical Report 53.

[20] Sincovec, R.F. and Madsen, N.K. (1975). Software for Nonlinear P.D.E.s. ACM Trans. Math. Soft., Vol. 1, No. 3, pp. 232-260.

[21] Skeel, R.D. (1981). Improving Routines for Parabolic Equations. Department of Mathematics, University of Manchester, Numerical Analysis Report 63.

[22] Skeel, R.D. et al. (1983). Improvements to the N.A.G. Library Parabolic Equations Code. (To appear).

DISCUSSION

Speaker: R. Furzeland

Yanenko: By using the ODE approximations which result from the Method of Lines, you cannot avoid and must consider the problems of stability and stiffness. It may be considerably more efficient to use a method which can use different time steps for different parts of the problems (decomposition of splitting). For example, in a combustion problem, you can use very simple methods for the diffusion part and use stiff ODE techniques for the stiff chemical reactions and thereby use different time steps for each of the decomposed subsystems.

Furzeland: I am aware of the splitting and decomposition possibilities and am interested in determining whether or not these will be more efficient.

Yanenko: I am sure that one must use both models and split the problem.

Sherman: The modular structure you propose is very attractive. However, I wonder if you will run into some unanticipated difficulties because conflicting basic assumptions of alternative modules for one specific task my require basic changes in the organizations of other tasks. In the construction of LSODES from LSODE, Alan Hindmarsh and I found the need to reorganize certain aspects of the overall integration procedure (particularly Jacobian handling) in order to efficiently exploit the problem sparseness implicitly assumed by the decision to use sparse linear algebraic methods in LSODES. We had originally expected that the designs of the linear algebra and time integration procedures would be entirely independent.

Furzeland: We have looked at the structure of your software and wondered what the reasons were for it.

Hindmarsh: We structured things partly because of historical reasons, but also because of the complexity of the return paths which would be required with a reverse communications approach. We feel that these complexities will present considerable difficulties and challenges - but may not be impossible.

Schönauer: It is attractive to separate the effects of spatial errors and time errors, but our experience has indicated that you really want to balance these errors and, in fact, we have found that they are closely coupled. If you were to adopt this philosophy, it seems to me that your interface module would have to be much more general.

Also, you have developed your interfaces and data structures in 1-dimension and then will proceed on to 2-dimensions and then on to 3-dimensions. We have found that proceeding in this manner led to data structures for 3-D which were not satisfactory. We have looked at the data structures in the reverse order. - beginning with 3-D and then working back to 2-D and 1-D and have found that this has been more effective.

Furzeland: I basically agree with your comments. I was particularly interested in your development of space and time error estimates and hope to incorporate some of these ideas in our package.

Hindmarsh: The differential-algebraic systems you have discussed are, in general, much more difficult than more linearized problems. Because of this complexity, little is available in the way of general purpose software. I have not seen in practical problems the type of nonlinear couplings in the time derivatives and so have concentrated my efforts on less general but easier problems. Are you aware of any physically realistic problems where your type of coupling (nonlinear in dy/dt) exists?

Furzeland: I have seen some wave propagation problems involving "N-waves" where this type of coupling exists. Also, I think that some problems, although based on conversation laws, may be subject to certain transformations which will result in this type of coupling.

Reid: In connection with reverse communication, I would like to comment that the Fortran committee has thought about this problem, which is really caused by the inflexibility of COMMON. The new language is unlikely to be in use for ten years, but then there will be a better mechanism for the user to access this data in a routine called by a library package. Note also the lack of safety in using reverse communication; the package's internal data structure is open to accidental corruption by the user.

Furzeland: Hindmarsh replied that often the more sophisticated user requests access to certain work storage spaces. I too have users who request this and one can usually rely on them not to corrupt the storage.

Young: Could you explain why you are not using iterative techniques?

Furzeland: In LSODE-type codes, one only recalculates and factors the Jacobian typically every 5 to 10 time steps. This offers a distinct gain in efficiency over iterative methods. However, if the Jacobian has to be recalculated more often, then iterative methods may be preferable. The program does, of course, have the flexibility of allowing the user to swap between direct and iterative methods. The prefactored Jacobian information is also used to form error estimates.

Rice: The structure you describe for your software was presented in terms of modular steps in solving the PDEs. The discussion suggests that sometimes it is difficult to change one module without affecting others. Do you plan to fix the interface between modules and focus on them in your software? More specifically, will you allow, in your "time control" program, someone to go from, say, interface 7 to interface 11? The advantage would be that, when necessary, someone could combine modules together for some special purpose or proceed in a manner not foreseen by your modular structure, or make "super elements" by combining the modules in certain ways.

Furzeland: Yes, the package does provide the tools and flexibility to achieve this. It would be an interesting and useful application of the package.

PDE SOFTWARE: Modules, Interfaces and Systems
B. Engquist and T. Smedsaas (eds.)
Elsevier Science Publishers B.V. (North-Holland)
© IFIP, 1984

ODE SOLVERS FOR TIME-DEPENDENT PDE SOFTWARE*

Alan C. Hindmarsh

Lawrence Livermore National Laboratory
Livermore, CA 94550
U.S.A.

Treatment of time-dependent PDE problems by the method of
lines produces ODE systems that are either explicit or
linearly implicit in the time derivatives. The size,
stiffness, and structure of these systems make heavy demands
on ODE initial value solvers, especially if used in automated PDE software. ODEPACK is a systematized collection of
general purpose ODE solvers developed with PDE problems in
mind (among others). It covers both explicit and implicit
systems, includes solvers with automatic stiff/nonstiff
method selection, and covers various Jacobian structures.

INTRODUCTION - PDE AND ODE SYSTEMS

We are concerned here with time-dependent partial differential equations,
including systems of such PDEs, with appropriate initial and boundary
conditions. If the PDEs are first-order in time and are given explicity, the
system can be written in the abstract form

$$\partial u / \partial t = F(u) \tag{1}$$

over some spatial domain, where u is a vector, t is time, and F generally
includes spatial differentiation operators. (Problems with higher-order time
derivatives or implicit occurrence of the time derivatives, if not easily
transformed to first-order explicit form, can nevertheless be treated by many
of the same techniques discussed here, but we will assume the form (1) for
simplicity.) Whatever the geometry or boundary conditions, it is assumed that
the vector u is known everywhere in its domain at the initial time $t = t_0$.

Often a system of PDEs that is partly time-independent can be altered to
one of the form (1), and can be solved more efficiently in that form. A
typical example is a system containing one or more parabolic equations of the
form $\partial u / \partial t = F(u,v)$ (F being an elliptic operator with respect to u), and

---

*This work was performed under the auspices of the U.S. Department of Energy
by Lawrence Livermore National Laboratory under contract No. W-7405-Eng-48,
and supported by the DOE Office of Basic Energy Sciences, Mathematical
Sciences Branch.

also one or more elliptic equations $0 = G(u,v)$ (G being elliptic with respect to v), where the latter is the result of invoking a quasi-steady state assumption on equations $\epsilon \partial v/\partial t = G$. It is usually easier (and equally accurate) to solve the system with the time-dependent form for the v equations. For an example, see [15], where a speedup by a factor of over 100 was realized. The extreme case is that of an elliptic system $F(u) = 0$, which can often be more easily treated by integrating $\partial u/\partial t = F$ to steady state than by other available means.

A highly popular and successful approach to initial-boundary value PDE problems is given by the <u>method of lines</u>. This is really a collection of similar methods, but the common feature among them is the discretization of the spatial variables (and of the boundary conditions), leaving ordinary differential equations (ODEs) in time, followed by the use of ODE solvers to integrate the initial value problem for that ODE system. For the present, it is important to divide the spatial discretizations into two groups:

(A) Finite differencing, including cases where the spatial grid is changed from time to time, and finite element treatments with "mass matrix lumping" all produce <u>explicitly</u> <u>given</u> <u>ODEs</u>. If the relevant discrete values of the components of u form a vector denoted by y, then the ODE system has the form

$$\dot{y} \equiv dy/dt = f(t,y) \ . \tag{2}$$

(In lumped mass finite element procedures, a nonsingular diagonal matrix multiplies $\dot{y}$ but can clearly be absorbed into f.) Initial conditions on u immediately yield an initial value vector $y_0 = y(t_0)$.

(B) Treatments with traditional Galerkin finite elements, with finite element collocation, or with other weighted residual methods, including the case where the grid changes with time, produce <u>linearly</u> <u>implicit</u> <u>ODE</u> <u>systems</u>. In terms of the vector y of unknown coefficients in the approximating function space, such a system can be written

$$A(t,y) \ \dot{y} = g(t,y) \ , \tag{3}$$

where A is a square matrix, and may or may not be singular. Interpolation or projection of the initial condition functions yields an initial value vector $y_0 = y(t_0)$. When A is nonsingular, it is often tempting to rewrite (3) in the form (2) with $f = A^{-1}g$, and then deal only with solvers for explicit ODEs. But in most cases, for reasons that will be clear shortly, this is much less efficient than treating (3) directly.

Once the discretization has been done by one of these approaches, what remains is the job of integrating the system (2) or (3) from $t = t_0$ forward in time as far as needed. If the spatial discretization has been automated in software form for a given class of PDE problems, the ideal situation is that in which an initial value ODE solver is available "off the shelf" for this integration job. ODE solvers that are suitable for this context are available in many cases, but more are needed.

The ODE systems that arise from time-dependent PDE problems tend to have certain features that are not typical of general ODE systems:

• They tend to be quite large, simply because of the number of spatial grid points or elements necessary to resolve the solution.

• They tend to be stiff, at least on parts of the solution, either from the existence of fast decay subprocesses in the PDE variables (e.g. fast chemical reactions) or from the spectrum of the discrete representation of the spatial operator (to the extent that it is diffusive).

• They tend to be nonlinear.

• The right-hand side or residual functions, i.e. f in (2) or g - A$\dot{y}$ in (3), tend to be expensive to evaluate, owing to the size and the nonlinearity of the problem.

• The coupling between the different equations in the system tends to be quite sparse (but often quite regular), in that the spatial discretization usually couples a given ODE variable only to the others at the same spatial point or element and to those at nearby points or elements. Note, however, that the sparse structure present in the implicit for (3) is lost if it is converted (A being nonsingular but not diagonal) to the explicit form (2); thus if the problem is stiff, it must be treated directly in its implicit form.

For the present, stiffness in an ODE system will be simply defined as the presence of one or more fast decay processes. On a stiff problem, a method that is not suitable for stiff systems will be constrained to small step sizes corresponding to the fastest decay mode present, even after that mode has decayed in the solution. The issues of stiffness and coupling are particularly important for the choice of ODE solver, because stiff systems are generally solved only with implicit methods, which take the coupling of the system into account. They therefore require considerably more effort, both in solution software and in computational cost. For linearly implicit ODE systems (3), the coupling given by A must be dealt with whether or not stiffness is present.

DESIRED PROPERTIES OF ODE SOLVERS

The ODE solver or solvers one uses for the automated method-of-lines solution of a class of PDE problems must meet the demands implied by the mathematical problem features listed above. In addition, there are factors in the solution environment associated with automatic PDE software that make certain demands on the ODE solvers to be used. Convenience, flexibility, economy, reliability, maintainability, and modifiability, all of which are desirable or essential for the PDE solver as a whole, translate into requirements of a similar nature on the ODE solver. An important difference, though, is that the "user" of the ODE solver is the PDE solver, not the problem poser. When all of these factors are taken together, we can form a list of the desirable properties of ODE solvers when used with PDE software for time-dependent problems:

(1) The solver should be able to handle reliably both stiff and nonstiff problems. Preferably, this should be automated so that the user is not required to specify whether (or where) the problem is stiff. Using a nonstiff method where the problem is stiff can result in prohibitive costs because of step size restrictions, while using a stiff method when the problem is nonstiff will entail greater expense than necessary on each step. A problem can be stiff along some parts of its solution and not others; typically a stiff problem has an initial transient solution that is best regarded as nonstiff (because step sizes must be restricted for reasons of accuracy).

(2) A wide range of sparsity structures must be expected and utilized. Problems in one space dimension will almost always have banded or block-banded coupling. Problems in higher dimensions may produce a regular block-tridiagonal structure, or may instead produce a sufficiently irregular (but very sparse) structure so as to require a general sparse matrix treatment. Whatever the structure, it must be efficiently exploited in any matrix operations the solver must do that involve the coupling in the system.

(3) When the solver must solve a linear algebraic system, it should interface to existing linear system software modules. Thus, for example, for the solution of a stiff system (2) using an implicit method and a modified Newton method, the solver should deal with the resulting structured linear systems by calling self-contained modules for such systems. These modules should exploit the fact that many right-hand side vectors may arise in succession for the same coefficient matrix. ODE solvers for the same problem type but for differing sparsity structures should share all modules other than those that directly related to the algebraic structure.

(4) Where stiff methods are to be invoked, and thus Jacobian matrices are involved in some way, the solver should allow the user to supply partial derivatives in closed form in optional routines (such as might be obtained by a symbolic processor), but it should also include the option of generating difference quotient approximations to all required partial derivatives.

(5) The solver should keep the number of evaluations of the right-hand

side function or residual to a minimum, for the sake of efficiency of the overall solution. Of course, tradeoff considerations have to be made between the cost of function evaluations and that of other operations in the solution.

(6) The solver should have widely flexible error control tolerances. Almost invariably, ODE solvers estimate and control the local discretization error (in time), and this process requires a definition of some weighted norm on error vectors. To accommodate arbitrary scalings in the PDE variables, the ODE solver must allow for relative or absolute tolerances, or any mixture of the two, including different mixing weights for different components.

(7) Throughout the solution algorithm, the solver should be as economical as possible in storage, not only in dealing with sparse Jacobian matrices and the like, but also with auxiliary vectors, history arrays, etc., as needed.

(8) The solver should allow for a variety of starting and stopping options. Stopping the ODE solution at a given output time is the usual choice, but stopping at each internal time step, or stopping on a root of a function of the solution may also be desirable. In any case, stopping should be done in such a way that a restart of the solver after intervening use of it is possible, such as for solution of a complex problem by an operator splitting approach. It should be possible to start up the solver so as to continue integrating the same ODE system with altered tolerance or other method-related inputs, and also to integrate an altered system, such as when spatial points or elements are added or deleted.

(9) Many of the method parameters and decisions that the ODE solver would normally take care of on its own need to be under the control of the user, at the user's option. For example, an appropriate maximum time step size may be computable from information in the PDE modules, and this data might enhance the performance of the ODE solver. The same is true of the maximum method order in an ODE solver based on a variable-order method, and also of the structure of sparse matrices involved. On the other hand, the solver should also be able to make reasonably correct decisions on step size, order, sparsity structure, etc., with no input from the user, if none is given.

(10) The solver should make available secondary information that is not normally requested by the user, but which might be useful in the method of lines strategy within the PDE solver. It should report back its best available error estimate (the local error at least, and the global error if available), and also any time derivatives of the solution available, as these might well be used in decisions to control both the spatial discretization error and the time integration error jointly. Also, function evaluation and matrix operation counts and counts of failed steps and of corrector convergence failures could be useful in decisions on grid alterations.

(11) There should be a means of passing data arrays (real and integer) from the module that calls the ODE solver to the user-supplied subroutines it calls, and in such a way that their length is dynamically variable. These would be useful for mesh or other information needed by the routines defining the ODE system but not otherwise relevant to the ODE solver.

THE ODEPACK COLLECTION OF ODE SOLVERS

General Information

The development of general purpose initial value ODE solvers has been very active at LLNL for over 15 years. Early solvers used Runge-Kutta and Adams methods predominantly. For stiff systems, C. W. Gear's solver [7] was adopted and rewritten as the GEAR package, and this and variants of it were used with much success on a wide variety of problems, many of them PDE-based [12,2]. These packages and their descendants are based on the Adams and Backward Differentiation Formulas (BDFs), in fixed-step form with interpolatory step size changing. Solvers based on truly variable-step forms of the BDFs were also developed, jointly with G. D. Byrne [1].

In either form, the BDF methods are very attractive for PDE-based stiff ODE systems, for several reasons:

• They constitute a series of stiffly stable methods of various orders, in which the order is easy to vary, as well as the step size.

• As linear multistep methods with convenient local error estimates, they require only a small number of function (or residual) evaluations per step (excluding any needed for Jacobian matrix approximations).

• For an ODE system of size N, they require the solution of only one nonlinear N x N algebraic system on each time step. This system is amenable to a modified Newton method, and this requires only one copy of an N x N Jacobian matrix to be stored at any one time.

• By the nature of the modified Newton iteration, the Jacobian matrix involved does not need to be very accurate, and thus partial derivatives need not be computed very accurately, nor at every time step.

• The nonlinear system to be solved allows for sparse structure in the system to be utilized in a direct manner.

Few other ODE methods have all of these properties. In the ODE solvers written at LLNL, and in PDE software that has made use of those solvers, these features of BDF methods have been exploited extensively.

In more recent years, various efforts have been made to write new ODE solvers and rewrite old ones so as to meet higher standards of flexibility, convenience, reliability, and commonality. The setting of standards for the user interface was undertaken within the U.S. Department of Energy laboratories [11], and a new series of solvers, called ODEPACK, has evolved from that effort. These solvers reflect a desire to meet not only the need for high quality ODE solvers in general, but also the demands posed by ODE problems that are based on time-dependent PDE problems.

ODEPACK is a "systematized collection," meaning that the solvers share, as much as possible, both external and internal features. Their user interfaces have in common almost all of their call sequence parameters, and internally they are highly modular and share many modules for common subtasks. Many, but not all, of the desirable properties listed above are met, specifically:

(1) Both stiff algorithms (BDF methods with modified Newton iteration) and nonstiff algorithms (Adams methods with functional iteration) are included. In two cases, there is automatic and dynamic selection between the two. In the case of the implicit problem form (3), the absence of stiffness is much less of an advantage, because the matrix A must be dealt with in any case.

(2) Structures allowed presently include full (dense), banded, general sparse, and block-tridiagonal structures. In all non-dense cases, sparsity is exploited when constructing and solving linear systems. Software combinations for other structures (where linear system solvers exist) are also possible.

(3) The solution of linear systems (within a modified Newton iteration) is always done with existing general purpose linear algebra packages. In the full and banded cases, LINPACK [4] is used. Wherever a direct method is used, it is in LU form (separate factorization and backsolution phases), so as to take maximum advantage of the occurrence of many right-hand side vectors for each matrix. There is much sharing of modules that do not involve matrix operations (e.g. for error estimation and for step and order selection), but there could be more. So far, only in-core linear system solvers have been used.

(4) When a Jacobian matrix is called for, the user has the option of supplying it in the form of a subroutine (which could be generated by an automatic symbolic processor), or of having the solver generate an internal difference quotient approximation. In the case of (3), the matrices involved are A and $\partial(g - A \dot{y})/\partial y$, and the latter Jacobian is approximated with difference quotients if not supplied by the user.

(5) The corrector iteration, in both Adams and BDF cases, is tuned in an attempt to keep the number of iterations (hence function evaluations) to a minimum; averages of 1.2 to 1.5 iterations per step are typical. Further, the algorithms used attempt to minimize Jacobian evaluations, and also the number

of extra function evaluations per difference quotient Jacobian evaluation.

(6) Flexible error tolerance parameters, which are standard throughout the collection, allow for any mixture of relative and absolute local error control, including options for tolerance choice that vary from one component of y to another. No assumptions are made about the problem being well scaled prior to solution by the solver.

(7) Work arrays used internally by the solvers (one real and one integer) are in the call sequence, and their size is set by the user. The sizes can be changed during the problem if solution parameters allow this, such as when the method is switched between stiff and nonstiff. Care has also been taken to keep array storage to a minimum in all cases (e.g. by avoiding the need to store two copies of a Jacobian or related matrix or of a history array).

(8) A variety of starting and stopping options are standard across the collection. Stopping options include returning (interpolated) answers at a given t value, stopping after each internal step, and stopping just short of a given critical time. In one case, a root stopping ability has been added. Starting options include continuing with a change in certain parameters (such as tolerances or matrix structure parameters). Stopping and restarting, as in overlay situation or in an operator splitting solution, is quite easy. Continuing with components removed from the ODE system is allowed, while continuing with added components is not normally allowed. Nevertheless, the latter has been successfully done with an ODEPACK solver in an adaptive grid solution of parabolic PDEs [18].

(9) There are convenient optional inputs, including maximum method order, maximum step size, and initial step size. In all cases, there are default values that are easily invoked.

(10) The estimated local error on each step is available on each return to the user as an optional output, and following any successful return, the user can call a routine that gives the derivative of the solution (with respect to t) at a specified output time, of any order up to the current integration method order. Other optional outputs include all relevant function evaluation counts, certain sparse matrix counts, and the current step size and order.

(11) There is a means of passing dynamic real and integer work space to the user-supplied routines without using altered call sequences. However, this is somewhat cumbersome, and a better solution to this problem requires either changes to the Fortran language or the use of reverse communication (which is not done in ODEPACK).

The capabilities and other important properties of the individual ODEPACK solvers are summarized below. The solvers are listed in two groups, corresponding to the two problem forms (2) and (3). Included in this list are solvers that are available now and also some that are still in development. Further details are available in [13,14].

Solvers for Explicit ODE Systems.

LSODE. The first of the ODEPACK solvers written was LSODE (Livermore Solver for Ordinary Differential Equations). It is based on the older GEAR and GEARB solvers and on the new user interface standard in [11]. It solves stiff and nonstiff systems $\dot{y} = f(t,y)$, with a method flag to specify the formula (Adams or BDF) and the corrector iteration method and matrix type. When a modified Newton iteration is specified, LSODE uses a full, banded, or diagonal Jacobian. Bandwidth parameters must be specified, but these can correspond to a banded matrix to which the true Jacobian is only roughly equal (allowing for a tradeoff between storage and convergence speed). When specified, the difference quotient approximation to a banded Jacobian is generated with a number of extra f evaluations equal to the bandwidth. The central routine in LSODE for taking each time step (with local error control) is independent of the Jacobian structure, and is shared with LSODES and LSODBI.

LSODA. This variant of LSODE was written jointly with L. R. Petzold (Sandia Natl. Labs., Livermore), and differs in one important respect: It switches automatically between stiff and nonstiff methods [17]. The user must still specify the type of matrix (full or banded, supplied or not). Typically, LSODA has an efficiency advantage over LSODE on stiff problems because it integrates the (nonstiff) fast transient (or transients) with the more efficient nonstiff method (Adams method with functional iteration). On nonstiff problems, however, LSODA can be somewhat less efficient because of the overhead of testing for stiffness.

LSODAR. This variant, also jointly written with L. R. Petzold, is an extension of LSODA with a root-finding ability [9] added. It will stop (and return to the user) at the root of any of a set of given functions $g_i(t,y)$ of the solution, or on any of the standard stop conditions, whichever comes first. LSODAR and LSODA share a central routine for taking each step.

LSODES. This is a variant of LSODE for the case of a general sparse Jacobian matrix, and was written jointly with A. H. Sherman (Exxon Production Research Co.), based on the older GEARS package. It uses the ODRV and CDRV modules from the Yale Sparse Matrix Package [5,6] for the linear systems. The sparsity structure can be determined from preliminary evaluations of f if no

Jacobian information is supplied. A column grouping method [3] attempts to minimize the number of extra f evaluations per difference quotient Jacobian. Jacobian evaluations are further minimized, without a penalty in storage, by use of the stored value of the Newton matrix $P = I - h\beta_0 J$ (which YSMP stores separately from its LU factors), to reconstruct a new Newton matrix when it appears that the old one has failed only because of changes in the value of $h\beta_0$. LSODES allows the sparsity structure to be changed in the middle of the problem (without restarting the integrator).

LSODBI. This is a variant of LSODE that is planned but not yet written. It will be based on an older and much used solver called GEARBI [10], and will use block-iterative treatment of the Jacobian. GEARBI has been very useful for PDE-based problems in two space dimensions with finite differencing on rectangular meshes [2].

Solvers for Linearly Implicit ODE Systems

LSODI. Motivated by PDE-based ODE systems using weighted residual methods on the spatial variables, LSODI was written (based on the older GEARIB package) jointly with J. F. Painter (LLNL), for the problem $A\dot{y} = g$. The matrices involved (A, $\partial g/\partial y$, and $\partial(A\dot{y})/\partial y$) are treated as either full or banded. LSODI allows A to be singular (and in that case requires the user to input a consistent value for the initial y vector), but much caution is needed when using LSODI to solve a differential-algebraic system [16], as its design is based on the case of non-singular A. (However, LSODI can solve the discretized form of some types of mixed parabolic/elliptic PDE system problems.) The user must supply a routine to compute the residual function

$r = g(t,y) - A(t,y)s$,

given t, y, and s (s is a current approximation to $\dot{y}$), and also a routine to add A into a given array. This part of the interface was designed to keep matrix storage and computational cost to a minimum; A need never be formed as a separate array, and r is often much more efficiently computable directly by the user than from given values of g, A, and s. LSODI uses the Jacobian $\partial r/\partial y$, and this can be either user-supplied or generated internally. The residual routine has a call parameter by which the user can either signal an illegal value of y or s (which LSODI will try to avoid), or force an interrupt of the problem. LSODI (or its predecessor) has been used to solve PDE systems with fixed finite elements, with adaptive (periodically changed) finite elements, and with moving (continuously) finite elements. It has also been surprisingly successful in solving hybrid parabolic/elliptic systems from applications such as incompressible Navier-Stokes equations, semi-conductor models, combustion models, hydrodynamic lubrication, and others. The difficulties anticipated from nilpotency analysis [16] seem to be avoidable with careful formulation of the equations.

LSOIBT. This is a variant of LSODI, written jointly with C. S. Kenney (China Lake Naval Weapons Center), which substitutes block-tridiagonal matrix solvers for the full and band solvers. It is nearing completion and will be available soon. It was motivated by ODE problems arising from the moving finite element method in one space dimension [8]. The block-tridiagonal solver is somewhat unique in that it allows nonzero elements in the (1,3) and (N,N-2) block positions (so as to accommodate 3-point boundary conditions). In all respects other than the matrix structure, LSOIBT and LSODI are virtually identical.

LSODIS. This is another variant of LSODI, written jointly with S. Balsdon (Univ. of Texas at Austin), with general sparse matrix treatment of the linear systems [19]. It was also motivated by PDE-based problems, namely problems in two space dimensions using a finite element spatial treatment with adaptive gridding. It uses the same YSMP modules as does LSODES (but does not reuse a saved Newton matrix the way LSODES does). In other respects, LSODIS has the same features as LSODI. LSODIS is also nearing completion.

Availability

The ODEPACK solvers listed above are available (or will be when completed) from the National Energy Software Center (NESC) at the Argonne National Laboratory (9700 South Cass Ave., Argonne, IL 60439, U.S.A.). (Requests from Western European countries are to go through the NEA Data Bank in GIF-sur-YVETTE, France.) The solvers are being distributed both individually and as a combined package, in either single or double precision versions. Requestors should deal with their NESC installation representative regarding costs and procedures.

DISCUSSION

It is possible to list many of the features that are desirable or essential in ODE solvers that are to be used in the automated solution of time-dependent PDE systems. The list given above is a general one, and could be expanded to better cover particular problem classes. Many ODE solvers available today, including those in the ODEPACK collection, have been designed with just such features in mind. But they do not meet the demand completely, by any means. Some desired capabilities, including various sparsity structures, have not yet been included. Or it may be that individual capabilities of interest each appear in one or more solvers, but not all in a single solver. Work is continuing on ways to provide arbitrary combinations of choices as to explicit vs. implicit problem form, sparsity structure, fixed vs. automatic method selection, and normal vs. root-defined stopping. Greater interchangeability of modules would be helpful. With continued efforts in the development and use of modern algebraic system solvers and in modular software design, ODE solvers should continue to come closer to meeting the needs of PDE software.

REFERENCES

[1] G. D. Byrne, The ODE Solver EPISODE, its Variants, and their Use, in: Proceedings of the ANS Topical Meeting on Computational Methods in Nuclear Engineering, Williamsburg, VA, April 23-25, 1979.

[2] J. S. Chang, A. C. Hindmarsh, and N. K. Madsen, Simulation of Chemical Kinetics Transport in the Stratosphere, in: R. A. Willoughby (ed.), Stiff Differential Systems (Plenum Press, New York, 1974), 51-65.

[3] A. R. Curtis, M. J. D. Powell, and J. K. Reid, On the Estimation of Sparse Jacobian Matrices, J. Inst. Math. Applic. 13 (1974), 117-119.

[4] J. J. Dongarra, J. R. Bunch, C. B. Moler, and G. W. Stewart, LINPACK User's Guide (SIAM, Philadelphia, 1979).

[5] S. C. Eisenstat, M. C. Gursky, M. H.Schultz, and A. H. Sherman, Yale Sparse Matrix Package: I. The Symmetric Codes, Int. J. Num. Meth. Eng. 18 (1982), 1145-1151.

[6] S. C. Eisenstat, M. C. Gursky, M. H. Schultz, and A. H. Sherman, Yale Sparse Matrix Package: II. The Nonsymmetric Codes, Research Report No. 114 (Dept. of Computer Sciences, Yale Universtiy, 1977).

[7] C. W. Gear, Numerical Initial Value Problems in Ordinary Differential Equations (Prentice-Hall, Englewood Cliffs, NJ, 1971), 158-166.

[8] R. G. Gelinas, S. K. Doss, and K. Miller, The Moving Finite Element Method: Applications to General Partial Differential Equations with Multiple Large Gradients, J. Comp. Phys. 40 (1981), 202-249.

[9] K. L. Hiebert and L. F. Shampine, Implicitly Defined Output Points for Solutions of ODE's, Sandia National Laboratories Report SAND80-0180 (February 1980).

[10] A. C. Hindmarsh, Preliminary Documentation of GEARBI: Solution of ODE Systems with Block-Iterative Treatment of the Jacobian, LLNL Report UCID-30149 (December 1976).

[11] A. C. Hindmarsh, A Tentative User Interface Standard for ODEPACK, LLNL Report UCID-17954 (October 1978).

[12] A. C. Hindmarsh, A Collection of Software for Ordinary Differential Equations, in: Proceedings of the ANS Topical Meeting on Computational Methods in Nuclear Engineering, Williamsburg, VA, April 23-25, 1979.

[13] A. C. Hindmarsh, ODE Solvers for Use with the Method of Lines, in: R. Vichnevetsky and R. S. Stepleman (eds.), Advances in Computer Methods for Partial Differential Equations - IV (IMACS, New Brunswick, NJ, 1981), 312-316.

[14] A. C. Hindmarsh, ODEPACK, A Systematized Collection of ODE Solvers, in: R. S. Stepleman (ed.), IMACS Trans. on Scientific Computation, Vol. 1, Scientific Computing (North-Holland, Amsterdam, 1983).

[15] S. H. Johnson and A. C. Hindmarsh, Numerical Dynamic Simulation of Solid-Fluid Reactions in Isothermal Porous Spheres, J. Comp. Phys. 52 (1983), 503-523.

[16] L. R. Petzold, Differential/Algebraic Equations are not ODEs, SIAM J. on Sci. and Stat. Computing 3 (1982), 367-384.

[17] L. R. Petzold, Automatic Selection of Methods for Solving Stiff and Nonstiff Systems of Ordinary Differential Equations, SIAM J. on Sci. and Stat. Computing 4 (1983), 136-148.

[18] W. E. Schiesser, Lehigh University, private communication (1982).

[19] M. K. Seager and S. Balsdon, LSODIS, A Sparse Implicit ODE Solver, in: Proc. of the IMACS 10th World Congress, Montreal, August 8-13, 1982.

DISCUSSION

Speaker: A. Hindmarsh

Schönauer: I was interested to see your presentation. For parabolic problems, at each time step you have to solve an elliptic problem and so you consider all possible combinations for solving elliptic PDEs (i.e., full, banded, sparse, iterative, etc.). This can be equally viewed in the opposite order. Also, you have only "in core" capability and this will be insufficient for 3-D problems. Would you comment on viewing the solution process in the reverse order?

Hindmarsh: In the long run, when a variety of linear and nonlinear algebra modules are available in combination with the ODE integrators, the two views become identical, i.e., one will be able to combine arbitrary ODE algorithms with arbitrary solvers for elliptic equations.

Simpson: I would like to comment further on one of the remarks of Professor Schönauer. I believe he pointed out that if you think of performing time discretization before space discretization for dynamic problems, you get a boundary value problem at each time level, with the forcing term depending on the solution (globally in space) at previous time levels. So, if you have a boundary value solver which provides a global solution, you do not need to couple the spatial discretization at subsequent time levels. I am pointing out that this may be a way to finesse the problems mentioned earlier that arise in moving mesh points from one time level to the next to provide a dynamic, adaptive spatial mesh. I have tried this in a small experiment on the standard shock tube test problem using the COLSYS BVP solver and the backwards differentiation time discretization.

I can say that the sophisticated spatial mesh distribution algorithms of COLSYS work using the forcing term involving (global, interpolated) past histories to move the mesh points with the waves in the solution; but, of course, it is very expensive.

Hindmarsh: This is an open question, as work on these alternative approaches is incomplete. The main issue is whether the BVP solver can benefit from information generated on prior time steps. I have had experience with one problem which consists of ODEs in time coupled to a time-independent spatial BVP. (The latter was a quasi-steady form of a parabolic PDE.) The solution using COLSYS alternating with a simple time stepping scheme took about 1 min per case on a Cray-1. The solution of the ODEs and parabolic PDE (finite-difference) using LSODE took less than 1/4 sec per case, and solved cases the first approach could not, especially in the presence of a steep moving front.

Gorenflo: You said that in some of your routines there is provision for fixing dependent variables which have reached steady state. You may interpret this as taking infinite step-length for such variables. A more general question: Do you know of any development of ODE schemes with individually varying step-lengths, i.e., large steps for slowly varying components of the solution vectors, short step-lengths for rapidly changing ones? Such schemes are useful, e.g., in celestial mechanics (evolution of star clusters with greatly varying distances between individual stars) and in simulation of a plasma by integrating the equations of motions of a mixture of many electrons and ions.

Hindmarsh: The idea of separate time steps, or multi-rate methods, is very appealing. Unfortunately, algorithms have not been developed that can be shown to be stable and robust. It is hard to know how to interrelate the slow and fast variables. A thesis by a student of Bill Gear's, and some work at Livermore have addressed these methods with only partial success.

Regarding steady state components - I do not generally recommend dropping components that have stopped changing because it is unsafe, as some periodic chemistry problems show (the "steady" component can become active again). However, the ODEPACK solvers do allow this reduction of the system size, and PDE solvers may need to make use of such a feature in the case setting of a changing mesh. More work is needed in the ODE solvers to give greater flexibility here.

Lawson: You mentioned certain difficulties with the reverse communication structures - do you use this type of structuring?

Hindmarsh: No we do not; we require user-supplied routines which the solvers call. An additional reason for this is the difficulty of explaining reverse communication to users. Very few users understand it (or like it). Fred Krogh, who once used it, now does not in his ODE solvers, and I understand this was his main reason.

Furzeland: I think gains can be made by use of reverse communication. I don't see why the user even needs to know about this internal structure.

Hindmarsh: It is true that reverse communication solves some shortcomings of ODE solvers. A major price for this is the complexity and loss of clarity of the solver. For example, think of the paths between the uses and the point 3 or 4 levels down where function values are needed for a difference quotient Jacobian approximation. Also, the user must be prepared to supply different quantities at different times (function, Jacobian, A matrix, etc.).

Reid: In connection with reverse communication, I would like to comment that the Fortran committee has thought about the problem, which is really caused by the inflexibility of COMMON. The new language is unlikely to be in use for ten years, but then there will be a better mechanism for the user to access this data in a routine called by a library package.

Hindmarsh: I am glad to hear this. The new and more flexible COMMON is just what is needed for the difficulty of user-defined data space.

Rice: I have seen multiple time scale (step) methods being used by several engineers.

Do you do any scaling of the problem before the linear equations are solved?

Hindmarsh: Not explicitly. A weight vector of scaling factors is formed from the user's input tolerance parameters, and this can vary during the problem. Any error-like quantity, as in convergence tests, is a weighted norm with these weights. There is no explicit multiplication by the scaling factors in saved vectors, though.

Rice: Then a badly scaled problem is just passed through?

Hindmarsh: Yes. If the scaling is extremely bad, then matrix ill-conditioning can degrade performance.

Rice: In LINPACK, no pre-scaling is used and we've found them sometimes unreliable. Do you use the LINPACK routines? I have an example problem that really needs scaling, but I don't know in advance how to scale it.

Hindmarsh: Yes, we use LINPACK in the full and band cases. I must leave to the numerical linear algebra experts the job of revising such solvers where bad scaling demands this. Some will argue that real problems never require rescaling, or require it only so rarely that revisions to solvers are not warranted.

Yanenko: These talks have made it seem very attractive to reduce all problems to ODEs - but for physical and mathematical reality, one must use at least two models: (1) cell model, and (2) particle model. The particle-in-cell (PIC) method and Buneman's efforts in plasma physics and chemical reactions are examples of this. It is necessary to use both models in good schemes and not just reduce problems to ODEs.

Young: What do you mean by "matrix-free" approaches? Is Purdue's sparse storage format an example of this? If you wanted to do SOR in this way - how would you do it?

Hindmarsh: Our experiments with matrix-free iterations (done jointly with P. N. Brown) are with the Incomplete Orthogonalization Method due to Y. Saad. Here one never stores a matrix, but instead, needs 5 to 10 working vectors. ODE systems from PDE systems tested so far show a 2 to 1 speedup and much greater reductions in storage. Storing the nonzeros in packed form does not qualify as matrix-free. If one has a large system with half a million nonzeros in the Jacobian, it is much preferable to have to store only 10,000 words, if the solution run time does not suffer. As to matrix-free forms of other methods, such as SOR, we have not worked these out, but are hopeful, and hope to get help on this from others such as yourself.

Kågström: When you talked about future developments of software for implicit ODE-systems $A\dot{y} = g$, you didn't say anything about the cases when A is singular or nilpotent. Is the reason that there are very few real problems that give rise to a singular (or nilpotent) A or is the problem too difficult to solve, especially when A is time-dependent? In [1] Gear and Petzold show that if the nilpotency is greater than or equal to 2, the BDF-method will almost always have a stability problem. (See reference below)

Hindmarsh: The reason is a mixture of the two. I agree that $A\dot{y} = g$ problems with singular A often arise, and I mentioned several cases. This happens as soon as one combines evolutionary (parabolic) equations and nonevolutionary (elliptic) equations in a coupled system, for example. But it seems to be the case that these problems can usually be formulated so that the nilpotency is not large, and solvers like LSODI can handle them. Admittedly, this depends on the skill of the modeler and person forming the semi-discrete system from the model. A friend of mine from General Motors Research Lab recently told me that he has solved numerous such differential-algebraic systems (he named four different applications), all with LSODI (or its predecessor), with no major difficulty.

Furzeland: You mentioned a root-finding stopping criteria for some integrators. Do these assume continuity across the stopping point? For discontinuities, this is not the case and it would, thus, be useful to relax this assumption.

Hindmarsh: Our solver assumes that the right-hand side of the ODE system is continuous, but that after the root is found and the solver is called again, the ODE may change discontinuously. This is the usual case. If the ODE cannot be posed in a continuous form (e.g., it involves the square root of a function that changes sign), one must work harder. Then, the ODE solver would have to take shorter steps on approaching the root, whereas, in the usual case, it does not.

Sherman: One way to handle this situation in a code such as LSODE is to make use of the existing capability to keep all evaluations to one side of a time t_0, while integrating up to t_0. One might try to estimato t_0 by extrapolating your (Furzeland's) switching function, which is assumed to be continuous in its variables.

Zlatev: How do you control and monitor stability in the ODE solver?

Hindmarsh: In LSODE and those variants where a fixed method is used, the stability is not directly monitored, but the local error control is sensitive to a violation of the stability limit and so, enforces it indirectly. In LSODA, the algorithm estimates the current Lipschitz constant, either directly when BDF is in use or by difference quotients when an Adam's method is in use, and the switching is based on this and the known stability boundaries of the Adam's methods.

Zlatev: Are you using the Shampine idea of assessing stability only through the error control?

Hindmarsh: Yes, basically, when the method is fixed (though the details are different). When the method is not fixed (the Petzold algorithm), the idea is quite different.

Zlatev: How do you handle the default values for the ODE package parameters?

Hindmarsh: A call sequence argument is set to zero if defaults only are desired. If not, the user loads a few elements of two input arrays.

Zlatev: Mention has been made that iterative methods are not attractive because of Jacobian evaluation and back solves. For a linear PDE, the Jacobian is just part of forming the right hand side and iterative methods should work well.

Hindmarsh: As we mentioned, we used block-iterative methods very successfully on MOL solutions of 2-D kinetics-transport problems (problem size N greater than 10,000). There the kinetics was nonlinear (and stiff) and a major savings was achieved by saving LU decompositions of the diagonal blocks (where the kinetics was the major contribution).

Ref. 1. C. W. Gear, L. R. Petzold: Differential/algebraic systems and matrix pencils, In Kågström, Ruhe, Matrix Pencils, Proceedings, Pite Havsbad, 1982, Lecture Notes in Math Vol. 973, pp. 75-89.

PDE SOFTWARE: Modules, Interfaces and Systems
B. Engquist and T. Smedsaas (eds.)
Elsevier Science Publishers B.V. (North-Holland)
© IFIP, 1984

COMMENTS ON THE VECTORIZATION OF A FRONTAL CODE

Iain Duff

A.E.R.E. Harwell
Computer Science and Systems Div.
Building 8.9
Oxford OX11 ORA
ENGLAND

The vectorization of frontal codes is discussed. It is shown
how the inner loops may be speeded up such that the performance is much higher than for general sparse codes. An illustration of the frontal code performance on a finite-element
Navier-Stokes solver is given.

Previous speakers (for example, Reid, Bjørstad and Sewell) have discussed frontal methods, and vectorization was considered by Schönauer and Bossavit inter
alia. If I can thus assume familiarity with these two notions, my task is
simply to marry them and I can be fairly succinct.

The feature of frontal codes which attracts us is that the arithmetic in the
innermost loop is performed using full matrix code. For example, the inner loops
of the Harwell MA32 package (Duff, 1981a, 1981b, 1983b) have the form

```
      DO 100 L = 1, LFRNT
      IF (PIVROW(L).EQ.ZERO) GO TO 100
      DO 50 K = 1, KFRNT
      A(K,L) = A(K,L) + PIVCOL(K)*PIVROW(L)        (1)
   50 CONTINUE
  100 CONTINUE
```

where it is evident that the inner loop (DO 50...) is a direct SAXPY viz.

$$a(.,l) \leftarrow a(.,l) + pivcol * pivrow(l).$$

Because two vector loads and one store are required for each set of two arithmetic operations, the asymptotic rate for a memory-to-memory SAXPY on the CRAY-1
is 50 Megaflops (millions of floating point operations per second).

If one considers that the best assembler code for an indirect SAXPY known to the
author has an asymptotic rate of 12.4 Megaflops (Dodson, 1981) then it is clear
that for problems where frontal codes are applicable, they should be much better
than general sparse codes, even if the general code has its innermost loop
written in assembler. Another factor favouring frontal codes is that the vector
length involved (KFRNT) is typically much higher than the $n_{1/2}$ value of the CRAY-1
(a value of 200 for KFRNT is common, whereas $n_{1/2}$ is about 10) whereas the vector
length in the sparse SAXPY may be only about 5 to 10.

We can, however, obtain a higher performance than the single memory-to-memory
SAXPY by observing that in the loops (1) we are performing a sequence of
SAXPYs of the form (2) with the vector pivcol remaining unchanged throughout
the sequence. Thus, if we can keep pivcol in the vector registers throughout
the sequence of SAXPYs we need only one load and one store for each two floating
point operations, yielding a maximum asymptotic rate of 75 Megaflops. A call to
this multiple-SAXPY CAL routine replaces both the innermost and next-to-inner-
most loops (all of (1)) in our frontal code.

It is possible to do even better. In any realistic problem, there are several
fully-summed rows and columns in the frontal matrix at each stage. If just two
elimination steps can be combined, then our inner loop can run at well over 100
Megaflops. This is done by loading the two pivotal columns into the vector
registers and chaining the load of the first non-pivotal column with the float-
ting point operations from the first pivotal column . The SAXPY operations from
the second pivotal column are then chained and the second non-pivotal column is simultaneously loaded from memory. The operations of the two pivot on columns on this
second non-pivotal column are then overlapped with the store of the first non-
pivotal column and the load of the third non-pivotal column respectively. We
continue in this way always keeping both arithmetic pipes busy, and so achieve
optimal performance. A prototype CAL code implementing this runs at over 90
Megaflops and it is hoped to improve this further.

Although the prospect of a fairly general sparse code whose inner loop runs at
well over 100 Megaflopgs on the CRAY-1 may raise one's pulse rate considerably,
a small caveat is in order. If we look in Table 1 at the ratio of inner-loop
time to total time for a problem obtained from a 16x16 grid of nine-node rectangular
elements with 5 variables per node, the values are .86 and .60 on the IBM 3081K
and CRAY-1 (using CFT) respectively reflecting the fact that the inner-loop time
is reduced much more than the rest of the code through vectorization. Thus, if we
speed up the inner loop even

	CPU time (seconds) Total	inner loop	% time in inner loop	% time selecting pivots
3081K	119	102	86	.9
CTF	12.6	7.6	60	9
CAL	7.5	3.7	49	16
"NEW ALG CAL"	5.8	2.0	35	21
Optimize pivot selection	4.7	2.0	43	1.5

Table 1   Effect of vectorization on matrix of order 5445.

more, this ratio will decrease further until the computation time in the inner
loop ceases to be dominant. This is a common phenomenon of vectorization and
is witnessed by the ratio of inner loop to total time reducing to .35 when CAL
is used. A corollary of this is that originally non-dominant parts of the code
may now be significant. This is seen dramatically in the last column where
the pivoting time which was negligible on the IBM now uses 21% of the CPU time.
It is relatively easy to vectorize this part of the code and the overall savings
in CPU time are not far short of 20% as is shown in row 5 of the table.

Another important lesson from these results is that, although it is conceivable
that the compiler could be smart enough to perform optimization to the level of
CAL (the third row in Table 1) further substantial gains can be attained by algorithmic redesign quite outwith the scope of any present day compilers.

We conclude by illustrating the performance of our frontal code in the solution
of nonlinear partial differential equations arising in fluid flow. A finite-
element method based on a Galerkin formulation of the velocity-pressure version
of the Navier-Stokes equations was used where the elements were nine-node isoparametric quadrilaterals with biquadratic interpolation for the velocities and
piecewise linear interpolation for the pressure. (Cliffe et al, 1983). Statistics
for the linearized problem are given in Table 2 where the version of MA32 using
multiple SAXPY's (but not two pivot columns) was employed.

The upper and lower grid sizes refer to the element grid before and after a backward facing step respectively.

Dimensions of grid of elements or equations	20x20 60x40
Order (degrees of freedom)	31282
Maximum front size	175
Total time in seconds for solution (including back substitution)	42.9
Time in innermost loop (in seconds)	16.9
Number operations in inner loop (in millions)	980
Inner loop megaflops Total megaflops	58 23

Table 2   Illustration of the performance of frontal code on the CRAY-1.

The complete solution of the nonlinear PDE required nearly 3 billion floating point operations and used 8 million words of data, the total time for solution including I/O being 4 minutes.

The overall simulation study of which this pde was one step took the theoretical physicists two days. They estimated that the same study would have taken two and a half months on the IBM 3081K. Although this is largely due to the job scheduling algorithms on the two machines, it is illustrative of the sort of problems and gains that can be achieved when running the frontal code on the CRAY-1. Further information on the vectorization of this code and of sparse codes in general is given by Duff (1983b).

References:

Cliffe, K.A., Jones, I.P., Porter, J.D., Thompson, C.P. and Wilkes, N.S. (1983). Laminar flow over a backward facing step: numerical solutions for a test problem. Harwell Report CSS 142.

Dodson, D. (1981). Preliminary timing study for the CRAYPACK library. Boeing Computer Services Memorandum G4550-CM-39.

Duff, I.S. (1981a). MA32 - A package for solving sparse unsymmetric systems using the frontal method. AERE Report R.10079, HMSO, London.

Duff, I.S. (1981b). Design features of a frontal code for solving sparse unsymmetric linear systems and out-of-core. To appear in SIAM J. Sci. Stat. Comput.

Duff, I.S. (1983a). The solution of sparse linears equations on the CRAY-1. AERE Report CSS 125 (Revised).

Duff, I.S. (1983b). Enhancements to the MA32 package for solving sparse unsymmetric systems. AERE Report R.11009, HMSO, London.

DISCUSSION

Speaker: I. Duff

Hockney (to Duff): Would you expand on your statement that the use of assembler language does not make the code any less portable.

Duff: We provide a standard FORTRAN equivalent subroutine for any of our assembler-coded routines so the recipient has merely to incorporate this to make the whole package portable. A good example of this is the BLAS where CRAY Inc. has coded some of them in their scientific library (SCILIB) in CAL, but standard versions are also available from IMSL as algorithms from ACM Transactions on Mathematical Software.

Sherman (to Duff): You gave times for the overall problem for the IBM 3081K code and the optimized CRAY code. What would the time have been for the unoptimized FORTRAN code on the CRAY? Is the difference between the CRAY code very significant, and, in any case, is not the degree of importance quite dependent on the particular computer installation?

Duff: The inner-loop time is more than halved and, as you saw in the presentation, accounted for 60% of the overall time in the non-optimized version so the solution time is reduced to about 2/3 of the time for vectorized CEF code. The main importance lies in the fact that many houndreds of systems will be solved in a lengthy computation so such savings at essentially the innermost loop are concial. The full impact is, of course, dependent on the policy governing scheduling of computing resources. In one case, our changes reduced the turn around time on the CRAY-1 by a factor of 10. I maintain this effect is common although the actual savings will be dependent on the value of various parameters in the system scheduling and billing software.

Zlatev (to Duff): This seems to be a useful modification of the frontal code program. Does it also apply to general sparse software?

Duff: We can modify general sparse software, but the effect will not be so significant. One way of doing this is to replace the innermost indirect SAXPY loop with assembler code, but this will at best speed up this loop by a factor of only 4 from 3 to about 12.4 Megaflops (asymptotically). But remember that the inner-loop accounted for 86% of the time in the frontal code. It may be much less for a general problem and so the effect of vectorization will not be so dramatic. For example, on our multifrontal codes the inner-loop (on the IBM 3081K) typically only accounts for 40-50% of the total time and the percentage time in the indirect SAXPY loop of a general code is often even less.

A simple way of speeding up general sparse codes on vector machines like the CRAY-1 is to switch to full code when the reduced matrix gets dense. It often pays to switch even when it is quite sparse and we have recorded reductions of a factor of 4 in overall solution-time by using this technique.

Hindemarsh (to Duff): To change the subject somewhat: most descriptions of the frontal method are in the context of elliptic problems. I wonder what is the state of frontal solvers for use on time-dependent problems, where one has multiple right-hand side vectors and one wants to use saved Jacobian information.

Duff: The MA32 package based on the work described in my talk applies to completely general problems. However, unless the structure is banded or nearly banded it may do badly. When resolving for subsequent RHS the I/O can dominate, since the data is read in and only used once.

Hindmarsh: So if I/O is dominant in the overall cost, can it be that solving for a second RHS is almost as expensive as the first?

Duff: Not quite, but it is expensive enough to contemplate changing one's algorithm to use and factorize a fresh Jacobian at each step. We only have to save a very few iterations to make this approach faster overall.

Rice (comment on Duff/Hindmarsh discussion): TWODEPEP uses the frontal method.

PDE SOFTWARE: Modules, Interfaces and Systems
B. Engquist and T. Smedsaas (eds.)
Elsevier Science Publishers B.V. (North-Holland)
© IFIP, 1984

DISCUSSION ON CONVERGENCE ACCELERATION AND MULTIGRID METHODS

Professor Yanenko opened this discussion with a summary of his ideas on iterative methods for elliptic equations, artificial viscosity and convergence acceleration.

Trottenberg to Yanenko: I did not quite understand which methods you used to accelerate convergence.

Yanenko: We applied the standard implicit iteration methods.

Brandt to Yanenko: What did you mean by saying that the timelike acceleration is like working on a coarse grid?

Yanenko: The coarse grid corresponds to artificial viscosity.

Brandt: But the convergence speed is not so good as with a coarse grid acceleration.

Yanenko: Yes, we did get a considerably better speed.

Brandt: It is true that the timelike acceleration gives good convergence but not as fast as solving a problem in a work equivalent to 5 relaxation sweeps.

Yanenko: This resembles approximating a viscosity term.

Brandt: Yes, artificial viscosity is good together with the non-elliptic part.

Yanenko: Yes, I agree.

Brandt (general comment on multigrid methods): Fast multigrid solvers in cases of small ellipticity (singular perturbation) introduce artificial viscosity to the relaxation process but not in calculating residuals to be transferred to the coarse grid.
The relaxation process requires a stable but low order approximation, whereas the residuals can have a non-stable and high order approximation. This results in an overall high-order approximation which is also stable.
For nonelliptic BVP you can most often avoid going through time evolution.

Sherman to Stüben: I have heard of an experiment at Colorado State University where AMG did not work well in a petroleum simulator model.

Stüben gave the word to Brandt.

Brandt: This is a development code which is extremely inefficient - a study code for us, not for time measurements.

Sherman: I heard of convergence troubles.

Brandt: That was not the AMG code but another MG code. I don't remember exactly what the problem was.

Sherman: Who wrote the code? Was it prepared by someone sufficiently expert in multigrid methods?

Brandt: It was written at Colorado State.

Duff (comment on Sherman/Brandt):   It would be very interesting to try AMG on the problem class Andy is suggesting. There is a real need to develop robust non-direct techniques for this class. Do you think AMG could be extended to solve such problems?

Brandt: Yes, it is suitable for such problems. The system you get at each timestep is suitable, with a few adjustments to the code.

Sherman: I would be happy to make experiments if you can send me the code. We can present our problems in an appropriate way.

Brandt: My impression of the oil industry is different. We proposed to consult them, but they wanted ready made programs.

Sherman: We cannot afford a large-scale effort to experiment with a special multigrid simulator. However, we would like to find out how promising AMG is. It is promising that it can exploit the anisotropic nature of the problem. I would be happy to participate in evaluation on real petroleum problems.

Brandt: We develop tools but are willing to cooperate with people interested in real world problems. In case of oil-reservoir simulators, my impression is that there is no pressing need there for advanced methods, basically because of the crudeness of the oil-field data.

Sherman: I would not go so far. We and other companies do a lot of cooperative research with universities. At present we are participating in a large joint project on iterative methods. However, it is extremely difficult to justify support for expensive efforts when the payoff is as uncertain as it has appeared in the past for geometric multigrid. I am aware of at least two independent negative evaluations of geometric multigrid in the oil industry. AMG seems to fit more naturally with the industry's simulation efforts and is, therefore, more attractive to us.

Gustafsson: Could we settle this question whether or not there will be any cooperation between Sherman and Brandt? --- If not, I suggest that we pass on to the next question.

Reid to Stüben: How do you choose coarser grids automatically?

Stüben: In point relaxation, smoothing is only in the direction of strong connections (consider the anisotropic operator, for example). Thus, roughly, the coarse grid is chosen so that fine-grid points are strongly connected to (enough of) the coarse-grid points.

Reid: Is this restricted to 2D problems?

Stüben: No, but no experiments have been made with higher dimensional problems so far.

Schönauer to Stüben: What about systems?

Stüben: In general, problems of this kind are not treated efficiently by the present version of AMG 01 (which is designed mainly for matrices with positive diagonal entries and non-positive off-diagonals).

Schönauer: You have to put in information about the blocks.

Stüben: Yes.

Rice to Stüben: When will AMG be available?

Stüben: Maybe in 1984.

PDE SOFTWARE: Modules, Interfaces and Systems
B. Engquist and T. Smedsaas (eds.)
Elsevier Science Publishers B.V. (North-Holland)
© IFIP, 1984

THE ARRAY FEATURES IN FORTRAN 8x

J.K. Reid

CSS Division
AERE Harwell
Oxon OX11 ORA U.K.

This note summarizes briefly the array features that
are currently planned for inclusion in Fortran 8x.
They will be extremely helpful for writing software
for solving partial differential equations,
particularly when the target machine has vector or array
facilities in its hardware.

1. INTRODUCTION

Several papers given on the first day of this conference made it
plain that array facilities are desperately needed in Fortran.
Several speakers began with vector or matrix operations, coded them as
DO loops, and then went to some trouble to ensure that the automatic
vectorizer treated the innermost loops in vector mode. Such coding
has been called "pornographic" by W. Kahan. Relief is on the way.
The full language is unlikely to be in use until the 1990s, but
vendors of vector and array machines are likely to implement subsets
of the array features as extensions to Fortran 77. For example Cray
have announced that they will include a conservative subset in their
new Fortran compiler (NFT).

In this note we summarize the principal array features that have
been passed by the committee. Some changes, particularly of the fine
details, are likely before final acceptance but it is my belief that
drastic changes are unlikely.

2. WHOLE ARRAY EXPRESSIONS AND ASSIGNMENTS

The most important extension is that whole array expressions and
assignments will be permitted. For example the statement

$$A=B+C*SIN(D) \tag{1}$$

where A,B,C and D are arrays of exactly the same shape is permitted.
It is interpreted elementwise, that is the sine function is taken on
each component of D, each result is multiplied by the corresponding
component of C, added to the corresponding component of B and finally
assigned to corresponding position in A. Functions, including user-
written functions, may be array-valued and may overload scalar
versions having the same name. All arrays in an expression or across
an assignment must "conform" that is have exactly the same "rank"
(number of dimensions) and "extent" (set of lengths in each
dimension), but scalars may be included freely and these are
interpreted as being broadcast to a conforming array. Expressions are
evaluated as a whole before assignment takes place.

Note that there is scope for a computer to fully exploit multi-
dimensional arrays in an expression such as (1), whereas if it is
rewritten in the form of nested DO loops, existing vectorization
techniques would vectorize only the inner-most loop.

3.   ARRAY SECTIONS

Wherever whole arrays may be used it is also possible to use rectangular slices called "sections". For example

$$A(:, 1:N, 2, 3:1:-1) \tag{2}$$

consists of a subarray containing the whole of the first dimension, positions 1 to N of the second dimension, position 2 of the third dimension and positions 1 to 3 in reverse for the fourth dimension. This is a bizarre artificial example chosen to illustrate the different forms. Of course, the most common use will be to pick out a row or column of any array, for example

$$A(:,J) \quad .$$

4.   WHERE AND FORALL STATEMENTS

There are two mechanisms for qualifying an array assignment. The where statement applies a conforming logical array as a mask on the individual operations in the expression and in the assignment. For example

$$WHERE \ (A.GT.O) \ B=LOG(A)$$

takes the logarithm only for positive components of A and makes assignments only in these positions.

The forall statement is used whenever it is convenient or necessary to have access to the actual subscript values in an array expression and assignment. For example

$$FORALL(I=1:N, \ J=1:N, \ I.GE.J) \ L(I,J)=A(I,J)$$

performs an array assignment over the lower triangular part of the leading NxN submatrix.

The where statement also has a block form.

5.   AUTOMATIC AND ALLOCATABLE ARRAYS

A major advance for our work will be the presence of "automatic" arrays, created on entry to a subprogram and destroyed on return, and "allocatable" arrays whose rank is fixed but whose actual size and lifetime is fully under the programmer's control through explicit "allocate" and "deallocate" commands. The declarations

```
SUBROUTINE X(N,A,B)
REAL WORK(N,N), HEAP(:,:)
```

are associated with an automatic array WORK and an allocatable array HEAP. Note that a stack is an adequate storage mechanism for automatic arrays, but a heap is needed for allocatable arrays.

6.   ARRAY CONSTRUCTORS

Arrays, and in particular array constants, may be constructed with "array constructors", exemplified by

[1.0, 3.0, 7.2]

which is an array of length 3,

[10[1.3,2.7], 7.1]

which has length 21 and contains [1.3, 2.7] repeated 10 times and

[1:N]

which contains the integers 1,2,...N. Only rank one arrays may be constructed in this way, but higher dimensional arrays may be made from them by calling the intrinsic function shape, see section 8, below.

7.   THE IDENTIFY STATEMENT

At its simplest, the identify statement permits the construction of subarrays that do not lie along the axes. As a simple example

IDENTIFY(I=1:N) DIAG(I)=A(I,I)

constructs a vector that overlays the main diagonal of A. After execution of such an IDENTIFY statement, the "virtual" array so constructed can be used wherever an array of the same shape might be used.

8.   INTRINSIC FUNCTIONS

All the Fortran 77 intrinsic functions and all the scalar intrinsic functions that have been added to the language have been extended to be applicable also to arrays. The function is applied element by element to produce an array of the same shape. In addition the following array intrinsics have been added.

i)   enquiry intrinsics

RANK   returns the number of dimensions

EXTENT returns an integer vector holding the lengths
       of the dimensions

SIZE   returns the total number of elements

UBOUND returns an integer vector holding the upper
       dimension bounds

LBOUND returns an integer vector holding the lower
       dimension bounds

ii)   array constructors

SPREAD   returns an array of increased rank by
          duplicating the array

REPLICATE   returns an array of the same rank by
            duplicating the array within a given dimension

SHAPE   alters the shape of an array

PACK   packs an array into a vector

UNPACK   unpacks a vector into an array

MERGE   merges two conforming arrays under the control
            of a conforming logical mask

CSHIFT   shifts circularly

EOSHIFT   shifts "end off", filling with a single default value

TRANSPOSE   transposes an array of rank two

iii) array manipulators

DOTPRODUCT returns the dot product of two vectors

MATMUL   multiplies two matrices

SUM   sums all the elements of an array or returns an
            array of dimension one less by summing along a
            given dimension. It may be qualified by a logical
            masking array

PRODUCT   is a similar function for products

MAXVAL   is a similar function for maximum values

MINVAL   is a similar function for minimum values

COUNT   counts the number of true values in a logical
            array or along a particular dimension

ANY   is a similar function for the logical operator any

ALL   is a similar function for the logical operator all.

9.   CONCLUDING REMARKS

This brief note is not intended to be comprehensive. For a full
definition the reader should refer to the committee's standing
document S7. Rather this should give a flavour of the proposed
facilities. I am certainly hoping to get some of the details changed,
but have avoided describing these. Your comments and constructive
criticisms will always be welcome.

Editors' comment: For the discussion, see pp. 360-363.

PDE SOFTWARE: Modules, Interfaces and Systems
B. Engquist and T. Smedsaas (eds.)
Elsevier Science Publishers B.V. (North-Holland)
© IFIP, 1984

SOFTWARE PARTS IN FORTRAN 8X

Brian T. Smith[*]

Mathematics and Computer Science Division
Argonne National Laboratory
Argonne, Illinois 60439

This paper briefly describes the data abstraction mechanisms that have been proposed by the Fortran Standards
Subcommittee X3J3 for Fortran 8x. With the proposed mechanisms, the building of software parts, that is, components of subroutine libraries, data bases, and program
packages, is greatly facilitated.

INTRODUCTION

Since 1978, when the work began on the next Fortran standard, the Fortran
Standards Subcommittee X3J3 has attempted to make Fortran more extensible to
meet the needs of its users. The subcommittee first focused on the concept of
preprocessors. This was rejected and later replaced by a new architecture for
Fortran that became known as the "core + modules" architecture The idea of core +
modules was to define and standardize a small core language that satisfied the
principles of good language design, such as orthogonality, consistency, and completeness. Later, as the need arose, extensions to the language would become
standardized as language extension modules or application modules, according to
what was most appropriate for each extension. In addition to these modules, a
compatibility module would retain features of the past standard that were likely
to be discarded in later revisions of the standard.

Within this core + modules architecture, extensions that required new statements
and were of general interest would likely be part of some language extension module, whereas extensions that were of limited interest to certain applications
would appear as application modules. For example, the complex data type, requiring
a specification statement, might appear within this model in a standardized
language extension model, whereas the collection of intrinsic functions for environmental inquiry might appear in a standardized application module. Some conceived that Fortran compilers would be partitioned in the same fashion as the
language modules, requiring that a program unit specify to the Fortran compiler
the modules that were being assumed.

However, in the past year, the subcommittee has revised its concept of modules.
Rather than permitting modules to specify new statements and arbitrary syntax,
the subcommittee feels that the core should be enhanced with an extensibility
mechanism that permits limited syntax extensions. This mechanism, using a new

[*]This work was supported by the Applied Mathematical Sciences Research Program
(KC-04-02) of the Office of Energy Research of the U.S. Department of Energy
and Contract W-31-109-ENG-38. Partial support was received from the Special
Interest Group on Numerical Mathematics of the Association for Computing Ma-
chinery for travel expenses to attend the X3J3 meetings.

program unit called a MODULE, permits the definition of "derived types" and
operations on these types. Using the MODULE program unit, software parts such as
components of subroutine libraries, data bases, and program packages [4,5] can be
readily implemented in Fortran 8x. As a result of this change, the subcommittee
believes that language extension modules are unnecessary, but does see the potential need for standardizing application modules based upon the language extension mechanism in the proposed Fortran 8x language.

This short note briefly introduces the Fortran 8x module. The module is similar
in one sense to the block data subprogram in that global data are being shared,
but it is based on a different principle of association, namely, an association
by name rather than an association by storage. Entities that can be shared include variables, arrays, derived types (or aggregates of data), operations on
the derived types, procedures (functions and subprograms), and procedure interfaces. Such entities may be referenced from any external program but, in contrast to COMMON blocks, are specified once only. A MODULE program unit consists
of specifications only and cannot itself be executed. However, a MODULE program
unit can contain executable statements which are, in fact, part of the specification of the internal procedures.

A MODULE PROGRAM UNIT

Within a MODULE program unit, the scope of the declared entities can be specified. For example, certain entities can be specified as private, that is,
available only to the procedures specified within the module and not available
to external subprogram units. Such entities are used to communicate values
strictly between the procedures within the module. In contrast, other module entities may be specified as public (which is, in fact, also the default), in which
case any external program unit can reference the module and will have access to
such entities.

A statement called a USE statement is used to reference a specified module and
particular entities within that module. The USE statement specifies the module by
name, and may specify by name the sharing of all, some, or most of the public entities in the module. To resolve name conflicts with local entities in the
referencing program unit, the USE statement permits the renaming of specified entities
from the module.

To visualize the module facility, consider creating a module (or a collection of
software parts) to perform linear algebra operations in a convenient operator notation. As described in [3], the multiplication operator * (asterisk) between
two conformable array operands results in an element-by-element multiplication of
the two arrays, producing an array result of the same shape as the operands. For
a linear algebra application, the more usual semantics (if the arrays were two
dimensional) would be to perform a matrix by matrix product made up of a series
of inner products of the rows of the first matrix with the columns of the second
matrix. With the MODULE program unit and the derived type mechanism, such a product can be written using the infix operator *.

With the understanding that the syntax below is incomplete and is strictly for
illustration purposes only, the following pseudo-code represents such a module:
```
    MODULE linear_algebra

   ! Define a "new type" called MATRIX

    "new type" MATRIX
   !   a real array of 2 dimensions
    end "new type"
```

```
! Define matrix product. Only the interface is given below.

FUNCTION matrix_by_matrix_product(A, B) RESULT(ANSWER) OPERATOR(*)

A, B, ANSWER: "new type" MATRIX

! Code to define matrix product as a sequence of inner products.
  :
  :
END matrix_by_matrix_product

! A reference to such a module may be:

USE /linear_algebra/

A, B, X: "new type" MATRIX
  :
  :
A = B * X
```

Widely used modules, such as might be expected for a linear algebra module, could be considered for standardization by the Fortran Standards Subcommittee as a collateral Fortran standard. The standardization process would, however standardize only the interface, the derived types, and the semantics of the operations; it would not standardize the method of implementation. (Thus, for efficiency, processors that used a paged environment might prefer to form the matrix product as a linear combination of the columns of the first operand, and not as an inner product.) Such a module is indeed what the subcommittee had in mind when it proposed an application module, and it seems possible therefore that such a module could become an intrinsic part of some Fortran compilers. Portability is not compromised as the user can always supply the necessary Fortran code as a MODULE program unit when the application module is not an intrinsic part of his Fortran compiler.

As well as providing software parts for well-established application areas, the MODULE program unit, the derived type mechanism, and internal procedures facilitate the definition of subroutine libraries, data abstraction modules, and program packages for more specific applications. For example, a module for defining an aggregate called a GRID and operations on instances of grids such as union (say, using the operator .UNION.) can be written. Such a module would be easier to define with the new facilities being proposed by X3J3 than with the use of COMMON and subprograms as illustrated in [1].

The Fortran subcommittee has proposed other features to facilitate the definition and use of software parts. Without going into details, the following is a list of such features

1) As mentioned above, internal procedures are permitted in a program unit. This mechanism can be used rather than "reverse communication" [2], since internal procedures can be passed as arguments to procedures. The data entities needed to evaluate the integrand, say, are readily available to the internal procedure.

2) An improved procedure interface facility is defined for both external and internal subprograms. The improved interface includes keyword actual arguments in a subprogram reference and optional arguments specified in the subprogram itself. Such a facility will be useful when long argument lists are required to provide the options for expert users where such a user can use keyword actual arguments to identify the appropriate argument. Users who want to use

the same subprogram as a black box need only supply the minimum number of
arguments while the remainder are given defaults by the designer of the subprogram.

3) Operator overloading is permitted. Thus the * operator, for instance, can be
   used for both element-by-element array multiplication and for matrix-vector,
   vector-matrix, and matrix-matrix multiplication. This will permit the programmer to use a convenient and familiar notation.

4) An interface specification block is optionally permitted. This block specifies
   the number, types, and dimensionality of arguments to subprograms in the
   calling program. Such blocks may conceivably be used by processors to check
   the validity of actual arguments supplied in reference to the subprograms.
   These interface blocks are permitted in MODULE program units so that references
   to compiled libraries can be validated.

DOCUMENTATION

The Fortran subcommittee has essentially three documents that describe its work
to date. The most readable and accessible document is the Fortran Information
Bulletin, which will be published simultaneously by CBEMA (Computer Business
Equipment Manufacturers Association, secretariat for the X3 committee) and the
FORTEC Forum, and possibly in SIGPLAN Notices in early 1984.   The document will give the major functionality of the proposed additions to Fortran 77
and the proposed syntax for the new facilities. It will however also include the
syntax for the existing language, and is expected to be approximately 35 pages.

The major working document of the X3J3 subcommittee has been the document
X3J3/S6. It is a detailed description of the additional feature proposed for the
language, with some simple examples. Updated in August 1983, it will no longer be
maintained by the subcommittee.

Replacing the S6 document is the document X3J3/S7. It is subcommittee's working
document which will eventually become the draft proposed standard.

SCHEDULE

The following schedule represents the subcommittee's goals for the next few
years. As such, they are subject to change.

By the spring of 1984, the subcommittee expects to publicly distribute the S7
document. It expects to present the document to the European Fortran Experts
Group in Geneva in April 1984. By the summer of 1985, X3J3 expects to complete
the S7 document and submit it to X3 for public review as a draft proposed
standard. The subcommittee then expects to use the next two years to revise and
update the document and respond to public comments. The revised draft proposed
standard will then be submitted for approval to X3 in 1987 or 1988.

CONCLUSIONS

Over the past year, the Fortran subcommittee has been preparing the early drafts
of the next proposed draft standard for Fortran. From numerous additions and deletions proposed for Fortran 77, the subcommittee is beginning to formulate an
extended Fortran 77 language that promises to be very useful in producing numerical software. Some of those features have been described above, and represent significant facilities for building software parts in Fortran.

Although it seems a long time before any of these features are likely to be in regular use, the Fortran subcommittee needs user comments now to help it produce a better standard. Fortran users are encouraged to obtain the various documents, read them, and express their opinions to the subcommittee.

REFERENCES

[1] Brandt, A., Ophir, D., GRIDPACK: Toward Unification of General Grid Programming, proceedings of this meeting, p 269-288.

[2] Lawson, C., Block, N., Garrett, R., Fortran IV Subroutines for Contour Plotting, Jet Propulsion Laboratory Section 914 Computer Memorandum 106, May 1965.

[3] Reid, J. K., The Array Features in Fortran 8x, proceedings of this meeting, p 351-354.

[4] Rice, J., Software Parts for Elliptic PDE Software, proceedings of this meeting, p 123-134.

[5] Rice, J., Interface Issues in a Software Parts Technology, to appear in Reusability in Software, E. Biggerstaff, ed., 1983.

DISCUSSION

Speakers: J. Reid , B. Smith

Duff to Reid: The other terms on your last slide were self-explanatory but what is ANY and ALL?

Reid: ANY and ALL apply the logical operations of "any" and "all" to a logical array to produce a scalar logical result.

Madsen to Smith: Why must it be such a long procedure to get a new standard?

Smith: It is indeed a long procedure.

Madsen: But compare with ADA. They reached a standard quickly.

Smith: Fortran has a large community of existing users, each with their own idea of how the language should develop. The many suggestions for additions to and deletions form Fortran 77 must be considered in the light of what is best for the entire language. Then, when changes are recommended by X3J3, it is required that they be reviewed by the Fortran user community. The process of reaching a consensus is therefore very time-consuming. In the future, the standard might come out piece-meal, particulary with respect to the application modules. In contrast, Ada was standardized by fiat. Ada developed through several versions over a period of 5 years or more. Each version was reviewed by those who had interests in language design, and the intended users in the U.S. Department of Defense, but not by a large collection of users who had experience with using the language. The standardization of Ada by the national standard association did not occur with the same kind of extensive public review that has been required for other languages such as Cobol and Fortran.

Schönauer to Reid: Will masking be possible in the new standard?

Reid: Yes. The WHERE statement makes it possible.

Rice (comment on Madsen): FORTRAN 8x was originally planned to be finished by now. But ordinary delays plus the need to reconsider some features have changed the schedule. For example, 2 years ago, when array facilities where presented at a WG 2.5 working conference, people revolted on certain proposed features. The working group voted to recommend that changes be made and offered to help. Several WG 2.5 people, especially John Reid, have since become involved with the FORTRAN committee. Furthermore compiler writers have their objections and you have to think of compatibility with earlier standards.

Delves to Madsen: ADA reached a standard quicker but it dosen't have all these features.

Madsen: Yes, it has.

Delves: No, it hasn't. For example it's impossible in ADA to refer to a row or a column of a multidimensional array, as a whole; that is, slicing of matrix objects is not available. This is a very big restriction for parallel processing algorithms.

Madsen: You can define a matrix as a vector of columns or rows and gain the access you need.

Schönauer to Smith: Is there free format in the new standard?

Smith: Yes. There is free format source form proposed for Fortran 8x. As far as free format input, there is in Fortran 77 a list-directed free format input/output facility. For Fortran 8x, a name-directed input/output (where the entity name appears on the input and output records) is proposed; in functionality, it is like the NAMELIST currently available in many Fortran compilers.

Perronet to Smith: Can comments appear on input records read by list-directed or name-directed input statements?

Smith: No. That has not been passed for either form of free format input records.

Huddleston to Smith: The standards subcommittee ought to meet with users (at least in linear algebra) to get a subset of standardized extension modules defined. These could then be released along with the new standard.

Smith: We have talked to different groups interested in preparing documents that standardize an extension module but without success. The problem in my opinion has been that the module concept has not been either clearly defined or adequate in the past. With the new ideas of a module, we have to wait and see whether it is adequate to permit the definition of useful application modules.

Hockney to Smith: Can one avoid the need to redefine COMMON everywhere a reference to it is needed.

Smith: Yes, using the MODULE program unit. In fact, if the MODULE program unit is used, only one declaration of anentity is allowed. Many USE statements, referencing the same MODULE programunit, are allowed.

Rice (comment on Huddleston):   There is a danger in the module approach. You can loose portability if several large groups make their own modules for, say linear algebra, so the numerical software community needs to produce a common and early proposal for standard application modules in their fields.

Smith: I agree with the need to have the numerical community agree on standard application modules. However, portability is not at stake here. The modules can be moved with the rest of the Fortran software, because all of the module-buildning facilities are within the core language. If your concern is that the modules will not be as efficient on some processors as others, because the module definitions are not intrinsic to the compilers, you have a valid point. Such a situation is analogous though to some processors having good optimizers and others not.

Rice: That is not quite so. Consider two large bodies of software that are written with different, but similar, linear algebra modules. Suppose now that they (or subsets of them) are to be combined into a larger package. You now have potential conflicts and confusion. The "name-hiding" mechanism of FORTRAN 8x will help to overcome these conflicts, but it would make life much simpler (and the software more reliable) to have only one linear algebra module.

Smith: But that's just similar to the conflict between IMSL and NAG software. They do not use the same algorithms or use the same interfaces for subroutines that solve the same problems.

Huddleston: If we don't create the modules, then the manufactures will. Then we will loose portability for sure.

Duff to Reid: Portable codes usually refer to PFORT and thus to a subset of FORTRAN 66, so FORTRAN 77 is not yet fully established. Perhaps we won't get

FORTRAN 8x until the year 2000? If, as you are hoping, CRAY implement some of the proposed array features in advance, use of these features would give non-portable code. I feel that few people would like to use those features before the standard is adopted. Do you think that they will be used?

Schönauer: CD has those features.

Duff: On the grounds of portability I wouldn't advice people to use them. Not all of CD's features even conform to the proposed standard.

Reid: The array features are desperatly needed.

Hemker: Why? You just wish to clean up a dirty language?

Delves: There's nothing wrong with that. People will use the array features when they see how they improve both performance and ease of development of parallel algorithms, even if they have not yet been adopted as a standard. They already do non standard things in the CRAY-1 to speed it up.

Reid: The standards committee has discussed the idea of adding the array features as an extension to the FORTRAN 77 standard. Does the audience consider this desirable?

Rice: Do you mean to take all those features on which there is a consensus?

Reid: No, only those array features on which there is a consensus.

Smith: To answer Iain Duff's question, "what are the consequences of not doing anything?" For example, people would move to other languages. The point is that we have no chance of influencing the design of any programming language in terms of obtaining features that we need to write numerical software unless we talk about them and propose solutions.

Duff: That was not my point. I am not suggesting that you abandon your efforts at improving and extending FORTRAN and I realize the value of your efforts. What I meant was that the new features will not be used before they are standard. Whenever we talked about portability in this conference, we meant portability in the sense of the verifier PFORT. So we don't even use FORTRAN 77 and it is now 1983. The new language will be, I believe, lucky to appear before 1990 and is much more complicated. Thus my prediction is for its use after the year 2000. If anything, I am encouraging you to get the new standard out as quickly as possible.

Delves: I want to make a different point. I believe that IDENTIFY is dangerous. I think that IDENTIFY is just a poor substitute for POINTER variables. I hope that POINTERs are coming into FORTRAN and that INDENTIFY will then go away again.

Reid: There are other problems with IDENTIFY, but this is not one; the example I gave defines a proper array which can be indexed with the help of a standard dope vector.

Rice: IDENTIFY is a dynamic EQUIVALENCE. The old EQUIVALENCE is sorted out because it was considered too dangerous and now they give us this instead. The IDENTIFY is needed in the FORTRAN 8x proposed, because there are things that need to be done, which are very clumsy unless you use it.

Delves: EQUIVALENCE is needed, but not like that.

Rice: They give people the means to hang themselves. This is in keeping with the philosophy of FORTRAN, as I see it, and does not bother me.

Delves: Pointers must come in and IDENTIFY be sorted out.

Schryer: PFORT is the only verifying tool for FORTRAN. The TOOLPACK group is trying to produce a verifier for a FORTRAN 77 subset. Talk to Brian Ford and other TOOLPACK people to put pressure on them.

Huddleston: The TOOLPACK board says that a verifier will be produced.

Madsen: Many of the proposed extensions make me happy. Can the US Department of Defense be turned to back up FORTRAN instead of ADA?

Smith: No, I don't think so. They appear not to be interested even in making interfaces from Ada to other languages. But Ada and Fortran are not on a collision course from my viewpoint, because they have different user communities in mind. The U.S. DoD will use Ada, but will anyone else? Ada will only be used by the non-coerced users if Ada compilers are widely available and are very good.

Madsen: Our problem is that we work for both.

Lawson: I heard the US National Bureau of Standards had issued a contract to have a FORTRAN 77 program verifier developed.

Delves: I think ADA compilers will be widely available soon, mainly because the money is there to provide them. ADA seems to me to be as inevitable as COBOL.

Sherman to Reid and Smith: One of the motivations for the array features in FORTRAN is to allow the compiler on each machine to compile code that is extremely efficient for that machine. This probably means that the order of the individual operations on array elements must be left unspecified in the standard. I am concerned that this may mean that identical code may have different effects on different machines, mainly due to the possibility of arithmetic exceptions. Has this been considered by the FORTRAN committee?

Reid: I think you are wrong. The operations are independent.

Sherman: I am thinking of the possibility of over-/underflow or other arithemetic exceptions.

Smith: No order is specified because we think that the order of the element operations in whole array operations should be determined by the optimizers. If the order of the element operations is critical to the correct execution of a whole array operation, the user can and should be using explicit statements (for example, explicit DO loops) to specify the order of the operations. A whole array operation in which the user needs to know at what point arithmetic exceptions have occurred is a good example where explicit statements should be used. But exception handling is a problem for the entire language anyway; the subcommittee has not addressed this issue even for the non-array operations.

Sherman: I just wonder whether users may hesitate to use array features adopted in advance if later decisions on other features (like exception handling) will affect the way array features operate.

Rice: (comment on ADA vs FORTRAN): The objective of ADA is not to replace FORTRAN, but to replace about 500 obscure languages used by the US Department of Defense. If you are not using one of those languages now, ADA can be completely successful and not affect you.

PDE SOFTWARE: Modules, Interfaces and Systems
B. Engquist and T. Smedsaas (eds.)
Elsevier Science Publishers B.V. (North-Holland)
© IFIP, 1984

LARGE NUMBERS ON SMALL COMPUTERS

J.J.H. Miller

Numerical Analysis Group
Trinity College, Dublin, Ireland

A. Sloane

Regional Technical College
Cork, Ireland

In several areas of engineering, problems arise in which the exponential function appears with large positive or negative arguments. Such areas include aspects of antenna design and solution of the semiconductor transport equations used in computer codes to simulate the operation of bipolar and MOS devices. This latter application involves the solution of the coupled set of nonlinear partial differential equations given in normalised form below.

$$-\Delta u + e^{u-v} - e^{w-u} = N(x,y) \qquad (1)$$

$$-\nabla.(\mu_n e^{u-v}\nabla v) = R(u,v,w) \qquad (2a)$$

$$-\nabla.(\mu_p e^{w-u}\nabla w) = -R(u,v,w) \qquad (2b)$$

The function u is the electrostatic potential, and v and w are, respectively, the electron and hole quasi-Fermi potentials. The function R describes recombination and generation effects, and the function N, commonly called the doping profile, specifies the net impurity concentration through the device. The values of $N(x,y)$ range over several orders of magnitude; typically $\pm 10^{15}$.

The simplest analysis of this system leads to a one-dimensional model using only the Poisson equation (1) above. A particular case of this model is considered by Polak et al [1]. Examination of the equations in [1] suggests that we may need to evaluate the exponential function over a range of -28000 to +28000. In other words we need to handle numbers with a range of magnitude of approximately 10^{-10000} to 10^{+10000}.

Several techniques are commonly used to deal with this difficulty. First, one can choose to use a computer which routinely allows such a range. However such facilities are not commonly available on 32-bit virtual memory minicomputers, the type of system which is increasingly used for engineering analysis (recent developments in both hardware and programming language design show promise of changing the situation [3]). A second approach is to modify the exponential function. The crudest method is simply to limit the value of the exponential. Suppose RMAX is the largest representable number, and $X_c = \log_e(RMAX)$. Then, if X is greater than X_c, set EXP(X) = RMAX. Such an approach is very easily implemented in FORTRAN or any other high-level language.

In practice the following refinement of the above method is often used. Suppose we know, a priori, an upper bound X_m on the value of the argument. Then choose a value X_c as indicated in the diagram below.

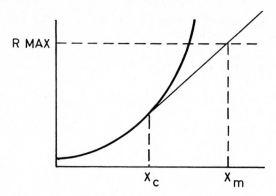

We replace the exponential function by the following procedure

$AEXP(X)$: if $X < X_c$ then $AEXP = EXP(X)$

else $AEXP = EXP(X_c)*(1 + X - X_c)$

We have assumed here that values of the argument are positive. The extension to negative values is clear. This second approach seems more desirable but, as can be seen from the diagram, may in fact result in modification of the exponential function over a wider range than the simple method. A further refinement of this technique is given by Schilders et al [2].

The major objection to any of these modifications of the exponential is that, in general, their effect on the set of equations being solved is not clear. On the other hand, however, it has been argued that the use of the exponential function itself is not completely justified since it arises from the assumption that Boltzman statistics are applicable, an assumption which is strictly valid only at equilibrium. Thus it is argued that the error in evaluation of the exponential is less than the error inherent in the mathematical model. Nevertheless if we choose a computer which allows a range substantially less than $10^{\pm 10000}$ it is unlikely that we could distinguish between the effects of mathematical tricks and the "true" behaviour of the solution. In addition we could not investigate fully the value of other, possibly more complex, physical models.

The authors have recently been concerned with the choice of a small computer for an EEC-funded Device Modelling Project. For our purposes a "small computer system" was defined by the following criteria:

(1) Approximately US$ 120,000 maximum cost including software and peri-
     pherals (e.g. colour and monochrome high resolution graphics terminals
     and inexpensive flat-bed plotter).

(2) Tolerant of environment, requiring minimal air-conditioning and
     temperature control.

(3) 32-bit virtual memory system.

(4) Reliable and efficient FORTRAN.

(5) No requirement for specialist support staff such as systems programmers
     or operators.

(6) Good networking facilities to enable use of the system as a pre- and post-processor for a large "number cruncher" or array processor.

Besides the points given above we also considered such issues as expandability of the system, upward compatibility with other computers in the range, and local hardware and software support.

These criteria led to a detailed evaluation of the following systems (these of course are not the only commercially available systems satisfying these require-ments):

Hewlett Packard	HP9000
Data General	MV/4000
DEC	VAX 11/730
PRIME	2250

In view of the foregoing discussion on the necessity of evaluating large and small numbers for our particular applications, we now show in Table 1 the range available for double precision floating point numbers on each of these four systems.

Machine	Range	Precision (number of decimal digits)
HP 9000	$2.2 \times 10^{-308} - 1.8 \times 10^{308}$	15-16 digits
MV/4000	$5.4 \times 10^{-79} - 7.2 \times 10^{75}$	16 digits
PRIME 2250	$10^{-9902} - 10^{9825}$	14 digits
VAX (D-format)	$0.29 \times 10^{-38} - 1.7 \times 10^{38}$	16 digits
VAX (H-format)	$0.84 \times 10^{-4932} - 0.59 \times 10^{4932}$	33 digits

Table 1. Double Precision Range and Precision

The VAX has also an "extended range double precision" (G-format) with an exponent range of ± 308. In addition to double precision each machine also offers single precision, sometimes with the same exponent range, sometimes with smaller.

It is perhaps interesting to compare the formats provided by the four systems with the draft IEEE standard on floating point arithmetic [4]. Each format is specified by the following parameters:

P   - the number of significant bits (precision)

E_{max} - the maximum exponent (binary), and

E_{min} - the minimum exponent (binary).

Parameter	Format			
	Single	Single Extended	Double	Double Extended
P	24	≥ 32	53	≥ 64
E_{max}	+127	$\geq +1023$	+1023	$\geq +16383$
E_{min}	-126	≤ -1022	-1022	≤ -16383
Exponent width in bits	8	≥ 11	11	≥ 15
Format width in bits	32	≥ 43	64	≥ 79

Table 2.　Summary of Format Parameters
(IEEE Draft Standard)

The Standard defines four formats: single; single extended; double; and double extended. Table 2 summarises the recommended format parameters, and Table 3 gives the values of the parameters for the formats specified in Table 1 above.

Parameter	Format				
	HP9000 Double Precision	MV/4000 Double Precision	PRIME 2250 Double Precision	VAX 11/730 D-Format	VAX 11/730 H-Format
P	52	54	47	55	112
E_{max}	+1023	+249	+32767	+127	+16383
E_{min}	-1022	-262	-32767	-127	-16383
Exponent width in bits	11	9	16	8	15
Format width in bits	64	64	64	64	128

Table 3.

It is seen from Table 1 that if we insist on evaluating exponentials exactly for a wide range of argument, we are restricted (for this set of machines) either to the PRIME or to H-format on the VAX. (The option of writing our own microprograms to implement extended range formats using a writable control store, as available on the MV/4000, was considered but regarded as impractical).

In evaluating the relative performance of the systems we employed two simple FORTRAN benchmarks developed by the Rutherford Appleton Laboratories. These programs primarily measure CPU speed, and do not measure efficiency of the virtual memory paging mechanism. The programs were run on a single user basis, both because of their design and also because such operating conditions would be the most usual for the project. It should be stressed that the benchmarks were designed to give a simple measure of the performance of a system under the load imposed by a typical Finite Element computation, and that variations of under 25% were not regarded as significant.

In Table 4 we show how the machines perform on the two benchmark tests. From this we see that the DG MV/4000 is the fastest machine. However, if we insist on the ability to handle the large numbers arising in our particular applications,

J.J.H. Miller and A. Sloane

the only options are the VAX 11/730 (H-format) and the PRIME 2250. From the table it is clear that the latter is significantly faster than the former.

Machine	Test 1	Test 2
HP 9000	134	110
DG MV/4000	82	58
PRIME 2250	160	102
VAX 11/730 (D-format)	162	158
VAX 11/730 (H-format)	637	336

Table 4. Benchmark Results

(CPU time in seconds)

References

(1) S.J. Polak, A. Wachters, Th. Beelen, P.W. Hemker, "A Mesh-Parameter-Continuation Method", Report NW 89/80, Mathematical Centre, Amsterdam, 1980.

(2) W. Schilders, S. Polak, C. den Heijer, "A Comparison of Subset Solving Algorithms", in Proceedings NASECODE III Conference, J.J.H. Miller (editor), Boole Press, Dublin, 1983.

(3) T.E. Hull, "The Use of Controlled Precision" in "The Relationship Between Numerical Computation and Programming Languages", J.K. Reid (editor), North-Holland, Amsterdam, 1982, pp. 71-84.

(4) "A Proposed Standard for Binary Floating-Point Artithmetic", Draft 10.0 of IEEE Task P754, December 2, 1982, IEEE P754/82-8.6

DISCUSSION

Speaker: J. Miller

Huddleston: The microcode for G floating format is very slow even on the VAX 11/780.

Einarsson: On some older VAX machines the G floating datum is not even in microcode but in software, which slows it down. The microcode is available as an option.

Edberg: At my institute, we have a problem with a program for antenna field transformations. The program was originally written for IBM. The DEC-10 which we use only has an exponent range of [-38,38] which in this case is not sufficient for our large problems. We have investigated the possiblity of using extended exponent arithmetic on a VAX, but apart from being slow, it requires extra hardware which is not included on the standard VAX computer.

Ford (to Miller): Have you really looked at the HP9000?

Schryer: A version of HP based on Motorola 68000 works very well on most cases. It meets the IEEE floating point requirements, except for comparison operations failing for small operands.

Schryer: I have an idea of how to get good advice: call up NPL, LLNL   - the large national laboratories. They have many small machines around and are usually very helpful.

Ford: There is a proposal in the UK to set up a service to check arithmetic and perhaps elementary functions. The intention is both to evaluate the floating point services of a given system and to check its continuing correct performance on a recurrent basis.

Smith: With IEEE floating point standard arithmetic, you can simulate in software very large exponent ranges using the extended registers and trapping modes. Using a similar floating point system on an IBM 7094-II, we were able to formulate algorithms that used large exponent ranges without a severe degradation in the running time. Have you looked into the various implementations of the IEEE floating point standard to see if they would meet your needs?

Dekker: I like to mention a technique for expanding the exponent range, which has been introduced long ago by Wilkinson & Reinsch in routines for calculating the determinant; in these routines the determinant is represented by two numbers d_1 and d_2 such that the determinant equals d_1 times 10 to the power d_2.

PDE SOFTWARE: Modules, Interfaces and Systems
B. Engquist and T. Smedsaas (eds.)
Elsevier Science Publishers B.V. (North-Holland)
© IFIP, 1984

THE APPLICABILITY OF GENERAL SOFTWARE
FOR REAL WORLD PROBLEMS
- A DISCUSSION

Introductory remarks by Jan van Welij

I work at the computer department at Philips. My function is to introduce
scientific software in our laboratories. In that work I am confronted with a
discrepancy between engineering practice and university work.

The "typical" engineer has the following "properties" (if I put it a bit provoca-
tively): he has never seen a computer, he has inverse problems with complex
geometries, he hardly knows what equations that ought to be solved and he knows
nothing about numerical mathematics. To provide him with constant help would be
too expensive, so what is needed is some good general software. This should
ideally be a "physical package", where the engineer could specify his problem
in the physical terms that he knows. Geometry, material constants and sources
should be possible to specify in a language that is "natural" to the engineer.
Everything else should be done within the package (as in a "black box").

Codes that are done at universities mostly deal with single rectangular domains,
linear problems, regular or even equidistant grids, or one space dimension. These
codes are not intended for engineers but for colleague mathematicians in order to
study the performance of the numerical methods. However, although about 85% of
the run time of a program may concern putting up the equations and solving them,
these program parts take only about 15% of the programming time. 70% of the
programming time concerns interface parts such as syntax, semantics and validity
checks and sorting out the problem structure. These parts of the program are
important in order to get good "black box" packages for engineers.

Concluding, I see the following issues that should be dealt with for people who
wish to do general software applicable for real world problems:

- as solving is a small part of the programming effort more work should be
  done on developing good interfaces to make "black boxes" for engineers

- practical problems have much more complex geometries than the ones that
  most university codes deal with and thus we have a gap here, that has to
  be bridged.

Introductory remarks by Robert E. Huddleston

I have been asked to make a few comments about the applicability of the material
presented at this conference to "real world problems." My comments will apply to
most, but certainly not all, of the talks given here.

First of all, it is not clear who the intended audience is for most of the talks
and for the software packages you have presented. Let me speculate on four
possibilities.

1. Yourself and fellow researchers at the conference
   Given the nature of the conference and the reasonably early stage of
   development for generalized software for PDE's this would be a reasonable
   audience.

2. Student level problems
   By this I mean those PDE problems which need to be solved by advanced
   undergraduate and beginning graduate students - specifically excluding
   the often quite complicated systems of non-linear PDE's that sometimes
   go along with Ph.D. dissertations.

   Much of the software presented here, and the packages that could easily
   be put together given these building blocks could serve students quite
   well. I believe that such packages would free up the non-numerical
   analysis students (engineers, physicists, quantum chemists) to study
   their own subjects instead of developing codes. These packages would
   encourage them to do parameter studies and thus gain more "engineering
   feel" (instruction) for their subject area. This would be most valuable.
   My only concern is that if these students go on to solving very difficult
   PDE's, the packages will not be there for them and they will have developed no skills in solution techniques.

3. "Real world" problems of moderate difficulty
   These problems are very closely related to the "student level problems",
   though somewhat more difficult. I believe the basic building blocks
   (pieces of software) are in existence or well understood to produce
   packages which would be a real boon to the engineering community. The
   final, complete packages must still be written and the documentation and
   teaching aids aimed at the right level must be produced, but the basic
   understanding of how to produce these packages is fairly complete (but
   known only to experts such as yourself).

   Let me interject at this point my excitement for the work of Achi Brandt
   in producing tools for "geometrical definition". These tools have the
   potential of automating an irritating, difficult and error prone task
   (see Brandt's paper in the proceedings).

4. Difficult problems
   As an example let us consider a structural failure in a component of a
   nuclear reactor. Here we have structures which may be subjected to
   mechanical forces large enough to cause deformation and shear,
   temperature high enough to cause flow, high neutron fluxes - all coupled
   with electro-mechanical devices which must activate under these emergency
   conditions. The large sets of non-linear PDE's and engineering
   "parameters" which define such problems at present are not to be solved
   by the building blocks presented at this conference. I would have been
   quite surprised at the conference had it been any other way. But the
   steps that are being taken now may very well lead to "standardized
   every day codes" which will solve these problems ten years from now.

Am I disappointed in the slowness of progress? Absolutely not. But then I have
worked on building general purpose mathematical subroutine libraries part time
for the last thirteen years. It took a very long time to build or collect quality
software, get it in a standard form, test it and then gain the confidence of the
user community so that they would use the library instead of their own archaic
methods which they kept tucked away in a card file and which they had written
years before when in graduate school. Still there are about 1% of incorrigibles
who maintain this practice.

More disturbing to me are about 5% of the users who cannot make use of the
library as much as they would like. These are the people who are solving really
large problems who end up doing their own out-of-core linear solvers, their
own disk I/O and who make engineering judgements about what parts of the
calculations must be kept or thrown out (or which parts must be solved accurately

and which parts need not be accurate). What disturb me about not being able to help these users more is that these 5% are the ones who use up 15% of the computer time. So while we have made a very large impact on saving labor (programming) for 95% of the people, we have made relatively little impact on saving computer time. (One exception to this is in the area of initial value problems for ordinary differential equations. The savings here due to vastly improved software is immense - so much so that we hardly remember the advances that have been made.) This situation of not being able to help the CPU time-consuming users with standard libraries though has its direct analogue with not being presently able to help the "Difficult Problem" (category 4 above) users in PDE's with the present building blocks. With new, standardized well tested out-of-core direct and iterative linear equation solvers becoming available, the math libraries will improve on helping our big users (but of course the problems posed will also become more difficult - think of it as job security). Likewise, I believe the PDE standard modules will progress to handling the present "Difficult Problems".

Such conferences as these show the progress being made and allow the necessary cross-fertilization amongst researchers.

Let me make one final observation. For the present and future difficult problems requiring large computers, the techniques that are being discussed will mean essentially nothing unless we come to grips with the problems of generating algorithms which are effective on multi-processors (see Yanenko's paper in these proceedings). Barring a real break through, most of the computing power advances that we are likely to see will come in the form of multi-processors. From my observations, the numerical analysis community is lagging behind these hardware advances. It is post time for a large effort in this area.

GENERAL DISCUSSION

<u>Rice</u>: University people should not develop software for real world problems. The grants I have are intended to support research and new ideas; any practical software that is developed should be accidental or "under-the-table". One does not obtain much academic recognition for such work; the only university people who should develop "real world" software (as defined by Huddleston)are those who intend to go into the software business.

There is also the question of the definition of real world software. Huddleston has used the definition: "software for the most difficult problems we can currently solve". This definition automatically excludes general purpose software from being real world software. However, problems that I worked on in the 1950's as real world problems can now be solved easily with several of the general purpose systems discussed here. The general purpose software will allow us to solve most of the "routine" problems quickly - and many of these arise in the real world.

A big question is: "Who is going to support the development of general software"? This software is very expensive if done well. We have heard that Exxon and some large national labs cannot afford it - then who can? It is clear to me that there would be a large savings from such software, but that savings is distributed over a wide community. No single member of this community can justify the expense and government agencys (at least in U.S.) are reluctant to fund this work.

<u>Schryer</u>: I agree with John. Universities should produce ideas to help people who shall solve real-world problems. We have experience when we tried general software that we have had to have the author of the inner loop there to tune it - even if it was good for the purpose it was written for.

No matter how good the general software is you will have trouble.

What can be useful is for academic and real-world people to interact - very good software and algorithms have come out of that.

<u>Ex</u>. D. Rose has made a successful frontal assault on semiconductor problems. A damped Newton method converging globally (if it comes from discrete PDE) came out of that.

Both sides have a lot to learn from collaboration. A battle side by side trying to understand the world - get the best out of each side.

<u>Duff</u>: I see two areas where work is much needed: In the solvers themselves (the "get somebody into the inner loop" of Schryer) and in user interfaces.

CAD is a beautiful example of user interface, as are some statistics packages, both of which are used extensively by non-mathematicians (the solution algorithm is maybe not always all that good, but the interface is).

I find engineering consultants would like to take our package and put an interface on top of it - and make money out of it. The interface is really the part of the package which determines how much it will be used.

<u>Andersson</u>: The packages are not general enough. They normally handle problems only in 2D and not in 3D. To be useable for industrial applications, they should be able to handle domains of solutions, the boundary of which is defined by splines in 2D and bisplines in 3D. Interfaces we can make ourselves.

Huddleston: We would certainly not put money into Ada. Thousands of manyears have gone into FORTRAN. We would rather support the FORTRAN standards committee.

Schönauer: I spent half of my time during two years to ask engineers what they do on the computer. Half of them did manage themselves, but they often used old methods and where nevertheless proud of their software. The other half was happy to get help. This motivated me to make software which gives information on the quality of the solutions.

The engineers are not fit for program parts. I am in favour of program parts, but they shall have black boxes. We should have "superprograms" that compose programs for them out of tools.

A problem arose when I asked for money for the development of a solver for nonlinear systems of PDEs. The project was nearly to be killed: the referee was a mathematician and he rejected my project because "there exist no mathematical proof of the existence of solutions to such systems".

However, what we did with the little money that we have was the best we could do. We could do much better with more money.

Trottenberg: In addition to that I have the impression that some interfaces between academic people and "the real world" are missing. Such an interface could be for example, a standard for the design of PDE software. If such a standard was available this would be a great help for academic groups who are interested in contributing certain modules to PDE software packages. We, the method builders, usually do not know what software design principles to adapt to. Different packages use different design principles and it takes a lot of time for us to change our programs if they should be incorporated into several packages. Perhaps the IFIP Working Group 2.5 could initiate some activity aiming towards a PDE software design standard. In such a standard the multigrid requirements should be taken into regard.

Sherman: I agree that the universities should not develop software that is immediately applicable to e.g. Exxon. Instead they should develop techniques that could then be adopted by industry.

Industry will attack the problems that are at the leading edge of computational technology, and if they are successful, they naturally don't want to share their results with their competitors. However, industry is willing to fund work in the universities that is not sufficiently "academic" to be sponsored by e.g. NSF. Such work can give high quality software that can be shared between different companies. A possible goal is for university developed software to be able to handle the fairly routine problems so that industry can devote most of its effort to the really difficult problems.

The large companies (such as Bell or Exxon) should help with money. On the other hand such influence has caused problems in the development of FORTRAN, so it can be bad if care is not taken.

Gustafsson: We must break the discussion here. We have not found any solutions, but everybody agree that this is a problem. Maybe it is just a question of time and money.

Certainly some will is also required to bridge the communication gap between mathematicians and computer scientists on one side and engineers on the other side.

PDE SOFTWARE: Modules, Interfaces and Systems
B. Engquist and T. Smedsaas (eds.)
Elsevier Science Publishers B.V. (North-Holland)
© IFIP, 1984

LOGICAL AND PHYSICAL REPRESENTATION OF AN OBJECT,

MODULARITY FOR THE PROGRAMMING OF FINITE ELEMENT METHODS

A. PERRONNET

Université Pierre et Marie Curie   I.N.R.I.A.
Laboratoire d'Analyse Numérique   Domaine de Voluceau Rocquencourt
4, place Jussieu   78153 LE CHESNAY CEDEX
75230 PARIS Cédex 05

ABSTRACT :

The programming of finite element methods needs

- an OBJECT REPRESENTATION from a logical point of view
  (object graph) and a physical point of view (data base)
- a good MODULARITY to reduce the program complexity, to
  allow easy extensions and deletions.

For each point, a proposition is stated and justified.

1. INTRODUCTION :

These last years, new disciplines appeared, about computer science : Computer
Aided Design (C.A.D.), Computer Aided Engineering (C.A.E.), Computer Aided
Manufacturing (C.A.M.). Each of them requires a different REPRESENTATION OF THE
OBJECT. The drawer's, the conceiver's or manufacter's point of view are very
different. The first defines the line, the form of the object. The second is
interested by its functionality, its strength. The third searches the best way
to construct it. Since the perception is not the same, the implementation of the
object varies. But, in view of a better communication between teams or programs,
it is tempting to have one and only one representation of the object but with
several points of view. The notion of DATA BASE (D.B.) is well adapted to it.
But, its programming requires a large programmers'team and large secondary
storages. Only the greatest aeronautical, car, naval factories or national
projects can afford them. Here, only the Data Structures (D.S.) used by Finite
Element Methods (F.E.M.) (in fact close to C.A.D. D.S.) are considered.

The current object is often complex. Its full perception is difficult. It is
natural to decompose it in simpler subobjects. All the repetitions (rotation,
displacement, symmetry,...) are taken into account. This splitting is written
in mathematical form with a graph, called here OBJECT GRAPH, where the nodes are
objects or subobjects and the edges are mathematical mappings.

The simplest objects, called "FIRST OBJECTS", are also decomposed from their
outlines : a volume from its surface, a surface from its lines, a line from its
vertices. The graph of a first object is then defined. These two graphs are
presented at the second paragraph.

In fact, the mathematical mappings shown previously often are theoretical and
cannot be used directly in practice. A numerical approximation must be applied.
The resulting approximate object graph is described at the paragraph 3.

These graphs must be implemented. A physical representation of the object in
terms of a small data base with its access ways is given at the paragraph 4.

Once the object is stored in the computer storage, the programming of the operators which work on it can begin. The writing of a large program must be modular
in order to be
  - realized simultaneously by several teams ;
  - divided into compartments to offer easy extensions and deletions ;
  - readable, understandable.

The notion of D.S., module, upper-module, defined at the paragraph 5, ensure
the modularity.

2. THE LOGICAL POINT OF VIEW OF THE OBJECT REPRESENTATION :

2.1. The object graph :

In order to minimize the complexity of the object and the costs, all of the
repetitivities, axis or plans of symmetry are taken in account. The object is
split, inducing the OBJECT GRAPH in which the nodes are simpler subobjects and
the edges are mathematical mappings. The simplest objects which are not decomposed, are called here FIRST OBJECTS. For instance, Fig. 1 shows the logical
splitting of an electric motor section and Fig. 2 the associated oriented graph
of this object. The user gives this oriented graph without problems because this
notion is clear, concise and follows the manufacturing steps of the object. The
F.E.M. may be used on the whole object or on a part of it. In both cases, the
treatment is done on a graph (the graph or a subgraph). The recursivity of graphs
is very useful here.

2.2. The first object graph :

In practice, two first objects may have a common boundary. A double description
of such a boundary is not only an additional expense but also a source of errors.
The simplest and surest way is to describe this boundary once and to refer to it
twice. The unicity of data is ensured and risks of errors reduced.

This method may be applied in terms of volumes with boundary surfaces, surfaces
with boundary lines, lines with boundary points. Hence, the first object is made
from a set of characteristic points, a set of lines bounded by these points,
a set of surfaces bounded by these lines, a set of volumes bounded by these
surfaces. Each item is described once and the user appreciates it.

More precisely, the graph of a first object consists of :
  - nodes : sets of volumes, surfaces, lines, points
  - edges : two types of mapping

  . $f : \mathbb{R}^{m-1} \to \mathbb{R}^m$ for   m = 2,3   (classical)
  . $g : \{\ell\} \to \overline{U\ell}$ where $\{\ell\}$ denotes the outline of $\overline{U\ell}$.

The example of Figure 3 describes such sets and mappings. This method is used
by the Club MODULEF to generate meshes (MODULEF 83, PERRONNET 83).

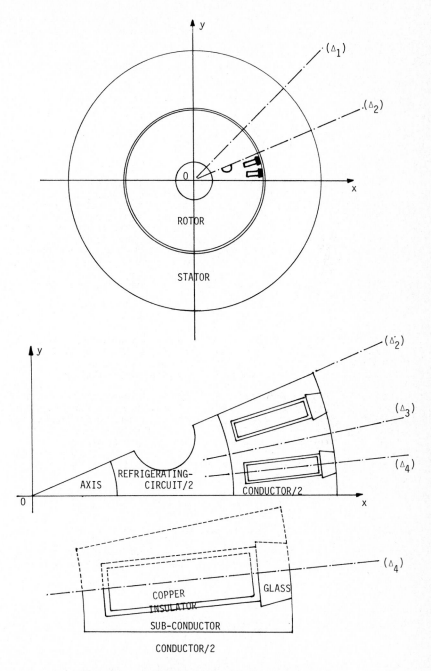

Figure 1 : A SECTION OF AN ELECTRIC MOTOR

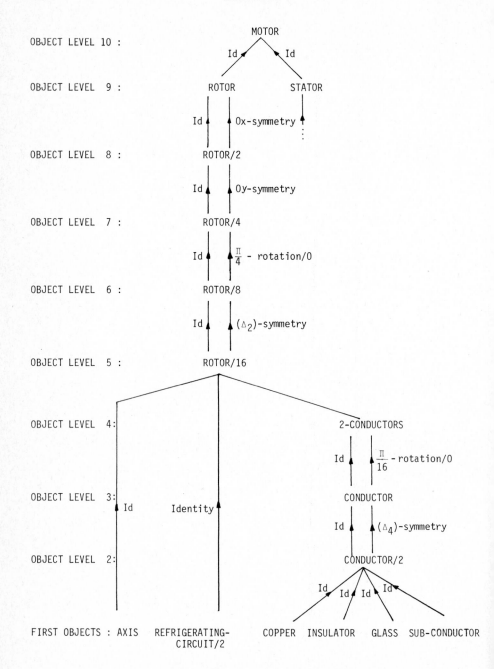

OBJECT LEVEL 10 :

OBJECT LEVEL 9 :

OBJECT LEVEL 8 :

OBJECT LEVEL 7 :

OBJECT LEVEL 6 :

OBJECT LEVEL 5 :

OBJECT LEVEL 4:

OBJECT LEVEL 3:

OBJECT LEVEL 2:

FIRST OBJECTS : AXIS   REFRIGERATING-   COPPER   INSULATOR   GLASS   SUB-CONDUCTOR
CIRCUIT/2

Figure 2 : THE ORIENTED GRAPH OF THE OBJECT : MOTOR

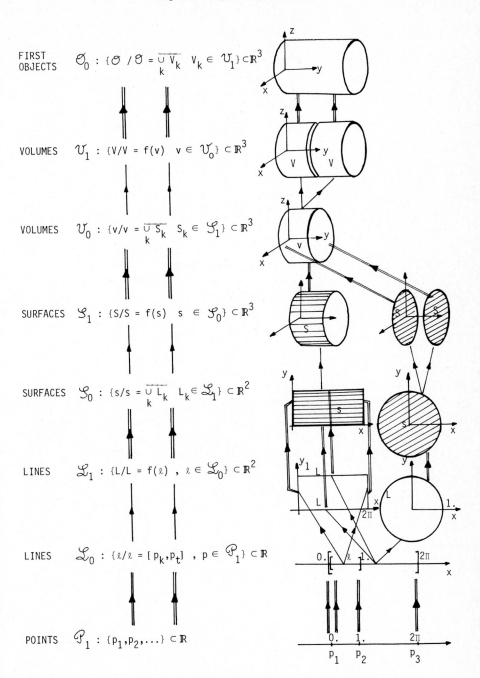

FIRST OBJECTS $\mathcal{O}_0$: $\{\mathcal{O} / \mathcal{O} = \overline{\underset{k}{\cup} V_k} \quad V_k \in \mathcal{V}_1\} \subset \mathbb{R}^3$

VOLUMES $\mathcal{V}_1$: $\{V/V = f(v) \quad v \in \mathcal{V}_0\} \subset \mathbb{R}^3$

VOLUMES $\mathcal{V}_0$: $\{v/v = \overline{\underset{k}{\cup} S_k} \quad S_k \in \mathcal{S}_1\} \subset \mathbb{R}^3$

SURFACES $\mathcal{S}_1$: $\{S/S = f(s) \quad s \in \mathcal{S}_0\} \subset \mathbb{R}^3$

SURFACES $\mathcal{S}_0$: $\{s/s = \overline{\underset{k}{\cup} L_k} \quad L_k \in \mathcal{L}_1\} \subset \mathbb{R}^2$

LINES $\mathcal{L}_1$: $\{L/L = f(\ell) \ , \ \ell \in \mathcal{L}_0\} \subset \mathbb{R}^2$

LINES $\mathcal{L}_0$: $\{\ell/\ell = [p_k, p_t] \ , \ p \in \mathcal{P}_1\} \subset \mathbb{R}$

POINTS $\mathcal{P}_1$: $\{p_1, p_2, \ldots\} \subset \mathbb{R}$

Figure 3 : THE ORIENTED GRAPH OF THE FIRST OBJECTS

3. THE GRAPH OF THE APPROXIMATE FIRST OBJECTS :

In fact, the above mathematical mappings f are not often defined by a known explicit expression. For instance, the intersection curve of two skew surfaces cannot be written exactly in terms of

$$x = F_1(\hat{x}) \; , \; y = F_2(\hat{x}) \; , \; z = F_3(\hat{x}) \quad \text{for} \quad \hat{x} \in [\,0,1\,] \; .$$

But, several points on this curve can be obtained thus defining an approximate curve $\tilde{\ell}$ passing through these points. In the same way, for a triangle or a quadrilateral (resp. a tetraedron, a pentaedron, an hexaedron) with skew sides known by an explicit expression, an approximate and explicit mapping $\tilde{s}$ (resp. $\tilde{v}$) exists from the outline to the surface (resp. volume). These mappings $\tilde{\ell}$, $\tilde{s}$ and $\tilde{v}$ are given in an annex.

Thus, the graph of the first objects may completed by the sets of approximate curves $\mathcal{L}_1^3$, surfaces $\mathcal{S}_1^3$, volumes and mappings $\tilde{\ell}$, $\tilde{s}$, $\tilde{v}$. It becomes the graph of the approximate first objects (Fig. 4).

If the shape of a first object is not one of the previous simple elements, then, it may be meshed with these elements which give as many new first objects.

The smallest example of a first object is a finite element. Consequently, it may be characterized in terms of volume, surfaces, lines, points or more exactly, volume, faces, edges, vertices. Therefore, the same management for first objects and finite elements may be used.

Alongside the graphs , other data may be stored : the physical characteristics, heat sources, strengths, matrices, displacement vectors, boundary conditions ; and the access must be easy. It is natural and efficient to associate these data to the point or line or surface or volume which is characterized by them. The displacement vector is associated to an object, the pressure to a surface, ...

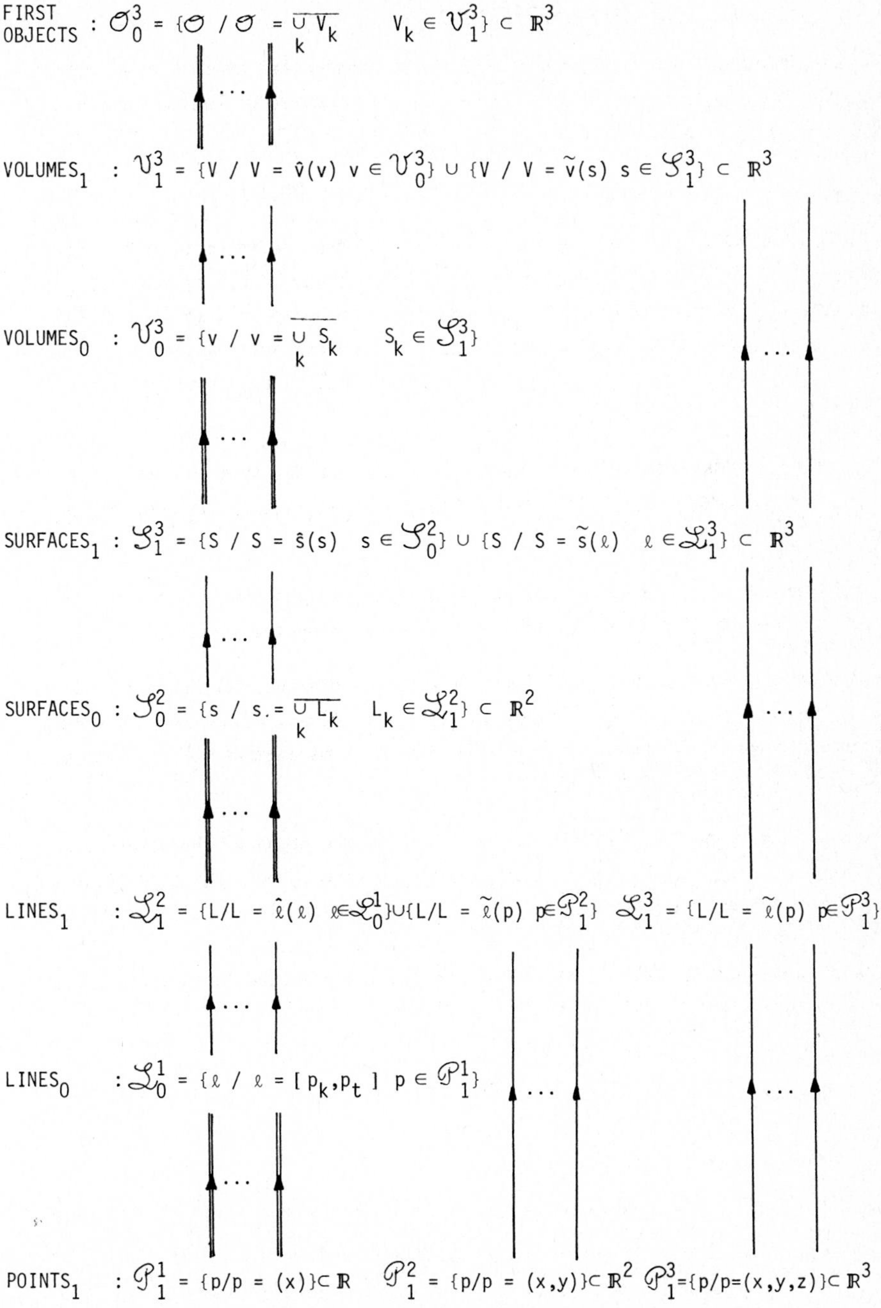

FIRST OBJECTS : $\mathcal{O}_0^3 = \{\mathcal{O} \ / \ \mathcal{O} = \overline{\underset{k}{\cup} V_k} \qquad V_k \in \mathcal{V}_1^3\} \subset \mathbb{R}^3$

$$\uparrow \quad \cdots \quad \uparrow$$

VOLUMES$_1$: $\mathcal{V}_1^3 = \{V \ / \ V = \hat{v}(v) \ v \in \mathcal{V}_0^3\} \cup \{V \ / \ V = \tilde{v}(s) \ s \in \mathcal{S}_1^3\} \subset \mathbb{R}^3$

$$\uparrow \quad \cdots \quad \uparrow \qquad\qquad\qquad\qquad\qquad\qquad\qquad\qquad\qquad$$

VOLUMES$_0$: $\mathcal{V}_0^3 = \{v \ / \ v = \overline{\underset{k}{\cup} S_k} \qquad S_k \in \mathcal{S}_1^3\}$

$$\uparrow \quad \cdots \quad \uparrow \qquad\qquad\qquad\qquad\qquad\qquad \uparrow \quad \cdots \quad \uparrow$$

SURFACES$_1$: $\mathcal{S}_1^3 = \{S \ / \ S = \hat{s}(s) \ s \in \mathcal{S}_0^2\} \cup \{S \ / \ S = \tilde{s}(\ell) \ \ell \in \mathcal{L}_1^3\} \subset \mathbb{R}^3$

$$\uparrow \quad \cdots \quad \uparrow \qquad\qquad\qquad\qquad\qquad\qquad\qquad\qquad$$

SURFACES$_0$: $\mathcal{S}_0^2 = \{s \ / \ s. = \overline{\underset{k}{\cup} L_k} \qquad L_k \in \mathcal{L}_1^2\} \subset \mathbb{R}^2$

$$\uparrow \quad \cdots \quad \uparrow \qquad\qquad\qquad\qquad\qquad \uparrow \quad \cdots \quad \uparrow$$

LINES$_1$: $\mathcal{L}_1^2 = \{L/L = \hat{\ell}(\ell) \ \ell \in \mathcal{L}_0^1\} \cup \{L/L = \tilde{\ell}(p) \ p \in \mathcal{P}_1^2\} \quad \mathcal{L}_1^3 = \{L/L = \tilde{\ell}(p) \ p \in \mathcal{P}_1^3\}$

$$\uparrow \quad \cdots \quad \uparrow \qquad\qquad\qquad\qquad\qquad\qquad$$

LINES$_0$: $\mathcal{L}_0^1 = \{\ell \ / \ \ell = [p_k, p_t] \ p \in \mathcal{P}_1^1\}$

$$\qquad\qquad\qquad \uparrow \quad \cdots \quad \uparrow \qquad\qquad\qquad \uparrow \quad \cdots \quad \uparrow$$

POINTS$_1$: $\mathcal{P}_1^1 = \{p/p = (x)\} \subset \mathbb{R} \qquad \mathcal{P}_1^2 = \{p/p = (x,y)\} \subset \mathbb{R}^2 \ \mathcal{P}_1^3 = \{p/p = (x,y,z)\} \subset \mathbb{R}^3$

Figure 4 : <u>THE ORIENTED GRAPH OF THE APPROXIMATE FIRST OBJECTS</u>

4. THE PHYSICAL POINT OF VIEW OF THE OBJECT REPRESENTATION :

All the graphs and the associated data must be implemented and the access at all levels must be as fast as possible.

The main difficulty is to define the simplest set of softwares which realizes that.(Simplicity in order to be accepted by the programmers.)

The trend, with good reasons, is to hide the physical support of the data : Main Storage (M.S.) or Secondary Storage (S.S.), and the transfers. The DATA BASE SYSTEMS (D.B.S.) take the place of files managed by the user. The relational model with its well-defined mathematical foundations (DELOBEL 83), its simplicity, its no-specification of access ways, its possible optimization of requests, its different views,... (BD3 83), seems the best method to day. But, at the present time, the D.B.S. have not the necessary characteristics to treat our graphs (FELIPPA 79), namely :

- fast accesses to data because essentially the waiting user is not the man but the computer

- lot of data to transfer (for instance a matrix usually contains several hundred thousands of variables)

- large complexity of data (scalars, character strings, arithmetic expressions, arrays, mappings, trees, graphs, drawings,..., of lengths often statically unknown).

A standard D.B.S. has at least two languages :

- the Data Description Language (D.D.L.) to describe the data and their relations

- the Data Manipulating Language (D.M.L.) to write the requests.

Within the framework of the F.E.M., the D.M.L. must be integrated into the programming language (FORTRAN,...) which has not been designed for this (BD3 83). Consequently, it is going to be reduced into some procedures called by the programming language.

The D.D.L. needs the management of attributes and relations. It must be adequate to find the values of the desired attributes. But a request implies a search into the list of attributes in order to obtain the address. The way among data of non constant length is difficult and expensive. So, if the access to the smallest information is often asked, the cost becomes very high.

Consequently, it seems more efficient

- to manage arrays (group of data which are likely to be used together) rather than variables ;

- to hide the physical support of arrays (file and record number)

- to realize small levels of software clear to understand and to use, simple to be accepted.

4.1. The management of arrays :

The M.S. is not large enough to contain all the data. The virtual storage (V.S.) is often not large enough or does not exist (CRAY1). The first idea may be to simulate a V.S. with a direct access file, subdivided into many pages, each one of constant length. The available M.S. is also subdivided into few pages. When a page is requested in M.S., it takes the place of the page which has the smallest probability to be used after (for instance, the oldest unused).

But, this method presents two disadvantages :
- every page has the same length ; consequently it often is too small or too large to contain an array
- all the variables of an array are not contiguous in M.S. thus causing many tests, chainings,... . Briefly, a complicated and expensive program !

Other choices are prefered :
- several direct access files are used ;
- the length of pages is not the same on different files ;
- all variables of an array are contiguous in M.S. ;
- the "name" of each array is stored and gives its address in S.S. and possibly in M.S.

(LEVESQUE 83) described a somewhat similar method.

The following use of files is consistent :
- The Multi-File (M.F.) declaration (to do one of course) where the number of files, the length of pages, the number of pages, the declaration of files are given.
- The M.F. opening where the transfer of the M.F. directory to M.S., the allocation of buffers and the opening of every file are done.
  . The array declaration where the allocation of its place in S.S. according to its length is done. If there is no place, then a new file is declared and opened.
  . The array opening where the allocation of its place in M.S., the update of its M.S. address, the transfer from S.S. into M.S. are done.· All variables are contiguous in M.S.

      Here, the handling of opened arrays is standard.

  . The array closing. After, all accesses are forbidden on M.S. without a new opening.
  . The array destruction where its name dissapears from the M.F. directory and its words in S.S. become free again.

- The M.F. closing where all arrays still in M.S. are transfered into their file, the M.F. directory is saved and all files are closed.
- The M.F. destruction where all files are deleted.

Some remarks :
. The M.F. and arrays have the same handling.
. The order of the statements is significant. An array must be opened before being used and closed. An array may be opened then closed several times.
. With Fortran, after its opening and through a call subroutine, the handling of an array becomes again standard.
. A closed array is not, without delay, put on a file. When there is no suffi-cient place in M.S. the closed array of the smallest length, but equal or greater than the request, is transferred in S.S.
. In the same way, choosing the file that supports an array minimizes the number of occupied pages and, if there are ties, minimizes the unused words number of the last page. In both cases, the algorithms minimize the number of occupied pages and inputs-outputs.

The 2.level of software i.e. the management arrays software uses
the 1.level of software which consists of

- a dynamic allocation of the M.S. ;
- a dynamic declaration, opening, closing, destruction of a file ;
- transfers between M.S. and S.S. without buffer.

These two last sets must be written with a computer dependent language.
The 3.level of software manages the graphs.

4.2. The management of object graphs - A small data base :

Four objectives must be achieved :

- an answer at the question : where are the data ? ;
- the unicity of data ;
- the easy accessibility at any level of graphs (objects and mappings) ;
- the simplicity to be accepted.

For that, the implicit recursivity of graphs is used. For instance, the printing
of the full object graph is done by two procedures.

procedure object-description (OBJECT)
write the character string 'OBJECT :' and the name of the OBJECT
if OBJECT is a first object then call volume-description (OBJECT)
                        else for each SUB-OBJECT of the OBJECT do
                            write 'SUB-OBJECT:' and the name of the SUB-OBJECT
                            write the mapping from the SUB-OBJECT to the OBJECT
                            call object-description (SUB-OBJECT)
                            end for
end object description

parameters "volume", "surface"
procedure "volume"-description (VOLUME)
  write the character string ' "volume" ' and the name of the VOLUME
  if VOLUME is defined by a mapping ^

        then write 'INITIAL-"volume"' and the name of the INITIAL VOLUME
            write the mapping from the INITIAL-VOLUME to the VOLUME
            for each SURFACE of the INITIAL-VOLUME do
            write '"surface":' and the name of the SURFACE
            call "surface"-description (SURFACE)
            end for
        else write the mapping ~ from the set of SURFACES to the VOLUME
            for each SURFACE of the set of SURFACES do
            write '"surface":' and the name of the SURFACE
            call "surface"-description (SURFACE)
            end for
end "volume"-description.

The parameters ("volume", "surface") replaced by (volume, surface), (surface,
line), (line, point) produces in fact three procedures.

The sequencialization of this recursivity implies the storage of several data
sets. Any data set is an array. Any array has a name. A name is, in fact, an
internal code. The graph is described by relations. A relation is done by a
pair : 'KEYWORD' : ARRAY-NAME.
'KEYWORD' is a character string which induces the knowledge of the associated
array address, whence the array.
The following notation
    'KEYWORD' : ARRAY-NAME = ARRAY —CONTENTS
denotes after the equal sign the significance of the array values. For instance,
the data sets of the objects and volumes are :

OBJECTS $\mathcal{O}$:

'OBJECT-NAME' : ARRAY-NAME = 'OBJECT-DEFINITION' : ARRAY-NAME = MAPPING + OBJECT,...

'FIRST'   : ARRAY-NAME = VOLUME,...

'STIFFNESS-MATRIX' : ARRAY-NAME = REAL,...

'DISPLACEMENTS'   : ARRAY-NAME = REAL,...

...

VOLUMES $\widehat{\mathcal{V}} = \{V \ / \ V = \hat{v}(v) \ \ v \in \mathcal{V}^3_0\}$:

'VOLUME-NAME' : ARRAY-NAME = 'VOLUME-DEFINITION' : ARRAY-NAME = (MAPPING $\hat{v}$ +
$$(\text{VOLUME OF } \mathcal{V}^3_0, ...))$$

'VOLUME-MESH'   : ARRAY-NAME = VOLUME-ELEMENT-
NUMBER,...

...

VOLUMES $\mathcal{V}^3_0 = \{v \ / \ v = \overline{\underset{k}{\cup\,S_k}} \quad S_k \in \mathcal{S}^3_1 = \vec{\mathcal{S}} \cup \vec{\mathcal{S}}\}$:

'VOLUME-NAME' : ARRAY-NAME = 'VOLUME-DEFINITION' : ARRAY-NAME = SURFACE OF $\mathcal{S}^3_1$,...

'VOLUME-MESH'   : ARRAY-NAME = VOLUME-ELEMENT-
NUMBER,...

...

VOLUMES $\widetilde{\mathcal{V}} = \{V \ / \ V = \tilde{v}(s) \quad s \in \mathcal{S}^3_1\}$:

'VOLUME-NAME' : ARRAY-NAME = 'VOLUME-DEFINITION' : ARRAY-NAME = (MAPPING $\tilde{v}$ +
$$(\text{SURFACE OF } \mathcal{S}^3_1, ...))$$

'VOLUME-MESH'   : ARRAY-NAME = VOLUME-ELEMENT-
NUMBER,...

...

VOLUME-ELEMENTS :

NUMBER = NUMBER_OF_FACES, ((FACE_ELEMENT_NUMBER + ORIENTATION +
NUMBER_OF_ROTATIONS_OF_THE_FACE_TO_OBTAIN_THE_
_ELEMENT_FACE),...),

NUMBER_OF_INTERNAL_POINTS, (INTERNAL_POINT_NUMBER,...),

NUMBER_OF_INTERNAL_NODES , (INTERNAL_NODE_NUMBER,...) ,

...

The data sets associated to the surfaces, lines and points are defined in the same way.

If a keyword does not exist (like 'FIRST') then its array does not exist.
With this method, in order to add a new data set, it is sufficient to

- find the adapted level (object, volume, surface,...)
- obtain its array-name, open its array (1) ;
- declare and open a new array (2)
- create a new pair 'keyword' : array-name
- add this pair in the array (1)
- transfer the new data set into the array (2).

Finally, the graphs offer us

- a good perception of different parts of the object ;
- an answer to the question : where are the data ? by
    . a logical location of data (a pressure implies a surface,
       i.e. a node of the graph) ;
    . an easy access of nodes by means of keyword array-name pairs ;
- a sufficiently simple set of standards to be accepted.

5. THE MODULARITY :

This intuitive notion is not well defined. For us, a program may be qualified
as a MODULAR PROGRAM when

- its execution has several logical steps ;

- at every step, all terms of one or several data sets, rather structured
  than not, receive a value ;

- every set is exhaustively described in a documentation where the significance and the access way of every data term are written.

Some definitions :

- such a set is called DATA STRUCTURE (D.S.) now on and may be logically
  treated as a block ;

- a MODULE is a translator from INPUT DATA STRUCTURE (I.D.S.) to OUTPUT
  DATA STRUCTURE (O.D.S.) ;

- an UPPER-MODULE is an interpreter of the user's language (LAUG 83).
  It reads the user's data and calls the module execution ;

- an ALGORITHM is a procedure where the mathematical formulas are treated.

The Figure 5 summarizes the program execution and the links between upper-
module, module and algorithm.

This structuration offers several advantages

- the algorithm, where the majority of computing operations are done, is
  written with the standard programming language without the data management ;
  consequently it does not slow down the algorithm ;

- the difficulties are dissociated : data management, algorithm, interpretation of user's statements ;

- the addition of a new module does not give problems if the D.S. are
  respected ;

- the suppression of a module, replaced by a faster one, does not disturb
  the totality ;

- the user's data cards only are read in upper modules. By a link of modules,
  written with the programming language, without data cards, a super-module
  can be written and called by a new upper-super-module... . The levels of
  modules stack up.

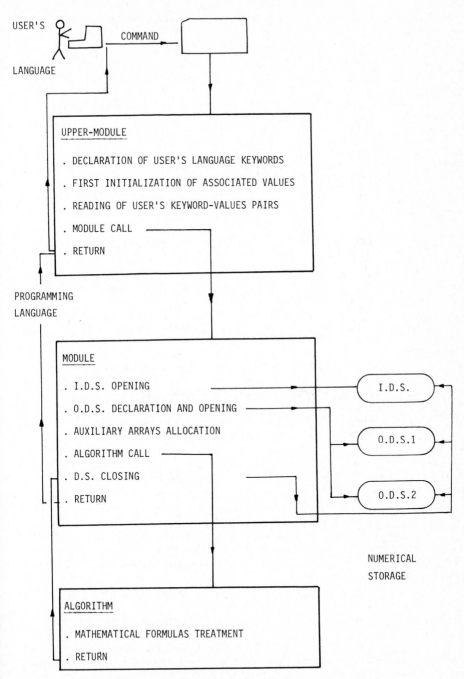

Figure 5 : THE PROGRAM EXECUTION

BIBLIOGRAPHIE :

(BD3 83)   Bases de données   Nouvelles perspectives
                Rapport du groupe BD3   janvier 1983
                INRIA et Agence de l'Informatique

(CIARLET 72)   P.G. CIARLET, P.A. RAVIART
                Interpolation theory over curved elements with applications
                to finite element methods
                Computer Methods in Applied Mechanics and Engineering 1,
                217-249   1972.

(DELOBEL 83)   C. DELOBEL, M. ADIBA
                Bases de données et Systèmes relationnels
                Dunod   phase spécialité   informatique 1983

(FELIPPA 79)   C.A. FELIPPA
                Data base management in scientific computing
                I. general description
                Computers & Structures   Vol. 10   pp. 53-61   1979

(GORDON 73)   J. GORDON, A. HALL
                Construction of curvilinear coordinate systems and application
                to mesh generation
                Int. Journal of Numerical Methods in Engineering
                Vol. 7   461-477   1973

(LAUG 83)   P. LAUG, A. PERRONNET
                MODULEF : Une expérience de programmation en éléments finis
                Int. Conference Tools, Methods and Languages for Scientific
                and Engineering Computation. May 17-19   1983   PARIS

(LEVESQUE 83)   J.R. LEVESQUE, H. NOE, M. PAOLILLO
                Méthode de gestion des objets de programme et organisation
                possible pour un code de calcul des structures
                Int. Conference Tools, Methods and Languages for Scientific
                and Engineering Computation   May 17-19   1983   PARIS

(MODULEF 83)   Présention du Club MODULEF
                Version 3.4   juin 1983   INRIA

(PERRONNET 83) A. PERRONNET
                Méfisto-Maillage   Version 1.2 du 01/03/83
                Manuel d'utilisation   83012
                Laboratoire d'Analyse Numérique
                4, place Jussieu - 75230 PARIS CEDEX 05

(ZIENKIEWICZ 71) : O.C. ZIENKIEWICZ
                The finite Element Method in Engineering Science
                Mc Graw-Hill   London

ANNEX

1. From a set of points, an approximation of a line :

Let

. L be a line in $\mathbb{R}^m$ m = 2, 3
. $\mathcal{P}^m_1$ a set of points in $\mathbb{R}^m$
. $\{p_i\}^n_{i=0}$ n+1 points of $\mathcal{P}^m_1 \cap L$
. $\hat{\ell}$: [0,1] $\to$ L a function

. find a function $\tilde{\ell}$: [0,1] $\to$ $\mathbb{R}^m$ that approximates $\hat{\ell}$ in the following sense

- $\tilde{\ell}$ passes by the n+1 points of L (LAGRANGE's interpolation)
- $\tilde{\ell}$ passes by the n+1 points of L and its differential form is continuous (HERMITE's interpolation)
- $\tilde{\ell}$ has a regularity (BERSTEIN-BEZIER's polynomials)
- ...

The list is too long to be given here. Only the simplest expressions follow :

1) At each $p_i \in \mathbb{R}^m$ is associated $\hat{p}_i \in [0,1]$ by the formula

$$\hat{p}_i = \begin{cases} 0 & \text{if } i = 0 \\[2mm] \sum_{j=1}^{i} |p_j - p_{j-1}| \Big/ \sum_{j=1}^{n} |p_j - p_{j-1}| & \text{if } i = 1,\dots,n \end{cases}$$

2) With $q^n_i(\hat{x}) = \prod_{\substack{j=0 \\ j \neq i}}^{n} (\hat{x} - \hat{p}_j) \Big/ \prod_{\substack{j=0 \\ j \neq i}}^{n} (\hat{p}_i - \hat{p}_j)$

$\tilde{\ell}$ is defined by

$$\tilde{\ell}^n(\hat{x}) = \sum_{i=0}^{n} q^n_i(\hat{x}) \, p_i$$

or

$$\tilde{\ell}(\hat{x}) = \tilde{\ell}^t(\hat{x}) \quad \text{if } \hat{x} \in [\hat{p}_{(r-1)t} , \hat{p}_{rt}] \qquad r = 1,\dots,n/t$$

or

...

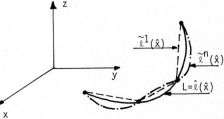

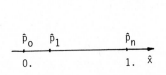

2. From a set of lines, an approximation of a surface :

Let

· S be a surface in $\mathbb{R}^m$ m = 2,3

· $\mathcal{L}_1^m$ a set of lines in $\mathbb{R}^m$

· $\ell_1,\dots,\ell_n$ n lines of $\mathcal{L}_1^m$, outline of S

· $\hat{\ell}_i$: [0,1] → ℓ_i i = 1,...,n   assumed known

· ê   a reference surface (triangle or quadrilateral)

· ŝ   the exact but unknown mapping from ê to S

· find $\tilde{s}$ an approximated mapping of ŝ which verifies

$\tilde{s}$ (side i of ê) = ℓ_i for   i = 1,...,n .

2.1. ê is the unity triangle (n = 3) :

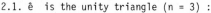

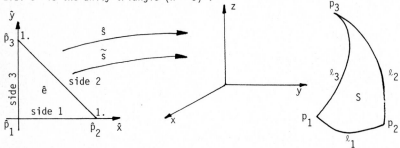

If p_i is the i-th vertex of the triangle S

$\hat{\lambda}_i(\hat{x},\hat{y})$ is the i-th barycentric coordinate of ê

i+1 , i+2 are computed modulo 3 on {1,2,3}

then, $\tilde{s}$ is defined by

$$\tilde{s}(\hat{x},\hat{y}) = \sum_{i=1}^{3} (\hat{\ell}_i(\hat{\lambda}_{i+1}(\hat{x},\hat{y})) - \hat{\lambda}_{i+1}(\hat{x},\hat{y})\, p_{i+1})\, \hat{\lambda}_{i+1}(\hat{x},\hat{y})/(1-\hat{\lambda}_{i+1}(\hat{x},\hat{y}))$$

or

$$\tilde{s}(\hat{x},\hat{y}) = \sum_{i=1}^{3} \hat{\Theta}_i(\hat{x},\hat{y})\, \hat{\ell}_i(\hat{\lambda}_{i+1}(\hat{x},\hat{y})) \, / \, \sum_{i=1}^{3} \hat{\Theta}_i(\hat{x},\hat{y})$$

with

$$\hat{\Theta}_i(\hat{x},\hat{y}) = \hat{\lambda}_i\, \hat{\lambda}_{i+1}(1+\hat{\lambda}_{i+2}) \, / \, ((\hat{\lambda}_i+\hat{\lambda}_{i+2})(\hat{\lambda}_{i+1}+\hat{\lambda}_{i+2}))$$

2.2. $\hat{e}$ is the unity square (n=4) :   (GORDON 73)

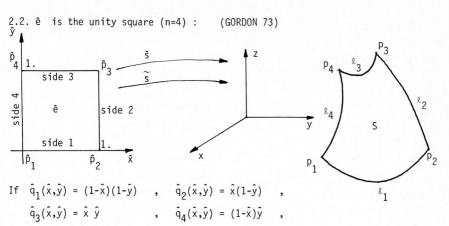

If $\hat{q}_1(\hat{x},\hat{y}) = (1-\hat{x})(1-\hat{y})$, $\hat{q}_2(\hat{x},\hat{y}) = \hat{x}(1-\hat{y})$,

$\hat{q}_3(\hat{x},\hat{y}) = \hat{x}\,\hat{y}$, $\hat{q}_4(\hat{x},\hat{y}) = (1-\hat{x})\hat{y}$,

then, $\widetilde{s}$ is defined by

$$\widetilde{s}(\hat{x},\hat{y}) = (1-\hat{y})\,\hat{\ell}_1(\hat{x}) + \hat{x}\,\hat{\ell}_2(\hat{y}) + \hat{y}\,\hat{\ell}_3(\hat{x}) + (1-\hat{x})\,\hat{\ell}_4(\hat{y})$$

$$- \sum_{i=1}^{4} \hat{q}_i(\hat{x},\hat{y})\,p_i \ .$$

Remarks :

. $\widetilde{s}$ may not be an injection without other assumptions on $\hat{\ell}_i$.

. In case 2.1., 2.2., if $\hat{\ell}_i$ is not exactly known, $\hat{\ell}_i$ may be approached by $\widetilde{\ell}$ defined at 1.

. If only $\widetilde{s}$ must verify $\widetilde{s}(\hat{p}_i) = p_i$ $i = 1,\ldots,n$
  then for the triangle $\widetilde{s}$ is defined by (CIARLET 72, ZIENKIEWICZ 71)

$$\widetilde{s}(\hat{x},\hat{y}) = \sum_{i=1}^{3} \hat{\lambda}_i(\hat{x},\hat{y})\,p_i$$

and for the quadrilateral

$$\widetilde{s}(\hat{x},\hat{y}) = \sum_{i=1}^{4} \hat{q}_i(\hat{x},\hat{y})\,p_i \ .$$

Others formulas exist for the tetrahedron, pentahedron, hexahedron. (ZIENKIEWICZ 71)

3. From a set of surfaces, an approximation of a volume :

Let

. V be a volume in $\mathbb{R}^3$

. $\mathcal{S}^3_1$ a set of surfaces in $\mathbb{R}^3$

. $s_1,\ldots,s_n$ n surfaces of $\mathcal{S}^3_1$, outline of V

. $\partial\hat{e}$ a reference element of surface included in $\mathbb{R}^2$
                         (unity triangle or square)

. $\hat{s}_i$ the mapping from $\partial\hat{e}$ on s_i $i = 1,\ldots,n$ assumed known

. $\hat{e}$ a reference volume (tetraedron, pentaedron, hexaedron)

. $\hat{v}$ the exact but unknown mapping from $\hat{e}$ to V

. find $\tilde{v}$ an approximated mapping of $\hat{v}$ which verifies

   $\tilde{v}$ (side i) = s_i for   i = 1,...,n

3.1. ê is the unity tetrahedron (n = 4) :

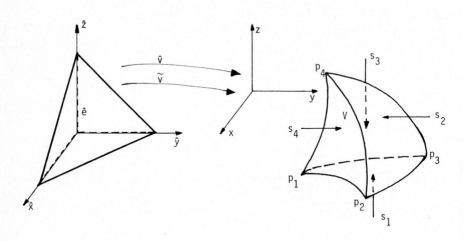

If $\hat{\lambda}_i(\hat{x},\hat{y},\hat{z})$ is the i-th barycentric coordinate of ê and

$\hat{\theta}_i(\hat{x},\hat{y},\hat{z}) = \hat{\lambda}_i \, \hat{\lambda}_{i+1} \, \hat{\lambda}_{i+2}(1-\hat{\lambda}_{i+3})/((\hat{\lambda}_i+\hat{\lambda}_{i+3})(\hat{\lambda}_{i+1}+\hat{\lambda}_{i+3})(\hat{\lambda}_{i+2}+\hat{\lambda}_{i+3}))$

then $\tilde{v}$ is defined by

$$\tilde{v}(\hat{x},\hat{y},\hat{z}) = (\hat{\theta}_1 \, \hat{s}_1(\hat{x},\hat{y}) + \hat{\theta}_2 \, \hat{s}_2(\hat{y},\hat{z}) + \hat{\theta}_3 \, \hat{s}_3(\hat{z},\hat{x}) + \hat{\theta}_4 \, \hat{s}_4(\hat{x},\hat{y}))/(\sum_{i=1}^{4} \hat{\theta}_i)$$

3.2. ê is the unity pentahedron (n = 5) :

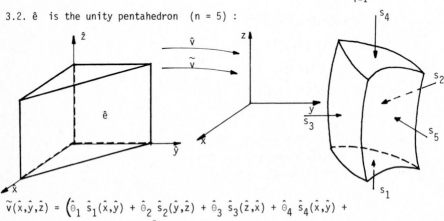

$$\tilde{v}(\hat{x},\hat{y},\hat{z}) = \Big(\hat{\theta}_1 \, \hat{s}_1(\hat{x},\hat{y}) + \hat{\theta}_2 \, \hat{s}_2(\hat{y},\hat{z}) + \hat{\theta}_3 \, \hat{s}_3(\hat{z},\hat{x}) + \hat{\theta}_4 \, \hat{s}_4(\hat{x},\hat{y}) + \hat{\theta}_5 \, \hat{s}_5(\hat{x},\hat{y})\Big) / \, (\sum_{i=1}^{5} \hat{\theta}_i)$$

$\hat{\Theta}_1(\hat{x},\hat{y},\hat{z}) = (1-\hat{z})(1-\hat{x}-\hat{y}) \ \hat{x} \ \hat{y} \ / \ ((1-\hat{x}-\hat{y}-\hat{z})(\hat{x}+\hat{y})(\hat{y}+\hat{z}))$

$\hat{\Theta}_2(\hat{x},\hat{y},\hat{z}) = (1-\hat{x}) \ \hat{z} \ (1-\hat{z})(1-\hat{x}-\hat{y}) \ \hat{y} \ / \ ((\hat{x}+\hat{z})(1-\hat{z}+\hat{x})(1-\hat{y})(\hat{x}+\hat{y}))$

$\hat{\Theta}_3(\hat{x},\hat{y},\hat{z}) = (1-\hat{y}) \ \hat{z} \ (1-\hat{z}) \ \hat{x} \ (1-\hat{x}-\hat{y}) \ / \ ((\hat{z}+\hat{y})(1-\hat{z}+\hat{y})(\hat{x}+\hat{y})(1-\hat{x}))$

$\hat{\Theta}_4(\hat{x},\hat{y},\hat{z}) = \hat{z} \ \hat{x} \ \hat{y} \ (1-\hat{x}-\hat{y}) \ / \ ((\hat{x}+1-\hat{z})(\hat{y}+1-\hat{z})(2-\hat{x}-\hat{y}-\hat{z}))$

$\hat{\Theta}_5(\hat{x},\hat{y},\hat{z}) = (\hat{x}+\hat{y}) \ \hat{z} \ (1-\hat{z}) \ \hat{x} \ \hat{y} \ / \ ((\hat{z}+1-\hat{x}-\hat{y})(2-\hat{x}-\hat{y}-\hat{z})(1-\hat{y})(1-\hat{x}))$

3.3. ê is the unity hexahedron (n = 6) :

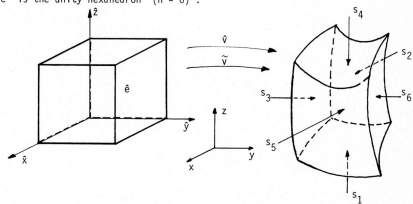

$\tilde{v}(\hat{x},\hat{y},\hat{z}) = (\hat{\Theta}_1 \ \hat{s}_1(\hat{x},\hat{y}) + \hat{\Theta}_2 \ \hat{s}_2(\hat{y},\hat{z}) + \hat{\Theta}_3 \ \hat{s}_3(\hat{z},\hat{x}) + \hat{\Theta}_4 \ \hat{s}_4(\hat{x},\hat{y}) + \hat{\Theta}_5 \ \hat{s}_5(\hat{y},\hat{z}) +$

$\hat{\Theta}_6 \ \hat{s}_6(\hat{z},\hat{x})) \ / \ (\sum_{i=1}^{6} \hat{\Theta}_i)$

with $\hat{x}_1 = \hat{x}$ $\hat{x}_2 = \hat{y}$ $\hat{x}_3 = \hat{z}$ and i+j computed modulo 3 on {1,2,3}

$\hat{\Theta}_i(\hat{x},\hat{y},\hat{z}) = (1-\hat{x}_{i-1}) \ \hat{x}_i \ (1-\hat{x}_i) \ \hat{x}_{i+1} \ (1-\hat{x}_{i+1}) \ /$

$((\hat{x}_i+\hat{x}_{i-1})(1-\hat{x}_i+\hat{x}_{i-1})(\hat{x}_{i+1}+\hat{x}_{i-1})(1-\hat{x}_{i+1}+\hat{x}_{i-1})$

$\hat{\Theta}_{i+3}(\hat{x},\hat{y},\hat{z}) = \hat{x}_{i-1} \ \hat{x}_i \ (1-\hat{x}_i) \ \hat{x}_{i+1} \ (1-\hat{x}_{i+1}) \ /$

$((\hat{x}_i+1-\hat{x}_{i-1})(2-\hat{x}_i-\hat{x}_{i-1})(\hat{x}_{i+1}+1-\hat{x}_{i-1})(2-\hat{x}_{i+1}-\hat{x}_{i-1}))$ i = 1,2,3

Remarks :

. $\tilde{v}$ may not be an injection without other assumptions on $\hat{s}_i$.

. If $\hat{s}_i$ is not exactly known, $\hat{s}_i$ may be approached by $\tilde{s}$ defined at 2.

. Any mesh on ê can be transfered on V .

DISCUSSION

Speaker: A Perronnet

Leaf: I am still a little confused by your definition of lines and surfaces. Can you explain further how the points in a surface are defined?

Perronnet: A surface is defined by it's edges, together with a mapping which then defines also the interior points of the surface, and which we choose in a way which exactly preserves the edges.

Rice: Is it possible for the user to give his own mapping to define a surface, or is he required to use the blending of the one-dimensional boundaries that is provided by the system?

As an example, to describe the surface of a sphere by blending the element boundaries requires that the surface be cut into many small elements. However, a user could cut the sphere in two and then give one mapping that describes an entire hemisphere with one simple formula.

Perronnet: You have to use the standard map provided in the package; but the examples which I gave on the slides indicate that the restrictions which this imposes are not as severe as you suggest.

Schönauer: You gave the description of whole objects. How can you derive from that a meshing, e.g. for a Finite Element method?

Perronnet: Suppose I compute the heat transfer through a whole object. This is not easy to do directly because of the physical interfaces. The natural way is to subdivide into homogeneous smaller objects, and to put a grid on each. The way this is done preserves the interfaces between objects, that is their outline which is what we store.

PDE SOFTWARE: Modules, Interfaces and Systems
B. Engquist and T. Smedsaas (eds.)
Elsevier Science Publishers B.V. (North-Holland)
© IFIP, 1984

AUTOMATIC ANALYSIS IN PDE SOFTWARE

B. Engquist and T. Smedsaas

Department of Computer Science
Uppsala University
Sturegatan 4B
S-752 23 Uppsala, Sweden

Automatic symbolic and numerical analysis can be of important
value in advanced software for partial differential equations.
We shall describe different applications of such analysis and
in particular discuss how analysis in the code can be used to
adjust the algorithm for the solution of a differential equation. The techniques will be exemplified by the presentation
of different software systems.

1. INTRODUCTION

A typical special purpose code for the numerical solution of partial differential equations (PDEs) very much uses special properties of the equations. This
is needed in order to produce a good approximation with a reasonable efficiency.
The necessity for using special properties and the existence of such a great
variety of different types of PDEs is the main obstacle for general purpose PDE
software.

In order to adapt the computational algorithm to the special features of a
class of differential equations and their solutions some sort of analysis is
needed. This is traditionally done by the person designing the algorithm and
the code.

With automatic analysis we mean both symbolic and numerical analysis which is
performed by a computer. We shall discuss those symbolic and numerical operations that are done to e.g. analyze and adjust the numerical algorithm and
not those that are done to produce the numerical solution.

The analysis can be elementary like an estimate of the local truncation error
by a divided difference with the simple result of adjusting the stepsize. It
can also be more elaborate and based on advanced theories, leading to a
variety of decisions on choice and form of the computational algorithm. It
would then be what sometimes is called an expert system.

The automatic analysis can be done within a general purpose or even a special
purpose PDE-code. It can also be done in special systems. In the latter case
the programmer interactively uses the system or the tool in the coding process.
An automatic formula manipulation program falls into this category.

The fully general purpose but still efficient PDE-code is out of reach at
present. The emphasis must be on generalizations of special purpose codes and
on making general purpose systems more reliable and efficient. We shall
discuss what kind of analysis could be useful in this context and give some
possible ways of its implementation. Our purpose is not to present a survey of
the field but to collect some ideas based on our experience with PDE software.

2. ANALYSIS IN THE COMPUTATIONAL PROCESS

There are different stages in the numerical process for which analysis is useful. Before the numerical calculation has started analysis of the differential equations and numerical algorithms are appropriate. During the calculation analysis is used to adjust the algorithm depending on the properties of the of the solution. This analysis is mainly numerical. Finally, after the calculation there is often a need for some sort of nontrivial processing of the output data.

2.1 Problem analysis

The aim of the problem analysis is to assist the user in formulating a well posed problem and to extract essential information for the later processing. Several features of a problem are best investigated by symbolic methods even if it is usually not possible to completely achieve the goals by such methods. The problem should then be specified in some nonprocedural, mathematical form instead of subroutines in ordinary programming languages. There are two reasons for this. First, this is more convenient for the user (provided the language is well designed) and, secondly, it facilitates the work for the symbolic analysis.

Assume, for this discussion, that we are working with time dependent systems of partial differential equations the following, general form:

$$\frac{\partial u}{\partial t} = f(x,t,u, \frac{\partial u}{\partial x}, \frac{\partial^2 u}{\partial x^2})$$

together with initial and boundary conditions. The following types of symbolic analysis of the problem have to be done:

- Syntactic analysis. The problem specification has to fulfill the rules of the specification language.

- Problem classification. Examples of essential information are: Number of equations, type of equations (order of derivatives, linear or nonlinear, constant or variable coefficients etc), type of boundary conditions and, for problems in several space dimensions, number of dimensions and type of geometry. During the problem classification simple errors, as for example unequal number of unknowns, equations and initial conditions, can be detected.

- Check for wellposedness. This is an intricate problem which often can not be completely answered by symbolic methods. It is, for example, not possible to check if a nonlinear problem is wellposed until the actual solution is calculated. However, the requirements can be stated and code for numerical checking during the computational process can be generated. It is also possible to see if a number of necessary conditions for wellposedness are fulfilled. This may give a good indication if e.g. the type of boundary conditions are correct.

- Problem transformation. We may desire to transform the domain, change coordinate system, scale the variables, rewrite the equations on conservation form etc. The equations can sometimes be simplified through substitutions. This may be a nontrivial task if e.g. an index of a differential algebraic equation is to be reduced.

During this phase various Jacobians are computed symbolically. They can later be used in the code for the numerical computations.

2.2 Algorithm selection and analysis

It is impossible to make the algorithm choice completely automatic since it often depends on which phenomena the user wants to study. Therefore, it is in may cases better to inform the user about the existing algorithms and their properties and leave the actual choice to him. Once the algorithms are selected, they can automatically be adapted to the actual problem.

During this phase, the user may be more or less involved in the development of the code. When the user is coding himself he may need a number of tools which also may include routines for analysis of algorithms. See e.g. the examples of software for roundoff analysis of matrix algorithms in [5] and the IBSTAB package for stability analysis of hyperbolic finite difference methods discussed below. A formula manipulation system for symbolic analysis is also very useful.

In the other extreme the user only gives the problem formulation together with some information of preferred methods and desired accuracy to the PDE software system. The system must then produce or choose code depending on the result of its own analysis. The result from the problem analysis phase regarding the type of equations, linear or nonlinear terms, constant or variable coefficients etc. are then of great importance.

2.3 Analysis during the numerical calculations

When the computations has started the solution is represented by an array of numbers and we have to rely on numerical analysis for adjusting the algorithm.

Let us consider a time dependent problem like a parabolic or hyperbolic equation solved over a domain Ω $(x \epsilon \Omega, t > t_0)$ Analysis can help us with the following two tasks.

- Determine if the problem still is correctly posed. If this is not the case the problem must be modified or an error message must be given.

- Update the algorithm to be efficient and accurate.

The first task is based on the theory of differential equations and usually involves the computation of eigenvalues of various Jacobian matrices of the function f in 2.1. Codes for these matrices must either be given by the user or better, be determined during the problem analysis phase.

The second task is usually to some extent performed in the PDE software today. It may consist of the following routines.

- Choice of time step based on (1) stability considerations - the von Neumann condition and (2) accuracy - estimates of the local truncation error.

- Choice of numerical order of approximation. The choice is based on accuracy and efficiency considerations and is common in method of lines code.

- Choice of boundary conditions. The type of boundary conditions that are appropriate for a nonlinear hyperbolic problem depends on the solution. An example is computation of fluid flow where the direction of the flow influences the boundary conditions. A local analysis can determine what form the boundary conditions must have at each time t and each point of the boundary of Ω.

- Rezoning and adaptation of the computational grid for the domain Ω. The decision on changing the grid or the form of the elements should be based on local error estimates and an estimate of how the local error influences the final result.

- Change of the algorithm. A major decision of this type is rare in present days codes but there are situations where it would be very useful to e.g. change from an explicit to an implicit method.

Most of these routines are similar for steady problems. The choice of time step can e.g. be compared with the choice of parameters for an iterative method.

2.4 Postprocessing of the output

In this final phase of the computational process the user has access to a file of numbers representing the solution of the differential equation. Printing and plotting routines are essential for presenting the data but quite often routines that, in a general sense, could be labeled analysis can also be applied.

The user may want to look at some functional of the solution like a norm or a derivative (approximated by a divided difference). A simple test if Richardson extrapolation gives an improvement or the computation of an a posteriori error estimate could be of interest.

These types of simple numerical analysis could have been in the main program as a part of the computation but sometimes it is difficult to anticipate which data is useful until one starts to look at the solution. It is therefore of value to extend the postprocessing printing and plotting routines to include the possibility of performing simple numerical operations on the data base representing the solution. This might save the users time and reduce the number of reruns of the main PDE-code. It is too often that "calculations by hand" are done because it is too time consuming to write a special code to perform the operation on the output data.

Other related operations are coordinate transformation of the dependent and independent variables. The simplest is just a scaling of a component in the solution.

3. IMPLEMENTATION STRATEGIES

According to the discussion above, we need to do analysis before, under and after and even completely apart from the numerical integration. This can be realized in different ways. We could add this processing to the code that performs the integration into a complete program or we could provide the facilities as separate tools. If we provide them as separate tools we could either use an existing environment (an operating system or a subsystem like VAXSYMA) or we could design an environment of our own.

Since many of these operations are much more problem independent than the numerical integration, we believe that they are often best provided as separate tools. However, we should define these tools and especially their interfaces so that they can work together in a consistent way. The question whether to use an existing environment or design a complete environment is of course very much a matter of money. Since the environment must include editors, formula manipulation, graphics, file system, numerical subroutine packages etc. it is much easier to utilize an existing environment.

However, portability is then a considerable problem. In a numerical code portability can usually be achieved through careful design and a few machine dependent constants. Unfortunately, this is not the case here. We are dealing with different operating system, file systems and terminal systems. We are also dealing with different types of equipment (terminals, plotters). Further, we want to use subsystems (graphic packages, symbolic manipulations, data bases) which usually are not portable.

The difficulties can be reduced, but not removed, by using standards, good design and transportability tools. However, in order to support all operating systems (or even only the major ones) we must set up severe restrictions which may make the price in reduced power, flexibility and friendlyness too high.

The LISP-F3 lisp interpreter (see [6]) used by the systems described in section 4 is useful for realization of advanced mathematical software. It makes the implementation of symbolic manipulation much easier since Lisp is a more powerful language than FORTRAN. Still, since LISP-F3 is written in FORTRAN it is transportable which usually is not the case with other lisp and formula manipulation systems. Furthermore, the FORTRAN base makes it easy to interface the system to numerical software like EISPACK and LINPACK libraries.

Many of the computers used for numerical computations have less developed operating systems. However, they are often accessed through front-end computers with much nicer operating systems. A possible approach is then to have the tools running on the front-end and let them generate code for the numerical integration to be run on the main frame or on a special purpose processor.

4. EXAMPLES OF PDE SOFTWARE SYSTEMS

At the Computer Science Department at Uppsala University we have developed three different general packages for PDE-problems: DCG, IBSTAB and NUTOIS. DCG is a system for problem analysis and code generation for time dependent PDEs. IBSTAB is a package for stability analysis of mixed initial boundary value problems and NUTOIS is postprocessor for analysis and graphics output of numerical solutions. We shall mainly discuss DCG and NUTOIS below. The IBSTAB package is described in detail elsewhere in this proceedings [8].

4.1 The DCG system.

In DCG, the user specifies a PDE problem in a nonprocedural specification language. DCG handles systems of nonlinear hyperbolic and parabolic PDEs in one or two space dimensions on general domains. DCG analyses the problem symbolically and generates FORTRAN code for numerical integration adapted to the problem.

DCG is implemented in FORTRAN and LISP. LISP is used for the symbolic analysis and the code generation and FORTRAN for the numerical calculations. The FORTRAN based LISP-F4 interpreter is used so the system is comparatively easy to transport. Figure 2 gives an overview of DCG. The system is described in [1]. For other general purpose systems see e.g. [4], [7].

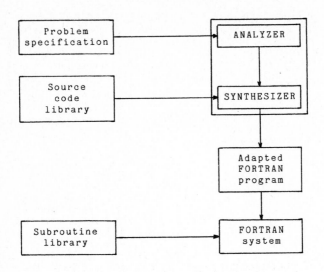

Figure 1. The DCG system.

Below is an (incomplete) example of a specification of a problem in DCG. The
notation is fairly self-explanatory. The dot denotes the differentiation
operator and the FORTRAN-section includes user supplied FORTRAN subroutines.

```
TITLE
     "Shallow water equations"

INDEPENDENT VARIABLES
     SPACE : X, Y;
     TIME  : T

EQUATIONS
     U.T   = -U*U.X - V*U.Y - G*PHI.X + F1 + A*(U.X.X + U.Y.Y);
     V.T   = -U*V.X - V*V.Y - G*PHI.Y + F2 + A*(V.X.X + V.Y.Y);
     PHI.T = -(PHI + H(X,Y))*(U.X + V.Y) -
             U*(PHI.X + HX(X,Y)) - V*(PHI.Y + HY(X,Y))

SHORTHANDS
     F1 = -R*U*SQRT(U**2 + V**2)/H(X,Y) + SX(X,Y);
     F2 = -R*V*SQRT(U**2 + V**2)/H(X,Y) + SY(X,Y);
     G = 9.81;
     R = 5.0E-3;
     A = 5.0E-2
```

```
INITIAL CONDITIONS
     U = 0.0;
     V = 0.0;
     PHI = P(X,Y)

GEOMETRY
     F(X,Y) > 0.0

BOUNDARY CONDITIONS
     U = 0.0;
     V = 0.0

FORTRAN
     FUNCTION SX(X,Y)
     ....
     END
     FUNCTION F(X,Y)
     ....
     END
     ....
 END
```

We have omitted some sections describing methods to be used, optional
information about the equations and the solution.

In the analysis, DCG calculates the Jacobian of the principal symbol. It is
used for the checking of wellposedness and the von Neumann condition and
construction of iteration matrices and numerical boundary conditions. DCG
investigates nonlinearities, space and time dependence in order to optimize
the code.

4.2 The IBSTAB system

IBSTAB is a tool for the numerical analyst to be used in the analysis and
design of difference approximations of hyperbolic mixed initial boundary value
problems. The user presents the problem in a specification language similar to
that in DCG.

The purpose of IBSTAB is to determine if the initial boundary value problem
for a set of difference equations is stable. See [2] for the appropriate theory
and stability definitions. In this theory, which is the normal mode analysis,
the problem of stability is transformed into conditions on the solution of
algebraic equations. The software package both performs the transformations and
solves the relevant algebraic equations. If the problem is simple it can be
solved directly by symbolic methods. If not, a Fortran program for a numerical
solution is produced. In the latter case the equations and the Jacobians
necessary to solve the problem are generated by IBSTAB.

IBSTAB has many parts in common with DCG. It uses the LISP-F3 interpreter and
the same symbolic manipulation routines as well as the code generation parts.
IBSTAB is not planned to be a part of a general purpose PDE solver but to help
the user during the phase of scheme design. See [8] for further description.

4.3 The NUTOIS system

NUTOIS is an interactive postprocessor which can perform various types of
elementary analysis and produce graphics output of a numerical solution to a
PDE problem. The idea is that a PDE-solver produces to much and often the wrong
type of data and that the user does not know in advance exactly what he wants
to see. Instead of printing the output the solver should store it in a data
base using some simple interface routines. NUTOIS works on the data base in
interaction with the user. Figure 2 contains an overview of the system.

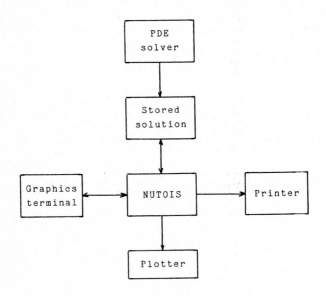

Figure 2. The NUTOIS system.

The user can print and plot the solution in different regions and coordinates,
search for extreme values, oscillations etc. and perform simple computations
like algebraic operations, extrapolations and norm calculations.

Some examples of the facilities are the following:

- Graphics output including contour, vector field and 3D plots.

- Comparison between different solutions (e.g. solutions calculated with
  different methods or different step sizes).

- Compute functions of the dependent variables using arithmetic operators and
  elementary functions. This feature can e.g. be used to scale the variables.

- Compute functionals of the dependent variables like extreme values,
  derivatives and norms.

- Combine values in different mesh points in order to make extrapolations, numerical differentiations, error estimates etc.

- Transform the domain. The physical domain may for example have been transformed in order to facilitate the computations. NUTOIS can put the solution back to the physical domain.

The operations can be performed on the whole domain or on a subdomain possibly of lower dimension. (Certain operations require certain domains - a contour plot require for example a two dimensional domain.)

The solution can be treated in two modes: numerical and analytical. In numerical mode, the solution is only defined in the mesh points where it has been calculated. All references to the solution are made at those points.

In analytical mode the meshpoints are hidden. The solution is regarded as continuously defined over the whole domain and NUTOIS performs the necessary interpolations.

NUTOIS is FORTRAN 66 based (although it uses interface systems which may contain assembler written routines). It uses the PLOT-10 TCS from Tektronix as interface to the graphic terminal but could fairly easy be completed with drivers for other equipment. All high level plot routines are device independent.

The other main obstacle for portability, the data base, is implemented using PIOS. PIOS is a Fortran based transportable file system which easily can be implemented. See [3].

REFERENCES

[1] Engquist, B. and Smedsaas, T., Automatic Computer Code Generation for Hyperbolic and Parabolic Differential Equations, SIAM J. Sci. Stat. Compute, Vol. 1, 1980, pp. 249-259.

[2] Gustafsson, B., Kreiss, H.-O. and Sundstrom, A., Stability Theory of Difference Approximations for Mixed Initial Boundary Value Problems II., Math. Comp., Vol 26, 1972, pp. 649-686.

[3] Hanson, D. R., The Portable I/O System PIOS, Dept. of Computer Science, The University of Arizona, Report no. TR 80-6a, 1980.

[4] Machura, M. and Sweet, R., A Survey of Software for Partial Differential Equations, ACM Trans. on Math. Software, Vol. 6, 1980, pp 461-488.

[5] Miller, W. and Wrathall, C., Software for Roundoff Analysis of Matrix Algorithms, Academic Press, 1980.

[6] Nordstrom, M., LISP-F3 User's Guide, Dept. of Computer Sciences, Uppsala University, Report no. DLU 78/4, 1978.

[7] Rice, J., ELLPACK: A Research Tool for Elliptic Partial Differential Equation Software, In Mathematical Software III, Academic Press, New York, 1977, pp. 319-341.

[8] Thune, M., A Software Package for Stability Analysis of Difference Methods, This proceedings, pp. 89-100.

DISCUSSION

Speaker: B. Engquist

Madsen: Most of your analysis appears to be performed either before the actual numerical calculations, or after. Do you ever do any analysis during the actual numerical solution process?

Engquist: Not much. We have put only four manyears into this package, and other groups do that kind of analysis - order changes, timestep changes etc - so that we have given it a lower priority.

Madsen: Does the state of existing PDE theory make it possible to use your analysis techniques for non-model problems?

Engquist: If you are talking about non-linear problems, the theory is not really there. But our analysis will apply to a linearised version of the non-linear problem, and may then be useful. When the theory is lacking, it is hard to do anything - e.g. mixed hyperbolic/parabolic problems.

Björck: You mention that you don't do as much checking as you would like. How would you add more?

Engquist: There are several things one can do, if one would like to add more things. The most important would be more aids to the production of the geometry. But this is a very hard work. Users would like help with constructing grids; boundary difference formulae; etc, etc.

Ford: You are obviously generating a FORTRAN program automatically from your analysis of the user's input. What tests do you carry out on this program for correctness?

Engquist: We test that it compiles, but really nothing else. Providing that our analysis is consistent, and our software bug-free, the program should be too.

Ford: Do you have any evidence that your analysis produces any inconsistencies?

Engquist: Any inconsistencies which we got to know about, we removed! Any that remain, we don't know about.

Schönauer: In our SLDGL program package, we deliver an error estimate to the user. We recommend the user to use this as a check of the program: to choose a test solution, put it into the PDE's and B.C's, get a residual, and subtract it. In this way we get a system whose solution is known. Then one should check the program's error estimate, by putting this system back into the program and running it.

If it is O.K., it is a rigorous test for the program, including the Jacobian matrices. Absolute terms do not change the consistency and stability. I had also an example of an engineer whose test failed, and it turned out his problem was not well posed because of wrong B.C's.

Engquist: That is very interesting. We have an option for the user to give an exact solution, and hence to produce "exact errors". But there is a pitfall in this: one is tempted to use "easy" solutions, which do not contain the difficulties in the actual problem.

If things do go wrong, our analysis tries to do a little more than just say that - it tries to help say why things have gone wrong.

Brandt: Quite often side conditions are needed to specify the problem and make it well posed. What can you do about such cases?

Engquist: These situations arise only when there is no strong (classical) solution. Our analysis strictly does not cover such cases, and the amount of theory available is rather low.

Andersson: Did you have to build a system for the symbolic calculation, or could you use existing ones such as REDUCE?

Engquist: The symbolic analyser is written explicitly here, because we know exactly the type of analysis needed. Systems like REDUCE are huge, and would be hard to embed in our system without unbalancing it.

Andersson: Ideas of this kind would be highly desirable within the domain of non-linear programming, where one often has to calculate gradients and Hessians analytically.

Engquist: Our analysis tests the problem for well-posedness. Even physicists need problems to be well-posed.

PDE SOFTWARE: Modules, Interfaces and Systems
B. Engquist and T. Smedsaas (eds.)
Elsevier Science Publishers B.V. (North-Holland)
© IFIP, 1984

DYNAMICALLY-ADAPTIVE GRIDS IN THE NUMERICAL SOLUTION
OF PARTIAL DIFFERENTIAL EQUATIONS

Joe F. Thompson

Department of Aerospace Engineering
Mississippi State University
Mississippi State, MS. 39762 USA

ABSTRACT

The construction of dynamically-adaptive curvilinear coordinate systems based on numerical grid generation and the use thereof is surveyed, and correlations are made among the various approaches. These adaptive grids are coupled with the physical solution being done on the grid so that the grid points continually move to resolve developing gradients in the solution. It is noted that dynamic grid adaption can remove the oscillations common when strong gradients occur on fixed grids, and that it appears that when the grid adapts to the solution all numerical solution algorithms work well.

INTRODUCTION

Numerical grid generation has now become a fairly common tool for use in the numerical solution of multi-dimensional partial differential equations on arbitrarily-shaped regions. This is especially true in computational fluid dynamics, from whence came much of the impetus for the development of this technique, but the procedures are equally applicable to all physical problems that involve field solutions.

Numerical grid generation is basically a procedure for the orderly distribution of observers over a physical field in a way that efficient communication among the observers is possible, and such that all physical phenomena on the entire continuous field may be represented with reasonable accuracy by this finite collection of observations. This technique frees the computational simulation from restrictions to certain boundary shapes and allows general codes to be written in which the boundary shape is specified simply by input. The boundaries may also be in motion, either as specified externally or in response to the developing physical solution. Similarly, the observers may adjust their positions to follow gradients developing in the evolving physical solution. In any case, the numerically-generated grid allows all computation to be done on a fixed square grid in the computational field. (Computational field here refers to the space of the curvilinear coordinates, i.e., where these coordinates, rather than the cartesian coordinates, serve as independent variables. This field is always rectangular by construction, being composed of contiguous rectangular blocks, as discussed by Ref. 1)

In an adaptive grid, the physics of the problem at hand must ultimately direct the grid points to congregate so that a functional relationship on these points can represent the physical solution with sufficient accuracy. The mathematics controls the points by sensing the gradients in the evolving physical solution, evaluating the accuracy of the discrete representation of the solution, communicating the needs of the physics to the points, and finally, by providing mutual communication among the points as they respond to the physics.

The basic techniques involved then are as follows:

(1) a means of distributing points over the field in an orderly
     fashion, so that neighbors may be easily identified and data
     can be stored and handled efficiently.

(2) a means of communication between points, so that a smooth
     distribution is maintained as points shift their positions.

(3) a means of representing continuous functions by discrete
     values on a collection of points with sufficient accuracy,
     and a means for evaluation of the error in this representation.

(4) a means for communicating the need for a re-distribution
     of points in the light of the error evaluation, and a means
     of controlling this re-distribution.

Considerable progress has been made in the past decade, especially in the last
few years, toward the development of these techniques and toward casting them
in forms that can be readily applied. A comprehensive survey of procedures
and applications through 1981 has appeared (Ref. 2), and two conferences
specifically in the area of numerical grid generation have been held, with
published proceedings (Ref. 3 & 4). Some expository papers included in the
latter proceedings (Ref. 4) supply some introduction to the area. A later
general survey has also been given, (Ref. 5), and three-dimensional elliptic
generation systems in particular have recently been surveyed in Ref. 6.

In the present discussion, some basic features of numerical grid generation,
particularly with regard to adaptive grids, are first noted. The minimization
of error by equidistribution of some solution quantity related to the error is
then discussed. (Impetus in this area has come initially from boundary-value
problems in ordinary differential equations.) It is noted that this equidistribution, which is the unifying feature of adaptive grids in general, is equivalent
to solving the Euler equations arising from a variational principle. The extension of this concept leads to the development of adaptive grids in multiple
dimensions, and the various approaches are discussed and correlated in this light.

SOME BASIC FEATURES

A numerically-generated grid is understood here to be the organized set of points
formed by the intersections of the lines of a boundary-conforming curvilinear
coordinate system. The cardinal feature of such a system is that some coordinate line (surface in 3D) is coincident with each segment of the boundary of the
physical region. This allows boundary conditions to be represented entirely
along coordinate lines without need of interpolation. The use of coordinate
line intersections to define the grid points provides an organizational structure which allows all computation to be done on a fixed square grid when the
partial differential equations of interest have been transformed so that the
curvilinear coordinates replace the cartesian coordinates as the independent
variables.

Probably the most important area of research in grid generation at present is the
development of dynamically adaptive systems in which the grid points move in
response to the developing physical solution being done on the grid. The point
distribution over the field thus readjusts dynamically to concentrate points in
regions of larger solution variation as they develop, without reliance on prior
knowledge of the location of such regions. Several considerations are involved
here, some of which are conflicting. The points must concentrate, and yet no
region can be allowed to become void of points. The distribution also must retain
a sufficient degree of smoothness, and the grid must not become too skewed, else

the truncation error will be increased (cf. Refs, 5, 7, and 8). This means that points must not move independently, but rather each point must somehow be coupled at least to its neighbors. Also, the grid points must not move too far or too fast, else oscillations may occur. Finally the solution error, or other driving measure, must be sensed, and there must be a mechanism for translating this into motion of the grid. The need for a mutual influence among the points calls to mind either some elliptic system, thinking continuously, or some sort of attraction (repulsion) between points, thinking discretely. Both approaches have been taken with some success, and both are discussed below.

With the time derivatives at fixed values of the physical coordinates transformed to time derivatives taken at fixed values of the curvilinear coordinates, no interpolation is required when the adaptive grid moves. The computation thus can be done on a fixed grid in the transformed space, without need of interpolation, even though the grid points are in motion in physical space. The influence of the motion of the grid points is registered through the grid speeds appearing in the transformed time derivative.

ONE-DIMENSIONAL ADAPTION

Equidistribution

A number of studies of numerical solutions of boundary-value problems in ordinary differential equations have shown that the error can be reduced by distributing the grid points so that some positive weight function, $w(x)$, is equally distributed over the field, i.e.,

$$\int_{x_i}^{x_{i+1}} w(x)dx = \text{constant} \qquad (1)$$

or, in discrete form,

$$h_i w_i = \text{constant} \qquad (2)$$

where h_i is the grid interval, i.e., $h_i = x_{i+1} - x_i$. It may be more appropriate in some cases to replace the equal sign in Eq. (1) and (2) with "less than or equal," and thus to "sub-equidistribute" the weight function.

This approach has also been applied to redistribute the grid points (or to add points) at each time step, or at certain intervals, in numerical solutions of initial/boundary-value problems in one-dimensional partial differential equations. Babuska & Rheinboldt (Ref. 9) note that the point distribution is asymptotically optimal if some error measure is distributed evenly, and that this optimum error is rather stable under perturbations of the point distribution. Thus it is not necessary to locate the grid points with excessive accuracy.

Since the discrete representation of higher derivatives is progressively less accurate and subject to computational noise, the actual truncation error and residual usually are difficult to evaluate accurately. Therefore, the most common approach has been to essentially equidistribute some derivative of the solution, as noted by Russell and Christiansen (Ref. 10) where a number of approaches are surveyed. Among the weight functions, $w(x)$, discussed by Russell and Christiansen are the following:

(1) $h^k||u^{(k+1)}||$.

(2) $\sqrt{1 + ||u_x||^2}$.

(3) h^k times the residual.

(4) truncation error divided by h^k.

Here $u^{(k)}$ indicates the k<u>th</u> x-derivative of the solution, u, and h is the local grid point spacing. (The solution, u, is in general the vector solution of a system of equations.) The integer k may range up to the order of the discrete representation. Methods using higher derivatives are ineffective, however, when the error is large. With k equal to the order, the first form above becomes the truncation error. Other applications of equidistribution appear in Ref. 11-17. A number of other studies have focussed on equidistribution in boundary-value problems in ordinary differential equations, and the present citations are not meant to represent coverage of this area. Rather this subject is introduced here to serve as a basis for adaption concepts in multiple dimensions.

Equidistribution by Transformation.

If the nonuniform point distribution is considered to be a transformation, $x(\xi)$, from a uniform grid in ξ-space, Eq. (2) can be represented as

$$x_\xi w(\xi) = \text{constant} \qquad (3)$$

But this is just the Euler equation for the minimization of the integral

$$I_1 = \int_0^1 w(\xi) \; x_\xi^2 d\xi \qquad (4)$$

which can be taken to represent the energy of a system of springs, with spring constants $w(\xi)$, spanning each grid interval, assuming all the points to have been expanded from a common point. The grid point distribution resulting from the equidistributions thus represents the equilibrium state of such a spring system.

An alternative viewpoint results from consideration of Eq. (3) in the form

$$x_\xi w(x) = \text{constant} \qquad (5)$$

This is now the Euler equation for minimization of the integral

$$I_2 = \int_0^1 \frac{\xi_x^2}{w(x)} \; dx \qquad (6)$$

which, since ξ_x can be considered to represent the point density, is a measure of the smoothness of the point distribution, with emphasis placed on smoothness in certain regions in inverse proportion to the weight function, $w(x)$. From this viewpoint the grid point distribution represents the smoothest distribution attainable.

The grid and solution may be determined separately, perhaps even in an iterative fashion. However, the transformation allows the grid and solution to be dynamically coupled so that both evolve together. With the spring analogy approach of Eq. (3), we have the following differential equation for the grid:

$$x_\xi w(\xi) = \frac{1}{\displaystyle\int_0^1 \frac{d\xi}{w(\xi)}} \qquad (7)$$

which supplies an additional differential equation to be solved simutaneously
with the differential equation system of the physical problem at hand, with the
grid point locations, x, added to the solution, u, as dependent variables, and
ξ taken as the independent variable. Similarly, with the smoothness approach
and Eq. (5) as the basis, the differential equation for the grid is

$$x_\xi w(x) = \int_0^1 w(x)\,dx \qquad (8)$$

In practice, the weight function is more likely to be expressed as an explicit
function of the solution variable and its derivatives, so that both Eq. (3) and
Eq. (5) become simply

$$wx_\xi = \text{constant} \qquad (9)$$

and either Eq. (7) or Eq. (8) can be applied. Thus the approaches defined by Eq.
(3) and (5), really differ only by the way the constant is evaluated, i.e.,
whether by integration over ξ or over x.

One-Dimensional Equations.

White (Ref. 18) followed the transformation approach and considered weight functions of the form

$$w = [\alpha + ||u^{(n)}||^2]^{1/2n} \qquad (10)$$

where α is a constant. With n = 1 and α = 0 this becomes

$$w = ||u_x|| \qquad (11)$$

which for a single equation yields, by Eq. (9)

$$u_\xi = u_x x_\xi = \text{constant} \qquad (12)$$

This choice thus places the points so that the same change in the solution occurs
over each grid interval. With this distribution, all higher derivatives of u
with respect to ξ vanish, of course, thus reducing the truncation error. Taking
n = 1 and α = 1 yields

$$w = \sqrt{1 + ||u_x||^2} \qquad (13)$$

which for a single equation gives, by Eq. (9)

$$\sqrt{1 + u_x^2}\, x_\xi = \text{constant} \qquad (14)$$

and thus produces a uniform distribution of arc length on the solution curve.

White also considered the form

$$w = [\alpha^2 + ||u_{xxx}||^2]^{1/2n} \qquad (15)$$

with n = 2 and 3, related to equidistributing the local truncation error and the
single-step truncation error (product of grid interval and the error), respectively. In the applications made, the solution arc length form was favored, and
the local trucation error form was the least successful.

The grid equation and the problem differential equations were solved simultaneously by White, using Newton iteration, with the grid equation in the form, wx_ξ
= θ, with the equation, $\theta_\xi = 0$, also added to the system. This corresponds to
Eq. (7), and hence to the spring analogy approach, since the constant is determined as a part of the solution.

This procedure was extended to one-dimensional initial/boundary-value problems by White in Ref. 19. An example of application to Burgers' equation is given, using the weight function based on the solution arc length, Eq. (13). The concentration of points in the shock as it develops is evident.

Ablow (Ref. 20), with a single ordinary differential equation, also used the solution arc length form, Eq. (13), and Ablow and Schecter (Ref. 21) applied a second transformation to cause the points to concentrate according to the solution curvature as well. Thus, to a transformation, $x(\bar{\xi})$, that equidistributes solution arc length (cf. Eq. (9) and (13)

$$\bar{\xi}_x = \frac{1}{C_1} \sqrt{1 + u_x^2} \qquad (16)$$

is applied a subsequent transformation, $\bar{\xi}(\xi)$, which equidistributes solution curvature:

$$\xi_{\bar{\xi}} = \frac{1}{C_2}(1 + \alpha|K|) \qquad (17)$$

where α is a constant and K is the curvature of the solution curve, i.e.,

$$K = \frac{u_{xx}}{(1 + u_x^2)^{3/2}} \qquad (18)$$

Combining Eq. (16) and (17) we have, as a single transformation, $x(\xi)$,

$$\xi_x = \xi_{\bar{\xi}}\bar{\xi}_x = \frac{1}{C}(1 + \alpha|K|) \sqrt{1 + u_x^2} \qquad (19)$$

The resultant weight function then is

$$w = (1 + \alpha|K|) \sqrt{1 + u_x^2} \qquad (20)$$

Here Eq. (9) was differentiated with respect to ξ to eliminate the constant, at the expense of an increase in order, and this equation was solved simutaneously with the problem differential equation. Larger values of α cause stronger concentration of points in regions where the solution curve has high curvature and thus decrease the error in such regions, at the expense of some increase in error elsewhere.

Adaption Along Fixed Lines.

Dwyer, et. al., (Ref. 22-27) has applied the one-dimensional transformation approach of Eq. (5), i.e., the smoothness form, to a two-dimensional curvilinear coordinate system, with the grid points constrained to move along one family of fixed coordinate lines. Although ultimately adaption should be used in all directions, many problems are well-suited to one-dimensional adaption, and there are fewer problems with severe grid distortions with the adaption limited to one family of lines. The weight function is taken in the form

$$w = 1 + \alpha|u_x| + \beta|f(u_{xx})| \qquad (21)$$

with x now understood to be arc length along the fixed coordinate curves. The form considered for $f(u_{xx})$ was the product of h^k and the difference expression for u_{xx}, with k = 0, 1, or 2. The strength of the second-derivative term decreases as k increases, and k = 1 was used in most of the applications. As noted above, the use of the second-derivative term may lead to oscillations when the solution is too rough for accurate discrete representation of this derivative. The use of this term is prompted, however, by the fact that a weight function based only on gradient will not concentrate points near a solution extremum.

Several problems in heat transfer, flame propagation, and fluid mechanics have been considered by Dwyer and his co-workers in the references cited. In some cases separate grids were used for different physical properties, with interpolation between the grids. In the combustion problem with separated flow (Ref. 26), the grid for the fluid mechanics was driven by the velocity gradient in the radial direction, while the grid for the flame was driven by the temperature gradient, the adaption being along fixed radial lines. The shock-boundary layer problem (Ref. 26) used adaption along fixed lines semi-parallel to the wall, with the pressure gradient as the driver.

Gnoffo (Refs. 28 and 29) also treated a two-dimensional system using adaption along one fixed family of coordinate lines in essentially the manner of Dwyer described above, the adaption being along lines between a body and an outer boundary. Here the spring analogy of Eq. (3) is explicitly invoked and the weight function (spring constant) is that of Eq. (21) with β = 0. The implementation differs from Dwyer, however, in that the time derivatives are not transformed, and the solution is implicit. At each time step, the grid was redone at certain intervals in the iteration for the solution, the new grid being calculated from Eq. (7). Since the integral in this equation depends on the grid, the solution of Eq. (7) for the new grid must itself be iterative. In an application to hypersonic viscous flow, the gradient of a single variable, e.g. energy, velocity, Mach Number, density, pressure, was used in the weight function. The concentration of points in the shock and shear layer regions is evident. Some attempts were also made at two-dimensional system with all points connected by springs (cf. Ref. 28), but problems with severe grid distortions were encountered.

The approach used by Tolstykh (Ref. 30) is also essentially the same as that of Dwyer above, using Eq. (21) for the weight function with β = 0, and using the gradient of the velocity magnitude in a viscous flow solution. Again a two-dimensional system was treated by adaption along one fixed family of coordinate lines, the fixed lines here being normal to the free flow. An example of the results for flow over a backward-facing step is given.

Another example of adaption along one fixed family in a two-dimensional system was given by Acharya and Patankar (Ref. 31), again using the weight function from Eq. (21), but now with α = 0 and $f(u_{xx})$ taken as simply u_{xx}. The application was to a parabolized viscous flow solution done by marching downstream, with adaption along lines normal to the free flow. All the flow variables were monitored, and the strongest was used in the weight function. The grid at each successive marching position was generated using the weight function evaluated from a preliminary flow solution on a course grid at that position. The use of the flow solution at the previous position to define the new grid line was found to lead to oscillation between the solution and the grid. Application was to flow in a channel with intermittent finite plates.

In the above procedures using adaption along a fixed family of coordinate lines, the fixed family may have been established by any means of grid generation. The simple expedient of connecting corresponding boundary points with straight lines has been used in some cases. Smoother grids can be obtained, however, by

generating the basic grid from a two (or three) dimensional grid generation system
that is designed to produce acceptable grids in its own right. The final grid
in the one-dimensional adaptions discussed above will, of course, be the result
of the grid point movement along the one family of fixed grids, and therefore
the smoothness of the original grid may not be preserved as the grid adapts.
Some restrictions on point movement have generally been necessary in order to
prevent excessive grid distortion.

MULTIPLE-DIMENSIONAL ADAPTION

In multiple dimensions, in general it is desirable to couple the adaption in the
different directions in order to maintain sufficient smoothness in the grid. One
approach to such coupling is to generate the entire grid anew at each stage of
the adaption from the basic grid generation system. The adaption then occurs
indirectly through changes in parameters in the grid generation system rather
than through direct changes in the grid point locations. The structure of the grid
generation system serves to maintain smoothness in the grid as the adaption proceeds

Grid generation systems are procedures for generating the curvilinear coordinate
system which defines the grid. These systems fall into two basic classes:
algebraic systems, in which the coordinates are determined by interpolation
between boundaries; and partial differential equation systems, in which the
coordinates are the solution of the differential equations. Both algebraic and
elliptic grid generation systems have been extensively surveyed in Ref. 2, and
both are discussed in some detail in Ref. 4. Elliptic generation systems for
three dimensions have recently been surveyed in Ref. 6. Other discussions appear
in Refs. 2, 5, 32 and 33, and a number of applications appear in Ref. 4. Applications to adaptive grids appear in Ref. 34-37. A natural extension of the
equidistribution concepts, expressed in terms of variational principles as
discussed above, to multiple dimensions can be made in the framework of elliptic
generation systems.

Variational Approach.

Considering the grid from a continuous viewpoint, it occurs that something should
be minimized by the grid rearrangement, and thus a variational approach is
logical. This is the natural extension of the equidistribution concept discussed
above to multiple dimensions. Such an approach is discussed by Brackbill and
Saltzman in Refs. 38-41. As noted in Ref. 7, there is a need for smoothness in
the grid in order to reduce certain terms in the truncation error of a solution
done on the grid. The quantity $\nabla \xi^i \cdot \nabla \xi^i$ represents the variation of the
curvilinear coordinates over the field, and thus is a measure of the roughness of
the grid. Therefore to maximize the smoothness of the grid it is appropriate to
minimize the integral of this quantity over the field.

Brackbill and Saltzman have noted that the Euler's variational equations for the
minimization of the sum of the Dirichlet integrals for the curvilinear coordinates
ξ^i, i.e.,

$$I_s = \iiint \sum_{i=1}^{3} \nabla \xi^i \cdot \nabla \xi^i dx_1 dx_2 dx_3 \quad (22)$$

yield the Laplace equations

$$\nabla^2 \xi^i = 0, \quad (i = 1,2,3). \quad (23a)$$

Here x_i (i = 1,2,3) and ξ^i (i = 1,2,3) are respectively the rectangular cartesian and the general curvilinear coordinates. Thus the smoothest grids are those for which the curvilinear coordinates satisfy the Laplace equations.

Emphasis on orthogonality and/or on concentration of grid lines can also be incorporated in the grid generation system by basing the system on the Euler equations for additional variational principles. Orthogonality can be emphasized by minimizing the integral I_o defined as

$$I_o \equiv \iiint [(\nabla \xi^1 \cdot \nabla \xi^2)^2 + (\nabla \xi^2 \cdot \nabla \xi^3)^2$$
$$+ (\nabla \xi^3 \cdot \nabla \xi^1)^2] g^{3/2} dx_1 dx_2 dx_3 \qquad (23b)$$

since each of these dot products vanishes for an orthogonal grid. The inclusion of the $g^{3/2}$, the cube of the Jacobian of the transformation, as a weight function in I_o is somewhat arbitrary, and was done to cause orthogonality to be emphasized more strongly in the larger cells. Finally, concentration can be emphasized by minimizing the integral I_w defined by

$$I_w \equiv \iiint w(x_1, x_2, x_3) \sqrt{g} \, dx_1 dx_2 dx_3 \qquad (24)$$

where $w(x_1, x_2, x_3)$ is a specified weight function. This causes the cells to be small where the weight function is large.

The generation system is then obtained from the Euler equations for minimization of the linear combination, I, of the smoothness, orthogonality, and concentration integrals given above:

$$I = \lambda_s I_s + \lambda_o I_o + \lambda_w I_w \qquad (25)$$

Larger values of the specified coefficients λ_s, λ_o, and λ_w place more emphasis on smoothness, orthogonality and concentration, respectively. These coefficients have been taken as constants in the results reported to date, but they could in general be taken to be variable over the field (and placed inside the integrals) in order to enhance the corresponding property locally. The resulting generation system is quasi-linear, being a linear combination of all the second derivatives, with coefficients which are nonlinear in the first derivatives. The weight function, w, is to be a function of some measure of the solution error or variation, so that the spacing will be reduced where the error or variation is large. In practice both smoothing and bounding was applied to the weight function to control grid distortion. The solution and grid were generated individually at each time step in an explicit manner. The time derivatives were transformed so that no interpolation was necessary. Some rather spectacular two-dimensional results of the grid adapting to a reflected shock are given in Ref. 40 and 41. Here the magnitude of the pressure gradient was used in the weight function.

Clearly, the integral, I_s, of Eq. (22) is the multi-dimensional generalization of the one-dimensional smoothness integral, I_2, of Eq. (6), without the weight function, and the integral, I_w, in Eq. (24) is the extension of the one-dimensional spring analogy, I_1, in Eq. (4) to multiple dimensions, with the spring extension, x_ξ, generalizing to the volume (the Jacobian, $\sqrt{g}$) in three dimensions (or area in two). This variational approach thus is a generalization of the one-dimensional equidistribution discussed above to multiple dimensions. All of the discussions of weight functions given above in regard to equidistribution therefore has relevance here to the weight function of the integral I_w in Eq. (24). (The role of the constant in the equidistribution weight function, e.g., α in Eq. (10), the one in Eq. (13), etc., which tends to produce a linear transformation, is taken by the smoothness integral, I_s in Eq. (22), which tends to produce an equally-spaced grid in multiple dimensions.)

A variational scheme which allows the grid some movement with a flow solution, but without strong distortions, was developed earlier by Yanenko, et. al. (Ref. 42, 43). Suppose the two-dimensional solution of a fluid flow problem with velocity components, u and v, is required. The idea of Yanenko, et. al., was to allow the mesh to move by minimizing a linear combination of three quantities. The first quantity measures the distortion in the mesh and is given by

$$h_1 = (\xi_x - n_y)^2 + (\xi_y + n_x)^2. \qquad (26)$$

When $h_1 = 0$, the mesh is conformal. The second measures the degree to which the grid moves with the fluid and can be expressed by the quantity

$$h_2 = (u - x_t)^2 + (v - y_t)^2. \qquad (27)$$

The third term is designed to give a fine mesh whenever the gradients of the flow variables become large. This expression could be problem dependent and take the general form

$$h_3 = q(\sqrt{g})^\alpha, \qquad \sqrt{g} = \frac{\partial(x,y)}{\partial(\xi,\eta)}$$

where $\sqrt{g}$ is again the Jacobian, q is a function of the flow gradients which may include density and energy as well as the velocity components, and α is a parameter to be selected. For the solution of gas dynamics problems, one might select q to be some linear combination

$$q = a_1|\nabla p| + a_2|\nabla u| + a_3|\nabla v| + a_4|\nabla e|, \qquad (28)$$

where in this equation $\nabla f = (f_\xi, f_\eta)$.

The grid is then to be constructed so as to minimize the functional

$$\Phi(\xi,\eta) = \iiint \psi \; dx \; dy \; dt, \qquad (29)$$

where

$$\psi = \varepsilon_1 h_1 + \varepsilon_2 h_2 + \varepsilon_3 h_3 \qquad (30)$$

and ε_1, ε_2, ε_3 are parameters. The Euler quations for this variational problem are then combined with the system of fluid flow equations to give a new system which determines the fluid variables and the coordinates of the grid points at each time step. This same technique can also be used when an error estimate is available, the moving mesh being then constructed so as to minimize the coordinate lines in the solution of flow over a blunt body. Although the procedure is formulated for general movement of the grid points, in the actual applications, the points were moved one-dimensionally along straight lines connecting the body and outer boundary. The resulting coordinate system gave good resolution of a boundary layer and shock wave.

Bell and Shubin (Ref. 44) used a similar variational approach for a one-dimensional problem. The integral to be minimized was essentially

$$I = \int [(1 + \lambda_a w(\xi)) x_\xi^2 + \lambda_b (x_\xi)_t^2] d\xi \qquad (31)$$

The first term is simply that used in the equidistribution procedures discussed above. The last term is expressed in practice as a time difference and serves to restrict the movement of the grid. The Euler equation is then

$$(1 + \lambda_a w) x_\xi + \lambda_b (x_\xi - x_\xi^{(n-1)}) = \text{constant} \qquad (32)$$

where $x_\xi^{(n-1)}$ is evaluated at the previous time step. The new grid is constructed from the integral of Eq. (32).

$$x(\xi) = \int_0^\xi \frac{C + \lambda_b x_\xi^{(n-1)}(\xi)}{1 + \lambda_a w(\xi) + \lambda_b} d\overline{\xi} \qquad (33)$$

where C is chosen such that x( ) is normalized to the interval (0,1) as usual.

Two forms for the weight function were tried, $w = |u_\xi|$ and $w = u_\xi^2$, and the former give better results. The solution and grid were generated individually at each time step, with transformed time derivatives. The weight function was smoothed before the new grid was calculated. Without the grid time derivative term in Eq. (31), the grid exhibited jerkiness and a longer time to converge. If this term was too large, however, the grid was unable to follow the shock in the application made.

Kovenya and Yanenko (Ref. 45) moved an initial coordinate system according to one-dimensional diffusion-type partial differential equations with the "diffusion" coefficients dependent on the magnitude of the gradient of the sum of the magnitudes of the physical solution quantities in one direction, and dependent on the magnitude of the body curvature in the other. Thus, with the body an η-line,

$$\frac{\partial y}{\partial t} = \frac{\partial}{\partial \eta} [(|\frac{\partial q}{\partial y}|^\beta + \varepsilon) \frac{\partial y}{\partial \eta}], \quad \frac{\partial x}{\partial t} = \frac{\partial}{\partial \xi} [(\delta |K|^{\beta_1} + \varepsilon) \frac{\partial x}{\partial \xi}] \qquad (34)$$

with q defined as the sum of the magnitudes of the physical solution quantities, K the body curvature, and β, β_1, δ, and ε being chosen constants. The problem treated was the blunt body shock. The coordinate system and physical solution were done in separate time steps, several steps of the former being taken between each step of the latter.

Examples were given of adaption to both the bow shock and the boundary layer. Grid oscillations occurring for high Reynolds number were countered by freezing the coordinate system as the steady state was approached. The generation system of Winslow (Ref. 37) is also in the form of diffusion equations.

Attraction Approach

A different approach to dynamically adaptive grids was taken by Rai and Anderson

(Ref. 46-49). Here instead of generating new grid point locations through the solution of partial differential equations, the grid points move directly under the influence of mutual attraction or repulsion between points. This is accomplished by assigning to each point an attraction proportional to the difference between the magnitude of some measure of error (or solution variation) and the average magnitude of this measure over all points. This causes points with values of this measure that exceed the average to attract other points, and thus to reduce the local spacing, while points with a measure less than the average will repel other points and hence increase the spacing. This attraction is attenuated by an inverse power of the point separation in the transformed field. The collective attraction of all other points is then made to induce a velocity for each grid point. Since each point is influenced by all other points this is effectively an elliptic generation system also.

A means of including terms that will induce rotational motion into the grid has been devised to cause the grid lines to align with lines of high gradients such as shocks. The adaptive grid essentially eliminated the postshock oscillations that occurred with the fixed grid. An example of alignment with a curved shock appears in Ref. 46.

Since this procedure has all grid points moving to cause some measure to approach uniformity over the field, it can be considered an iterative approach to the equidistribution of this measure over the field. This procedure does not exercise any control over either the smoothness or orthogonality of the grid, so that distortion is possible. Collapse of points into each other is, however, impeded because the attraction will become repulsion as the points approach each other, since the measure which drives the motion will drop below the average as the spacing decreases. Collapse is further impeded by the fact that the grid velocities decrease with the spacing. It has been found necessary to apply some limits and some damping of the grid speeds to prevent grid oscillation and distortion. In practice, the computed grid speeds were scaled so that the maximum over the field was a set value, but with the maximum scaling also limited. Provision was also made for exponential damping of the grid speeds according to the ratio of the maximum Jacobian to a specified value.

A Relaxation Procedure

Eiseman (Ref. 50) gives a relaxation procedure to implement adaption in both directions of a two-dimensional system. This procedure is equivalent to an iterative adjustment of the grid points to achieve equidistribution individually along each family of coordinate lines with the weight function

$$
w^{(i)} = (1 + \sum_j \alpha_j M_j) A \sqrt{1 + u_s^2 s_{\xi^i}} \qquad (i = 1,2) \qquad (35)
$$

with s being arc length along the lines on which ξ^i varies, and A being the area on the solution surface, and thus is also elliptic in nature, the M_i are solution properties, e.g. curvature, and the α_i are constants. With no solution properties, M_i included, this becomes a generalization of the solution arc length form of White (Ref. 18), cf. Eq. (13) above, while with only the solution curvature included as an M_i, this is a generalization of the curvature form of Ablow and Schecter (Ref.21), cf. Eq. (20) above.

Moving Finite Elements

The moving finite element method of Miller (Ref. 51, 52) is a dynamically-adaptive finite element grid method in which the grid point locations are made additional dependent variables in a Galerkin formulation. The solution is expanded in piecewise linear functions, in terms of its values at the grid points and those of the grid point locations on each element. The residual is then required to be orthogonal to all the basis functions for both the solution and the grid. The grid point locations are thus obtained as part of the finite element solution. An internodal viscosity was introduced to penalize the relative motion between the grid points. This does not penalize the absolute motion of the points. An internodal repulsive force was also introduced in Ref. 52 to maintain a minimum point separation. Both of these effects are strong but of short range. A small long range attractive force was also introduced to keep the nodes more equally spaced in the absence of solution gradients. Small time steps were used in the initial development of the solution. The results show that the oscillations typically associated with shock with fixed grids are removed with the adaptive grid. Results for several problems are given in Ref. 52 and 53. In Ref. 53 some tests were conducted with the moving finite element method which show that dispersion and dissipation are essentially eliminated. Square waves are convected exactly as is shown in comparison with other methods. Numerous other examples are given for various equations. An order of magnitude increase in stability is realized over conventional methods. This work makes it clear that the key to reducing dispersion is adaptive grids.

CONCLUSION

The ultimate answer to numerical solution of partial differential equations may well be dynamically-adaptive grids, rather than more elaborate difference representations and solution methods. It has been noted by several authors that when the grid is right, most numerical solution methods work well. Oscillations associated with cell Reynolds number and with shocks in fluid mechanics computations have been shown to be eliminated with adaptive grids. Even the numerical viscosity introduced by upwind differencing is reduced as the grid adapts to regions of large solution variation. The results have clearly indicated that accurate numerical solutions can be obtained when the grid points are properly located.

It is also clear that there is considerable commonality among the various approaches to adaptive grids. All are essentially variational methods for the extremization of some solution property. The explicit use of variational principles allows effective control to be exercised over the conflicting requirements of smoothness, orthogonality, and concentration, and this is probably the most promising approach in multiple dimensions. The adaptive grid is most effective when it is dynamically coupled with the solution, so that the solution and the grid are solved for together in a single continuous problem. The most fruitful directions for future effort thus are probably in the development and direct application of variational principles and in intimate coupling of the grid with the solution.

REFERENCES

1. Thompson, Joe F., "General Curvilinear Coordinate Systems," Numerical Grid Generation, Ed. Joe F. Thompson, North-Holland 1982.

2. Thompson, J. F., Warsi, Z. U. A. and Mastin, C. W., "Boundary-Fitted Coordinate Systems for Numerical Solution of Partial Differential Equations - A Review," Journal of Computational Physics, Vol. 47, 1982, pp. 1-108.

3. Smith, Robert E., Numerical Grid Generation Techniques, NASA Conference Publication 2166, NASA Langley Research Center, 1980.

4. Thompson, Joe F., Numerical Grid Generation, Ed. Joe F. Thompson, North-Holland, 1982.

5. Thompson, J. F., "A Survey of Grid Generation Techniques in Computational Dynamics," AIAA-83-0447, AIAA 21st Aerospace Sciences Meeting, Reno, January 1983.

6. Thompson, Joe F. and Warsi, Zahir U. A., "Three-Dimensional Grid Generation from Elliptic Systems," AIAA Computational Fluid Dynamics Conference, Danvers, Massachussets, July, 1983.

7. Thompson, Joe F. and Mastin, C. Wayne, "Order of Difference Expressions on Curvilinear Coordinate Systems, "Advances in Grid Generation", ASME Fluids Engineering Conference, Houston, June, 1983.

8. Mastin, C. Wayne, "Error Induced by Coordinate Systems," Numerical Grid Generation, Ed. Joe F. Thompson, North-Holland, 1982.

9. Babuska, I. and Rheinboldt, W. C., "A-Posteriori Error Estimates for the Finite Element Method, "International Journal for Numerical Methods in Engineering, Vol. 12, 1978, p. 1597.

10. Russell, R. D. and Christiansen, J., "Adaptive Mesh Selection Strategies for Solving Boundary Value Problems," SIAM J. Numer. Anal., Vol. 15, 1978, p. 59.

11. Pereyra, V. and Sewell, E. G., "Mesh Selection for Discrete Solution of Boundary-Value Problems in Ordinary Differential Equations," Numer. Math., Vol. 23, 1975, pp. 261-268.

12. Lentini, M. and Pereyra, V., "An Adaptive Finite Difference Solver for Nonlinear Two-Point Boundary Problems with Mild Boundary Layers," SIAM J. Numer. Anal., Vol. 14, 1977, p. 91.

13. Davis, Stephen F. and Flaherty, Joseph E., "An Adaptive Finite Element Method for Initial-Boundary Value Problems for Partial Differential Equations, "SIAM J. Sci. Stat. Comput., Vol. 3, 1982, pp. 6-27.

14. Carey, Graham F., "Adaptive Refinement and Nonlinear Fluid Problems," Computer Methods in Applied Mechanics and Engineering, Vol. 17/18, 1979, pp. 541-460.

15. Carey, Graham F. and Humphrey, David L., "Mesh Refinement and Iterative Solution Methods for Finite Element Computations," International Journal for Numerical Methods in Engineering, Vol. 17, 1981, pp. 1717-1734.

16. Rheinboldt, Werner C., "Adaptive Mesh Refinement Process for Finite Element Solutions," International Journal for Numerical Methods in Engineering, Vol. 17, 1981, pp. 649-662.

17. Denny, V. E. and Landis, R. B., "A New Method for Solving Two-Point Boundary-Value Problems Using Optimal Node Distribution," Journal of Computational Physics, Vol. 9, 1972, pp. 120-137.

18. White, Andrew B., Jr., "On Selection of Equidistributing Meshes for Two-Point Boundary-Value Problems," SIAM J. Numerical Analysis, Vol. 16, 1979, p. 472.

19. White, Andrew B., Jr., "On the Numerical Solution of Initial Bounday-Value Problems in One Space Dimension," SIAM J. of Numer. Analysis, 1982, p. 683.

20. Ablow, C. M., "Equidistant Mesh for Gas Dynamic Calculations," Numerical Grid Generation, Ed. Joe F. Thompson, North-Holland, 1982.

21. Ablow, C. M. and Schechter, S., "Campylotropic Coordinates," Journal of Computational Physics, Vol. 27, 1978, pp. 351-363.

22. Dwyer, Harry A., Smooke, Mitchell D. and Kee, Robert J., "Adaptive Griding for Finite Difference Solutions to Heat and Mass Transfer Problems," Numerical Grid Generation, Ed. Joe F. Thompson, North-Holland, 1982.

23. Dwyer, H. A., Kee, R. J. and Sanders, B. R., "Adaptive Grid Method for Problems in Fluid Mechanics and Heat Transfer," AIAA J., Vol. 18, 1980, p. 1205.

24. Dwyer, H. A., Raiszadah, F. and Otey, G., "A Study of Reactive Diffusion Problems with Stiff Integrators and Adaptive Grids," Lecture Notes in Physics, Vol. 141, 1981, p. 170, Springer-Verlag.

25. Dwyer, H. A., Kee, R. J., Barr, P. K. and Sanders, B. R., "Transient Droplet Heating at High Peclet Number," J. of Fluids Engineering, Vol. 105, 1983, p. 83.

26. Dwyer, H. A., "Grid Adaption for Problems with Separation, Cell Reynolds Number, Shock-Boundary Layer Interaction and Accuracy," AIAA Paper No. 83-0449, presented at AIAA 21st Aerospace Sciences Meeting, Reno 1983.

27. Dwyer, H. A., Sanders, B. R. and Raiszadeh, R., "Ignition and Flame Propagation Studies with Adaptive Numerical Grids," to appear in Combustion and Flame.

28. Gnoffo, Peter A., "A Vectorized, Finite-Volume, Adaptive-Grid Algorithm for Navier-Stokes Calculations," Numerical Grid Generation, Ed. Joe F. Thompson, North-Holland, 1982.

29. Gnoffo, P. A., "A Vectorized Finite-Volume, Adaptive Grid Algorithm Applied To Planetary Entry Problems," AIAA Paper 82-1018 presented at AIAA/ASME 3rd Joint Thermophysics, Fluids, Plasma, and Heat Transfer Conference, St. Louis, Missouri, 1982.

30. Tolstykh, A. I., "Condensation of Grid Points in the Process of Solving and Using High-Accuracy Schemes for the Numerical Investigation of Viscous Gas Flows," USSR Comput. Math. Math. Phys., Vol. 18, 1979, p. 134; see also Lecture Notes in Physics, Vol. 90, 1979, p. 507, Springer-Verlag.

31. Acharya, S. and Patankar, S. V., "Use of An Adaptive Grid for Parabolic Flows," AIAA Paper 82-1015, presented at the AIAA/ASME 3rd Joint Thermophysics, Fluids, Plasma and Heat Transfer Conference, St. Louis, Missouri, 1982.

32. Thompson, Joe F., "Elliptic Grid Generation," Numerical Grid Generation,
     Ed. Joe F. Thompson, North-Holland, 1982.

33. Warsi, Z. U. A., "Basic Differential Models for Coordinate Generation,"
     Numerical Grid Generation, Ed. Joe F. Thompson, North-Holland 1982.

34. Hindman, R. G. and Spencer, J., "A New Approach to Truly Adaptive Grid
     Generation," AIAA Paper 83-0450, presented at AIAA 21st Aerospace Sciences
     Meeting, Reno, January 1983.

35. Hindman, R. G., Kutler, P. and Anderson, D., "Two-Dimensional Unsteady
     Euler-Equation Solver for Arbitrarily Shaped Flow Regions," AIAA Journal,
     Vol. 19, 1981, pp. 424-431.

36. Freeman, L. Michael, The Use of an Adaptive Grid in a Solution of the
     Navier-Stokes Equations for Incompressible Flows, Ph.D. Dissertation,
     Mississippi State University, 1982.

37. Winslow, Alan M., "Adaptive Mesh Zoning by the Equipotential Method,;
     UCID-19062, Lawrence Livermore Laboratory, 1981.

38. Brackbill, J. U. and Saltzman, J. S., "Adaptive Zoning for Singular Problems
     in Two Dimensions," Journal of Computational Physics, Vol. 46, pp. 342-368,
     1982.

39. Brackbill, J. U., "Coordinate System Control: Adaptive Meshes," Numerical
     Grid Generation, Ed. Joe F. Thompson, North-Holland 1982.

40. Saltzman, Jeffery and Brackbill, Jeremiah, "Applications and Generalizations
     of Variational Methods for Generating Adaptive Meshes," Numerical Grid
     Generation, Ed. Joe F. Thompson, North-Holland 1982.

41. Saltzman, J., "A Variational Method for Generating Multi-Dimensional Adaptive
     Grids", Report DOE/ER/03077-174, Courant Mathematics and Computing Laboratory,
     New York University, New York 1982.

42. Yanenko, N. N., Kovenya, V. M., Lisejkin, V. D., Fomin, V. M. and Vorozhtsov,
     E. V., Comput. Method. Appl. Mech. Eng., Vol. 17/18, 1979, p. 659.

43. Yanenko, N. N., Kroshko, E. A., Liseikin, V. V., Fomin, V. M., Shapeev, V. P.
     and Shitov, Y. A., "Methods for the Construction of Moving Grids for Problems
     of Fluid Dynamics with Big Deformations," Lecture Notes in Physics, Vol. 59,
     1976, p. 454, Springer-Verlag.

44. Bell, J. B. and Shubin, G. R., "An Adaptive Grid Finite Difference Method
     for Conservation Laws," to appear, 1983.

45. Kovenya, V. M. and Yanenko, N. N., USSR Comput. Math, Math, Phys., Vol. 19,
     1980, p. 178.

46. Anderson, Dale A. and Rai, M. M., "The Use of Solution Adaptive Grids in
     Solving Partial Differential Equations," Numerical Grid Generation, Ed.
     Joe F. Thompson, North-Holland, 1982.

47. Rai, Man Mohan and Anderson, D. A., "Grid Evolution in Time Asymptotic
     Problems," Journal of Computational Physics, Vol. 43, 1981, pp. 327-344.

48. Rai, M. M. and Anderson, D. A., "Application of Adaptive Grids to Fluid-Flow
     Problems with Asymptotic Solutions," AIAA Journal, Vol. 20, 1982, pp. 496-502.

49. Anderson, Dale A., "Solution Adaptive Grids for Partial Differential Equations," in ARO Report 82-3, <u>Proceedings of 1982 Army Numerical Analysis and Computer Conference</u>, Vicksburg, MS 1982.

50. Eiseman, P. R., "Adaptive Grid Generation by Mean Value Relaxation," ASME Applied Mechanics, Bioengineering and Fluids Engineering Conference, Houston, June 1983.

51. Miller, Keith and Miller, Robert N., "Moving Finite Elements I," <u>SIAM J. Numer. Anal.</u>, Vol. 18, 1981, pp. 1019-1032.

52. Miller, Keith, "Moving Finite Elements II," <u>SIAM J. Numer. Anal.</u>, Vol. 18, 1981, pp. 1033-1057.

53. Gelinas, R. J., and Doss, S. K., "The Moving Finite Element Method: Applications to General Partial Differential Equations with Multiple Large Gradients", <u>Journal of Computational Physics</u>, Vol. 40, 1981, pp. 202-249.

DISCUSSION

Speaker: J. Thompson

Yanenko: It is not always possible to construct a unique grid for a very complex domain. Then it is necessary to subdivide and construct a partial grid on each subdomain. Have you any comments on this?

Thompson: I agree. This is especially important in three space dimensions, and I would always recommend that three-dimensional calculations make provisions for subdivision of the whole domain. This also helps to take into effect changes in the type of equation in different parts of the domain.

Yanenko: I believe that such adaptive grid techniques are very well worthwhile, especially for complex flow problems. The attached figures (slides were shown here) show two calculations which we performed, giving an example of the benefits; one is an example of a jet, and the other of a flow with a sharp barrier. In both cases it was possible to calculate a satisfactory grid.

Brandt: There is a decision to be made, whether to move grid points around or to add extra grid points in places where there is trouble. You gave quite a strong argument against adding new points by showing that this can lead to additional sources of truncation error, if it is not done right. Have you thought about how to do it right?

Thompson: I have not really thought about that, because using a moving grid you actually work with a fixed, transformed grid. Hence the number of points is constant. I do not think you can say that one approach is always better than the other; but you should certainly take into account the truncation errors coming directly from the non-uniform spacing, whether you generate that by moving the grid or by adding extra points.

Brandt: I believe you have to add pieces of grid to do it right.

Thompson: I agree; the idea of segmenting the region effectively does that. I also might mention that I believe multigrid techniques are equally applicable to curved and moving grids; and I am sure you will agree with me there!

Schönauer: If we have complicated systems of PDE's, as in compressible fluid mechanics with chemical reactions, and we use non-orthogonal grids, we get a lot of additional terms, with mixed derivatives. Would it not be better to retain the orthogonality of the grid?

Thompson: I believe not. Often the "additional terms" are already in the equations; but even if not, the penalty is well worth paying in terms of the error reduction achieved.

Young: How do you solve the equations? Do you consider the original differential equations and the grid equations separately, or do you consider them all together?

Thompson: It has been done both ways; and, rather commonly, simultaneously. Point S.O.R seems particularly well suited to generating the grid solution, but I don't think that anyone has shown that one way is better than another.

Stetter: In hyperbolic systems, can you generate a grid of characteristics?

Thompson: Effectively, yes. It is possible to get the grid to follow the characteristics if you set up the grid equation suitably.

PDE SOFTWARE: Modules, Interfaces and Systems
B. Engquist and T. Smedsaas (eds.)
Elsevier Science Publishers B.V. (North-Holland)
© IFIP, 1984

THE $n_{1/2}$ METHOD OF ALGORITHM ANALYSIS

Roger W. Hockney

Computer Science Department
Reading University
Reading, Berks, RG6 2AX
U.K.

The parameter $n_{1/2}$ measures the effect of vector length on the performance of a parallel computer, and varies from zero for a serial computer to infinity for an infinite parallel array. Given the serial and parallel operations' counts of the algorithm, the parameter $n_{1/2}$ can be used to select quantitatively the best algorithm to use on a particular parallel computer. The $n_{1/2}$ method of algorithm analysis is a straightforward and natural extension of the traditional method which is based solely on the serial operations' count. The results of such analyses are given for a number of problems including solving tridiagonal systems and Poisson's equation.

I.   INTRODUCTION

The advent of the new generation of parallel computers presents the numerical analyst with new problems. After questions of numerical convergence and accuracy have been satisfactorily answered, there remains the question of the selection of the best algorithm to solve a particular problem on a particular computer. If we consider "best" to be synonymous with the least execution time, then it is necessary to take into account the timing characteristics of the computer involved. The simplest assumption to make is that an algorithm is a sequence of vector instructions, and that the time to execute a vector instruction is linearly dependent on the length of the vectors involved. In this case, the timing can be characterized by two parameters: r_∞, the asymptotic performance for infinitely long vectors; and $n_{1/2}$, the vector length necessary to achieve half the asymptotic performance. These parameters are defined and their significance discussed in section II. Although conceived in terms of pipelined vector computers, it is shown in this section how the characterization can be interpreted to apply also to arrays of processors and even to MIMD computers.

In order to time an algorithm on the serial computer it is only necessary to know its total amount of arithmetic - often called the work or serial operations' count - because the computer time is directly proportional to this number. On a parallel computer, however, the work is collected into a smaller number of vector operations, in each of which many elemental arithmetic operations are executed in parallel by either pipelining or the simultaneous use of many arithmetic units. There is a timing overhead associated with the initiation of each of these parallel or vector operations. This overhead is proportional to the $n_{1/2}$ of the computer and must be included in the timing comparison. In fact parallel computers differ more in the extent of this overhead than they do in their asymptotic performance. In estimating the timing of an algorithm on a parallel computer it is therefore necessary to know, and include the effect of, both the

serial and parallel operations' count. The general formulae for doing so are
derived in Section III.

The choice of the best algorithm on a particular computer clearly depends only on
the $n_{\frac{1}{2}}$ of the computer and the serial and parallel operations' counts of the
algorithms. Quite obviously the value of r_∞ does not affect the choice because it
multiplies the time of all algorithms by the same factor.

The performance of an algorithm, that is to say the inverse of its time of
execution, can be expressed as a relation between some measure of the size of the
problem, n, and the $n_{\frac{1}{2}}$ of the computer. It is natural therefore to consider the
relative performance of competing algorithms on a phase plane defined by n and $n_{\frac{1}{2}}$,
or scaled values of these variables. For every pair of values for these
variables it is possible to compute which of a menu of possible algorithms has the
least execution time, and to mark that point of the phase plane as belonging to
that algorithm. In this way the whole phase plane can be marked into regions in
which different algorithms have the least execution time. These regions are
divided by lines of equal performance between the algorithms lying to either side
of the line. Such phase diagrams are given for a number of problems and
algorithms in Section IV.

One of the problems facing the writers of software packages for PDEs on parallel
computers is the choice of the most suitable algorithm and its optimal parameters.
We present the $n_{\frac{1}{2}}$ method of algorithm analysis as a rational way of introducing
the characteristics of the parallel computer hardware into the method of choice.
Since $n_{\frac{1}{2}}$ can be used to characterize a wide variety of computer designs (see
Section II) including pipelined, array and MIMD computers, it is a unifying
concept that greatly simplifies the problem of choosing algorithms. There is no
reason why the choice of algorithm and its parameters should not be made automatically by the software using the formulae obtained from the $n_{\frac{1}{2}}$ analyses of the
available algorithms.

II.   THE PARAMETERS r_∞ and $n_{\frac{1}{2}}$

It has been shown by Hockney and Jesshope [1] how both pipelined vector computers
like the CRAY-1 and Cyber 205, and array-like computers such as the ICL DAP, can
be compared on a common basis by considering the timing equation for a vector
operation. If this is given the generic form:

$$t = r_\infty^{-1}(n+n_{\frac{1}{2}}) \tag{1}$$

then the two parameters $n_{\frac{1}{2}}$ and r_∞ completely characterize the timing behaviour.
The parameters are defined as:

r_∞:   (maximum or asymptotic performance) the maximum number of elemental
        arithmetic operations (i.e. operations between pairs of numbers) per
        second, usually measured in megaflops. This occurs for infinite
        vector length on the generic computer.

$n_{\frac{1}{2}}$:   (half-performance length) the vector length required to achieve half
        the maximum performance

Alternatively, for array-like computers, the timing expression is more usefully
written as:

$$t = \pi^{-1}(1+n/n_{\frac{1}{2}}) \tag{2}$$

π: (specific performance) is defined as the ratio $r_\infty/n_{\frac{1}{2}}$.

An array-like design such as the ICL DAP [1] with N processors is included in the formalism by taking either $n_{\frac{1}{2}}=N/2$ if n>N, or $n_{\frac{1}{2}}=\infty$ if there are always enough processors, i.e. when n<N. The value of π is the inverse of the time for one parallel operation of the array.

The significance of the above parameters is as follows:

$n_{\frac{1}{2}}$: measures how parallel the computer appears to the user, and varies from $n_{\frac{1}{2}}=0$ for a serial computer, to $n_{\frac{1}{2}}=\infty$ for an infinitely parallel array. It includes the effect of any timing overhead associated with the initialization of the operation. It is the parameter that measures the effect of vector length on the performance of an algorithm, and therefore determines the choice of the best algorithm on a particular computer.

r_∞: measures the performance of a computer on long vectors (i.e. those for which $n>n_{\frac{1}{2}}$).

π: measures the performance of a computer on short vectors (i.e. those for which $n<n_{\frac{1}{2}}$). Note that for an array-like computer with enough processors (n<N), $n_{\frac{1}{2}}=\infty$ and all vectors are short.

The parameter $n_{\frac{1}{2}}$ can also characterize the behaviour of MIMD computers such as the Denelcor HEP [2], if it is appropriately defined. For such computers the main overhead is that due to synchronization, and unlike a vector computer the arithmetic operations performed in parallel do not have to be the same; indeed they may be quite unrelated programs. Accordingly the definition of $n_{\frac{1}{2}}$ is generalized to mean the total amount of arithmetic that must be included between two successive synchronization points in an MIMD program in order to achieve half the maximum performance of the computer [3]. The synchronization points are, for example, the FORK that initiates several independent processes to be executed by separate instruction streams possibly on separate processors, and the corresponding JOIN at which the control program waits for all the processes to finish. The total amount of arithmetic is the total of all the arithmetic operations between pairs of numbers in all the processes. A theoretical analysis of the timing of the Denelcor HEP is given in [3], and confirmed by measurements of r_∞ and $n_{\frac{1}{2}}$ reported in [4].

The above characterization of computer performance using two parameters naturally leads to plotting computers as points on the $(n_{\frac{1}{2}},r_\infty)$ parameter plane. Computers can usually operate in several different modes which are characterized by different values for the parameters. A computer then appears as a constellation of points on such a diagram, which is known as the "Spectrum of Computers". Several such diagrams have appeared in references [1],[3],[5] and [6], and two are reproduced here in Figs. 1 and 2. Because of the greater programming flexibility of an MIMD computer, the values of $n_{\frac{1}{2}}$ for SIMD and MIMD are not directly comparable. Generally speaking much larger values of $n_{\frac{1}{2}}$ are acceptable on MIMD computers, because very large sections of code can be executed in parallel. This easily gives very large values of n in Eqn. (1), and the desirable condition that $n>>n_{\frac{1}{2}}$.

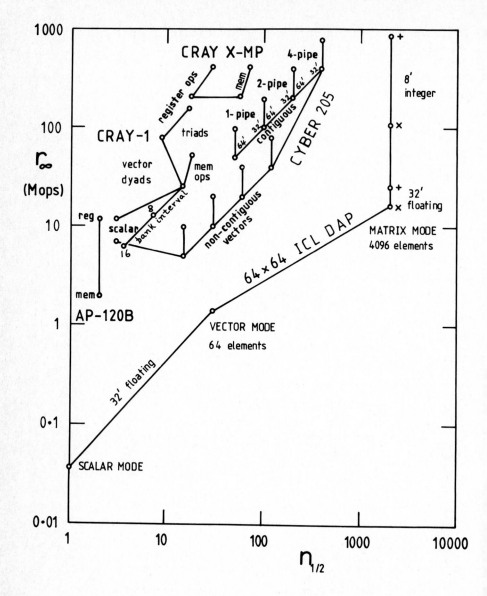

Fig. 1. The spectrum of SIMD computers, showing the Cray-1, Cray X-MP, CDC Cyber 205, ICL DAP, and FPS AP-120B. (From reference [3], courtesy of Springer-Verlag.)

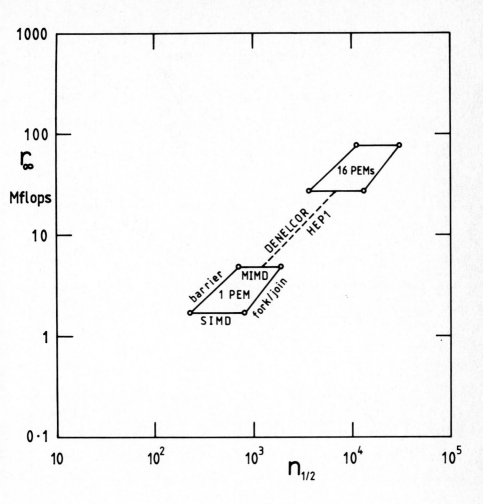

Fig. 2. The spectrum of MIMD computers, showing the Denelcor HEP. Drawn from the measurements of Hockney and Snelling [4]. SIMD refers to element-by-element vector multiply as in Fig. 1. MIMD refers to a more typical MIMD program containing the conditional evaluation of sine/cosine and exponential functions.

III.   CHARACTERIZING PARALLEL ALGORITHMS

To a first approximation an algorithm may be considered as a sequence of parallel operations, each of which obeys the timing relation (1). For SIMD computers, whether pipelined vector computers or processor arrays, the parallel operation means a vector instruction and the variable n is the number of elements in each vector involved. For MIMD computers the parallel operation is all the work between a pair of synchronization points, and the variable n is the total amount of arithmetic within such a pair, as previously explained. Using the definition of n that is appropriate in any particular case, the time T for the execution of an algorithm can be written:

$$T = \sum_{i=1}^{i=q} r_\infty^{-1}(n_i + n_{\frac{1}{2}})$$
(3)

where

q is the number of parallel operations making up the algorithm

n_i is the amount of arithmetic in the ith parallel operation

If the parameters r_∞ and $n_{\frac{1}{2}}$ are approximately the same for all the operations, or suitable average values are taken, then r_∞ and $n_{\frac{1}{2}}$ may be taken out of the · summation, and Eqn. (3) may be written:

$$T = r_\infty^{-1}(s + n_{\frac{1}{2}}q)$$
(4)

where

$s = \sum_{i=1}^{i=q} n_i$ is the total amount of arithmetic in the algorithm, or serial

operations' count.

Much work on parallel algorithms for MIMD computers is concerned with dividing the problem into, p, independent parallel instruction streams between points at which synchronization is unavoidable. Each stream is given to a separate process or processor and ideally all such processes should finish at the same time, because otherwise some processes will become idle. The effectiveness with which this is achieved is measured by the EFFICIENCY, E_p, as defined by Kuck [7], and this can be included in the timing formula as follows:

$$T = r_\infty^{-1}(s/E_p + n_{\frac{1}{2}}q)$$
(5)

Alternatively the time for the execution of an algorithm can be written in terms of the average length, $\bar{n}$, of a parallel operation in the algorithm, either as

$$T = r_\infty^{-1}q(\bar{n}/E_p + n_{\frac{1}{2}})$$
(6a)

where $\bar{n} = s/q$, or as

$$T = r_\infty^{-1}s(E_p^{-1} + n_{\frac{1}{2}}/\bar{n})$$
(6b)

The expression in parenthesis in Eqn. (6b) is the factor by which a traditional serial complexity analysis, $r_\infty^{-1}s$, is in error when applied in a parallel environment. It also shows that it is not the absolute value of $n_{\frac{1}{2}}$ which is important, but its ratio to the average length of a parallel operation in the algorithm: i.e. the ratio $n_{\frac{1}{2}}/\bar{n}$.

If the parallel operation is a single vector operation, the independent instruction streams are all identical and comprise a single arithmetic operation. Such a simple operation is performed with unit efficiency by assigning one process to each element of the vector, because all processes finish at the same time and none become idle. The timing is then given by Eqn. (4), which is the timing equation for a pipelined vector computer. Thus we regard Eqn. (4) as a special case of Eqn. (5): a case which applies for vector computation when $E_p = 1$.

When algorithms are compared on the same computer, we take the ratio of two timing expressions of the form of Eqn. (5). The algorithm is fully described by giving the operations' counts s and q (or n and s or q) and, if necessary, the efficiency E_p. The computer is described by the two parameters r_∞ and $n_{\frac{1}{2}}$. In taking the ratio of two timing expressions to determine the best algorithm, the value of r_∞ cancels out, since it affects both algorithms equally. Thus we find that the choice of the best algorithm on a particular computer depends only on the $n_{\frac{1}{2}}$ of the computer.

When comparing algorithms, equal performance lines play a key role. If $T^{(a)}$ and $T^{(b)}$ are the execution times for algorithms (a) and (b) respectively, then the equal performance line is defined by the condition that $T^{(a)} = T^{(b)}$, from which we obtain:

$$n_{\frac{1}{2}} = \frac{s^{(b)}/E_p^{(b)} - s^{(a)}/E_p^{(a)}}{q^{(a)} - q^{(b)}} \qquad (7)$$

Because of the nature of the characterization, $n_{\frac{1}{2}}$ always appears linearly in equations for equal performance lines. It may therefore be set explicitly on the left-hand-side of such equations. It is a property of the computer, as seen through the compilers and assemblers that are used. The right-hand-side, however, depends only on the operations' counts and efficiencies of the two algorithms, and is likely to be a complicated non-linear function of the size of the problem n. This might be the order of the matrices in a matrix problem, or the number of mesh points along a side in a finite difference approximation to a PDE problem.

The manner of presenting the results of an algorithm comparison is important. Formulae such as Eqn. (7) contain the result, but cannot be used without extensive computation, and in complicated cases, tables of numbers soon become unmanageable. Clearly a graphical presentation is to be preferred, which will allow the choice of algorithm to be made directly from the information that defines the problem. Such a presentation can be made by plotting equal performance lines between pairs of algorithms on the $(n_{\frac{1}{2}}, n)$ plane. These lines divide the plane into regions in which each of the competing algorithms has the best performance. We call such a presentation a "Phase Diagram" in analogy with such diagrams in physical chemistry. In the case of the chemical phase diagram, the value of parameters describing the conditions (e.g. temperature and pressure) determine a point in a parameter plane that is divided into regions in which the different states of matter have the lowest energy. One could say that nature then chooses this state from all others as the best for the material. In the case of the algorithmic phase diagram, parameters describing the computer and problem size determine a point in a parameter plane that is divided into regions in which each algorithm has the least execution time. This algorithm is then chosen as the best.

It is helpful to adopt certain standards in the presentation of such algorithmic phase diagrams, in order to make comparisons between them easier. It is good practice to make the x-axis equal to or proportional to $n_{\frac{1}{2}}$, and the y-axis equal

to or proportional to the problem size n. In this way algorithms suitable for
the more serial computers (small $n_{\frac{1}{2}}$) appear to the left of the diagram, and
those suitable for the more parallel computers (large $n_{\frac{1}{2}}$) to the right.

Similarly, algorithms suitable for small problems are shown at the bottom of the
diagram, and those suitable for large problems at the top. A logarithmic scale is
usually desirable for both axes, and in the simplest case of the $(n_{\frac{1}{2}},n)$ plane,
the horizontal axis specifies the computer and the vertical axis the problem size.
Some examples of algorithmic phase diagrams are given in Figs. 3 to 5, and
explained in the next section.

We have seen in Eqn. (6b) that the ratio $n_{\frac{1}{2}}/\bar{n}$ is more important in the timing of
an algorithm than $n_{\frac{1}{2}}$ itself. Similarly we find that algorithmic phase diagrams
are usually more compactly drawn if the x-axis is equal to the ratio of $n_{\frac{1}{2}}$ to
problem size: i.e. $n_{\frac{1}{2}}/n$. This ratio, rather than $n_{\frac{1}{2}}$ itself, determines whether
one is computing in a serial environment (small values) or parallel environment
(large values). It also has the additional advantage of being independent of
the units used to measure n.

IV.   SOME EXAMPLES OF PHASE DIAGRAMS

The first example considered is the solution of tridiagonal systems of equations
using scalar cyclic reduction (Hockney [5]). Two alternative formulations
present themselves, the SERICR and PARACR algorithms. In the SERICR variant
which is designed for serial computers, the total number of arithmetic operations,
s, is kept to a minimum. The vector length starts at n/2, where n is the number
of equations, halves itself at each reduction stage of the algorithm, and finally
becomes one if n is a power of two. At this point the solution for one variable
is found. The values of the other variables are then computed in an expansion
phase in which the vector length doubles at each stage, finally returning to a
vector length of n/2.

Because the vector length becomes very short for part of the algorithm, SERICR
is not well suited for computation on highly parallel computers. For this reason
the alternative formulation, PARACR, was devised. This maximizes the vector
length, keeping it at n throughout the algorithm. At the last stage of reduction,
the solution for all the variables is obtained in one parallel operation, hence
there is no need for the expansion phase. PARACR minimizes the number of parallel
operations, q, at the expense of increasing the total amount of arithmetic, s.

PARACR is clearly suited for computation on highly parallel computers, and the
question arises: "how parallel (as measured by $n_{\frac{1}{2}}$) does your computer have to be,
before it is advantageous to use the PARACR algorithm instead of the SERICR
algorithm?". Such a question is answered by computing the equal performance line
between the two algorithms, and drawing the algorithmic phase diagram shown in
Fig. 3. The equal performance line is given by:

$$n_{\frac{1}{2}} = 2.4n(1-1.42/\log_2 n) \tag{8}$$

In order to compress the phase diagram it is advantageous to scale the x-axis and
use the parameter plane $(n_{\frac{1}{2}}/n,n)$. This makes the diagram less easy to interpret,
but is really unavoidable if a compact presentation is desired.

Lines of constant $n_{\frac{1}{2}}$, corresponding to a particular computer, are vertical in
the $(n_{\frac{1}{2}},n)$ plane. However in the scaled axes these lines lie at 45 degrees to the
axes, running from the top left to the bottom right. The diagonal bisecting

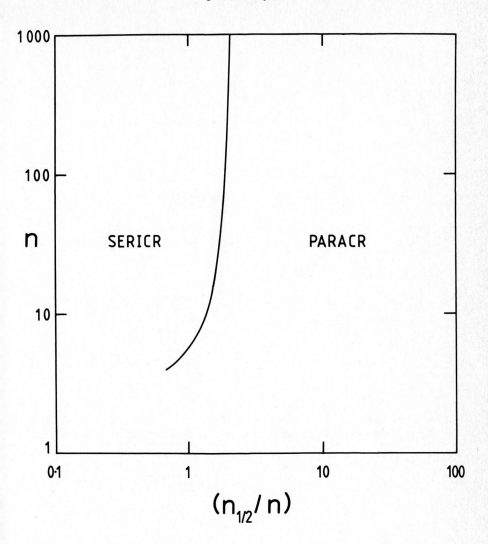

Fig. 3. The algorithmic phase diagram for the solution of a single tridiagonal system of n equations using cyclic reduction. The parameter plane is divided into regions in which either the serial form of the algorithm (SERICR) or the parallel form (PARACR) has the least execution time. (From Hockney [5], courtesy of North-Holland.)

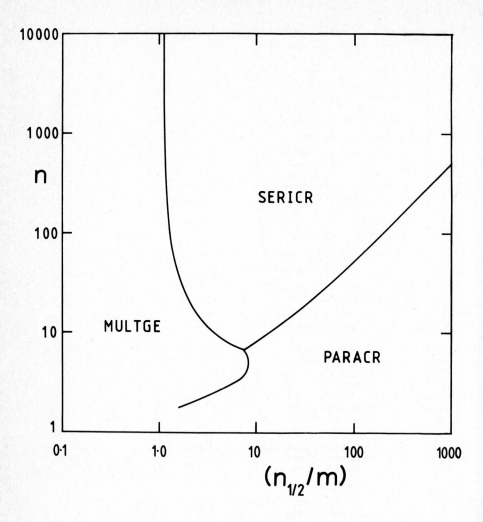

Fig. 4. The algorithmic phase diagram for the solution of multiple tridiagonal systems of n equations. The method indicated is applied to the m systems in parallel. MULTGE refers to Gaussian elimination. (From Hockney [5], courtesy of North Holland.)

Fig. 3 corresponds to $n_{\frac{1}{2}}$=100, that is to say to computers with characteristics similar to the CDC Cyber 205 (see Fig. 1). The phase diagram predicts that for tridiagonal systems shorter than about n=55 the PARACR algorithm should be used, whereas longer systems should be solved with SERICR. The CRAY-1 has $n_{\frac{1}{2}}$=10, and the prediction is that SERICR should be used for all systems longer than about 10, that is to say for all systems of practical interest.

For large n there is an asymptote, showing that PARACR should be used if $n_{\frac{1}{2}}$/n>2.4 and SERICR otherwise. The fact that the ratio $n_{\frac{1}{2}}$/n appears as the determining parameter has a natural explanation. This ratio measures how parallel the computer appears to the problem. If it is large, the computer appears highly parallel to the problem, and parallel algorithms like PARACR are the best. If, however, the ratio is small, the computer appears serial to the problem, and serial algorithms like SERICR are best. This may be so even if the computer is quite parallel. What matters is not how parallel the computer is in any absolute sense, but how parallel it is compared to the vector lengths in the problem; and this is measured by the ratio $n_{\frac{1}{2}}$/n.

Regarded in another way, $n_{\frac{1}{2}}$ is proportional to the overhead of initiating a parallel operation. If $n_{\frac{1}{2}}$/n is small this overhead is negligible compared with the time spent on arithmetic ($\propto$n), and it is as though one was computing on a traditional serial computer. On the other hand, if $n_{\frac{1}{2}}$/n is very large the time is dominated by the initialization of parallel operations, and it is as though one is using an infinitely parallel computer.

We consider next the problem of solving multiple independent tridiagonal systems. Both the SERICR and PARACR algorithms can be applied to the m systems in parallel, increasing the vector length by the factor m at all stages of the algorithms. There is however a third alternative, namely to apply Gauss-elimination to the m systems in parallel. We call this the MULTGE algorithm. The algorithmic phase diagram for these three alternatives is shown in Fig. 4, where it is convenient to use the axes ($n_{\frac{1}{2}}$/m,n). The plane is now divided into three regions, in each of which one of the three algorithms has the least execution time. The phase diagram even has a "triple point" at which all three algorithms have the same performance. The prediction is that computers with small values of $n_{\frac{1}{2}}$ compared to m should use MULTGE which has the least amount of arithmetic. Highly parallel computers with large values for the ratio $n_{\frac{1}{2}}$/m should use PARACR, and the SERICR algorithm is appropriate in an intermediate zone. Thus, although the problem of choosing the best algorithm for multiple systems is more complex, the results can still be clearly presented on a single phase diagram.

An even more complicated example concerns the optimization of a class of direct Poisson solvers, and is shown in Fig. 5. The method of Fourier Analysis and Cyclic Reduction, FACR(ℓ), is fully described in reference [8]. As with the solution of tridiagonal systems, two implementations are discussed: SERIFACR that minimizes the arithmetic and PARAFACR that minimizes the number of vector operations. In both cases the parameter ℓ, which is the number of levels of cyclic reduction that are performed before Fourier analysis takes place, can be optimized to minimize the execution time.

A two dimensional finite-difference mesh is considered with n points along each side. If the $n_{\frac{1}{2}}$ of the computer is less than about half n, the computer does not "look" parallel to the problem, and serial implementation, SERIFACR, is recommended. Within this region, we find that more levels of cyclic reduction

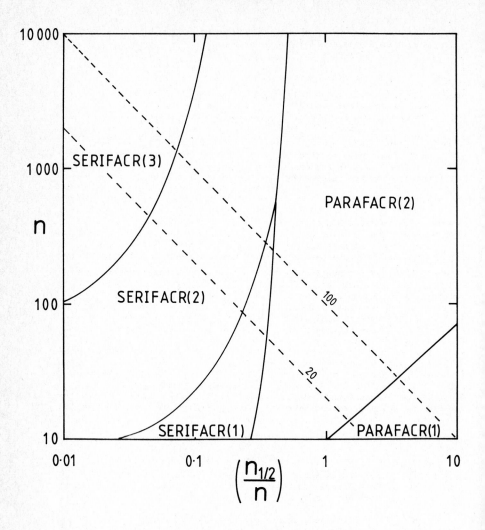

Fig. 5. The algorithmic phase diagram for the solution of Poisson's equation on
an (n×n) mesh using the FACR(ℓ) algorithm. The optimum form of the algorithm and
the optimum value of ℓ are shown throughout the parameter plane. The dotted lines
are for constant values of $n_{\frac{1}{2}}$, and correspond to the properties of the Cray-1 (20)
and Cyber 205 (100). (From Hockney [8], courtesy of IEEE.)

should be made as the number of mesh points increases, but that for practical cases (i.e. less than a million mesh points), it is never desirable to use more than three levels of reduction.

On the other hand, if $n_{\frac{1}{2}}$ exceeds about half n, then the computer does "look" parallel to the problem, and the PARAFACR implementation is recommended. Again more levels of reduction should be used as the number of mesh points increases, but not more than two for practical meshes. The dotted lines in Fig. 5 are drawn for constant values of $n_{\frac{1}{2}}$=20 and 100, which correspond respectively to the behaviour of the CRAY-1 and CDC Cyber 205. These results suggest that it is quite possible for the choice of algorithm to depend not only on the computer, but also on the problem size. In the cases shown no less than five different versions of the FACR algorithm are recommended depending on the mesh size.

V. CONCLUSIONS

We have described a method of algorithm analysis which takes into account the parallelism of the computer on which the algorithm is to run. We find that the half-performance length of the computer is the parameter which determines the choice of algorithms on a particular computer. The results of such $n_{\frac{1}{2}}$ analyses of algorithms can be conveniently displayed in algorithmic phase diagrams. The examples given show how increasingly complex situations can be summarized in a single diagram, ending with the choice between five different versions of the FACR Poisson-solver. It is hoped that this, or a similar, method of analysis will be adopted by numerical analysts in order to help assess the relative merits of their algorithms on the wide variety of parallel computer architectures that are now becoming available.

ACKNOWLEDGEMENTS

The author wishes to acknowledge useful discussions with Chris Jesshope, Jim Craigie, Knut Morken and Dave Snelling during the development of the ideas in this paper.

REFERENCES

[1] Hockney, R.W., and Jesshope, C.R., Parallel Computers - Architecture, Programming and Algorithms (Adam Hilger, Bristol, 1981). Distributed in North and South America by Heyden & Son, Philadelphia.

[2] Smith, B.J., A pipelined, shared resource MIMD computer, Proc. 1978 Intl. Conf. on Parallel Processing, (IEEE, Silver Spring, 1978) 6-8.

[3] Hockney, R.W., Performance of parallel computers, in: Kowalik, J.S. (ed.), Proc. NATO Advanced Research Workshop on High-Speed Computation, Jülich, Germany (Springer-Verlag, Heidelberg, 1983).

[4] Hockney, R.W. and Snelling, D.F., Characterization of MIMD computers: e.g. the Denelcor HEP, in: Feilmeier, M., Joubert, G.R., and Schendel, U. (eds.), Proceedings Parallel Computing 1983 (North-Holland, Amsterdam, 1983).

[5] Hockney, R.W., Characterization of parallel computers and algorithms, Comput. Phys. Commun., 26 (1982) 285-291.

[6] Hockney, R.W., Characterization of parallel computers, in: Ruschitzka, M.,
     Christensen, M., Ames, W.F. and Vichnevetsky, R. (eds.), IMACS Trans. on
     Scientific Computation, 2 (North-Holland, Amsterdam, 1983).

[7] Kuck, D.J., Computers and Computations (Wiley, New York, 1978).

[8] Hockney, R.W., Characterizing computers and optimizing the FACR(ℓ) Poisson-
     solver on parallel unicomputers, IEEE Trans. Comput. (1983) to appear.

DISCUSSION

Speaker: R. Hockney

Smith: It seems counter-intuitive that as the problem size increases, the best choice of algorithm is usually the serial algorithm. Can you give an intuitive argument why this is the case?

Hockney: As N increases, the ratio $N/n_{1/2}$ increases, so $n_{1/2}$ looks more and more like zero; i.e. the computer looks more and more serial. This does not mean that its vector capacity is not used, just that it's startup time becomes negligible.

Rice: Your results show that, if we are to build software parts for vector processors, we shall need to build hybrid algorithms together with quite a complicated mechanism for switching between the sub-algorithms.

Hockney: I agree.

Sherman: You show how to use $n_{1/2}$ to choose an algorithm on a particular machine, but some of us have to choose a machine as well an an algorithm. Have you any comments on how to do that?

Hockney: You need to measure $n_{1/2}$ and also put the relative speeds and costs into the analysis. The relevant algebra is in the paper, but I have not done any specific calculations. They will depend on what type of problem you expect to run.

Duff: You have been talking of a single value of $n_{1/2}$ for a particular machine. However, as we all know and as you said in your talk, this is not constant but depends on the algorithm. Are you justifying the single value on the basis that, for a particular machine, the $n_{1/2}$ value is fairly constant? Could you give an indication of the $n_{1/2}$ range for the Cray-1 and the Cyber-205?

Hockney: I did show that you have to take averages when $n_{1/2}$ is not constant; but in practice, the spread in $n_{1/2}$ shown by a given computer is relatively small, and unlikely to affect the rather coarse analysis we are doing here. For example, $n_{1/2}$ lies between 10 and 20 for the Cray-1.

Sherman: Can you comment on the difficulty of determining the $n_{1/2}$ parameter for new machines? Have you found the manufacturer's estimates to be truly indicative of what you find in practice?

Hockney: I have asked manufacturers; Fujitsu, for example. I find that, first of all, they are amazed at the question; they seem not to have thought of it before. Then however they have, so far anyway, been very cooperative. For example, Fujitsu are now, I believe, measuring $n_{1/2}$ for their machine.

Huddleston: Seeing these diagrams is very nice, and they do allow a comparison of algorithms. But most of us don't have a chance to play with different machines; we may however need to choose between machines, with no idea what our workload will be after the machine is delivered.

Hockney: That is a tough problem.

Schönauer: We should not forget that the present vector computers have a relatively small main store compared to the processing speed. If the problems become larger, we are bound to the limit of the I/O speed. Could you please comment on this.

Hockney: The I/O is very important, and can be analysed in just the same way as we have analysed arithmetic operations. The timing curve is linear, and hence we can define $r_{infinity}$ and $n_{1/2}$; one finds $n_{1/2}$, which represents the latency time for the backing store device, to be very high for transfer to backing store – maybe 15000 or so. But it can be analysed in the same way.

Brandt: There is another complication. In choosing a computer, $n_{1/2}$ is helpful; but different computers differ in their ability to move data around store, or from store to vector registers etc, rapidly. How do you allow for this?

Hockney: If data routing is important, then you need to know $n_{1/2}$ and $r_{infinity}$ for these routing operations, and then you can allow for them as just a part of the total algorithm, and in just the same way as the arithmetic operations.

LIST OF POSTERS

Computer Demonstration of the SESAM' 80 FEM Package
P. BJØRSTAD

Code Harwell MA32 for Frontal Solution of Unsymmetric Problems
I. DUFF

Demonstration of the Ericsson step/one Personal Computer
B. EINARSSON

Solution of Almost Block Diagonal Linear Systems
G. FAIRWEATHER

Phase Diagrams and Spectrum of Computers
R. HOCKNEY

Software System DISPL2 for One and Two Dimensional Kinetics - Diffusion problems
G. K. LEAF

CLUB MODULEF Information
A. PERRONNET

Algorithm 593 (A Package for the Helmholtz Equation in Nonrectangular Planar Regions) and its use as an ELLPACK Module
W. PROSKUROWSKI

ELLPACK examples
J. R. RICE

NAG Fortran Library Software for Solving Certain Almost Block Diagonal Linear Systems
D. K. SAYERS

IMSL'S TWODEPEP
G. SEWELL

Online Demonstration of the COM Teleconferencing System
G. SKÖLLERMO

Interactive Raster Graphics Analysis of PDE Results
G. VOLPI

LIST OF PARTICIPANTS

R. ANDERSSON
Volvo Data
Department 2372
S-405 08 Göteborg
Sweden

O. AXELSSON
University of Nijmegen
Department of Mathematics
Toernooiveld
NL-6525 ED Nijmegen
The Netherlands

Å. BJÖRCK
University of Linköping
Department of Mathematics
S-581 83 Linköping
Sweden

A. BOSSAVIT
Electricité de France
Service I. M. A.
1, Avenue du General de Gaulle
F-92141 Clamart
France

F. CHATELIN
University of Grenoble
IMAG, Tour des Mathematiques
B. P. 68
F-38402 St. Martin d´Heres Cedex
France

W. M. COUGHRAN, Jr
Bell Laboratories
Computing Mathematics 2C-469
600 Mountain Avenue
Murray Hill, NJ 07974
U.S.A.

L. M. DELVES
The University of Liverpool
Department of S. C. M.
Brownlow Hill, Victoria Building
Liverpool L69 3BX
England

E. EDBERG
National Defence Research Institute
Department 3
Box 1165
S-581 11 Linköping
Sweden

B. ARLINGER
SAAB-SCANIA
Department KLU
S-581 88 Linköping
Sweden

D. E. BATCHVAROV
Institute for Industrial
Cybernetics and Robotics
Acad. Bontchev Street Bl . 2
Sofia 1113
Bulgaria

P. BJØRSTAD
Det Norske Veritas
FDIV
P. O. Box 300
N-1322 Høvik
Norway

A. BRANDT
The Weizmann Institute of Science
Department of Applied Mathematics
P. O. Box 26
Rehovot 76 100
Israel

T. M. CHRISTOV
Institute for Industrial
Cybernetics and Robotics
Acad. Bontchev Street Bl. 2
Sofia 1113
Bulgaria

Th. J. DEKKER
University of Amsterdam
Department of Mathematics
Roeterstraat 15
NL-1018 WB Amsterdam
The Netherlands

I. S. DUFF
A.E.R.E. Harwell
Computer Science and Systems Div.
Building 8.9
Oxford OX11 ORA
England

B. EINARSSON
University of Linköping
LIDAC
S-581 83 Linköping
Sweden

B. ENGQUIST
University of Uppsala
Department of Computer Science
Sturegatan 4B, 2tr
S-752 23 Uppsala
Sweden

B. FORD
Numerical Algorithms Group
Mayfield House
256 Banbury Road
Oxford OX2 7DE
England

R. M. FURZELAND
Shell Research Ltd.
Department of Computing and Math.
Thornton Research Centre
P. O. Box 1
Chester CH1 3SH
England

R. GORENFLO
Free University of Berlin
Department of Mathematics
Arnimallee 2-6
D-1000 Berlin 33
Federal Republic of Germany

M. HAMINA
University of Oulu
Faculty of Technology
Department of Mathematics
Linnanmaa
SF-90570 Uleåborg 57
Finland

A. C. HINDMARSH
Lawrence Livermore National Lab.
Mathematics and Statistics Div.
L-316, P. O. Box 808
Livermore, CA 94550
U.S.A.

HUANG HONG-CI
Academia Sinica
Computing Center
P. O. Box 2719
Beijing
People's Republic of China

K. E. KARLSSON
ASEA
Department KYT
S-721 83 Västerås
Sweden

G. FAIRWEATHER
University of Kentucky
Department of Mathematics
Patterson Office Tower
Lexington, KY 40506-0027
U.S.A.

L. FUNKQUIST
Swedish Meteorological
and Hydrological Institute
Box 923
S-601 19 Norrköping
Sweden

C. GROSSMANN
Technical University of Dresden
Sektion Mathematik
Mommsenstrasse 13
DDR-8027 Dresden
German Democratic Republic

B. GUSTAFSSON
University of Uppsala
Department of Computer Science
Sturegatan 4B, 2tr.
S-752 23 Uppsala
Sweden

P. W. HEMKER
Mathematisch Centrum
Kruislaan 413
NL-1098 SJ Amsterdam
The Netherlands

R. W. HOCKNEY
Reading University
Department of Computer Science
White Knights
Reading RG6 2AX
England

R. E. HUDDLESTON
Sandia National Laboratories
Computer Systems Division 8335
P. O. Box 969
Livermore, CA 94550
U.S.A.

B. KÅGSTRÖM
University of Umeå
Department of
Information Processing
S-901 87 Umeå
Sweden

C. L. LAWSON
Jet Propulsion Laboratory
MS 171-249
4800 Oak Grove Drive
Pasadena, CA 91103
U.S.A.

B. LINDBERG
Royal Institute of Technology
Department of Computer Science
S-100 44 Stockholm
Sweden

M. MACHURA
Institute of Atomic Energy
Computing Center
PL-05-400 Otwock-Swierk
Poland

Z. B. MARCHEV
Institute for Industrial
Cybernetics and Robotics
Acad. Bontchev Street Bl. 2
Sofia 1113
Bulgaria

O. NEVANLINNA
Helsinki University of Technology
Institute of Mathematics
SF-02150 Esbo 15
Finland

J. OPPELSTRUP
The Swedish Institute
of Applied Mathematics
Box 5073
S-102 42 Stockholm
Sweden

A. PRIDOR
Tel-Aviv University
Department of Matehmatical Sciences
Ramat Aviv, P. O. Box 39040
Tel Aviv 69978
Israel

J. K. REID
A.E.R.E. Harwell
Computer Science and Systems Div.
Building 8.9
Oxford OX11 ORA
England

G. K. LEAF
Argonne National Laboratory
Mathematics and Computer Science
Division
9700 South Cass Avenue
Argonne, IL 60439
U.S.A

M. LINDGREN
The Swedish Institute
of Applied Mathematics
Box 5073
S-102 42 Stockholm
Sweden

N. K. MADSEN
Lawrence Livermore National Lab.
Department of Electronics Eng.
L-156, P. O. Box 5504
Livermore, CA 94550
U.S.A

J. J. H. MILLER
University of Dublin
Numerical Analysis Group
39 Trinity College
Dublin 2
Ireland

D. OPHIR
The Weizmann Institute of Science
Department of Mathematics
P. O. Box 26
Rehovot 76 100
Israel

A. PERRONNET
University of
Pierre and Marie Curie
Laboratorie Analyse Numerique
4, Place Jussieu
F-752 30 Paris Cedex 05
France

W. PROSKUROWSKI
University of Southern California
Department of Mathematics
University Park, DRB 306
Los Angeles, CA 90089-1113
U.S.A

J. R. RICE
Purdue University
Department of Computer Science
West Lafayette, IN 47907
U. S. A

J. SARANEN
University of Oulu
Faculty of Technology
Department of Mathematics
Linnanmaa
SF-90570 Uleåborg 57
Finland

W. SCHÖNAUER
University of Karlsruhe
Rechenzentrum
Postfach 6380
D-7500 Karlsruhe 1
Federal Republic of Germany

G. SEWELL
University of Texas at El Paso
Department of Mathematics
El Paso, TX 79968
U. S. A

R. B. SIMPSON
University of Waterloo
Department of Computer Science
Waterloo, Ontario N2L 3G1
Canada

T. SMEDSAAS
University of Uppsala
Department of Computer Science
Sturegatan 4B 2tr
S-752 23 Uppsala
Sweden

H. J. STETTER
Technical University of Vienna
Department of Numerical Mathematics
Gusshausstrasse 27-29
A-1040 Vienna
Austria

K. STÜBEN
Gesellschaft fuer Mathematik
und Datenverarbeitung
Schloss Birlinghoven, Postfach 1240
D-5205 St. Augustin 1
Federal Republic of Germany

H. TAMVEL
Volvo Flygmotor
Department 361
S-461 81 Trollhättan
Sweden

D. SAYERS
Numerical Algorithms Group
Mayfield House
256 Banbury Road
Oxford OX2 7DE
England

N. L. SCHRYER
Bell Laboratories
Computing Mathematics Research
600 Mountain Avenue
Murray Hill, NJ 07974
U. S. A

A. H. SHERMAN
Exxon Production Research Company
P. O. Box 2189
Houston, TX 77001
U. S. A

G. SKÖLLERMO
Stockholm University
Computing Center QZ
Box 27322
S-102 54 Stockholm
Sweden

B. T. SMITH
Argonne National Laboratory
Mathematics and Computer Science
Division
9700 South Cass Avenue
Argonne, IL 60439
U. S. A

E. I. STOILOV
Institute for Industrial
Cybernetics and Robotics
Acad. Bontchev Street Bl. 2
Sofia 1113
Bulgaria

D. SUNDSTRÖM
The Swedish Institute
of Applied Mathematics
Box 5073
S-102 42 Stockholm
Sweden

J. F. THOMPSON
Mississippi State University
Department of Aerospace Engineering
Drawer A
Mississippi State, MS 39762
U. S. A

M. THUNÉ
University of Uppsala
Department of Computer Science
Sturegatan 4B 2tr
S-752 23 Uppsala
Sweden

G. VOLPI
IBM Italy
Rome Scientific Center
Via Giorgione 129
I-00147 Rome
Italy

J. WALSH
University of Manchester
Department of Mathematics
Oxford Road
Manchester M13 9PL
England

K. WITSCH
Gesellschaft fuer Mathematik
und Datenverarbeitung
Schloss Birlinghoven, Postfach 1240
D-5205 St. Augustin 1
Federal Republic of Germany

N. N. YANENKO
Institute for Theoretical
and Applied Mechanics
Institutskaya ul. 4/1
630090 Novosibirsk 90
USSR

Z. ZLATEV
National Agency of Environmental
Protection
Air Pollution Laboratory
Risø National Laboratory
DK-4000 Roskilde
Denmark

U. TROTTENBERG
Gesellschaft fuer Mathematik
und Datenverarbeitung
Schloss Birlinghoven, Postfach 1240
D-5205 St. Augustin 1
Federal Republic of Germany

M. A. VOUK
University Computing Centre (SRCE)
Engelsova b.b.
YU-41000 Zagreb
Yugoslavia

J. VAN WELIJ
Philips
Department ISA
Building SAQ
Eindhoven
The Netherlands

M. H. WRIGHT
Stanford University
Department of Operations Research
Systems Optimization Laboratory
Stanford, CA 94305
U. S. A

D. M. YOUNG, JR.
The University of Texas at Austin
Center for Numerical Analysis
RLM 13.150
Austin, TX 78712
U. S. A

LIST OF AUTHORS